ARKANSAS BIRDS
Their Distribution and Abundance

FRONTISPIECE: Willow Flycatcher, the only species of bird that first became known to science through its discovery in Arkansas. It was found and first described by John James Audubon at Arkansas Post in 1822. *David Plank*

with illustrations by David Plank
and Sigrid James Bruch

Douglas A. James and Joseph C. Neal

ARKANSAS BIRDS
Their Distribution and Abundance

THE UNIVERSITY OF ARKANSAS PRESS

FAYETTEVILLE 1986

The authors wish to express their gratitude to members of the Arkansas Game and Fish Commission whose assistance, both personal and financial, has brought this fifteen-year project to its successful realization: Steve N. Wilson, Andrew H. Hulsey, Carl Hunter, Duncan W. Martin, Richard Broach, and Perry Max Johnston. Further special encouragement was willingly and generously granted by George M. Purvis, whose wisdom, patience, and foresight concluded the task.

∞
The paper used in this publication meets the minimum requirements of the American National Standard for Permanence of Paper for Printed Library Materials Z39.48—1984.

Designer: Joyce Kachergis Book Design & Production
Typeface: Linotron 202 Palatino
Typesetter: G&S Typesetters, Inc.
Printer: Kingsport Press
Binder: Kingsport Press

LIBRARY OF CONGRESS CATALOGING-IN-PUBLICATION DATA
James, Douglas A. 1925–
  Arkansas birds.
  Bibliography: p.
  Includes index.
  1. Birds—Arkansas—Identification.   I. Neal, Joseph C. 1946–   .   II. Title.
QL684.A8J36   1986   598.29767   85-20835
ISBN 0-938626-38-8

Contents

Illustrations, Maps, and Tables

Dedication

This book is dedicated to Frances C. James,
whose efforts spurred its initiation,
to George M. Purvis who encouraged its completion,
and to the many observers of birds
in Arkansas whose records made it possible.

Acknowledgments

A book of this kind, that draws on so many records and diverse sources of information, is by its very nature dependent upon the support of many people, agencies, and institutions, and would not have been possible without their cooperation and assistance. The primary source of support during manuscript preparation and publication was the Arkansas Game and Fish Commission. Funds for various activities associated with compiling information for the book and for preparing the completed edition were provided through grants from the National Institutes of Health, the Frank M. Chapman Memorial Fund of the American Museum of Natural History, the Arkansas Audubon Society Trust, Northwest Arkansas Audubon Society, the U.S. Army Chemical Corps, the National Park Service, the National Science Foundation in the form of both direct grants and institutional grants to the University of Arkansas Research Reserve Fund. The Arkansas Audubon Society allocated funds for maintaining the state bird record files, and the Department of Zoology at the University of Arkansas, Fayetteville, provided space for housing the files.

Several state and federal agencies as well as private institutions supplied necessary information, including the U.S. Fish and Wildlife Service, the Arkansas Game and Fish Commission, the Arkansas Natural Heritage Commission, the Arkansas Nature Conservancy, and the National Wildlife Federation. Use of the computerized file of Christmas Bird Counts established by Carl E. Bock at the University of Colorado was greatly appreciated. Information for the Appendix on Arkansas bird specimens existing in museums was obtained from the U.S. National Museum, the American Museum of Natural History, the Field Museum of Natural History, the Royal Ontario Museum, the Museum of Comparative Zoology, the University of Michigan, the University of Kansas, and Louisiana State University. Most of the museum catalogues were searched by Douglas James and Frances James, but searches at the Field Museum of Natural History and the National Museum of Natural History at the Smithsonian Institution were performed by William M. Shepherd and Ruby G. Crews, respectively. We are grateful for their help and for the assistance offered by Jon C. Barlow in completing the search at the Royal Ontario Museum.

The fine artwork which adds immeasurably to the book is credited throughout. We are particularly grateful to Sigrid James Bruch and David Plank for generously donating their fine color paintings for use as illustrations. David Plank's line drawings of birds were done in the field at specific sites around Arkansas; Sigrid Bruch also works with live birds, primarily in zoo collections. The Arkansas Audubon Society Trust, the Northwest Arkansas Audubon Society, and Ruby G. Crews assisted financially with the preparation of the color paintings for publication. We also thank Ruby G. Crews and Dr. and Mrs. G. D. Nichols for making their Bruch paintings available; the Library of Congress, Robert D. Wheeler and Eloise Baerg-King for the photographs of Arthur H. Howell, Harry E. Wheeler, and William T. Baerg, respectively. Credits are given to the following photographers who so generously provided their photographs of birds and habitats in Arkansas: William Brazelton, Fred L. Burnside, Neil Compton, Thase F. Daniel, Levi Davis, Thomas L. Foti, Edith M. Halberg, Larry Higgins, Charles Mills, Max Parker, William F. Pell, George M. Purvis, J. H. Rettig, William M. Shepherd, and Howard S. Stern. Additionally, we wish to acknowledge the excellent photographs of bird effigy pottery that were offered by Mary McGimsey of the University of Arkansas museum, Fayetteville.

Several people provided various kinds of data analyses for material used in the book, and others read chapters relating to their fields of expertise. Some gave generously of their time to critically read substantial portions of the species accounts in draft form, which resulted in a strengthening of the manuscript. Others provided editorial assistance. Some performed many of these tasks. For this we thank Elizabeth M. Adam, Eloise Baerg-King, B. William Beall, Jeannine S. Becker, Robin Rhinehart Buff, Edward E. Dale, Jr., Thomas L.

Foti, Frances C. James, Edith M. and Henry N. Halberg, Earl L. Hanebrink, John G. Hehr, Phillip W. Mattocks, Jr., Walter L. Manger, Cynthia Marks, Charles Mills, Helen L. and Max D. Parker, William F. Pell, Cecilia M. Riley, Terry Root, Vivian B. Scarlett, William M. Shepherd, H. H. "Shug" and K. Luvois Shugart, Herman Henry "Hank" Shugart, Jr., Kimberly G. Smith, Jane E. Stern, Connie Sweeney, Lloyd O. Warren and Robert D. Wheeler. Charles Mills additionally provided advice and assistance concerning Arkansas bird records kept during the past decade when he was curator of the files on bird sightings for the Arkansas Audubon Society. For their assistance with the chapter on birds and prehistory in Arkansas, the help of Hester Davis and John House of the Arkansas Archeological Survey; Mary Printup, past librarian for the Survey; and Michael P. Hoffman of the University of Arkansas museum are gratefully acknowledged. Miller Williams, Katharine Villard, and Brenda Zodrow of the University of Arkansas Press were of immeasurable assistance in the final stages of producing the book and are thanked for their help.

We especially thank the good friends who have faithfully submitted their Arkansas bird sightings. Without this cooperative and herculean effort there would have been little to write about. In fact, so many people have become involved in keeping records since the 1950s it is impossible to name them all. The following list includes those who deserve special appreciation: Harold E. Alexander, Carl Amason, M. Ruth Armstrong, Curt Adkisson, Sam Barkley, Irving T. Beach, B. William Beall, Pamela J. Blore, Thurman W. Booth, William Brazelton, John M. Briggs, David Brotherton, Luanne Brotherton, Bobby W. Brown, Jimmie J. Brown, Robin Rhinehart Buff, Fred L. Burnside, Jr., George T. Clark, W. G. Click, Ben B. Coffey, Jr., Lula Coffey, Lana Cook, Roberta Crabtree, James M. Dale, Herbert H. Daniel, Thase F. Daniel, Levi Davis, David M. Donaldson, Wayne Easley, Elizabeth Fleener, Marty Floyd, E. P. "Perk" Floyd, Thomas L. Foti, Ralph D. Fox, Charles L. Gardner, Lois M. Giles, Sue H. Glass, J. C. Glover, M. E. Glover, Lynn Goodwin, Gary R. Graves, Jane Gulley, Thomas M. Haggerty, Edith M. Halberg, Henry N. Halberg, Justine Hamm, Earl L. Hanebrink, Josephine Hanna, Nona Herbert, J. B. Herring, Jewel E. Herring, George Hoffman, Arnold J. Hoiberg, Truston H. Holder, Vernon Howe, Peter J. Van Huizen, David R. Hunter, Philip E. Hyatt, Thomas A. Imhof, Frances C. James, Atha S. Jamison, Ross L. Jamison, David M. Johnson, Martha Johnson, Paul Johnson, Robert T. Kirkwood, Vernon Kleen, Bret D. Kuss, Sterling S. Lacy, Norman Lavers, Jack Logan, Almyra Love, Florence Mallard, Larry E. Mallard, Horace N. Marvin, Clyde Massey, Philip W. Mattocks, Jr., Richard McCamant, Paul K. McCoy, Sophia L. McCoy, Raymond R. McMaster, M. Brooke Meanley, Charles Mills, Michael A. Mlodinow, Peter A. Money, Bobby G. Moore, Clementine Moore, James S. Mulhollan, Ellen Neaville, Jean M. Niemyer, Helen Parker, Max Parker, Helen Pfeifer, Dorabelle Purifoy, Andrew G. Pursley, Iola M. Rae, Jo Anne Rife, Robert Sanger, Vivian B. Scarlett, William P. Scarlett, W. M. Shepherd, Sr., William M. Shepherd, H. H. "Shug" Shugart, Herman Henry "Hank" Shugart, Jr., K. Luvois Shugart, Don R. Simons, Kimberly G. Smith, Virginia G. Springer, Richard Stauffacher, Jane E. Stern, Joseph Stockton, Vivian Stockton, Keith Sutton, Bruce L. Tedford, Ruth H. Thomas, Merritt G. Vaiden, Mel White, J. Edward White, Patsy R. White, Eugene J. Wilhelm, Jr., Janette O. Wilson, Thomas B. Wilson, and Charlie W. Wooten. We extend a sincere and heartfelt thank you to all who participated and apologize if deserving names have been inadvertently omitted.

James thanks his wife, Elizabeth M. Adam, for organizing the material for several parts of the book and for help with proofreading. Neal gratefully acknowledges his wife, Nancy Monteith Edelman, for her patience and support during the book's completion.

Prefatory Note

Arkansas Birds is directed to a wide group of people, ranging from the casual observer to the serious student of ornithology, and should appeal equally to those who feed or watch birds, members of naturalist, wildlife, and conservation organizations, bird and garden club enthusiasts, classroom teachers and students, and sportsmen in the field.

Although this book does not provide information on the identification of birds, it may be used in conjunction with any popular guide that offers specific details on birds of the region.

ORNITHOLOGY
IN ARKANSAS

Chapter 1

INTRODUCTION

By providing a current appraisal of the distribution and abundance of 366 species of Arkansas birds, this book makes a significant contribution to the ornithological knowledge of the state. Specifically, the present volume gives information on distribution patterns, abundance levels, seasonal occurrences, habitats, changes in status, nesting seasons, and migrational movements of birds occurring in Arkansas.

It is not the first such treatise on Arkansas birds, but because of the vast accumulation of new information and spectacular recent advances in the study of birds, it is possible to introduce for the first time new material on avian distribution and concurrent population data relating to avian abundance. The book is also unique in including Arkansas data on migrational movements provided by bird banding recoveries. Documentation of breeding schedules of birds in Arkansas is the most thorough ever presented.

The opening chapters discuss avian ecology in Arkansas, birds in prehistory, and the history of Arkansas ornithology as well as offering suggestions on where to find birds in the state. An exhaustive bibliography of Arkansas ornithology and a listing of most of the specimens of Arkansas birds held in museums in the United States and Canada completes the volume. What this book lacks that was once included in the four previous monographs devoted to Arkansas birds is a section on their economic value. The obvious change in public attitude that permits this omission should be applauded. It is now possible to enjoy birds for their own sake, which everyone really always did, and it is no longer necessary to indicate whether or not they are economically beneficial.

Although two decades or less elapsed between each of the former monographs, more than thirty years have passed since the previous volume on Arkansas birds was published. Since then there has been a tremendous increase in the knowledge of birds on state, national, and international levels. This is the result of a rising interest in ornithology and its development and is especially due to an increased awareness of birds by the general public, which in turn has generated a proliferation of local bird clubs composed of people expert in the identification of birds in the field. In Arkansas this phenomenon led to a density of observers statewide that left few areas uninvestigated. This coverage was greater in intensity and uniformity than previous coverage.

The Bird Record File

In May of 1955, the Arkansas Audubon Society was formally established in ceremonies held at Petit Jean State Park. The impetus for the formation of the Society had been initiated when M. Ruth Armstrong, who had founded the Fort Smith Audubon Society, wrote to Herbert H. Daniel, then president of the Pulaski

County Audubon Society centered in Little Rock, suggesting the need for a state organization (Armstrong 1975). At the charter meeting, Herbert Daniel was elected president of the new Arkansas Audubon Society and stayed in office for five years.

In 1953, Douglas A. James was invited to join the zoology faculty at the University of Arkansas as professor of zoology. He reached Fayetteville in the fall of the same year and taught ornithology for the first time during the spring semester of 1954. James immediately began collecting information on a systematic basis, and as more and more observers participated in recording birds, and as new sources of original data became available, he was able to document the distribution and abundance of birds sighted and identified within the state. James became the first curator of records for the Society and started incorporating sightings made by others into his personal card file of Arkansas bird records begun in 1953. The Society soon generated a network of bird observers around the state who contributed reports to what then became the Arkansas Audubon Society file of bird records. The Audubon file now contains approximately 40,000 bird observations, constituting the primary source of new information for this book. (In compiling the book records through 1985 were used.)

James' tenure in maintaining the file extended from 1955 to 1973, during which period it received support from the Arkansas Audubon Society and University of Arkansas. Edith M. Halberg and then Charles Mills curated the files for the Society from 1974 to 1983, when Joseph C. Neal became curator. (Over the years the most significant records deposited in the bird file were mentioned in "The Changing Seasons" section of *American Birds* and its predecessor *Audubon Field Notes* published by the National Audubon Society.)

When the bird file was first begun, James made a special effort to incorporate the past field notes from ornithologists particularly active in Arkansas, whose observations extended the records to dates earlier than 1953. These included the following: M. G. Vaiden, southeastern Arkansas, back to 1913; Ben B. Coffey, Jr., statewide but primarily eastern and northeastern Arkansas, mainly 1950s and 1960s and back to 1929; Arnold J. Hoiberg, south central

Arkansas, 1948 to 1952; M. Brooke Meanley, the lowlands of eastern Arkansas, 1951 to 1962; B. W. (Bill) Beall, to the early 1950s in northwestern Arkansas; Charles L. Gardner, old nest records in southwestern Arkansas; in addition to summaries of the bird record files from the Big Lake National Wildlife Refuge for the 1940s, '50s, and '60s.

In the bird file, individual reports of each species were normally kept on a separate card. Records through 1973 were also positioned on state outline maps, a separate map for each species showing precise locations of each observation, coded to show seasonal distributions and migratory dates. The maps and the individual record cards were extremely useful in preparing the species accounts for this book. It was decided to omit observers' names (except in unusual circumstances) when listing bird records in the species accounts. As on labels for museum specimens upon which the collector is named, cards in the file may be consulted if the observer of a record needs to be identified. It is anticipated that at least part of the bird files and the map book used in preparing this book will be deposited with the Special Collections Department of the University of Arkansas Libraries at Fayetteville. In addition, there is a file of documentation forms providing written descriptions of difficult or unusual bird sightings found in the bird card system. These will also become the responsibility of the University Museum.

Lastly, the zoology graduate program in ornithology and ecology has generated many studies and papers on birds in Arkansas. Among the contributions offered by doctoral students in this program, those by Frances C. James were especially significant. The continuing field studies, undertaken by Douglas James, which focus upon avian ecology, have also brought valuable knowledge and expertise to the present volume.

Preparing the Book

As new and substantial information accumulated, the need for a fresh approach to Arkansas birds became obvious. A decision to produce an up-to-date volume was reached in the late 1960s, and in 1969, Douglas and Frances James, with the aid of commission member P. M. Johnston, presented a proposal to the Arkansas Game and Fish Commission suggesting support for a new Arkansas bird book. The commission and its then director, Andrew H. Hulsey, were favorably receptive to the idea and the project was approved by the following year. Designed as a joint effort by Douglas and Frances James, Joseph Neal's involvement began in 1980, after Frances James had left the project.

Joseph C. Neal graduated from the University of Arkansas in 1968 and pursued a career in writing while developing a keen interest in field ornithology. During recent years he has contributed many valuable bird records for inclusion in this book, with a special focus on records of birds in the western Arkansas Ozarks.

In writing the book, James coordinated the gathering of bird records and related information, and directed the project. Based upon data collected and some preliminary summaries produced by Frances C. James, Neal prepared drafts of the bird species accounts. These drafts were reviewed and critiqued by Douglas James, who suggested or provided revisions. New drafts were then written by Neal and after further review final drafts were developed. Chapters preceding the species accounts were written by James with the exception of "Arkansas Birds in Prehistory," which was written by Neal. James also organized the bibliography with the assistance of Neal and others over many years. The Appendix on bird specimens was produced through joint effort by Douglas and Frances James, again assisted by others. Neal provided broad stroke generalizations in the overall synopses, while James tenaciously pursued accuracy in the nagging details. The two authors agree that although their approaches to the project differed, the difference was complementary in an important way.

During the several years taken to prepare a draft manuscript, the authors were continually surprised by new and important records being submitted concerning new bird species for the state, new finds in diverse areas, and changing distributions in areas previously well covered. Viewing this against past history documented in the previous works on Arkansas birds, it is evident that change is a conspicuous aspect of

avian existence. That is why efforts such as this one and its predecessors are needed not only to upgrade and update the general state of knowledge but especially to monitor changing patterns.

Many new sources of information on birds in Arkansas have become available during the past three decades through the rising involvement of experienced bird watchers participating in organized projects. This has been augmented by a flourishing program of avian research in the state conducted by ornithologists and students of ornithology.

Sources of Information

In addition to the Audubon Society file of bird records described above, the four previous monographs on Arkansas birds (Howell 1911, Wheeler 1924, Baerg 1931, 1951), all titled *Birds of Arkansas,* were important sources of information. Several more recent publications concerning seasonal distributions of birds in various local areas in the state were very helpful in updating regional patterns. Pamphlets now exist for south central Arkansas (Mattocks and Shugart 1962), the Fort Smith area (Armstrong and Beall 1962), Faulkner County in central Arkansas (Johnson 1979), northeastern Arkansas (Hanebrink 1980), and northwestern Arkansas (Neal 1983). In addition, the pages summarizing seasonal bird distributions in the Arkansas Audubon Society newsletter were consulted, although most of these records are also found in the Society's bird record file. All the available published literature on birds in Arkansas was searched for useful information. The bibliography in this book includes an exhaustive listing through 1979, plus additional titles up to 1985, of published references on bird life in Arkansas whether or not entries are actually cited in the text.

Various organized bird counts, censuses, and surveys provided important information on avian abundance. Thus, the annual Christmas Bird Counts conducted nationwide under the auspices of the National Audubon Society and published in *American Birds* (formerly *Audubon Field Notes*) were an indispensable source of bird population values used in estimating average winter densities of birds in various parts of Arkansas. Especially useful were composites of a decade of recent Christmas Bird Counts from various localities in all regions of the state. These compilations, submitted by volunteers, provided a view of recent trends in winter bird populations in Arkansas. The listing provided by Vivian B. Scarlett summarizing all Christmas Bird Counts held in the state from 1948 to 1961 was consulted, and extensive use was made of the 1962–71 compilation and summary of the counts for Arkansas maintained in the computerized file of Christmas Bird Counts organized by Carl E. Bock at the University of Colorado. Individual Arkansas counts, particularly those conducted in recent years, were frequently consulted.

The Winter Bird Population Studies (Anon. 1950, Kolb 1965), also coordinated and published by the National Audubon Society, provided another important source of information on wintering bird populations in Arkansas. These studies are less extensive but more precise than the Christmas Bird Counts, and in Arkansas have not been conducted for many years. The winter bird population studies conducted and summarized by Arnold J. Hoiberg were often consulted. These studies, made in the 1950s, took place near El Dorado in south central Arkansas. Results of other winter bird population studies for Arkansas were used when appropriate.

Abundance levels of summer birds were determined from the results in Arkansas of the nationwide annual breeding bird survey coordinated by the U.S. Fish and Wildlife Service. The Arkansas results of these June counts conducted from 1967 to 1972 were used in addition to a summary of Arkansas surveys for the ten year period from 1967 to 1977. There are twenty-nine roadside survey routes positioned around the state, information from which was supplemented by the Arkansas results of the annual *Breeding Bird Censuses* (Anon. 1950, Hall 1964), coordinated and published by the National Audubon Society. Like the winter bird population studies, these plot censuses of breeding birds are limited in number and have not been conducted in Arkansas during recent years. The studies completed by Arnold J. Hoiberg near El Dorado in the 1950s were used extensively.

Previously unpublished results were used concerning both breeding censuses and winter population studies conducted by Douglas James in the northwestern Ozarks and in central Arkansas near Pine Bluff. Previously unpublished graduate thesis results compiled by Katherine W. Collins for summer and winter birds in northeastern Arkansas were also used (Collins 1960). A study in the Ozarks by Shugart and James (1973) provided the basic data for breeding bird populations with respect to ecological succession.

Extensive midwinter waterfowl surveys conducted over the years jointly by the U.S. Fish and Wildlife Service and the Arkansas Game and Fish Commission were used in determining the abundances of ducks and geese wintering in the state. The annual winter blackbird-starling roost survey coordinated in recent years by Thurman W. Booth for the U.S. Fish and Wildlife Service was a primary source of information on numbers of various blackbird species and associated birds that enter large communal nocturnal roosts in Arkansas each winter. The Arkansas colonial bird rookery survey conducted cooperatively in 1980, compiled by Thurman W. Booth, provided data on numbers of various herons and associated species that form nesting colonies in the state. Wild Turkey population data was obtained from the annual results of turkey hunting seasons compiled by the Arkansas Game and Fish Commission. Numbers of both wintering Bald and Golden Eagles were available in the annual results of the midwinter Bald Eagle survey sponsored by the National Wildlife Federation and conducted in Arkansas jointly by the U.S. Fish and Wildlife Service and Arkansas Game and Fish Commission. Sam Barkley of the Commission was the area eagle survey coordinator. Additionally, files of several federal, state, and other organizations for bird data were consulted. These included searching the narrative files of the Big Lake and White River National Wildlife refuges and inspecting waterfowl survey results for these refuges plus the Holla Bend and Wapanocca National Wildlife refuges. Avian information was also obtained from the files of the Arkansas Game and Fish Commission, the Arkansas Natural Heritage Commission, and the Arkansas Nature Conservancy.

Additional sources of information include specimens of Arkansas birds kept in the collection at the University of Arkansas Museum and at various other museums in North America. A grant awarded in 1960 to Frances C. James from the Frank M. Chapman Memorial Fund of the American Museum of Natural History made possible a search of some major museum catalogues in the United States and Canada. From this activity and from other endeavors, entries of Arkansas specimens were found in the following collections: National Museum of Natural History (Smithsonian Institution), American Museum of Natural History (New York City), Field Museum of Natural History (Chicago), Royal Ontario Museum (Canada), Museum of Comparative Zoology (Harvard University), University of Michigan, University of Kansas, Louisiana State University, University of Oklahoma, and Cornell University.

The egg collection in the University of Arkansas Museum was used extensively in conjunction with more recent sightings of nests in Arkansas in determining nesting dates of Arkansas birds. The eggs in the museum were mainly part of the Harry E. Wheeler collection but included other smaller Arkansas collections such as the Tomlinson and Luther collections. It was found that in Wheeler's book (1924) on nesting birds in Arkansas, many egg dates he had documented in his collection were not mentioned in the text even though they must have been collected prior to the publication of his book, after which he left the state.

A grant from 1964 to 1967 awarded to Douglas James by the National Institutes of Health enabled a search to be done through June 30, 1963, of the federal bird banding files for records of banding recoveries associated with Arkansas. This provided data from 18,000 band recoveries for analyzing patterns of migratory movements of Arkansas birds based on banding results. Other grants awarded to James by the Frank M. Chapman Memorial Fund of the American Museum of Natural History, the National Science Foundation, and the National Park Service, and by the University of Arkansas Research Reserve Fund produced important information concerning avian ecology in Arkansas. Finally, a major source of information on rare and endangered species of birds in Arkansas comprised the material furnished by Frances C. James (1974) in the *Arkansas Natural Area Plan* published by the Arkansas Department of Planning in 1974.

Ornithological Progress

If it can be suggested that the number of species found is a rough gauge to the extent of ornithological knowledge of an area, one can measure progress in this regard by comparing the number of species reported between past and current books devoted to birds in Arkansas. The matter is confused, since previous volumes also listed subspecies in the totals, whereas the present study contains only species. Furthermore, extensive taxonomic revisions have been made over the years, causing some taxa to be merged and thus reducing the number of species, while others have been split, resulting in an increase. The subspecies problem was solved by eliminating them from former lists; however, no attempt was made to adjust for changes in species numbers due to revised taxonomic considerations. Former books also listed some species that had not been reported in Arkansas but were included anyway because of occurrences in nearby states. These too were deleted. One other problem remained. Harry E. Wheeler listed some species in italics that were included "only upon meager evidence" (Wheeler 1924). In perusing these it became evident that many were ones that Arthur H. Howell claimed had not yet been found in Arkansas and were mentioned only because of close proximity to the state. On the other hand, some of the birds named in italics were species Howell actually found in Arkansas but had been based on only one or a few known records. No attempt was made to sort out this situation. In final analysis, Howell in 1911 listed 242 species of birds occurring in Arkansas; Wheeler in 1924 showed 272 species (only 224 if those inappropriately shown in italics are omitted). William J. Baerg's original edition in 1931 showed 277 species and his revised edition in 1951 named 324. The volume at hand describes 366 species of Arkansas birds. Thus, over about three-quarters of a century (from Howell's first summary of Arkansas birdlife to the present book), new discoveries in the state have resulted in a 50 percent increase in the number of bird species. This may be attributed primarily to increased ornithological activities rather than to a steady influx of new birds into the state, although there have also been some new avian range extensions into Arkansas.

Chapter 2
HISTORY OF ORNITHOLOGY IN ARKANSAS

Written history of Arkansas may be dated from the arrival of De Soto's army on the banks of the Mississippi in 1541. Records of this Spanish expedition provide details about the Indians with whom we now associate bird effigy pots and other cultural traces. The use of bird feathers is mentioned in connection with the Spanish as they were preparing to cross the Mississippi River. A great Indian chief came to look them over accompanied by "two hundred canoes filled with men, having weapons. They were painted ochre, wearing great bunches of white and other plumes of many colours, having feathered shields in their hands, with which they sheltered the oarsmen on either side, the warriors standing erect from bow to stern, holding bows and arrows" (Phillips, et al. 1951).

After an uncontested crossing of the Mississippi into what is now Arkansas, the Spanish visited an impressive and prosperous town with five hundred large houses, a temple mound, and a plaza, all surrounded by a palisade and connected to the Mississippi River by a wide canal. Extensive agricultural fields and smaller towns and villages lay beyond.

Early Exploration

Birds are mentioned in the accounts of the first adventurers who came to Arkansas, and are detailed in Deaderick's (1941) description of the history of Arkansas ornithology. These include accounts by the French explorers Louis Jolliet and Father Jacques Marquette, who descended the Mississippi River in 1673 to the mouth of the Arkansas River and named the first two birds ever reported in Arkansas, the bobwhite and the now extinct parakeet (Thwaites 1896–1901). Further mention of birds by seventeenth and eighteenth century French travelers came from La Salle's party at Arkansas Post in 1687 (Joutel 1966), from the journeys of La Harpe (Lewis 1932) in 1721–22, Captain Bossu of the French marines (Bossu 1771) in 1751 along the Arkansas River, and from Le Page du Pratz (1763).

John James Audubon (1785–1851) was evidently the first person with primarily ornithological interests to visit Arkansas. Embarked upon a voyage of exploration and discovery, he created magnificent and carefully detailed paintings of birds in their natural habitat capturing the special glory of wild birds with an eloquence which would bring knowledge of American birds to the world. Years before he won international fame with *The Birds of America*, Audubon floated down the Mississippi

River in a keelboat (Audubon 1929). Between November 26 and December 20, 1820, he explored the shoreline of the river forming the eastern boundary of the newly created Arkansas Territory. Daily entries in his journal for this period record approximately fifty species of birds, further documented in his *Ornithological Biography* (Audubon 1831–1839).

Audubon came to Arkansas at least one more time, since his illustration of the Traill's Flycatcher, *Muscicapa Traillii* (Audubon 1828, *Birds Amer.*), represented a bird he found in prairie lands near the Fort of Arkansas on April 17, 1822 (Audubon 1831, *Ornith. Biog.*), a locality in southeastern Arkansas later called Arkansas Post, near the Arkansas River (presently Arkansas Post National Monument). The significance of the Traill's Flycatcher, now named the Willow Flycatcher, *Empidonax traillii* (Amer. Ornithologists' Union 1983), is that the species was unknown to science until Audubon found it, and is the only species of bird that first became known to ornithologists by its discovery in Arkansas. In commemoration of this event, a modern painting of the Willow Flycatcher by David Plank was chosen for the frontispiece of this book.

Audubon named the bird after a British gentleman whom he met in 1826 when he was in England arranging for the publication of his illustrations of American birds (Ford 1967). He wrote, "I have named this species after my learned friend Dr. Thomas Stewart Traill of Liverpool, in evidence of the gratitude which I cherish towards that benevolent gentleman for all his kind attentions to me" (1828, *Ornith. Biogr.*). Dr. Traill was a Scottish naturalist and professor at the University of Edinburgh and an editor of the Encyclopedia Britannica (Coues 1882).

Audubon said he collected his Traill's Flycatchers on April 17th and that the female had partly formed eggs (Audubon 1831, *Ornith. Biogr.*). This is puzzling because the date is well before the earliest migration arrival date in Arkansas ever reported since then for this summer resident species, besides being late enough in the season to show indications of nesting and egg laying. There seems no satisfactory solution to this discrepancy.

Thomas Nuttall (1786–1859) was also one of the first naturalists to visit Arkansas. In 1819 he traveled down the Mississippi River, following the Arkansas River up to Fort Smith and beyond. Although Nuttall was also an ornithologist, on that trip his botanical interests took precedence and his journal, published in 1821, contains only a few references to birds. His manual of ornithology published in 1832 similarly mentions very few birds from Arkansas.

Other observers of local avian life in the state who made expeditions during the first half of the nineteenth century included Arfwedson (1834), Featherstonhaugh (1835, 1844), Hidreth (1842), Lawrie (1844), and Mollhausen (1858, also see Kennerly 1859). What these travelers, including Audubon and Nuttall, all reported in common was that they often saw the now extinct Carolina Parakeet (McKinley and James 1984).

During the last half of the nineteenth century a smattering of articles on Arkansas birds involving short notes on bird distribution and habits appeared in a variety of journals including *Forest and Stream*, the *Oologist*, the *Auk* (published by the American Ornithologists' Union), and the *American Naturalist*. C. E. Pleas and his wife of Clinton, Arkansas, and D. B. Wier of Crockett's Bluff were the most prolific writers of this period. For the first time people residing in the state were reporting on its avifauna. Professor Francis LeRoy Harvey, another Arkansas resident writing about local birds, became the first chairman of the Biology Department at the University of Arkansas in Fayetteville (Reynolds and Thomas 1910). He stayed in Arkansas from 1875 to 1885 where he enjoyed a distinguished career in botany. He was also the first observer to submit bird records to Professor Wells W. Cooke (Howell 1911) for Cooke's series of articles on bird migration beginning in the late 1800s and extending into the early 1900s. Professor Harvey was later joined by a few other observers in the state, including Mr. Pleas, who submitted information to Professor Cooke (Howell 1911). Deaderick (1941) provides added details concerning this interesting early period of Arkansas ornithology.

One of Cooke's observers deserving special mention is Louise M. Stephenson of Helena, Arkansas, who was truly the "mother" of Arkansas ornithology (Deaderick 1940a, 1941). She held the longest tenure among Cooke's observers, from 1894 until her death in 1916, and was the second Arkansas member of the American Ornithologists' Union. She initiated the legislative act that became, on March 15, 1897, the first comprehensive law protecting nongame birds and their eggs in Arkansas. She campaigned to establish a Bird Day in the public schools, a proposal successfully enacted in 1897. Furthermore, she wrote regular articles on birds for the Helena *World*. Deaderick (1941) described her as "Arkansas' first resident ornithologist, who outranked all who preceded her and most of those who followed."

Consolidation Period

The complete history of ornithology as it applies to Arkansas is contained in the bibliography of this book. In summary, Arkansas ornithology may be divided into three periods: 1) the period of early exploration and discovery in the nineteenth century, 2) the period of consolidation and exposition in the first half of the twentieth century, and 3) a time of greatly increased activity and rapidly expanding knowledge since approximately 1950. Of course, these categories are not sharply divided. Thus, due to an ever increasing interest in birds, the realm of discovery is still thriving and new information is being consolidated.

Because of their significant contributions in compiling information on birds throughout the state, it will be of interest to provide brief profiles of three persons who previously published books about Arkansas birds, all of whom, incidentally, were members of one of the oldest scientific societies in North America, the American Ornithologists' Union. These authors provided important summaries of ornithological knowledge in Arkansas in the first half of the twentieth century.

Arthur H. Howell (1872–1940) was born and raised in New York state, and was a biologist in federal employment throughout his professional career, stationed in Washington, D.C. (Schantz 1940). He was with the former U.S. Biological Survey when he conducted his brief field study of Arkansas birds in 1910, then returned to his office to incorporate his findings into a collected body.

Howell's *Birds of Arkansas* was subsequently

FIGURE 2-1 Arthur H. Howell, author of the first monograph entitled *Birds of Arkansas*, published in 1911. *Photograph courtesy of the Library of Congress*

published in 1911 and marked the beginning of the period of consolidation and exposition. His book was the first attempt to describe the avifauna of the entire state and incorporated all of the material available at the time. This included accumulated literature, collected specimens, and field notes from his own studies supplemented by those submitted by others. Howell provided a carefully detailed account of his "sources of information," which in fact covered the complete history of Arkansas ornithology, but occupied only two pages of text! The brevity with which he could dispose of this subject at that early date indicates how little attention the Arkansas region had received during its initial period of avian discovery. Howell's work on his Arkansas bird book was associated with the need for collecting information within the state as part of a larger project involving the mapping of biological life zones along the Mississippi Valley for the U.S. Biological Survey. He wrote that "no detailed study of the avifauna of the state has hitherto been made and very little in its animal life has been published" (Howell 1911). The frontispiece of his book illustrated for the first time the life zones of Arkansas. The author of two other state bird books, the *Birds of Alabama* and *Florida Bird Life,* Howell's career in ornithology and mammalogy was very distinguished.

Harry E. Wheeler (1874–1958), originally from Alabama, attended Lehigh University as a science major, transferred after two years to Southwestern University at Clarksville, Tennessee, and then entered the theological division of Vanderbilt University and ultimately became a Methodist minister (Harris 1958, Abbott 1973). He apparently came to Arkansas around 1910 (Anderson 1935). He served in several Arkansas cities and thus was able to observe birds in a wide area. He also assembled an impressive egg collection. These factors, together with notes contributed by a few other observers, provided the data on Arkansas birds subsequently offered in his book.

Possibly because of his activities with Methodist Sunday schools and his role as one of the earliest U.S. scoutmasters, Wheeler was stimulated to write *The Birds of Arkansas,* which he viewed largely as an educational enterprise to provide information about birds to teachers and students, and also to enhance general interest

FIGURE 2-2 Harry E. Wheeler in clerical attire, probably during his late twenties. He wrote the second monograph on birds in Arkansas, published in 1924. *Photograph courtesy of Robert D. Wheeler*

in the appreciation of birds, to promote their protection, and to encourage the study needed to complete the knowledge of birds in the state (Wheeler 1924). Wheeler wrote that he had "kept definitely in mind the needs of the amateur student" and that the book was "planned as a reference book for public schools, to answer questions most commonly asked, and to furnish some material for class study." As a result, the book contained many illustrations intended for use in bird identification plus general avian life-history information obtained from outside sources. This second summary of Arkansas birds, published in 1924, appeared thirteen years after the Howell study. Wheeler provided details only about the birds that nested in Arkansas, but included a total list of species for the state. The new information and emphasis on nesting birds reflected his avid interest in egg collecting, and his collection is now in the University of Arkansas museum. He also used bird records by a few new observers. It is not well recognized that Wheeler's book contains a "Bibliography of Arkansas Birds" with annotations prepared by Arthur H. Howell. This was the first exhaustive avian bibliography for the state and included citations from the 1800s to approximately 1923.

Wheeler's ministerial career came to a close at the time he finished *The Birds of Arkansas* since he soon withdrew from the church (Anderson 1935). He took a position with the Field Museum in Chicago, 1924–1925, then became curator-in-charge of the Alabama Museum of Natural History at Tuscaloosa, 1925–1928, and subsequently held other museum and related positions (Abbott 1973). In Alabama he distinguished himself as a conchologist (Abbott 1973) and continued his interest in birds (Imhof 1962:x, 586).

William J. Baerg (1885–1980) was born and raised in Kansas, where he graduated from the University of Kansas before earning a doctoral degree from Cornell University (Warren 1980). His entire professional career was spent at the University of Arkansas where he was the head of the Department of Entomology for thirty-three years, from his arrival in 1918 until his retirement in 1951. Baerg's publications were mainly concerned with economic entomology and arachnology but included thirteen titles in ornithology. The studies he made concerning tarantulas are well known (Peck 1981). His in-

terest in natural history, his increasing interest in bird life, and his concern for the importance of birds in consuming noxious insects led him to develop a course in ornithology taught in the Department of Entomology for more than twenty years, from the mid-1920s to the late 1940s (James 1980). However, it was the Dean of Education who asked Baerg to instruct teachers during a summer school session that provided the stimulus for the course, first taught in 1925 (Baerg 1984; E. Baerg-King, pers. comm.). Baerg eventually produced two editions of a manual for the class (Baerg 1937, 1941), and this instruction quite possibly stimulated his desire to write a new *Birds of Arkansas*. Published in 1931, this third summary of Arkansas bird life was designed "to give such information on the birds of Arkansas as will be useful to teachers of nature study, students of birds, and everybody else interested in birds." It followed Wheeler's effort by seven years. Baerg was able to build on the foundations provided by Howell and Wheeler, and also took advantage of an expanding literature and information compiled from an increased number of observers around the state.

Demand for the book persisted when its original edition was exhausted. This encouraged Baerg to write a revised second edition twenty years later (Baerg 1951), which included a number of birds that had been added to the state list in the interim. The economic importance of birds was highlighted in both versions but the author always maintained that "from an aesthetic viewpoint birds may be even more important" (Baerg 1931).

Cordiality between Baerg and Wheeler was diminished by Baerg's enthusiasm for the conservation of birds which Wheeler's zest for egg collecting seemed to counter. In fact, it is said that Wheeler once denounced the university professor from the pulpit over this issue.

Meanwhile, between Baerg's two editions, William H. Deaderick, a physician at Hot Springs, Arkansas, published in 1940 an important and comprehensive annotated bibliography of writings on Arkansas ornithology inclusive through the 1930s. The bibliography contained in the present book, *Arkansas Birds*, includes everything written through the 1970s, plus selected titles into 1986, and is the first complete listing since Deaderick's work.

FIGURE 2-3 William J. Baerg, author of the third monograph dealing with birds in Arkansas, published in 1931 and revised in 1951. *Photograph courtesy of Eloise Baerg-King*

Expanding Knowledge

Knowledge of birds in Arkansas has been further enhanced during the present century by several individuals whose active interests in ornithology have resulted in diverse publications. Two who were active before the middle of the present century were Albert Lano and John D. Black.

Albert Lano, a pharmacist from Minnesota, moved to Arkansas in 1912 (Deaderick 1941, *Daily Democrat,* Fayetteville, Arkansas, 5 July 1928). Though blind in later life, Lano nevertheless continued his longtime interest in birds, prepared a modest collection of bird skins, and published six short papers between 1913 and 1927 about birds found in the state. He often joined field trips, and both William J. Baerg and John D. Black (Deaderick 1941) have said that Lano was extremely gifted in identifying birds by their sounds. He even participated in the first Christmas Bird Count at Fayetteville in 1920 (Bates et al. 1921), which was the third such count ever conducted in Arkansas. Lano and his group repeated the count yearly through 1925.

John D. Black, raised in the Ozarks at Winslow, published seventeen papers on birds in Arkansas between 1922 and 1935 prior to earning his bachelor's degree at the University of Kansas. Between obtaining a master's degree at the University of Indiana and a doctoral degree at the University of Michigan, he taught in the Department of Zoology at the University of Arkansas, Fayetteville, during the 1937–1938 academic year. Black's professional career led from his first writings in ornithology to later publications on fishes, amphibians, reptiles, and mammals, and two books on conservation. He enjoyed a 25-year teaching career at Northeastern Missouri State University in Kirksville, where he now resides in retirement.

Ornithological efforts undertaken by Ruth H. Thomas and Ben B. Coffey, Jr., were significant in bridging the first and second halves of the 1900s. They each published papers and represented a break from the former specimen-collecting approach to bird study. Both were bird banders.

Ruth Thomas (1900–1973) pursued a form of bird study represented by patient backyard observation of avian habits often based on recognizing banded individuals (Anon. 1973). She published nine papers between 1941 and 1952, including the first comprehensive life history of the Eastern Bluebird (Thomas 1946c). She was a friend of Margaret Morse Nice, an internationally known ornithologist, and published in collaboration with her (Nice and Thomas 1948) a paper based on data obtained when Nice visited Arkansas. However, Nice's description of her Arkansas journey (Nice 1948) mistakenly places the site where she saw a Red-cockaded Woodpecker as being northwest of Little Rock, rather than in its correct location 15 or 20 miles to the south at a place where the species is still present (James et al. 1981). Referring to Nice and Amelia R. Laskey of Nashville, Tennessee, Thomas once reported to Douglas James that there was a special tie felt among the three women in a field that was then dominated by men. (All three were members of the American Ornithologists' Union.)

For forty years, between 1933 and 1973, Thomas wrote a Sunday column on nature and natural history for the *Arkansas Gazette*. "The Country Diarist" commonly contained interesting information derived from observations of birds in her own yard, birds that nested or fed there, or birds she had banded. This weekly article became a focal point for people in the state who were devotees of nature, natural history, and bird life. It often contained news of events in Arkansas that was of general interest to avid bird watchers and backyard birders alike, and frequently took tough stands on important conservation issues. "The Country Diarist" thus generated an interest that ultimately resulted in the formation of the Arkansas Audubon Society. As this statewide interest in birds was aroused it promoted the creation of other local bird and nature organizations. Thomas participated in the formation of the Arkansas Audubon Society (Armstrong 1975) and frequently boosted the organization in her column. Without this stimulus, the proliferation of bird information would probably have been much delayed.

Ben Coffey epitomizes the tireless field investigator in his extensive and intensive travels through Arkansas and the mid-south section of the United States. As a result of salient observations documenting distributional patterns of birds in the region, Coffey published seventeen papers between 1938 and 1964 about Arkan-

sas birds. He also organized Christmas Bird Counts in the state, and edited and issued a newsletter entitled "Mid-South Bird Notes" from 1952 to 1956, covering a multi-state area including Arkansas (Coffey 1981). He now resides in Memphis, retired from a professional career as a fire protection engineer, but remains active in ornithological pursuits.

The most prolific writer on Arkansas birds is M. Brooke Meanley. He was a representative of the U.S. Fish and Wildlife Service investigating the blackbird situation in the rice growing area of the Grand Prairie region from the early 1950s to the early 1960s. From 1951 to 1976 he authored over two dozen titles directly or indirectly concerned with bird life in the state. These papers dealt with bird distribution, breeding ecology, population levels, and related subjects, and consequently provided a grand beginning to the surge in ornithological knowledge that has occurred since mid-century.

In 1950, when Howard Young joined the Department of Zoology in Fayetteville, he became the first person hired by the University of Arkansas as an ornithologist. He arrived just as William Baerg was about to retire. Young first taught ornithology in the zoology curriculum during the spring of 1951, marking the transfer of the course from the Department of Entomology. Douglas James arrived in 1953 after Young's resignation and has continued to teach the course to the present. (Subsequently a course in ornithology has been taught at five different institutions in the state.)

Another center of ornithological studies was organized by Earl L. Hanebrink at the Arkansas State University at Jonesboro in the mid-1960s. He and his students have produced numerous papers that have contributed much to the knowledge of birds in northeastern Arkansas.

Arnold J. Hoiberg's studies on breeding and winter bird populations in the mid-1950s should also be mentioned (see bibliography). They deserve recognition not only because his studies are the most extensive censuses of this kind ever conducted in Arkansas, but because they stimulated two school students in El Dorado to continue the effort. Herman Henry Shugart, Jr., and Phillip W. Mattocks, Jr., not only conducted their own censuses but then compiled a distributional list of the birds of south central Arkansas (Mattocks and Shugart

FIGURE 2-4 Douglas A. James (left), and Joseph C. Neal (right), authors of the present book. *Robert M. Lowe, Jr.*

1962) and later embarked on professional careers in biology.

Henry N. and Edith M. Halberg have for many years observed birds in the Little Rock and Grand Prairie areas of central Arkansas, and Mrs. Halberg was curator of the bird files for several years. Besides editing the newsletter for the Audubon group in central Arkansas, Mr. Halberg spearheaded the establishment of the Arkansas Audubon Society Trust founded on October 28, 1972. The trust is an organization independent from the Arkansas Audubon Society and has used its funds over the years to award small grants, many of which have supported important studies on Arkansas birds.

William M. Shepherd, Jr., has been a longtime contributor from central Arkansas, and ever since his association began with the Arkansas Natural Heritage Commission he has been very helpful in providing information on the distribution of special bird species in the state. Thomas L. Foti has been helpful in this regard also. Others who have been active in central Arkansas include Gary R. Graves, especially for shorebirds on the Grand Prairie; William P. and Vivian B. Scarlett; Virginia G. Springer (the last two being very adept at finding nests); Ross L. and Atha S. Jamison; and Iola Rea.

During her lifetime, M. Ruth Armstrong contributed many bird records from the Fort Smith area, and B. W. (Bill) Beall has been active there too and was curator for a brief time of the state bird files. H. H. Shugart and Luvois Shugart have been mainstays in submitting reports from south central Arkansas and have been especially interested in investigating the distribution of Red-cockaded Woodpeckers in southern Arkansas. Jimmie Brown (Mrs. W. Milton Brown), Carl R. Amason, Josephine Hanna, Dorabelle Purifoy, and, in their youth, Herman Henry Shugart, Jr., and Phillip W. Mattocks, Jr., have all been helpful in the El Dorado area. Arnold J. Hoiberg made his field notes available for the years he was there in the 1950s.

In the western part of southern Arkansas, Sterling S. Lacy has sent reports from the Magnolia area, as has Charles L. Gardner from the Texarkana region. Many records from the western Ouachita Mountains came from Aileen Mc-Williams. Jane E. Stern coordinated activities in the Pine Bluff area, and Irving T. Beach and Mr. and Mrs. Thomas H. Wilson sent reports from the Clarksville area in the Arkansas River Valley. Earl L. Hanebrink has been the organizer of records originating from northeastern Arkansas.

Reports from Charles Mills at Millwood Lake in southwestern Arkansas have added immeasurably to the knowledge of water birds in the state. Mills was curator of the bird files for the Arkansas Audubon Society during several years prior to 1983. The tireless efforts of Max D. and Helen L. Parker have produced a wealth of reports from the Arkadelphia area. Parker acted as state coordinator for the annual Breeding Bird Survey in Arkansas for many years. (Douglas James was the first coordinator when the routes were originally established in 1967, and continued to 1972.)

Christmas Bird Counts

Because data from the Christmas Bird Counts are used extensively in this book, it is of interest to trace the history of these counts in the state. The first count in Arkansas was taken at Monticello on December 26, 1910 (Cavaness 1911), ten years after the counts were begun in New York City. That first count at Monticello recorded 19 species and 165 individual birds. The single observer was afield between 1 p.m. and 3 p.m. The second Arkansas count was conducted on December 20, 1917, at Dewitt, by Alexander Wetmore (Wetmore 1918), who later became the dean of American ornithology. Between 8 a.m. and noon he found 40 species, comprising 1463 individuals, mostly Rusty Blackbirds and Mallards. The third Arkansas count was at Fayetteville, December 29, 1920 (Bates et al. 1921), and is the oldest count that is still in existence today, although it has not been conducted continuously since 1920. Some 23 species and 247 individual birds were found between 12:30 p.m. and 4:30 p.m. Other counts still existing today that had early initial dates are, in order of date: Texarkana, 1924 (Boyce 1925), the fourth state count, Little Rock, 1930 (Baugh et al. 1931), and White River National Wildlife Refuge, 1939 (Miller and Ax 1940). After Texarkana, the fifth count in the state was at Rush in 1928 (McKnight 1929). (Rush is now an abandoned mining town within the boundaries of the Buffalo National River in the Ozarks.) The sixth count was at Mammoth Spring in 1929 (Coffey 1930), marking the threshold of Ben Coffey's long career in Arkansas ornithology. From these beginnings in the 1920s the number has progressively increased until now there are approximately twenty counts conducted around the state each winter, usually at locations where they have been repeated for many years in succession.

Chapter 3

ARKANSAS BIRDS AND THE ENVIRONMENT

Birds are distributed in the landscape according to their ecological requirements. To find these appropriate conditions birds seek characteristic vegetational habitats, which are determined by climate and terrain. Physiographic features of a region are determined by the interaction of geologic structure, soil types, climate, vegetation, land forms, and exposure. Despite the inland location, modest state boundaries, and limited topographic relief, the Arkansas climate still exhibits a fifty-day difference in the growing season from northwestern to southern parts of the state. Yet the climate is uniform enough to permit growth of deciduous forest all over the state. Geologically, however, Arkansas is very diverse. Thus, physiographic variation plays an important role in determining the nature of vegetational patterns and land use practices that affect avian ecology. This chapter will discuss the climate in Arkansas, and more fully explore the geographic terrain, habitat types, and associated avian community ecology.

Climate

The Arkansas climate is rather mild, having long warm summers with periodic heat waves, and short cool winters with some very cold weather, particularly in the northwest. Rainfall shows a pronounced spring maximum and smaller peak in early fall, particularly in the northwest, and less so in the southeast but still averaging around three or more inches each month in most places, climbing to five and six inches at some localities, although hot weather in late summer and early fall often produces droughty conditions. The ample rainfall and long mild growing season create conditions that favor the growth of woodland, particularly a broad-leafed deciduous forest. These general climatic conditions have important implications for birds in Arkansas. Because of the forest-favoring climate, bird life across the state originally included mainly woodland species with open country birds in the scattered prairie areas, but as people have progressively cleared the forest, particularly in the eastern lowlands (Holder 1970), open country birds have become more abundant. Insectivorous land birds predominate in the long growing season but granivorous species are characteristic in winter. Many insect eating birds have to migrate south from Arkansas during cold weather or substitute other forms of food such as seeds. The mild winters in Arkansas encourage overwintering of several species that usually nest to the north. Many birds simply use Arkansas as a temporary hospitable stopover during north and south migration.

Average annual temperature is just below 60°F

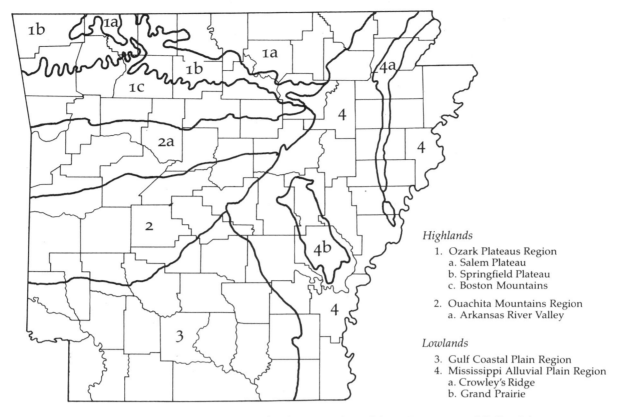

FIGURE 3-1 Map of the physiographic regions of Arkansas (adapted from Foti 1974 and Pell 1983).

Highlands
1. Ozark Plateaus Region
   a. Salem Plateau
   b. Springfield Plateau
   c. Boston Mountains

2. Ouachita Mountains Region
   a. Arkansas River Valley

Lowlands
3. Gulf Coastal Plain Region
4. Mississippi Alluvial Plain Region
   a. Crowley's Ridge
   b. Grand Prairie

in the north and around 65°F in the south, with July temperatures averaging in the high 70's along the northern border and low 80's over the rest of the state. January averages fall around 36°F in the north and to 46°F in the south. In summer the western uplands (Ozark Plateaus and Ouachita Mountains) are cooler than the rest of the state and interrupt the north to south temperature zonation, but there is little topographic effect in winter. Maximum temperatures can exceed 100°F anywhere in the state during summer heat waves. In the northwestern tier of counties, winter extremes often drop below 0°F, but across the southern third of the state winter lows average between 10°F and 15°F. The growing season between killing frosts averages 180 days in the northwestern corner of Arkansas, 200 days in the northeastern corner, and around 230 days in the southern tier of counties.

In some regards, average daily maximum and minimum temperatures are more informative than overall averages. In summer, July maximum* temperatures average from the mid-80's (°F) to the low 90's in the Ozark highlands of northwestern Arkansas and in the low 90's over most of the rest of the state. Southwestern Arkansas and the Arkansas River Valley, averaging over 94°F, have the highest July temperatures in the state. Minimum July temperatures average from the mid- to high 60's in the northern and western triangle of the state occupied by the Ozark and Ouachita highlands (Figure 3-1) to the low 70's in the lowland plains of eastern and southern Arkansas and the Arkansas River Valley. In winter, January maximum temperatures average in the high 40's across the northern quarter of the state, increasing evenly southward to the high 50's along the southern boundary. Minimum January averages range

*Maximum temperatures are usually, but not always, reached in the daytime, and minimum temperatures are usually nighttime occurrences.

from below freezing (mid-20's) in the north to above freezing (mid-30's) in the south.

Annual precipitation is around 50 inches per year throughout eastern Arkansas, in the central Boston Mountains of the southern Ozarks, and across the Ouachita Mountains. Most of northwestern Arkansas receives precipitation averaging from a low to high 40-inch range, as does the southwestern corner of the state. Precipitation is predominantly in the form of rain, but snowfall is regular and sometimes heavy in the Ozarks. In southern Arkansas snowfall is light and not common. Ice storms are regular occurrences in winter throughout the state. Precipitation in southwestern Polk County, where the geologically southern boundary of the Arkansas Ouachitas crosses into Oklahoma, has averaged over 60 inches a year in certain decades.

Storms in Arkansas significantly affect the birdlife. Winter storms accompanied by snow and ice followed by prolonged freezing temperatures occur periodically in northern Arkansas, especially in the Ozarks, and often adversely affect wintering insectivorous birds. The Carolina Wren population often drops dramatically after such severe winter weather. Similarly, prolonged cold and rainy weather in the spring is associated with massive failures in the early nesting of birds such as the Blue Jay, Northern Mockingbird, and American Robin. The passage of cold fronts and simultaneous arrival of adverse northern winds during spring migration, especially in May, are often marked by the massive grounding of overhead migrants. These fronts are particularly effective when they pass at night, the time when most birds migrate. Grounded migrants await more favorable weather to continue their northward progress, but in the meantime the halted parade of various species proves a delight to bird watchers. Another effect of storms upon Arkansas birdlife results when waning hurricanes move inland to the state from the Gulf Coast. Winds sometimes transport sea birds such as the Magnificent Frigatebird, Sooty Tern, and Black Skimmer northward to Arkansas from the Gulf of Mexico region.*

*Climate information for Arkansas was taken from *Climate and Man, the 1941 Yearbook of Agriculture*. U.S. Department of Agriculture; and "Climates of the States: Arkansas" by R. O. Reinhold, published in 1969 in *Climatography of the*

Physiographic Regions

Arkansas is roughly square in overall shape, and a diagonal running between the upper right to lower left corner separates the state into two major geographic divisions (Figure 3-1). The highlands in the northwestern triangle, and the lowlands in the southeastern half are themselves comprised of two physiographic regions. The lowlands include the Mississippi Alluvial Plain extending from the northern to the southern state boundaries in eastern Arkansas, and the Gulf Coastal Plain occupying the south central and southwestern parts of the state. Crowley's Ridge (Figure 3-1), a narrow finger of raised land projecting southward through the northern half of the eastern lowlands, is a subdivision of the Mississippi Alluvial Plain. The Grand Prairie (Figure 3-1) is another subdivision. Centrally located, it was originally named for its treeless character in the heavily forested lowlands.

Whereas the lowlands are flat or rolling with mostly deep alluvial soils or unconsolidated sandy or gravelly substrates, rocky outcrops are commonplace in the highlands, and the local relief is rugged, with soils frequently thin. The Ozark Plateaus region occupies the northern part of the highlands, extending from the western boundary nearly across the state. The Ouachita Mountains comprise the remaining highlands extending from central Arkansas to the western border. The Arkansas River Valley (also called Arkoma Basin) is between the Ozarks and the Ouachitas, but because the valley is structurally more similar to the Ouachitas than the Ozarks, it has been considered a subdivision of that physiographic region. (The Ouachitas and Ozarks, often collectively called the Interior Highlands, represent the only extensive "mountainous" topography at the Arkansas latitude between the Appalachian Mountains to the east and Rocky Mountains to the west.)

The surface of the Mississippi Alluvial Plain across the lowlands of eastern Arkansas is mainly composed of recent alluvial and older terrace deposits. The higher terraces are former bottomlands of the Pleistocene age (Cenozoic era), and lower levels are more recent alluvial

United States No. 60-3 by the U.S. Department of Commerce, ESSA, Environmental Data Service.

deposits formed along major waterways such as the Mississippi, St. Francis, Cache, Black, White, and Arkansas rivers. The region has the lowest overall elevation (under 250 feet) and by far the most level terrain due to recent erosion by major rivers.

The dominating effect of river activity has given the Mississippi Alluvial Plain a deep alluvial soil with both coarse sand and fine silt, thus varying in permeability from fast to slow. Low wetlands once characterized the area, namely various types of swamps and other bottomland deciduous forests. Eventually many of the wetlands were drained and forests removed to permit development of agricultural lands which have become the most intensively farmed areas in Arkansas. By 1970 only 20 percent of the original forested area still remained (Holder 1970). Where forest birds once predominated, open country species associated with agriculture now favor the area. Much wetland remains, but less than before, in the form of forested swamps. Instead there are open marshes, oxbow lakes, and reservoirs used in agriculture, particularly in rice growing. The region thus attracts more water birds than any other part of the state.

Crowley's Ridge is a prominent raised upland, jutting about 150 miles southward in Arkansas through the northern half of the Mississippi Alluvial Plain (Figure 3-1). It represents an old divide between the Mississippi and Ohio rivers in the geological past when the Mississippi flowed west of the ridge, and the Ohio east of it. They joined near present-day Helena, where the terminus of the ridge now exists. Subsequently, the Mississippi was rerouted into the Ohio drainage in the vicinity of southern Illinois, but the old divide still remains. It varies from an average of about three miles wide and 100 to 150 feet above the adjacent flatlands along the southern half, to around ten miles wide and a maximum of 250 feet in elevation above the surrounding terrain in the northern half. The deep soil is composed mainly of wind-deposited Pleistocene silts having moderate permeability, capping subsurface beds of Pliocene age. Crowley's Ridge has been less intensively cleared for agriculture than surrounding parts of the Mississippi Alluvial Plain. The St. Francis National Forest is located in the southern portion. Upland oaks and hickory forests

are characterized on better soil by the unique presence of the Tuliptree (*Liriodendron tulipifera*), and are joined by Shortleaf Pine (*Pinus echinata*) at sandy sites. Overgrown clearings and the forest edge attract some breeding birds that are unusual in eastern Arkansas, such as the Whip-poor-will, Prairie Warbler and Rufous-sided Towhee.

In contrast, the Grand Prairie subdivision, a treeless expanse in the center of the Mississippi Alluvial Plain (Figure 3-1), continues to exist in this form. Vegetation was formerly dominated by tall grass prairie, although trees did occur in wet depressions and along drainages (Foti 1971). The lack of trees was apparently due to hostile conditions produced by an impervious subsoil layer composed of dense clay, commonly called "hardpan." The soil remains too saturated for tree roots in spring, and becomes too desiccated for trees in the late summer months. These conditions once favored prairie grasses, but today few prairie patches remain (Foti 1971). The land has been developed for rice, a commercially important grass agriculture. When the prairie existed, Greater Prairie-Chickens were abundant, but have now disappeared. The Willow Flycatcher was common where small trees dotted the prairie, having been first discovered for science there by John James Audubon. It too may now be gone.

The Gulf Coastal Plain division occupies most of southern Arkansas except the southeasternmost corner (Figure 3-1). It consists mostly of Cenozoic deposits, mainly Eocene but also Pleistocene in age, with a variety of Cretaceous beds in the northwestern sector. The topography is low and rolling, composed primarily of poorly consolidated sand and clay, with recent alluvium along the southerly flowing waterways that cross the region. The lowest elevation in Arkansas (54 feet above mean sea level) occurs where the Ouachita River leaves the Gulf Coastal Plain and flows into Louisiana.

The soils are well drained, deep sandy or silty clay loams, which support extensive forests. The region is still well forested with mixed stands of various hardwoods and pines on the elevated areas (both Loblolly, *Pinus taeda*, and Shortleaf Pines) tending toward mixed bottomland hardwoods along the major rivers. The forests of the Gulf Coastal Plain are a valuable resource intensively managed for pine production by the forest products industry. This selection for pine species has produced a habitat where pineland birds such as the Pine Warbler and Brown-headed Nuthatch reach their greatest abundance, and in certain circumstances, even the rare and endangered Red-cockaded Woodpecker is favored (James and Burnside 1979a, 1979b).

The fine calcareous particles weathered from Cretaceous chalks and marls have produced tight blackland prairie soils along the northern rim of the western part of the Gulf Coastal Plain and account for scattered prairie areas there. Much cleared agricultural land also exists in the Gulf Coastal Plain.

The two divisions of the highlands, although similar in geological age, are structurally quite different. The Ozark Plateaus or Ozark Dome is just that, a raised dome eroded into a series of three plateaus. The bedrock strata are essentially horizontal, and drainage patterns are not determined by inherent geological structure. Instead, Ozark streams radiate in all directions showing the pattern characteristic of such eroded lands.

The highest Ozark plateau, known as the Boston Mountains (Figure 3-1), is also the youngest in geological age (Pennsylvanian period of the Paleozoic era). Elevation generally ranges between 1500 and 2300 feet. Much of the region is over 2000 feet, with some higher points, such as in the headwaters of the Buffalo River in southwestern Newton County, that reaches 2578 feet. Because it is the youngest geologically, and therefore lies atop the older strata buried beneath, this plateau has long been exposed to erosional forces, and is thus relatively small in area compared to the entire Ozark region (including adjoining states) and has the most rugged topography. The Boston Mountains lie at the southern rim of the Ozark Plateaus, extending from east to west just north of the Arkansas River Valley. Sandstone and shale of the Atoka Formation dominate the surface geology of the range, and the derived soils are sandy and clay loams, medium in texture, usually well-drained, and frequently shallow in nature. The Boston Mountains are still extensively forested with upland oak-hickory forests, including a mixture of Shortleaf Pines on the dry sandy south-facing slopes extending from the divide into the Arkansas River Valley. The

Ozark National Forest encompasses approximately one million acres mostly in the Boston Mountains. The whole region is rich in woodland birds, particularly nesting warbler species. Birds with more northern affinities, such as the Whip-poor-will, Ovenbird, and Scarlet Tanager, nest at the higher elevations.

The level below the Boston Mountains is the Springfield Plateau, a geologic band crossing the Ozarks to the north, and including all of the northwestern corner of the state (Figure 3-1). It varies from approximately 1000 to 1500 feet or higher in elevation and appears very flat in profile. Surface geology is composed mainly of chert and limestone of the Boone Formation (Mississippian period of the Paleozoic), and particularly on slopes where erosion can be severe, soil is very thin and strewn with a rocky rubble preventing agriculture. Extensive upland oak-hickory forests thus prevail in areas having rolling terrain, but where there are broad flat uplands agriculture is well developed. Some of these uplands originally had tall grass prairie vegetation, possibly because of tight, poorly drained soil formed from the fine particles produced from weathering chert and limestone. The earliest descriptions of habitats in northwestern Arkansas (Owen 1858, and Lesquereux 1860) mention extensive prairie areas scattered across the northwestern tier of the state, but only a few small, isolated prairie acreages exist in the region today.

The Salem Plateau forms the lowest level of the Ozarks, exhibiting elevations from about 500 feet to under 1000 feet. It lies north and mainly east of the Springfield Plateau (Figure 3-1). Surface geology is formed by the oldest rocks of the Ozark Plateaus (Ordovician age of the Paleozoic), largely dolomites and primarily Cotter dolomite. Like the Springfield Plateau, it is very level in profile, rolling in places, and supports a mixture of upland oak-hickory forests and agriculture.

The upland oak-hickory forests of both the Springfield and Salem plateaus generally lack pines except on the persistent escarpment of the Boone Formation. Wherever the edge of the Boone slopes down from the Springfield Plateau to meet the Salem Plateau, the physiography and geology combine to form a steep rocky rubble substratum with meager dry topsoil. These conditions apparently cause hardwoods to struggle and enable pines to compete successfully. Therefore, Shortleaf Pines are mixed with the oaks and hickories on the Boone escarpment or "fall line" where it occurs, which is in the vicinity of the White River near Beaver Lake and Eureka Springs in northwestern Arkansas and again further east where the White River returns to the Arkansas Ozarks, including the lower end of the Buffalo River. Where dolomitic bedrock lies close to the surface, soils are thin and conditions are xeric. This encourages the formation of extensive cedar "glades," or forests of Eastern Redcedar (*Juniperous virginiana*), a species favoring dry limestone sites. Upland tall grass prairie patches also occur on these thin soil areas.

The Ouachita Mountains form the rest of the interior highlands (Figure 3-1). Unlike the Ozarks, the Ouachitas have undergone extensive folding and faulting of the earth's crust. Therefore, the exposed layers of bedrock are usually steeply tilted, not horizontal as in the Ozark region of plateau uplift. The northern half of the Ouachita Mountains contains the same Atoka rocks (Paleozoic and Pennsylvanian, composed of sandstone and shale) that characterize the Boston Mountains. Older rocks exist to the south with Ordovician strata forming the core of the Ouachitas flanked by surface rocks of Silurian, Devonian, Mississippian and Pennsylvanian periods, but still consisting mainly of shales and sandstones.

The mountain forming process in the Ouachitas produced a series of directional folds evident today in the east-west ridges that cross the region. The drainage pattern is therefore very regular with major streams flowing mostly from west to east between the ridges. This physiographic pattern produces an extremely diverse landscape of repeated slopes, valleys, and ridgetops. The ridges are narrow and long compared to the Ozarks, and much less high country is above 2000 feet. Nevertheless, the highest points are in the Ouachitas: Magazine Mountain, at 2753 feet elevation, the highest point in Arkansas; Rich Mountain, 2681 feet; and Blue Mountain, 2623 feet high in the western Fourche Mountain region. The east-west coursing ridges produce different microclimates on the northern and southern slopes. The south-facing slopes are exposed to summer sun and hot dry summer winds that prevail from the southwest. The desiccating summer condi-

tions apparently help pines compete well with hardwoods. Thus, south-facing slopes are covered with mixed oak-hickory-pine forests from the valley floor well up the slopes and often to the summits. (As in the Ozarks, only the Shortleaf Pine occurs naturally in the Ouachitas.) In contrast, the north-facing slopes, shielded from summer sun and wind, have a moist climate conducive to the growth of oaks, hickories, and other hardwoods, and pines are often absent. Valley floors along stream beds support mixed hardwood bottomland forest. This diversity in forest communities over short distances produces a correspondingly rich avifauna. The Ouachitas are still heavily forested, and lumbering is a major industry. The Ouachita National Forest occupies over 1.5 million acres in Arkansas and southeastern Oklahoma.

The Arkansas River Valley is a major physiographic subdivision of the Ouachita mountain region (Figure 3-1). Geologically it is called the Arkoma Basin and contains the youngest Paleozoic rocks in the state. This wide depression along the northern limits of the Ouachitas is a structural basin extending from Fort Smith to Searcy, Arkansas. The river flows eastward through the valley until it turns southward between Conway and Little Rock. The east to west coursing low ridges and small valleys produced by folding and faulting are similar to the structure of the higher Ouachitas. Some high structures, such as Magazine Mountain, Mount Nebo, and Petit Jean Mountain, lie in the valley. The Arkansas River Valley was once heavily forested with upland oaks and hickory, including Shortleaf Pine in the eastern part, and bottomland hardwood trees, especially along the Arkansas River, but extensive tall grass prairie areas occurred in the western part near Fort Smith. The whole valley is now extensively cleared for agriculture although some upland forest remains on major ridges and prominences, and many prairie remnants persist. Because of this early clearing and occurrence of former prairies, the Arkansas River Valley has provided a route for open country birds of western affinities to enter the state, such as the Greater Roadrunner and Scissortailed Flycatcher.*

*Information concerning the physiographic regions of Arkansas was taken mainly from Thomas L. Foti, 1974, "Natural Divisions of Arkansas," pp. 11–34, in: *Arkansas Natural Area Plan*, Ark. Dept. of Planning, Little Rock; also

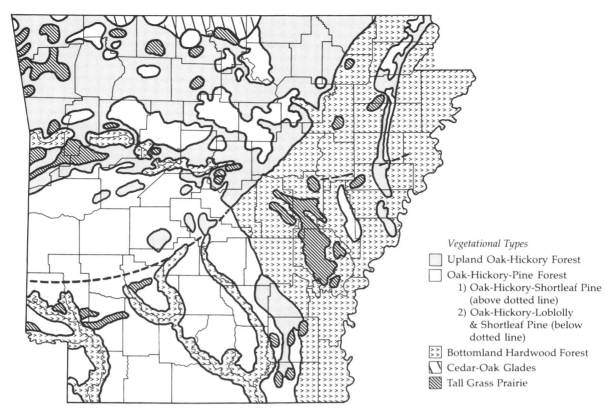

FIGURE 3-2 Map of the original vegetation of Arkansas (compiled from various sources: Allred and Mitchell 1955, Foti 1974, Kuchler 1964, Arkansas State Game and Fish Commission 1948, and Arkansas Forestry Commission).

Vegetational Types

☐ Upland Oak-Hickory Forest

☐ Oak-Hickory-Pine Forest
   1) Oak-Hickory-Shortleaf Pine (above dotted line)
   2) Oak-Hickory-Loblolly & Shortleaf Pine (below dotted line)

⟩⟩ Bottomland Hardwood Forest

\ Cedar-Oak Glades

▨ Tall Grass Prairie

Vegetational Habitats

Because bird species seek certain vegetational habitats, the nature of available environments is important in affecting the distribution of birds. Due to climatic characteristics, Arkansas was primarily forested with deciduous trees when European settlers arrived, and many regions are still heavily wooded in this manner. A map of the state's original vegetational patterns (Figure 3-2) reflects various types of forest regions. Forest stands in the Ozark Plateaus and Arkan-

sas River Valley are mainly upland hardwood trees dominated by various species of oaks and hickories (Figures 3-3 and 3-4). The apparent climax type on superior moist soils is White Oak (*Quercus alba*) in association with other oaks and various hickories. In the northern Ozarks, Black Oak (*Q. velutina*) is an important codominant, with Northern Red Oak (*Q. rubra*) prevailing at the highest elevations, and Southern Red Oak (*Q. falcata*) becoming important southward and at lower elevations. Depending upon the quality of the site, Black Hickory (*Carya texana*), Mockernut Hickory (*C. tomentosa*), Shagbark Hickory (*C. ovata*), and Bitternut Hickory (*C. cordiformis*) can comprise the hickory component of this forest type. Poorer quality drier soils support oak-hickory associations consisting of Black Oak, Post Oak (*Q. stellata*), Blackjack Oak (*Q. marilandica*) and Black Hickory, tree species that can survive in drier, less fertile sites. These

from George T. Clark, "A Preliminary Ecological Study of Crowley's Ridge," pp. 213–241 in the same publication; Nevin M. Fenneman, 1938, *Physiography of Eastern United States,* McGraw-Hill; Walter L. Manger, 1983, "The Geologic Provinces of Arkansas," *Ark. Naturalist* 1(7):1–6, and "Landsat Imagery of Arkansas," *Ark. Naturalist* 1(10):5–8, 13; John A. Sealander, 1979, *A Guide to Arkansas Mammals,* River Road Press, Conway, Ark.; plus various other sources including geological and topographic maps.

FIGURE 3-3 Oak-hickory upland forest—Ozark Plateaus (overview). *D. James*

FIGURE 3-4 Oak-hickory upland forest—Ozark Plateaus (interior). *D. James*

FIGURE 3-5 Beech-maple cove forest (interior). *Neil Compton*

conditions are especially common on southern and southwestern-facing slopes that receive the full force of hot sunshine and intercept desiccating southerly winds in summertime. Winged elm (*Ulmus alata*) is frequently found in the younger stands of this forest type.

Although the oak-hickory forest formation has its center of distribution in the Ozark Plateaus region and can be considered as the climax vegetation there, a remnant of the eastern moist forest exists in protected cool damp north-facing ravines (Figure 3-5). This is the cove forest characterized by the presence of Carolina Beech (*Fagus grandifolia*) and to some

extent Sugar Maple (*Acer saccharum*), which includes elements of the eastern mixed mesophytic forest from the Appalachian Mountains. This forest, left behind in the Ozarks in the protective cove environment, is thought to be a relic from the geological past when conditions were cooler and moister, and eastern forests spread westward.

The driest Ozark forests contain conifers such as the Shortleaf Pine (*Pinus echinata*), Eastern Redcedar (*Juniperus virginiana*) and some Ashe Juniper (*J. ashei*). Thus, Shortleaf Pine is abundant in the dry oak-hickory stands on the sandy south-facing slopes of the Boston Mountains ex-

FIGURE 3-6 Cedar glade. *D. James*

tending into the eastern lowlands of the Arkansas River Valley. In the northern Ozarks, however, pines are usually absent except on the thin rock-strewn soils of the Boone Formation escarpment where the Springfield Plateau meets the Salem Plateau. Cedar glades, which are dry forests composed mainly of Eastern Redcedar (Figure 3-6), occur primarily on the Salem Plateau where dolomitic limestone bedrock is near the surface, thus producing a thin dry limestone-derived soil (whereas wet limestone substrates in the higher Ozarks support Sugar Maples). Limestone cliffs sometimes support Ashe Juniper.

Shortleaf Pine is a regular constituent of upland hardwood forests covering the Ouachita Mountains (Figures 3-7 and 3-8). The oak-hickory stands occurring there are very similar to those in the Ozarks but characteristically include pine. The long narrow east-west ridges throughout the Ouachitas produce local climatic differences affecting forest composition. The south-facing aspects of these ridges, which in summer receive the dry hot southerly winds and intense sun radiation, have the driest, warmest forest environments. Shortleaf Pines are therefore numerous on the south-facing slopes, extending from the valley floor to ridgetop, or near ridgetop. Conditions on north-facing slopes, which are shielded from the drying effect of wind and sun, are cooler and moister and favor hardwoods. So pines are usually absent in the oak-hickory forests on the north sides of ridges except near the bases of the slopes. Some of the higher Ouachita ridges, such as Rich Mountain and neighboring Black Fork Mountain in northern Polk County, support only dwarf forests with trees stunted as a result of exposure to environmental rigors. Also, the forest atop Magazine Mountain in the Arkansas River Valley consists of trees with noticeably smaller growth form than those at

FIGURE 3-7 Oak-hickory-pine upland forest—Ouachita Mountains (overview). *George Purvis*

FIGURE 3-8 Oak-hickory-pine upland forest—Ouachita Mountains (interior). *J. H. Rettig*

FIGURE 3-9 Gulf Coastal Plain forest (overview). *Bill Pell*

FIGURE 3-10 Red-cockaded Woodpecker habitat—Gulf Coastal Plain (interior). *Levi Davis*

lower elevations and springtime tree leafing is seasonally much delayed there.

The pine element continues in the hardwood forests of the Gulf Coastal Plain (Figures 3-9 and 3-10), not just Shortleaf Pine, but here Loblolly Pine (*Pinus taeda*) is especially abundant. Definitely a pine of the Gulf Coastal Plain, Loblolly extends only a very short distance onto the foothill rocks of the southern rim of the Ouachita Mountains. The best Coastal Plain soils in elevated sites tend to have pure oak-hickory stands including White Oak, Southern Red Oak, sometimes Shumard Oak (*Quercus shumardii*), Shagbark Hickory, Mockernut Hickory, and Bitternut Hickory. The less supe-·rior soils support the Black Oak-hickory-pine forest of the mountains, including, of course, the Loblolly Pine, but also Shumard Oak and Sweetgum (*Liquidambar styraciflua*). The poorest soils support oak-pine forests containing the xeric Post and Blackjack Oaks plus the two pine species. Bottomland forests in the Gulf Coastal Plain are extensions along major rivers from the adjoining Mississippi Alluvial Plain.

The Mississippi Alluvial Plain is dominated by two main types of bottomland hardwood forests (Figures 3-11 and 3-12). The lowest floodplain level, subject to inundation 20 to 40 percent of the time, supports woodlands composed of Water Hickory (*Carya aquatica*) and Overcup Oak (*Quercus lyrata*) in association with other wetland trees such as Sugarberry (*Celtis laevigata*), Water Locust (*Gleditsia aquatica*), Green Ash (*Fraxinus pennsylvanica*), Bald-cypress (*Taxodium distichum*) and Water Tupelo (*Nyssa aquatica*). The higher river terraces, flooded only 10 to 20 percent of the time, are characterized by forests containing Willow Oak (*Quercus phellos*), Nuttall Oak (*Quercus nuttalii*) and Sweetgum, along with species common to the lower bottoms, plus Water Oak (*Quercus nigra*), Pecan (*Carya illinoensis*), Honey Locust (*Gleditsia triacanthos*), Box Elder (*Acer negundo*) and others. The river terrace woodlands are very rich in tree species.

The lowest areas of the Mississippi Alluvial Plain, permanently flooded or nearly so, contain swamp forests composed of Bald Cypress and Water Tupelo (Figure 3-13). The highest elevations in the region, found on Crowley's Ridge (Figure 3-1), have upland oak-hickory forests similar to those of the Ozark and Oua-chita uplands. The sandy sites include Short-leaf Pine; the wetter ones contain Carolina Beech and Tuliptree. White Oak, Northern and Southern Red Oak, and Black Hickory occur at all sites. The only other place where pines are found on the Alluvial Plain are on the river terrace sediments of eastern Monroe and adjoining northwestern Phillips counties (Figure 3-2). The pines there are Loblolly, and it is the only site outside the Gulf Coastal Plain where this species occurs naturally in Arkansas.

Tall grass prairie originally existed in Arkansas in all physiographic divisions of the state (Allred and Mitchell 1955, Eyster-Smith 1983), wherever compact or thin soils produced moisture conditions adversely affecting tree growth. Dominant grasses were Big Bluestem (*Andropogon gerardi*), Indian Grass (*Sorghastrum nutans*), Switchgrass (*Panicum virgatum*) and Little Bluestem (*Andropogon scoparius*). The biggest expanse of original prairie in Arkansas grew on impervious claypan subsoils of the central Mississippi Alluvial Plain, and was called the Grand Prairie (Figures 3-1 and 3-14), once covering around 1000 square miles in most of Prairie and Arkansas counties over a region about 65 miles long and up to 25 miles wide (Foti 1971). A few tree "islands" existed within its precincts. Due to rice agriculture today only a few small patches of this original prairie remain, some of which are under protection. Other smaller prairie areas originally existed north of the Grand Prairie, scattered across northeastern Arkansas.

Prairies on blackland soils produced on Cretaceous limestone bedrock once existed in the northwestern part of the Gulf Coastal Plain in Arkansas. These have all but disappeared. There were additional prairie areas in Ashley, Drew, Bradley, and Cleveland counties in the eastern part of the Coastal Plain. A few small prairies still exist there, one of which is protected (Figure 3-15).

Rather extensive stands of prairie formerly occurred in the western Arkansas River Valley of the Ouachita Mountains division extending eastward mainly south of the Arkansas River to the vicinity of present day Clarksville. Segments of this prairie can still be found, particularly near the Oklahoma border. A few smaller patches of prairie originally existed eastward in the valley running into Faulkner County.

FIGURE 3-11 Bottomland hardwood forest—Mississippi Alluvial Plain (overview). *Bill Shepherd*

FIGURE 3-12 Bottomland hardwood forest—Mississippi Alluvial Plain (interior). *George Purvis*

FIGURE 3-13 Cypress swamp. *George Purvis*

FIGURE 3-14 Grand Prairie. *Larry Higgins*

Expanses of tall grass prairie were common in the northwestern Ozarks when settlers arrived (Owen 1858, 1860; Lesquereux 1860). Smaller prairie areas were distributed across the northern Ozarks to the center of the region of what now comprises Baxter, Marion, and Searcy counties.

In the Ozark and Ouachita interior highlands, the forests bordering rivers (Figure 3-16) have a unique character compared to surrounding upland forests. Riverside sand and gravel bars have pioneer willows (*Salix*), followed by Sycamore (*Platanus occidentalis*) or Eastern Cottonwood (*Populus deltoides*), with the addition of River Birch (*Betula nigra*), Silver Maple (*Acer saccharinum*), American Elm (*Ulmus americana*), Slippery Elm (*Ulmas rubra*), Sweetgum, Green Ash, Pecan, and other trees on the higher river terraces. These species-rich forests on the flat terraces often have a dense understory of Cane (*Arundinaria gigantea*).

Forest clearing and the development of agriculture have greatly modified natural habitats statewide. This process has been especially severe in the Mississippi Alluvial Plain where in 1970 only about 20 percent of the original forest acreage still remained (Holder 1970), and where forest clearing activities have increased significantly since that time. No part of the state has been exempt from this phenomenon. Open agricultural lands, forest clearings caused by timber operations, and the growth of urban areas are all factors now so widespread that they must be considered when addressing the subject of avian habitats within the state. Although forest clearings are designed for rapid return to tree production, management favors a greater predominance of pines than originally occurred in Arkansas. Cleared agricultural lands in the Ozark and Ouachita highlands feature mainly pastures and hayfields, although in the past crops were common too. Row crops and grain-

FIGURE 3-15 Warren Prairie. *Bill Shepherd*

FIGURE 3-16 Riverine forest—Ouachita Mountains. *Fred Burnside*

fields now dominate the Mississippi Alluvial Plain and parts of the Arkansas River Valley. The many new open habitats created favor open country birds often at low population densities, but sometimes attract large numbers of starlings and blackbirds. In the Ozarks, Ouachitas, and Gulf Coastal Plain, forests cleared for timber industry operations have opened large areas especially attractive to open country birds, including the Bachman's Sparrow in the Ouachitas.

A definite advantage to having open country environments is that they provide habitats for a rich avifauna consisting of grassland, shrubland, and forest edge birds. Many of these species are backyard birds that enhance Arkansas towns. Admittedly, extensive tracts of agricultural land have rather meager avifaunas except sometimes in winter when waste grains attract large flocks of blackbirds, sparrows, finches, and other species. On the other hand, fallow farms returning slowly to forest through ecological succession produce overgrown grassy and shrubby fields (Figures 3-17 and 3-19) that attract an abundance of both nesting and wintering birds. Such abandoned farmlands and unmanaged pastures are now especially numerous in the Ozark and Ouachita highlands. The old field succession in Arkansas that progresses on these sites (Shugart 1968, Shugart and James 1973) begins with characteristic herbaceous plants that are soon invaded and dominated by grasses, especially Broom Sedge (*Andropogon virginicus*). Low woody species gradually invade these fields, especially blackberry (*Rubus*), sumac (*Rhus*), and early successional saplings such as Common Persimmon (*Diospyros virginiana*), Sassafras (*Sassafras albidum*), and Winged Elm (*Ulmus alata*). Redcedar too can be an important component of old field succession, and in southern parts of the state pines and Sweetgum are common early trees. Oaks and hickories characterizing the woods of the region slowly become established in the next stage and eventually transform the fields to forest. Various stages in this successional sequence can persist (Shugart and James 1973),

and the return from farm to natural forest in the Ozarks takes around 150 years.

Although trees are uprooted when woods are cleared for farmland, this is not always the case when cutting forests for timber operations. Therefore, on some forest industry lands, succession is greatly accelerated due to the rapid resprouting of woody vegetation plus the planting of pines. Before people were directly involved in land clearing in Arkansas, natural fires and violent windstorms cleared forests. Natural forces still prevail, but human activity has become a more important factor in this regard.*

*Information concerning the vegetational habitats of Arkansas was taken from the following: E. Lucy Braun, 1950, *The Deciduous Forests of Eastern North America*; Thomas L. Foti, 1974, "Natural Divisions of Arkansas," pp. 11–34, in: *Arkansas Natural Area Plan*, Ark. Dept. Planning, Little Rock; also from George T. Clark, "A Preliminary Ecological Study of Crowley's Ridge," pp. 213–241 in the same publication; "Wildlife and Cover Map of Arkansas" prepared in

FIGURE 3-17 Old field. *D. James*

FIGURE 3-18 Cypress swamp at Grassy Lake. *Fred Burnside*

Aquatic Environments

Aquatic environments also provide important habitats for water birds. Before settlement in Arkansas, rivers and streams, associated ox-bow lakes, and flooded bottomland forests

1948 by the Arkansas Game and Fish Commission in cooperation with the U.S. Fish and Wildlife Service; the pertinent citations listed in Edward E. Dale, Jr., 1963, *Literature on the Vegetation of Arkansas,* Ark. Acad. Sci. Proc., v. 17, pp. 40–49; Dwight M. Moore, 1972, *Trees of Arkansas,* Ark. Forestry Comm., Little Rock; plus the sources cited in the text. The terminology for the trees was taken from the Moore publication.

provided the only aquatic habitats. Flooded wetland forests and Cypress swamps (Figure 3-18) were extensive in the Mississippi Alluvial Plain, in the Arkansas River Valley, and along major rivers in the Gulf Coastal Plain. Since then, although many of the natural wetlands have been drained, particularly in the Mississippi Alluvial Plain (Holder 1970), many new aquatic environments have been created. These include small farm ponds all over the state, large deep reservoirs on dammed mountain rivers in the highlands, and agricultural reservoirs mainly associated with rice culture in the

FIGURE 3-19. Old Field. *D. James*

Mississippi Alluvial Plain. The Arkansas Game and Fish Commission has been preeminently active in establishing large wildlife management areas (Ark. Game and Fish Comm. 1979), especially for waterfowl in the lowlands, and has constructed numerous public lakes (Ark. Game and Fish Comm. 1982) for fishing throughout the state. These lakes also attract many water birds. The six national wildlife refuges in Arkansas were especially planned to attract a variety of waterfowl. Federal, state and private fish-raising operations in the state also attract water birds, as do wastewater treatment ponds. Finally, the rivers themselves, without including overflow areas, are frequented by water birds and were a main habitat for ducks, herons, kingfishers, and other water birds before the recent development of new aquatic habitats.

Marsh habitat is rare in Arkansas. Apparently, it was once rather extensive in Big Lake

in northeastern Arkansas (Mississippi County), where this "sunken land" lake formed in association with seismic activity along the New Madrid fault. Marshland disappeared there following waterway channelization developments. An extensive marshland still exists in Grassy Lake in southwestern Arkansas (Hempstead County) where marsh birds such as the Pied-billed Grebe, Least Bittern, Purple Gallinule, Common Moorhen, and American Coot nest. Other small patches of marshland can be found in unmanaged parts of shallow rice reservoirs, fish hatcheries, and farm ponds, and in wet roadside ditches. Faulkner Lake in Pulaski County (central Arkansas), which has open lily pad habitat, supports summering Least Bitterns, King Rails, Purple Gallinules, Common Moorhens, and various herons and egrets.

Two aquatic areas in Arkansas deserve special attention because of the vast numbers of waterfowl, shorebirds, and other water birds attracted during migration and in winter. The area that has been studied longest is at Lonoke in the Grand Prairie where large private and state fish-raising ponds and rice water reservoirs have long existed. In fact, the whole Grand Prairie region, including surrounding forested wetlands, has proved so attractive to wintering waterfowl that it provides a focal point for the nation's overwintering Mallard population. The other area is Millwood Lake in southwestern Arkansas, a rather recent impoundment resulting from dam building activities by the U.S. Army Corps of Engineers. Most of the Corps' reservoirs in Arkansas are located in the mountainous highlands, thus inundating deep mountain valleys and attracting a few deepwater seeking birds such as the Common Loon, Horned Grebe, Common Goldeneye, Bufflehead, and Red-breasted and Common Mergansers. Millwood Lake on the other hand is a broad shallow body of water situated on the Gulf Coastal Plain. Apparently the aquatic habitat is ideal, and its position on migratory routes between the northern wetlands and Gulf Coast area is perfect, since the variety of water birds attracted is spectacular, including many rarities for the state, such as three species of jaegers, Glaucous and Sabine's Gulls, and Red Phalarope, to name a few.

Forest Bird Populations

Since most of Arkansas was originally forested, forest land birds constitute the basic avifauna of the state, so it is appropriate to analyze their populations in various Arkansas regions. In each area studied, upland and bottomland forest bird communities are treated separately and analyzed in both nesting and winter seasons (Tables 3-1, 3-2, 3-3, and 3-4). Study sites were located in northwestern, northeastern, central, and southern Arkansas. Bird populations were censused using techniques recommended by the National Audubon Society for conducting the *Breeding Bird Censuses* and *Winter Bird Population Studies* (Anon. 1950, Hall 1964, Kolb 1965), which are based on the spot mapping or Williams' (1936) method.

The upland area studied in northwestern Arkansas was located in the Boston Mountains

TABLE 3-1

Breeding bird populations in upland forests of Arkansas

Bird species	Number of birds per 100 acres			
	NW Ark.	NE Ark.	Cent. Ark.	South Ark.
Ovenbird	33	—	—	—
Cerulean Warbler	13	—	—	—
Northern Parula	8	—	—	—
Scarlet Tanager	2	—	—	—
Whip-poor-will	2	—	—	—
Rufous-sided Towhee	—	17	—	—
Northern Bobwhite	—	3	—	—
Great Horned Owl	—	1	—	—
Worm-eating Warbler	4	—	+	—
Brown Thrasher	—	—	+	—
Hairy Woodpecker	—	—	+	—
Chuck-will's-widow	—	30	4	—
Hooded Warbler	8	—	—	2
Red-eyed Vireo	32	1	7	35
Tufted Titmouse	5	11	16	20
Carolina Chickadee	4	7	5	10
Blue-gray Gnatcatcher	2	1	2	6
Wood Thrush	2	1	+	6
Yellow-billed Cuckoo	3	5	6	4
Downy Woodpecker	2	5	3	3
Acadian Flycatcher	11	—	1	16
Yellow-throated Vireo	4	—	3	7
Black-and-white Warbler	10	—	5	+
White-breasted Nuthatch	2	—	+	+
Northern Cardinal	—	23	3	23
Carolina Wren	+	10	2	18
Kentucky Warbler	—	1	4	16
Blue Jay	—	8	8	10
Eastern Wood-Pewee	—	11	2	10
Summer Tanager	—	10	3	9
Great Crested Flycatcher	—	7	5	4
Brown-headed Cowbird	+	8	4	+
Red-bellied Woodpecker	—	5	+	+
Pine Warbler	—	—	1	19
Mourning Dove	—	17	—	+
Northern Flicker	—	1	—	+
Pileated Woodpecker	2	—	1	+
Northern Mockingbird	—	—	—	+
American Robin	—	—	—	+
Red-shouldered Hawk	—	—	—	+
Chipping Sparrow	—	—	—	3
Indigo Bunting	—	—	—	3
Yellow-breasted Chat	—	—	—	3
Common Yellowthroat	—	—	—	2
Yellow-throated Warbler	—	—	—	2
Prairie Warbler	—	—	—	2
White-eyed Vireo	—	—	—	2
Brown-headed Nuthatch	—	—	—	2
Ruby-throated Hummingbird	—	—	—	2
Louisiana Waterthrush	—	—	—	1
Eastern Bluebird	—	—	—	1
TOTAL PER 100 ACRES	149	183	85	241
NUMBER OF SPECIES	21	22	26	39

+ indicates species present but less than 1 per 100 acres, not included in total population figure.

TABLE 3-2
Winter bird populations in upland forests of Arkansas

Bird species	Number of birds per 100 acres			
	NW Ark.	NE Ark.	Cent. Ark.	South Ark.
Eastern Screech-Owl	—	+	—	—
American Woodcock	—	+	—	—
Mourning Dove	—	3	—	—
Great Horned Owl	—	+	+	—
Pileated Woodpecker	2	2	+	—
Northern Bobwhite	—	12	+	—
White-breasted Nuthatch	3	—	1	—
Loggerhead Shrike	—	+	—	+
American Crow	—	2	—	+
Dark-eyed Junco	—	3	—	22
White-throated Sparrow	—	+	—	15
American Goldfinch	—	+	—	10
Ruby-crowned Kinglet	—	2	—	8
Northern Cardinal	—	3	—	3
Eastern Bluebird	—	3	—	1
Hairy Woodpecker	4	2	+	+
Tufted Titmouse	3	7	20	11
Carolina Wren	4	7	3	10
Carolina Chickadee	4	12	11	8
Golden-crowned Kinglet	1	3	11	6
Downy Woodpecker	6	5	6	4
Red-bellied Woodpecker	1	2	5	2
Northern Flicker	3	2	2	2
Blue Jay	—	10	7	8
American Robin	—	3	1	3
Yellow-rumped Warbler	+	—	+	6
Brown Creeper	1	—	2	2
Pine Warbler	—	—	1	9
Purple Finch	—	—	+	1
Hermit Thrush	1	—	2	2
Barred Owl	+	—	—	+
Winter Wren	1	—	—	2
Yellow-bellied Sapsucker	1	+	—	1
Song Sparrow	—	—	—	+
Rufous-sided Towhee	—	—	—	+
Red-shouldered Hawk	—	—	—	+
Brown-headed Nuthatch	—	—	—	8
Cedar Waxwing	—	—	—	3
Field Sparrow	—	—	—	2
Common Grackle	—	—	—	1
TOTAL PER 100 ACRES	35	83	72	150
NUMBER OF SPECIES	16	25	19	33

+ indicates species present but less than 1 per 100 acres, not included in total population figure.

in the Ozark National Forest at an approximate 1800 foot elevation just a few miles north of Cass in Franklin County. Findings are the previously unpublished results of seven censuses from December 14, 1958, to February 17, 1959, and nine censuses from March 31 to June 7, 1959, conducted by James. The bottomland site was located near Savoy, Washington County, on the flood plain along the east side of the Illinois River in the Wedington district of the Ozark National Forest. The surveys there, results also previously unpublished, consisted of seven censuses from December 13, 1958, to February 7, 1959, and from April 2 to May 31, 1959, all conducted by James.

The census areas in northeastern Arkansas were located near Jonesboro in Craighead County (Collins 1960). These bird population findings are the results of an unpublished master's thesis by the late Kathryn W. Collins. The upland site was on Crowley's Ridge and the bottomland area was on the lowland level of the Mississippi Alluvial Plain.

Study areas in central Arkansas were forest stands north of Pine Bluff in Jefferson County (James 1955, 1956a, 1956b). They were located on the Gulf Coastal Plain on the west side of the Arkansas River, but adjacent to the Mississippi Alluvial Plain, and also fairly close to the Ouachita Mountains. Bird population results from central Arkansas are from published data (James 1955, 1956a, 1956b) except for the breeding birds of the bottomland forest there, which come from unpublished results of nine censuses conducted by James between April 1 and May 30, 1956.

The upland and bottomland forest areas studied in southern Arkansas were situated in the Gulf Coastal Plain near El Dorado, Union County, in the south central part of the state (Hoiberg 1957b, 1957c, A. J. Hoiberg and J. A. Hoiberg 1957, A. J. Hoiberg and S. Hoiberg 1957). These studies were repeated annually. Consequently, the bird population values used (Tables 3-1, 3-2, 3-3, and 3-4) represent five-year averages for the upland forest and six and seven-year averages for the bottomland forest. All the other population studies in the state were single year efforts. Pines were conspicuous in the upland forests at the central and southern Arkansas sites, and in the bottomland in southern Arkansas, but were absent in the

TABLE 3-3
Breeding bird populations in bottomland forests of Arkansas

Bird species	Number of birds per 100 acres			
	NW Ark.	NE Ark.	Cent. Ark.	South Ark.
Chuck-will's-widow	5	—	—	—
American Crow	5	—	—	—
Mourning Dove	—	3	—	—
Hairy Woodpecker	—	1	—	—
Yellow-crowned Night-Heron	—	1	—	—
Indigo Bunting	2	1	—	—
Kentucky Warbler	2	—	4	26
Common Yellowthroat	5	—	7	4
Brown-headed Cowbird	19	2	4	+
Red-eyed Vireo	19	5	33	78
Carolina Wren	26	8	8	35
Tufted Titmouse	10	11	12	34
Northern Cardinal	36	17	11	29
Acadian Flycatcher	19	5	17	26
American Redstart	19	1	9	16
Carolina Chickadee	5	3	4	14
Prothonotary Warbler	10	+	4	14
Louisiana Waterthrush	5	1	2	14
Blue-gray Gnatcatcher	5	11	2	13
Downy Woodpecker	10	12	2	9
Red-bellied Woodpecker	+	6	2	9
Summer Tanager	—	6	1	12
Blue Jay	—	5	10	11
Eastern Wood-Pewee	—	13	2	9
Pileated Woodpecker	—	3	1	2
Barred Owl	—	1	2	1
Hooded Warbler	—	—	4	23
Wood Thrush	—	—	4	14
Red-shouldered Hawk	—	—	2	2
Ruby-throated Hummingbird	—	—	2	1
Northern Parula	—	—	+	13
Yellow-throated Vireo	—	—	—	13
Great Crested Flycatcher	—	12	—	10
Northern Flicker	—	1	—	1
White-eyed Vireo	—	—	—	18
Yellow-billed Cuckoo	—	—	—	11
Pine Warbler	—	—	—	9
Yellow-throated Warbler	5	—	—	9
White-breasted Nuthatch	—	—	—	5
Black-and-white Warbler	—	—	—	1
Brown-headed Nuthatch	—	—	—	1
TOTAL PER 100 ACRES	207	129	149	487
NUMBER OF SPECIES	19	24	25	35

+ indicates species present but less than 1 per 100 acres, not included in total population figure.

TABLE 3-4
Winter bird populations in bottomland forests of Arkansas

Bird species	Number of birds per 100 acres			
	NW Ark.	NE Ark.	Cent. Ark.	South Ark.
European Starling	—	2	—	—
Mallard	—	2	—	—
Loggerhead Shrike	—	1	—	—
Northern Bobwhite	—	—	10	—
American Goldfinch	24	—	—	18
Red-winged Blackbird	—	22	—	+
Swamp Sparrow	—	+	—	+
Red-headed Woodpecker	—	+	—	+
Common Grackle	—	+	—	140
Rusty Blackbird	—	12	—	44
Mourning Dove	—	+	—	2
Winter Wren	5	1	—	12
Dark-eyed Junco	22	1	—	6
Song Sparrow	1	1	—	4
Hairy Woodpecker	3	5	3	+
White-throated Sparrow	3	12	214	121
Tufted Titmouse	10	18	15	22
Carolina Wren	19	5	16	16
Northern Cardinal	19	15	14	15
Carolina Chickadee	20	8	15	12
Northern Flicker	3	13	5	12
Blue Jay	1	15	28	11
American Robin	1	5	18	11
Red-bellied Woodpecker	6	14	9	11
Ruby-crowned Kinglet	1	+	8	9
Downy Woodpecker	14	12	8	8
Golden-crowned Kinglet	10	2	31	4
Brown Creeper	3	7	6	4
Pileated Woodpecker	1	7	2	3
Eastern Bluebird	2	5	+	3
Rufous-sided Towhee	—	—	17	27
Yellow-rumped Warbler	4	—	3	5
Purple Finch	3	—	2	2
Barred Owl	—	2	2	+
Hermit Thrush	—	2	7	7
Yellow-bellied Sapsucker	—	2	1	5
Fox Sparrow	—	+	7	3
American Crow	—	25	1	1
Red-shouldered Hawk	—	2	1	1
Brown Thrasher	—	—	4	2
Northern Mockingbird	—	—	+	1
Brown-headed Cowbird	—	—	—	+
Eastern Phoebe	—	—	—	+
Cooper's Hawk	—	—	—	+
Wood Duck	—	—	—	+
White-breasted Nuthatch	1	—	—	5
Cedar Waxwing	—	—	—	4
Pine Warbler	—	—	—	3
Brown-headed Nuthatch	—	—	—	3
Red-breasted Nuthatch	—	—	—	1
Field Sparrow	—	—	—	1
TOTAL PER 100 ACRES	176	218	447	559
NUMBER OF SPECIES	23	34	28	47

+ indicates species present but less than 1 per 100 acres, not included in total population figure.

study areas of northwestern and northeastern Arkansas.

The tables of bird populations (Tables 3-1, 3-2, 3-3, and 3-4) are arranged by season, i.e. breeding birds and wintering birds, and by site, i.e. upland as opposed to bottomland. Locations are listed in sequence starting in northwestern Arkansas and progressing to the southern portion of the state. The bird species order is arranged so that birds common to all four areas are listed centrally in the tables, species that are essentially exclusive to the northern part of the state are at the top, and species exclusive to southern Arkansas are listed at the bottom. Species that were observed flying over the study sites, such as vultures and certain hawks, were omitted.

Differences between species occurring seasonally in upland sites around Arkansas (Tables 3-1 and 3-2) are due to the occurrence of summer resident birds in the breeding season that depart upon the arrival of winter resident species. These migrants augment permanent resident birds such as the Downy Woodpecker, Carolina Chickadee, Tufted Titmouse, and Carolina Wren characteristic of all areas in all seasons. The presence of old field and forest edge birds at the upland site in southern Arkansas (Tables 3-1 and 3-2) was due to tree thinning operations and the existence of a small field in the forest study plot (A. J. Hoiberg and J. A. Hoiberg 1953a). These open country species include the Eastern Bluebird, Prairie Warbler, Common Yellowthroat, Yellow-breasted Chat, Rufous-sided Towhee, Indigo Bunting, Chipping Sparrow, Field Sparrow, and Song Sparrow. The influence of pine trees found in the forests of central and southern Arkansas, but not in the northern study areas, was evidenced by the presence of Brown-headed Nuthatches at the southern site and Pine Warblers in both the southern and central areas. Breeding season forest birds with northern affinities were found only in the Boston Mountains of northwestern Arkansas where the upland study site, having by far the highest elevation (around 1800 feet), was located. These species were the Whip-poor-will, Ovenbird, and Scarlet Tanager. Besides common permanent resident birds named previously, the Yellow-billed Cuckoo, Blue-gray Gnatcatcher, and Red-eyed Vireo occurred at all upland forests in Arkansas in sum-

mer. A number of other species were present in summer at three of the upland forest sites from northern to southern Arkansas (Table 3-1). In winter the Red-bellied Woodpecker, Hairy Woodpecker, Northern Flicker, and Golden-crowned Kinglet were present in all upland study plots (Table 3-2), in addition to the Downy Woodpecker, Carolina Chickadee, Tufted Titmouse, and Carolina Wren. The kinglet is the only one that has strictly winter resident status, others being permanent residents, or partially so. On this list, the presence of woodpeckers in the upland forests of Arkansas during winter is conspicuous.

All the bottomland forests of the state were also inhabited throughout the year by the Downy Woodpecker, Carolina Chickadee, Tufted Titmouse, and Carolina Wren (Tables 3-3 and 3-4), but in both summer and winter there were more species that were common to all four bottomland forests than in the upland sites. When comparing upland and bottomland sites in each region by season, the four primary species named above tend to be more abundant in bottomland areas than in corresponding upland ones (Tables 3-1, 3-2, 3-3, and 3-4). The same trend is reflected by comparing population totals of upland and bottomland study areas on both seasons. Seven out of the eight paired comparisons show markedly higher bird numbers in bottomland areas than in upland ones. In winter the number of species was much higher too in the bottomlands of various parts of the state, but in summer these corresponding areas were nearly equal in total species. These findings generally confirm what field observers in Arkansas commonly notice: numbers of birds are rather sparse in upland compared to bottomland forests, especially in winter.

The great scarcity of birds in upland forests in winter is further corroborated by comparing total population levels in winter and summer at each upland study area (Tables 3-1 and 3-2). In each of the four paired comparisons, populations were higher in summer than in winter, and the same holds for three out of the four pairings with respect to total numbers of species. The reverse was true for bottomland forests (Tables 3-3 and 3-4) in which populations usually were higher and more species were present in winter. Remembering that in bottomlands birds are more numerous than in the uplands, a shift to a higher winter population in the bottomlands further accentuates the depleted nature of upland avifaunas in that season.

Comparing forest types within each season across the state shows that total bird populations and total numbers of species were always highest in southern Arkansas (Tables 3-1, 3-2, 3-3, and 3-4). Study areas there may have been the most heterogeneous due to forest thinning practices and the presence of open areas (A. J. Hoiberg and J. A. Hoiberg 1953a, A. J. Hoiberg and S. Hoiberg 1957), and this may account for the increased numbers and diversity of birds. High numbers of birds in the south, declining to low numbers in the north, is a pattern illustrated by bottomland forest areas in winter (Table 3-4). The same gradation is shown with respect to the number of bird species in the breeding season for both upland and bottomland forests (Tables 3-1 and 3-3). This sequence, however, is not clearly evident for either total populations or species in any of the other areas or seasons, primarily due to the low numbers found in central Arkansas.

Synopses of the forest habitat structure of each study area appear in Tables 3-5 and 3-6. The same sampling techniques were used at all sites to insure uniformity. The procedure was introduced in central Arkansas by James (1955), who subsequently used it in the northwest and even visited the Hoiberg areas in southern Arkansas to analyze vegetation there. Collins (1960) used essentially the same procedure in the northeast. In all cases approximately 5 percent of the forest study areas were subjected to vegetational sampling.

Birds and Their Habitats

The preceding material has drawn attention to forest birds because of the extensive woodland that originally covered most of Arkansas. However, subsequent forest clearing has resulted in an increase of areas that attract open country birds. Various degrees of habitat openness develop when pasture and cropland are abandoned and allow a gradual return to forest through intermediate stages starting with open

TABLE 3-5
Vegetational habitats of forest study areas used for upland bird population investigations

| | Study area location | | | |
Vegetational factor	NW Ark.	NE Ark.	Cent. Ark.	South Ark.
DOMINANT TREES *(percent of total number of trees)*				
Shortleaf Pine *(Pinus echinata)*	—	—	15%	7%
Loblolly Pine *(Pinus taeda)*	—	—	15%	72%
Shagbark Hickory *(Carya ovata)*	3%	—	—	—
Mockernut Hickory *(Carya tomentosa)*	—	25%	5%	—
Black Hickory *(Carya texana)*	8%	4%	—	—
White Oak *(Quercus alba)*	33%	30%	7%	—
Post Oak *(Quercus stellata)*	—	19%	15%	7%
Northern Red Oak *(Quercus rubra)*	32%	3%	—	—
Southern Red Oak *(Quercus falcata)*	—	5%	35%	3%
Sweetgum *(Liquidambar styraciflua)*	—	—	—	3%
Red Maple *(Acer rubrum)*	6%	—	—	—
Blackgum *(Nyssa sylvatica)*	4%	5%	—	—
TREE SIZE *(diameter breast high)*				
3 to 6 inches	60%	39%	60%	66%
6 to 9 inches	18%	31%	22%	14%
9 to 12 inches	12%	19%	9%	8%
12 to 15 inches	6%	7%	6%	2%
over 15 inches	4%	4%	3%	10%
Number of trees per acre	272	275	276	237
Tree canopy height *(feet)*				
Range	30–75	85–95	40–75	30–75
Average	51	—	60	48
Forest overstory closure	73%	60%	53%	43%
Forest understory closure	75%	52%	76%	63%
Number of shrub and sapling stems per acre	1655	4212	2941	3269

TABLE 3-6

Vegetational habitats of forest study areas used for bottomland bird population investigations

Vegetational factor	Study area location			
	NW Ark.	NE Ark.	Cent. Ark.	South Ark.
DOMINANT TREES *(percent of total number of trees)*				
Loblolly Pine *(Pinus taeda)*	—	—	—	11%
Bitternut Hickory *(Carya cordiformis)*	—	—	3%	—
Shagbark Hickory *(Carya ovata)*	—	5%	—	—
Mockernut Hickory *(Carya tomentosa)*	—	21%	—	—
American Hornbeam *(Carpinus caroliniana)*	—	—	12%	14%
Carolina Beech *(Fagus grandifolia)*	—	—	—	4%
White Oak *(Quercus alba)*	—	13%	9%	—
Post Oak *(Quercus stellata)*	—	5%	—	—
Overcup Oak *(Quercus lyrata)*	—	11%	—	—
Swamp Chestnut Oak *(Quercus michauxii)*	—	—	—	5%
Black Oak *(Quercus velutina)*	—	4%	—	—
Water Oak *(Quercus nigra)*	—	5%	12%	4%
Willow Oak *(Quercus phellos)*	—	11%	6%	—
American Elm *(Ulmus americana)*	—	3%	—	—
Slippery Elm *(Ulmus fulva)*	28%	—	—	3%
Winged Elm *(Ulmus alata)*	—	13%	—	—
Hackberry *(Celtis occidentalis)*	3%	—	—	—
Sweetbay *(Magnolia virginiana)*	—	—	—	21%
Sweetgum *(Liquidambar styraciflua)*	—	3%	33%	14%
American Sycamore *(Platanus occidentalis)*	9%	—	—	—
Honeylocust *(Gleditsia triacanthos)*	4%	—	—	—
Silver Maple *(Acer saccharinum)*	26%	—	—	—
Boxelder *(Acer negundo)*	13%	—	—	—
Blackgum *(Nyssa sylvatica)*	—	—	7%	9%
Green Ash *(Fraxinus pennsylvanica)*	8%	—	—	—
TREE SIZE *(diameter breast high)*				
3 to 6 inches	53%	37%	48%	42%
6 to 9 inches	27%	23%	21%	21%
9 to 12 inches	13%	18%	16%	16%
12 to 15 inches	5%	11%	7%	10%
over 15 inches	2%	11%	8%	11%
Number of trees per acre	325	321	273	183
Tree canopy height (feet) Range	15–70	55–85	61–96	55–75
Average	44	—	77	65
Forest overstory closure	65%	79%	81%	60%
Forest understory closure	84%	77%	62%	62%
Number of shrub and sapling stems per acre	969	718	1657	3373

weedy grasslands that are subsequently invaded by shrubs and old field trees (Figure 3-17 and 3-19). This process leads eventually to the return of mature forest that characterizes the region, a sequence of change called ecological succession. The ultimate plant community formed is the climax forest of the region. The succession of vegetational communities produces a variety of habitats attracting a particular group of bird species ranging progressively from open country to forest birds. Even within the forest there are subtle differences in the habitats occupied by different species of woodland birds. The following treatment of birds and their habitats in Arkansas will focus on terrestrial birds since they comprise the dominant avifauna in the state, but some attention to various types of non-forest habitats will also be given.

The only detailed study of changes in bird communities during stages of ecological succession in Arkansas was conducted in Benton County in the Ozark highlands, and concerned nesting birds (Shugart 1968, Shugart and James 1973, 1975). The findings of this study (Table 3-7) showed that the earliest stage, consisting of open grassy hayfields still mowed annually and thus still managed for agriculture, were inhabited mainly by Horned Larks, Eastern Meadowlarks, and Grasshopper Sparrows. These grassland birds were sparse or absent in the unmanaged early successional fields dominated by Broom Sedge grass (*Andropogon virginicus*) and invaded by various shrubs, sapling trees, and blackberry(*Rubus*) thickets. Birds that entered this habitat persisted through later progressive growth of tree clumps that gradually shaded out the grasses (persimmon grove and woody field study areas in Table 3-7). Birds that characterized these open old field stages included the Northern Bobwhite, Prairie Warbler, Yellow-breasted Chat, Rufous-sided Towhee and Field Sparrow. The Northern Cardinal was an element in the old fields, but it also occurred in all but one of the field and forest stages, reaching peak numbers in the forest edge habitat. It is joined there by the Blue Jay, Carolina Wren, Blue-gray Gnatcatcher, Northern Mockingbird, Blue-winged Warbler, Black-and-white Warbler, Summer Tanager, and Indigo Bunting among others, including the Northern Bobwhite, Prairie Warbler, Yellow-breasted Chat, Rufous-sided Towhee, and Field Sparrow. Two groups of birds inhabited three forest stages that terminate the successional sequence (Table 3-7). One group was composed of widespread forest birds found in more than one stage (dry, intermediate, and moist forest); the other consisted of specialized species confined to the moist forest. Widespread forest generalists included the Red-bellied Woodpecker, Eastern Wood-Pewee, Great Crested Flycatcher, Blue Jay, Tufted Titmouse, Carolina Chickadee, White-breasted Nuthatch, Carolina Wren, Red-eyed Vireo, Black-and-white Warbler, and Northern Cardinal. Moist forest specialists included the Acadian Flycatcher, Wood Thrush, Northern Parula, Cerulean Warbler, Worm-eating Warbler, Ovenbird, Kentucky Warbler, and American Redstart.

Of course, the successional communities of breeding birds will differ somewhat in other parts of the state compared to northwestern Arkansas, but similarities will be more striking than differences. The successional study by

Shugart and James (1973) confirmed for Arkansas some ecological phenomena that have been shown to exist in other parts of the world: 1) bird populations increase as ecological succession progresses, 2) avian diversity also increases through succession, and 3) if the vegetation in two areas in a region is very similar, then the corresponding bird communities will be similar too, and vice versa. In presenting this analysis (Table 3-7) it needs to be emphasized that the burned field, cedar glade, and to some extent forest edge habitats are not regular components in the direct path of ecological succession in the Ozarks (Shugart and James 1973), but the other habitats shown listed in successional sequence are in regular progressive stages. Open country stages take around fifty years to pass before terminal forest stages begin to develop (Shugart and James 1973) and full maturation of climax forest can take an additional one hundred years or more.

Although it is meaningful to determine the composition of avian communities occurring in major habitats, an alternative way to distinguish between various avian habitats is to find birds and analyze the vegetation in the vicinity of each individual. Habitat samples can then be grouped by species, analyzed, and compared. Frances C. James used this approach to avian ecology when she studied forty-six common breeding birds at locations across Arkansas (James 1971). For each singing bird encountered she obtained information concerning ten aspects of the vegetation within a tenth-acre circle surrounding the bird. Data obtained were subjected to a multivariate statistical technique called principal components analysis, which identifies important ecological factors. The analysis arranged the birds with respect to the habitat variables (Figure 3-20). Birds on the left end of the horizontal axis are open field birds such as Prairie Warbler, Bell's Vireo, Yellow-breasted Chat, Eastern Kingbird and Field Sparrow. Deep forest species are on the right end of the axis, such as Wood Thrush, Red-eyed Vireo, Black-and-white Warbler, Ovenbird and Acadian Flycatcher. Species near the middle of the axis are shrubby old field and forest edge birds such as the White-eyed Vireo, Northern Cardinal, Brown-headed Cowbird, and Blue-gray Gnatcatcher. Other species lie between these habitat positions. This presentation shows

TABLE 3-7
Ozark bird communities arranged in sequence of ecological succession

Species	Territorial males per 100 acres in study plots									
	HF	BF	BS	PG	WF	CG	FE	DF	IF	MF
Loggerhead Shrike	3	—	—	—	—	—	—	—	—	—
Horned Lark	13	+	—	—	—	—	—	—	—	—
Grasshopper Sparrow	38	19	—	—	—	—	—	—	—	—
Eastern Meadowlark	59	19	6	—	—	—	—	—	—	—
Common Nighthawk	+	+	+	+	+	+	+	+	+	+
Mourning Dove	2	2	+	—	—	—	14	3	+	—
Northern Bobwhite	2	6	13	9	25	13	29	—	2	—
Northern Harrier	—	+	—	—	—	—	—	—	—	—
Ruby-throated Hummingbird	—	+	—	—	—	—	—	—	—	—
Northern Mockingbird	—	6	—	—	—	—	14	—	—	—
Eastern Bluebird	—	6	—	—	13	—	—	—	—	—
Bell's Vireo	—	6	2	—	—	—	—	—	—	—
Northern Oriole	—	2	—	6	—	—	—	—	—	—
Dickcissel	—	21	—	—	+	—	—	—	—	—
American Crow	—	+	—	—	+	—	—	—	+	—
Brown Thrasher	—	6	—	3	25	—	—	—	—	—
American Goldfinch	—	6	—	13	25	—	—	—	—	—
Northern Flicker	—	2	—	—	6	—	—	2	6	—
Eastern Kingbird	—	6	6	6	+	—	—	—	—	—
Yellow-breasted Chat	—	6	6	13	50	25	7	—	—	—
Rufous-sided Towhee	—	6	12	19	25	—	57	6	—	—
Field Sparrow	—	19	44	69	50	25	21	—	—	—
Northern Cardinal	—	9	6	9	25	25	61	29	41	29
Common Barn-Owl	—	—	+	—	—	—	—	—	—	—
Prairie Warbler	—	—	22	28	—	18	21	—	—	—
Blue Grosbeak	—	—	—	3	—	—	—	—	—	—
Painted Bunting	—	—	—	3	—	—	—	—	—	—
Blue-winged Warbler	—	—	—	6	—	—	14	—	—	—
Indigo Bunting	—	—	—	3	+	+	25	14	—	—
Yellow-billed Cuckoo	—	—	—	+	—	—	—	—	—	—
Blue Jay	—	—	—	9	12	—	14	—	13	14
American Robin	—	—	—	—	25	—	—	—	—	—
Red-winged Blackbird	—	—	—	—	+	—	—	—	—	—
Wild Turkey	—	—	—	—	+	—	—	—	+	—
Greater Roadrunner	—	—	—	—	—	+	—	—	+	—
Eastern Wood-Pewee	—	—	—	—	—	25	—	—	9	7
Red-bellied Woodpecker	—	—	—	—	—	6	—	7	6	4
Carolina Chickadee	—	—	—	—	—	25	—	8	28	14
Tufted Titmouse	—	—	—	—	—	25	—	12	38	29
Blue-gray Gnatcatcher	—	—	—	—	—	13	14	8	9	43
Summer Tanager	—	—	—	—	—	—	14	4	9	—
Great Horned Owl	—	—	—	—	—	—	+	+	+	+
Chuck-will's-widow	—	—	—	—	—	—	+	+	+	+
Carolina Wren	—	—	—	—	—	—	14	—	6	7
Black-and-white Warbler	—	—	—	—	—	—	14	6	14	29
Hairy Woodpecker	—	—	—	—	—	—	—	4	—	—
Great Crested Flycatcher	—	—	—	—	—	—	—	4	—	7

Species	Territorial males per 100 acres in study plots									
	HF	BF	BS	PG	WF	CG	FE	DF	IF	MF
Red-eyed Vireo	—	—	—	—	—	—	—	4	—	50
White-breasted Nuthatch	—	—	—	—	—	—	—	4	9	4
Red-tailed Hawk	—	—	—	—	—	—	—	—	+	—
Downy Woodpecker	—	—	—	—	—	—	—	—	6	—
Pileated Woodpecker	—	—	—	—	—	—	—	—	—	+
Acadian Flycatcher	—	—	—	—	—	—	—	—	—	14
Gray Catbird	—	—	—	—	—	—	—	—	—	7
Wood Thrush	—	—	—	—	—	—	—	—	—	7
White-eyed Vireo	—	—	—	—	—	—	—	—	—	14
Worm-eating Warbler	—	—	—	—	—	—	—	—	—	14
Northern Parula	—	—	—	—	—	—	—	—	—	14
Cerulean Warbler	—	—	—	—	—	—	—	—	—	14
Ovenbird	—	—	—	—	—	—	—	—	—	14
Kentucky Warbler	—	—	—	—	—	—	—	—	—	14
American Redstart	—	—	—	—	—	—	—	—	—	14
Scarlet Tanager	—	—	—	—	—	—	—	—	—	7
TOTAL NUMBER OF SPECIES	7	22	12	17	18	13	18	18	22	27
TOTAL MALES PER 100 ACRES	117	147	115	199	281	200	333	115	196	370
DIVERSITY INDEX (Shannon formula)	1.19	2.59	1.85	2.21	2.26	2.24	2.52	2.44	2.33	2.91
PLOT SIZE (acres)	16	16	16	16	4	4	7	24	16	7

After Shugart and James 1973, 1975. Numerals indicate territorial males per 100 acres, a plus shows that a bird was present on a plot, but it was not possible to determine actual density per 100 acres. HF indicates mowed hayfield plot; BF, burned field plot; BS, broomsedge field plot; PG, persimmon grove field plot; WF, woody field plot; CG, cedar glade plot; FE, forest edge plot; DF, dry forest plot; IF, intermediate forest plot; MF, moist forest plot.

the average habitat designation for each species rather than grouping a set of species into avian communities by habitat categories. This approach stresses subtle differences in avian habitats. Shugart and James (1973), on the other hand, emphasize associations of species by general habitat categories. For example, in Figure 3-20 it is apparent that the Prairie Warbler is on the average a more open country bird than the Yellow-breasted Chat and Field Sparrow. In the Shugart and James (1973) approach, these birds were all part of the same Broom Sedge old field community. Other comparisons of this type between species along the axes in Figure 3-20 are valid "on the average." There is much overlap between adjacent species when variation within species is considered.

The front to back axis in Figure 3-20 arranges birds mainly with respect to habitat shrubbiness, decreasing in shrubbiness from front to back. A second component in this axis pertains to the number of medium-sized trees, a greater number at the back, and fewer in front. Thus, one finds that the Gray Catbird and Orchard Oriole are both rather open country birds on the first axis (left end of the horizontal axis), but the catbird is found where shrubby thickets occur, and the oriole inhabits areas free from thickets but having scattered trees of medium size. Compare also the White-eyed Vireo and Red-headed Woodpecker, both of which are usually found in moderately open country, the vireo in dense thickets, the woodpecker in open groves of maturing trees. Going to the forest end of the horizontal axis, the Carolina Wren is found in forest thickets, the Wood Thrush in more open forests. An advantage in having the overall presentation or ordination of

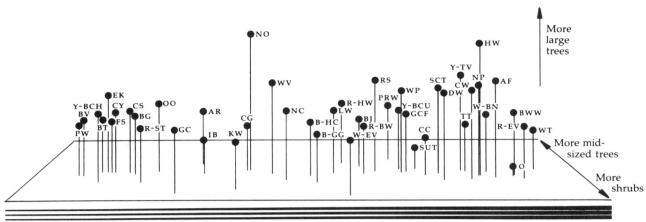

FIGURE 3-20 Habitat relationships of 46 species of Arkansas birds (dots atop lines) arranged left to right from open country birds through shrubland birds to forest birds, from front to back according to decreasing shrub density and increasing number of medium sized trees, and the greater heights of the vertical lines show the increasing presence of large trees (after James 1971). The alphabetic order of bird abbreviations is as follows:

AF	Acadian Flycatcher	FS	Field Sparrow	R-BW	Red-bellied Woodpecker
AR	American Robin	GC	Gray Catbird	R-EV	Red-eyed Vireo
BG	Blue Grosbeak	GCF	Great Crested Flycatcher	R-HW	Red-headed Woodpecker
B-GG	Blue-Gray Gnatcatcher	HW	Hooded Warbler	R-ST	Rufous-sided Towhee
B-HC	Brown-headed Cowbird	IB	Indigo Bunting	SCT	Scarlet Tanager
BJ	Blue Jay	KW	Kentucky Warbler	SUT	Summer Tanager
BT	Brown Thrasher	LW	Louisiana Waterthrush	TT	Tufted Titmouse
BV	Bell's Vireo	NC	Northern Cardinal	W-BN	White-breasted Nuthatch
BWW	Black-and-White Warbler	NO	Northern Oriole	W-EV	White-eyed Vireo
CC	Carolina Chickadee	NP	Northern Parula	WP	Eastern Wood-Pewee
CG	Common Grackle	O	Ovenbird	WT	Wood Thrush
CS	Chipping Sparrow	OO	Orchard Oriole	WV	Warbling Vireo
CW	Carolina Wren	PW	Prairie Warbler	Y-BCH	Yellow-breasted Chat
CY	Common Yellowthroat	PRW	Prothonotary Warbler	Y-BCU	Yellow-billed Cuckoo
DW	Downy Woodpecker	RS	American Redstart	Y-TV	Yellow-throated Vireo
EK	Eastern Kingbird				

species is that one can simultaneously determine their relative habitat characteristics.

The remaining axis in Figure 3-20, the vertical axis or length of the lines below the black circles, pertains to the presence or absence of large trees. Long vertical lines indicate the presence of large trees, short ones their absence. Northern Orioles seem to require larger trees than Kentucky Warblers in the same moderately open habitat. Similarly, in the forest, the Ovenbird is not as dependent upon big trees as is the Hairy Woodpecker. This ordination shows that not only do birds exhibit interesting differences in open country habitats, but the same pertains to forest birds, a situation related to the Shugart and James' (1973) findings in which some birds were specialists in certain types of forests, while others overlapped several forest

habitats. The complicated ordination analysis (which requires computer assistance) also shows that the arrangement of nesting land birds in Arkansas habitats is broadly determined by three relatively simple vegetational relationships: 1) degree of forest vs. open country, 2) development of shrubby thickets contrasted to the presence of medium-sized trees, and 3) the presence or absence of large trees.

The ordination approach to avian habitat analysis (James 1971) was later applied exclusively to old field birds in northwestern Arkansas (Posey 1974) and to Ozark forest birds (Smith 1975, 1977). The Posey study was conducted in the same area as the one by Shugart and James (1973). He measured twelve vegetational factors for seventeen birds nesting in old fields, and based on principal components analysis, birds were arranged in the following order from open country (Eastern Bluebird) to dense shrubland inhabitants (White-eyed Vireo):

1. Eastern Bluebird
2. Eastern Kingbird
3. Eastern Meadowlark
4. Northern Mockingbird
5. Field Sparrow
6. Dickcissel
7. Brown-headed Cowbird
8. Northern Bobwhite
9. Indigo Bunting
10. Brown Thrasher
11. Yellow-breasted Chat
12. Prairie Warbler
13. Northern Cardinal
14. Bell's Vireo
15. Rufous-sided Towhee
16. Common Yellowthroat
17. White-eyed Vireo

This list contains six species not included in the James (1971) ordination, and the two studies show some differences in species sequence (Figure 3-20). Posey's results may be more accurate for old field species because forest habitats were not included in the analysis. Using multiple discriminant analysis, which emphasizes the vegetational factors that best separated the avian habitats, Posey found the ordination of species from open country to dense shrubland differed from the above in some details:

1. Dickcissel
2. Eastern Kingbird
3. Eastern Meadowlark
4. Eastern Bluebird
5. Northern Mockingbird
6. Brown-headed Cowbird
7. Brown Thrasher
8. Field Sparrow
9. Northern Bobwhite
10. Indigo Bunting
11. Northern Cardinal
12. Yellow-breasted Chat
13. Prairie Warbler
14. Rufous-sided Towhee
15. Bell's Vireo
16. Common Yellowthroat
17. White-eyed Vireo

In the species accounts that form the bulk of this book, a brief habitat synopsis is given for many of the birds. These synopses can be used with the ordination information provided in this section to obtain a rather precise comparison between the subtle differences in species' habitats.

Four studies of birds and their habitats have been conducted along the Buffalo National River in the central Ozark Plateaus, mainly in the headwaters country of Newton County where the Boston Mountains meet the Springfield Plateau (Smith, 1975, 1977; Hunter et al. 1979; James et al. 1979, 1980; Rhinehart 1984). This is an area where protected coves harbor moist forests dominated by Carolina Beech (*Fagus grandifolia*), and the exposed dry slopes are covered with forests containing mainly Post Oak (*Quercus stellata*) and Black Hickory (*Carya texana*). Smith (1975, 1977) analyzed summer bird distribution with respect to this moisture difference. Among the eight common forest birds there, he found that none showed a great affinity toward the dry oak-hickory forest and only the Tufted Titmouse used the dry forest very much at all. The Hooded Warbler, Acadian Flycatcher and Ovenbird, in that order, sought the moist forest the most; the Downy Woodpecker, White-breasted Nuthatch and Red-eyed Vireo were the closest to the Tufted Titmouse; and the Blue-gray Gnatcatcher was between these two groups.

Working in Smith's study area, Rhinehart (1984) attempted to ascertain whether or not sizes and abundances of arthropods were associated with the differential usage of forest habitats there. She added an intermediate site dominated by White Oak (*Quercus alba*) to her study of dry Post Oak and moist Carolina Beech forests. She found that although all three areas contained about twenty species of breeding season birds, population levels of birds and the abundance-size index of arthropods were the lowest in the dry forest. On the other hand, the moist forest had the highest numbers of birds, but the intermediate forest contained the highest arthropod abundance-size index. Rhinehart concluded that arthropod distribution was not a strong factor affecting forest bird distribution.

This same relative avoidance of dry forests was substantiated by a study on the Ozarkian

Springfield Plateau in Washington County by Wooten (1982). The dry Post Oak forest there had both lower total bird populations and number of species than a nearby more moist forest dominated by Black Oak (*Quercus velutina*) and White Oak. The Tufted Titmouse was by far the most common species among those that were abundant in both forest types. It was joined by several other birds, including the Downy Woodpecker and Carolina Chickadee, that were also common in both dry and moist forests. The Acadian Flycatcher was confined to the moist forest, as were other species, and several birds trended strongly in that direction, including the Blue-gray Gnatcatcher and Red-eyed Vireo. No bird was confined exclusively to the dry forest, but there were four such species in the moist one.

Returning to the avian ecology of the upper Buffalo River in the Ozarks, the different habitats occurring there were studied for Breeding Bird Populations (Hunter et al. 1979). The three most common species in order of abundance in these primary habitats are as follows:

Old Fields	*Oak-hickory Forest*
Indigo Bunting	Red-eyed Vireo
Field Sparrow	Blue-gray Gnatcatcher
White-eyed Vireo	Tufted Titmouse
Cedar Glades	*Floodplain Forest*
Blue-gray Gnatcatcher	Kentucky Warbler
Tufted Titmouse	Northern Parula
Indigo Bunting	Indigo Bunting
Oak-Pine Forest	*Beech Forest*
Yellow-throated Warbler	Acadian Flycatcher
Common Grackle	Red-eyed Vireo
Blue-gray Gnatcatcher	Ovenbird

Considering all habitats combined, the most common bird in the area was the Indigo Bunting, followed in decreasing order of abundance by the Red-eyed Vireo, Tufted Titmouse and Blue-gray Gnatcatcher. These birds are plentiful throughout Arkansas in summer.

The final study for consideration, conducted at the Buffalo River, was an evaluation of avian community ecology in winter and summer. Using data showing only the presence or absence of 105 bird species in various habitats (James et al. 1979), it was possible to perform analyses that showed how closely related the various habitats were to each other based on their respective avifaunas (James et al. 1980). Several open country environments as well as different forest types were studied. Results showed that in summer the habitats contained more bird species that were confined to one or a few habitats than in winter, whereas in winter more birds used several habitats than in summer. Therefore, habitats were more alike in winter based on their bird communities than in summer. This phenomenon is further emphasized as follows: in winter when only 57 species were found in the area, the average number of species per habitat was 30, whereas in summer when the species per habitat decreased slightly to 25, the total avifauna increased markedly to 83 species. Considering the widespread distribution in Arkansas and elsewhere of the avian species involved, this case of habitat specialization in summer, and the shift to lack of specialization in winter, is probably a common ecological event.

While the presence of certain birds in Arkansas is attributable to accidental circumstances (like the single Lesser Goldfinch that appeared at a feeder in Benton County), most birds are distributed in the state in a relatively predictable manner according to their ecological requirements. The best indicators of these requirements are the habitats where each species is the most abundant. Knowledge of the distribution and abundance of birds in Arkansas is basically an understanding of avian habitat requirements.

Chapter 4
ARKANSAS BIRDS IN PREHISTORY

The first human inhabitants of Arkansas were small migratory bands of hunters and gatherers called Paleo-Indians, who entered Arkansas perhaps as early as 11,500 years before the present (Morse 1982). The land must have abounded with prairie chickens on the grasslands, turkeys in the woods, and flocks of migratory waterfowl in the Mississippi River Valley. Some of the earliest and most reliably dated records of birds associated with people in Arkansas were obtained by John House of the Arkansas Archeological Survey, who directed excavations at the Powell Canal site in Chicot County, a site dated to A.D. 600 (House 1982). In this camp site or seasonal village, bones belonging to four species of birds were identified (Carr 1982). Another very early record linking birds and people in Arkansas was provided by archeologist Dan Morse, who recently stated that the earliest deposits in the Zebree site in Mississippi County have been dated to about A.D. 600–800. These early deposits contain the remains of at least eleven species of birds (pers. comm. 1984).

Time and cultural evolution separate Paleo-Indians from the later inhabitants of Chicot and Mississippi counties. Those who occupied the Powell Canal site, for example, cultivated a few crops to supplement their subsistence. The people occupying the Banks site in Crittenden County became even more accomplished at farming, as the intensive cultivation of maize (corn) brought new economic prosperity to a human society. "It was the gradual shift to substantial dependence on agriculture for food that tied the societies to specific localities, emphasized territoriality and ownership of land, provided a supply of storable food that allowed marked increase in population, permitted specialization of labor, provided markets for the exchange of goods, and led to the development of elaborate religious ceremonies" (Griffin 1967). These societies, making up a cultural complex called "Mississippian," began to form in the fertile river bottoms of the Mississippi River Valley as early as A.D. 700–900, reaching a pinnacle of development by A.D. 1200, and declining rapidly after the arrival of Europeans in the 1500s.

The inhabitants of Powell Canal predated the Mississippian culture, whereas the people of the Banks site probably typified it. Though separate in time and culture, these peoples shared the habit of exploiting wild birds (Figure 4-1). In Arkansas there is abundant evidence of bird bones closely associated with human occupations. More than fifty species of birds have been identified by bones found at middens in Arkansas (Table 4-1). For example, in the Banks site alone more than twenty-six species have been identified (B. D. Smith 1975).

During the Mississippian period, farms, vil-

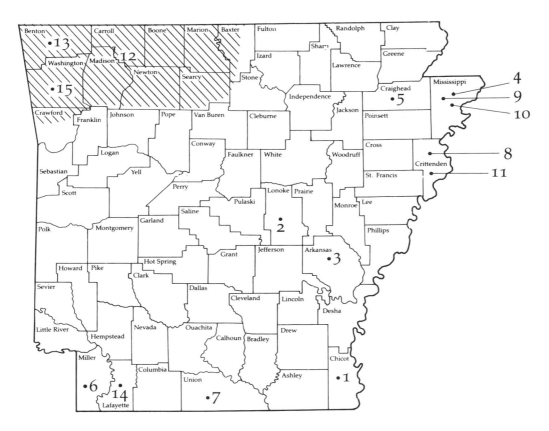

1. Powell Canal *ca. A.D. 600* Carr 1982
2. Toltec *A.D. 500–900* Hoffman 1981, Rolingson 1982
3. Roland Mound *A.D. 500–1000* Butsch 1971
4. Zebree *A.D. 600–1100*
   Roth 1977, Guilday and Parmalee 1971, 1977
5. Lawhorn *A.D. 1100–1400* Parmalee 1962
6. Haley *A.D. 1200–1400* Perino 1967
7. Shallow Lake *ca. A.D. 1300*
   Rolingson and Schambach 1981
8. Banks *A.D. 900–1600* B. D. Smith 1975

9. Knappenberger *A.D. 1400–1600* Bogan 1974
10. Pecan Point *A.D. 1400–1600* Moore 1911
11. Rhodes Place and Bradley Place *A.D. 1400–1600*
    Moore 1911
12. Ozark bluffs *Prehistoric Period*
    Cleland 1965, Thomas 1969
13. Albertson *6600 B.C.–A.D. 1500*
    Hoffman 1983, Sabo et al. 1982
14. Cedar Grove *A.D. 1670–1730* Styles and Purdue 1984
15. Ridge House *Historic Period* Jurney 1978

FIGURE 4-1 Some archeological sites in Arkansas with identified bird bones.

TABLE 4-1
Some Archeological Bird Remains in Arkansas

	Powell Canal	Toltec	Roland Mound	Zebree	Lawhorn	Haley	Shallow Lake	Banks	Knappenberger	Pecan Point	Rhodes & Bradley	Ozark bluffs	Albertson	Ridge House	Cedar Grove
Pied-billed Grebe		*													
Eared Grebe			■												
Double-crested Cormorant			*					*	*						
Great Blue Heron								*							
Great Egret								*							
Tundra Swan								■							
Trumpeter Swan								*							
swan species									■	*	*				*
Snow Goose			*					*	*		*				
Canada Goose		*	*	■		*		*	*	*	*				*
Wood Duck	*	*	*	*				*							
Green-winged Teal			■					*	■						*
Mallard, or American Black Duck	*	*	*	*		*		*	*			*	*		
Northern Pintail			*					*							
Blue-winged Teal			■					*							
Northern Shoveler			■												
Gadwall			*					*							
American Wigeon			*					*							
Canvasback		*													
Redhead			*												
Ring-necked Duck or Lesser Scaup			*	*		*		*							
Greater Scaup			■												
Bufflehead								*							
Hooded Merganser		*	*					*							
Common or Red-breasted Merganser								*							
Turkey Vulture								*				*			
Bald Eagle								*							*
Northern Harrier								*							
Red-tailed Hawk			*					*							
American Kestrel			*												
Peregrine Falcon			■												
hawk species			*									*	*		*

	Powell Canal	Toltec	Roland Mound	Zebree	Lawhorn	Haley	Shallow Lake	Banks	Knappenberger	Pecan Point	Rhodes & Bradley	Ozark bluffs	Albertson	Ridge House	Cedar Grove
Greater Prairie-Chicken				*	▪									*	
Wild Turkey	*	*		*	*		*	*	*	*	*	*	*		*
Northern Bobwhite		*		*									*		
King Rail					*										
American Coot				*				*							
Sandhill Crane				*				*							
Whimbrel				*											
Short-billed Dowitcher				▪											
Passenger Pigeon		*		*						*				*	
Yellow-billed or Black-billed Cuckoo						*									
Barred Owl				*											
Red-headed Woodpecker		*													
Pileated Woodpecker		*													
American Crow				*				*							
Red-eyed Vireo or vireo species						*									
Summer or Scarlet Tanager						*									
Common Grackle				*											
passerines or songbirds	*			*		*							*	*	

Site names are shown at the top of the table. Dates of occupation, location, and bibliographic reference are shown in Figure 4-1. The * indicates the presence of a species in the site; the ▪ or listing of two names indicates difficulty in separating osteologically similar species. Most sites also have unidentified bird bones. Nomenclature and taxonomic order follows the sixth edition of the *Check-list of North American Birds* (American Ornithologists' Union 1983).

lages, and towns were established in the river valley and along the lakes or larger stream bottomlands where there was fertile and easily tilled soil. Recent archeological work in the Ozarks has shown that Mississippian peoples utilized the region's relatively small stream bottoms as well as bluff shelters or rock overhangs (Sabo et al. 1982). These bluff shelters were also occupied in a much earlier time period by people long predating the Mississippians. It is not unreasonable to speculate that archeologists may yet uncover evidences of avian and human life that predate both the Mississippians and the peoples at Powell Canal.

The rise of the Mississippian society draws our attention to the relationship between birds and people that showed the development of an extraordinary culture. This was expressed artistically through the production of objects made from clay, copper, shell, and other materials reflecting considerable knowledge about birds as well as skill in crafts.

The meat from larger birds, especially turkeys and waterfowl, was a ready source of protein, and feathers played a functional role in both clothing and as quills on arrow shafts. Images of birds were depicted on pottery, engraved on shell, and used in other artistic ways. The language of the Mississippians included the names of many birds. Their religion and magic were enriched by birds and creatures with highly specific bird-like attributes, including enigmatic bird-man figures.

Speaking in purely functional terms, the bones of waterfowl—especially the Mallard, Wood Duck, and several species of geese—plus bones of the Wild Turkey and Passenger Pigeon, have been identified with enough regularity in archeological sites (Table 4-1) to make a convincing case for their importance in the protein base of aboriginal societies in Arkansas. At the Toltec mounds area in Lonoke County, it was estimated that 25 percent of the non-deer animal subsistence was derived from birds (Hoffman 1981). And although species were not identified, bird bones constituted approximately one percent of the total bone material recovered from the Roland mound in Arkansas County (Butsch 1971).

The importance of migratory waterfowl is strongly evident in the Zebree site at Big Lake in Mississippi County. Of 813 bird bone fragments identified there, 585 were those of waterfowl. The greatest number of identifiable bones belonged to Mallards (or American Black Ducks), with 174 fragments (Guilday and Parmalee 1977). Big Lake National Wildlife Refuge still remains an important stopping place for migratory and wintering waterfowl, and visitors to the Big Lake area today can easily see why waterfowl were so important to the prehistoric inhabitants.

In the Ozarks, which had no extensively flooded prairies, marshes, or natural oxbow lakes like those of the eastern and southern lowlands, there was relatively little habitat to attract flocks of migratory waterfowl. As a result, there is a predictable difference in the bird species whose bones are found among human artifacts in archeological sites. A survey of bone fragments recovered from fifty-seven bluff shelters in the Arkansas Ozarks showed that among the total of forty-two species of animal and bird bones represented in the shelter deposits, only those of deer were more abundant than those of Wild Turkey. Mallard bones were also found, but in insignificant quantities. Bones of turkeys were recovered from two-thirds of the shelters surveyed (Cleland 1965). It is evident that in the forested Ozark highlands, turkeys replaced Mallards (and other species of waterfowl) in the Indians' diet.

Bluff shelters in the Ozarks have also provided information concerning the purely functional ways in which Indians used birds. Dry conditions in some of the shelters protected artifacts from total deterioration over long periods of time. Among artifacts found have been feathered robes which were constructed by attaching the soft downy feathers from turkeys onto natural fiber threads (Harrington 1960).

It would be a mistake, however, to view the relationship between birds and people in prehistoric time in purely functional terms: so much meat for the pot, so many feathers for a robe. In this respect, Indian artwork provides us with much information about cultural realities in Arkansas and adjacent areas during Mississippian times.

The turkey's importance is expressed in artistic ways. In the Ozarks, Indians pecked or abraded what appear to be turkey tracks on sandstone outcroppings above streams. These bird petroglyphs, carved or inscribed on rock, have been documented in Johnson and Independence counties (Fritz and Ray 1982). Folk traditions of Indians in the southeastern United States maintain that in certain tribes warriors mimicked the turkey gobble, and that the black, hairlike "beard" of an adult male turkey symbolized a scalp (Hudson 1976). The turkey's influence can also be seen on pottery. Bowls and other ceramic objects with effigies or images of birds have been recovered from Mississippian graves in the lowlands of eastern and southern Arkansas, the Arkansas River Valley, and adjacent Mississippian areas beyond the borders of modern Arkansas. While numerous animals, including people, are the subjects of these effigies, birds are most often depicted. Some pottery designs found at modern day Helena are probably of stylized birds dating as far back as the 200-year period from approximately 0 to 200 A.D. (per. comm. Dan Morse).

In the University of Arkansas museum at Fayetteville there are approximately 115 bird images on ceramic pieces, mainly rim effigy bowls (Table 4-2). Most notable in this collection are waterfowl, including Wood Ducks, geese, and swans; also Wild Turkeys, birds of prey, and forms which combine characters of several birds species. Though so-called "primitive" art is often stylized, many of the bird pictures (as well as those of other animals) are

FIGURE 4-2 Wood Duck effigies often showed the short bill, rounded chest, and eye pattern characteristic of the species. (Univ. Ark. cat. no. 32-74-36 B & C)

TABLE 4-2
Bird effigy pottery in the University of Arkansas museum

Swan: 32-74-79A, 33-4-21B, 33-5-73B

Goose: 32-65-17A

Wood Duck: 29-30-17, 32-5-242B, 32-74-36, 32-80-4, 32-153-1B, 33-3-371B, 47-6-141, 47-6-151, 59-34-9, 59-49-1

Hooded Merganser (?): 47-71-2, 59-45-37

Various stylized forms, possibly Wood Duck or Hooded Merganser: 29-64-2, 30-2-458, 32-5-224A, 32-65-668, 32-70-38, 32-95, 32-101-49C, 32-113-4B, 32-131-35A, 33-3-64D, 33-3-120B, 33-3-207A, 33-4-40A, 33-5-34B, 33-5-46B, 34-65-1, 40-2-434, 47-6-92, 47-6-136, 47-6-102, 55-14-20, 55-14-13, 59-45-19, 59-46-23, 59-46-43, 59-46-82, 59-49-23, 67-266-122

Other waterfowl forms: 27-11-177, 27-20-1, 32-104, 33-4-56B, 47-6-93, 47-6-127, 59-64-26

Vulture: 31-12-19, 32-103-45A, 32-153-2A, 47-6-180, 47-6-255

Raptors with falcon-like facial markings: 32-5-309B, 32-103-20B, 47-21-5, 59-60-56

Grouse, prairie chicken, or bobwhite: 30-1-3, 32-103-71, 59-89-9

Wild Turkey: 32-65-28A, 32-132-28C, 33-3-417C, 33-3-450B, 33-5-30A, 47-6-663, 59-46-94, 59-64-27

Owl, species with "ears" or "horns": 33-3-500A, 33-5-87, 47-6-162

Owl, species without "ears" or "horns": 47-6-64, 59-46-152

Forms with large, split crests, like kingfishers: 32-70-24, 33-5-39B, 33-5-44B, 59-90-6

Woodpecker-like forms: 32-98, 47-57-4, 59-46-98, 59-49-21

General bird forms: 32-5-20A, 32-70-86, 32-74-68C, 32-74-95B, 32-94-24, 32-115, 33-3-464A, 33-4-8B, 47-6-110, 47-6-124, 47-6-135, 47-6-142, 47-6-235, 47-6-377, 47-32, 47-57-2, 59-49-9, 59-60-24, 59-60-54

Forms combining birds and mammals: 32-94-15A, 33-3-7A, 33-3-78A, 33-3-327B, 33-3-1053, 33-4-9B, 33-4-82B, 33-4-101B, 33-5-80C, 47-6-250, 47-9-1, 47-41-1, 59-46-2

The University of Arkansas museum catalogue numbers are given in numerical order. Identification is based upon reasonably apparent "field marks" of birds occurring or known to have occurred in Arkansas.

rendered in careful detail. This is an eloquent testimony to the observational and artistic skills of these artists.

Among the Wood Ducks in the University of Arkansas collection is a literal representation of a bird with a short bill, rounded crest, and an eye pattern (Figure 4-2). A host of imaginative stylizations (Table 4-2) suggest the term "wood duck" might refer to either the Wood Duck or Hooded Merganser, which occur throughout the year in Arkansas and nest in tree cavities in the forested bottomlands and wooded swamps of the state. Based upon faunal evidence recovered from Arkansas sites (Table 4-1), most of these birds may be Wood Ducks.

Swan effigies were especially beautiful. One image was so grandly elegant it is easy to imagine the living bird as it was seen hundreds of years ago during migration or winter on an oxbow lake or large river (Figure 4-3). Other swans have been depicted in a resting position, their long necks extended along the side of the bowl (Figure 4-4).

Examples of gallinaceous (or chicken-like) birds were commonly depicted on Mississippian pottery. The "field marks" evident on several effigy pots in the University of Arkansas museum collection will be as familiar to bird watchers today as they were when Mississippian culture was at a peak.

Turkey effigies often show a stout and roughly conical bill, a lumpiness in the neck, and a protuberance at the base of the upper

FIGURE 4-3 Swans were sometimes depicted in a swimming position.
(Univ. Ark. cat. no. 32-4-21B.)

FIGURE 4-4 This swan appears to be in a resting or sleeping position.
(Univ. Ark. cat. no. 33-5-73B.)

FIGURE 4-5 Mississippian period patterns frequently reflect the Wild Turkey as a subject for artistic reproduction. (Univ. Ark. cat. no. 32-65-28A.)

FIGURE 4-6 The short, broad wings of this effigy bowl suggest that the subject was a Northern Bobwhite. (Univ. Ark. cat. no. 30-1-3.)

FIGURE 4-7 The subject of this effigy bowl may have been a Greater Prairie-Chicken, once a common species on Arkansas grasslands. (Univ. Ark. cat. no. 59-89-9.)

mandible (Figure 4-5). The model for a plump looking bird with short, broad wings (Figure 4-6) may have been a grouse, prairie chicken, or bobwhite. On another effigy pot (Figure 4-7) the wattles above the eyes, a long and carefully crafted tail, and chicken-type bill seem characteristic of a grouse or prairie chicken.

The majority of these effigy bowls were "grave goods," buried with the deceased, and the art associated with them clearly has a religious aspect. The predominance of avian life in the images suggests that birds occupied a high place in Indians' beliefs about the universe, and often figured directly in their creation stories.

Several bowls in the University collection (Figure 4-8) depict a bird with a hooked bill, caruncles incised on the head, and large talons, which is probably a vulture. In Arkansas this could be either a Black or Turkey Vulture. According to a story in the Cherokee tradition, a Great Buzzard (vulture) flew down to the earth when the land was "soft and new." A valley

was formed when the vulture's wings touched the ground, and a mountain arose when its wings were raised (Hudson 1976). The same traditions inform us that a priest who could cure a wound was entitled to wear a Turkey Vulture feather. Vultures, which feed on carrion, seemed to the Indians unaffected by exposure to death and impurity, and hence symbolized healing (Hudson 1976). The role of vultures in removing flesh from dead bodies suggests that vulture effigy pots may have been associated with mortuary rites.

Several fierce looking hawks with a forked eye pattern are seen among the effigies (Figure 4-9). This facial pattern typifies hawks of the family *Falconidae*. Various species of hawks were recognized by Indians. The Quapaws, a tribe living at the mouth of the Arkansas River in early historic times, identified and had specific names for at least five hawks (Dorsey 1891–1894). The Quapaw reflect upon the origins of hawks in their fable "Stars Sisters." Female star beings (gods) came down to the earth

FIGURE 4-8 Vultures were sometimes depicted on effigy bowls. (Univ. Ark. cat. no. 47-6-180.)

FIGURE 4-9 Some effigy bowls feature the forked pattern around the eye that is characteristic of several falcons. (Univ. Ark. cat. no. 32-5-309B.)

FIGURE 4-10 A species of owl with ear tuft feathers seems to have inspired this pot. (Univ. Ark. cat. no. 33-3-500A.)

in a basket. After many attempts a Quapaw managed to catch one of these female gods, and made her his wife. By and by a son was born to the couple, and later the star being took her son home to the upper world. Later she sent back to earth for her Quapaw husband. With him he brought from earth the claws of beasts and the wings of birds. Each star being then chose a claw or a wing, becoming a beast or bird. The wife, husband, and child took hawk wings, and became hawks (Dorsey 1891–1894).

In the University of Arkansas collection, owls are depicted on both statue-like bottles and bowls. The horned owl type appears (Figure 4-10) as well as the non-horned owl type (Table 4-2). In Pemiscott County, Missouri, which is part of the "bootheel" jutting into

northeastern Arkansas, a carved bone owl effigy pendant was found in a grave (Klinger 1975–1978). Three species of owls were identified by the Quapaws (Dorsey 1891–1894). Among some of the Mississippian tribes, only priests were entitled to wear the feathers of Great Horned Owls in their headdress. Some priests actually carried a stuffed owl as part of their professional equipment. A priest was also presumed to have extraordinary night vision (Hudson 1976).

The importance of owls in the Mississippian tradition is emphasized by the persistence of certain beliefs about them. At Fayetteville in 1982, Carrie Vee Wilson-Jones, a Quapaw woman, told about certain taboos concerning owls. The Quapaw listen to owls because other beings talk through them. A screech owl calling

FIGURE 4-11 Copper ornament from a Mississippian period site west of Fort Smith combines human and falcon features. (Univ. Ark. cat. no. 62-84.)

three times warns of impending death. Shortly after her son was born, Wilson-Jones heard an owl calling in this manner and told her mother, who immediately came to the house and purified the dwelling with cedar smoke (pers. comm.).

Effigy bowls are but one aspect of the relationship between birds and people in matters of religious or spiritual significance. For example, in Miller County colorful birds found in graves "may have been offerings put on top of pottery groups" (Perino 1967). At three sites in Mississippi and Crittenden counties, wing and other bones from swans, geese, turkeys, and a duck were found in association with human burials (Moore 1911, Perino 1966). A Wood Duck effigy bowl was recently recovered from the grave of an infant in northeastern Arkansas (Morse 1984). A medicine bag or sacred bundle recovered from a bluff shelter in the Ozarks included a bird's bill and several other bird bones (Harrington 1960). In Newton County, the humerus bone of a Common Raven (*Corvus corax*) was found in a cave with human bones (U.S. Nat. Mus. 1949).

The Bald Eagle, chosen as a symbol of the United States, was also held in special regard by Mississippians. In a burial in Miller County, three large effigy pipes were recovered from one grave (Durham and Kizzia 1964). One pipe featured the forked eye pattern associated with falcons. A second pipe was molded in the shape of a vulture, with a human skull in its bill. The third pipe had a strong bill whose shape was much like that of an eagle. Also in Miller County, a recent archeological project resulted in the recovery of a burial in which an apparently entire Bald Eagle was interred with or near a child (Styles and Purdue 1984).

Among some of the Indians of the Mississippian period, the Bald Eagle symbolized peace, and its tail feathers were greatly valued because they were essential for some rituals. Only men with the highest social ranking, for example, were allowed to carry these feathers at a dance (Hudson 1976).

Other striking evidence linking birds and people in prehistoric times comprises bird-man figures associated with several Mississippian areas (Hudson 1976). Unique, stylized bird-man representations have been recovered at Spiro, Oklahoma, a few miles west of Fort

Smith, Arkansas, in a loop of the Arkansas River. Spiro reached its pinnacle of power and influence approximately 600 to 800 years ago. Composite figures of birds and people, and birds or parts of birds, have been discovered on numerous artifacts from the area (Phillips and Brown 1978).

Several copper plaques in the collection at the University of Arkansas Museum feature an apparently human form in a costume that includes the typical forked eye markings associated with falcons, a hooked bill, long tail feathers, and wings (Figure 4-11). Similar forms were engraved on conch shell. These composite figures have been referred to as "masked eagle dancers" (Griffin 1967), "winged beings" (S. Williams 1968), and the familiar bird-man. It is not known if they were Indians wearing costumes, mythical birds assuming humanlike forms, or actual gods. To one writer, they seem to be invested with "mythic, ritual, or even political significance" (Wilson 1981). However, there is room for many possibilities. Among the Quapaw a story was told about the son of Rabbit who told his father that he desired some fine clothing. Rabbit "made an owl-skin headdress for him. He made garments which had bird-skins sewed all over them, and moccasins that had owl-skins on them. At every step which the son took, the birds said 'Hu! Hu! Hu!' He made the owls hoot as he walked, and all the birds used to make a great noise by crying out" (Dorsey 1891–1894).

Some descendants of Mississippian Indians living today in Oklahoma continue to celebrate the Greencorn Ceremony, which offers a feather dance in honor of the birds. "Each man holds a length of rivercane with two or three white feathers attached to the end. One man stands atop the earthen mound and whoops to call the birds. At different parts of the dance they shout the turkey-gobble war whoop. This dance over, they sweep away the ashes of the old year's fire and strike flint to kindle a new fire . . ." (Hudson 1976).

Birds played a significant role in the lives of prehistoric and early historic Indians both culturally and economically. It is impossible to think of these people without also reflecting upon their relationship with birds. Much is now known about the birds and people of this prehistoric time, but much also remains to be learned. In the future, archeological bird watching will continue to add to our knowledge of birds and people in prehistoric as well as early historic Arkansas.

Chapter 5
FINDING BIRDS IN ARKANSAS

Visitors to Arkansas and residents who move into the state from other localities are often impressed with the numbers of birds they may see, especially in settled urban areas. An abundant bird life speaks well for the quality of environment found in Arkansas, and birds may be enjoyed here everywhere. In summer, wooded urban neighborhoods attract a variety of nesting birds and characteristically Arkansas towns are filled with morning birdsong. Winters are mild enough for sizeable populations to remain throughout the cold weather, since food is available naturally and many birds are attracted to backyard feeding stations.

Discovering birds in Arkansas means one can go just about anywhere that suitable habitat exists and find birds in abundance. Bird enthusiasts are especially pleased by large tracts of public land contained in national forests situated in the western highlands, including several units of the Ozark National Forest in the Ozark Plateaus, the Ouachita National Forest in the Ouachita Mountains, and the smaller St. Francis National Forest on the southern end of Crowley's Ridge in the Mississippi Alluvial Plain in eastern Arkansas. These areas are delineated on highway maps issued by the Arkansas State Highway and Transportation Department. National forests have ample public recreational facilities and offer fine access to ideal environments for forest birds. The Buffalo National River, a national park extending across the center of the southern Ozark Plateaus, is a splendid place for upland and river land forest birds. Another favorable site is Hot Springs National Park in the forested highlands of the Ouachita Mountains.

The National Park Service administers several other areas that provide excellent bird watching, such as Pea Ridge National Military Park in Benton County in the Ozarks, where forest and open country birds may be found; Arkansas Post National Monument, near the Arkansas River in Arkansas County in the southeastern part of the state, and Louisiana Purchase National Monument in Lee County, where bottomland forest birds may be seen.

There are six national wildlife refuges in Arkansas including Big Lake and Wapanocca in the northeastern quadrant, White River and Felsenthal and Overflow in the southeastern part of the state, and Holla Bend in the Arkansas River Valley. These are managed especially for waterfowl and are thus most valuable for seeing birds during winter months and throughout the waterfowl migratory periods when these birds assemble in the state. There are considerable areas of forest lands on some of the refuges that provide habitat for forest birds, particularly the lowland forest at the White River National Wildlife Refuge, and the lowland and upland forest at the Felsenthal refuge. The oak-pine uplands at Felsenthal support a local abundance of Red-cockaded Woodpeckers (James and Burnside 1979a).

Large impoundments administered by the U.S. Army Corps of Engineers are another type of federally supported project visited by birds. These are large deep lakes located mostly in the highlands that attract deepwater birds in winter. Millwood Lake in southwestern Arkansas has a different character. Being quite shallow, it has become a primary site attracting a great variety of water birds, including herons, waterfowl, and shorebirds, gulls, and terns, during migratory and wintering periods.

The Arkansas Game and Fish Commission maintains a large number of wildlife management areas especially designated for use by the hunting public, but which are often well timbered lands attractive to a variety of forest birds. Access to some of these areas can be difficult. A booklet entitled *Wildlife Management Areas Guide*, which describes individual districts and how to reach them, is available from the Commission. Most of the districts in eastern Arkansas are seasonally flooded and managed for waterfowl. Wildlife management areas in other parts of the state have upland forests. The Commission has also constructed a number of public lakes, many of which are attractive to waterfowl in winter. Descriptions and locations of these lakes are given in a booklet entitled *Public Owned Fishing Lakes,* obtainable from the Commission.

The Arkansas Department of Parks and Tourism maintains a system of state parks, many of which are ideal for birds, and especially forest birds. Particularly abundant in bird life are Crowley's Ridge and Village Creek state parks in northeastern and eastern Arkansas; Devil's Den, Lake Fort Smith, and Withrow Springs in the western Ozarks; Petit Jean in the Arkansas River Valley; and Queen Wilhelmina at Rich Mountain in the Ouachitas. Other state parks also offer excellent opportunities for finding birds.

An easy way to locate the national forests, parks and monuments, national wildlife refuges, Corps of Engineers impoundments, state wildlife management areas, and state parks is to consult the state highway map issued by the Arkansas State Highway and Transportation Department in Little Rock.

A number of favorite places exist that have been visited frequently over the years by bird watchers. In northwestern Arkansas favorable birding areas include Pea Ridge National Military Park, lands adjacent to and bordering upon Beaver Lake, and around the state fish hatchery at Centerton, all in Benton County. In adjacent Washington County, prime areas include Lake Fayetteville, north of the city; the Wedington unit of the Ozark National Forest; Devil's Den State Park; and part of the White River near Greenland. Franklin County offers a circuit through the Ozark National Forest that includes Redding, White Rock Mountain, and Shores Lake recreation areas. It is a favorite route for finding upland and riverine forest birds. Along the Arkansas River, from Fort Smith to Pine Bluff and southward, flooded agricultural fields, river levees, and lock and dam sites provide good vantage points for viewing birds.

In northeastern Arkansas the Nettleton wastewater ponds near Jonesboro regularly attract water birds, and the Jonesboro airport is good for finding grassland birds. Other places in the region productive to bird watchers include Crowley's Ridge and Village Creek State Parks, Big Lake and Wapanocca national wildlife refuges, plus several state wildlife management areas. These and other sites are described by Hanebrink (1980). In the vicinity of Conway in central Arkansas, Beaver Fork Lake north of the town, and the lower portion of Lake Conway to the south are both good for land and water bird observation. These and other areas are described by Johnson (1979). In the Little Rock vicinity large city parks on both sides of the Arkansas River attract numerous land birds, and birds are also plentiful at nearby Pinnacle Mountain State Park. Lake Maumelle and Faulkner Lake should be visited by those in search of water birds. At Lonoke the state and private fish hatcheries and nearby rice field reservoirs have been visited for many years because of the prolific and diverse numbers of water birds, particularly shorebirds, during migration. Stuttgart airport in Prairie County has been a favorable site for grassland birds in winter.

In the Ouachita Mountain region shorebirds are found at proper seasons at the state fish hatchery at Lake Hamilton in Garland County and at wastewater treatment ponds at Mena in Polk County. Recreational areas in the Ouachita National Forest provide substantial numbers of upland forest birds, and near Mena, the slopes of Rich Mountain and Wilhelmina State Park are excellent bird watching environs. On the Gulf Coastal Plain, Lake Earling in Lafayette County is also worth a visit to see pineland birds at picnic and campground areas, where a favorite bird is the Red-cockaded Woodpecker. Residents of El Dorado find quantities of land birds attracted to the city wastewater treatment ponds, and at appropriate seasons water birds may also be seen. Calion Lake northeast of the town is another fine area for viewing land and water birds. The vicinity of Lake Georgia Pacific near Crosset is favorable for pineland and water birds, especially during migratory months. In extreme southeastern Arkansas near Lake Village, Lake Chicot State Park is rewarding to observers of both water and land birds.

Local bird enthusiasts in Arkansas who are familiar with the most favored areas may be contacted through their appropriate bird clubs. Organizations exist throughout the state: the Audubon Society of Central Arkansas (Little Rock and vicinity), Columbia County Audubon Society (Magnolia), Fort Smith Audubon So-ciety, Garland County Audubon Society (Hot Springs), Greers Ferry Audubon Society, Hope Audubon Nature Club, Hot Springs Village Audubon Society, Little Red River Audubon Society (Fairfield Bay), Mena Nature Club, Northeast Arkansas Audubon Society (Jonesboro area), Northwest Arkansas Audubon Society (Bentonville, Fayetteville, Rogers, and environs), Ouachita Caddo Audubon Society (Arkadelphia), Ozark Audubon Society (Mountain Home), Petit Jean Audubon Society (Conway, Morrilton, and vicinity), South Arkansas Audubon Society (El Dorado), Texarkana Audubon Society, and Three Rivers Audubon Society (Pine Bluff region). Officers of these organizations are regularly changed so it would not be useful to publish addresses here. However, many of the places also have Christmas Bird Counts, and local count compilers would be good contacts for reaching club members. In the July issue each year the names and addresses of current compilers are published in *American Birds* magazine, which may be obtained from the National Audubon Society, 950 Third Avenue, New York, N.Y. 10022. Persons interested in communicating with local bird clubs in Arkansas may consult this annual Christmas Bird Count issue for current information.

THE SPECIES
ACCOUNTS

INTRODUCTION

The following accounts of 366 species of Arkansas birds give a brief synopsis of each species, denoting where and when the bird has been observed in the state, its relative abundance, and the habitat in Arkansas where it may be found. The remainder of each account provides specific details based on data from the bird file maintained by the Arkansas Audubon Society, combined with other records.

Information on migration, nesting, and winter status is presented in an appropriate sequence. For a winter resident such as the Hermit Thrush, for example, the sequence begins with its arrival in the state during fall; records for the winter season are then summarized, and the account concludes with information concerning spring migration when the species departs from Arkansas for its northern breeding grounds. This sequence is reversed for a summer resident such as the Wood Thrush, which arrives in Arkansas on northward migration during spring, nests, and then departs southward in the fall. For birds such as the Northern Cardinal, present in the state throughout the year, information is arranged for the different seasons in a sequence chosen for clarity. Some species, like the Passenger Pigeon, are treated primarily by historical narrative.

In referring to bird abundances, the text has followed ordinary English usage rather than attempting to propose rigid definitions. For instance, if the Gray Catbird is "common" in Arkansas it implies that if an observer visits suitable habitat at the right time of the year, there is a strong likelihood that a Gray Catbird will be present. Brown-headed Cowbirds are "abundant" because they are numerous throughout the year in Arkansas in a variety of habitats, and at certain times of the year they congregate in extraordinary numbers. On the other hand, the term "rare" is used in discussing the Rufous-crowned Sparrow because it is present in Arkansas in very small numbers and has been found in the state only in a limited geographical area. Terms used to designate increasing levels of abundance range from *rare, uncommon, fairly common, common, very common,* to *abundant.* When data was available, actual numbers of birds or population values were cited, as was possible for most species.

Although the terminology describing seasonal occurrences of birds is fairly uniform in the ornithological literature, some variation does exist. To avoid confusion terms are hereby defined: a "summer resident" bird is a species such as the Indigo Bunting that nests in Arkansas but is absent in the non-breeding season; a "winter resident" such as the White-throated Sparrow is regularly present somewhere (in this case everywhere) in Arkansas throughout the cold months but is absent during the nesting season. The Northern Cardinal is an example of a "permanent resident" that is present throughout the state in all seasons. Some migratory or partially migratory species can also qualify as "permanent residents." For example, the Rufous-sided Towhee is present in some parts of the state all year but is apparent in other parts only during the cold months. The seasonal situation is reversed with the Chipping Sparrow, which is a "permanent resident" in much of the state but appears only in the breeding season in northern sections. This situation can be even more complex, as in the case of the "permanent resident" House Wren, which is found only in winter in southern

FIGURE 6-1 Arkansas counties and principal cities mentioned in the text.

Arkansas, and only in summer in northern Arkansas. This bird is not found year-round at any given locality in the state, but is present statewide all year. The adjective "transient" has generally been reserved for a species like the Nashville Warbler that passes briefly through the state in migration during spring and fall, but does not remain for a lengthy period of time and does not nest or overwinter. The term "migrant" was usually applied to a bird such as the Blue Jay that, while present during summer, winter, or both seasons, nevertheless performs notable migrations. The term "migrant" has also been used for species such as the Indigo Bunting or Yellow-rumped Warbler, which are at least sometimes observed in flocks during spring and fall migratory periods, and which also remain in Arkansas for a lengthy period during summer (the bunting) or in winter (the warbler). Migration in resident birds was recognized by population peaks in usual habitats, influxes into new areas, mi-

gratory flocks seen passing overhead by day, or birds striking high obstructions while migrating at night, and for summer and winter residents, arrival and departure dates. The term "visitor" is similar to both "migrant" and "transient," but used in reference to certain species, such as some herons and egrets, which perform post-breeding movements or wanderings that actually precede the southward migration. Also described as "visitors" are the species that appear irregularly in Arkansas, such as the Red Crossbill. (Notice that summer resident and winter resident birds are also migrants, and so are some permanent resident species.)

A variety of terms are used to describe where birds may be found in Arkansas. The Northern Cardinal, for example, occurs "throughout" the state, and this means that it can be found during appropriate times (in this case all year) and in appropriate habitat in each of the physiographic regions (Figure 3-1). Many of the key records are identified by county, city or town, or by important land features (Figures 3-1, 6-1 and 6-2). In some cases it has been convenient to employ generalizations about large sections of the state such as the "northeast" or the "south." The "northeast" in Arkansas includes parts of such diverse physiographic regions or subregions as the Mississippi Alluvial Plain, Crowley's Ridge, and the Ozark Plateaus, and the "south" includes the Coastal Plain and part of the Mississippi Alluvial Plain. The terms "highlands" and "lowlands" are used frequently. The former refers to the interior highlands, or combined Ozark Plateaus and Ouachita Mountains, the physiographic regions comprising the northwestern half of the state. The "lowlands" is a collective term for the Mississippi Alluvial Plain and the Gulf Coastal Plain occupying the southeastern half of Arkansas.

Giving precise first arrival and last departure dates, as exhibited by migratory species, was usually avoided since specific dates were just chance sightings, indicating a general period of time. In fact, such sightings have a high probability of occurring on weekends when bird

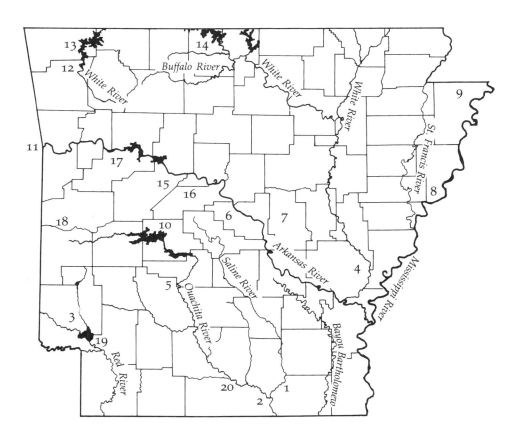

1. Lake Georgia-Pacific
2. Felsenthal National Wildlife Refuge
3. Millwood Lake
4. White River National Wildlife Refuge
5. DeGray Lake
6. Lake Maumelle
7. Lonoke area
8. Horseshoe Lake
9. Big Lake National Wildlife Refuge
10. Lake Ouachita
11. Arkansas River bottoms, Moffett, Oklahoma
12. Lake Fayetteville
13. Beaver Lake
14. Bull Shoals Lake
15. Holla Bend National Wildlife Refuge
16. Petit Jean Mountain
17. Magazine Mountain
18. Rich Mountain
19. Grassy Lake
20. Calion Lake

FIGURE 6-2 Arkansas rivers, impoundments, national wildlife refuges, and other features mentioned in the text.

watchers are afield in the largest numbers. Arrival and departure times are therefore referred to by the week of the month in which the sighting occurred, the four weeks of a month being divided into days 1–7, 8–14, 15–21, and 22–31.

Considerable bias exists in the way records are accumulated, and this bias is unavoidably transmitted to books such as the present one, concerned as it is with bird distribution. As may be expected, a denser human population in the larger towns and cities produces a large number of bird watchers, while in isolated rural areas fewer people means fewer birds reported. Sparsely settled areas in Arkansas that still remain rather neglected by bird watchers include the north central Ozarks, the northern Ouachitas (just south of the Arkansas River Valley), and southeastern Arkansas. Future study of birds in these interesting regions is encouraged.

Range maps are included for species that are not distributed over the whole state. These maps show a single black dot centered in the counties where there have been one or more reports of a species based on the records in the Audubon Society file, the literature, and the Breeding Bird Surveys. Where possible a dashed line is included to indicate probable range limits.

Maps showing overall movements based on the recovery of banded birds (James 1967) are included for each species that had at least seven recoveries. Straight lines connect individual banding and recovery locations in species with relatively few recoveries (Figure 6-3). It is not assumed that the birds necessarily flew these straight courses; in fact, the many birds that survived more than a year between banding and recovery obviously did not. Nevertheless, the pattern of the lines does show overall trends in migratory direction. The symbols used at the ends of the lines are defined on the maps and indicate the seasons of banding and recovery: breeding period (solid circle), migratory period (open diamond), or wintering period (open circle). The dates of these periods had to be determined separately for each species based upon differing phenologies (James 1967). (Note that there is no indication concerning the ends of the lines where the birds were banded as opposed to recovered. This detail is not of biological significance.)

When there were around 150 recoveries or more for a species, lines became crowded and confusing and spoke diagrams were employed (Figure 6-15). Spoke diagrams show sixteen radii centered on Arkansas. The thicknesses of radiating lines, or spokes, are proportional to the numbers of banded or recovered birds recorded in the various compass directions at various distances from Arkansas. The sixteen directions actually represent 22.5 degree directional sectors (James 1967), the first sector spanning compass directions from zero degrees to 22.5 degrees, the second 22.5 degrees to 45 degrees, etc. The distances along the spokes are divided into 500 mile units centered on Arkansas. Thus, all banding-recovery records within 500 miles of the center of Arkansas are represented by the relative width of the spokes in the first distance zone. The second distance increment is 500 to 1000 miles away, and so forth. The numbers of birds represented by the thicknesses of the spoke lines are shown on the figures and vary from species to species.

In the species accounts, population level information is often provided based on the Christmas Bird Counts, the Breeding Bird Surveys, Breeding Bird Censuses, and Winter Bird Population Studies. Each Christmas Bird Count contains a total number for each species seen and counted by a number of observers during one day afield in a specified area during late December or early January. The observers often form groups called field parties and each field party records the number of hours afield. These are summed to give the total party hours for each count. Since the number of field parties varies from count to count, the data presented for each count in the species accounts that follow are standardized to birds per party hour. This was done by dividing the total number for a species by the total party hours for the particular count. Ten party hours are roughly equivalent to a full day afield, so multiplying the number of birds per party hour by 10 gives an estimate of how many individuals of that species one could expect to find in a day's outing.

The Breeding Bird Surveys are roadside counts conducted in June. The observers travel the same 24.5 mile routes annually by automobile, stopping every half mile and recording from each stopping point the number of each species seen or heard during a three minute period. The total for each bird on each route is then summed across all fifty stops (the first stop being the starting point). These totals represent relative population levels and in the species accounts are usually expressed as average values for a number of survey routes in a physiographic region.

Both the Breeding Bird Censuses and Winter Bird Population Studies are conducted by establishing a study plot of fixed size and homogeneous habitat and repeatedly counting birds and mapping their locations over the study areas. In the breeding bird studies the number of territorial males of each species per study area is determined from the combined data (Hall 1964); in the winter studies the average number of birds per species regardless of sex or age seen per visit to the study areas is calculated (Kolb 1965). Because the various study plots vary in size, the population data is standardized by converting all numbers to birds per 100 acres, and this is how the population levels are expressed in the species accounts.

The species accounts were originally going to include information on avian subspecies occurring in Arkansas, and in anticipation of this, Arkansas bird specimens existing in major museums were located. Soon, however, investigations by Frances C. James cast considerable doubt on the validity of the subspecies concept (James 1970a, 1970b). Her study included several common Arkansas birds. More recently, her new findings (James 1983) further erode the basis for designating subspecies. Therefore, no attempt was made to assign subspecies names to bird specimens collected within the state. The museum specimens, however, are listed in the Appendix for use by future researchers. The only mention of subspecific variation in the species accounts refers to those few morphological patterns that are conspicuous when seen in the field, such as is shown by pattern and color variation in the Red-tailed Hawk, Northern Flicker, and Rufous-sided Towhee. (Some of the museum specimens represented unusual records and interesting distributions, and this important information was incorporated in the species accounts.)

Most of the species of Arkansas birds are common and widespread enough to be well recognized components of the avifauna. Some birds, however, are very rare and have been seen only a few times, or only once in the state. These species have been included in the book only after careful evaluation of the evidence concerned. Thus, rarities were accepted only after approval of a properly documented specimen or photograph, or submitted written description.

Taxonomy, nomenclature, and order of species follow the 6th edition of the *Check-list of North American Birds* published in 1983 by the American Ornithologists' Union. The species accounts are grouped into avian family and subfamily categories. The common names assigned to these categories usually follow recommended usage (Amer. Ornith. Union 1983), but in some cases they were tailored to the Arkansas avifauna, or simply made more understandable to the average person. For example, since Arkansas only has kinglets and gnatcatchers in the "Old World Warbler" group, the subfamily Sylviinae was called "Kinglets and Gnatcatchers." In another example, the name "Emberizines" was rejected for the subfamily Emberizinae and "New World Sparrows" was used instead.

Order GAVIIFORMES

Family Gaviidae Loons

RED-THROATED LOON, *Gavia stellata* (Pontoppidan)

Rare transient and winter visitor.

Red-throated Loons are found primarily along the Atlantic and Pacific coasts, but they are also found inland on occasion (AOU 1983). In Arkansas there are fewer than ten records, and these are for fall, winter, and spring. All involved single birds. A bird was seen in the "sunken lands" of Poinsett County during the winter of 1888–89 (Pindar 1924). A specimen was collected in Phillips County on November 5, 1933 (Deaderick 1935). There were reports at Lake Maumelle in central Arkansas on January 12, 1963, and on January 25, 1969. A bird was seen at DeGray Lake in Clark County between October 23 and 24, 1976. There was a report at Lake Millwood in the southwest on November 10, 1979, and another there on December 9, 1981. The only spring record in the Audubon Society file is from Pine Bluff on April 5, 1974.

COMMON LOON, *Gavia immer* (Brunnich)

Fairly common migrant, local and uncommon winter resident, locally on the larger lakes and impoundments in all regions. Several summer records.

FALL MIGRATION: Common Loons have arrived in Arkansas as early as the third week in September, but the species is seen primarily after the second week of October. Arrivals in Garland County on Lakes Hamilton and Catherine occurred between October 5 and 24 (Deaderick 1938), and the birds were said to be fairly common there in migration. In the north-eastern counties fall migrants have been recorded between mid-October to the end of November, with scattered sightings thereafter (Hanebrink 1980). At Lake Millwood in southwestern Arkansas, a peak of 11 birds was reported on October 31. A flock of 10 was among 21 birds counted on Lake Maumelle near Little Rock on November 8. The single largest one-day count was on Lake Ouachita in Garland County where 40 were observed along 18 miles of the lake on November 17, 1985.

WINTER: These birds are present regularly in the state during winter, but there appears to be considerable variation from year to year. While they utilize all types of open water in migration, they are confined at this season to the larger, deeper reservoirs and lakes, and thus have probably benefitted from the construction of large reservoirs in the state since World War II. In recent years Common Loons have been found regularly all winter in good numbers at Lake Maumelle where as many as 18 have been counted in late January. The species is found with regularity on the Christmas Bird Count at Lake Georgia-Pacific, where 10 were reported in 1981 (the usual number is about two). As many as five have been reported on the Christmas Count at Arkadelphia (DeGray Lake), and a similar number has been reported on Beaver Lake in the western Ozarks. However, in some years the numbers are low: only three were reported on the Christmas Bird Count statewide in 1984. The distinctive calls of these birds are sometimes heard during winter in Arkansas.

SPRING AND SUMMER: Small numbers of Common Loons are present until the last regular spring date, often in the second week of May. Members of the Audubon Society of Central Arkansas counted 13 at Lake Maumelle on March 19. The six at Lake Millwood on April 12 was also a large number for spring, as were the six at DeGray Lake on May 5. Some of these spring birds had already acquired the distinctive dark head and checkered back of the nuptial plumage.

On very rare occasions Common Loons are present after May. Each record between June and August involved single birds. There were June 1 reports at Lake Dardanelle in Logan County, and at Cherokee Lake in Sharp County. One was caught on a trotline at Greer's Ferry Lake in Cleburne County on June 23. A Common Loon was seen at Mammoth Spring in Fulton County on July 4. The fifth sighting involved a single bird swimming near the Beaver Lake dam during the period July 22 to August 3.

Order PODICIPEDIFORMES

Family Podicipedidae Grebes

PIED-BILLED GREBE, *Podilymbus podiceps* (Linnaeus)

Permanent resident. Common migrant and winter resident in all regions. Local summer resident at a few places in the lowlands.

FALL MIGRATION: While some Pied-billed Grebes remain in the state throughout the year, their presence in places where they do not occur in summer indicates that the fall migration into Arkansas has begun. These migrants are sometimes seen as early as late August, but more often during September, with major influxes in October and November. Fall arrivals in Garland County were recorded between August 2 and September 6 (Deaderick 1938). The 79 birds on Lake Fayetteville on September 25 was an unusually large number for the Ozarks. Files at Big Lake Refuge in Mississippi County showed that Pied-billed Grebes began to arrive there in early October, with an unusually large peak one year of 400 at mid-November. The 212 on Lake Ouachita in Garland County on November 24, 1960, was also a large number.

WINTER: Pied-billed Grebes are locally common in appropriate habitat in all regions of the state during winter, with the largest numbers generally in the southern lowlands. The state-wide mean number on Christmas Bird Counts was 0.1 birds per party hour, and means of up to 0.4 per hour were recorded in central and southern Arkansas. At Fayetteville in the northwest as many as 33 have been recorded on the Christmas Count, but the usual number is much lower, and very low numbers have been found in years with prolonged cold and freezing. In the south there are several records of 40 to 50 on Christmas Counts. Peak totals of 17 to 27 birds on the 1980 Christmas Count were all reported from participating locales in the southern lowlands.

SPRING MIGRATION: While some birds remain to nest in Arkansas, the vast majority move north into their breeding areas during the period of spring migration: March, April, and the first few weeks of May. The latest record at Fayetteville in the Ozarks, where the birds do not nest, is in the third week of May.

BREEDING SEASON: The breeding season in Arkansas gets underway while other Pied-billed Grebes are still migrating north. Nesting activity has been observed from early April until the arrival of frost in late October. Nesting occurs in the southern and eastern lowlands where there are shallow stable ponds, reservoirs, or flooded fields with marsh or marsh-like vegetation. There is no suitable habitat for nesting birds in the Ouachita Mountains or in the Ozarks, and nesting has not been reported in the Arkansas River Valley above Little Rock even though there are some places that seem to have the appropriate habitat.

The extreme records of nesting activity include a nest with two eggs on an oxbow lake associated with the Little Red River in Miller County on April 17 (Audubon Society file), and in Lonoke County a bird incubated four eggs from October 12 until the onset of freezing weather in the last week of the month (Meanley and Neff 1953a). The peak date for eggs in twenty-five nests in the Audubon Society file is in May, with the earliest date for hatching in early June, after which time adults have been seen with zebra-striped young of various sizes. The breeding season continues throughout the summer.

Five of the best known breeding colonies have been observed at the state fish hatchery in Lonoke County, near Hilleman in Woodruff County, Booker Reservoir in Crittenden County, Bayou Meto in Arkansas County, and on ponds four miles north of Grady in Lincoln County. There were ten nests, nine of them with two to ten eggs, in an eighty-acre abandoned rice field near Grady on May 31, 1955. Other colonies have been found in Ashley and Miller counties (Howell 1911, Wheeler 1924, file), and elsewhere in the lowlands. They have nested successfully in neglected or abandoned ponds associated with rice fields and commercial fish farms, as well as ditches and borrow pits.

Recent nesting records include two nests and adults with three batches of small young at Anderson's Minnow Farm in Lonoke in late August and early September of 1983. The birds have nested recently in borrow pits along the Arkansas River levee near Linwood, in Jefferson County, in shallow ponds and borrow pits near the Terry Lock and Dam on the Arkansas River in Pulaski County, and at Faulkner Lake in the same county. Nesting attempts at the Port of Pine Bluff sewer lagoon seem to depend upon the height of the water there.

While Arkansas has probably never had a large breeding population of Pied-billed Grebes, the dependence of the birds on natural marshes, many of which have been drained in recent years, and on artificial ponds that are subject to considerable change from year to year, has caused concern about its future as a breeding species in the state (James 1974).

HORNED GREBE, *Podiceps auritus* (Linnaeus)

Fairly common migrant and winter resident in all regions. Observed during migration on a variety of bodies of water, but in winter usually confined to the larger, more open lakes or reservoirs.

FALL MIGRATION: In the Audubon Society file there are scattered records of Horned Grebes arriving as early as the third week of August and occasionally during September, but these are isolated events. The usual time of arrival is in early October with migration apparently continuing throughout November. At Lakes Hamilton and Catherine in Garland County it arrived between October 1 and 15 (Deaderick 1938). In the northeastern counties, where the species does not regularly overwinter, there are only scattered reports after late November (Hanebrink 1980). Seven birds were counted at the Jonesboro wastewater treatment ponds on November 4. A total of 21 were at the Beaver Lake dam site in the western Ozarks on November 14. A conservative estimate of 250 Horned Grebes were seen during the course of an 18-mile boat trip (9 miles each way) on Lake Ouachita on November 17, 1985.

WINTER AND SPRING: Horned Grebes have been observed in winter on the larger reservoirs and lakes in all regions. At DeGray Lake near Arkadelphia they have been seen regularly on Christmas Bird Counts, with reports of 10 or more birds several times during the 1970s (peak of 18 on the 1975 Christmas Count). Large numbers are also reported at Lake Conway: on Christmas Bird Counts at Conway between 1968 and 1982, 20 or more Horned Grebes were reported for seven count years (peak of 30 in 1972). A total of 70 were seen above Beaver Lake dam in the western Ozarks on January 4. The largest number ever seen in the state involved 150 reported at Lake Millwood on the 1976 Christmas Count.

SPRING MIGRATION AND SUMMER: The birds are found with fair regularity in late winter and early spring through March, with only scattered records thereafter in April and May. The 28 at DeGray Lake on February 6 was a large number there, as was the 20 at Lake Maumelle on March 19. At Calion Lake near El Dorado, a flock of Horned Grebes first observed on February 10 was last seen on March 24. On Lake Conway the species is of regular occurrence until March 24 (Johnson 1979). In the northeast there are spring reports between mid-March and about the third week of May (E. Hanebrink, pers. comm.). The five birds seen at the mouth of the White River in Desha County on April 4 was a relatively large number so late in the season.

Single birds have been reported on two occasions during summer by reliable observers on the large reservoirs in the north: June 6 and 7, 1975, at Bull Shoals Lake, and July 29 and August 2, 1979, at Beaver Lake. It is not clear why these birds, which normally migrate far to the north for nesting, were present in Arkansas at that time, but it is not unreasonable to speculate that injuries or some other abnormality prevented them from making the normal migration.

RED-NECKED GREBE, *Podiceps grisegena* (Boddaert)

Three sight records.

Pindar (1924) found the species in northeastern Arkansas during the winter of 1888–89. One was seen at Geridge in Lonoke County on October 21, 1951. The third record is from near Roland in Pulaski County, where one was reported on December 5, 1970.

EARED GREBE, *Podiceps nigricollis* Brehm

Uncommon migrant and winter resident in all regions. Sometimes fairly common locally in migration. Much less numerous than the Horned Grebe.

FALL MIGRATION: This grebe of western North America has arrived in fall as early as mid-August, but the usual early fall arrival date seems to be in the first week of September, with numbers increasing thereafter. Many reports in the Audubon Society file for a day have involved one or two. The 10 birds at Lake Millwood on October 25 and the four at Lonoke on October 31 are suggestive of important migration times. In the Audubon Society file there are several reports involving five to seven birds in the latter part of November (Jonesboro on November 21 and Calion Lake near El Dorado on November 28), which are also suggestive of migratory influxes. Eared Grebes and Horned Grebes utilize similar habitats in Arkansas.

WINTER: Reports in the file do not indicate an obvious dividing line between fall and winter Eared Grebe populations; however, smaller numbers are seen between mid-December and mid-February than at other times. Many reports in this period have involved single birds or sometimes two in a day, and the species is rarely ever reported in large numbers on Christmas Bird Counts. At Lake Georgia-Pacific in southern Arkansas, for example, there are irregular reports of one or two on the Christmas Count, with one highly unusual peak of six in 1971. The three reported on DeGray Lake on the 1981 Arkadelphia Christmas Count was also unusual.

SPRING MIGRATION: Reports in the file between late February and early May are suggestive of the northward migration period. The six birds on wastewater treatment ponds at Jonesboro on February 20 had apparently just arrived. The reports for this period are highly concentrated during April. Several peak numbers and localities in the file are twelve birds on the Pine Bluff wastewater treatment ponds on April 4; seven at Lake Millwood on April 12; nine on Lake Conway on April 20; and four in breeding plumage at Grassy Lake in Hempstead County between April 19 and 26.

WESTERN GREBE, *Aechmophorus occidentalis* (Lawrence)

Rare and irregular transient and winter visitor.

This species of western North America has been reported approximately fifteen times since the mid-1960s. These reports span the period from the second week of October to late April. The only record in the Audubon Society file that involves more than a single bird was for three found frozen on the ice near Piggott in Clay County in January 1977. Western Grebes have been observed at Lake Millwood in the southwest (two sightings), on a fish pond in Craighead County, on Lake Maumelle near Little Rock (sightings in 1971, 1975, 1976, 1978 and 1985), on DeGray Lake in Clark County, and on Beaver Lake and Budd Kidd Lake, both in the western Ozarks.

In several instances observers have noted the color phase of the bird seen, and in each of these cases the bird in question was the dark phase type.

Order PELECANIFORMES

Family Pelecanidae Pelicans

AMERICAN WHITE PELICAN, *Pelecanus erythrorhynchos* Gmelin

Regular migrant in all regions. Additionally, there are a few records in summer and winter.

SPRING MIGRATION: White pelicans have been seen during the northward migration period, primarily late March to mid-May, with a peak in numbers usually noted by mid-April. One unusually early flock involving 100 birds was seen in Columbia County on March 2. At Pine Bluff 900 were counted on April 14. The two most impressive recent records in the Audubon Society file were 1300 birds at DeGray Lake in Clark County on April 12, 1980, and three flocks totalling 2200 at Lake Millwood in Little River County on April 17, 1985. These large birds may settle onto the larger lakes or reservoirs in the state, or be observed in flocks as they alternately flap and glide overhead. A few are seen even on some of the smaller lakes in the state, such as Sequoyah in Washington County. The flocks that are seen in Arkansas may sometimes remain for several days or even several weeks in one area.

FALL MIGRATION: The southward migration period involves the months of September, October, and November, and flocks with at least 100 individual birds have been reported from the last week of September to late October. At Lake Millwood there were 550 birds on September 27, 1980. Immense fall flocks containing more than 1000 birds were recorded on two occasions near the Mississippi River in 1954 and 1960, but were not found during fall in the state again until September 27, 1985, when approximately 1000 birds were observed by Don Simons on Lake Chicot in Chicot County.

Banding records demonstrate that birds passing through Arkansas in fall are associated with populations that nest in the northern prairie states and the prairie provinces of Canada, 950 to 1500 miles north-northwest of Arkansas (Figure 6-3). Most of the thirty-seven banding recoveries involved birds banded as nestlings and recovered on their first fall migration. Three birds lived over ten years and one over fifteen years between banding and recovery.

WINTER AND SUMMER: Occasionally a few stragglers remain in the state after the main migration period. Baerg (1951), for example, reported a bird at Rogers, Benton County, on December 26. A single apparently uninjured white pelican was observed during the 1963 Fayetteville Christmas Bird Count. More recently, single birds have been seen on Lake Chicot in Chicot County (January 24, 1977), on the Arkansas River at Fort Smith (January 7, 1978), on the 1983 Christmas Count at Mena, and there are two records in December 1984 (Pine Bluff and Fayetteville).

On July 2, 1985, 54 pelicans were observed on a 15-acre sandbar in the Arkansas River in Sebastian County. The presence of these birds in Arkansas during the middle of summer was surprising, but there was no indication whatsoever that the birds were nesting. There are also midsummer records for the large impoundments in neighboring Oklahoma (Sutton 1967).

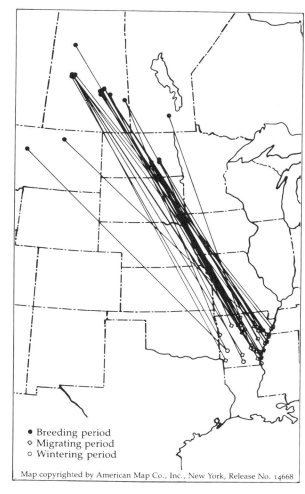

- ● Breeding period
- ◇ Migrating period
- ○ Wintering period

Map copyrighted by American Map Co., Inc., New York, Release No. 14668

FIGURE 6-3 Movements of the American White Pelican based on banding records.

BROWN PELICAN, *Pelecanus occidentalis* Linnaeus

Two records.

A single Brown Pelican appeared at Big Lake Refuge in Mississippi County in April 1947 during a severe storm (Baerg 1951). A single bird was seen near Magnolia in Columbia County on March 20, 1971, and was found dead the following day. The skin was preserved and is in the University of Arkansas Museum collection.

Family *Phalacrocoracidae*
Cormorants

DOUBLE-CRESTED CORMORANT, *Phalacrocorax auritus* (Lesson)

Common migrant on larger bodies of water in all regions. Observed in winter in the Arkansas River Valley and the southern lowlands. No recent breeding record.

FALL MIGRATION: These birds sometimes arrive from breeding areas north of Arkansas by late August, with large numbers observed from mid-September and thereafter, and migration continues through November and early December. In Garland County fall arrivals were noted between September 16 and 25 (Deaderick 1938). Records in the Audubon Society file sometimes involve only one or a few birds seen in a day, but larger numbers are not unusual. Approximately 500 were seen at Lake Francis near Siloam Springs in the western Ozarks on October 21, 1984. As many as 1500 to 2000 have been counted in a day during fall at Lake Millwood. The numbers at Lake Millwood remain high throughout November and even later, with the population thinning out after the arrival of the coldest weather.

Banding recoveries associated with Arkansas show that the birds are derived from breeding areas 700 to 1450 miles to the north-northwest (Figure 6-4). Each of the 45 birds was banded as a nestling, and most recoveries involved immatures on their initial southward migration. Two lived over ten years, and one over sixteen years, between banding and recovery.

WINTER: Most birds leave the state after the arrival of severe, prolonged cold and freezing

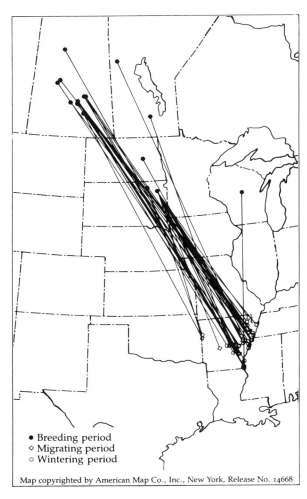

FIGURE 6-4 Movements of the Double-crested Cormorant based on banding records.

- Breeding period
◇ Migrating period
○ Wintering period

temperatures, but sometimes (especially in recent years) large numbers are still present at the time of the Christmas Bird Counts in the second half of December. Pindar (1924) considered them "fairly common" in Poinsett County during the early part of 1889. Very few were reported on Christmas Counts in the state from 1948 to 1961. More have been seen in recent years, and now they seem to be present locally in small numbers in winter in the southern areas of the state. The 410 at Lake Millwood in 1977, for example, was not an exceptionally large number there for the Christmas Count. Previous to 1982, the largest number reported on the long-standing Christmas Count at Fort Smith was six. In 1982, however, 229 were counted at the junction of the Arkansas and Poteau rivers, and an additional 125 were seen near Lock and Dam 13 on the Arkansas River. The large numbers seen at Pine Bluff, Lake Millwood, Fort Smith, and elsewhere in recent years may be attributable in part to the impoundment of large amounts of water. Of equal importance, this species may be recovering from population declines that were noticed in Arkansas at least by the 1960s (see "Former Breeding" below).

SPRING MIGRATION: Huge numbers of Double-crested Cormorants have been reported on several occasions in the past on large natural lakes in the eastern lowlands during February and March. At Horseshoe Lake in Crittenden County (near the Mississippi River), 2000 were seen on February 6, 1939, and twice that number were at Big Lake Refuge in Mississippi County on March 25, 1946. Certainly by late March the birds are beginning their northward migration that will carry them to their nesting areas, and this movement extends through May. In Garland County arrival dates for spring ranged between March 26 and April 18, and departures were recorded to mid-May (Deaderick 1938).

FORMER BREEDING: In past years some Double-crested Cormorants remained to breed locally in Arkansas. Howell (1911) visited a large rookery at Walker Lake in Mississippi County. During the first week of May in 1910, he saw birds on more than one hundred nests atop tall cypress trees out in the lake. There were three or four nests in many of the trees. By the time Wheeler (1924) wrote, however, Walker Lake had been drained and the rookery had disappeared. Young were seen at Old Town

Lake in Phillips County in 1913. The last known nesting in the state was at Grassy Lake in Hempstead County in 1951.

Certainly the potential for breeding in Arkansas has become greatly limited by the loss of cypress swamps and other remote swampy places that have been turned into plantations of cotton, soybeans, and rice. In addition, these birds, like other fish eating species (including the Osprey, Bald Eagle, and others), were affected by the presence of DDT and its derivatives. The gradual reduction of DDT in the food chain may allow populations of these birds to recover. The most significant summer record since 1951 was at Lake Millwood where 30 birds were seen in 1982. No evidence was found, however, that these birds were nesting.

Family Anhingidae Anhingas

ANHINGA, *Anhinga anhinga* (Linnaeus)

Locally common to uncommon migrant and summer resident in small numbers on a few swampy oxbow lakes and rivers in the lower regions of the Mississippi Alluvial Plain and on the Coastal Plain. Rare winter visitor in the extreme south. Very rare at any time in the highlands and unreported in the Ozarks.

SPRING MIGRATION: Arkansas is at the northern limit of the nesting range for this species (AOU 1983). Migrants have arrived in spring as early as the third week of March at Bois D'Arc Wildlife Management Area in Hempstead County, but most records in the Audubon Society file indicate that birds reach their nesting colonies during April, with breeding activity underway shortly thereafter.

BREEDING SEASON: The most complete nesting study of this species in Arkansas involved the former mixed-species rookery at Swan Lake in Jefferson County, about fifteen miles east of Pine Bluff (Meanley 1954). The nesting area utilized by Little Blue Herons, Snowy Egrets, Great Egrets, Green-backed Herons, Anhingas, as well as other smaller birds, occupied twenty acres of buttonbush and swamp privet in an oxbow lake associated with an old channel of the Arkansas River.

Meanley wrote that during the three years of his observations, 1951 to 1953, twenty to twenty-five pairs of Anhingas were present

FIGURE 6-5 Anhinga. *Howard Stern*

during the nesting season. Usually the birds arrived during the first week of April. Sometimes Anhingas built their own nests, other times they appropriated materials or whole nests from other herons and egrets. Egg laying was observed as early as April 24, but some nests still had eggs on June 6. The clutch size varied from two to five eggs, with the number often four or five. The nests were about eight feet high in standing water that averaged three feet in depth. Anhingas had departed from the rookery by mid-July.

The 1980 U.S. Fish and Wildlife Service's colonial bird rookery survey included reports of nesting in Hempstead, Lafayette, and Little River counties. A single nest was observed in Drew County in 1980. At Grassy Lake in Hempstead County, where some of the best swampy habitat remains in the state, 15 birds and about fifty nests with young were observed during June of 1980. In Lafayette County, sixty adults and several immature birds in nests were seen in cypress trees in an oxbow lake on July 14, 1981. In the Audubon Society file there are summer records scattered widely in the state's lowlands. Single birds have been observed in recent years in Saline, Lonoke, Pulaski, and Hot Spring counties, but these sightings have not been associated with nests.

In the early 1900s, Howell (1911) wrote, "The water turkey or 'snake bird' is fairly common locally in the swamps of eastern Arkansas." He listed nesting localities that included Helena in Phillips County, Wilmot in Ashley County, and Walker Lake in Mississippi County. Baerg (1951) added Grassy Lake in Hempstead County, and a heronry in Arkansas County. Besides Swan Lake, Meanley (1954) observed Anhingas nesting at Cypress Bayou near Tichnor in Arkansas County as well as at "several" rice field reservoirs near Stuttgart.

Many of the colonies listed by Howell (1911) have disappeared, as has the one Meanley studied in the early 1950s. Coffey (1981) states the Swan Lake site was in use continually between 1929 and 1955. Like the nesting populations of Double-crested Cormorants in Arkansas, Anhingas have suffered a population decline due to a combination of former hunting pressure and continuing drainage of the forested lowlands and swamps for agricultural development (James 1974).

LATE SUMMER, FALL, AND WINTER: Banding recoveries show that Anhingas wander north of their nesting sites after the breeding season. Four birds recovered in Arkansas in July and August had been banded in early summer in western Mississippi. (A fifth bird banded at the same time was recovered in Arkansas much later, in April.) The common banding site for all five birds was in western Mississippi, 37 to 151 miles from the recovery sites in Arkansas. The longest duration between banding and recovery was just under three years.

Anhingas largely depart the state during October, and very few are seen even as late as the end of November in the extreme southern lowlands. Nevertheless, a few individuals sometimes linger through December. The 14 Anhingas observed on the 1979 Christmas Bird Count at Texarkana was very unusual, as was one on the same count in 1984.

Family *Fregatidae* Frigatebirds

MAGNIFICENT FRIGATEBIRD, *Fregata magnificens* Mathews

Rare visitor usually associated with major weather disturbances on the Gulf of Mexico.

With their eight-foot wingspan and habitual soaring, these huge birds are sometimes carried far inland after storms. At the time of Hurricane Carla, for example, one bird was sighted at Horseshoe Lake in Crittenden County on September 13, 1961. "It was the first record of this coastal bird in the state. Obviously, it had been displaced by the hurricane, which had struck the Gulf Coast of Texas" (James 1964). The day after Hurricane Betsy, September 11, 1965, one bird was photographed in Grant County, and the photograph is on file with the Arkansas Audubon Society. A bird observed on the Fayetteville Christmas Bird Count in 1967 had presumably been carried north by a strong frontal movement associated with high winds from the Gulf of Mexico. Documentation associated with this sighting is in the Audubon Society file. The most recent observation involved a single bird that soared over the wastewater treatment ponds at El Dorado on May 2, 1984, after a night of abnormally heavy rains.

Order CICONIIFORMES

Family Ardeidae Herons

AMERICAN BITTERN, *Botaurus lentiginosus* (Rackett)

Transient observed in small numbers in low wet places with extensive marsh or marsh-like vegetation including flooded fields with tall grass primarily in the lowlands, but elsewhere in the state as well. Several records for summer and winter.

SPRING MIGRATION: There are scattered records during March, April, and May in all regions, with about half of these sightings on the Grand Prairie, including Lonoke, Arkansas, and Prairie counties. The species has been seen in appropriate habitat across the Coastal Plain in the southern lowlands, with spring records at Lake Bois d'Arc (3 there on April 13) in Hempstead County, and at Calion Lake in Union County. In the Arkansas River Valley the birds have been observed at Little Rock, at Lake Conway in Faulkner County, in the Fort Smith area. In the northeastern counties it has been seen with the greatest regularity at the Claypool Reservoir in Poinsett County. A single bird was seen at Mena in Polk County on May 1. In the western Ozarks there are scattered spring records. When these birds are found, most reports for a day's outing involve one or two birds. Four were seen on Sullivan's Island at Little Rock on March 26, ten at Lonoke in Lonoke County on May 2, and five at the Claypool Reservoir on May 31.

BREEDING SEASON: Arkansas lies south of the regular breeding range of this species (AOU 1983), and the only actual instances of nesting that have been reported are from Lonoke, where young were about to leave the nest on June 15,

and in Benton County (Baerg 1951). The species was also said to be a "summer resident" at Newport in Jackson County in 1895 (Howell 1911). Based upon the one known nesting date (Lonoke County), the presence of the birds in late May in Arkansas, Poinsett, Prairie, and Pulaski counties suggests that the birds might sometimes nest in these areas as well.

FALL MIGRATION: Fall reports are concentrated during October and November. At Lonoke, 11 birds (including one group of 10) were seen on November 16. The only record for the Ouachita Mountains involved a bird killed by hunters on November 17 (Deaderick 1938). In the western Ozarks there is one recent report from Washington and Benton counties, and an old record from the Fayetteville area on December 1 (Baerg 1951).

WINTER: In the Audubon Society file there are a small number of reports in December, January, and February involving single birds in Pope, Arkansas, Prairie, Union, and Crittenden counties. The fact that American Bitterns have been seen in every season in the eastern lowlands, especially on the Grand Prairie, suggests that they may be permanent residents in small numbers there.

LEAST BITTERN, *Ixobrychus exilis* (Gmelin)

Local summer resident in small numbers at a few places in the lowlands and the Arkansas River Valley, and generally a rare transient elsewhere. Inhabits natural and artificial marshes.

SPRING MIGRATION: A single bird found dead after striking a utility wire in Jefferson County on March 11 is the earliest spring arrival date for Arkansas. Otherwise, most spring "first" reports are in April and May. In the

FIGURE 6-6 Least Bittern. *Fred Burnside*

northwestern region, where the species is a rare transient, there are approximately four reports between April 19 and May 25 (file, Baerg 1951, Callahan 1953).

BREEDING SEASON: In the eastern lowlands nesting birds have been reported in Jefferson, Arkansas, Lincoln, Lonoke, and Phillips counties, and in Miller and Hempstead counties on the Coastal Plain. Recently two calling birds were reported at Faulkner Lake in Pulaski County, where they have been found previously in summer. There are nesting records for Faulkner County (Johnson 1979) and in the northeastern counties (Hanebrink 1980). The presence of Least Bitterns in summer in the Moffett bottoms of the Arkansas River in Oklahoma, three miles west of Fort Smith, Arkansas, suggests that the birds are nesting there. Probably the healthiest population in the state nests under natural conditions at Grassy Lake

in Hempstead County, where 20 birds were counted in June of 1980.

The peak period for nesting activity occurs during June. Nest construction has been observed as early as May 18 in Jefferson County. Records of nests with eggs in the Audubon Society file are dated as early as May 26 (Miller County) and as late as July 13 (Woodruff County). Some nests already have young by early June, such as the nest with five eggs that hatched on June 7 at Stuttgart in Arkansas County. Least Bitterns usually nest in small, loose colonies. Ben Coffey (1981) counted 11 birds at the state fish hatchery in Lonoke on July 11, 1954.

Shallow standing water and tall grasses, cattails, and other aquatic vegetation occurs in all the places where Least Bitterns have been found. Nests found at Lonoke by Vivian Scarlett in 1955, 1956, and 1957, were about two feet high in reeds in shallow water. Four nests in 1955 were near the edge of open water at the state fish hatchery.

Even though extensive amounts of natural marshlands in Arkansas have been lost as a result of conversion to agricultural production, some of this loss is compensated when reservoirs, rice fields, and commercial fish ponds are allowed to develop cattails, reeds, and other marsh vegetation. The birds have shown a willingness to adapt to this change, but the subsequent intensification of agricultural activity and the clearing of vegetation from fish ponds has been accompanied by a decline in the number of these birds in the state (James 1974). On the other hand, new habitats are sometimes created. Channel stabilization and navigation projects along the Arkansas River have created backwater habitats suitable for cattails and other aquatic vegetation. Summer records of Least Bitterns in the late 1970s and early 1980s at Arkansas Post in Arkansas County, Willow Beach on the Arkansas River at North Little Rock, and at Pine Bluff (Lake Langhofer slackwater harbor) are attributable to these artificial marshes and suggest that the birds are now present in areas not available to them in the past.

FALL MIGRATION: There are relatively few sightings after July. A Least Bittern was seen at Calion in Union County on October 7, and one was observed at Centerton in Benton County on October 10. The only report thereafter involved a single bird that was killed upon impact with a building in Little Rock on December 4.

GREAT BLUE HERON, *Ardea herodias* Linnaeus

Common permanent resident in all regions. In winter, somewhat more numerous in the southern lowlands. The "crane" of folk idiom.

BREEDING SEASON: Nesting activity has been observed as early as the middle of February and may continue in some colonies throughout June. One of the first indications of the commencement of the breeding season is the arrival of Great Blue Herons in their colonial nesting areas and the refurbishment of old nests used in previous years, or the beginnings of new ones. In Washington County in the northwest, birds have been seen standing in nests as early as the third week of February.

The peak of the season occurs during April and May. At a colony in Hot Spring County in the Ouachitas, feathered nestlings were seen in some nests on May 13, but incubation of eggs was still underway in other nests.

Observers who participated in the 1980 colonial bird rookery survey reported colonies in ten counties scattered in all regions of the state, and nesting doubtless occurs elsewhere. These colonies may vary from a few individuals and one or a few nests up to several hundred. Nests are often placed over dry land in the tallest trees growing in large, undisturbed bottomland forests near streams or other large bodies of water. Great Blue Herons return to these colony sites year after year. At Malvern in Hot Spring County, eighty-six active nests were recently counted seventy to ninety feet high in the large pine trees growing in a hardwood swamp. Only rarely are the colonies found in upland sites, like the one with sixteen adults and eight active nests in a single sycamore tree on a hillside "bench" above Lee Creek in Washington County. One of the best examples of a colony over water is the long-existing one in the cypress swamp at Grassy Lake in Hempstead County, where by the second half of April there have been as many as 200 birds associated with nests in the cypress. Although occasionally nesting with other species, Great Blue Herons characteristically nest in separate colonies, particularly in dry land sites.

Populations in the highlands have apparently remained stable over the years, but the loss of bottomland forests and suitable shallow water feeding habitat in the Mississippi River region seems to have reduced numbers there. One of the greatest colonies ever reported in the state involved several hundred pairs of birds at Walker Lake in Mississippi County. Subsequently, the lake was drained and the colony disappeared. Illegal shooting also continues to be a problem. In May 1981, a colony in the northwestern highlands was "shot up" by a man and two boys "out for some fun." At least twenty-nine adults were killed, as were many nestlings and unhatched eggs.

FALL: After the breeding season large numbers of Great Blue Herons may congregate in prime feeding areas, including shallow waters of open lakes or reservoirs and associated mud-

FIGURE 6-7 Great Blue Heron.
Howard Stern

flats. At Big Lake Refuge, where several hundred birds sometimes nested, the population reached 500 birds during September, a peak in numbers there. The more than one dozen birds seen on mudflats at Lake Sequoyah in the western Ozarks during September is a peak in numbers there.

Banding recoveries for Arkansas show the presence of birds here that have wandered north from heronries to the south, plus records of birds migrating southward into the state from breeding areas in the north. Four of the five recoveries were initially banded as birds of the

year in Wisconsin, 650 to 800 miles north. The fifth bird, after the breeding season in Texas, had traveled 400 miles north into Arkansas.

WINTER: Great Blue Herons are observed on Christmas Bird Counts in all regions, with the highest numbers generally recorded in the Arkansas River Valley and the southern lowlands. Unprecedented large numbers were reported in the state during the 1983 Christmas Count period, with peaks of 135 at Lonoke (previous high there in a thirty-year period was 80), and 91 at Pine Bluff. The birds are seen most, if not all years in the western Ozarks,

FIGURE 6-8 Great Egret. *Charles Mills*

where as many as 28 (also in 1983) have been reported on the Christmas Count at Fayetteville.

GREAT EGRET, *Casmerodius albus* (Linnaeus)

Local summer resident breeding in small numbers in the lowlands and in the Arkansas River Valley. Regular transient and post-breeding season visitor in all regions. Irregular winter visitor in the lowlands. Observed in flooded fields, along major rivers, in the shallow waters of lakes and reservoirs. Formerly called "American" and "Common" Egret.

SPRING MIGRATION: Northward moving Great Egrets generally reach Arkansas during the second half of March, with migrants seen in all regions during April and May. The first arrivals often were seen during the third week of March at Big Lake Refuge in Mississippi County and also at the former Swan Lake heronry in Jefferson County (Meanley 1955).

BREEDING SEASON: Most nesting records are from the lowlands, especially the Mississippi River region. Great Egrets once nested in the "sunken lands" area of Walker Lake in Mississippi County (Howell 1911); at the Old Town

Lake in Phillips County (Audubon Society file); at Cypress Bayou in White County (file record for 1951); in the former mixed-species heronry at Swan Lake (Meanley 1955); at White River Refuge; and in the former mixed-species heronries at Luxora and later at Burdette in Mississippi County (file, Hanebrink 1968, Singleton 1973). Great Egrets have nested for years at Grassy Lake in Hempstead County, and in small numbers since the 1970s in the mixed-species heronry in the Ouachita River bottomlands near Malvern in Hot Spring County. Since 1980 nesting has been confirmed at Grassy Lake, in a newly established mixed-species heronry near Lake Conway in Faulkner County, in the Red River bottoms of Lafayette County, at the Malvern heronry, at Burdette (although this site was abandoned by 1983), and in a mixed-species heronry at Van Buren in Crawford County. There are additional breeding season records, but no specific evidences of nesting, in all regions of the state.

Nesting activity has been observed from late March to mid-July, but chiefly in April, May, and June. At Grassy Lake, the birds have commenced "nesting" (presumably nest construction) as early as March 24. The month of April is devoted to nest construction, egg laying, and incubation. Nests have been observed as high as eighty feet in cypress trees over water at Grassy Lake and also high in trees at Cypress Bayou, in thick lakeshore bushes as they were at Swan Lake, or in moderately tall trees over dry land at the Luxora heronry. Anhingas have nested among the Great Egrets at Grassy Lake, but both species were somewhat removed from the section of the heronry where the Cattle Egrets and Snowy Egrets nested. By the middle of May some of the Great Egret nests have young, and by late June at Grassy Lake nearly all the Great Egrets have left their nests. The breeding schedule may be somewhat later further north. At Old Town Lake, for example, many juveniles were still being fed by adults in the last week of June, and active nests have been observed in Mississippi County at mid-July.

Great Egret populations in Arkansas have undergone considerable fluctuations. Howell (1911) found only four pairs at Walker Lake in 1910, down from what was described as a "large colony" only twenty years before, no doubt a result of shooting by plume hunters who then sold the feathers of dead birds to the millinery trade. The birds were so reduced in numbers throughout the United States by around 1910 that hunting ceased, and public awareness of the importance of protection for nongame species resulted in legal protection.

In more recent years there has been a great reduction in the amount and extent of suitable swampy lowland habitat for nesting. This is a result of land clearing operations associated with the expansion of agriculture in eastern Arkansas. This habitat loss and the increased application of pesticides to farmland have paralleled another overall decline in the numbers of Great Egrets in Arkansas, and the species has been added to the unofficial "red list" of birds whose breeding populations are thought to be threatened or endangered in the state (James 1974).

FALL MIGRATION: Beginning in July, Great Egrets (and other colonial waders) can be seen feeding in shallow reservoirs and flooded fields in the eastern lowlands and elsewhere. In the western Ozarks, for example, these post-breeding birds have been seen as early as the second week of July, and they are regular visitors in the highlands during August and September, though in smaller numbers than in the lowlands. Certainly the numbers seen in fall in recent years have been lower than at any time since the early 1960s.

Legal protection from shooting allowed the birds to recover so that during the 1940s and 1950s considerable numbers, up to 1000 or more, were reported in late summer and early fall roosts at Big Lake and generally throughout the rice country. Even as late as 1958, over 245 birds were present at the White River Refuge in July. By the early 1970s, however, experienced observers were hard pressed to find even a dozen birds anywhere in eastern Arkansas. Almost certainly this downward trend in numbers is related to factors discussed above (see BREEDING SEASON). The 87 birds seen in Desha County on August 3, 1974, comprised an exceptionally large number in recent years. During the drought year of 1980, a highly unusual number of 208 were concentrated at a single roadside pond of moderate size in Little River County. Similar peak counts in the western Ozarks in recent years have involved no more than 12 to 15 birds.

There are seventy-four recoveries of banded Great Egrets associated with Arkansas. All of these recoveries are associated with the fall season, and all consistently demonstrate the fact that after the breeding season this species moves northward from the places where they were hatched or nested before heading south again for the winter season (Figure 6-9). The distances between banding and recovery ranged up to 262 miles. Of the seventy-four records, 50 birds were recovered within three months following banding as nestlings. One bird lived almost sixteen years between banding and recovery.

Only a few Great Egrets remain in the state after October. Files at Big Lake showed most birds were gone by the end of October, with the latest record on November 20.

WINTER: Most observations of Great Egrets in Arkansas during December, January, and early February have involved single birds in the southern or southeastern lowlands. Rarely are they seen at this time in the Arkansas River Valley or in the northeast, and there are no records for the Ozarks between November and early April. While it is therefore of irregular occurrence in the state in winter, there are some reports of unusual concentrations: 68 at Lake Millwood on the 1980 Christmas Count; 30 in Arkansas County in the southwest on February 16, 1961; and 51 at Horseshoe Lake in Crittenden County on February 24, 1952.

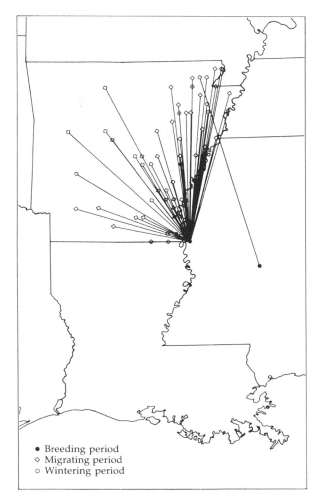

● Breeding period
◇ Migrating period
○ Wintering period

FIGURE 6-9 Movements of the Great Egret based on banding records.

SNOWY EGRET, *Egretta thula* (Molina)

Uncommon migrant and post-breeding season visitor in all regions. Uncommon local summer resident in small numbers in a few mixed-species heronries in the lowlands and in the Arkansas River Valley.

SPRING MIGRATION: Spring migrants have been reported from late March to the middle of May. At the former Swan Lake heronry in Jefferson County, Snowy Egrets arrived during the third to last week of March (Meanley 1955), and there is a similar arrival record in the Audubon Society file for Grassy Lake in Hempstead County. Otherwise, most arrivals have been reported in early April and thereafter.

BREEDING SEASON: Snowy Egrets nest with other colonial birds, but always in small numbers in Arkansas. M. G. Vaiden reported the presence of many juveniles being fed by adults at Old Town Lake in Phillips County on June 25, 1913 (Audubon Society file). The species nested in the former mixed-species heronry at Swan Lake in Jefferson County (Meanley 1955). Two birds were seen at the mixed-species heronry at Lollie in Faulkner County on May 18, 1957. Snowy Egrets have nested for a number of years at Grassy Lake, and twenty adults and one nest were seen there in June 1980. Five pairs of Snowy Egrets first nested at the former Luxora heronry in Mississippi County in 1968. When this heronry moved to Burdette in the same county, 10 birds were seen in 1972 (Hanebrink 1980, Singleton 1973). Snowy Egrets did not nest at Burdette in 1982, and the entire heronry was abandoned in 1983. Other than the recent nesting records for Grassy Lake, the only other confirmed breeding records are from Lafayette County in 1981, and from Van Buren in Crawford County in 1982, 1984, and 1985.

There are only a few actual nesting dates available for this species in Arkansas. At Swan Lake the birds began nesting in the second week of April in 1951. At Grassy Lake in 1960, eggs were seen in some nests on May 14, and construction was still underway on others. At the same place in 1967, Snowy Egrets were said to be "fighting constantly with Cattle Egrets at nest" in the first week of June. The report from Old Town Lake (see above) stated that juveniles were still being fed by adults in the last week of June. The low numbers that currently nest in Arkansas have led to its being placed on an unofficial "red list" of birds whose breeding populations are considered to be threatened or endangered in the state (James 1974).

FALL MIGRATION: Even though some Snowy Egrets may still be engaged in nesting activity, by late June or during July they begin to move from their nesting colonies and may then be seen anywhere in the state. Information derived from banding studies shows that Snowy Egrets wander northward from their breeding areas. Five birds recovered in Arkansas (four of them on the Mississippi Alluvial Plain) had been banded as nestlings in Mississippi, 58 to 185 miles south, and all five were recovered during their first summer in age. Most post-breeding season records have involved small numbers of birds, often one or two, but there are a few larger counts. In Jefferson County, 100

were seen on Bayou Meto on July 16, 1954. And while most peak fall records, even in prime areas of the southern lowlands like Lake Millwood, usually amount to only a dozen birds seen on one day in the field, more are seen under special circumstances. For example, in the drought year of 1980, when most aquatic feeding areas were dried up, a concentration of 40 Snowy Egrets was observed at Lake Millwood in mid-July along the Okay levee. There are few records for the state after September, and the latest involved a single bird at Stuttgart in the second week of October.

LITTLE BLUE HERON, *Egretta caerulea* (Linnaeus)

Common transient in all regions. Summer resident, breeding near a few major lakes and rivers, principally in the lowlands and the Arkansas River Valley; and present to some extent in all regions in summer. Rare and irregular visitor in the southern lowlands in winter.

SPRING MIGRATION: Little Blue Herons begin to arrive from their wintering areas from mid-March to late April, mainly in late March. At Grassy Lake in Hempstead County, 1300 birds were present on March 24, 1968.

BREEDING SEASON: The nesting season begins as soon as the birds arrive in the wooded moist bottomlands where they form colonies. Records in the Audubon Society file for the heronries at Malvern in Hot Spring County and at Grassy Lake in Hempstead County, plus the former heronry at Luxora in Mississippi County (Hanebrink 1968c) and the former heronry at Swan Lake in Jefferson County (Meanley 1955), show a fairly uniform nesting season. Nest construction may sometimes occur as early as the third week of March (Meanley 1955), but usually in late March and early April. Most nests have eggs by mid-April, and incubation continues through May. At Swan Lake, the peak period of hatching of eggs was in the second week of May. By the second half of May the adults are feeding nestlings, and by June most of the young have fledged. A nesting cycle of secondary importance involves some nests with eggs as late as the first half of July, but by early August these young have fledged. By late August the heronries are abandoned and the birds have begun to disperse widely on their post-breeding season movements.

FIGURE 6-10 Heronry at Malvern in June: Little Blue Herons and Cattle Egrets. *David Plank*

Nests have been found in Arkansas at heights ranging from three to fifty feet above the ground, usually in small trees or shrubs growing on moist ground or in shallow standing water. A recently established colony in the western Ozarks was in a thicket on an upland site. At Swan Lake, fifty-eight nests ranged in heights from three to twenty-five feet, with an average of eight feet. At Luxora, the nests ranged from five feet in height to "the tops of the trees" but the smaller trees were preferred. Even though many nests used in the previous year's nesting season may still be intact, Little Blue Herons seem to prefer to construct entirely new nests (Meanley 1955). The clutch sizes at Swan Lake ranged from three to five eggs, chiefly four.

The 1980 Arkansas colonial bird rookery survey showed active nesting colonies in eight counties in the central and southern regions and also in the northeastern lowlands. More than 1000 adult birds have been counted in the principal nesting colonies in the cypress swamp at Grassy Lake (Hempstead County), in a mixed oak-sweetgum bottomland forest associated with the Ouachita River at Malvern, and at Burdette in Mississippi County. In the 1984 season an estimated 5000 adults and young were present at a mixed-species heronry in southwestern Pulaski County (P. Floyd, Arkansas Natural Heritage Commission file). In 1982 an estimated 150 birds nested near the Arkansas River at Van Buren, and in 1983 some 300 birds nested in a mixed-species colony near Lake Conway in Faulkner County. The Burdette heronry was abandoned in 1983. The Van Buren heronry was active in 1984 and 1985, but the noise and odors associated with a large, mixed-species heronry became a source of considerable frustration for local residents who forced the birds to move. Nests and young found near Lincoln in Washington County in May 1985 were the first confirmed breeding reports for the western Arkansas Ozarks.

POST-BREEDING SEASON: By the last week of May some Little Blue Herons begin to leave the immediate environs of the colonies and range over a wide area. From late May or early June

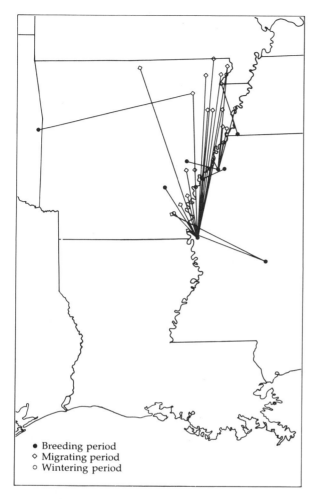

- ● Breeding period
- ◇ Migrating period
- ○ Wintering period

FIGURE 6-11 Movements of the Little Blue Heron based on banding records.

and then throughout the fall, the species can be observed in wet open fields, along streams, on ponds, and on mudflats associated with reservoirs in all regions. These post-breeding season birds may include the slaty blue adults, the mottled blue-and-white second year birds, and the pure white juveniles. At Big Lake Refuge several hundred birds maintained a post-breeding season roost from early July until mid-September. By late September or early October the bulk of the population has moved south of the state.

The post-breeding season dispersal is well documented. Many of the 37 birds banded in their nests in states bordering Arkansas were subsequently recovered in the state, with the distance traveled often about 100 miles north of the banding site, and the maximum distance being 234 miles (Figure 6-11). Most were recovered three months after banding, but one had survived six and one-half years between banding and recovery.

Reports after late October are rare and widely scattered, and most records for "winter" are single individuals in Union, Miller, and Hempstead counties in December. At least one of these records involved a slightly injured bird that was caught and examined in hand.

NOTE: Despite the impressive numbers of Little Blue Herons that annually nest in the state, its status is subject to considerable change. Disturbance in nesting areas is one problem. After nesting in one location in Hot Spring County for ten years, the colony moved a quarter mile away, apparently as a result of harassment by gunners. The important heronry in Mississippi County, one of the few large colonial nesting areas in the vast expanse of cleared land on the Mississippi Alluvial Plain in Arkansas, was swept by fire in 1981 and later abandoned. These problems are brought into focus by the continued loss of forested wetland habitat. This loss deprives the birds of lands where they have historically nested and it also deprives them of lands suitable for the establishment of new colonies when the old sites are lost due to land clearing or have become unsuitable for other reasons.

TRICOLORED HERON, *Egretta tricolor* (Müller)

Rare and irregular summer resident that has bred a few times at two locations in the lowlands. Rare transient in other regions. Formerly called "Louisiana Heron."

BREEDING SEASON: Arkansas is without coastal salt marshes, the favored habitat of this species. Nevertheless, a few pairs have nested at the former mixed-species heronry at Burdette (Mississippi County) in the northeast not far from the Mississippi River, with sightings in that region from early April through August (Hanebrink 1980). In 1982 the birds were not seen at Burdette, and in 1983 the site was abandoned by all the colonial nesting birds. The only other breeding record involved a juvenile in a nest on an old meander scar lake in the Red River bottoms (Lafayette County) of southwestern Arkansas on July 14, 1981.

OTHER RECORDS: Records of sightings from late June to early November have involved other areas of the state. In Garland County, one or two birds were seen on three occasions during August (Deaderick 1938), the only records for the highlands. There are no records for the Ozarks in Arkansas. A single bird was observed from July 29 to August 23, 1956, in the Arkansas River bottomlands west of Fort Smith near Moffett, Oklahoma. The four birds at Lake Millwood on August 21, 1977, seemed to be associated with Wood Storks, and another bird was there November 4, 1984. A single bird was seen October 2, 1983, at Lake Chicot State Park in Chicot County. Fall 1985 brought an unprecedented number of Tricolored Heron records in the state. In addition to several records in central Arkansas, a total of seven were seen by Bob Sanger and others along the Okay levee at Lake Millwood on September 2, 1985.

CATTLE EGRET, *Bubulcus ibis* (Linnaeus)

Common to fairly common migrant and summer resident in all regions, but primarily in the lowlands and the Arkansas River Valley. Present irregularly in winter in small numbers in the south.

SPRING MIGRATION: While a few Cattle Egrets are present in the southern lowlands during February and March, they do not move into the more northerly regions of the state until mid-March or early April (Johnson 1979, Hanebrink 1980) and may not arrive in breeding areas until early May.

BREEDING SEASON: A flock of Cattle Egrets reported in Florida during 1942 was the first record for the United States. They were first reported in Louisiana in 1955 (Lowery 1974), in Oklahoma in 1962 (Sutton 1967), and in Arkansas in 1962 when a single bird was observed in Clark County near Arkadelphia between November 15 and 17 (James 1964). The following year there were reports in Lonoke, Miller, Crittenden, and Mississippi counties. Nesting was confirmed at Grassy Lake in Hempstead County in 1964, and by 1968 more than a hundred pairs were engaged in nesting activities at two large mixed-species heronries in Mississippi and Hempstead counties.

The U.S. Fish and Wildlife Service's colonial bird rookery survey in 1980 showed the species nesting in Mississippi, Saline, Hot Spring, Hempstead, Lafayette, and Little River counties. The birds nested at Sweet Home in Pulaski County in 1976, between 1982–85 at a mixed-species heronry at Van Buren in Crawford County and in 1983 at Lake Conway in Faulkner County. The heronry in Hot Spring County in 1983 included almost 3000 Cattle Egrets, 1500 Little Blue Herons, and much smaller numbers of Great Egrets, Green-backed Herons, Snowy Egrets, and Great Blue Herons. An estimated 5000 adults and young were observed in a mixed-species heronry in southwestern Pulaski County in 1984. A small heronry with about fifty nests in Washington County found in 1984 was the first definite nesting record for the Arkansas Ozarks.

Cattle Egrets apparently begin their nesting activities later than other herons and egrets (Audubon Society file, Hanebrink 1968c). Although present near the heronries in April, they do not begin to build their nests until May. This was the case at Lake Conway in 1983, where the birds began to arrive in early May and did not reach their full number (1200) until two weeks later. At Grassy Lake there is a record of these birds "all fighting for sticks" during June, but by the end of June most nests have young. Young were still in nests in Washington County in the last week of August, but this late nesting may have been a result of shooting that disrupted the normal nesting cycle.

LATE SUMMER AND FALL: After the breeding season Cattle Egrets wander from the breeding areas, and by late summer they may be observed in pastures, on pond flats, and in open fields where they feed on insects (and where they may be confused with Little Blue Herons which are also white in their juvenile plumage). In recent years flocks of Cattle Egrets numbering up to 300 to 400 birds have been seen at Anderson's Minnow Farm in Lonoke County, apparently attracted by the cattle there. Over 200 roosted at Lake Sequoyah in Washington County in August and September of 1982, and an estimated 1000 "plus" roosted near Lincoln in the same county in August 1984. The 1200 seen flying at Lake Millwood on October 6, 1976, was not considered an unusually high number for that area. The birds are present regularly in the state until about mid-October, especially in the southern lowlands, and numbers decline sharply thereafter.

WINTER: A few birds, usually one or two, are seen somewhere in the state, often the southern lowlands or occasionally in central Arkansas, during December. A highly unusual number of 21 were counted along the Okay levee in Howard County during the 1978 Lake Millwood Christmas Bird Count. A total of 37 birds were seen on four Christmas Bird Counts in 1984.

GREEN-BACKED HERON, *Butorides striatus* (Linnaeus)

Common migrant and summer resident along streams and lakes in all regions. Several December records. Formerly called "Green Heron."

SPRING MIGRATION: Green-backed Herons sometime arrive in the lowlands of southern Arkansas in March (earliest report, one bird on the El Dorado wastewater treatment ponds on March 7), but most "spring first" sightings in the south occur during the last week of March and generally few are observed until the first and second weeks of April, after which it becomes common. There is also one record of a bird in Greene County on February 26.

BREEDING SEASON: They are common in appropriate habitat during the nesting season throughout the state. The average annual mean numbers per route in each region on the Breeding Bird Survey was 2.6 on the Coastal Plain, 0.7 on the Mississippi Alluvial Plain, and 1.3 in the highlands, including the Arkansas River Valley.

Nesting activity has been observed from late April to early August. The extreme nesting records are a nest with three eggs in Arkansas County on April 25 and three young in a nest in Washington County on August 4. In the Wheeler Collection there are two clutches of eggs that were taken from nests on April 27 and May 14. One of these nests had five eggs, and the heights of the nests were nine and fifteen feet above the ground. Heights of nests in the Audubon Society file have varied, from as low as the nest holding four eggs found by Charles Gardner in a willow tree on April 26, only four feet above ground, to as high as the nest mentioned in connection with Wheeler (above). Clutch sizes of nests in the file have varied from two to four eggs. Green-backed Herons nest as solitary pairs or in small colonies. The nest site may be a thicket of small trees like willows near a lake or stream, or a woodlot or cedar grove a considerable distance from water. Some pairs have been found in mixed-species heronries. At the former Swan Lake heronry in Jefferson County, for example, fifteen pairs nested in the same area as other colonial birds (Meanley 1954).

LATE SUMMER AND FALL: After the breeding season relatively large numbers may gather at such places as fish ponds. Considerable numbers have been reported during the second half of July and thereafter to early September, after which numbers in the state begin to decline. At least 18 birds were observed around several ponds at the state fish hatchery in Garland County on July 20, and 19 were seen at Anderson's Minnow Farm in Lonoke County on August 12. Some of these birds seen in fall are derived from populations that breed north of the state. One bird recovered in August along the Mississippi River in Arkansas had been banded almost 200 miles away in Missouri during June of the previous year.

A few birds are seen in the state until late October. Several December records associated with Christmas Bird Counts suggest that on occasion a few isolated individuals straggle behind the normal period for migration.

FIGURE 6-12 Black-crowned Night-Heron. *Sigrid James Bruch*

BLACK-CROWNED NIGHT-HERON,
Nycticorax nycticorax (Linnaeus)

Migrant in all regions in small numbers. Local summer resident in small numbers in southern lowlands, and perhaps elsewhere in the lowlands. A few irregular winter records. Observed much less often than Yellow-crowned Night-Heron.

SPRING MIGRATION: Single birds have arrived in the state as early as mid-March. The four birds at Grassy Lake in Hempstead County on March 24 is the earliest spring arrival record involving more than one bird; most other "spring first" sightings occurred in the first half of April. At Big Lake Refuge in the northeast, for example, the species was usually observed in the second week of April. The few spring records for the Ozarks involve the month of April. There is one spring banding record: a bird recovered in northeastern Arkansas in April had been banded nearly ten years before during July in Minnesota, almost 700 miles away.

BREEDING SEASON: There are breeding records or breeding season sightings for the White River Refuge, at Lake Chicot in Chicot County, at the former mixed-species heronries (Luxora and Burdette) in Mississippi County, at Grassy Lake, at Booker in Crittenden County, and at Village Creek State Park in Cross County. The species was formerly reported nesting at Newport in Jackson County (Howell 1911); it nested at the former mixed-species heronry at Swan Lake in Jefferson County as late as 1953 (file); and nested in a "small colony" on Gold Creek in the Palarm bottoms in Faulkner County (Wheeler 1924). The 1980 Arkansas colonial bird rookery survey reported nestings at Grassy Lake and at Burdette in Mississippi County (the Burdette site has since been abandoned).

Eggs or young have been observed from the second week of April into the second half of July. The earliest record that involved "nesting" was at Swan Lake on April 10. The first indication of nests with eggs involves two records at Grassy Lake where incubation was underway at mid-May. The latest nesting date is from Mississippi County, where two nests with two young each were seen on July 18. In addition to the records already mentioned, the following records indicate ranges of nesting heights and number of eggs or young in nests: a clutch of three eggs collected from a nest fifty feet high in an oak tree on June 14, and a nest with five young was also found (Wheeler 1924); a nest with three eggs eight feet high in a cypress on May 15 at Grassy Lake.

Since this species has often been found nesting with other colonial birds, the general disappearance of heronries in the state has presumably hurt the Arkansas population of Black-crowned Night-Herons. This loss of appropriate nesting habitat compounds other problems known to affect birds that feed in wetlands, including pesticide pollution, drainage of wetlands, and channelization of streams (James 1974).

FALL AND WINTER: From July until about mid-October, mixed groups of immature and adult birds may be observed feeding in open areas with shallow water, especially on the Mississippi Alluvial Plain. Peak fall counts include 74 birds around reservoirs at England in Lonoke County on October 12, 1958, and more recently, 58 or more at Anderson's Minnow Farm (also at Lonoke) in early September of 1977. During the early 1980s there have been several fall records in the western Ozarks involving one or two birds from late August to mid-October, but the birds are uncommon or somewhat rare in the Arkansas highlands at any season.

Some birds seen in fall have come from long distances: one banded in July in Saskatchewan, Canada, was recovered in October of the same year in Arkansas, over 1000 miles away. Few birds are seen after mid-October, but there are three records involving single birds in Pulaski, Lonoke, and Miller counties in December and January.

YELLOW-CROWNED NIGHT-HERON,
Nycticorax violaceus (Linnaeus)

Migrant and summer resident in wooded swamps, lakes, and stream bottomlands in all regions. Locally common at a few colonial nesting areas on the Coastal Plain and at a few prime, post-breeding season feeding areas in the lowlands. Uncommon elsewhere in the state.

SPRING MIGRATION: There is one record in the Audubon Society file of a single bird in extreme southern Arkansas in early March, but there are no additional sightings other than scattered individuals until the second week of April, after which time the species seems to move north throughout the state, arriving in the northeastern counties by early May.

BREEDING SEASON: Reports in the Audubon Society file show that the species is present in all regions during summer, with nesting activity underway as early as the second week of April, and continuing during May and June. The earliest report in the file involved 30 birds and six nests in the Ouachita River bottoms in Calhoun County near Calion on April 10. Several records that indicate the season extends through June include an adult flushed from a nest in Perry County on June 1 and a nest with eggs at Grassy Lake in Hempstead County on May 30. Nests have been observed in both pine and deciduous trees, eight to twenty feet high, and usually near or over water. At Sweet Home in Pulaski County, for example, five nests were twenty feet high in open pine woods, with the nests in pine trees near a slough.

Observations published in the 1980 Arkansas colonial bird rookery survey showed nesting colonies in Arkansas, Calhoun, Faulkner, and Hempstead counties. The size of these colonies ranged from three nests in Faulkner County southwest of Conway in the Arkansas River Valley to another with thirty nests, eighty to one hundred young, and twenty-five to fifty adults in Calhoun County on the Coastal Plain. Several recent additional reports of colonies are from the Bayou Meto Wildlife Management Area east of Pine Bluff where there were twenty-three nests and 50 birds in 1980, and one in Clark County where there were six adults and three nests in 1981.

Colonies have been located exclusively in the lowlands of the southern half of the state, or in the Arkansas River Valley up to Faulkner County, where there is very similar habitat. In the northeast the species occurs regularly in the Black River bottoms near Corning in Clay County, and older records indicate its presence all summer at Big Lake. The scattered summer records from the Ozarks and the Ouachitas have usually involved one or two birds and single nests.

LATE SUMMER AND FALL: By mid-July the breeding season is past, and in a few places such as Lonoke, where there is an abundance of open, shallow water feeding habitat, large congregations of these birds are sometimes seen. Of 25 birds seen there on August 2, 1980, 21 were immatures. By the middle of September the species is no longer present in the north, and occurs only very rarely after mid-October anywhere in the state. The six at Lonoke on November 16 was unusual.

There is one banding recovery associated with Arkansas. A bird banded as a nestling in Mississippi near the Mississippi River was recovered near the same river in Arkansas, 92 miles away and five and one-half years later.

Family *Threskiornithidae* Ibises

Subfamily *Threskiornithinae* Ibises

WHITE IBIS, *Eudocimus albus* (Linnaeus)
Rare late summer and early fall visitor, primarily in the lowlands.

As is the case with the Wood Stork, the White Ibises observed in Arkansas have wandered far north of the wooded swamps where they nest. In the Audubon Society file there are records for the post-breeding period between the second week of June and September, primarily mid-July through August. Most of these sightings have involved one or two birds, but sometimes a relatively large flock is seen. Such was the case at the White River Refuge in the southeast where 25 were reported on June 29, 1956. Thirty immature birds were reported in Lonoke County during early August of 1981.

While most of these sightings have occurred in southern and southeastern Arkansas, there is also a record at Little Rock, and two records from the northeastern counties. There are also two highly unusual spring reports: one bird among a flock of Little Blue Herons at Lonoke on April 26, 1961, and another single bird in Jefferson County on May 28, 1974.

GLOSSY IBIS, *Plegadis falcinellus* (Linnaeus)
Rare migrant and irregular summer resident that bred in northeastern Arkansas near the Mississippi River in the 1960s and 1970s. Otherwise, its status is uncertain. Several additional reports for the genus *Plegadis*.

SPRING MIGRATION: A single Glossy Ibis in Mississippi County on April 24 is the earliest record in the Audubon Society file. Otherwise, the earliest date for the northeastern counties is early May (Hanebrink 1980).

BREEDING SEASON: Hanebrink and Cochran (1966) found six Glossy Ibises and three nests at the old heronry at Luxora in Mississippi County during May and June 1965. This was the first Arkansas record for the Glossy Ibis and the first reported nesting in the interior of the United States. The heronry, which included approximately 2000 Little Blue Herons and 75 Great Egrets, occupied eight acres of lowland deciduous woods three miles from the Mississippi River, and was one of the last large mixed-species heronries to survive massive timbering and land clearing operations on the Mississippi Alluvial Plain of Arkansas. The Glossy Ibis nests were placed in low trees with a heavy entanglement of vines. An egg collected on June 1 was estimated to be over one week old. A female collected for a study specimen had been feeding on small clams. During the summer of 1972, seven adults with four young were observed at a heronry in Burdette, also in Mississippi County, which formed at the time the Luxora site was abandoned. Glossy Ibises were not found at Burdette in 1982, and the site was abandoned by all colonial nesting birds in 1983.

FALL: There are a few fall records for most regions of the state involving the genus *Plegadis* (see the following species account), but because of confusion with the White-faced Ibis these records cannot be definitely assigned to either species. However, there are several reliable Glossy Ibis records for fall. In the northeast the latest date for Glossy Ibis in fall is in mid-September (Hanebrink 1980). The presence of a single bird at Lonoke, September 25, 1984, was well documented. A single bird at Lake Millwood was observed repeatedly November 30 to December 21, 1981.

WHITE-FACED IBIS, *Plegadis chihi* (Vieillot)
Two definite records, plus eight additional sightings for the genus *Plegadis*.

This species breeds locally primarily to the west of Arkansas (including both the northwestern and southwestern directions) and winters west and south of the state (AOU 1983). A single bird identified as a White-faced Ibis was observed on the Arkansas River in Jefferson County on May 20, 1971. This is the only spring record. An adult bird observed at Lake Millwood on September 17, 1980, was identified as this species.

The eight additional sightings involving the genus *Plegadis* could not be identified as to species, but they might have involved transients associated with breeding populations of White-faced Ibises west or south of the state. These records are from all regions between the second week of September and late November. Each involved single birds except for the two at Budd Kidd Lake in Washington County on September 9, 1983.

Subfamily Plataleinae Spoonbill

ROSEATE SPOONBILL, *Ajaia ajaja* (Linnaeus)
Rare fall visitor.

Seven sightings in Arkansas between mid-July and mid-October, primarily involving the southwestern counties, are presumably the result of birds that have wandered far north of the Gulf Coast nesting areas after the breeding season. The first record involved a single bird at a swampy lake near the Red River in Miller County on September 20, 1959. A single bird was observed at Lake Millwood in the southwest from July 16 to 19, 1966, and another was seen nearby on the Red River on September 10, 1972. Two immature birds were observed at a puddle in an agricultural field in Jefferson County between September 8 and 16, 1973. A

single bird was among a large flock of egrets observed by two employees of the Arkansas Game and Fish Commission at Sulphur River Wildlife Management Area in Miller County on October 18, 1978. The fall of 1985 brought the largest number of Roseate Spoonbills ever recorded in the state. A number of observers in central Arkansas saw at least nine birds near Galloway in Pulaski County on August 17, and 10 were observed at the Okay levee by Lake Millwood on September 2.

Family Ciconiidae Storks

WOOD STORK, *Mycteria americana* Linnaeus
Uncommon visitor, primarily in fall, in the lowlands. Formerly called "Wood Ibis."

STATUS IN ARKANSAS: Northward wandering post-breeding season birds from breeding areas south of Arkansas have been observed from the second week of June to the first week of November, but there are few reports prior to July or after early October. Reports for the state (chiefly in the 1950s and 1960s) indicate that peak numbers can be expected between the second week of July and the last week of September. In earlier years Wood Storks were sometimes seen in conspicuous flocks as they flew overhead, roosted in trees, or fed on muddy flats of drained ponds, reservoirs, or along the Mississippi River. Of the highest numbers seen recently, between 6 and 50 birds appeared at Lake Millwood from early August to early October of 1977. Charles Mills, who saw these birds, states that Wood Storks are rare though fairly regular visitors in southwestern Arkansas and have been seen at Lake Millwood in 1974, 1976, 1977, 1978, 1982, 1983, and 1985, with counts of individuals varying from 1 to 50. There are also three spring reports in the file from Union, Pope, and Pulaski counties during April and May. The 25 counted August 4, 1984, in the Ouachita River bottoms of Bradley County was a relatively large number. The birds were also seen regularly in the same area of Bradley County during late summer and fall of 1985. An estimated 30 to 40 were seen at Lake Chicot State Park in Chicot County on September 8, 1985.

CHANGE IN STATUS: Prior to the mid-1960s, many reports of this species involved flocks of

20 or more birds, and sometimes more than 200. Records at Big Lake Refuge in Mississippi County between the early 1940s and early 1960s showed that Wood Storks reached peak numbers of 150 to 200 birds during August and September, and in 1941 approximately 2000 were there. The birds are no longer seen at Big Lake. Since the 1960s there have been considerably fewer sightings in Arkansas than was the case previously, and when seen the flocks are much smaller. Doubtless the situation in Arkansas is the result of large reductions in the breeding populations. Between 1960 and 1975, for example, the breeding population in the United States declined by an estimated 41 percent, and this was attributed primarily to "loss of feeding habitats coupled with a reduction in the fish biomass or food availability in remaining wetlands" (Ogden and Nesbitt 1979). In February 1984, the Wood Stork was placed on the list of endangered species maintained by the U.S. Fish and Wildlife Service.

Order ANSERIFORMES

Family Anatidae

Subfamily Anserinae Swans and Geese

FULVOUS WHISTLING-DUCK,
Dendrocygna bicolor (Vieillot)

Rare fall visitor in the southern lowlands. Formerly called "Fulvous Tree Duck."

When these birds are found in Arkansas they are far north of their usual breeding range, which is no closer to Arkansas than central and eastern Texas and the Gulf Coast in Louisiana (AOU 1983). The first records involved the Lonoke area in September of 1950 (Baerg 1951). Reports in the Audubon Society file show that these birds were seen on several occasions between mid-September and mid-October, with a peak of 51 on October 14. As many as 25 were seen at Lonoke in early September of 1952 (Coffey 1981), and a flock of eight was seen and a male collected there on September 17 (Meanley and Neff 1953a). There were no further reports for almost thirty years, then four were seen at Lake Millwood on August 14, 1980. An undated, mounted specimen of a bird apparently shot at Grassy Lake in southwestern Arkansas is in the possession of Mrs. Justine Hamm.

BLACK-BELLIED WHISTLING-DUCK,
Dendrocygna autumnalis (Linnaeus)

One record.

Five immature Black-bellied Whistling-Ducks were seen at Lake Millwood in Hempstead County on September 3, 1982. Written documentation is on file with the Arkansas Audubon Society.

TUNDRA SWAN, *Cygnus columbianus* (Ord)

Rare migrant and winter visitor in small numbers, chiefly in the lowlands and the central Arkansas River Valley. Formerly called "Whistling Swan."

Prior to 1950 the only record of this species in Arkansas was a flock of "some 12 or 15" in the St. Francis River "sunken lands" in early 1889 (Pindar 1924). In 1950 a single bird was found among a flock of Canada Geese in Arkansas County on November 21. Subsequently there have been observations between late November and late March, often on the national wildlife refuges at Holla Bend in central Arkansas and in the eastern lowlands. Besides Holla Bend, these birds have been seen at Big Lake Refuge, White River Refuge, and several large reservoirs or flooded fields in all regions except for the Ouachita Mountains. Most reports have involved one or two birds or occasionally small flocks that usually are present for a few days or a few weeks. A dozen Tundra Swans were seen among large flocks of Snow Geese south of Valley View in Craighead County on March 2 and 3, 1975, and 16 were seen in Arkansas County between January 29 and February 10, 1962. The flock of four adults and three immatures at Holla Bend between late November and early March, 1960–61 was the second consecutive year a flock had remained all winter on the refuge. The four birds seen in a flooded rice field near Forrest City in St. Francis County in mid-November of 1977 remained in the area until mid-December (three were seen there in the fall of 1978). The three that remained a few days at the state fish hatchery in Benton County in late November of 1981 is the only report for the

Ozarks. Single birds were observed at Lake Millwood in January of 1974 and during January and February of 1977. During late winter and early spring of 1985 small flocks were seen in flooded fields in Jefferson and Lincoln counties.

TRUMPETER SWAN, *Cygnus buccinator* Richardson

Extirpated from the state with no reports in at least seventy years.

Trumpeter Swans formerly wintered well to the south of Arkansas, including the Gulf Coast and the Mississippi Valley (AOU 1983). The earliest record for the state involved Trumpeter Swan bones recovered from an archeological site in Crittenden County (B. D. Smith 1975). Audubon (1831–1839) shot a Trumpeter Swan near the mouth of the Arkansas River. Pindar (1924) considered the species "very rare" in the St. Francis River bottoms area of Poinsett County during his visit there between late January and early March of 1889. Howell (1911) stated that the species was seen occasionally at Mud Lake in St. Francis County, "but in recent years has become very rare. . . ." There have been no subsequent records.

MUTE SWAN, *Cygnus olor* (Gmelin)

One record.

Two birds were seen by Ben Coffey and other experienced observers on May 26, 1971, at Benwood Lake (formerly Lake Alpe) near West Memphis in Crittenden County. The birds were thought to be wild transients because they were not seen at this frequently observed location before or after the above date. This introduced domesticated species does breed in the wild, resulting from former escapees from captivity (AOU 1983). (The lake where the birds were seen, and where other bird records were obtained over the years, no longer exists.)

GREATER WHITE-FRONTED GOOSE, *Anser albifrons* (Scopoli)

Fairly common migrant in all regions and winter resident chiefly in the lowlands. Least common of the geese that occur regularly in Arkansas, but now increasing in numbers.

FALL MIGRATION: This species has arrived in the state as early as the last week of September, but most migrants are seen from the first week of October to the end of November. Many sightings have involved only small numbers, but relatively large flocks have been seen in recent years. Some of the peak counts and locations are: 35 at Lake Sequoyah in Washington County on October 6, 1983; approximately 50 on the Arkansas River at Little Rock on October 10, 1978; an estimated 55 in Monroe County on October 13, 1976; 63 at Lake Millwood in Little River County on October 14, 1979; and 60 at Holla Bend Refuge in Pope County on November 30, 1980.

WINTER: Many winter records have involved no more than one to eight birds either at the national wildlife refuges or at other locations in the eastern lowlands. Certainly numbers seen in the state have increased in recent years. At White River Refuge, for example, the species was very rarely reported on the Christmas Bird Count between the late 1940s and the early 1970s, but thereafter it has been found with regularity, and 50 to 100 have been reported on four counts since the late 1970s. The largest number reported in the state involved 900 birds at the Banefield Reservoir in Desha County on January 31, 1981.

SPRING MIGRATION: The northward migration of spring seems to involve the period between late February and early April, with the latest Arkansas sighting at the end of April. The peak of migration occurs during March. Some peak counts have included "several hundred" at Claypool Reservoir in Poinsett County on March 3, 1977; 82 at Lake Millwood on March 11, 1979, and 43 on the same day in 1983 at the state fish hatchery in Benton County; 27 or more at Big Lake Refuge on March 14, 1981; 80 or more at Holla Bend Refuge on March 16, 1975; and more than 100 associated with Snow and Canada Geese in a flooded field at Moffett, Oklahoma, just west of Fort Smith, Arkansas, in early March of 1984.

SNOW GOOSE, *Chen caerulescens* (Linnaeus)

Regular migrant in all regions. Winter resident in the largest numbers on the national wildlife refuges and in the eastern lowlands,

FIGURE 6-13 Snow Geese. *Bill Brazelton*

but seen in winter in all regions. Both the blue morph (formerly the "Blue Goose") and the white morph are observed.

FALL MIGRATION: Early fall migrants sometimes arrive in late September, but few are generally seen until the time of the first big masses of polar air, in late October or early November, at which time large numbers of Snow Geese move south from their breeding areas in Canada and Alaska. At Big Lake Refuge records between the 1940s and the early 1960s showed that the fall peak occurred between late October and early November, with the birds departing the refuge no later than the first half of December. Records in Arkansas have involved small flocks containing a few individuals and much larger flocks comprised of hundreds of birds. Many flocks include both the blue and white morphs. At Big Lake the blue morph greatly outnumbered the white morph, but the

reverse may be true elsewhere in the state, especially in the western areas. Generally the greatest concentrations of birds are seen at the national wildlife refuges, but large numbers are sometimes seen elsewhere, such as the estimated 500 birds in one flock that flew over Lake Fayetteville during a big cold front on November 23, 1983.

WINTER: Considerable changes in the populations of these birds have been noted in the state. At Big Lake, for example, there were fall peaks of upwards to 2000 birds in the 1940s, but these peaks had fallen drastically by the late 1950s. Winter season counts in recent years, especially since the 1970s, suggest that conservation measures have begun to pay off in larger populations. Peak numbers present statewide at midwinter in the 1970s ranged from fewer than 1000 up to about 30,000, and more than double that number were seen on surveys in the state in 1981, 1982, and 1983. In the mild winter weather of January 1983, survey personnel from state and federal conservation agencies reported an unprecedented 178,000 Snow Geese in Arkansas, primarily on the national wildlife refuges and in the rice growing areas of the Mississippi Alluvial Plain. Much lower numbers are reported in other areas of the state during winter.

SPRING MIGRATION: Northward moving spring migrants pass through the state between late February and early April with the peak during March. The main northward movement seems more concentrated than the fall migration. Certainly few people have had the opportunity to see a concentration such as the one estimated at 16,000 blues and 4000 whites that passed over the Grand Prairie at Stuttgart on March 8, 1962. All able-bodied birds make the spring migration, and records after mid-April usually involve a few scattered birds that are injured.

BANDING: Banded Snow Geese recovered in Arkansas demonstrate the long distances they travel. Six recoveries of white morph birds were banded as close to the state as northwestern Missouri and as far away as 1800 to 2100 miles in such places as South Dakota and Hudson Bay (Figure 6-14). None of these birds survived as long as 2.5 years after banding. Ten recoveries of blue morph birds were banded on their breeding grounds in Hudson Bay, and on their wintering grounds on the Gulf Coast of Louisiana. One lived just over nineteen years between banding and recovery.

ROSS' GOOSE, *Chen rossii* (Cassin)

Four records.

This western migrant sometimes strays eastward. One immature Ross' Goose was seen on a farm pond near Fayetteville in Washington County on December 12, 1973, and remained until April 18, 1974. Photographs of this bird were published in the March 15, 1974, Arkansas Audubon Society Newsletter and in the Arkansas Gazette for January 31, 1974. There is a second documented record from Holla Bend Refuge, on January 21, 1978. A Ross' Goose shot in Prairie County on January 19, 1985, was placed on display in the Pine Bluff Public Library. There is also a record of an adult goose

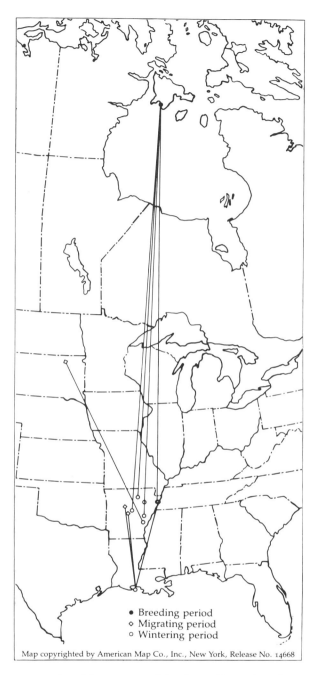

● Breeding period
◇ Migrating period
○ Wintering period

Map copyrighted by American Map Co., Inc., New York, Release No. 14668

FIGURE 6-14 Movements of the Snow Goose based on banding records.

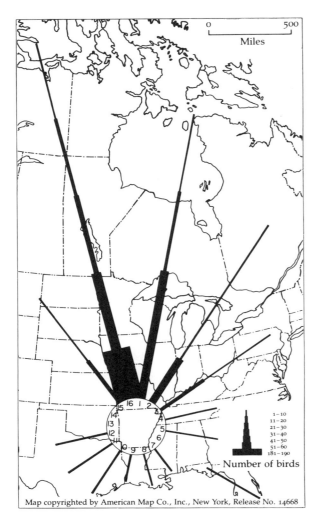

FIGURE 6-15 Movements of the Canada Goose based on banding records.

banded August 17, 1979, on Southampton Island, Canada, at the northern end of Hudson Bay, and found dead near Springdale, Arkansas, in late October 1983.

CANADA GOOSE, *Branta canadensis* (Linnaeus)

Common migrant in all regions. Winter resident or visitor in all regions, especially numerous in the eastern lowlands. Both the large and small forms of the Canada Goose have been reported.

FALL MIGRATION: Canada Geese occasionally arrive during September (there are scattered reports involving small numbers throughout the month), but few are generally seen until the passage of major cold fronts, usually during October and November. At Big Lake Refuge, for example, there is an arrival record during the last week of September, but the usual time is mid-October or later, with a peak at the end of the month. Certainly the very largest numbers of Canada Goose can be seen at the national wildlife refuges, or in open fields nearby, but their "honking" and the lines and wedges of birds overhead are characteristic of fall in all regions of the state.

WINTER: Winter food and protection from disturbance attracts these birds to refuges, where hundreds and sometimes thousands may be seen during winter. At the White River Refuge large numbers are seen every year on the Christmas Bird Count, and more than 6000 were counted in 1977 and 1981. An estimated 25,000 were at Wapanocca Refuge in Crittenden County on February 4, 1984. Coverage of prime waterfowl areas in the state during the 1970s showed a statewide population varying from over 50,000 one year to less than 2000 in another. The annual average during the decade was 14,000. While the population is concentrated in the refuges and nearby areas, the birds are seen elsewhere. At Fayetteville in the western Ozarks, for example, 162 were reported on the 1979 Christmas Count, and there are midwinter records from Christmas Counts in all regions.

SPRING MIGRATION: Northward-moving spring migrants are seen during March and in the first few weeks of April, occasionally later (see RESIDENT FLOCKS below). At Big Lake the peak occurred during late March, but as many as 1000 were seen on the refuge on April 10 one year. Off the refuges the counts tend to be lower.

BANDING: There are almost five hundred recoveries of banded birds associated with Arkansas (Figure 6-15). Almost 75 percent were banded in Arkansas and recovered during spring, north-northwest of the state. Over half the recoveries had traveled up to 425 miles, but some had gone 2000 miles. About half were adults when banded, and the bulk of the recoveries occurred within two years. However, 27 survived longer than five years, and two longer than seven years between banding and recovery.

RESIDENT FLOCKS: According to information in the January 1983 Arkansas midwinter waterfowl survey, there were 60 resident Canada geese at Holla Bend Refuge, 300 on the Arkansas River between Clarksville and Morrilton, and 400 (captive migrants) at the Cummins Unit of the state penitentiary in Lincoln County. In addition there are scattered small flocks at other lakes in the state.

Subfamily Anatinae Ducks

WOOD DUCK, *Aix sponsa* (Linnaeus)

Permanent resident. Common migrant and summer resident in the larger forested stream bottoms and forested swamps throughout the state. Common in winter primarily in the southern lowlands.

SPRING MIGRATION: Spring migrants are seen from mid-February through April. In Faulkner County, where the birds usually do not winter in numbers, they become "regular" after mid-February (Johnson 1979). An unusually high total of 33 was reported on March 15 at Moffett, Oklahoma, near Fort Smith. It appears that some migrants are still passing through the state while local nesting is already underway: a flock of at least 10 males in breeding plumage was observed at Lake Sequoyah in Washington County on April 29 not far from where an adult pair was escorting a brood of young across open water.

BREEDING SEASON: Records in the Audubon Society file indicate that nesting occurs pri-

marily between April and July. Extreme records in the file include young "less than half-grown" accompanied by adults in a shallow, quiet cove at Lake Sequoyah in late April, and young in a similar stage of development during the second half of July at the state fish hatchery in Benton County. Nesting usually occurs near or over quiet, undisturbed bodies of water, with cavities in hollow trees or nesting boxes three feet or higher above the ground. A nest with fourteen eggs on April 26 in Lawrence County was unusually high at fifty feet.

While Wood Ducks are still common in the state, they were formerly very widespread and abundant in the eastern lowlands. Files at Big Lake Refuge showed that there were 1000 to 5000 young and adults present during summer in the 1940s, but only 500 in the 1950s, and many fewer yet in the 1960s. This drastic decrease in numbers was due, no doubt, to overhunting and massive land clearing and drainage of forested swamps. Conservation efforts seem to be helping somewhat to stabilize the bird populations. At Big Lake, for example, a nesting box program is said to have produced 3000 young in 1971. At the White River Refuge the nesting box program was discontinued because the extensive forested bottomlands there are now believed to have enough natural nesting cavities to accommodate the estimated summer population of 3000 birds. It also appears that some dams constructed on rivers may have benefitted Wood Ducks by flooding forested coves and other low-lying areas. At Fort Smith Wood Ducks were considered rare prior to the damming of the Arkansas River in the late 1960s. Today the birds can be found regularly there.

Occasionally Wood Ducks with young are seen right in the middle of towns, some distance from any major body of water. It is not clear what eventually happens to the young in such situations.

FALL AND BANDING: Activities associated with fall, ranging from small flocks congregating on mudflats and shallow ponds to larger flocks of 100 or more birds, are reported from August and thereafter to November. Wood Ducks are uncommon in the western Ozarks in winter, and relatively few are generally seen after October. However, during the mild fall of 1983, 100 or more birds were observed on several occasions during October and early No-

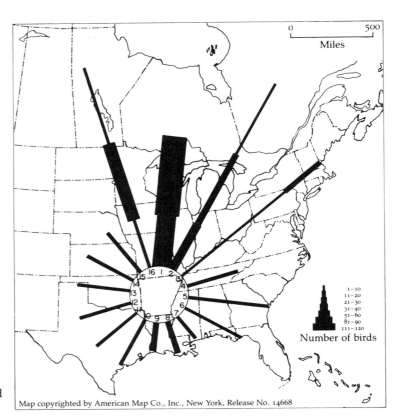

0   500
Miles

1–10
11–20
21–30
31–40
51–60
81–90
111–120
Number of birds

FIGURE 6-16 Movements of the Wood Duck based on banding records.

Map copyrighted by American Map Co., Inc., New York, Release No. 14668

vember as they flew into the Lake Fayetteville area at dusk, presumably in order to feed on the abundant seeds of the American Lotus.

Banding recoveries associated with 435 Wood Ducks showed that during different times of the year this species traveled in every direction relative to Arkansas, but the main pattern of movement involved the breeding areas around the Great Lakes region (Figure 6-16). Distances between banding and recovery ranged from 50 miles to almost 1300. No bird lived as long as six years between banding and recovery.

WINTER: Wood Ducks are rare or very uncommon in the northern areas during winter, but large numbers are seen with regularity in the southern lowlands. At White River Refuge, for example, 400 to 1000 were reported on four Christmas Bird Counts between 1950 and 1982, but the usual number was well under 100. Several other peak winter counts have included 227 at El Dorado in 1975, 448 at Lake Georgia-Pacific in 1981, and 70 at Little Rock in 1975. The largest winter record at Fayetteville in the north was six birds on the 1981 count.

GREEN-WINGED TEAL, *Anas crecca* Linnaeus

Common migrant and winter resident, usually in moderate numbers, in all regions. Numerous in winter in a few places, especially in the southern lowlands.

FALL MIGRATION: These birds have arrived in Arkansas from their breeding grounds to the north as early as the end of August, but few are generally seen until October. The 17 at the Jonesboro wastewater treatment plant ponds on September 25 was an early high number. By mid-October large numbers are observed: 120 near Keo in Lonoke County on October 12, and 150 to 200 counted by a party of observers at Calion Lake near El Dorado on October 18. At Big Lake Refuge a fall peak involving as many as 200 to 1500 birds has been noted between mid-October and early November, with the bulk of these migrants departing by late November or early December. As many as 1500 have been counted on fish ponds in the Lonoke area during fall, but in most areas the numbers seen are lower, often 25 or fewer during a day.

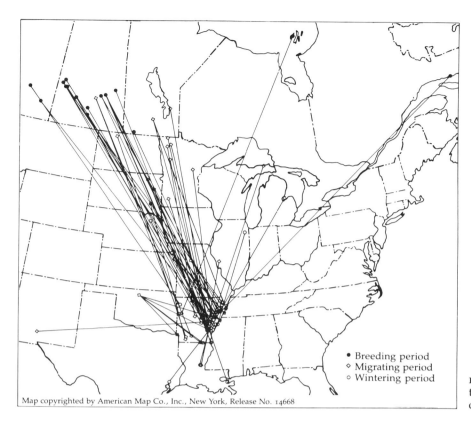

- Breeding period
◊ Migrating period
○ Wintering period

Map copyrighted by American Map Co., Inc., New York, Release No. 14668

FIGURE 6-17 Movements of the Green-winged Teal based on banding records.

WINTER: Green-winged Teal seem to remain in relatively large numbers until the onset of sharp, prolonged cold which freezes ponds and other shallow water habitats where they feed. Thereafter, relatively few are seen in the northern areas. At Big Lake sometimes as many as 50 to 150 birds remained for the winter, but usually all birds departed by early December. At the White River Refuge, however, data between 1950 and 1982 show that hundreds are typically present there during the Christmas Bird Count period, and in eight years (during the 32 years) as many as 550 to 5400 were reported. As many as 1000 have been reported during December and January at Lake Georgia-Pacific in the extreme south. Such large numbers are unusual. In the western Ozarks the species can be found with fair regularity at Lake Fayetteville during winter, with numbers seen on Christmas Bird Counts there usually falling within the range of 10 to 20. These numbers are more typical for the state as a whole than the huge concentrations sometimes seen in a few places.

Midwinter surveys of prime waterfowl areas in Arkansas in the 1970s showed the totals varying widely from a high of 18,500 one year to a low of only 1000.

SPRING MIGRATION: A spring influx of northward-moving birds is noted as early as mid-February, and relatively large numbers have been reported in the state until the second half of April. Scattered May or June records usually involve singles. In Faulkner County, the spring peak occurs between mid-February and the third week of March (Johnson 1979). Hanebrink (1980) had only one isolated record for the northeast after March. Records at Big Lake show departures all during April, but the spring peak occurred in the second half of March.

BANDING: Most of the recoveries of Green-winged Teal involved birds banded on their breeding grounds in the prairie provinces of Canada, and the prairie states, north-northwest of Arkansas (Figure 6-17). Hence, these migrants had traveled roughly 1200 to 1500 miles upon recovery. Over two-thirds were banded as

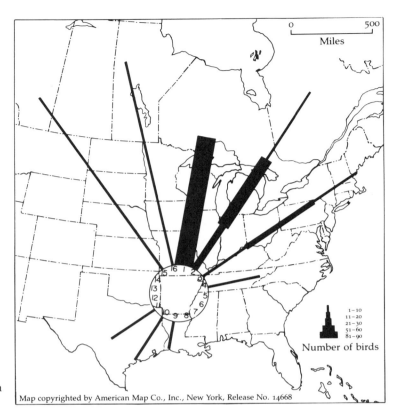

FIGURE 6-18 Movements of the American Black Duck based on banding records.

adults, and none had lived longer than four years between banding and recovery.

AMERICAN BLACK DUCK, *Anas rubripes* Brewster

Migrant and winter resident seen primarily at a few national wildlife refuges in the eastern lowlands, and rarely elsewhere.

FALL MIGRATION: American Black Ducks have arrived during August (eight in Critten-den County on August 13), but few are generally seen until October and thereafter. Files at Big Lake Refuge in Mississippi County in the 1940s, 1950s, and early 1960s showed that a peak involving 600 to 3000 black ducks occurred during the second and third weeks of November. Records there in the 1970s and early 1980s indicate arrivals in different years between September and December, but usually in October or November. The 150 birds at Holla Bend Refuge on November 3, 1965, was a fall peak, as were the 200 at Big Lake in November of 1980. These reports are unusual; most records

in the Audubon Society file have involved single birds or small flocks, and outside of a few refuges the birds are not seen often at all.

WINTER: During the 1970s and early 1980s there were several population peaks at Big Lake that involved as many as 1500 to 2500 black ducks during January, and similar numbers have been reported on the midwinter waterfowl surveys at White River Refuge and Wapanocca Refuge, both in the eastern lowlands. At White River Refuge the numbers reported on Christmas Bird Counts have varied considerably. Between 1966 and 1976, 100 to 1000 were reported in six years, but otherwise most of the Christmas Counts there between 1950 and 1982 involved fewer than 25. Statewide midwinter surveys of Arkansas's prime waterfowl areas in the 1970s showed numbers ranging from a low of 1000 to a high of 11,000.

SPRING MIGRATION: Recent records at Big Lake show that black ducks are usually last seen in February or March, and unusually as late as April. Records at Holla Bend and White River Refuge showed that the large numbers present during December and January had declined sharply by early March. The only report in the Audubon Society file after mid-April involves a single bird in the second week of May.

BANDING: There are 317 recoveries of American Black Ducks associated with Arkansas, and the distances between banding and recovery ranged from approximately 300 to a maximum of 1400 miles (Figure 6-18). This population associated with Arkansas is derived from breeding and migration areas mainly to the north and east of the state. About half of these birds were banded as immatures, and most recoveries occurred within fourteen months after

banding. Still, three survived longer than ten years, and one over seventeen years.

MALLARD, *Anas platyrhynchos* Linnaeus

Permanent resident. Abundant migrant throughout the state. Common winter resident that is abundant especially in the eastern lowlands. The most numerous duck in the state. Mallards have nested in the state but the status of these birds is not clear.

FALL MIGRATION: Mallards are present in Arkansas all year, but the few seen between April and August become thousands and tens

FIGURE 6-19 Mallards at the White River National Wildlife Refuge in January. *David Plank*

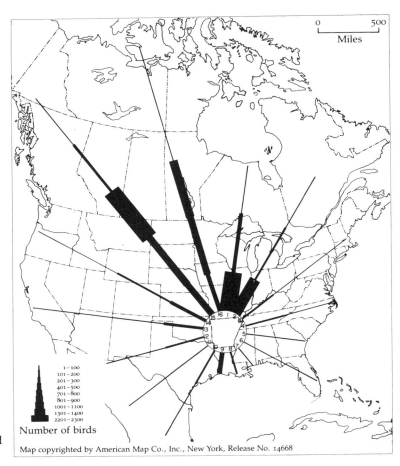

1-100
101-200
201-300
401-500
701-800
801-900
1001-1100
1301-1400
2201-2300

Number of birds

FIGURE 6-20 Movements of the Mallard based on banding records.

of thousands between October and March. Fall migrants trickle into the state beginning in September. Records at Big Lake Refuge, for example, showed that Mallards usually arrived between mid-September and mid-October in different years, with the numbers increasing dramatically at the time of the big cold fronts in late October, and peak numbers ranging from 20,000 to 115,000 during November. Fall migrants rest and feed on ponds, lakes, and rivers throughout the state in October and November, with the largest concentrations in those areas having appropriate vegetation submerged in shallow water.

WINTER: Statewide coverage of prime waterfowl areas during the 1970s showed an average of more than one million Mallards annually, varying from 1.5 million in 1970 to 0.5 million in 1979. Because of these huge numbers, lands have been purchased to provide habitat and to facilitate hunting for which the Grand Prairie, especially, is nationally famous. Smaller but still impressive numbers are seen elsewhere in winter. During severe winter freezes in the western Ozarks, Mallards congregate by the hundreds in the few areas with open water.

SPRING MIGRATION: The northward migration gets underway during February and continues through March with a sharp decline in numbers obvious by April. At Big Lake Mallards were seen through the month of April. At the White River Refuge, over 700,000 birds present one year during January had diminished to 10,000 by mid-February. On the Grand Prairie, two-thirds of the wintering population were said to have departed by early March (Audubon Society file).

BANDING: Arkansas-associated recoveries of Mallards have involved nearly all of North America, but the main directions of travel between banding and recovery have included areas to the northwest, north and northeast of Arkansas, extending from the midwestern United States to the prairie states and the prairie provinces of Canada (Figure 6-20). A significant number of the nearly 13,000 birds had traveled about 1000 miles between banding and recovery, with 2300 miles being the longest such distance. Many adult and young birds were banded, and most of the recoveries occurred within four years following banding. Thirty-five survived ten years or more between banding and recovery, five more than fifteen years, one nearly nineteen years, and another just over nineteen years.

BREEDING: Three broods at Big Lake in the summer of 1940 were thought to be from cripples left over from spring migration. Two males, one female, and four half-grown ducklings were seen at Van Buren in Crawford County on May 27, 1960; the presence of the drakes suggests these were not completely wild birds. At the state fish hatchery in Benton County, Mallard hens on nests "flushed like wild birds," but again the drakes were present. There are records of this sort from all areas of the state. Certainly some summering Mallards are cripples, and some nesting birds, perhaps most, are feral, i.e., domesticated birds that have returned to a free existence.

NORTHERN PINTAIL, *Anas acuta* Linnaeus

Common to abundant migrant and winter resident chiefly in the eastern lowlands. Present during the same periods elsewhere, but gener-

FIGURE 6-21 Northern Pintail. *Sigrid James Bruch*

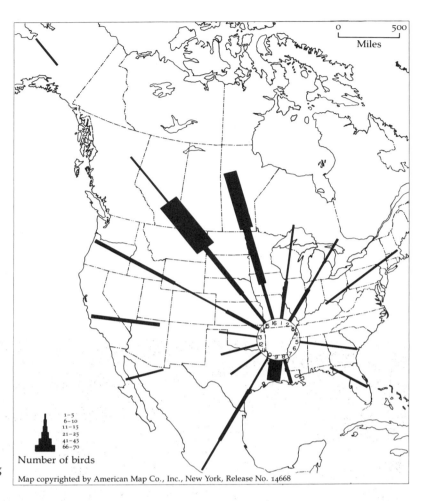

1-5
6-10
11-15
21-25
41-45
66-70

Number of birds

Map copyrighted by American Map Co., Inc., New York, Release No. 14668

FIGURE 6-22 Movements of the Northern Pintail based on banding records.

ally in lower numbers, and largely absent from the highlands in winter.

FALL MIGRATION: While small flocks of pintails may be observed in late August and early September, the large number signaling the main southward migration arrive during October and November. The 1400 at Keo in Lonoke County on September 29 were early migrants. Records at Big Lake Refuge showed the peak movement between the end of October and throughout November, often late in the month. More than 1500 pintails have been seen during the peak, and once 6000. Few observers have seen a concentration as large as the 10,000 at Lonoke on November 26. During migration they are seen on prairie ponds, rivers, shallow reservoirs, and lakes. In the highlands, where

there is much less of this shallow water, open country habitat, the counts tend to be much lower.

WINTER: The abundance and distribution of this species in winter in Arkansas is illustrated by two Christmas Bird Count areas in eastern Arkansas. At Lonoke, for example, 500 or more were reported nine years on Christmas Counts between 1952 and 1982, with a peak of 15,000 in 1961. During this same period, 100 or fewer were seen in eleven of the count years. A similar pattern is apparent at the White River Refuge, where during the same period 500 or more were counted in six of the years (peak of over 3000 in 1961) and 100 or fewer in twelve of the years. It would seem that in some years the bulk of the birds reaching Arkansas in fall depart for the south before the Christmas Count period, but in other years they remain longer. Midwinter surveys of prime waterfowl habitats in Arkansas during the 1970s showed that pintail populations statewide varied from 120,000 in 1975 to under 4000 in 1979. In many places in the state pintails are never really common. At Fayetteville, for example, the species is rarely seen during the Christmas Bird Count period, and is not seen in large numbers at any time of the year.

SPRING MIGRATION AND SUMMER: An influx of pintails is sometimes noticed as early as late January, but more often during February and March. The 76 on Lake Fayetteville in Washington County on February 8 was a large number for the western Ozarks. "Hundreds" were seen at Clarksville in Johnson County on February 28, and large numbers are seen elsewhere in shallow open ponds of the Arkansas River Valley. At Big Lake an overwinter peak was observed in late January, with the birds remaining on the refuge until the last week of March or mid-April. Certainly by mid-April the population has moved north of the state toward their breeding areas (see BANDING). Nevertheless, there are several records in the Audubon Society file of pintails between May and July, including one late record involving 10 at Lonoke on May 30, and scattered reports usually involving one or two birds in the eastern lowlands throughout the summer. There is no evidence that any of these birds nested.

BANDING: The 309 Arkansas-associated recoveries of banded pintails show patterns of movement relative to the state in nearly every direction (Figure 6-22), but the main pattern involves the Louisiana coast (wintering population) and the northern prairie states and the prairie provinces of Canada (breeding population). Distances between banding and recovery varied from a low range of under 600 miles, to a high range of over 3000 miles. Both adults and immatures were banded, with frequent recoveries through the fourth year. One bird lived over twelve years between banding and recovery.

GARGANEY, *Anas querquedula* Linnaeus
    One record.
    This widespread Old World counterpart of the Blue-winged Teal is a rare vagrant across North America (AOU 1983). One was seen in Arkansas on April 1, 1984, by a skilled observer who found it among other waterfowl in a shallow pond near the Arkansas River just northwest of Little Rock. The bold white head stripe and other critical field marks were seen and well described in written documentation on file with the Arkansas Audubon Society. Both the Garganey and nearby Blue-winged Teal were seen as they swam, and later as they flew.

BLUE-WINGED TEAL, *Anas discors* Linnaeus
    Common migrant in all regions. Rare winter resident. Records for every month of the year, including three apparently isolated instances of nesting.
    FALL MIGRATION: Blue-winged Teal are the earliest migrant waterfowl to reach Arkansas in fall, with arrivals as early as mid-July. The species becomes numerous in open shallow ponds, flooded fields, and on associated muddy areas by late August and early September. The 600 at Lake Sequoyah in Washington County on August 29, 1963, was a large number for the western Ozarks, but reports of 100 in a day are not rare anywhere in the state where there is sufficient habitat. During this period peak counts on the Grand Prairie in the eastern lowlands frequently involved hundreds, sometimes a thousand or more, birds in a day. At Big Lake Refuge, records showed that as many as 1000 to 6000 were present on the refuge during the fall peak. By late November or early December all but a highly exceptional few have moved south into their usual wintering grounds, which includes the Gulf Coast, Middle America, and South America (AOU 1983).
    WINTER: Inexperienced observers frequently exhibit difficulty in distinguishing the two species of teal in Arkansas. Since the common wintering teal is the Green-winged, it must be assumed that some winter records of Blue-winged Teal involve mis-identifications. Nevertheless, there are some valid "winter" records. Many perhaps are like those in the Jonesboro area where the species has been reported on five of thirteen recent Christmas Bird Counts, with as many as 129 in one year (Hanebrink 1980). Earl Hanebrink (pers. comm. 1983) stated that when the Christmas Count is held in December before there is any severe, prolonged

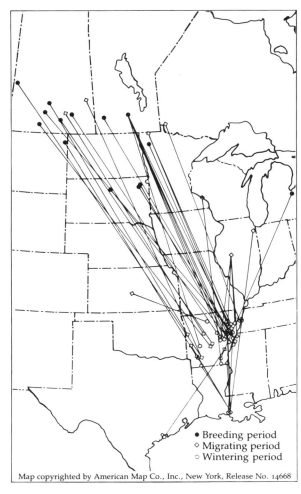

• Breeding period
◇ Migrating period
○ Wintering period

Map copyrighted by American Map Co., Inc., New York, Release No. 14668

FIGURE 6-23 Movements of the Blue-winged Teal based on banding records.

cold, a few birds usually can be found on waste-water treatment plant ponds. There are no records for the area in January.

SPRING MIGRATION: At Big Lake Refuge, where there were no fall records after mid-December, northward-moving birds returned by early March, with a peak of 200 to 700 between mid-March and mid-April. The birds were frequently present on the refuge all during May, with one record of 200 in late May. In the Lonoke area, some birds are still present in the rice fields during the first half of June. A male and a female seen at Lonoke on June 4 were able to fly and were therefore not cripples straggling behind the migration.

BREEDING SEASON: An adult female and one half-grown duckling were seen on the Mississippi River of Phillips County on May 17, 1980. Near Big Lake in Mississippi County, an adult female was killed as she incubated nine eggs in late April of 1973. One female, nine down-covered young, and six adult males were seen on wastewater treatment plant ponds in El Dorado on May 7, 1983.

BANDING: There are forty recoveries of banded Blue-winged Teal associated with Arkansas that demonstrate patterns of movement into the northern prairie states and the prairie provinces of Canada, as much as 1300 miles north-northwest of the state (Figure 6-23). Four birds lived five or six years between banding and recovery.

CINNAMON TEAL, *Anas cyanoptera* Vieillot
   Rare transient.

While this species is common in western North America, the first Arkansas record involved Arkansas County where two or three were seen on April 16, 1949 (Baerg 1951). Four were seen in Union County on September 21, 1967. A single male was reported in Clark County on March 10, 1971. Three males were seen at Lake Millwood on October 3, 1977. A single male was seen in a shallow pond at Moffett, Oklahoma, just across the Arkansas River from Fort Smith, Arkansas, on February 28, 1984. Two male Cinnamon Teals and two probable females were observed at the state fish hatchery in Benton County on March 24, 1984.

NORTHERN SHOVELER, *Anas clypeata*
Linnaeus

Common migrant observed in open, shallow water habitats in all regions. Common in winter especially in the eastern lowlands, but observed in all regions.

FALL MIGRATION: Shovelers have arrived as early as the last week of August. Numbers increase through September and October with a peak by early November. The seven birds seen on the Arkansas River in Crawford County on August 23 were early migrants. The 250 birds at Lonoke on November 2 was a fall peak on the Grand Prairie. Records at Big Lake Refuge showed that the birds arrived on an irregular basis, between mid-September and even as late as mid-November. A peak involving as many as 200 to 300 was observed there between late November and mid-December. The 24 shovelers at Lake Fayetteville on November 23 arrived along with a major cold front that also involved large numbers of geese and other species of ducks.

WINTER: Shovelers are common during most winters in the eastern lowlands. At the White River Refuge up to 100 have been reported on several Christmas Bird Counts since the late 1960s. Large numbers are sometimes reported at Lonoke, with 100 or more sixteen times on Christmas Counts since 1952, and peaks of almost 800 for two years. More than 1000 were reported at Pine Bluff on the 1980 Christmas Count. Elsewhere the species is seen in small numbers in winter. At Arkadelphia fewer than 10 are reported most years on the Christmas Count. There are few Christmas Count reports of any sort at Little Rock, Fayetteville, and other places in central and western Arkansas. Statewide surveys of prime waterfowl habitats during the 1970s showed an average of 4500 birds annually.

SPRING MIGRATION AND SUMMER: Spring migration seems to take place between mid-February and the second half of April, with a peak frequently observed during March, and small numbers occasionally during May. Departure dates at Big Lake varied from mid-March to the second week in April. The 2500 on Pine Bluff's wastewater treatment ponds on February 16, 1974, were present all of February. The 77 birds at Lake Fayetteville on April 3 was an exceptional number for the highlands. In the

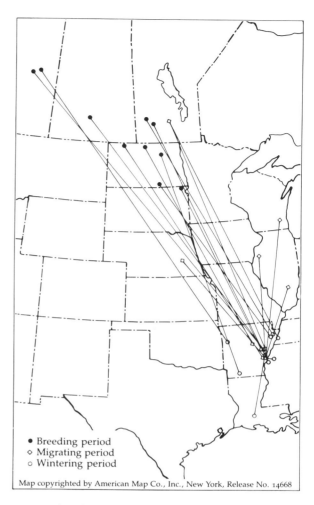

● Breeding period
◇ Migrating period
○ Wintering period

FIGURE 6-24 Movements of the Northern Shoveler based on banding records.

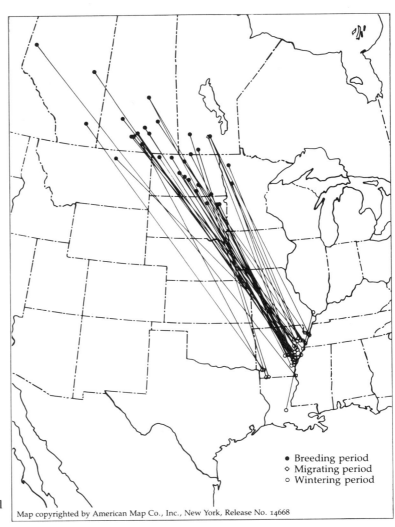

- ● Breeding period
- ◇ Migrating period
- ○ Wintering period

FIGURE 6-25 Movements of the Gadwall based on banding records.

Audubon Society file there are records of injured and uninjured single individuals, mostly drakes, during May and through the summer in Lonoke County, but there is no indication that any of these birds were nesting.

BANDING: The nineteen Arkansas-associated recoveries of banded shovelers show the main direction of movement relative to the state is north-northwest into the northern prairie states and the prairie provinces of Canada (Figure 6-24). The most common distance between banding and recovery was 1100 miles, and the longest was over 1600 miles. None survived over three years between banding and recovery.

GADWALL, *Anas strepera* Linnaeus

Common migrant and winter resident in all regions, with the largest numbers in the eastern lowlands. Observed in a variety of shallow water habitats with submerged vegetation.

FALL MIGRATION: Gadwalls begin to arrive in Arkansas in numbers usually by the second week of October, with migration continuing throughout the month and during November. The nine birds at Anderson's Minnow Farm in Lonoke County on August 31, and the nine at Lake Sequoyah in Washington County on September 6, were both early fall reports. Some peak counts during fall are 400 at Lonoke on

October 12; 76 on wastewater treatment ponds at Jonesboro on October 18; 900 near Keo in Lonoke County on October 20; and 85 at Lake Fayetteville on November 1. At Big Lake Refuge the birds arrived no earlier than the first week of October, and the peak involving 1000 to 4000 occurred during the last two weeks of November.

WINTER: Statewide surveys in the 1970s showed that the number of this species wintering in prime waterfowl areas varied from nearly 59,000 in 1971 to just over 5000 in 1976. At Big Lake, the usual wintering number was about 500, but in some years as few as 25 were present. Gadwalls are commonly reported on those Christmas Bird Counts in the state where there is a sufficiency of suitable habitat. Several hundred or more have been reported on Christmas Counts at Fayetteville, Pine Bluff, Lake Georgia-Pacific, White River Refuge, Lonoke, and elsewhere. An unusually high peak of 8540 was reported on the 1983 Christmas Count at Texarkana.

SPRING MIGRATION AND SUMMER: Relatively large numbers of Gadwalls are still present during March and April. Near the state fish hatchery in Lonoke County 350 were counted on March 16, and 144 were counted on Grassy Lake in Hempstead County on March 24. Numbers reported during April tend to be smaller, with the 29 males and 25 females on Lake Sequoyah in Washington County on April 14 being a large late number. At Big Lake the birds usually departed in April, but nine stayed one year until May 14. In the Audubon Society file there are several records, often of single birds, in eastern Arkansas during June and July. Five birds were seen on two occasions at Anderson's Minnow Farm in June 1972. One of two females seen in the same area in June 1971 was wounded.

BANDING: There are thirty-nine banding recoveries of Gadwalls associated with Arkansas, and most were banded as birds of the year in the northern prairie states and the prairie provinces of Canada, mainly about 1000 miles from Arkansas, but once up to 2000 miles away (Figure 6-25). Most birds were recovered within six months following banding, but one survived into its sixth year.

AMERICAN WIGEON, *Anas americana* Gmelin

Common migrant and winter resident in all regions. Most numerous in the eastern lowlands.

FALL MIGRATION: Wigeons, or "Baldpates," have arrived as early as the first week in August and as many as five birds have been seen at Lonoke on August 31. Generally, however, few are seen until the latter part of September, with major influxes in the second week of October and thereafter through much of November. At Big Lake Refuge, American Wigeons arrived in different years between September 24 and October 20, with a peak in numbers that varied from 200 to 12,000 between mid-October and mid-November. Some other peaks have included 100 birds near Keo in Lonoke County on September 29; an estimated 175 at Lake Fayetteville in Washington County on October 13 (a very high count for the western Ozarks); 1500 near Keo on October 20; and 200 seen on open ponds near Jonesboro on November 18.

WINTER: Wigeons have been found in all parts of the state during winter, but they are not reported frequently on the Christmas Bird Counts anywhere except at the national wildlife refuges in the lowlands. Hundreds are often reported on the Christmas Count at White River Refuge and as many as 100 to 3000 were reported there three years between 1967 and 1975. Hundreds have also been reported at Lonoke, with a peak of 1500 on the 1975 Christmas Count. Several large counts have occurred at Lake Georgia-Pacific and at Texarkana, including 3756 at the latter place on the 1983 Christmas Count. The species overwintered at Big Lake, with a peak during January that involved as many as 200 to 500. Much smaller numbers are seen on ponds and lakes in other places. The largest number reported on a Christmas Count at Fayetteville was 25 in 1983. This unusually high winter count for Fayetteville was presumably the result of freezing temperatures that caused most ponds, streams, and lakes in the area to freeze over, concentrating waterfowl upon those few places with patches of open water.

The statewide midwinter survey of prime waterfowl areas during the 1970s showed Ameri-

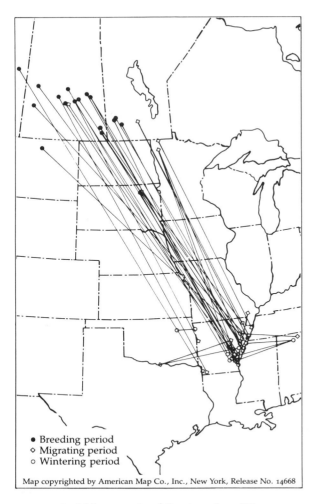

● Breeding period
◇ Migrating period
○ Wintering period

Map copyrighted by American Map Co., Inc., New York, Release No. 14668

FIGURE 6-26 Movements of the American Wigeon based on banding records.

can Wigeon populations ranging from a high of almost 50,000 birds in 1971 to only 11,000 in 1976.

SPRING MIGRATION AND SUMMER: A buildup in numbers during February signals the beginning of the northward migration. At Holla Bend Refuge a maximum count of 425 was observed in the first half of February 1963, and steadily declined thereafter to near zero at mid-March. At Big Lake all wigeons had departed between the last week of March and mid-April. The 300 wigeons at Lake Fayetteville on March 24, 1956, was a large number for the highlands. Few of these birds are seen after mid-April, but there is one report in the Audubon Society file of 10 in Conway County on April 29, and five in Lonoke County on June 8. Most reports after mid-April and during the summer have involved one to three uninjured birds or cripples, usually in the Lonoke area.

BANDING: Based upon 37 recoveries, American Wigeons in Arkansas are derived from breeding populations over 1000 miles north-northwest of the state (Figure 6-26). Only a single bird survived as much as five years between banding and recovery.

CANVASBACK, *Aythya valisineria* (Wilson)

Migrant and winter resident, usually in small numbers, in all regions. Sometimes locally common, especially in the lowlands.

FALL MIGRATION: Canvasbacks have arrived as early as mid-October, but sightings are unusual until late in the month and thereafter. At Big Lake Refuge arrival dates varied from late October (earliest October 20) through November, with peak numbers varying from a single individual in some years, to as many as 75 to 200 birds during other years. Approximately 800 were observed in one flock at Lonoke on September 29, 1985, an unusually high number. A total of 378 were found on three lakes in Crittenden County on November 24, 1963. While these high numbers are sometimes seen in the eastern lowlands, reports for other regions are often much smaller, often less than 10 in a day.

WINTER: Canvasbacks have been observed in all regions during winter, but in those areas with only limited amounts of appropriate habitat they are not seen with regularity and only in small numbers. Consistently high numbers, on the other hand, have been observed on the Christmas Count at Lonoke, often 100 or more, and as many as 224 to 778 were reported on five of the counts there between 1964 and 1982. A few other peak numbers on Christmas Counts are 280 at Lake Millwood, 200 at Pine Bluff, 81 at Fayetteville, 65 at Jonesboro, and 90 at White River Refuge. Surveys or prime waterfowl habitats in Arkansas during the 1970s showed that Canvasback populations varied from a peak of 9000 one year to one of 300 in another. The average for the decade was over 4350 annually.

SPRING MIGRATION: Departure dates at Big Lake showed considerable variation, ranging from late February through late April. More than 100 birds were seen on Horseshoe Lake in Crittenden County on February 29. The 24 males at Lake Fayetteville on March 10 was a peak for the western Ozarks. The 40 at Lonoke on May 3 was a late, large number. In the Audubon Society file there is only one later report, a single male at Lonoke on June 20.

BANDING: Of seven banded Canvasbacks associated with Arkansas, five had traveled 1100 to nearly 1300 miles between banding and recovery, and this documents movements to the breeding areas on the northern prairies and wintering grounds south to the Gulf of Mexico (Figure 6-27). Only one bird survived as long as two and one-half years between banding and recovery.

REDHEAD, *Aythya americana* (Eyton)

Migrant, usually in small numbers, in all regions. Winter resident that is irregular except at a few places in the lowlands.

FALL MIGRATION: The three Redheads seen at the Jonesboro wastewater treatment plant ponds on October 7 were relatively early arrivals. Generally few are seen until the last week of October and thereafter, with a peak during November. At Big Lake Refuge they frequently arrived in the second and third weeks of November, with a peak as high as 25 in the last week of the month. Many reports in the Audubon Society file have involved one to seven birds in a day, even during the peak. The 28 at Lake Millwood on October 25 was a high number, as were the 21 at Jonesboro on November 7. The 16 male and female Redheads at Lake

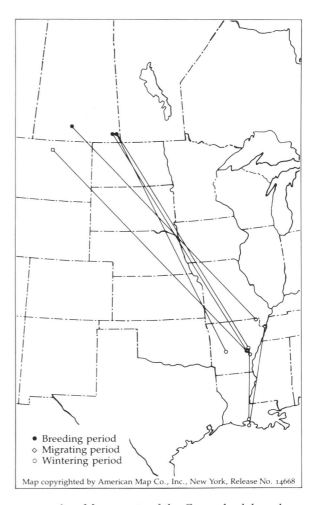

- Breeding period
- Migrating period
- Wintering period

Map copyrighted by American Map Co., Inc., New York, Release No. 14668

FIGURE 6-27 Movements of the Canvasback based on banding records.

FIGURE 6-28 Redhead. *Fred Burnside*

● Breeding period
◇ Migrating period
○ Wintering period

Map copyrighted by American Map Co., Inc., New York, Release No. 14668

FIGURE 6-29 Movements of the Redhead based on banding records.

Fayetteville on November 10 were part of a huge raft of ducks (including Lesser Scaup, Ring-necked Ducks, Buffleheads, and other species) that arrived along with the first snowfall of the season.

WINTER: This species winters chiefly south of Arkansas, but some are found in the state each winter. At Big Lake, Redheads were sometimes completely absent by late December, but more often 25 to 75 remained during winter. Redheads have been found in midwinter in all regions of the state. On twelve recent Christmas Bird Counts at Fayetteville, they were reported three times, with a peak number of 10 in 1976. The species has been found with the greatest consistency and generally in the highest numbers on the Christmas Count at Lonoke. Even there the numbers present have often been fewer than 40, but there have been peaks of 92 (1969) and 78 (1976). The midwinter survey of prime waterfowl areas in the state during

the 1970s showed the total number of Redheads ranging from as few as 50 one year to as many as 2600 in another.

SPRING MIGRATION: At Big Lake Refuge the birds departed between the second week of March and early April, often by late March. The 13 males and females at Lake Fayetteville on March 9 was a spring peak, and all but a single female had departed by the following day. The species is rare after the first week of April, and there are no records of sightings in the Audubon Society file later than the three birds at Calion Lake near El Dorado on April 24.

BANDING: There are sixteen recoveries of Redheads associated with Arkansas (Figure 6-29). Most were banded as juveniles on the breeding grounds up to 1200 miles north-northwest of Arkansas in the northern prairie states and southern Manitoba, Canada. None survived as long as a year between banding and recovery.

Order Anseriformes   121

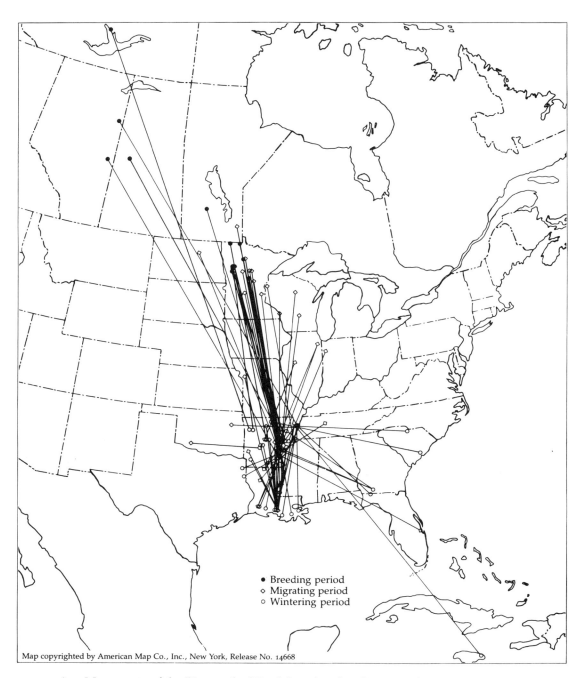

FIGURE 6-30 Movements of the Ring-necked Duck based on banding records.

RING-NECKED DUCK, *Aythya collaris*
(Donovan)

Common migrant and winter resident in all regions. Especially numerous in winter in the southern and southeastern lowlands.

FALL MIGRATION: Ring-necked Ducks sometimes have been seen in the state in late summer or early fall, but these sightings are unusual, and few are seen until the second half of October, especially from the last week and thereafter. At Big Lake Refuge in the northeast the birds arrived in late October (earliest October 20) or early November, with a fall peak involving 100 to 500 in the second half of November. The 40 on ponds of the Jonesboro wastewater treatment plant on October 23 was a large early number, as were the 31 on the De-Gray Lake regulation pond in Clark County on October 21. The 220 seen on Cave Lake in Logan County on November 27, 1964, was a very large number outside the prime areas in eastern Arkansas.

WINTER: Ring-necked Ducks are common in the state during winter. Even in the highlands, the species is seen on many Christmas Bird Counts at Fayetteville, though the numbers are usually small. In lowland areas the numbers are sometimes impressive. At Lonoke there have been several counts (1965 and 1969) in the range of 1000 to 2000 birds, and many counts of 100 or more. Over 2500 were seen at Texarkana on the 1983 Christmas Count. At the White River Refuge there are two records (1972 and 1975) of 800 or more. The birds are also seen regularly and in impressive numbers in the Arkadelphia area, where several Christmas Count peaks (1970 and 1978) have reached the range of 250 to 300. On the statewide 1980 Christmas Count, the species was reported in twelve of the seventeen count areas, with peaks of 90 to 200 in the lowlands. Surveys of prime waterfowl habitats in Arkansas during the 1970s showed annual numbers ranging from 2000 to 10,000.

SPRING MIGRATION AND SUMMER: By late April or early May most birds have departed for their breeding grounds to the north. At Big Lake, however, 15 were present on the refuge one year until mid-May. Thereafter, there are only scattered reports that usually involve one or two birds on the Grand Prairie. One male and one female were seen on the old millpond at Boxley in Newton County in late June and

early July of 1978. In the Audubon Society file there is one highly unusual record of 10 at Lonoke on July 28. Presumably these birds were not "summering," and so it seems they must have been extremely early fall migrants.

BANDING: Recoveries involving 89 Ring-necked Ducks associated with Arkansas indicate directions of travel that include breeding populations in Minnesota and central Canada, and the wintering grounds on the Louisiana Gulf Coast (Figure 6-30). Distances of travel ranged from less than 500 miles to a maximum of 2000 miles between banding and recovery. While one survived almost eight years after banding, there was a good distribution of ages up to five years in the remaining birds.

GREATER SCAUP, *Aythya marila* (Linnaeus)

Status unclear. Infrequently reported migrant and winter visitor.

Even though Arkansas lies well within the known migration and wintering range of this species (AOU 1983), it has been identified infrequently here. Probably the numbers present are small, since Arkansas is without the "open marine or brackish situations" said to be their preferred wintering habitat (AOU 1983). They have been seen between early October and early April (Audubon Society file, Deaderick 1938, Baerg 1951, Hanebrink 1980). The most significant reports in the Audubon Society file are from Lonoke County and Lake Millwood. Approximately 40 were seen on December 23, 1973, at Anderson's Minnow Farm in Lonoke County. According to a description written by Gary Graves, flocks of Lesser Scaups were flying in and out of the ponds, and each flock contained several Greater Scaups. The largest number seen at one time was 18 to 20. A total of 43 Greater Scaups were seen at Lake Millwood on February 27, 1977, and 30 were seen on the ponds at the state fish hatchery in Lonoke on March 5, 1972. Five were seen at Budd Kidd Lake in Washington County on March 13, 1984, and two were carefully identified at the same location on November 16, 1985. The observers noted the differences in size, head shape, and wing stripes that separated Greater Scaups from the Lesser Scaups in the same small flock. Because of the difficulty in confidently separating Greater and Lesser Scaups in the field, it is

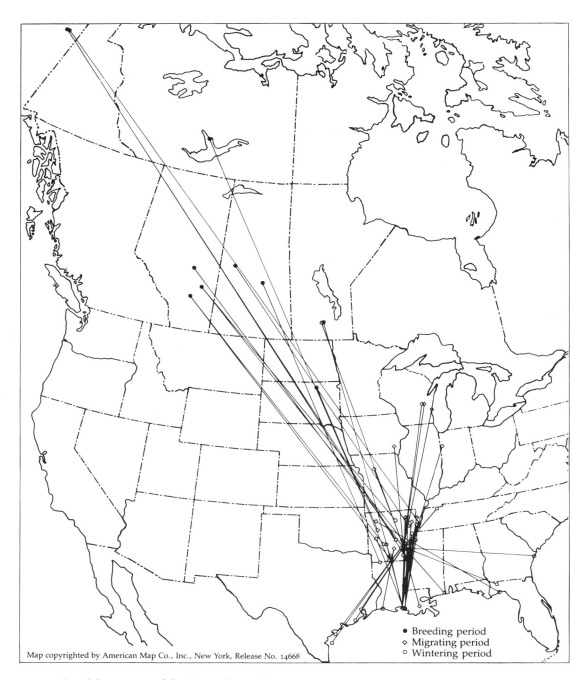

FIGURE 6-31 Movements of the Lesser Scaup based on banding records.

Legend:
- ● Breeding period
- ◇ Migrating period
- ○ Wintering period

not clear whether Greater Scaups are or are not of regular occurrence in the state. According to Lowery (1974), in Louisiana "the comparative scarcity of records for this species in the state is attributable in part to the difficulty of distinguishing it from its smaller relative. One's tendency to call all scaups 'lessers' probably leads to correct identification in the vast majority of instances."

LESSER SCAUP, *Aythya affinis* (Eyton)

Common migrant and winter resident in all regions; especially numerous in the lowlands.

FALL MIGRATION: Lesser Scaups have arrived as unusually early as late September, but few are generally seen until the last week of October and thereafter, with a peak during November or early December. The 69 birds at the Jonesboro wastewater treatment plant ponds on October 23 was a high early number; two weeks later (November 6) the number observed in the same place had increased to 365. The 215 at Lake Fayetteville on November 23, 1983, were all in a raft with other species of ducks that arrived along with a major cold front. At Big Lake Refuge a fall peak involving as many as 400 to 600 Lesser Scaups occurred during late November and early December.

WINTER: These birds winter in impressive numbers in all regions, with the highest counts usually recorded in the eastern lowlands. As many as 800 have been reported on the Christmas Bird Count at Pine Bluff, 400 at the White River Refuge, and over 1000 on several occasions at Lonoke. Large numbers are also observed in other areas of the state at this time. In the western Ozarks there is one winter record of 600 (Baerg 1951), and as many as 500 have been reported on the Christmas Count at Arkadelphia. Surveys of prime waterfowl habitats in Arkansas during the 1970s showed that there was an annual average of 9000 in the state at midwinter, with a high-low variation of between 1000 and 17,000.

SPRING MIGRATION AND SUMMER: Large numbers suggestive of the northward spring migration have been observed primarily during March and April, with only scattered reports after the end of May. A spring peak involving 68 was observed at Lake Fayetteville on March 15, and 30 females and 48 males were seen at the same place in a different year on April 3. At Lake Conway an estimated 225 were present on April 20, 1956, a large late peak in numbers. Reports during May tend to involve small numbers, usually fewer than 10 in a day.

Even though most Lesser Scaups depart for breeding grounds north of the state by late April, a few sometimes remain behind. In the Audubon Society file there are several reports between June and September involving one or two birds that were apparently uninjured. Most such reports are from the Lonoke area, but all regions of the state are represented. In the summer of 1968 Mark Block reported as many as five individuals in a day in the Lonoke area. He reported that even though some were flightless from molting none appeared to be injured. Ben Coffey saw three males and one female at Mammoth Spring in Fulton county on July 29, 1956. There is no evidence that any of these birds were nesting.

BANDING: Recoveries of Lesser Scaups indicate numerous directions of travel relative to Arkansas, chiefly involving breeding areas in the prairie provinces of Canada and beyond, even to Alaska, and movements south including wintering grounds on the Gulf of Mexico (Figure 6-31). Distances between banding and recovery ranged from less than 100 miles to over 3000 miles. While most of the 56 birds were recovered within two years of banding, five survived over five years. The longest survival was just over thirteen years.

OLDSQUAW, *Clangula hyemalis* (Linnaeus)

Very uncommon to somewhat rare migrant and winter visitor, mainly on the Mississippi Alluvial Plain, with additional sightings in the other regions. Observed on lakes and reservoirs, shallow impoundments, and on the Mississippi River.

This long-tailed duck of the far north winters in North America primarily along the northern Pacific coast, across Canada, along the Atlantic Coast and as far south as South Carolina, and on the Great Lakes (AOU 1983). A few winter further south on a casual basis, and it is to these birds that the Arkansas records are presumably attributable. Observations in the Audubon Society file span the period from mid-November to late April, with a concentration from late November through January. Many of these involved single birds, but four or more have been seen on several occasions: four on the 1980 Christmas Bird Count at Fayetteville; four in Lincoln County on January 12, 1967; eight in Prairie County on January of 1962 during the annual midwinter waterfowl survey; and 20 near Pastoria in Jefferson County in January of 1963. Each of the three reports from the northeast have involved birds at the Jonesboro wastewater treatment plant ponds in late November. The birds reported on a Christmas Count at Fayetteville were seen several times thereafter on Lake Fayetteville, where there are several additional records.

BLACK SCOTER, *Melanitta nigra* (Linnaeus)

Rare transient. Formerly called "Common Scoter."

Black Scoters, as well as species of scoters listed below, winter primarily along the coasts of the Atlantic and Pacific and on the Great Lakes (AOU 1983). In the Audubon Society file there is a record of two Black Scoters on the wastewater treatment ponds at Jonesboro between October 28 and 30, 1969. A single female was seen at Lake Maumelle near Little Rock on November 11, 1971. Two females were seen at Lake Millwood on November 22, 1981. A lone female was present on Horseshoe Lake in Crittenden County on February 22, 1970. Each of these observations has occurred during periods when waterfowl migration is especially heavy in the state.

SURF SCOTER, *Melanitta perspicillata* (Linnaeus)

Rare transient.

While this species is primarily coastal (and on the Great Lakes) in its usual winter distribution, it also occurs along the Gulf Coast south of Arkansas (AOU 1983). It has been seen in the state primarily in fall between the last week of October and the last week of November. The first report involved a bird that was collected in Union County on April 26, 1966. One was seen on wastewater treatment ponds in Clark County on November 6, 1971. In recent years there have been four records from Washington County in the western Ozarks: an adult female at Lake Fayetteville on November 10, 1981; an immature bird in the same place ten days later on November 20,

1981; an immature bird at Budd Kidd Lake near Prairie Grove, November 19–26, 1983; and two birds, both in immature plumage, on Lake Fayetteville, October 15–25, 1985. A single bird was observed on the Nettleton sewage ponds near Jonesboro, October 25, 1984, and one was photographed in Union County on November 27, 1984.

WHITE-WINGED SCOTER, *Melanitta fusca* (Linnaeus)

Somewhat rare transient and winter visitor. Most regions are represented in these sightings. This is the scoter most often seen in the state.

White-winged Scoters have been reported thirteen times in Arkansas between the last week of October and the third week of March. Half the sightings in the Audubon Society file have occurred during November. Additionally, there are five sightings between December and February, and one in March. Most reports involved one or two birds, but three were seen at Lake Millwood in Hempstead County on January 15, 1977, and three at Lake Maumelle in Pulaski County on March 19, 1977. The species has been reported in three different years at Lake Millwood, and in two different years on the wastewater treatment ponds near Jonesboro, and twice at El Dorado. Additionally, there have been single sightings at Lonoke on a fish pond, at Lake Mena in Polk County, at Lake De Soto in Garland County, on the Arkansas River at Pine Bluff, on De Soto Lake in Phillips County (where two were taken in fishing nets), and on Lake Maumelle.

COMMON GOLDENEYE, *Bucephala clangula* (Linnaeus)

Uncommon migrant and winter resident in all regions and sometimes common locally. Many sightings have involved deep water impoundments.

FALL MIGRATION AND WINTER: Goldeneyes have arrived as early as the second week of November. The three males and nine females at Lake Fayetteville on November 14 was a fairly large number so early in the fall. First arrivals at Big Lake Refuge were recorded as late as the second week of December, and the fall peak, often about 50 birds, occurred from mid-to-late

December. About the same number remained during the winter, with one unusual peak of 150. The 200 "plus" goldeneyes in one large rafting flock at Lake Maumelle in Pulaski County on December 28 was possibly a migratory peak, and perhaps the same can be said for the 63 at Lake Millwood in Hempstead County, also on December 28 of a different year. Several other peaks in numbers have been recorded on Christmas Bird Counts, including 103 at Lonoke in 1982, 98 at Conway in 1980, and 33 on Lake Francis in 1981 (Siloam Springs Christmas Count).

Statewide midwinter surveys of prime waterfowl areas during the 1970s showed that Common Goldeneyes were present only in relatively small numbers at that time. In seven of ten years the survey showed extremely small numbers, and the peak number was only 1000 in one of the remaining three years.

SPRING MIGRATION: At Big Lake the birds departed either by late March or early April. The latest departure date there, April 18, is also the latest departure date on file. The 30 birds at Lake Maumelle on February 4 was a large number for that month, as was the 20 (9 males, 11 females) at Lake Fayetteville on March 9. Other than the records at Big Lake, there is only one report in the file after March.

BUFFLEHEAD, *Bucephala albeola* (Linnaeus)

Fairly common migrant and winter resident, usually in small numbers, on the larger open bodies of water in all regions.

FALL MIGRATION: Buffleheads arrive later than many other ducks. They have been seen no earlier than the last week of October, but few are generally present until the second week of November and thereafter. The 35 birds near Jonesboro on November 8 was an early large number. The total of 200 seen in a day on Booker, Porter, and Horseshoe lakes in Crittenden County on November 24 was an unusually large number. Records at Big Lake Refuge showed the birds arrived in different years between the last of October and early December, with a peak that involved 100 to 200 often in mid-November. Buffleheads are usually seen in small flocks rather than in large rafts.

WINTER: Buffleheads are seen in all regions during winter. The species is reported regularly on the Christmas Bird Count at Conway.

Often the number found there is 40 or fewer, but 72 were seen on the 1982 count. The species is also regular at Lonoke where as many as 100 have been seen several times, and 501 on the 1960 Christmas Count. Small numbers are present on Lake Fayetteville in the western Ozarks every winter, but the birds were absent from the lake after prolonged cold and freezes in late December of 1983 and early 1984. On the statewide 1980 Christmas Counts, Buffleheads were reported at about half of seventeen count locales, with peaks of about 100 at Lake Georgia-Pacific and Lake Millwood, both in the southern lowlands. Midwinter surveys of prime waterfowl areas in Arkansas during the 1970s showed that relatively small numbers remained in the state, with a peak one year of 1300.

SPRING MIGRATION: The period of northward flight seems to range between late February and about mid-April. A migratory movement is suggested by a report from Horseshoe Lake, where the 293 birds present on February 23 had declined sharply several days later. The last birds were seen at Big Lake between late March and mid-April. The latest regular sightings for the state have involved single birds in different years on April 21. Thereafter, there are several reports in the lowlands involving one or two birds in May and the first two weeks of June. The 12 birds at Lake Fayetteville on April 11 was a large number for so late in migration.

HOODED MERGANSER, *Lophodytes cucullatus* (Linnaeus)

Permanent resident. Migrant in all regions. Summer resident chiefly at a few national wildlife refuges on the Mississippi Alluvial Plain. Winter visitor in all regions, but chiefly in the southern lowlands. Observed on quiet wooded lakes and swamps, and along wooded shorelines of large impoundments.

SPRING MIGRATION: Migrants and late departing wintering birds are seen during February, March, and April. At Big Lake Refuge in Mississippi County, files maintained through 1961 showed a peak of 100 to 200 birds in late January and early February, with some late departure dates in the second week of April. The latest regular sightings in the western Ozarks range into the second half of February. Records after mid-January in Faulkner County are scattered into early March (Johnson 1979). The birds have been seen into the third week of April at Lake Millwood in the southwestern counties. Most spring migration sightings in the Audubon Society file have involved one or two birds. The 17 Hooded Mergansers on the White River at Cotter in Baxter County on January 21 were probably migrants, as were the 75 at Lonoke on February 1.

BREEDING SEASON: Some Hooded Mergansers remain to nest in Arkansas. Records of nests of young are primarily from Big Lake and the White River Refuge, both on the Mississippi Alluvial Plain. There are also confirmed nesting records in Arkansas, Jefferson, Benton and Hot Spring counties. In addition to these, adults have been observed in summer in Lonoke, Washington, and Clark counties.

Howell (1911) saw "strong-flying young" at Big Lake on June 22. "Nesting" was reported in Arkansas County on July 5 (Baerg 1951). At the White River Refuge, an estimated ten pairs of Hooded Mergansers nested in Wood Duck boxes in the mid-1970s. Even though the Wood Duck nesting box program has been discontinued there, the summer population of Hooded Mergansers is estimated now at 150 to 200 birds. Almost 400 young Hooded Mergansers have been produced in Wood Duck boxes in one season at Big Lake, and sometimes mixed broods have resulted when Wood Ducks and Hooded Mergansers lay eggs in the same box. Hooded Mergansers have also nested in Wood Duck boxes in Jefferson County. Records not apparently involving nesting boxes have included a female with young on Beaver Lake in Benton County on June 2, 1965, and a female with nine young in Hot Spring County on May 2, 1979.

The nesting habitat suitable for this species has been restricted in recent years by the widespread destruction of bottomland forests and swamps throughout the region of the Mississippi River (James 1974).

FALL MIGRATION: Hooded Mergansers sometimes arrive in the state from the north as early as the first of October, but records of this sort mainly involve the period from the latter part of October to early November and thereafter. One Hooded Merganser recovered in Arkansas along the Mississippi River in mid-November had been banded in August of the previous year almost 800 miles north, in Michi-

gan. A peak involving 100 to 400 birds was observed at Big Lake in the second half of November. Only small numbers of Hooded Mergansers are seen in most places in Arkansas. Flocks of 17, 4, and 24 at Grand Lake in Chicot County on November 27 produced a high count.

WINTER: While this species is sometimes very common in the lowlands of southern Arkansas in winter, they are very uncommon in northern Arkansas (there are only a few Christmas Count reports at Jonesboro and Fayetteville). Hooded Mergansers have been reported with fair regularity on the Christmas Counts at Conway and Little Rock, but always in small numbers. Large numbers are occasionally reported on Christmas Counts in the southern lowlands. At Arkadelphia there are several reports of 20 or more since 1980. At the White River Refuge there is one report of 100 (1968). A total of 119 were reported at Pine Bluff (1983). At Lake Georgia-Pacific, 100 or more have been counted in four years since 1977, including a highly unusual peak of 456 on the 1978 Christmas Count, and 100 "plus" were seen at Lake Chicot in Chicot County on January 22, 1985.

COMMON MERGANSER, *Mergus merganser* Linnaeus

Uncommon migrant and winter visitor in small numbers on the larger lakes and reservoirs in all regions.

Common Mergansers have arrived in Arkansas as early as the last week of October, but few are seen until mid-November and thereafter, with peak numbers between late December and February. There are scattered records during spring to early April. At Lake Fayetteville in the northwest, 13 birds in male type plumage were seen on November 14, and 11 (also in the male plumage) were seen on November 30 of a different year. The birds are usually reported only in small numbers on Christmas Bird Counts. The seven, eight, and eleven birds reported on counts in different years at Lake Millwood, Pine Bluff, and Fayetteville were all high numbers. Peak numbers seem to occur later, and usually in the northern half of the state. A total of 22 was reported in the Bull Shoals Lake area of Boone County on January 16, and 50 were seen on Horseshoe and Porter lakes in Crittenden County on January 21. Some other peak counts

FIGURE 6-32 Ruddy Ducks at the state fish hatchery at Lonoke in January. *David Plank*

have included 20 at Holla Bend Refuge in Pope County on February 2, and 30 seen by a party of observers at Horseshoe Lake on February 22. Reports after late February have involved smaller numbers. The two males and two females seen on Lake Sequoyah in Washington County on March 21 was a late report.

RED-BREASTED MERGANSER, *Mergus serrator* Linnaeus

Uncommon migrant and winter visitor in small numbers on lakes, reservoirs, and large rivers in all regions.

FALL MIGRATION: Red-breasted Mergansers sometimes arrive in Arkansas from their northern breeding grounds as early as the fourth week of October, but most sightings occur during November and thereafter. The fall peak seems to occur during the second, third, and fourth weeks of November. Several fall peak reports include: 10 seen on the wastewater treatment ponds near Jonesboro on November 13; 32 on Calion Lake near El Dorado on November 15; 13 at Lake Millwood on November 23; and 14 at Lake Fayetteville on the same day in a different year. In Garland County, where the species was considered an "uncommon fall transient," fall arrivals were noted between October 24 and November 14 (Deaderick 1938).

WINTER AND SPRING: There have been sightings in December, January, and early February in all regions, but the small numbers involved suggest that all but a very few Red-breasted Mergansers migrating through Arkansas moved south of the state by December. The peak numbers for this midwinter period were six at Lake Maumelle near Little Rock on February 10, and 10 in Jefferson County on January 2. The 20 birds counted on Horseshoe and Porter lakes in Crittenden County on February 25 may have been spring migrants. As many as seven birds have been reported at El Dorado on March 30, and the same number in Sharp County in early April. During spring most birds have departed by the second week of April. Thereafter, all sightings in the Audubon Society file have involved single birds, and only two of these sightings occurred after May 8.

RUDDY DUCK, *Oxyura jamaicensis* (Gmelin)

Common migrant and winter resident in all regions, with the largest numbers on the Mississippi Alluvial Plain. Rare summer resident that has nested in the eastern lowlands.

FALL MIGRATION: Fall migrants have been reported as unusually early as mid-September, but few are seen until early October, with numbers increasing with the arrival of cold fronts in mid-to-late October and during November. The birds arrived regularly during October at Big Lake Refuge, with peak numbers of 100 to 500 during mid-November. The 6400 at Horseshoe and Porter lakes in Crittenden County on November 10, 1963, and 3200 in Chicot County on November 25, 1966, are the largest fall peak records in the Audubon Society file. In the western Ozarks there are no arrival dates before mid-October, and the peak of 23 birds was reported on November 28.

WINTER: Ruddy Ducks are present in fair numbers most winters. They have been reported with fair regularity on the Christmas Bird Count at Fayetteville in the western Ozarks, with one peak of 48. At Conway the numbers on the Christmas Count usually vary between 20 and 40. Huge concentrations involving over 2000 Ruddy Ducks have been reported on several occasions since the 1970s at both Pine Bluff and Lonoke. Midwinter surveys of prime waterfowl areas in the state during the 1970s showed a population that varied from over 10,000 one year to less than 1000 in another.

The one banding record associated with Arkansas involved a bird banded in summer over 900 miles north in Minnesota and recovered in Arkansas during winter more than two years later.

SPRING MIGRATION: As judged from large concentrations, influxes of spring migrants occur as early as late February, with most birds departing by mid-April, and only a few stragglers remaining after early May. At Lonoke, where Christmas Bird Counts have usually involved at most a few hundred of this species, 1000 were seen on February 26, and 1200 on March 17. In the western Ozarks, the 15 at Lake Fayetteville on April 13 was a peak.

BREEDING SEASON: In summer 1968 several pairs were observed on ponds at Lonoke and Keo in Lonoke County. Courtship displays were seen and two ducklings collected September 30. Two of the three nests found contained abandoned Ruddy Duck eggs. There are several other summer records from grassy or weed-covered ponds in eastern Arkansas that could have indicated breeding, but no other confirmed records.

Order FALCONIFORMES

Family Cathartidae New World Vultures

BLACK VULTURE, *Coragyps atratus* (Bechstein)

Permanent resident in small numbers in the open country of the Coastal Plain and on the southern half of the Mississippi Alluvial Plain; scarce and or very local elsewhere. Generally much less numerous than Turkey Vultures.

BREEDING SEASON: Reports of Black Vultures in the Audubon Society file are concentrated in the lowlands of southern and southeastern Arkansas, with scattered records elsewhere. The average annual mean number per route of Black Vultures in each region on the Breeding Bird Survey in Arkansas was 1.1 on the Coastal Plain, 2.1 on the Mississippi Alluvial Plain (mainly Chicot County), and 0.4 for the highlands (including the Arkansas River Valley). Peak means of 0.8 to 4.2 were reported mainly on the Coastal Plain and the eastern edges of the Ozarks bordering the Mississippi Alluvial Plain.

Nesting activity has been observed in March and April. The earliest nest involved two eggs found on the ground in a thick canebrake in Arkansas County on March 1. Young estimated to be ten days old were observed there on April 14. An adult was flushed from a nest with two eggs in a slight depression under a bluff at Petit Jean State Park in Conway County on March 15, and there is a similar record for Devil's Den State Park in Washington County. In the University of Arkansas museum (Fayetteville) there are three clutches of two eggs each that were collected between March 27 and April 15 from nests in the cliffs above Rock Creek near Mena in Polk County. A nest with eggs was found on April 5 at the long-established vulture roost site near Rudy in Crawford County.

Black Vultures were said by one observer to be a fairly common permanent resident on the Grand Prairie in eastern Arkansas, but they are not truly common anywhere in southeastern Arkansas, and they are difficult to find in the heavily forested regions further north. There is a nesting record for northeastern Arkansas (Hanebrink 1980); this record came from Batesville in Independence County, which is in the eastern Ozarks rather than in the lowlands. Black Vultures were said to be a "fairly common permanent resident" in Garland County in the Ouachitas, but Turkey Vultures outnumbered Black Vultures six to one (Deaderick 1938). In heavily forested areas, such as in the Ozarks, the species is highly local, and only small numbers are observed. Black Vultures have nested regularly near Rudy in Crawford County, which is near the open country of the Arkansas River Valley bordering the Ozarks.

WINTER AND OTHER RECORDS: While this species is considered to be largely resident (rather than migratory as in the Turkey Vulture), there are several records that show the birds move fairly long distances and that they concentrate in impressive numbers at times other than in winter. Three birds banded in winter in coastal Louisiana were recovered in later winters due north in southeastern Arkansas near the Mississippi River, 219 to 289 miles from the banding place. The concentration of 75 birds along the Buffalo River in Marion County on March 26 was unusual for the Ozarks.

FIGURE 6-33 Black Vulture at Grassy Lake near Saratoga in early May. *David Plank*

One of the most notable features of the winter season are the large roosts. There were 100 Black Vultures with 300 Turkey Vultures at Grassy Lake in southwestern Arkansas on November 11. An estimated 70 were roosting in three trees in Lincoln County on February 22. At Grassy Lake, 80 were still present March 24. In the highlands and in the Arkansas River Valley the species is seen at midwinter on a somewhat irregular basis. None are found on the Christmas Bird Counts for this region some years. The roost of 45 birds reported on the 1984 Fayetteville Christmas Count was unusual. At Arkadelphia on the Coastal Plain, on the other hand, the species is seen annually on the Christmas Count. Often 15 or less are reported, but there is one peak of 27 birds. These numbers seem fairly typical for the lowlands except for the northeastern counties.

TURKEY VULTURE, *Cathartes aura* (Linnaeus)

Common to fairly common permanent resident in all regions except for the northeastern lowlands.

SPRING MIGRATION: Spring migration has been observed during March and April. Near Natural Dam in Crawford County, 69 birds were strung out across a valley and slowly drifting north on March 2. At least 32 birds were seen as they soared above Devil's Den State Park in the western Ozarks on April 5.

BREEDING SEASON: Data in the Audubon Society file and Breeding Bird Surveys show that during the nesting season this species is most often found in the highlands (especially the Ozarks) and on the Coastal Plain. The average annual mean number per route in each region reported on Breeding Bird Surveys was 3.0 for the Coastal Plain, 0.7 for the Mississippi Alluvial Plain, and 2.5 for the highlands (including the Arkansas River Valley). The peak means involving 5.1 to 9.2 birds per survey were reported in Dallas County on the Coastal Plain, and Van Buren, Izard, and Carroll-Boone-Newton counties in the Ozarks. In the northeastern counties the species is rare, and is generally recorded only from Crowley's Ridge and on the edge of the Ozarks (Hanebrink, Sutton, and Posey 1978).

Nesting activity has been observed in April, May and June. In the Wheeler Collection there are four clutches of two eggs each that were collected between April 2 and June 5 on high bluffs (100 to 200 feet above streams) in Faulkner, Pope, and Yell counties. Several pairs were said to be nesting on a bluff above the Arkansas River in Franklin County on May 26. Howell (1911) reported two half-grown young in a cave near the top of a steep bluff above the White River at Cotter (Baxter County) on June 8. "In Crawford County . . . a large number of birds formerly bred in the cliffs above Frog Bayou, but so persistently were they persecuted . . . that not a pair now returns to this once favored retreat" (Wheeler 1924). This site, which is near Rudy, has been reoccupied for several decades by both species of vultures. Its historical nature, and the fact that it provides suitable habitat, make it one of the most important such locations in the state.

FALL MIGRATION: Fall migrants are seen during September, October, and November. At least 15 Turkey Vultures were associated with other species of southward moving raptors in Washington County on September 17. Observers atop Magazine Mountain counted 21 Turkey Vultures as they slowly drifted southward on October 1. On November 2 in Faulkner County, 132 birds were migrating at sunset, soaring upward and then circling on thermals. At Grassy Lake in southwestern Arkansas, 300 were in a roost on November 11, 1967. At Winslow in Washington County, Turkey Vultures were said to "retire" from the high elevations (2200 feet) to below 1500 feet in early December, and to "reascend" toward the end of February (Smith 1915).

WINTER: Turkey Vultures and Black Vultures form winter roosts that are sometimes impressively large. One of the best known locations in the state is north of Rudy in south central Crawford County. Birds have used this location in Lancaster Valley at least since the 1920s (Wheeler 1924). As many as 100 to 200 vultures (primarily Turkey Vultures) use this roost, which is on the east side of a 300-foot bluff. In the Audubon Society file there are some other unusually large winter records, including 200 birds in Yell County on January 1.

The ten-year statewide mean number of Turkey Vultures per party hour on Christmas Bird Counts varied from 0.6 to 1.3 on the Coastal Plain, 0.0 to 0.1 on the Mississippi Alluvial Plain, and 0.0 to 1.3 in the highlands (including the Arkansas River Valley). On the 1980 statewide Christmas Counts, three-fourths of the 437 Turkey Vultures reported were in southern Arkansas, with peaks of 58 to 94 birds at Lake Millwood, Magnolia, Mena, and Texarkana. There are no Christmas Count reports for Turkey Vultures at Jonesboro, and the birds are virtually absent or occur locally in small numbers in the Ozarks during the sharpest cold of winter.

NOTE: Both species of vultures are well-known for their quick response to feeding opportunities. In Prairie County, where enormous flocks of blackbirds assemble in winter roosts, vultures have been observed feeding on the accumulation of dead birds. An estimated 100 birds fed on fish killed by sewage pollution on the White River below Fayetteville, and on mussels killed during a "drawdown" of Lake Sequoyah in Washington County. Small numbers sometimes occur at disposal sites for dead chickens from poultry houses.

Family Accipitridae

Subfamily Pandioninae Ospreys

OSPREY, *Pandion haliaetus* (Linnaeus)

Common to fairly common transient observed on larger rivers and other large open bodies of water in all regions. Rare winter visitor sometimes observed in the southern lowlands. Several recent summer records, including one successful nest.

FALL MIGRATION: Ospreys are usually seen in Arkansas from early September to the fourth week of October. They usually do not arrive until the second or third week of September, and few are seen after the middle of October. Most of the scattered sightings after late October involved single birds on the Coastal Plain. An Osprey recovered in southwestern Arkansas during mid-September had been banded in late July of the same year in Wisconsin, 860 miles away.

WINTER: December through February reports are irregular and unusual. There are several reports from the Union County area in the extreme south, and other reports, all involving single birds, from eight counties in the lowlands, and two counties in the Arkansas River Valley (Audubon Society file, Hanebrink 1980, Johnson 1979).

SPRING MIGRATION: Occasionally Ospreys are seen in Arkansas as early as mid-March, but few are reported before the first week of April, with a concentration of sightings from the second week of the month and thereafter until the first week of May. Most sightings in the Audubon Society file for spring involve single birds, rarely as many as three in a day.

SUMMER SEASON: Bendire (1892) states that Ospreys nested on sandstone bluffs above the Little Red River in central Arkansas. Howell (1911) considered Ospreys "a common summer resident along the larger rivers of the state, but of late years it has become scarce." He did not speculate concerning the cause of this apparent decline. Deaderick (1938) stated the species was a "fairly common summer resident" at Lake Hamilton in Garland County. Baerg (1931) says Ospreys were "reported nesting in various localities, Fort Smith, Osceola, Newport and elsewhere" but no dates are given. In his 1951 edition Baerg mentions Deaderick's observation of summering birds (see above), but the only mention of actual nesting pertains to Sharp County (Baerg 1951), and again no date is given. Based on this information it may be surmised that the Sharp County nesting occurred sometime in the 1930s or 1940s (the time span between Baerg's two editions), which is the last report of definite Osprey nesting in Arkansas until the unsuccessful attempts in 1982 and 1983 (see below).

Although Osprey nests were not reported in Arkansas between Baerg's last nesting report and the early 1980s, there were a few summer sightings of Ospreys: single birds were observed in Searcy County along the Buffalo River on June 16, 1963, at Lake Maumelle in Pulaski County on July 28, 1953, and in Poinsett County on August 4, 1964. Prior to 1961 Ospreys were seen regularly during several summers at DeVall's Bluff along the White River in Prairie County. At Beaver Lake in Benton County, two Ospreys (one of them was missing feathers from the wing) were seen in late June and early July of 1982 in the Prairie Creek area, and the birds were observed as they caught fish and repeatedly carried them off in the same direction. Again in the summer of 1983, at least one Osprey was observed repeatedly in the same area.

Osprey nests found at Big Lake Refuge in 1982 and 1983 were the first nests seen in Arkansas in three to five decades. Ospreys built two nests at Big Lake in 1982, but no eggs were laid in either nest. Both nests seemed to be built by the same birds. In 1983 one of these nests was rebuilt and one egg laid, but it did not hatch. Later in 1983 another new nest was built, but no eggs were laid.

The alarming decline in the number of Ospreys in the United States, and the fact that it was no longer breeding in Arkansas, caused it to be placed on an unofficial "Black List" for the state (James 1974). Reproductive failure in Ospreys was positively linked to the ingestion of DDT and its derivatives, which Ospreys obtained through fish, its principal food (Ames and Mersereau 1964). The fact that Ospreys are apparently returning to nest again in Arkansas suggests that the ban on DDT in the United States is working to reduce stress on these birds.

Finally in 1984 Ospreys built a nest during early April at Mallard Lake, adjacent to Big Lake. Three eggs were laid and young three to four weeks old were seen during the first week of July. The presence of numerous fishermen in the area of the nest did not seem to disturb the nesting pair.

Subfamily *Accipitrinae* Kites, Eagles, and Hawks

AMERICAN SWALLOW-TAILED KITE, *Elanoides forficatus* (Linnaeus)

No record since the 1940s.

While Howell (1911) did not see this species during his trip through Arkansas, he published reports that it had bred at Newport in Jackson County in 1884 and in Little River County in 1890. He stated further that before 1900 it was "doubtless at that time . . . fairly numerous in the lowlands of the State, nesting chiefly in the cypress swamps. At present this interesting and useful species must be extremely rare." Smith (1915) stated that residents in the Winslow area of Washington County described the birds to him "minutely." One was seen there by a resident on October 8, and there were additional reports of several birds together. Baerg (1951) published two secondhand reports: one from Newport in 1935, and another record involving two birds seen on July 10, 1949, in Newton County. There are no reports in the Audubon Society files.

BLACK-SHOULDERED KITE, *Elanus caeruleus* (Desfontaines)

Three records. Formerly called "White-tailed Kite."

The range of this species has greatly expanded since 1960 (AOU 1983). The three Arkansas records can presumably be attributed to this expansion. The first observation involved a single bird at Old River in Miller County on December 12, 1976. Two birds were seen near the college campus at Russellville (Pope County) on April 14, 1978. A single bird was photographed by Max and Helen Parker at Arkadelphia in Clark County on March 7, 1981.

Written documentation is available for each of these sightings, and a duplicate slide is on file with the Arkansas Audubon Society for the March 7 sighting.

MISSISSIPPI KITE, *Ictinia mississippiensis* (Wilson)

Migrant and summer resident that is locally common on the larger forested rivers and bayous in the lowlands, along the Arkansas River to Faulkner County, and in the Ouachitas at the border of the lowlands.

SPRING MIGRATION: Arrivals have been reported primarily between the third week of April and early May, with several records involving peak numbers in the last week of May. Thirty were seen in Chicot County along the Mississippi River on April 22, and 50 were present in the same place one week later. The earliest positive arrival date for the state involved two birds at Little Rock on March 23. A single bird seen along the White River in eastern Washington County from late May into June 1985 was the first record for the western Ozarks in over forty years.

BREEDING SEASON: Most breeding season records are from the lower Arkansas, Mississippi, mid-to-lower Ouachita, and lower Red rivers, with sightings either directly along the rivers or nearby. Some of the largest numbers have been observed along the Mississippi River. In Phillips County, 15 birds were seen in mid-May of 1983. On Brandywine Island in the Mississippi River in Crittenden County, 75 to 80 birds were counted as they hovered over large trees in late June of 1980 (Ark. Natural Heritage Comm. 1983). In the northeastern lowlands the birds are common near Wilson and Luxora, both near the Mississippi River in Mississippi County. There are no breeding records for the Ozarks. In the Ouachitas they have been found during summer in the Ouachita River bottoms just north of Arkadelphia in Clark County where the Ouachita Mountains meet the Coastal Plain.

Nesting activity has been noted from late April to August. The earliest nest, eighty feet high, was under construction at Boyle Park in Little Rock on April 29 in a sweetgum tree. The latest nesting activity recorded in the Audubon Society file involved an adult feeding a fledgling near Camden in Ouachita County on August 19. The earliest date fledglings have been reported is at mid-June, but a nest was under construction at Wilson in Mississippi County as late as June 29. On the Grand Prairie, where the species was said to be "fairly common," most of fourteen nests one year were "high up in tall bottomland cottonwoods" (Meanley and Neff 1953a). Several observers have reported that these birds use the same nests in successive years.

FALL MIGRATION: The peak of the fall migration seems to occur during mid-to-late August, with a sharp decline in numbers after early September. There are several reports involving sightings of 20 to 30 birds in a day during this period, but none top the report of 68 individuals in flocks of 8 to 10 observed along the Arkansas River in extreme southeastern Arkansas on August 13. Single birds seen in Union County during the second and third weeks of October in different years were late reports for the state.

NOTES ON FEEDING: On a trip up the Mississippi River in June of 1819, Audubon saw Mississippi Kites in the vicinity of the mouth of the St. Francis River (Audubon 1929). In his journal he wrote, "the Mississippi Kite Were Busily Employed in Catching small Lizards off the Bark of Dead Cypress Trees, this effected by Sliding beautifully by the Trees and suddenly Turning on their Side and Graple the prey. . . ." Jane Stern noted that in Jefferson County a bird brought a rodent to the female, who tore it up, taking a few bites for herself, but feeding most to the nestlings. The birds have also been seen during May and June catching dragonflies in rice fields adjoining bottomland forests in southeastern Arkansas (Meanley and Neff 1953a). In northwestern Arkansas one was seen apparently capturing and consuming periodical cicadas during the 1985 cicada emergence there.

BALD EAGLE, *Haliaeetus leucocephalus* (Linnaeus)

Fairly common, local migrant and winter resident on larger bodies of water including reservoirs, lakes, and rivers in all regions. Recent nesting records at the White River National Wildlife Refuge. The eagle most often seen in the state.

FALL MIGRATION: Bald Eagles sometimes ar-

rive from their nesting areas north of the state during the period from late August through October, but few are seen until November, especially late in the month. The 16 seen on the Little Red River below Greers Ferry Dam in Cleburne County on November 27, 1977, is a peak count for the fall migration period.

WINTER: The construction of large reservoirs in the state in recent years seems to have provided new winter habitat for this species. Around some of these big reservoirs the birds appear almost common. A summary of the 1981 Mid-winter Eagle Survey sponsored by the National Wildlife Federation showed over 500 birds in the state, with peak numbers as follows: Bull Shoals Lake, 87; Lake Millwood, 66; the Arkansas River in central Arkansas, 57; Lake Ouachita, 50. The birds are not limited to big lakes or rivers, either. Poultry farmers in several regions of the state have in recent years taken hundreds of dead chickens from their big poultry houses and disposed of them in open pastures. At some locations this is an attraction to Bald Eagles and other raptorial birds. Up to over 50 Bald Eagles have been seen in one small pasture area. (There is no evidence that Bald Eagles attack livestock.)

Some recent recoveries in winter of Bald Eagles banded north of Arkansas during the summers since 1977, illustrate migration into the state. Three birds banded in the nest in June in Wisconsin were recovered up to two and one-half years later at Lake Millwood, at the Buffalo River in northern Arkansas, and in Pope County. Three birds banded in nests in June in Ontario, Canada, were recovered about six months later in southeastern Arkansas (two birds) and in northern Arkansas (one bird).

SPRING MIGRATION: Most Bald Eagles have departed from the state by late March. The 40 birds from a wintering population in a study area in Benton County present on March 18, 1985, declined to four birds one week later. Some birds seen in late spring or early summer may be northward wanderers from nesting areas south of Arkansas. A juvenile Bald Eagle banded in April in central Florida was recovered in late May of the same year in Arkansas. This northward wandering might also account for a single immature bird seen at Lake De Soto in Garland County on June 30, 1979.

HISTORY AND PRESENT STATUS OF BREEDING BIRDS: Bald Eagles nested regularly in

FIGURE 6-34 Bald Eagle. *Sigrid James Bruch*

Arkansas during the past until about the mid-1950s, by which time they had become threatened or endangered throughout much of their range in the United States due to loss of nesting habitat and the concentration of pesticides in food consumed by eagles. Then, after about twenty-five years in which no Bald Eagle nests were seen in Arkansas, a pair successfully raised young in a nest at the White River Refuge in 1982 and another successful nesting was reported at the same location in 1984.

One of the first detailed records of nesting Bald Eagles in Arkansas was made by Audubon who observed them while passing along the eastern border of Arkansas during his trip down the Mississippi River in the winter of 1820–1821 (Audubon 1929). In his journal he wrote of seeing courtship, including copulation and nest building, during early December of 1820:

I saw this afternoon Two Eagles Coatiting—the femelle was on a Very high Limb of a Tree and squated at the approach of the Male, who came Like a Torrent, alighted on her and quakled shrill until he sailed off the femelle following him and zig zaging herself through the air.

Between the 1920s and 1950s, Bald Eagle nests were observed at several locations on the Mississippi Alluvial Plain (Wheeler 1924, Ganier 1932), and the birds were said to be a "permanent resident" in Saline County (Deaderick 1936a). One of the best known nesting sites was an old oxbow of the Mississippi River in Crittenden County where Wheeler said "several pairs" were nesting, "fortunately protected by the Five Lakes Hunting and Fishing Club." Several years later, Ganier (1932) and others found four nests there on March 9, 1930, with fully grown young in all three nests. Wheeler collected two eggs from a nest at Big Lake in Mississippi County on March 5, 1923 (Wheeler 1923b), and published a picture of the nest, which was six feet wide and 72 feet high in "a very large and old cypress." Another nesting site mentioned by Wheeler was in Phillips County between the Arkansas and Mississippi rivers where the birds were said to have been nesting "for many years."

Files maintained at the White River Refuge showed that occupied Bald Eagle nests were seen as late as the early 1950s at Old Goose Lake, Big Island, and Swan Lake. Refuge Mana-

ger Peter Van Huizen saw two nests, probably in 1952, in cypress trees on Eagle Nest Lake and East Moon Lake (Mallard, pers. comm. 1983). As late as 1956 refuge files showed two immature birds seen in late April. A pair of adult birds was seen near a nest at Peckerwood Lake in Prairie County in 1957, but no eggs or young were seen there, and the nest tree was later blown down.

Over two decades elapsed before there was any further indication that Bald Eagles were nesting in Arkansas. In 1980 the birds built a nest at Big Lake Refuge, but eggs were not laid in it. Also in the early 1980s, other unsuccessful nesting attempts occurred at Lake Millwood and at Wapanocca Refuge. Finally in 1982 there appeared a successful nest.

According to personnel at the White River Refuge, the 1982 nest was sixty feet high in a cypress tree. The adult pair was first sighted on March 3. Observations of the young indicated that hatching of the two eggs occurred in the second half of April. Two nestlings were observed in late April, but one subsequently disappeared. The adults were not seen in the area after June 10, but the fledgling was still near the nest on July 16. A second nest was also found that year, and an adult bird was seen nearby, but no other activity was observed.

While Bald Eagles apparently did not nest at White River Refuge in 1983, explorations of the most remote regions of the refuge resulted in the discovery of two additional nests, but birds were not seen in their vicinity, and it is not known when the nests were actually constructed. Both nests were huge—six to eight feet across and four to five feet deep (Mallard, pers. comm. 1983). Two eaglets were found in a nest on the refuge in April 1984.

In 1985 there were seven Bald Eagle nests in Arkansas, but only one produced young. These nests were located at Bayou Meto Wildlife Management Area east of Pine Bluff, Grassy Lake in southwestern Arkansas, on Big Island in Desha County, and at the White River Refuge. Four of the seven nests were at the White River Refuge, and one of them produced young—the same nest that has produced young since 1982.

The construction of nests and the fledging of young are hopeful signs. Among recent efforts designed to encourage Bald Eagle nesting in the state are attempts to introduce young eagles

FIGURE 6-35 Northern Harriers on the Mississippi Alluvial Plain at Lonoke in late January. *David Plank*

on the Buffalo River (Barkley 1984). This project, a joint effort between the Arkansas Game and Fish Commission, the U.S. Fish and Wildlife Service, and the National Park Service, has been launched in hopes that when these Bald Eagles reach maturity they may return there to nest. A Bald Eagle released along the Buffalo River in the summer of 1985 was found dead in September 1985 on an island in Lake Champlain in Vermont, 13 miles south of the Canadian border. This bird had originally been taken from a nest in Minnesota at the age of six weeks and released along the Buffalo River in Arkansas. It appears to have starved to death after its wing became entangled in a tree limb.

Habitat protection, gradual reduction of pesticides in the environment, and various protective efforts have all coincided to promote the recovery of Bald Eagle populations. Nevertheless, serious problems remain. According to

personnel of the U.S. Fish and Wildlife Service, during the winters from 1980 to 1982, 29 Bald Eagles were killed or seriously wounded in Arkansas as a result of illegal shooting, and the actual totals may be twice that high. On the other hand, the public is becoming more aware of these problems. An excellent example of public spirited activity was offered by Mrs. Jane Gulley whose Eagle Awareness program was presented to more than 100,000 Arkansans by early 1982.

NORTHERN HARRIER, *Circus cyaneus* (Linnaeus)

Migrant and winter resident in all regions, especially common in the lowlands. Rare summer resident. Formerly called "Marsh Hawk."

FALL MIGRATION: Harriers sometimes arrive from breeding areas north of the state by mid-to-late August (Audubon Society file, Black

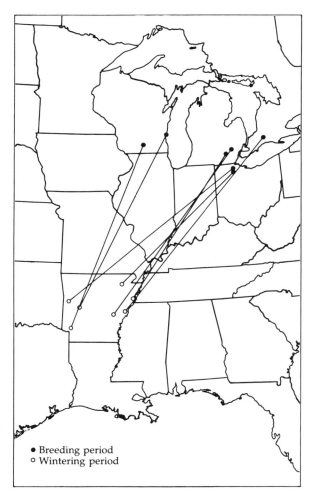

- Breeding period
○ Wintering period

FIGURE 6-36 Movements of the Northern Harrier based on banding records.

1935a, Hanebrink 1980), with numbers increasing thereafter. The three birds flying south in Washington County on October 17 were migrating with a Red-tailed Hawk. In Union County, 50 harriers were seen on October 30, and 15 were seen in the Lonoke area on November 23.

WINTER: Northern Harriers winter in large numbers in the rice areas of eastern Arkansas. Brooke Meanley considered it the most common hawk in Arkansas County during winter. In the northeastern lowlands, harriers were the second most numerous wintering hawk (Hanebrink, Sutton, and Posey 1978). At Lonoke, 50 or more have been reported on many of the Christmas Bird Counts, with a peak of 114. The birds are seen in smaller numbers elsewhere. They are regularly seen during winter in the Arkansas River Valley, and somewhat less regularly in the western Ozarks. The ten-year statewide mean on the Christmas Count was 0.3 harriers per party hour. On the Coastal Plain this mean varied from 0.0 to 0.2, on the Mississippi Alluvial Plain from 0.3 to 0.7, and in the highlands (including the Arkansas River Valley) from 0.0 to 0.2.

Banding recoveries show that Northern Harriers wintering in Arkansas come from populations that nested 550 to 850 miles north and northeast of the state (Figure 6-36). Of seven recoveries, four survived less than a year after banding. The longest survival period was over five years.

SPRING MIGRATION: During spring harriers are seen with fair regularity through March, with only scattered records thereafter until the second week of April. In Craighead County, 24 birds were reported on February 10. The nine birds seen in Lafayette County on March 23 was a large late count. Reports of birds during May raise the possibility of summering (see below).

BREEDING SEASON: Howell (1911) reported nesting near the White River in Jackson County in 1884. A nest with six eggs was discovered at Fort Chaffee in Sebastian County on March 24, 1954; inexplicably, the eggs disappeared in late May. More recently, a nest with four nearly grown young was found near Alma in Crawford County on June 24, 1982. The nest and young were accidently destroyed by a harvesting machine.

There have also been sight records during

summer that involved single birds in Sebastian County (prior to 1982); in Clark County; at Holla Bend Refuge and at Russellville, both in Pope County; and at Stuttgart.

SHARP-SHINNED HAWK, *Accipiter striatus* Vieillot

Regular migrant and winter resident or visitor in small numbers in wooded areas in all regions. Several recent summer records, but no evidence of nesting.

FALL MIGRATION: Sharp-shinned Hawks begin arriving from breeding areas north of Arkansas by mid-September, with numbers increasing by late September and during October. In the northeastern counties the birds are seen from the second week of October through December, with records scattered in winter and in spring (Hanebrink 1980). In the south central region the species is most numerous during fall and early winter (Mattocks and Shugart 1962). Four birds were seen during a hawk migration watch from the west end of Magazine Mountain on October 1. The highest numbers reported in the Audubon Society file involved 10 near Calion in Union County on October 10, and 11 birds seen from Magazine Mountain on October 14.

WINTER: Even though Sharp-shinned Hawks are seen in small numbers every year on Christmas Bird Counts in the state, composite summaries from each of the regions show that the birds are not seen every year on any single Christmas Count. In the El Dorado area, for example, there are only five records on Christmas Counts in the past two decades. At Arkadelphia, the birds have been seen on about half of fifteen recent Christmas Counts. Most records in late December have involved one, occasionally three birds on a Christmas Count. The 1979 Christmas Count was fairly typical: 18 birds for the state, with reports from all regions, and two or three birds at four of the participating communities. During January and February the birds are relatively scarce in the state. Sometimes in winter Sharp-shinned Hawks are seen near home bird feeders, where they catch small birds and are sometimes themselves killed when they fly against large plate glass windows.

SPRING MIGRATION: Sightings for the northward migration are relatively numerous from late March through April and into the first half of May. There are no large peak counts during spring, and no clear demarcation exists between winter residents and spring migrants. One bird recovered in Arkansas in spring had been banded in Wisconsin during the autumn three years previously.

BREEDING SEASON: There are several recent June sightings in Madison, Cleburne, Saline, and Union counties, but none of these involved nests or dependent young. Wheeler (1924) had no nesting records. Howell (1911) published secondhand breeding reports for Van Buren County in 1890, and Jackson County, but he had no firsthand knowledge of nesting birds in the state. There is also a June record for Washington County (Baerg 1931).

COOPER'S HAWK, *Accipiter cooperii* (Bonaparte)

Migrant and winter resident in small numbers in woodlands in all regions. Formerly at least fairly common as a summer resident, but now uncommon to somewhat rare in summer, with no recent confirmed nesting records.

SPRING AND FALL: The paucity of records in the Audubon Society file between late April and early August suggests that spring migrants that will nest north of the state usually depart by the second half of April and perhaps earlier, and that birds migrating through Arkansas during the southward migration, or that are planning to winter in the state, begin to arrive in late summer or early fall, especially from mid-September and thereafter. The migratory status of the species, however, is greatly complicated by the fact that the birds once nested regularly in the state, and are still present irregularly and in small numbers during summer. Most reports at any time of the year have involved single birds. The three seen from Wildcat Mountain in Fort Smith on September 28 was a one day peak count, and two were seen during a hawk migration watch from atop Magazine Mountain on October 1.

BANDING: There are two banding records that illustrate migratory movements relative to Arkansas. One bird banded in Wisconsin in spring was recovered over 600 miles south-southwest in Arkansas in winter nearly three years later. Another, banded in fall in Wisconsin, was recovered 570 miles south in winter of the same year.

WINTER: While most sightings in the file have involved single Cooper's Hawks, larger numbers are sometimes tallied on Christmas Bird Counts when many observers are in the field all day in late December or early January. At Arkadelphia, for example, records for this species have generally involved one to three birds on a Christmas Count, but eight were found in 1982. The species shows up regularly on Christmas Counts in all regions of the state.

BREEDING SEASON: Based upon relatively sparse nesting data for Arkansas, birds seen during May and June could be summer residents. Howell (1911) reported a nest in Pike County. Wheeler (1924) found nests in Washington, Sebastian, Pope, Faulkner, and Yell counties, all in the northwestern quarter of the state. He further stated that the species was as common in summer as the Red-shouldered Hawk. Smith (1915) and Black (1935a) both found the species common in summer in the rugged, heavily forested Boston Mountain region around Winslow in Washington County. According to Baerg (1951), "In Arkansas it is relatively common in the northwestern counties; elsewhere it is reported as uncommon." In the file there is a confirmed nest for Hempstead County (Grassy Lake). At Big Lake Refuge, Cooper's Hawk was a permanent resident as late as 1961. There are additional May or June records in Craighead and Cleburne counties, and in 1983, two birds were seen in Hot Spring County on June 22 and one in Hempstead County on June 11. There were additional similar reports for Hot Spring and Hempstead counties in 1984, and Washington County in 1985. There are several additional records of fully grown immature birds in July and August.

There are confirmed nesting records for March, April, and May. Charles Gardner found a nest with three eggs that was seventy-five feet high in a cypress tree at Grassy Lake on March 29, 1942. In the Wheeler Collection, five Arkansas nests (see locations above) with either three or four eggs were dated from April 22 to May 19, and the nests ranged in height thirty-five to seventy feet above the ground. Baerg (1951) states that incubation of eggs at Fayetteville continued forty-two to forty-four days after the laying of the first egg.

NORTHERN GOSHAWK, *Accipiter gentilis* (Linnaeus)

Rare winter visitor.

This woodland hawk of the northern and western regions of North America winters irregularly south of its usual range (AOU 1983). The first definite record involved an adult female taken at Winslow in Washington County on November 5, 1926 (Black 1935a). Baerg (1931) stated that a specimen was taken "not far from Fayetteville during the winter of 1928–29." A goshawk was killed in Sharp County on December 7, 1981, and the specimen was donated to the Museum of Science and History in Little Rock. According to information obtained from the U.S. Fish and Wildlife Service, a bird was shot in Saline County on November 30, 1982, and another was shot near Jerusalem in Conway County on December 12, 1982. A bird with a damaged wing was found at Conway in Faulkner County on January 11, 1983. Additionally, there are several other sight reports in the Audubon Society files.

RED-SHOULDERED HAWK, *Buteo lineatus* (Gmelin)

Permanent resident usually in small numbers, in extensive forests, especially mature forested bottomlands, in all regions.

BREEDING SEASON: Red-shouldered Hawks are found regularly in all the larger forested bottomlands in the state. Reports of one to three birds are not uncommon on those Breeding Bird Surveys with sufficient suitable habitat, and as many as five or six have been reported on the surveys in the Ouachita Mountains and on the Coastal Plain. This species was once said to be the most common of the hawks in Arkansas (Smith 1915, Wheeler 1924). Its numbers seem to have been reduced as a result of extensive clearing of mature, bottomland forest, its favored habitat (James 1974).

Breeding activity has been reported from late February through June. The earliest and latest such records involve a bird using a nest at De-Vall's Bluff in Prairie County on February 25 and young were still present in several nests as late as the second half of June at Boyle Park in Little Rock. In the Wheeler Collection, records of seven nests with eggs are dated from March 29 to June 23, but only one record is later than

FIGURE 6-37 Broad-winged Hawk in the Ozarks southeast of Harrison in early May. *David Plank*

April. The clutch sizes in the Wheeler Collection ranged from two to four eggs. Nest heights in the Audubon Society file and in the Wheeler Collection generally ranged from forty to sixty feet from the ground, and involved both pine and deciduous trees. At Boyle Park, Vivian Scarlett observed a nest in a pine tree that was used three years in succession.

FALL AND WINTER: While numbers of these birds seem fairly stable throughout the year, there are several records involving migration. Two birds banded in June in Wisconsin were recovered the following October almost 600 miles south in northwestern Arkansas. Red-shouldered Hawks were among a mixed-species flock of migrating hawks observed at Little Rock on September 18.

The ten-year statewide mean of 0.1 Red-shouldered Hawks per party hour on Christmas Bird Counts was exceeded at Texarkana and Arkadelphia, both on the Coastal Plain, with 0.2 birds per party hour. On the statewide 1980 Christmas Counts, peak numbers of seven to twelve birds were reported only in the Ouachitas and on the Coastal Plain. Data from Christmas Counts at Fayetteville and Jonesboro, both in the north, indicate that the species occurs in these areas with fair regularity in winter, but in low numbers.

BROAD-WINGED HAWK, *Buteo platypterus* (Vieillot)

Migrant in all regions. Local summer resident in small numbers where there are extensive upland forests such as in the highlands.

SPRING MIGRATION: A single Broad-winged

Hawk seen at Lake Millwood in the southwest on March 15 is the earliest spring arrival date in the Audubon Society file. Otherwise, few birds are seen until the end of March or early April, with numbers increasing thereafter. The spectacular migrations for which this species is justifiably famous have been observed during April. Bill and Janis Beall saw 585 in ten minutes near Van Buren in Crawford County on April 22, and in Franklin County over 40 flew north on a good tail wind on April 19.

BREEDING SEASON: Reports in the file show that these woodland hawks have been seen during summer in all regions, but occur rarely in summer in places where there has been extensive deforestation. Unfortunately there are relatively few reports on the Breeding Bird Surveys, certainly not enough to draw any firm conclusions about their numerical distribution in the state in June.

Breeding activity has been observed from early April through July. A nest with three eggs was found forty feet high in a sweetgum in Miller County on April 2. A bird was observed at Boyle Park in Little Rock as it went to a nest thirty feet up in a pine tree on April 13. Two eggs were collected from a nest thirty feet high in "deep woods" of Pope County on May 21 (Wheeler 1924). Three young were seen in a nest at Fort Smith on June 27. At the Shady Lake campground in the Ouachita National Forest (Polk County), one nestling was seen in a nest sixty to eighty feet high in a pine tree on June 28. At Hamburg in Ashley County a nest was under construction in a deciduous tree on June 10, and two young fledged from the nest on July 30.

FALL MIGRATION: The peak period for fall migration occurs between the third week of September and the first week of October, especially during the last week of September. Over 2000 Broad-winged Hawks were counted at Lake Millwood on September 19. At Little Rock, more than 4300 were seen in fifteen minutes on September 24. More than 1000 were seen in Union County on September 26. There are only a few scattered reports for the state after the first week of October. A single bird seen at Fort Smith in early November is the latest record.

SWAINSON'S HAWK, *Buteo swainsoni* Bonaparte

Very uncommon transient reported in small numbers primarily in the west. One summer record.

SPRING MIGRATION: Swainson's Hawk is seen more often in spring than in fall. Sightings for the northward migration period range between the last week in March and the last week of May, with sightings in many of the western counties, and secondarily in the central and eastern regions. Many of these records have involved one or two birds, but occasionally a few more are seen. Three, for example, were seen at Des Arc in Prairie County on April 22, 1984, and six at Holla Bend Refuge in Pope County on April 18 of the same year.

FALL MIGRATION: The earliest sighting associated with the southward migration occurred in the third week of September, and few have been seen after late October and mid-November. Most of the reports are from the northwestern quarter of the state and involved single birds, or occasionally two. The record published by Baerg (1951) that Swainson's Hawk was "abundant" in Arkansas County on November 8, 1949, unfortunately cannot now be verified.

OTHER RECORDS: There are three sight records in the file that involve the period between December and February, and the one dated December 1 in the south was especially well-documented by experienced observers. A summer record was submitted by Tom Foti, who photographed two Swainson's Hawks at the state fish hatchery in Benton County on June 8, 1969. These birds were seen repeatedly in the open country of Benton County that year until September, but attempts to locate a nest were not successful.

RED-TAILED HAWK, *Buteo jamaicensis* (Gmelin)

Common permanent resident in open country in all regions. Numerous especially during winter.

MIGRATION: Southward moving fall migrants often begin to arrive in numbers about the time of the first big cold fronts, usually in late October or early November. However, a total of 25 Red-tailed Hawks were counted during a mi-

FIGURE 6-38 Red-tailed Hawks in Benton County in early May. *David Plank*

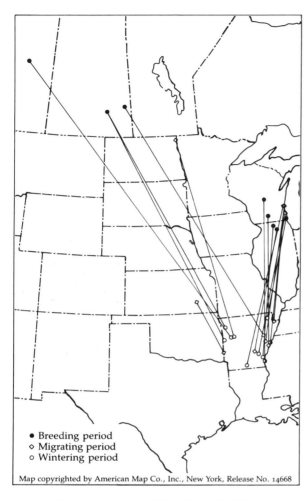

• Breeding period
◇ Migrating period
○ Wintering period

Map copyrighted by American Map Co., Inc., New York, Release No. 14668

FIGURE 6-39 Movements of the Red-tailed Hawk based on banding records.

gration watch from atop Magazine Mountain on October 1. The northward migration of these hawks through Arkansas seems to be largely completed by the end of February, at which time the resident hawks have already begun nesting activities. An unusual concentration of at least 50 birds was seen on a forty-acre field in Washington County on February 12. A study made in northeastern Arkansas showed that this species peaks in numbers during the months of November and February (Hanebrink, Sutton, and Posey 1978).

Migrants and wintering birds are derived from populations that breed to the north (Figure 6-39). Of sixteen recoveries in Arkansas, six were banded about 550 to 700 miles away, and the remainder about 1500 miles. Birds overwintering in eastern Arkansas show strong affinities to populations of the form *B. j. borealis* that nest in the midwestern states. However, birds recovered in western Arkansas trend strongly toward the breeding population of the western forms *calurus* and *kriderii* of the northern prairie states. All but six birds were recovered within thirteen months of banding. One lived nine years, another ten years after banding.

BREEDING SEASON: Records in the Audubon Society file and those taken on the Breeding Bird Surveys show that these birds are present in modest numbers in all regions in summer, with little apparent variation in numbers from region to region. Interestingly, the average annual mean number per route reported on Breeding Bird Surveys was slightly lower than the mean numbers of Red-shouldered Hawks (which nest in forested bottomlands). Red-tailed Hawks were once rare in the state (Howell 1911), although the Red-shouldered Hawk was common (Howell 1911 and others). This apparent population reversal is due, in large part, to extensive deforestation that is often beneficial to Red-tailed Hawks, but detrimental to Red-shouldered Hawks.

Nesting activity has been noted primarily from late February through May, but a full grown and still dependent juvenile was observed as late as the first half of July. The peak period involving incubation occurs in March and April. Nests on file were situated in deciduous trees, thirty to fifty feet high. Three nests observed in 1982 in the northwest were all in tall trees associated with fencerows or remnant woods surrounded by large open fields.

WINTER: Certainly this is the most often reported hawk in the state in winter, and is numerous in the cold months in open country wherever this habitat is found. On the 1980 Christmas Bird Count the number of birds reported in the various count areas varied from 2 to 71, with 30 or more at Jonesboro, Lonoke, Fayetteville, Village Creek State Park (Cross County), and the White River Refuge. At Lonoke rarely as few as 40 are reported on the Christmas Count, at least 60 is a common report, and there is a peak of 155. At Fayetteville numbers in recent years have varied from 23 to 139 birds, with 90 or more on four Christmas Counts. The ten-year statewide mean on Christmas Counts was 0.5 birds per party hour. This varied on the Coastal Plain from 0.1 to 1.7, in the Mississippi Alluvial Plain from 0.5 to 0.9, and in the highlands (including the Arkansas River Valley) from 0.2 to 0.6.

PLUMAGES: There is considerable plumage difference in this species, and this extensive variation causes problems in correct field identification. Most Red-tailed Hawks do, but some do not, have red tails as adults. Immatures regularly lack red tails. Some birds do and others do not have the pattern of dark ventral marks that form "belly bands," and there is tremendous variation in the lightness and darkness of these patterns. Some birds are lightly colored, and others are very dark. While Red-tailed Hawks frequently hunt from a perch, they are also observed hovering over open fields in the manner of Rough-legged Hawks (Lavers 1979).

A study of "Harlan's Hawk" (now a subspecies of the Red-tailed Hawk) was based in large part on specimens collected in northwestern Arkansas (Wood 1932). This study showed that two very dark, often completely black-looking, subspecies of Red-tailed Hawks are present regularly in the state in winter. One, *Buteo jamaicensis calurus*, the western Red-tailed Hawk, has a red tail as an adult, dark tail when immature. The other, now *Buteo jamaicensis harlani*, has enough white in the tail when adult (and very little or no red) that novice observers frequently mis-identify it as a dark

phase Rough-legged Hawk. Whereas *calurus* body plumage is usually uniformly dark black or deep brown, *harlani* is usually heavily flecked with white on the otherwise very dark plumage.

A roadside survey conducted in northeastern Arkansas between 1974 and 1977 resulted in sightings of 864 Red-tailed Hawks (Hanebrink, Sutton, and Posey 1978). Of this number, 26 were the light colored *kriderii* and 31 melanistic or *harlani*.

A study in Benton County of mature Red-tailed Hawks showed that light colored birds use open perch sites, while dark colored hawks more frequently occupy perch sites characterized by dark patterns (dense stem cover). The author suggests that the birds seek perch sites that best conceal them from their prey (Preston 1978, 1980).

SOARING BEHAVIOR: Red-tailed Hawks find their prey while perched rather than when soaring. It was found in a study in northwestern Arkansas that soaring activity contributes significantly to territorial defense, and courtship activity is a prominent function of soaring in late winter (Ballam 1981). A second study, also in northwestern Arkansas, showed that the percentage of hawks observed soaring increased significantly as relative humidity and cloud cover decreased, and as wind velocity and solar illumination increased. Wind velocity was the most important factor associated with soaring (Preston 1981). The birds use thermal updrafts for soaring in spring and summer, and shift to declivity currents—those produced when wind blows over an obstacle such as a hill—during fall and winter (Ballam 1981). In short, the birds utilize declivity updrafts to soar under conditions not conducive to thermal soaring.

FERRUGINOUS HAWK, *Buteo regalis* (Gray)
   One record.
   One Ferruginous Hawk was observed in Prairie County on January 3, 1965. Details were provided on a documentation form that is on file with the Arkansas Audubon Society.

ROUGH-LEGGED HAWK, *Buteo lagopus* (Pontoppidan)

Rare transient and winter visitor. Reports from open country in all regions.

MIGRATION AND WINTER: These birds have been seen in Arkansas between late October and the end of February, with most sightings during the period of severe winter cold, mid-December to mid-February. Most reports have involved single birds. An unusually high number of four birds, all in light phase plumage, was seen in Craighead County on December 23, 1977. Three birds, also all in the light phase plumage, were seen in Washington and Benton counties on December 23, 1983, one of which was photographed by Kimberly Smith. A statewide total of five were reported on the 1983 Arkansas Christmas Bird Count. The relatively large numbers in Arkansas during the winter of 1983–84 may be attributable to an unusually harsh and prolonged period of ice and snow.

A study in northeastern Arkansas (Hanebrink, et al. 1978) emphasizes the relative scarcity of these birds. Between 1974 and 1977 hawks were counted along 20,000 miles of roadsides. Among the species reported were 864 Red-tailed Hawks and only 15 Rough-legged Hawks.

Most reports placed a file with the Arkansas Audubon Society in the past unfortunately did not indicate whether the Rough-legged Hawks were of the light or dark phase. Where color phase was indicated, most reports were for the light phase. A study of plumage variation in this species (Cade 1955) showed that the percentage of dark phase birds in the breeding populations in Canada and Alaska was relatively small, less than 20 percent. It is not, therefore, unreasonable to suspect that most birds reaching Arkansas in winter should be light phase birds, and that some reports of dark phase birds may actually represent misidentifications of dark-plumaged Red-tailed Hawks that are fairly common in some areas of Arkansas in winter (see below).

FIELD IDENTIFICATION: Questions concerning the abundance and distribution of this species in Arkansas are complicated by the regular presence in winter of two subspecies of the Red-tailed Hawk that have melanistic color phases, *Buteo jamaicensis calurus* and *B. j. harlani.*

The dark phases of both species bear a close resemblance to the dark phase *lagopus.* In the dark plumage all three taxa share a general dark to black appearance. When seen from below each shows a considerable contrast between the dark wing linings and the light color of the flight feathers. Each may be seen in open country, and each may sometimes hover. As the name implies, Rough-legged Hawks have legs that are feathered to the toes. The presence of visible, unfeathered lower legs would therefore eliminate *lagopus,* but this feature is seen only under the most favorable circumstances.

Observers in Arkansas have sometimes identified dark phase *lagopus* primarily on the basis of the general dark appearance of the bird coupled with a tail which, when seen from below, is white with a dark terminal band. This description, in fact, better fits "Harlan's Hawk," which is a regular winter resident in the state. An inspection of specimens in major museums showed that the tail of the dark phase *lagopus* when seen from below has a great deal of variation, ranging from very dark to very light, with or without assorted combinations of dark bands often against a background of gray similar to the shade of gray in the flight feathers of Turkey Vulture. When the tail is seen from above, however, it is uniformly dark. This whole situation is further complicated by the fact that immatures of dark phase Red-tailed Hawks have dark tails with barring similar to many dark Rough-legged Hawks.

Other clues may aid in correct identification of dark hawks. Rough-legged Hawks have proportionately longer wings than Red-tailed Hawks. When the birds are perched at close range the relatively small bill and feet may be seen in Rough-legged Hawks. However, it must be concluded that the tremendous amount of plumage variation in Red-tailed Hawks, and the large numbers of these birds present in the state in winter, means that all large forms of *Buteo* cannot be accurately identified in the field.

GOLDEN EAGLE, *Aquila chrysaetos* (Linnaeus)

Rare migrant and winter resident in small numbers in all regions. Several older possible nesting records, but none recently. Much less often found than the Bald Eagle.

MIGRATION AND WINTER: In the Audubon Society file there are reports of Golden Eagles between mid-September and the second week of April, with very few after early March. Reports generally have involved single birds, and these are scattered throughout the state except for the White River Refuge, where Golden Eagles have been reported with regularity on the Christmas Bird Count and other winter population surveys. A composite of the Christmas Count there between 1949 and 1982 showed that at least one or two birds were seen most years. A peak of 11 was reported in 1959, and as many as four to six were reported in six other years there. Between 1979 and 1982 an approximate average of 500 Bald Eagles were reported in Arkansas on the statewide Mid-winter Bald Eagle Survey. By comparison, only an average of about 30 Golden Eagles were reported in the survey. The largest single number of Golden Eagles observed in one locale during this survey period was the 20 at the White River Refuge in 1981. Presumably the Golden Eagles are attracted by the relatively large numbers of waterfowl on the refuge.

BREEDING SEASON: The breeding range of this species lies primarily to the west of Arkansas, but there are also records east of the state (AOU 1983). The only breeding records from Arkansas are two reported by Wheeler (1924), but it appears these reports are based upon secondhand information. He states that he saw a bird in Fort Smith in 1923 that "was probably reared on the Big Mulberry Creek, north of Ozark, where a pair of eagles have been known to nest." Also, a pair of "eagles" were said by Wheeler to have nested near Ruddles on the White River in Jackson County. Unfortunately, there is now no way to independently verify these records.

Family Falconidae Falcons

AMERICAN KESTREL, *Falco sparverius* Linnaeus

Permanent resident in all regions. Summer resident in small numbers in open country in all regions. Much more numerous in winter than in summer. Formerly called "Sparrow Hawk."

BREEDING SEASON: Reports in the files of the Audubon Society show that this species has been seen in all regions during the nesting season, with reports from nearly every community where there are active bird watchers. Reports on the Breeding Bird Surveys are relatively sparse, with the largest numbers in the highlands (including the Arkansas River Valley), and a peak annual mean of 2.7 birds on the survey route in Benton County.

The nesting season has been observed from early March through June. On the University of Arkansas campus (Fayetteville), the species has nested for years in one of the towers in Old Main (Baerg 1951, Audubon Society file) or in an oak tree nearby. A pair of kestrels arrived at Old Main in mid-February of 1982, and were observed in early March as they copulated and investigated a nesting site in an eave of the building forty to fifty feet high. During June the fledgling birds were being fed in trees near Old Main, and by July all the birds were gone. In the Wheeler Collection there is a clutch of four eggs that was collected from a nest twenty-five feet high on May 29. Wheeler (1924) stated that a pair had nested for years in the belfry at Hendrix College in Conway. In Miller County, four eggs were collected in an old flicker cavity nine feet high in a telephone pole on June 3. At Little Rock, Vivian Scarlett observed nests in the support for a drive-in theatre screen, a ledge under a roof, and in a hollow tree in Boyle Park.

MIGRATION AND WINTER: A fall migratory influx involving birds that nested north of Arkansas is apparent in the state after mid-September; thereafter, and through winter to the end of February, kestrels are commonly seen as they perch on wires or in snags in open country wherever this habitat occurs. There are five recoveries of banded kestrels associated with Arkansas. These birds were banded during the breeding season or in early fall 550 to 700 miles north or northeast of the state, and were recovered in Arkansas during fall, winter, and spring. The longest period between banding and recovery was less than two years.

While kestrels are certainly scarce in those areas with little open country, their numbers

FIGURE 6-40 American Kestrel. *Sigrid James Bruch*

are impressive elsewhere. On the 1980 Christmas Bird Count, peak numbers involving 25 to 54 birds were reported at Fayetteville, Jonesboro, Lonoke, Pine Bluff, and Texarkana. They seem fairly evenly distributed during winter with little variation from region to region. The statewide ten-year mean on Christmas Counts was 0.2 kestrels per party hour. On the Coastal Plain this mean varied from 0.1 to 0.7, on the Mississippi Alluvial Plain from 0.3 to 0.5, in the highlands, including the Arkansas River Valley, 0.1 to 0.5.

MERLIN, *Falco columbarius* Linnaeus

Somewhat rare migrant and winter visitor in all regions. Formerly called "Pigeon Hawk."

This open country falcon breeds well to the north and northwest of Arkansas (AOU 1983). A small number enter the state annually and are usually reported from places such as reservoirs, rice fields, and other large open expanses that attract the small birds upon which it feeds. There are sightings in the Audubon Society file from late August to the second half of April, mainly mid-September to mid-February. Most reports have involved single birds. Two were seen at Fayetteville in Washington County on December 20. One was observed regularly at El Dorado in Union County as it fed on sparrows between December 15 and December 29. At least three specimens have been collected in Arkansas at Winslow in the western Ozarks on September 12 (Black 1935a), another on September 22 (Smith 1915), and Brooke Meanley took one at Gillett in Arkansas County on September 24 (Audubon Society file).

PEREGRINE FALCON, *Falco peregrinus* Tunstall

Rare migrant and winter visitor chiefly in the southern and southeastern lowlands. One old breeding record. Formerly called "Duck Hawk."

FALL MIGRATION: Peregrine Falcons have been observed as early as the second week of September. At Big Lake Refuge, reports between the 1940s and 1960s showed that it was not seen every year, but when present as many as four to ten might be observed during spring and fall migrations. Fall arrivals there usually occurred in late October or early No-

vember with a peak in the last week of November and the first week of December. In the Audubon Society file the largest number of reports are dated between mid-September and mid-October, and most are single birds in the southern half of the state. Two were seen at Lake Georgia-Pacific in the southeast on September 10, 1970. At Anderson's Minnow Farm in Lonoke County individuals have been seen on several occasions hunting and capturing shorebirds during the month of September. There are also a few fall records for the Ozarks in northern Arkansas.

WINTER: Based upon the Big Lake data, winter sightings probably involve the period from late December through January. On Christmas Bird Counts in Arkansas from 1948 to 1961, there were only two records, both of single birds at White River Refuge. There have been approximately ten additional winter sightings since then, all single birds chiefly from Union County and from locations in southeastern Arkansas, and one record each from Mississippi and Clark counties. In Union County one immature bird was observed repeatedly from December 29, 1959, until January 23, 1960, as it perched on top of an oil derrick.

SPRING MIGRATION: At Big Lake the birds were not present at mid-winter, but spring migrants were seen in February and early March, with a peak in February. In the Audubon Society file there are eleven reports from March to mid-May, and six of them are in the last week of April. There is also one banding record. One bird banded as a nestling in April at Reelfoot Lake in northwestern Tennessee was recovered a month later in northwestern Arkansas, 242 miles west of the banding site.

FORMER BREEDING: In Cleburne County, Peregrine Falcons were said to nest on the sandstone bluffs along the Little Red River where they were seen in spring 1888 (Bendire 1892). There are no other such records for the state. The Peregrine Falcon *F. p. anatum* is on the list of endangered species compiled by the U.S. Fish and Wildlife Service. Its decimation was linked to nesting failures associated with the ingestion of pesticides, which the Peregrine obtained through the flesh of its prey (Hickey 1969). This has probably been a major factor in the decline of the number of birds migrating through Arkansas in recent years. While it appears the eastern population in the U.S. was completely extirpated, reintroductions of birds from other areas into some former breeding locations have been accomplished.

PRAIRIE FALCON, *Falco mexicanus* Schlegel
Four records.

This large western falcon was first reported for Arkansas by Brooke Meanley, a biologist for the U.S. Fish and Wildlife Service, who saw one at Hazen in Prairie County on February 9, 1951 (Baerg 1951). The second sighting occurred near Flippin in Marion County on November 29, 1981. A third acceptable report involved a bird in Miller County on December 21, 1982. The fourth was a bird seen in Cleburne County on November 22, 1984. Documentation is on file with the Arkansas Audubon Society for the three most recent sightings.

Order GALLIFORMES

Family *Phasianidae*

Subfamily *Tetraoninae* Grouse

RUFFED GROUSE, *Bonasa umbellus* (Linnaeus)

Largely or completely extirpated from Arkansas by 1900. Recently reintroduced into the Ozark Plateaus.

PREVIOUS RECORDS: There are relatively few records for this forest bird in Arkansas. Ruffed Grouse were among bird and other bones recovered from the Conrad Fissure near the Buffalo River in Newton County (Shufeldt 1913, Wetmore 1940, Wetmore 1959). These bones were dated to the mid-Pleistocene, or roughly half a million years before the present. When Pindar (1924) visited eastern Arkansas in 1888 and 1889, he found Ruffed Grouse were "rare" in Phillips County (but was told it had "formerly been common" there), and was absent from Poinsett County. In his article Pindar mentions the upland areas associated with Crowley's Ridge in Phillips County. Presumably it was this upland forest habitat where he found Ruffed Grouse. Howell (1911) was aware of only one record from Fayetteville, where Ruffed Grouse were said to be "very scarce" by 1883.

Roberts, Branner and Owens (1942) indicated that Ruffed Grouse were once very common in the Ozarks, but had disappeared there during the 1880s. Holder (1951) stated that there were no records for Arkansas after 1900, and he described the species as formerly occurring only in northern Arkansas. A range map in a definitive treatise on the Ruffed Grouse (Bump, et al., 1947) shows one record for the Ozarks during the quarter century between 1900 and 1925,

and the same map shows four records in the same period for the Ouachita Mountains. These records for the Ouachitas are the only known published records for that region. The post-1900 occurrence for the Ozarks, and these occurrences in the Ouachita Mountains, were not mentioned either by Holder (1951) in his authoritative game survey of the state, nor in the earlier analysis of the disappearance of the Ruffed Grouse in Arkansas (Roberts, et al., 1942). Since the sources of the records in question were not cited (Bump, et al., 1947) we contacted the personnel who helped conduct the Arkansas game survey (Holder 1951) and also consulted with wildlife personnel in the Ozark and Ouachita National Forests. No one knew of Ruffed Grouse records in Arkansas after the 1880s nor of any sightings ever reported in the Ouachita Mountain region.

Based upon the above information, it can be concluded that Ruffed Grouse were once permanent residents in the forests of the Ozark Plateaus, ranging down the upland forests of Crowley's Ridge in eastern Arkansas.

CAUSES OF EXTIRPATION: Roberts, et al. (1942) stated that "although the grouse was the finest game bird in the Ozarks, it could not survive the slaughter of 30 to 40 birds that many hunters killed per day." It may also be that the destruction of forest habitat in the grouse range contributed to its extinction. Holder (1951) stated that "vast changes in the amount and type of forest cover occurred about the time the grouse disappeared" from Arkansas. "Destruction of timber, burning, changes in vegetation, and intensive grazing are believed to be the principal factors which contributed to extermination."

REINTRODUCTIONS: The Arkansas Game and Fish Commission restocked Ruffed Grouse during 1948, 1949, and 1950 (Holder 1951). Though these pen-reared birds persisted for several years in Stone County, they quickly disappeared in the other stocked area at Black Mountain in Franklin County, and later also disappeared from Stone County. In 1981 a cooperative effort by the Arkansas Game and Fish Commission, the National Park Service (Buffalo National River), and the U.S. Forest Service (Ozark National Forest) was undertaken to restock several areas in northern Arkansas with wild-trapped birds from the Cumberland Gap National Historic Park at the Kentucky-Virginia border (Pharris, et al., 1983, Pharris 1983). These birds were released near Ponca at the Buffalo National River in Newton County. Additional trapping was undertaken at the Shenandoah National Park in Virginia for further releases at Ponca, and birds trapped in Ohio and Minnesota were released in the Ozark National Forest north of Hagarsville in Johnson County. A total of 117 birds were released at the two sites between 1981 and 1983.

Follow-up activities demonstrated that the wild-trapped birds were persisting (Pharris, et al., 1983). Winter censuses and spring drumming surveys showed survival rates of 20 to 24 percent in the two release sites. The presence of unbanded juveniles indicated that the birds were reproducing. It is not yet clear if this reproduction will ultimately be sufficient to support an expansion of the Ruffed Grouse population in the Arkansas Ozarks.

GREATER PRAIRIE-CHICKEN,
Tympanuchus cupido (Linnaeus)

Extirpated from the state.

The Prairie Chicken or Prairie Hen was once locally common on prairies in Arkansas (Howell 1911). On his trip through the upper White River region of the Ozarks during 1818 and 1819, Schoolcraft (1821) noted that "The prairie-hen, notwithstanding the cold, rose up in flocks before us. . . ." An observer at Fayetteville in 1883 noted that the species was "formerly plentiful but now rare." It was exterminated by hunters in Hempstead County around 1876 (Alexander and Kirby 1943). And though these birds were said to be "abundant" in 1899 near

Stuttgart in Arkansas County, none could be found there in 1900. A Prairie Chicken was killed west of Fayetteville on November 15, 1919, but "no others were observed. Undoubtedly it was a straggler. The species is extremely rare in the state. Have not had reports of its occurrence in the past eight years" (Lano 1921a). The last bird reported in eastern Arkansas was apparently shot on the Konecny farm in Prairie County in 1938 (Foti 1971), and the last records for the prairies in the western Ozarks of Arkansas were in 1939 (Baerg 1951). Roberts, et al. (1942) states that the Arkansas General Assembly attempted to control hunting of these birds during the breeding season as early as 1889, and totally closed the season in 1893, stating that "the breaking of the prairies for growing rice hastened the destruction of the prairie chicken in Arkansas County and adjacent counties." Certainly hunting pressure was an early cause for the bird's decline, but it is now clear that widespread conversion of the native prairies for other purposes has been detrimental to numerous species of plants and animals in the state (Ark. Dep. Plan. 1974).

Subfamily Meleagridinae Turkeys

WILD TURKEY, *Meleagris gallopova* Linnaeus

Permanent resident. Locally common to uncommon in extensive woodlands in all regions. Current widespread population is largely the result of restocking.

HISTORY AND DISTRIBUTION: In his journal of travels through Arkansas in the early 19th century, Schoolcraft mentions that on Christmas Day 1818, hunters in the upper White River country killed 14 birds in two hours (Schoolcraft 1821). By 1910 Wild Turkeys were still "numerous in the wilder parts of the heavily timbered bottoms in the eastern counties" but "practically extirminated" in the Ozarks and in all the "thickly settled regions" of the state (Howell 1911).

A survey in the Arkansas Ozarks in 1957 showed a residual population of the original stock in the Ozarks totalling an estimated 128 birds in six counties (James and Preston 1959). This low population in the Ozarks was attrib-

FIGURE 6-41 Wild Turkey in late January at the White River National Wildlife Refuge on the Mississippi Alluvial Plain. *David Plank*

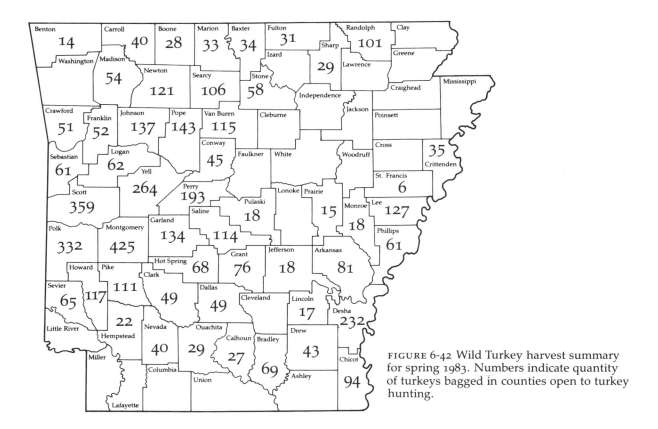

FIGURE 6-42 Wild Turkey harvest summary for spring 1983. Numbers indicate quantity of turkeys bagged in counties open to turkey hunting.

uted to land use practices, including excessive lumbering and subsequent agricultural practices. Wild Turkeys continued to be relatively numerous in the southeastern lowlands. In August 1954, 112 birds were counted as they fed along a 12-mile stretch of the lower White River (Meanley 1956c). Examination of stomachs of turkeys taken along the lower White River showed they were eating seeds, fruits, and herbaceous leaves.

Restocking with birds from other parts of North America began in Arkansas in 1932 (Holder 1951), but major success in rehabilitating populations resulted from shifting of Arkansas birds from one area to another in the state (James, et al., 1983). Data on the legal kill provided by the Arkansas Game and Fish Commission has shown a steady increase: from 150 taken in 1950 to over 1000 in the early 1970s and over 6000 by the late 1970s (Figure 6-42). Recent data from the Commission shows that

the largest numbers of turkeys are taken in the western Ouachitas and the southeastern lowlands with peak numbers in Montgomery County.

BREEDING SEASON: The nesting season seems to extend from March through July. An "old nest" with three broken eggs was found in Desha County in late March. Wheeler (1924) states that males begin to gobble in March and mentioned an old record at Fort Smith in which turkeys were reportedly nesting in the first week of April (see Chapman 1932). An adult with 22 "chicken-sized" young were seen on a dry pine slope in Logan County on May 30. At the White River Refuge, 20 young turkeys were seen in the last week of July.

A study in the Ozarks showed that there was an average of eight birds per flock "throughout the year" in Crawford and Franklin counties (James and Preston 1959).

FIGURE 6-43 Northern Bobwhite near Marshall in the Ozarks in mid-June. *David Plank*

Subfamily *Odontophorinae* Quail

NORTHERN BOBWHITE, *Colinus virginianus* (Linnaeus)

Common permanent resident. Observed in open fields with brush piles, fencerows, thickets, and other types of cover, also in bushy forest edge adjoining clearings and forest margins.

BREEDING SEASON: Bobwhites are numerous and widely distributed in the state during the nesting season, with little difference in the numbers present from region to region. The average annual mean number per route in each region reported on the Breeding Bird Surveys varied only from 26.8 to 29.9. Peak numbers involving 30 to 50 birds were reported on at least one survey in each region.

The presence of coveys in late winter and early spring indicates the breeding season has not begun (coveys become rare by April). The early days of the breeding season are marked by single singing males or male and female pairs. In southern Arkansas the characteristic singing of male Northern Bobwhites has been heard in mid-February. Singing is heard normally from late March or early April until early September with a peak in June (Baerg and Warren 1949). Nests or eggs have been observed from April through September. In the Wheeler Collection there are four clutches of eggs taken from nests between June 5 and 25. These clutch sizes involved 9, 18, 15, and 23 eggs. In the file there are seven nesting records that indicate the presence of 12 to 19 eggs (or young), often around 15. There is also one very late nesting record involving juveniles in Monroe County in the first week of November.

Several summer population studies have been conducted in the state. Baerg and Warren (1949) indicated there were as many as five to seven coveys on a two hundred-acre farm with "excellent" bobwhite habitat in Greene County, but no more than two coveys per square mile in an area with "poor" habitat in Ashley County. In the western Ozarks of Benton County, it was found that as many as 25 to 29 territorial males occupied a hundred acres of the best habitat, characterized as open field with scattered small woody plants grading to forest edge habitat (Table 3-7). The 1982 spring quail call count conducted by personnel of the Arkansas Game and Fish Commission in late May and early June showed statewide population levels varying from 5.5 to 7.4 birds heard per mile, with highest counts in the Ozarks and the Coastal Plain.

WINTER: This non-migratory species is common throughout the state during winter. Sightings of coveys with a dozen or more individuals are common from September through early spring. The ten-year statewide mean on the Christmas Bird Counts was 0.7 birds per party hour, with peaks of 1.6. At Little Rock, where the ten-year mean was slightly higher than that for the state as a whole, an average of 50 bobwhites has been reported on the Christmas Count, with the numbers counted ranging from lows of 20 or fewer and highs of 80 or more. These kinds of fluctuations are observed on Christmas Counts throughout the state.

Order GRUIFORMES

Family Rallidae Rails

YELLOW RAIL, *Coturnicops noveboracensis* (Gmelin)

Status is unclear. Apparently transient and winter visitor in small numbers.

Although Arkansas lies between its breeding and wintering ranges, this secretive species has been reported fewer than ten times in Arkansas. The few records involve spring, fall, and winter seasons. For spring there are two reports, both in the second week of May in Arkansas County. There are four sightings for fall from late September through October. Five birds were seen, and one collected, in Cleburne County in the last week of September in 1976. One was observed in a rice stubble field south of Stuttgart, Arkansas County, on October 9 (Meanley and Neff 1953a). A single bird was seen in Garland County on October 22, 1978. One adult and one immature were killed when they struck a tower in Jefferson County on October 18, 1981. All three of the winter reports have involved the month of January. One bird was caught by a dog at Booneville, Logan County, on January 5, 1963. (This bird was banded and released.) In White County a melanistic bird (much darker than the usual plumage) was collected in January of 1963. This bird is now in the University of Arkansas museum collection. A hunter in Sevier County flushed a "flock" of these birds, and shot one, on January 1, 1975. A bird that was collected on Spavinaw Creek in what was then thought to be northwestern Arkansas (Howell 1911) was actually in Delaware County, Oklahoma (Tomer 1959).

BLACK RAIL, *Laterallus jamaicensis* (Gmelin)

Status unclear. Four sight records.

This tiny, secretive species of rail resembles in some respects the juveniles of several of the more common species. Two sight records published by Baerg (1951) were from Arkansas County and involved single birds on October 7, 1939, and September 13, 1948. Unfortunately, no further details are available on these sightings. During a special search for rails in the rice fields of Crittenden County, a Black Rail was said to have been found on October 19, 1952 (Coffey 1981). Gary Graves saw one at close range September 19, 1972, at the state fish hatchery in Lonoke County. Written documentation submitted for several possible additional sightings has not been of a conclusive nature.

KING RAIL, *Rallus elegans* Audubon

Local migrant and summer resident in small numbers in the rice field region of the Mississippi Alluvial Plain, especially the Grand Prairie, with additional summer records scattered in the lowlands including Pulaski County. Apparently irregular winter resident on the Grand Prairie. Rare or undetected elsewhere.

SPRING MIGRATION: Brooke Meanley (1969a) collected extensive data on King Rails in the rice fields of the Grand Prairie near Stuttgart in Arkansas County. The period of study ranged from 1948 to 1962, primarily the early 1950s. He found that some birds remained throughout the winter, but this resident population was swelled by an influx of migrants from mid-February through March. All the birds observed in March 1952 were already paired. In the Audubon Society file there are also recent April records in Pulaski, Sevier, Craighead, and Desha counties.

BREEDING SEASON: Based upon records of forty-nine nests, Meanley (1969a) found that the chief months of the nesting season were April, May and June, but eggs were seen in nests from April 1 to August 29. The clutch sizes in sixteen nests were nine to fourteen eggs, usually ten to twelve eggs. The nests were found primarily in flooded rice fields, wet grassy ditches, canals, and pond edges. The round, elevated platform was often less than one foot above water. He found 22 King Rails on a six-mile roadside census in April 1955. There is one banding record associated with the breeding season in Arkansas: an incubating bird banded on the nest on May 6 was recaptured a year later on another nest only thirty feet away (Meanley 1969a).

There are a number of additional records in the Audubon Society file and from other sources. Files at Big Lake Refuge maintained up to 1961 indicated that the species nested there annually in "fair numbers." At Old Town Lake south of Helena in Phillips County, five vacated nests and many young were seen on June 25, 1913 (file). On the Coastal Plain there are summer records in Hempstead, Columbia, Clark, and Saline counties. For the state as a whole, nests, eggs, or young have been seen in Pulaski, Prairie, Lonoke, Saline, Phillips, and Arkansas counties. Since the early 1970s there have been summer records from Jackson and Prairie counties, and at Faulkner Lake in Pulaski County. The five King Rails on the 1976 Breeding Bird Survey in Prairie County was one of the highest numbers reported in summer in recent years.

FALL AND WINTER: At Stuttgart, Meanley (1969a) found that migrants departed the rice fields from mid-October to mid-November. The only record for King Rails in Faulkner County was in late September (Johnson 1979). There is also an October record for northeastern Arkansas (Hanebrink 1980). In five years in the rice fields, Meanley never found a King Rail in mid-winter in Arkansas, but mink trappers told him that they caught them every year in January. For the Ozarks there are two records: one at the state fish hatchery in Benton County on Oc-

tober 10, and one found dead at Batesville in Independence County on December 14. One bird killed by a hunter in Garland County on December 22 was the only record there in any season (Deaderick 1938). While King Rails have been found in winter in the past at Lonoke, the 3 found on the 1978 Christmas Bird Count was the first such record there in twelve years.

CHANGING STATUS: When Meanley returned to the rice fields in the middle of the 1960s, he was unable to locate birds or nests in those areas where they had been so common only a decade before. This has raised concern about its status in Arkansas (James 1974). Certainly during this period agricultural activity has greatly intensified, including the use of chemicals. Meanley (1969a) found that King Rails eat mainly crayfish, fish and insects. "Studies made elsewhere show that persistent pesticides applied to crops are eventually concentrated through aquatic food chains and may reach toxic levels in the tissues of secondary consumers such as herons, rails, ospreys, and eagles" (James 1974).

VIRGINIA RAIL, *Rallus limicola* Vieillot

Generally a rare transient in all regions that is occasionally common locally in prime marsh or marsh-like habitat. Very local and apparently irregular winter resident on the Grand Prairie. One summer record.

SPRING MIGRATION: Most spring reports have involved single birds between late April and the end of May. Two sightings for this period suggest peak times of movement. Members of the Audubon Society of Central Arkansas found five Virginia Rails at Lonoke on April 20, and five birds were observed on Sullivan's Island near Little Rock on April 26. In the western Ozarks there are spring reports between April 28 and May 11. Since the Ozarks have no extensive marshes, these birds may be found in wet open fields and other unexpected places. There is an April record for the northeastern counties (Hanebrink 1980).

BREEDING SEASON: The two Virginia Rails that were reported between May and July of 1977 in Cleburne County comprise the only summer record for Arkansas. Arkansas lies within the recognized area where this species has been known to breed (AOU 1983), but no nests or young have yet been found in the state.

FALL MIGRATION: Reports for fall migration are scattered from the second week of August through November. Peak numbers include four birds in a Crittenden County rice field on October 19, and five killed upon collision with a tower in Jefferson County on September 22. There are two records from Little Rock, both in September, in which domestic cats were chasing (or had captured) Virginia Rails. The only fall record for the northeast is in September (Hanebrink 1980), and the only fall record for the western Ozarks is on November 11.

WINTER: During the 1950s Brooke Meanley considered Virginia Rails a "common winter resident" seen and heard regularly at a blackbird roost near Hazen in Prairie County (Audubon Society file), and Meanley reported that in the same area a trapper caught both Virginia and King Rails. Small numbers of Virginia Rails (one or two) have been reported irregularly on the Christmas Bird Count at Lonoke. The few other winter season reports are from Sebastian and Union counties.

SORA, *Porzana carolina* (Linnaeus)

Fairly common to common migrant in all regions. Abundant locally in rice fields. Irregular winter visitor or resident in the southern lowlands. Inhabits natural marshes, artificial marshes associated with rice fields, rank moist vegetation in drained impoundments, and wet grassy ditches in extensively open areas.

FALL MIGRATION: During the southward migration Soras are seen primarily during September and October, but there are early fall records from the rice areas in the second week of July and scattered thereafter. The latest record for the western Ozarks, where the species is not known to winter, is in late October. Large numbers are sometimes reported from the rice areas. In the Audubon Society file there are a fair number of reports involving 20 to 30 Soras flushed in front of rice combines, and 400 were flushed in a five-acre field in Arkansas County on September 21 (Meanley 1960). The four birds found at Fort Smith on September 21 was a large one-day total for that area, as were the eight flushed from moist dense weeds at the state fish hatchery in Benton County on October 9. A nighttime migrant,

Soras sometimes strike objects and may thus be found in unlikely places. One was once found dead on Bluff Avenue in Fort Smith on September 28.

WINTER: Soras winter primarily south of Arkansas (AOU 1983), but the birds have been found often enough on Christmas Bird Counts to indicate that at least a few remain past the normal migration period, and some actually may overwinter. Soras have been reported irregularly on the Christmas Count at Lonoke (five reports during the 1970s). There were seven reports at Lake Georgia-Pacific on the Christmas Counts between 1972 and 1983, and as many as four or five were seen there in three of those years. Single birds have also been reported once on Christmas Counts at Arkadelphia and Little Rock. A Sora was found in the stomach of a bobcat killed near Beebe in White County on February 15.

SPRING MIGRATION: Spring migrants have been reported from late March through May, and especially from mid-April to mid-May. There are fewer reports for spring than fall, and most involved single birds flushed during a day in the field. Peaks in migration are suggested by the 10 "plus" Soras flushed at Lonoke on April 20, and the 25 or more seen on Sullivan's Island in the Arkansas River at Little Rock on April 26.

PURPLE GALLINULE, *Porphyrula martinica* (Linnaeus)

Local migrant and summer resident in small numbers in the lowlands including Pulaski County. Absent from the highlands. Observed on quiet, cattail-lined lilypad ponds, or in flooded fields and ditches with suitable vegetation.

MIGRATION: Spring arrivals have been observed in late April or early May. At Grassy Lake in Hempstead County, at least 10 have been seen by the third week of April, and there is an arrival record at Glenwood, Pike County, on April 26.

There is relatively little information about fall migration, but the species seems to depart from the state by September, with no report on file after September 20.

BREEDING SEASON: There are relatively few nesting reports in the file for Purple Gallinules,

FIGURE 6-44 Purple Gallinule. *Sigrid James Bruch*

and these few involve the months of May, June and July. Egg dates range from May 28 at Grassy Lake to June 12 at Lonoke. Clutch sizes ranged from four to six eggs. The nesting season may extend a little later: one young bird was seen in a nest at Lonoke on July 5, and adults were observed as they accompanied a brood of five young at Eudora in Chicot County on August 11.

The habitat favored by this species on the Grand Prairie has been primarily shallow open ponds originally constructed for rice and fish culture, then later allowed to fall into disuse, with a subsequent development of marshy vegetation. Elsewhere, nesting has occurred under natural conditions in open marshy lakes, such as Grassy Lake in Hempstead County, Horseshoe Lake in Crittenden County, Faulkner

Lake in Pulaski County, and elsewhere. In the Memphis area, Coffey (1943b) found the species regularly and in small numbers in levee borrow pits associated with the Mississippi River.

During the 1970s and the 1980s adults and or young have been seen during the breeding season in Lafayette, Pulaski, Lonoke, Jefferson, Columbia, and Hempstead counties. A colony of 40 birds was observed at Grassy Lake in June 1980. Adults with at least three broods were seen at Faulkner Lake in 1984. Large numbers have been seen in the past on the Grand Prairie. At Stuttgart, sixty young were seen in a rice field on August 26, 1954, but there have been no reports of similar magnitude from the Grand Prairie in recent years, presumably because the many ponds and shallow reservoirs formerly abandoned and subsequently developing marsh-like conditions have now been returned to agricultural production, reducing the amount of suitable habitat. The species has been informally listed as an endangered breeding bird in Arkansas because of habitat restrictions (James 1974).

COMMON MOORHEN, *Gallinula chloropus* (Linnaeus)

Migrant and summer resident locally in small numbers primarily in the lowlands. Permanent resident at Grassy Lake in Hempstead County. Inhabits quiet, shallow ponds with lily pads and marshy vegetation. Formerly called "Florida Gallinule" or "Common Gallinule."

SPRING MIGRATION: Common Moorhens have arrived in the state as early as the second week of March, but few are seen until the second half of April or until the first two weeks of May. At Grassy Lake, the "hundreds" there in the third and fourth weeks of April in 1968 suggested a large increase in numbers over the usually much smaller wintering population. Outside of Grassy Lake there are only scattered spring records. The three single birds seen in Crawford County between April 30 and May 12 are the only reports for this species in the western Arkansas River Valley. In Pulaski County Common Moorhens have been reported by the second week of May, and there are similar records on the Grand Prairie in Lonoke and Arkansas counties. There are no spring records for the Ozarks or the Ouachitas.

BREEDING SEASON: Common Moorhens have definitely nested at Grassy Lake and in the marshy edges of fish ponds in Lonoke County, at Faulkner Lake in Pulaski County,

FIGURE 6-45 Common Moorhen at Grassy Lake near Saratoga in early May. *David Plank*

and have been reported during summer at Stuttgart, near Pine Bluff (immature birds), south of Grady in Lincoln County, at Hunter in Woodruff County, near Calion in Calhoun County, at North Little Rock, and in Columbia County near Southern Arkansas University farm. The nesting range for Arkansas therefore seems to include much of the lowlands in the southern half of the state. Since the birds seem to require natural marshes like those at Grassy Lake or artificial marshes like those that develop where impoundments are built for fish culture, the summer population will be affected by changes, such as the clearing of marsh vegetation from ponds, or the drainage or alteration of natural marshlands.

The nesting season has been reported from May through September. The earliest nests in the Audubon Society file are from Grassy Lake where Charles Gardner found two nests in different years on May 30. One nest held nine eggs and was eight inches over water, and the other nest held thirteen eggs. The nesting season continues until September. On fish farms in the Lonoke area a nest with six eggs was seen on September 9, and four downy young not more than a week old were seen on another farm on September 17 (Meanley and Neff 1953a). Some of the 35 birds seen at Grassy Lake on October 28 were not fully grown, suggesting that they hatched late in the season.

FALL MIGRATION: Common Moorhens are still present in breeding areas in the state during September (see "Breeding" above) but they seem to migrate southward shortly thereafter, with the last sightings in the Pulaski and Lonoke County areas occurring in the fourth week of October. The only fall records for the highlands are from the Fayetteville area where migrants were seen as late as October 30 (Baerg 1951).

WINTER: This species apparently winters regularly at Grassy Lake, where as many as 17 birds have been observed in late December. In the past few years they have been found in the marsh-like habitat on the Georgia-Pacific mill pond which is included in the Lake Georgia-Pacific Christmas Bird Count area.

AMERICAN COOT, *Fulica americana* Gmelin
Common to locally abundant migrant and winter resident in all regions. Local summer

resident in small numbers in a few marshy lakes or reservoirs in the lowlands.

FALL MIGRATION: Coots are present in Arkansas in every month of the year, but are numerous only during migration and winter. They begin arriving from breeding areas north of Arkansas in September, with many first sightings for the fall in late September or early October, and some large flocks are present as early as the second week of October. The estimated 175 at Lake Fayetteville on October 12 was an early fall peak for the northwestern highlands, as was the more than 2000 at Lonoke on October 8 for the eastern lowlands. There is a steady increase in numbers during October, building to a peak in November. At Big Lake Refuge in the northeast, arrivals were observed from mid-September to mid-October, with a fall peak in numbers ranging from 500 to 17,000 during November. Rafts of over 1000 or more birds are sometimes observed on the larger lakes and reservoirs of the lowlands, and smaller numbers are observed widely in all regions.

WINTER: Coots are numerous and well distributed in the state during winter, with reports on Christmas Bird Counts from most places where there is at least a modest sized lake or reservoir. More than 3.0 birds per party hour were reported on some Christmas Counts in all regions of the state, and the ten-year mean at Lonoke was 32.3 per party hour. Almost 7000 were seen on the 1979 Christmas Count at Lonoke, and in the same year more than 600 were reported in several communities in southern Arkansas on the Christmas Count. Midwinter waterfowl surveys in the 1970s showed numbers of coots in prime waterfowl areas varying from 3000 to 28,000. Mild weather probably encourages large numbers of coots to winter in the state, but severe and prolonged cold forces them further south. Many birds froze to death at Big Lake during the winter of 1939–40, and after a mild fall at Lonoke in 1962, many coots were killed during a period of extreme cold in December. The more than 100 coots at Lake Fayetteville in December 1983 dropped to fewer than 20 in January 1984 after severe winter weather.

SPRING MIGRATION: As judged from peak numbers, northward moving spring migrants pass through the state from early March into

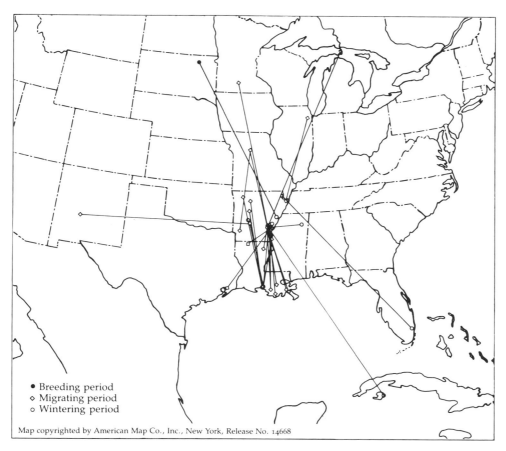

- • Breeding period
- ◇ Migrating period
- ○ Wintering period

FIGURE 6-46 Movements of the American Coot based on banding records.

the second week of May. A few birds are seen in places where breeding is not known, as late as the end of May (Johnson 1979). At Lake Fayetteville, peak numbers for spring are evident during April, when as many as 175 birds have been seen in the second week of the month, and as many as 28 in the second week of May. At Big Lake, the spring peak involved 200 to 500 birds from early March to early April, with no records after the second week of May.

BANDING: There are 27 recoveries of coots associated with Arkansas, and about half of these birds were banded in the state (Figure 6-46). This helps explain the wide scattering of directions. Main directions involved coastal regions to the south, where coots winter, and areas north of Arkansas. Many birds had traveled from 275 to 425 miles between banding and recovery, with the maximum distance being over 1000 miles. About half were recovered near the end of the first year following banding, and one lived slightly more than five years between banding and recovery.

BREEDING SEASON: The vast majority of the birds that winter in Arkansas migrate to breeding grounds north of the state, but a few remain and are seen during summer in the dense vegetation of natural marshy lakes, and shallow reservoirs with similar vegetation in the lowlands. There are summer records in the file, some of them involving definite breeding, from Crittenden, Woodruff, Lonoke, Jefferson, and Lincoln counties on the Mississippi Alluvial Plain, and from Saline, Union, Calhoun, and Hempstead counties on the Coastal Plain. There is a summer record from Big Lake (Howell 1911) and one from Faulkner County in the Arkansas River Valley (Johnson 1979).

Nesting activity has been observed from late

May to early September. The earliest nest record on file involved eight eggs in a nest two feet above water in marsh grass at Grassy Lake in Hempstead County found by Charles Gardner on May 30. The latest such reports are from Hilleman in Woodruff County, where nests with four and six eggs were seen on a marshy lake on July 13 (one egg was hatching) and from Lincoln County north of Grady, where a nest with eight eggs was found on July 15. Adults with three half-grown young and another adult with six downy young were observed on September 7 in shallow reservoirs south of England in Lonoke County.

It is not clear how many of the adults present in the state during summer are actually nesting. Only three young were seen with thirty-four adults in Lonoke County in August of 1962. In 1974 at Lonoke, only 15 coots could be found on fish ponds during the nesting season, even though the usual summer population has in previous years ranged from 60 to 200 birds. Certainly the birds require natural marshes or marshy conditions in reservoirs. The lack of either or both habitats will reduce the number of coots that can successfully nest in the state.

Family Gruidae Cranes

SANDHILL CRANE, Grus canadensis (Linnaeus)

Rare and irregular transient and winter visitor in the lowlands, and at Holla Bend Refuge in the Arkansas River Valley.

There are five older records that involve the period from late November to early April in Arkansas, Poinsett, Jackson, and Pike counties, and along the Mississippi River (Wier 1881, Howell 1911, Pindar 1924, Audubon 1929). Pindar (1924) considered them "rather common latter part of February and first of March" in Poinsett County during the period of 1888–89. A flock of 20 was seen at Delight in Pike County on March 12, 1911 (Howell 1911). During Au-

dubon's trip down the Mississippi (Audubon 1929), he saw a "large flock" on November 30, 1820, while in the area of the present state. During the past half century there have continued to be scattered reports. A single Sandhill Crane was collected on June 20, 1932, at Pendleton Ferry (where Arkansas Highway 1 now crosses the Arkansas River between Desha and Arkansas counties). A single bird was also seen at Pendleton Ferry on May 20, 1953. At Holla Bend Refuge a single bird was seen on February 17, 1967. At Grassy Lake in Hempstead County a single bird was reported on January 5, 1970, and another single bird was observed north of Hoxie in Lawrence County on September 27, 1970. During the month of January in both 1976 and 1979, one or two birds were seen in the Holla Bend area, and during the winter of 1980–81, reports of up to a maximum of four birds were received from either Holla Bend Refuge or the surrounding area in Yell and Pope counties. Three birds were seen in the same locale between February 2 and March 16, 1985.

WHOOPING CRANE, Grus americana (Linnaeus)

Three or four old records.

The two "large white cranes with black tips" seen by Audubon (1929) in the vicinity of modern day Helena on December 6, 1820, may have been Whooping Cranes. Pindar (1924) stated that Whooping Cranes were "Very rare, and only in the Sunk Lands" of the St. Francis River in Poinsett County when he was there between late January and early March in 1889. A single Whooping Crane is said to have been seen near Crocketts Bluff in Arkansas County on November 5, 1882 (Wier 1882c). There was also a report at Corning in Clay County on April 22, 1914 (Allen 1952). This extremely rare crane is listed as an endangered species by the U.S. Fish and Wildlife Service. Careful management may eventually rescue it from the brink of extinction.

Order CHARADRIIFORMES

Family Charadriidae Plovers

BLACK-BELLIED PLOVER, *Pluvialis squatarola* (Linnaeus)

Transient, observed in small numbers in all regions. Rare in spring, uncommon but regular in fall. Several winter records.

SPRING MIGRATION: Reports for spring migration in the Audubon Society file range from mid-March through May, with a concentration of reports from late April through the third week of May. At Moffett, Oklahoma, just west of Fort Smith, Arkansas, there are four reports involving 26 to 63 Black-bellied Plovers between May 12 and 16 in different years. A total of 11 were seen near Claypool Reservoir in Poinsett County on May 14. There is an additional record, not obviously associated with spring or fall, involving a single bird in winter plumage on a Mississippi River sandbar in Crittenden County on June 24.

FALL AND WINTER: Sightings for the southward migration, when this species is seen more often in the state than in spring, span the period from late July to early December, and some individuals occasionally linger beyond that time. Many of the fall sightings have involved single birds or small flocks of up to eight individuals. The 30 at Lake Millwood on October 14 was a high number, as were the "many" in Poinsett County between November 11 and 19.

There are several observations involving one or two Black-bellied Plovers in late December or January. A single bird was seen at Lonoke on December 23, 1972. Birds were seen on the Christmas Bird Counts at Lake Millwood on December 17, 1977, and on December 21, 1980. The latter record involved two birds, present until January 3. There is also a recent late February record at Lonoke.

LESSER GOLDEN-PLOVER, *Pluvialis dominica* (Müller)

Common to locally abundant spring transient in appropriate habitat in all regions. Much less numerous in fall than spring. Frequently observed in large open shortgrass pastures and fields, as well as on drained pond mudflats.

SPRING MIGRATION: Lesser Golden-Plovers pass through the state during spring primarily from March through May, unusually as early as late February or as late as the first half of June. The peak migration period occurs between mid-March and the end of April. Spring sightings may sometimes involve single birds, but flocks, some of them very large, are fairly common. During a peak reported in Crittenden County on March 28, one observer saw them sixteen times, including one flock of 60, for a one-day total of over 300. Also on March 28, 1000 were seen in Miller County near Texarkana. At Moffett, Oklahoma, near Fort Smith, 1700 were observed between April 1 and 5. A large, late peak in numbers is indicated by the presence of "several hundred" at Tyronza in Poinsett County on April 21. The single Lesser Golden-Plover in nuptial plumage at the state fish hatchery in Lonoke County on June 14 is the only record for June in the Audubon Society file.

FALL MIGRATION: There are reports in the file for the southward migration between mid-August and mid-December, with the peak period between late September and early December. Many sightings involve only one to three birds, and never large flocks. The handful of reports that have involved as many as eight to twelve birds are all from the Mississippi Alluvial Plain. The single bird seen during the 1977 Christmas Bird Count at Lake Millwood was "late."

SNOWY PLOVER, *Charadrius alexandrinus* Linnaeus

Two records.

One was seen in Lonoke County on August 11, 1961. A second bird was seen in the same area, at Anderson's Minnow Farm, on August 17, 1974, by three experienced observers. Written documentation for this sighting is on file.

SEMIPALMATED PLOVER, *Charadrius semipalmatus* Bonaparte

Common transient in all regions, especially in fall.

SPRING MIGRATION: In the Audubon Society file there are spring reports from mid-April into the second half of May, and rarely into June. While most records for a day in the field have involved only one to three birds, 26 were seen in the Moffett bottoms in Oklahoma, just west of Fort Smith on April 28, and 20 were seen at Centerton in Benton County on May 23. There are fewer sightings in spring than fall. This is partially due to the fact that the kinds of places where observers find these birds—drained ponds, drawn down reservoirs, and other types of artificial mudflats—are less available in spring than in fall.

FALL MIGRATION: The species arrives in Arkansas on its southward migration as early as the second week of July, and there are regular sightings through September, with stragglers thereafter, once as late as the third week in December. The peak has been reported between late July and early September. As many as five or ten birds are sometimes seen on extensive, open mudflats. A party of observers counted 25 on the banks of the Mississippi River in Desha County on August 31. In the Scott-Lonoke area of central eastern Arkansas, as many as 44 birds were counted in the last week of August (Graves 1972). In 1974 at Anderson's Minnow Farm in Lonoke, as many as 55 birds were observed on field trips during the

peak period, from late July to the second week of August (summary on file).

PIPING PLOVER, *Charadrius melodus* Ord

Rare transient in all regions. An endangered species.

SPRING MIGRATION: There are only five spring records in the Audubon Society file. All involved one or two birds seen between mid-April and the first week of May at Lonoke, at Moffett, Oklahoma (just west of Fort Smith), and along the Okay levee in Howard County near Lake Millwood.

FALL MIGRATION: Most of the approximately 25 reports in the file involve fall migration and are scattered between mid-July and mid-October. An unusually large number of 10 was observed along the Mississippi River in Desha County on August 11, 1963. One observer considered them "common along the sandbars of the Mississippi River" in late summer (Vaiden 1964). One or two Piping Plovers were observed daily between September 5 and 20, 1980, at Lake Millwood. There are two records for this species in the western Ozarks: a single bird at the state fish hatchery in Centerton (Benton County) on September 24, 1968, and a single bird September 16 and 17, 1982, on mudflats exposed when the water level at Lake Sequoyah (Washington County) was lowered. A specimen collected in Garland County on August 10 (Deaderick 1938) is the only record from the Ouachita Mountains. The majority of the records in the file are from the Mississippi Alluvial Plain, especially the Lonoke area.

NOTE: The populations of this species are declining, apparently due to loss of and disturbances in its sandy beach nesting habitat (Russell 1983).

KILLDEER, *Charadrius vociferus* Linnaeus

Common permanent resident in open country. Uncommon in the north during severe cold. Local populations are swollen by migrants during spring and fall.

SPRING MIGRATION: Flocks seen during winter begin to break up with the arrival of the first warm weather in late February or during March. After this time, observers usually report one to five birds during a day's outing, with frequent sightings of pairs. These paired birds are separate from the flocks of migrants seen on drained ponds or in pastures.

BREEDING SEASON: Records in the Audubon Society file show that Killdeers are common during the breeding season in all regions. Breeding Bird Surveys indicate that the species is most numerous on the Mississippi Alluvial Plain. The mean number of birds per route reported on surveys in Chicot, Lincoln, Poinsett, Woodruff, and Randolph counties varied from nearly seven to over ten annually over a ten-year period.

Breeding activity has been observed from early March to early July. The extreme records are: a nest with one egg at Stuttgart on March 3, and a nest with two eggs in gravel in Lonoke County on July 4. While there are several March nesting records, there is no evidence of hatching until after mid-April. Clutch sizes have ranged from one to four eggs, often two to four. Nesting sites have included many types of flat, gravelly places including roofs in cities, graveled drives and parking lots, and gravel bars along streams as well as grassy yards, golf courses, airports, and agricultural fields.

At Little Rock, Vivian Scarlett watched as young birds hatched on May 3, and she noted that the hatchlings "both ran away at once." Even though young Killdeers may appear to be unattended or abandoned, the adults are almost always somewhere nearby. The young should be left alone.

FALL: Killdeers begin to congregate in flocks on drained ponds, reservoirs, and large fields as early as July. These flocks may often involve more than 25 birds, and later in the fall it is not uncommon to find 100 or more Killdeers in a relatively small area with favorable habitat.

WINTER: After the arrival of severe cold weather Killdeers usually become relatively scarce in the northernmost areas. The ten-year statewide mean on the Christmas Bird Counts in the state was 1.4 Killdeers per party hour. Fayetteville and Jonesboro in the north at 0.9 to 0.5 per party hour, were well below this mean; Christmas Counts at Hot Springs, Lonoke, and Texarkana all exceeded the mean. Unusual numbers of Killdeers were seen on Christmas Counts in 1971. The 853 at Lonoke and the 196 at Fayetteville were nearly twice the previous Christmas Count peaks, and in the same year an amazing 1300 were seen at Texarkana.

MOUNTAIN PLOVER, *Charadrius montanus* Townsend

One record.

The only Arkansas record for this western species was reported by biologist Brooke Meanley who saw two in a field of lespedeza in Arkansas County on December 16, 1951 (Baerg 1951). Unfortunately it was not possible to collect a specimen (Meanley, pers. comm.).

Family Recurvirostridae Stilts and Avocets

BLACK-NECKED STILT, *Himantopus mexicanus* (Müller)

Rare spring visitor.

The first Arkansas record involved a single bird seen by a number of observers from Texarkana on May 9, 1960, at the shallow edge of a marshy place along a highway near Fulton in Hempstead County. Subsequently, a single bird was seen at Anderson's Minnow Farm in Lonoke County on April 4, 1975, two birds at the same place on July 3, 1981, and 3 on May 12, 1984. One was seen on an island in the Arkansas River at Little Rock on May 18, 1982. A single bird observed by Bill Brazelton in flooded fields near the Arkansas River at Moffett, Oklahoma, just west of Fort Smith, Arkansas, on May 22, 1984, was subsequently seen by a number of members of the Fort Smith Audubon Society on the following three days and was photographed. In 1982 and 1984 pairs of Black-necked Stilts nested in the Memphis area across the Mississippi River from Arkansas (Martha Waldron, pers. comm.).

AMERICAN AVOCET, *Recurvirostra americana* Gmelin

Uncommon but regular transient in all regions, with more records for fall than spring.

SPRING MIGRATION: American Avocets have been reported during the northward migration period between the second week of April and the second week of May, usually during the second half of April. Most reports in both the spring and fall seasons have involved one or two birds observed during a day. Therefore, the 15 seen at Bull Shoals Lake on April 10 was unusual, as were the approximately 30 in breeding plumage that were photographed at the waste-water treatment ponds at Mena on April 21, 1984.

FALL MIGRATION: Avocets are seen with regularity in Arkansas during fall, but even in especially good shorebird habitat like that found in the Lonoke area, the species is seen only once or a few times during the season, and the report usually involves three or fewer birds. Fall sightings have been reported between the second week of July and late December, primarily between September and mid-November. On several occasions unexpectedly large numbers have been seen in the fall. Peak counts of 9 to 23 avocets have been reported between late September and the fourth week of October at Lake Millwood, Lake Fayetteville, at Calion Lake near El Dorado, and the White River Refuge. The most unusual observation is from Greenwood in Sebastian County where flocks of 34 and 10 were seen on October 21.

Family Scolopacidae

Subfamily Scolpacinae Sandpipers

GREATER YELLOWLEGS, *Tringa melanoleuca* (Gmelin)

Fairly common transient in all regions. Several winter reports. Less numerous than Lesser Yellowlegs.

SPRING MIGRATION: Spring migrants are observed chiefly between the second week of March and the second week of May, with peak numbers from late March through April. The 90 birds at Stuttgart on March 27 were all in one flock. The 139 Greater Yellowlegs seen by Edith and Henry Halberg at Lonoke on March 29, 1964, was a very large number. A few individuals sometimes linger to early June.

FALL AND WINTER: There are reports involving the fall migration from early July through December, chiefly late August through November, with a peak in numbers from late October to mid-November. The latest fall record for the western Ozarks is in mid-November. While many reports in the file have involved one to six birds observed on a day's outing, 100 were seen by the Halbergs at Lonoke on October 22,

1961. The species is not often seen in the state after November, but there are several reports during December, especially in the Lonoke area, involving as many as 33 birds. These late season observations suggest that migrants tend to linger in the Lonoke area and that there are occasional late spurts in migration. In addition, three sightings in January and February involved single birds on the Mississippi Alluvial Plain. Greater Yellowlegs do not normally winter in Arkansas.

LESSER YELLOWLEGS, *Tringa flavipes* (Gmelin)

Common, sometimes locally abundant, transient in all regions. Observed in large, open, flooded fields as well as shallow reservoirs, ponds, and lake margins.

SPRING MIGRATION: There are some records in the Audubon Society file for the Mississippi Alluvial Plain as early as mid-February, but most Lesser Yellowlegs pass through Arkansas on the northward migration between the fourth week of March and the second week of May, with some sightings through May and into June. There are no spring reports for the western Ozarks before late March. Many observations in the file have involved one to five birds, but there are also several instances where observers have counted 50 to 200 or more during a day in the field. At Lake Sequoyah in Washington County, "several hundred" were seen on May 9. An estimated 500 were observed several miles west of DeVall's Bluff in Prairie County on April 26. The 3600 at Lonoke on April 27, 1973, is the largest number ever reported in the state.

June records for this species, and other species of shorebirds, fall between the late spring migration period and the early fall migration period. The gap of several weeks between sightings of Lesser Yellowlegs in the early and late weeks of June suggests that this is the demarcation line between the two seasons.

FALL MIGRATION: There are reports for the southward migration period, chiefly between the fourth week of July and the end of October, with some records in the Lonoke area in December. The intensity of migration declines significantly after mid-November. There are no reports for the north after late November. While single birds are sometimes reported in fall, flocks of five to twenty are fairly common, and larger flocks are not rare. The 610 at Lonoke on July 21, 1968, however, was an unusually high number for fall. The 58 at drained ponds at Anderson's Minnow Farm (Lonoke County) on June 28 were presumably early "fall" transients.

SOLITARY SANDPIPER, *Tringa solitaria*
Wilson

Common to fairly common transient in all regions, frequents margins of small ponds and streams.

SPRING MIGRATION: Spring transients have been reported from the first week of March to the fourth week of May, mainly late March to mid-May. For the northern regions there are no reports before the first week of April. While most sightings in the Audubon Society file have involved single birds, two or three are sometimes seen during a day in the field. The five in Benton County southwest of Rogers on April 21 was a relatively large report. Solitary Sandpipers can sometimes be observed along the forested edges of streams, far from the open mudflats where shorebirds are usually found.

FALL MIGRATION: Fall transients are seen between the first week of July and the first week of October, occasionally through November. The species is not necessarily solitary during migration. Of 13 birds seen along the Arkansas River levee in Crawford County on August 23, 11 were together. A single bird reported in Pulaski County on January 7 is the only report after November in the file.

WILLET, *Catoptrophorus semipalmatus*
(Gmelin)

Uncommon to somewhat rare transient observed in small numbers in all regions, with the largest numbers seen in the west.

SPRING MIGRATION: There are records between late March and May for spring, with peak numbers from the last week of April to mid-May. Most reports have involved small numbers, often only one or two birds. The larger counts are from the west: 40 to 45 in flooded fields just west of Fort Smith at Moffett,

Oklahoma, on April 25; flock of 38 in wet, grassy vegetation at Lake Sequoyah in Washington County on April 27; 32 in a flock on a Buffalo River gravel bar in Marion County on April 29; 14 at El Dorado on May 2. There is also a count of at least five birds from DeGray Lake in Clark County.

FALL MIGRATION: Reports for the southward migration period range chiefly from the second week of July to the fourth week of September. Most of these have also involved one or two birds. The six at Lonoke on August 23 is the largest number ever found in that generally highly productive shorebird region. Thirty-six were seen on July 7 at Lake Millwood in the southwest. The seasonal status of a single bird seen at Fort Smith on June 28 is not clear.

SPOTTED SANDPIPER, *Actitis macularia*
(Linnaeus)

Common transient in all regions. Rare winter visitor chiefly in the southern lowlands. Among several summer reports are two instances of breeding. Frequents shorelines.

SPRING MIGRATION: Spring transients are seen primarily during April and May. There are some early reports in March, and a few birds are observed annually during early June. Most reports involve small numbers or solitary birds. The 21 counted along the Buffalo River shoreline on April 26 was a large number. Some of the highest counts have occurred at wastewater treatment ponds in El Dorado where several counts as high as 30 to 40 were made in a day during mid-April, and an astounding 300 "plus" were seen there on May 2, 1984, after the passage of a very heavy rainstorm.

While there are some rare sightings scattered throughout the summer, the discernible gap between early and late June seems to separate the late spring transients from the early fall transients.

FALL MIGRATION: Fall transients are seen from the second week of July to early October, with some reports into early November. There is only one unusual record for the western Ozarks after mid-October. Several reports in the file indicate a fall peak in numbers between late July and mid-to-late August. At Lake Millwood, 65 Spotted Sandpipers were seen from July 13 to October 26, 1980, with a peak of 12 on August 26.

BREEDING SEASON: The only confirmed nesting records for the state are from the Boston Mountains section of the western Ozarks. Black (1935a) stated, "I have observed one family of young, just out of the nest, one mile north of Winslow, and another at Schaberg, five miles south of Winslow." A probable courtship display was reported on June 8, 1963, at the old mill pond near Boxley (Newton County). There are other summer records, but none that apparently involved the discovery of nests or young (Audubon Society file, Baerg 1951, Callahan 1953).

WINTER: Most of the few scattered winter sightings are from the southern lowlands. One bird was seen repeatedly at the Arkadelphia wastewater treatment ponds between November 1970 and March 1971, and two to three birds remained on wastewater treatment ponds at El Dorado in Union County between mid-October 1982 and mid-April 1983. The only winter report in the Ozarks involved a single bird that overwintered on a "hot water" lake associated with the Flint Creek power plant in Benton County during 1982–83 (Smith 1985). Each of these sightings involved habitats where the water (and hence the shoreline) is warmer than under normal conditions.

UPLAND SANDPIPER, *Bartramia longicauda* (Bechstein)

Uncommon transient, usually in small numbers, in all regions, with the largest numbers in the lowlands. Observed on grassy flats, in pastures and in croplands. Formerly called "Upland Plover."

SPRING MIGRATION: Spring transients have been reported between the last week of March and mid-May. Most records in spring or fall involve small numbers, usually fewer than five on a day's outing, but larger numbers are sometimes found. The following peak counts are in the Audubon Society file: 100 near Richwood Community in Clark County on March 30, 1978; 150 in Jefferson County, two miles north of Sherrill, on April 3, 1956; 43 near Texarkana in Miller County on April 10, 1977; 27 in Clark County at Arkadelphia on April 11, 1981; 26 on April 20, 1974, and 21 on April 27, 1973, both at Scott in Lonoke County. Howell (1911) states, "This famous game bird—the 'papabotte' of the Southern States—was formerly very abundant in migration on the prairies of the Mississippi Valley, but the terrible slaugther to which it is subjected every spring . . . has greatly diminished its numbers." The species is no longer legally hunted in the United States.

FALL MIGRATION: There are sightings primarily between the third week of July and the second week of October, with peak numbers apparently in the second half of August. Almost all the sightings in the file for fall have involved one or two birds. In Garland County, the species was seen between August 10 and September 5, including one flock of 22 (Deaderick 1938). Other peaks have included 13 observed by members of the Tennessee Ornithological Society near Horseshoe Lake in Crittenden County on August 13, 1950; 30 at Eudora in Chicot County on August 16, 1961; a total of 95 in several flocks on grassy embankments around Lake Millwood on August 21, 1980; and eight at Scott in Lonoke County on August 22, 1972. The seasonal status of the small flock in Benton County on June 30, 1940 (Baerg 1951), is unclear.

ESKIMO CURLEW, *Numenius borealis* (Forster)

One record.

The species was reportedly seen at Fayetteville on March 31, 1883 (Howell 1911). In publishing this record, Howell noted that "within the last 15 years . . . [the species had] become nearly or quite extinct." Unfortunately, there is no additional information available on this sighting.

WHIMBREL, *Numenius phaeopus* (Linnaeus)

Rare transient. Formerly called "Hudsonian Curlew."

The first record for Arkansas was a single bird seen by Brooke Meanley at a fish hatchery in Lonoke County on September 9, 1952. Twenty years later a bird was discovered by Henry and Edith Halberg at a fish pond, also in Lonoke County, on September 3, 1972. (This bird was seen by several additional observers on the following day.) A single bird was seen by Max and Helen Parker a few miles south of Helena on the Mississippi River levee in Phillips County on May 15, 1983. The bird was photographed, and written documentation concerning the sighting included a statement about the field marks that allowed the observers to separate this species from several species of curlews that have a similar appearance. The bones of a Whimbrel were recovered from the Zebree archeological site at Big Lake in Mississippi County (Guilday and Parmalee 1977). Two Whimbrels were observed at Budd Kidd Lake in Washington County on May 23, 1984.

LONG-BILLED CURLEW, *Numenius americanus* Bechstein

Rare transient.

This species from the western United States and Canada was first reported in Arkansas by Audubon (1831–39) who collected a specimen during his visit to the state. Since the 1820s, there have been four subsequent records: two birds at Lonoke on October 5, 1934; one in Miller County on December 9, 1961; one in Arkansas County near Stuttgart on November 18, 1967; and one in Clark County on April 21, 1980.

HUDSONIAN GODWIT, *Limosa haemastica* (Linnaeus)

Regular transient observed in small numbers primarily in the spring, and usually in wet agricultural fields or on mudflats associated with drained fish ponds and reservoirs in the central and western regions. Of the two godwits seen in Arkansas, this is by far the more numerous.

SPRING MIGRATION: During spring Hudsonian Godwits migrate principally through the central interior of the United States, north from Texas and Louisiana into Canada (AOU 1983). Spring sightings in the file range between mid-April and late May. Fewer than half the spring sightings for Arkansas are from the Lonoke area in the central-eastern lowlands, and most of the remainder are from the western regions, including the western Ozarks and the Fort Smith area. Most records in the Audubon Society file have involved one to three birds, but there are several reports involving larger numbers including nine at Holla Bend Refuge in Pope County on April 27, and nine at Lonoke on May 27. The single most productive area for this species is the flooded field terrain in the Arkansas River bottomlands at Moffett, Oklahoma, approximately two miles west of Fort Smith, Arkansas. As many as 10 to 20 Hudsonian Godwits have been observed by members of the Fort Smith Audubon Society there between mid-April and mid-May. Bill Brazelton, who has been along on many of these outings, stated that Hudsonian Godwits were "not at all rare in the Moffett area. We see them every year there." A flock of 26 was present at Centerton in Benton County on May 12, 1984.

FALL MIGRATION: In the file there are only two fall sightings, and both are from Lonoke: three on August 22, and one on August 21.

MARBLED GODWIT, *Limosa fedoa* (Linnaeus)

Rare transient.

SPRING MIGRATION: One bird was seen in association with a flock of Willets at Lake Maumelle in Pulaski County on April 28, 1963; one was near Cash in Craighead County on May 11, 1980; and one occurred in flooded fields at Moffett, Oklahoma, two miles west of Fort Smith, Arkansas, on May 11, 1983.

FALL MIGRATION: There are six fall records, all in August or September, and each involving single birds. Most sightings have occurred in Lonoke County, often at Lonoke where there is an abundance of habitat attractive to shorebirds, including large, drained fish ponds and wet agricultural fields. The Marbled Godwit seen by Vivian Scarlett, Virginia Springer, and others on September 13, 1956, was the first record for the state; this bird was seen repeatedly by numerous observers until September 21 (James 1960). Subsequently, single birds have been seen at Lonoke on August 23, 1970; September 11, 1973; and August 24, 1976. Near Farlow, also in Lonoke County, a single bird was seen between August 14 and 17, 1982. The other fall record involved a bird at Lake Millwood on August 21, 1980.

RUDDY TURNSTONE, *Arenaria interpres* (Linnaeus)

Uncommon but fairly regular transient in small numbers with reports from all regions. Reported more often in spring than fall.

SPRING MIGRATION: Sightings for the northward migration period have taken place between the second week of May and the first week of June. Peak records of six birds in a day are from Lonoke (May 14) and from flooded fields in the Arkansas River bottomlands west of Fort Smith at Moffett, Oklahoma (May 16). Also at Moffett reports of three or four birds have occurred on May 11, 12, and 28 in different years, and there are reports of one or two birds at Lock and Dam 3 on the Arkansas River at Pine Bluff, and on drained fish ponds at Centerton in Benton County.

FALL MIGRATION: Fall transients have been reported between late July and the end of September. Most of these reports are from the Lonoke area and Lake Millwood. There are additional records from drained ponds at the state fish hatcheries at Lake Hamilton (Garland County) and Centerton (Benton County), at Lake Pine Bluff (Jefferson County), from Calion near El Dorado, and from Desha County where the Arkansas River flows into the Mississippi. Most of these sightings have involved single birds. At Lake Millwood in 1980, a year when the water level was drawn down exposing large mudflats, 13 Ruddy Turnstones were seen between September 6 and 17, with a peak of four on September 13. Other peak counts have included four birds in Desha County at the northern mouth of the Arkansas River on July 29, and seven at Lonoke on September 4.

RED KNOT, *Calidris canutus* (Linnaeus)

Rare fall transient.

Red Knots migrate primarily along the Atlantic and Pacific coasts, but a few birds also migrate on a casual basis through the interior of the United States (AOU 1983). There are records in the Audubon Society file for Arkansas from early September to early October. At Lonoke there have been six reported sightings since 1972. At Lake Millwood in 1977, a year when the lake was drawn down exposing large mudflats, one to six Red Knots were seen between September 15 and October 1. In 1980, another draw down year at Lake Millwood, one to ten birds were seen on almost a daily basis between September 5 and 21. The only other report in the file involved a single bird seen repeatedly in Washington County at Lake Sequoyah (which was also drawn down, exposing large flats) between September 1 and 10, 1983. All of the birds seen so far in Arkansas have been in first winter plumage. Baerg (1951) pub-

lished the report by Dean Crooks for a bird in Benton County on April 30, 1947.

SANDERLING, *Calidris alba* (Pallas)

Generally an uncommon to somewhat rare transient in all regions, but regular in small numbers at Lonoke and locally uncommon to common at Lake Millwood in years when water levels were lowered, exposing mudflats.

SPRING MIGRATION: There are fewer than ten spring records in the Audubon Society file, all between late April and late May. Most involved single birds. Two birds, one in breeding plumage, were seen at Lonoke on May 26, and three were seen at Lonoke (Anderson's Minnow Farm) on May 19 of a different year. There are two other sightings at Lonoke. There is also a record from the Southern Arkansas University farm in Columbia County, from the Jonesboro wastewater treatment plant pond in Craighead County, and from Moffett, Oklahoma. (There is one other sighting, discontinuous in time from the others, involving a single bird at Lake Millwood on February 3.)

FALL MIGRATION: Sanderlings are seen much more often in fall than spring, at least in part because there are so many more mudflats associated with fish ponds and drained reservoirs at that time of the year. From the 1930s to the early 1970s, there were about fourteen records for this species in the state, all involving one or two individuals from August through October (file, Deaderick 1938). In recent years the birds have been observed in surprisingly large numbers at Lake Millwood during the draw down years. In 1977 Sanderlings were observed regularly there from September 11 to October 25, with daily totals varying from one to eleven birds, and a peak during September. In 1980, another draw down year at Millwood, the birds were seen from August 21 to November 9, with a peak of 54 at mid-September. According to Charles Mills, who has been involved in most of these sightings, many of the birds seen in both draw down years were in their first winter immature plumage. As many as three to five birds have been reported a few times at Lonoke, and three were seen at Lake Sequoyah in Washington County on August 29 when water levels were low and mudflats exposed.

SEMIPALMATED SANDPIPER, *Calidris pusilla* (Linnaeus)

Fairly common to sometimes locally abundant transient in all regions, especially during spring.

SPRING MIGRATION: Most reports for the period of northward migration fall between late April and the second week in June, but occasionally the species is seen as early as the first half of April. Many observations in the file have involved small numbers, but spring flocks are common and numbers in this season tend, on the average, to be higher than those in fall. At Anderson's Minnow Farm in Lonoke a thorough survey on May 26, 1979, turned up a count involving over 2000 Semipalmated Sandpipers, almost three times any similar effort for fall in the same place. The 128 birds in the same area on June 8 was a large number so late in the season. Smaller numbers have been reported elsewhere in the state. An estimated 100 at the state fish hatchery in Centerton, Benton County, on May 12, was a high count for the highlands.

There is a break in sightings between mid-June and mid-July. This suggests a dividing line between the late spring transients and early fall transients.

FALL AND WINTER: During the southward migration period the species is seen primarily between mid-July and mid-October, but there are sightings into the first half of November, and a few questionable ones even later. A study conducted in the Scott-Lonoke area (Graves 1972) showed that the largest numbers were present between August 22 and September 10, with a peak of 345 on September 5. A similar study at Anderson's Minnow Farm showed 150 or more present regularly between July 17 and August 27 (which was the terminal date for the study), and a peak of 790 observed on August 12.

While as many as 100 Semipalmated Sandpipers have been seen at the state fish hatchery in Lonoke in the first week of November, there are only four records thereafter and no more than three birds were involved in any single sighting. Since the species is not known to winter north of southern Florida (AOU 1983), all winter season sight records must be held in suspicion. Certainly this species cannot always be reliably separated from the Western Sandpiper, which is known to winter abundantly along the Gulf Coast in Louisiana (Lowery 1974) and has been reported in numbers during December in the Lonoke area.

WESTERN SANDPIPER, *Calidris mauri* (Cabanis)

Transient in all regions. Common and regular in fall, and much less common in spring.

SPRING MIGRATION: The relatively few spring observations in the Audubon Society file are scattered from the last of April into the first week of June, chiefly during May. Most of these reports involve one to six birds seen during a day, but there is one report of 50 at Lonoke on June 3. There are spring reports in the file from Lonoke, Prairie, Union and Benton counties, and from flooded fields in the Arkansas River bottomlands just west of Fort Smith.

The division between spring and fall migration is evident in a break in sightings between early June and early July.

FALL MIGRATION: Western Sandpipers are seen in all regions during fall, sometimes in large numbers. There are records in the file primarily from the second week of July through October, with a few scattered sightings through December primarily in the Lonoke area. In the western Ozarks there are no sightings after late September. Observers sometimes see single individuals, small flocks of two to seven birds, or sometimes more. M. G. Vaiden said Western and Stilt Sandpipers were "about the most common sandpiper that drops in on us" along the Mississippi River in Desha County with the species seen regularly in 1963 from July 19 to September 16 (file). A shorebird study in the Scott-Lonoke area (Graves 1972) showed that the largest numbers, 70 to 250 birds, were present from August 22 to September 10, with the peak on August 25. A similar study involving Anderson's Minnow Farm at Lonoke (summary on file) conducted July 17 to August 27 showed more than 200 of these birds were present on most field trips, with a peak of 735 on August 12. Lower numbers are seen in other areas. The 24 at Lake Sequoyah in Washington County on August 31 was a peak for the Ozarks, as was the 52 at the Lake Hamilton fish hatchery in Garland County on July 7 for the Ouachitas.

FIGURE 6-47 Least Sandpiper in October on mudflats in ponds at Lonoke. *David Plank*

Almost all reports in the file after October are from the Lonoke area (the rest are in the lowlands also), and are mainly in December. Because there is no particular evidence that this species overwinters regularly in the state, it must be presumed that the 24 birds seen at Lonoke on December 23 were probably late fall transients. There is also one record of a single bird at Lonoke in early January, but otherwise no later record for January, nor any for February or March.

LEAST SANDPIPER, *Calidris minutilla* (Vieillot)

Migrant in all regions. Common to locally abundant in fall, and much less numerous in spring. Winter resident in the southern lowlands. Characteristically found on exposed mudflats.

FALL MIGRATION: Fall migrants are common by mid-July and have been seen as far north as the western Ozarks as late as the second week of December. Large numbers are seen at almost any time during this period. In the Audubon Society file there are records involving 100 to nearly 1000 Least Sandpipers before the month

of August, and an estimated 1000 birds were seen at the Delta Fish Farm in Drew County on December 7, 1965. A study in the Scott-Lonoke area (Graves 1972) showed the species was present in numbers varying from 3 to 700 from the second half of July to the second week of November (end of the study period), with peaks from the second half of August into November. On a drained fish pond in Craighead County, Least Sandpipers were seen regularly from October 24 to November 18 (the entire period of the study) with a peak of 50 birds on the final day (Hanebrink 1969b). The 36 birds at Lake Sequoyah in Washington County on September 13 was a peak for the Ozarks.

WINTER: Since these birds feed by probing mud, their distribution in Arkansas during late fall and early winter is presumably governed by the presence of unfrozen mudflat areas. In the Ozarks, Least Sandpipers may be present throughout November and into the first half of December, but their numbers decline sharply upon the arrival of hard freezes and extended cold. Further south, in the Arkansas River Valley, the birds are sometimes reported on Christmas Bird Counts, but really large numbers during winter are seen only in the lowlands, especially in the Lonoke area. Typical reports on the Christmas Count at Lonoke involve 100 to 300 Least Sandpipers, and 900 were reported in 1971. In the file there are records for all the winter months at Lonoke, and flocks have been seen there even in the coldest months.

SPRING MIGRATION: While Least Sandpipers winter regularly in southern Arkansas, they have begun to be seen in places where wintering is not known to occur during March, especially late in the month. These records suggest the beginning of spring migration through the state. Thereafter, transients are seen wherever there is available habitat during April and May, occasionally in early June. Numbers seen during spring are considerably lower, as a rule, than those of fall. In prime shorebird habitat at Lonoke, there are several peak counts involving as many as 50 to over 150 birds, usually during May. The 40 there on June 6 were late.

Least Sandpipers are seen in Arkansas in every month of the year, but a gap in records from mid-June to the second week of July suggests the dividing line between spring and fall migrants.

WHITE-RUMPED SANDPIPER, *Calidris fuscicollis* (Vieillot)

Locally common spring transient, less common in fall. Observed on typical shorebird mudflats and in wet or flooded fields.

SPRING MIGRATION: Spring transients have been observed from the second week of April to mid-June in all regions. Many reports in the Audubon Society file have involved fewer than 10 birds, but in the Lonoke area especially, larger numbers have been reported with some frequency. Records there between the second half of May and the first week in June have involved 25 to 100 birds, and 1300 were seen in a drained fish pond on May 17, 1979. The 184 birds at the state fish hatchery ponds at Centerton (Benton County) on May 28 was a high count. Members of the Fort Smith Audubon Society who visit flooded agricultural fields in the Arkansas River bottoms at Moffett, Oklahoma, just west of Fort Smith, have found these birds with some regularity there in spring, with counts between 21 to 42 during the first two weeks of May. It appears that in at least certain areas White-rumped Sandpipers are common locally during spring.

FALL MIGRATION: There are fewer than ten reports for the southward migration period, and these are scattered from mid-August through October. None of these reports involve more than four birds.

BAIRD'S SANDPIPER, *Calidris bairdii* (Coues)

Uncommon but fairly regular transient in all regions. More often seen in fall than spring. Observed on mudflats, in flooded fields, and sandbars of major rivers.

SPRING MIGRATION: The relatively few spring sightings range from the second week of March to the first week of June. Many reports in the Audubon Society file have involved single birds, but there are three reports involving at least 10: 12 on a drained catfish pond near the Red River in Lafayette County on March 30; 64 or more on a drained fish pond in Lonoke on April 20; and 10 on a drained fish pond at the state fish hatchery in Benton County on May 15. There is no spring record for the northeast (Hanebrink 1980) or for Faulkner County (Johnson 1979).

FALL MIGRATION: There are sightings for the southward migration period between the last week of July and mid-November, with a peak often during September. In Desha County, Baird's Sandpiper was said to be common on a big sandbar near the mouth of the Arkansas River during September, and 13 were seen on September 3 (file). In a shorebird study in the Scott-Lonoke area (Graves 1972), Baird's Sandpiper was present between July 30 and October 7, with a peak of seven birds on September 24 (Graves 1972). At Lake Millwood peaks of 10 to 17 birds have been observed from mid-September to mid-October. At Lake Sequoyah in Washington County, the species was present during the first three weeks of September in 1983, with a peak of five birds on September 14.

PECTORAL SANDPIPER, *Calidris melanotos* (Vieillot)

Common to locally abundant transient in all regions. Reports for every month of the year, but only a rare few are seen outside the normal migration period. Most numerous during fall. Frequents wet grassy fields and mudflats.

SPRING MIGRATION: Pectoral Sandpipers are

seen during the northward migration period primarily between the second week of March and the end of May, with a few unusual records in June. Many reports for a day's outing in this period have involved up to 20 or 30 birds, and only rarely as many as 100. Peak numbers are usually seen in late March or April. All the large counts involving 500 or more birds are from Lonoke, and an estimated 2080 were seen at Anderson's Minnow Farm there on April 6, 1975. Peak counts outside the Lonoke area invariably involve 100 or fewer Pectoral Sandpipers. Among these peaks are 54 at Conway in Faulkner County on March 26; 100 in Lafayette County on March 27; and 76 in Craighead County on April 4. The six birds in Jefferson County on February 20 were unusually early.

FALL MIGRATION: Fall migrants are seen from the first week of July to the fourth week of December, but there are only scattered records in the state after the second week of November. The major peak in numbers occurs in the third or fourth weeks of July and during August with a sharp drop in numbers after September. Reports after mid-November have generally involved single birds. Pectoral Sandpipers are numerous in prime shorebird habitats such as drained fish ponds during fall. The really large numbers are seen primarily in the Lonoke area, but more than 100 have been seen during August and early September in the western Ozarks, at Stuttgart in Arkansas County, and in a few other places.

In the Lonoke area there are several records during August in different years where observers have found more than 1000 Pectoral Sandpipers in one day. On August 13, 1978, Henry and Edith Halberg estimated that there were about 1000 Pectoral Sandpipers in a flock of about 2000 shorebirds that included twelve other species, primarily Lesser Yellowlegs and Least Sandpipers. In a 1974 study at Anderson's Minnow Farm (summary on file), Gary Graves and others counted nearly 700 to over 8000 on field trips between July 17 and August 20, with the big peak on August 1.

There are four reports in December and January. All involved single birds in Lonoke County (three records) or Benton County.

PURPLE SANDPIPER, *Calidris maritima* (Brünnich)

One record.

One Purple Sandpiper was observed on November 29 and 30, 1976, but was not found thereafter, in the Hopefield Chute area off Crittenden County, immediately west of the main channel of the Mississippi River along the Arkansas-Tennessee state line (Holt 1979).

DUNLIN, *Calidris alpina* (Linnaeus)

Regular transient in small numbers in all regions. More reports for fall than spring.

SPRING MIGRATION: Dunlins have been reported from the second week of April through May, with unusual records in the fourth week of March and the first week of June. While some reports involve single birds, Dunlins are more often seen in small flocks, often six to eight birds together, and occasionally more. At Lonoke, 23 were observed on April 18 in drained fish ponds. On May 27, 17 Dunlins were feeding in a rice field at Stuttgart in Arkansas County. At Holla Bend Refuge in Pope County, 20 birds were observed as late as May 28. As many as 21 to 35 Dunlins have been counted in the first half of May in flooded fields at Moffett, Oklahoma, just west of Fort Smith, Arkansas.

FALL MIGRATION: Dunlins are generally among the latest of the shorebirds to reach Arkansas, with reports primarily from the second week of October into the last week of December. There are a few unusual records as early as the third week of July. While many of the fall records in the file involved one or two birds, small flocks of about a dozen birds are not rare, and have been found in most regions of the state. Information in the shorebird survey of the Scott-Lonoke area (Graves 1972) showed that Dunlins were not seen until October 7 and were observed regularly thereafter with as many as 75 counted at the end of the study period in the first half of November. There are December records for Garland, Crittenden, and Lonoke counties, but most records are from the Lonoke area where the species is present throughout the month. As many as 15 have been seen there in the fourth week of December. The well-documented sighting of a single bird at Lake Millwood in February, 1978, is the only record in Arkansas for the period between Christmas and early spring.

STILT SANDPIPER, *Calidris himantopus* (Bonaparte)

Fairly common to common transient in most regions, especially in fall.

SPRING MIGRATION: For the northward migration period there are scattered reports from the last of March into the early days of June, chiefly in May. Many reports have involved one or two birds. Peak records include 118 at the state fish hatchery in Benton County on May 14, and 31 in flooded fields at Moffett, Oklahoma, just west of Fort Smith, Arkansas, on May 13.

FALL MIGRATION: Stilt Sandpipers seem to be fairly common during the fall migration in those areas of the state where there is suitable habitat, principally drained fish ponds and very shallow or drained reservoirs. The 141 birds, most of them still in summer plumage, at Lonoke on July 19 was an early and large peak in numbers for the state, but over 200 have been seen at Lonoke as late as October 8. In the western Ozarks there have been regular fall sightings, with reports of 50 or more birds (up to 84) in late August and early September. An estimated 100 Stilt Sandpipers were seen between August 23 and September 16 along the Mississippi River in Desha County, and the observer noted the species was, in that area, "our most common sandpiper" (Audubon Society file). There are reports from the first week of July to the first week of November, but most birds are seen between mid-July and mid-October.

BUFF-BREASTED SANDPIPER, *Tryngites subruficollis* (Vieillot)

Fairly common fall transient in all regions. Rare spring transient. Usually observed on shortgrass flats above the muddy flats utilized by other shorebirds; also uses sandbars along rivers and agricultural fields.

SPRING MIGRATION: This species has been found in only a few locations in the state during spring. At Anderson's Minnow Farm in Lonoke, five birds were seen on May 10, and 10 were found in the same place two days later. There have also been several sightings in flooded fields in the Arkansas River bottoms at Moffett, Oklahoma, just west of Fort Smith, Arkansas, between April 21 and May 19. The five birds seen in a flooded field in Benton County on May 12 is the only report in spring for the Ozarks.

FALL MIGRATION: Observations for the southward migration span the period from late July to early October. Most reports have involved only a few, or sometimes as many as a dozen birds during a day in the field in appropriate habitat, but more are sometimes seen in places like Lonoke where there is an unusual abundance of moist, open grassy flats. A study in the Scott-Lonoke area (Graves 1972) showed that Buff-breasted Sandpipers were present regularly from August 19 to September 30 with peak numbers between the fourth week of August and the fourth week of September; 98 birds were counted in the area on August 30. During the 1980 draw down at Lake Millwood, a peak of 91 birds was reported on September 12. Peak counts in other areas of the state with much less suitable habitat have usually involved about a dozen of these birds. In Garland County, the species was seen between August 8 and September 13, with one flock of 13 (Deaderick 1938). In the northeastern counties 12 birds were seen in a field near the Jackson-Craighead County line on August 31. There is a similar record for Lake Sequoyah in Washington County in mid-September.

RUFF, *Philomachus pugnax* (Linnaeus)

One well-documented record.

A Ruff was seen at the state fish hatchery ponds in Lonoke County on August 7, 1974. It was observed over a period of three hours and was compared directly to Pectoral Sandpipers, Upland Sandpiper, and Lesser Yellowlegs. Written and photographic documentation is on file with the Arkansas Audubon Society.

SHORT-BILLED DOWITCHER, *Limnodromus griseus* (Gmelin)

Transient in small numbers in all regions. Rare in spring. Fall status unclear, but observed more often than in spring, and in much smaller numbers than the similar appearing Long-billed Dowitcher.

All three reports in the Audubon Society

file for spring migration involved birds in the first half of May. Two of the records were from Lonoke, and one was from a drained fish hatchery pond in Benton County. The 35 birds identified by call notes at Anderson's Minnow Farm in Lonoke on May 10 was a peak. During fall, the species is seen primarily from the second week of July to the third week of October. Many reports in the file for this period involve one or two birds seen in a day, but larger numbers are reported, especially in the Lonoke area. In 1968, Henry and Edith Halberg saw 48 on September 7, and 67 on October 12. (Both records are high numbers for Arkansas.) In breeding plumages, the two dowitcher species can usually be separated in the field by experienced observers. However, there is much overlap in the winter plumages (the ones most often seen in Arkansas) and this makes their separation difficult in the field on the basis of plumage characters alone (see Pitelka 1950, for a full discussion). Field observers in Arkansas must sometimes settle for calling the birds in question "dowitcher species" (see Long-billed Dowitcher below).

LONG-BILLED DOWITCHER, *Limnodromus scolopaceus* (Say)

Fairly common transient in fall, and rare transient in spring. Reported several times in late December at Lonoke.

SPRING AND FALL MIGRATION: There are three spring records in the Audubon Society file: one bird in Washington County on March 26; two in Crittenden County under the Mississippi River bridge on April 23; one at Lonoke on May 13. During the fall southward migration period the species is seen much more often, and in fairly large numbers. While many reports in the file have involved single or a few birds, records of small flocks of five or a few more birds are not rare and have been reported from all regions. As in the case of so many other species of shorebirds in Arkansas, the big peak numbers are reported from the Lonoke area where large acreages of drained fish ponds provide an abundance of suitable habitat. The peaks at Lonoke usually occur in October and early November (250 at Anderson's Minnow Farm on November 5), but there is at least one record of 50 birds at Lonoke as early as August

6. Reports for the state range primarily between the third week of July and late November, with extreme early and late records in the second week of July and the last week of December. Two late December records at Lonoke involved three to six birds. There is also an early December record at Lake Millwood involving two birds.

DOWITCHER SPECIES: Since the two dowitcher species cannot always be accurately separated, there are entries in the Audubon Society file for "dowitcher species." For spring migration these birds have been reported from the third week of March into the first week of May. The peak record involved flocks of 18, 40, and 30 birds at Lonoke on April 26. Fall records are primarily between the second week of July and the first week of December, with a concentration from the third week of August and the third week of November. At Lonoke, 10 to 20 have been reported on several occasions, and a party of observers counted 239 there on November 2. There are a few rare midwinter records in southern Arkansas.

COMMON SNIPE, *Gallinago gallinago* (Linnaeus)

Common, sometimes locally abundant, migrant in all regions. Winter resident in all regions. Additional reports in all months of the year. Frequents wet grassy habitat in open area.

FALL MIGRATION: Snipes do not often arrive in Arkansas before early September, and these early September records often involve individuals or small flocks. They begin to arrive in numbers in late September and the first half of October. From this time until the onset of hard freezes (often in December), snipes are numerous on drained fish ponds, rice fields, wastewater treatment ponds, and wet grassy fields in all regions. Fall peak counts may involve upwards to 100 birds in the better habitats, and sometimes more. An estimated 1000 were seen on a drained fish pond in Drew County on December 7.

WINTER: Snipes can be found in winter in all regions where there is suitable, unfrozen habitat. Analysis of the statewide Christmas Bird Counts show them most numerous at Lonoke, White River Refuge, Hot Springs, and Texarkana, all in the southern half of Arkansas

FIGURE 6-48 Common Snipe. *Bill Brazelton*

FIGURE 6-49 American Woodcock. *Edith Halberg*

and mainly in the lowlands. The ten-year mean number of birds on Christmas Counts was 0.9 snipes per party hour. This mean was exceeded at Lonoke and the White River Refuge, but the average mean in the state was much lower, often 0.2 snipes per party hour or less. At Fayetteville in the northwest, the usual number reported on Christmas Counts is fewer than 20 birds, but there is one peak of 102. At Conway in the Arkansas River Valley the usual number found is fewer than 10, with a peak of 15. At Lonoke, 100 or more are frequently reported, and there is a peak of over 400. The birds are driven out of northern Arkansas by severe and prolonged cold which freezes the soft ground where they feed.

SPRING MIGRATION AND SUMMER: Numbers of spring migrants are seen in places where they did not overwinter, about the time of the first warming trends, often in March, and they continue to move through the state until mid-April, after which few are seen. Spring peak numbers are lower than those in fall, with often no more than 10 to 20 even in prime habitats. The 85 seen in one field in Crittenden County on March 9 was an unusually large number for the season.

There are scattered reports from May through August that presumably involved non-breeding stragglers who did not, for reasons unknown, make the northward migration.

AMERICAN WOODCOCK, *Scolopax minor* Gmelin

Migrant and permanent resident, usually in small numbers, in all regions. Sometimes flushed from low damp woods, but seen more frequently during the nuptial flights of late winter and early spring.

MIGRATION: Most reports in the Audubon Society file involve the period between mid-October and late March, or roughly the periods of migration and winter. Many reports have involved single birds, but six were flushed in a small area of Dallas County on October 23, and four in Van Buren County on November 19. Hollister (1902) found the species common during November in the southeastern lowlands. At the White River Refuge woodcocks were said to be present regularly in winter, but much more numerous during migrations in early December and late February (Mendall and Aldous 1943). The sparseness of the record after late March or early April suggests that by this time local breeding woodcocks have begun nesting, and those that will breed north of Arkansas have already passed through the state.

There are numerous records in the file for February and March that suggest this as the peak time for northward migration. However, since many of these reports involve nuptial flights, it is not known if these birds are merely performing on migration, or are preparing to nest locally. At Lake Fayetteville in Washington County, 10 or more woodcocks were displaying in a small field in late February, but this number had declined to one bird by early April. These courtship flights seem to occur year after year in the same fields, but often these fields do not involve areas where woodcocks have been found in summer. This suggests that the nuptial flights commonly are performed by males during stops in northward migration.

Nine woodcocks banded in Louisiana during winter were recovered in Arkansas one month, three months, and up to one or two winters following banding (Figure 6-50). Distances between banding and recovery ranged from 200 to 400 miles.

BREEDING SEASON: Spectacular nuptial flights associated with courtship have been observed in the state from midwinter to early April. Some of the 10 birds seen in Union County on December 30 were performing these flights far in advance of any known nesting activity. In the western Ozarks nuptial flights do not get underway until February, but thereafter may continue for nearly two months. Near Fayetteville in March, three males were seen

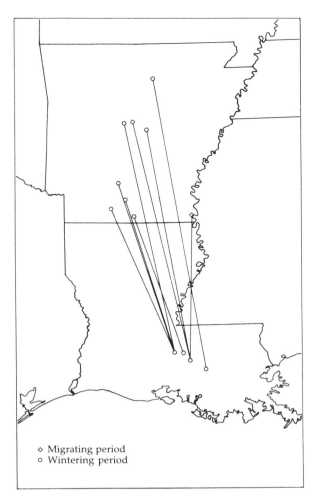

◇ Migrating period
○ Wintering period

FIGURE 6-50 Movements of the American Woodcock based on banding records.

performing their flights in the moonlight over a field covered with snow.

Nests or young have been reported between mid-February and early May. Eggs hatched in Yell County by February 15 (Pettingill 1936). A nest found at Hamburg in Ashley County on February 13 had hatchlings on March 8. Four highly incubated eggs were found in Yell County on March 1 (Pettingill 1936). Eggs hatched at Lake Nimrod in Yell County on March 15. A nest was found just south of Little Rock on March 15. An adult and four chicks were seen in Dallas County on March 23. An adult carrying young was seen at Fayetteville on April 1 (Harvey 1882). Nesting was reported on Rich Mountain in Polk County on April 3. An adult and two juveniles were seen in Desha County on April 4. One adult and one immature were seen in Saline County on April 11, and 10 birds not obviously associated with nesting activity were in the same area between April 30 and May 10. An adult and four young were on an upland area in Newton County on April 15. An adult and five flying young were seen in the eastern Ozarks near Batesville on April 16. An adult and four almost fully grown young were seen at Devil's Den State Park in Washington County on May 2 (Sutton 1967).

In the Audubon Society file there are summer reports for counties other than those already listed including Phillips, Sebastian, Grant, Union, Ouachita, Prairie, Ashley, and Calhoun. There is also a summer report for Faulkner County (Johnson 1979).

WINTER: Hollister (1902) considered woodcocks common in Lonoke, Prairie, and Arkansas counties during January. A tabulation of questionnaires sent to game officials showed the birds were common in winter in east central and southeastern Arkansas (Mendall and Aldous 1943), essentially the same area covered by Hollister. Woodcocks have been reported on Christmas Bird Counts primarily in the lowlands in the southern half of the state, including the Arkansas River lowlands in central Arkansas. The species has not been reported with much regularity at Little Rock, but there are several records of three and four on the Christmas Count there, and the same can be said for the count at Lonoke, just east of Little Rock. There are several records of five or six at Lake Georgia-Pacific, and at Arkadelphia the birds have been seen annually on the Christmas Count since 1974, with one peak of seven. As many as 10 have been reported at El Dorado (December 30), and H. H. Shugart of that city was told by hunters that in December of 1962 they killed one or more birds every day throughout the month.

Subfamily Phalaropodinae Phalaropes

WILSON'S PHALAROPE, *Phalaropus tricolor* (Vieillot)

Fairly common transient in all regions. The phalarope most often observed in Arkansas. Reported in flooded agricultural fields, drained ponds (including fish and wastewater treatment ponds), and reservoirs.

SPRING MIGRATION: During spring Wilson's Phalarope has been reported between the third week of March and late May, mainly between the second week of April and the third week of May. Most reports in the Audubon Society file for a day have involved one to three birds, but 32 were counted at the state fish hatchery in Benton County on May 20. Counts of seven or eight were reported at Holla Bend Refuge on April 30, at Lonoke on May 13 (four males, three females), and at Lake Sequoyah in Washington County on May 18. As many as 11 to 17 have been counted at Moffett, Oklahoma, between April 11 and May 6 in the flooded fields near the Arkansas River. More than 40 were seen at Lonoke on May 8.

FALL MIGRATION: There are sightings for this period between the third week of July and the second week of October. Peak numbers in the Lonoke area involving six to eleven birds have been reported from the second week of August to the second week of October. The five at Arkadelphia on August 30–31 was a high number for the state outside the Lonoke area. At Anderson's Minnow Farm in Lonoke, Wilson's Phalarope was reported regularly from July 29 to August 27 (which was the end of the study period), with peaks as high as 34 birds on both August 12 and 27 (summary on file).

FIGURE 6-51 Wilson's Phalarope. *Bill Brazelton*

RED-NECKED PHALAROPE, *Phalaropus lobatus* (Linnaeus)

Somewhat rare transient.

SPRING MIGRATION: There are fewer than ten reports in the Audubon Society file for the northward migration period, May 22 to May 30. Most of these reports are from the Lonoke area, but a single bird was also seen on the flats of a drained pond at the state fish hatchery in Benton County. Usually single birds have been seen, females reported more than males.

FALL MIGRATION: There are approximately 25 reports in the file between the second week of August and the first week of October. The only report that involved more than one or two birds was from the wastewater treatment plant ponds at El Dorado, where six were seen together on September 27. Most fall reports are from Lonoke, but there are also reports from the Fort Smith area, from the Red River in Little River County, from the wastewater treatment ponds at Arkadelphia, and of course from Union County.

RED PHALAROPE, *Phalaropus fulicaria* (Linnaeus)

Rare transient. Seen much less often than the Red-necked or Wilson's Phalaropes.

Though principally a pelagic (seagoing) migrant, this species also migrates less commonly but regularly through the interior of western North America (AOU 1983). The first of fewer than ten records for Arkansas involves a single individual in winter plumage at Anderson's Minnow Farm in Lonoke on August 24, 1973. A single bird, possibly the same bird, was seen in the same place until September 18. Subsequently, there have been six documented sightings of single birds, chiefly at Lake Millwood in southwestern Arkansas (five sightings between 1976 and 1980) and at Lake Hamilton in Garland County, all between mid-September and late November. The Lake Millwood records have involved adults in winter plumage and juveniles in the first winter plumage. Photographic and written documentation is on file for some of these sightings.

Family Laridae

Subfamily Stercorariinae Jaegers

POMARINE JAEGER, *Stercorarius pomarinus* (Temminck)

One record.

An adult light phase Pomarine Jaeger was first discovered at Lake Millwood on August 21, 1983, and was photographed repeatedly by several observers until last seen during the first week of October, almost two months later. Charles Mills found that this bird (and other jaegers seen at Lake Millwood) seemed to prefer the eastern region of the lake where the greatest concentration of ducks, gulls, and terns is usually found.

PARASITIC JAEGER, *Stercorarius parasiticus* (Linnaeus)

Three records. Several additional records of *Stercorarius* spp.

Records from Lake Millwood in southwestern Arkansas dated September 12, 1982, and October 13–17, 1982, involved juvenile Parasitic Jaegers, and an adult bird was seen there in late September of 1984. Additionally, two other records, dated September 1, 1974, and December 3–18, 1976, were not identified as to species, though both sightings were suspected by Charles Mills of being Parasitic Jaegers on the basis of several plumage and behavioral characteristics. Written and photographic documentation is on file with the Arkansas Audubon Society.

LONG-TAILED JAEGER, *Stercorarius longicaudus* Vieillot

One record.

A bird observed by Charles Mills and others between September 29 and October 4, 1974, at Lake Millwood in southwestern Arkansas, was identified as a subadult Long-tailed Jaeger. Written and photographic documentation is on file with the Arkansas Audubon Society.

Subfamily *Larinae* Gulls

LAUGHING GULL, *Larus atricilla* Linnaeus

Rare fall visitor in southern Arkansas.

This very common coastal species is rare in Arkansas, but apparently is sometimes carried far inland by storms. Three birds seen at Lake Millwood in late August and early September of 1980 were probably attributable to Hurricane Allan, which struck the lower Texas Gulf Coast approximately two weeks before these sightings occurred. Two Laughing Gulls at Lake Millwood on August 22, 1983, may have been driven inland by Hurricane Alicia which struck the Texas coast at that time. The eight records in the Audubon Society file from Lake Millwood have involved sightings between the second half of August and early December. There are also two records from the Grand Prairie area in eastern Arkansas. Laughing Gull records have involved single birds except for two on August 22, 1983 (above), and two adults on October 3, 1976. According to Charles Mills, who has seen all the Laughing Gulls at Lake Millwood, in two instances Franklin's Gulls were available for direct comparison. Arkansas records have involved birds in adult, first-winter, and second-winter plumages. Written and or photographic documentation is available for each of the Lake Millwood sightings.

FRANKLIN'S GULL, *Larus pipixcan* Wagler

Regular migrant in all regions, seen more often in fall than spring, most common in the central and western areas. Several extra-seasonal records.

SPRING MIGRATION: In the Audubon Society file there are sightings for the northward migration period between the third week of March and June 7, with a modest concentration of sightings in April and early May that is suggestive of a peak. Flocks involving as many as 40 and 41 birds have been seen in Lonoke County and at Lake Millwood during the second week in April. In each case the birds were already in their summer plumage. An estimated 77 birds were seen at Lake Millwood on May 4, and 75 at Moffett, Oklahoma, near Fort Smith, Arkansas, on May 6. An exception to the apparent peak period involved 22 Franklin's Gulls at Lonoke on June 6. There is also one

much later report that involved a bird with a broken wing in the Norfolk Dam area of Baxter County on July 6.

FALL MIGRATION: During the southward migration period Franklin's Gull has been found primarily between the last week of September and early November, but there are sightings as early as mid-August. The peak seems to occur during October and early November. A flock of over 200 was seen at Centerton in Benton County on October 9, and an estimated 200 circled Lake Fayetteville on October 27. At Lake Millwood in the fall of 1979, counts involving 29 to 386 Franklin's Gulls were obtained between September 23 and November 4 with a peak on October 26. More than 400 were seen there on November 9 of the following year. It is seen with much less frequency in eastern Arkansas. Therefore it was a big surprise to find 50 or 60 as they followed a plow in St. Francis County on November 2 (Coffey 1947). There are also two later records from Lake Millwood that involved single birds on December 4, 1977, and January 4–7, 1976.

LITTLE GULL, *Larus minutus* Pallas

A record of two birds.

Two individuals of this small gull species were found at Lake Millwood on November 22, 1985, and both were still present the next day. One bird was in adult winter plumage and was well described by Max Parker, the other was in second winter subadult plumage and was photographed by Charles Mills. The subadult bird was present until December 8. Written and photographic documentation are on file with the Arkansas Audubon Society. There are scattered records of this Old World gull on both coasts and at interior locations in North America, where it began nesting in the Great Lakes region in 1962 (AOU 1983).

BONAPARTE'S GULL, *Larus philadelphia* (Ord)

Regular migrant, usually in small numbers, observed along major rivers, and larger open bodies of water in all regions. Winter visitor or occasional winter resident in small numbers chiefly in the Arkansas River Valley and further south.

FALL MIGRATION: Bonaparte's Gulls seem to

arrive in Arkansas with fair regularity during October, especially from about the last week of the month and thereafter during November. At Lakes Catherine and Hamilton in Garland County, birds were seen on five occasions between October 1 and November 7, with a peak of 60 on October 31 (Deaderick 1938). There are several reports in the Audubon Society file for September, and a highly unusual report for two birds at Lonoke that were seen by skilled observers in late July. The fall peak in numbers for the state involved 105 birds at Lake Millwood on November 27.

WINTER: Bonaparte's Gulls are seen in fair number during much of December, though numbers decline thereafter until the spring influx in late March and in April. Several peak counts in December include the 26 at Little Rock, 60 at Fort Smith, and more than 100 for several years at Lake Millwood in southwestern Arkansas. There are also additional winter records for the state.

SPRING MIGRATION: The species is modestly widespread from mid-March through April, with the latest report in the first week of May. Occasionally a few of the birds seen in the northward migration period have already acquired their summer plumage. Most reports for spring, as in fall and winter, have involved five or fewer in a day, but sometimes more are seen. There are several reports of peak flocks during April involving as many as 25 to 30 in a day at Lake Millwood and Lake Francis near Siloam Springs.

RING-BILLED GULL, *Larus delawarensis* Ord

Common migrant and winter resident in all regions. Observed on larger bodies of water, especially around the tailwaters of dams.

FALL MIGRATION: Ring-billed Gulls begin trickling into Arkansas during September. An occasional individual is seen early during August or even mid-July. Large numbers are present by the second week of October and thereafter, with migration continuing during November. At Lakes Catherine and Hamilton in Garland County, arrivals were recorded between August 21 and November 2 (Deaderick 1938). The 100 birds at Horseshoe Lake in Crittenden County on October 8 was an early large number, as was the 100 at Calion Lake near El

Dorado on October 18. The 134 birds at Lake Francis in the western Ozarks on November 13 declined sharply by early December.

WINTER: Ring-billed Gulls are present in winter essentially throughout the state where there is appropriate habitat, often a large river, lake or reservoir. Especially large congregations of these gulls occur around the spillways and tailwaters of dams, or where there are significant mortalities in small fish. At Little Rock between 1961 and 1983, the numbers of these birds reported on the Christmas Bird Count varied from 8 to 714, with 100 or more found in thirteen of those years, and 400 or more in six years. At Conway in Faulkner County, as many as 200 to 300 have been reported on several Christmas Counts, and at Lonoke there is one Christmas Count record of 400 (1977). A total of 750 were seen at Horseshoe Lake on February 24.

BANDING: Four Ring-billed Gulls have been recovered that were banded outside of Arkansas when they were nestlings, juveniles, or immature birds. Two banded in North Dakota were recovered twenty-two and twenty-four months later in Arkansas. A bird banded in northern Michigan was recovered twenty-two months later in Arkansas. The fourth bird was recovered in Arkansas in December, having been banded in Wisconsin during the preceeding June.

SPRING MIGRATION: Ring-billed Gulls are common in the state during March, and to a somewhat lesser extent during April and early May (latest May 25). The 145 birds at Little Rock on March 4 was a major spring peak, as were the 100 or more at the state fish hatchery in Lonoke County on March 12. There are two reports in the file involving flocks with as many as 30 to 50 individuals during April and in the first week of May.

HERRING GULL, *Larus argentatus* Pontoppidan

Uncommon migrant in small numbers in all regions. Rare winter visitor except for a few places, especially along the Arkansas River, where larger numbers are sometimes seen. Rare in all seasons in the Ozarks. Observed in the same places as Ring-billed Gulls, but almost always in much smaller numbers.

MIGRATION AND WINTER: Herring Gulls

FIGURE 6-52 Ring-billed Gull. *Charles Mills*

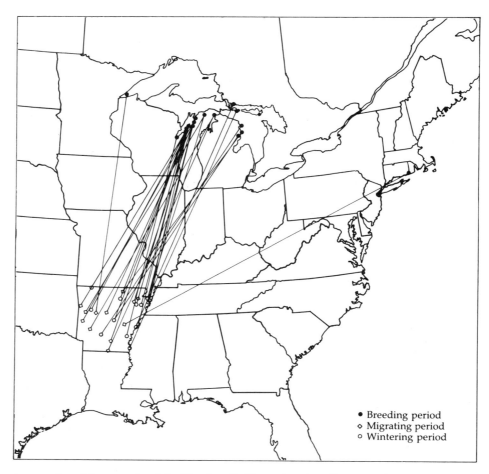

FIGURE 6-53 Movements of the Herring Gull based on banding records.

have been seen in Arkansas between the second week of August and the second week of June. However, most observations on file with the Audubon Society have occurred between the third week of September and the third week of March. At Lakes Hamilton and Catherine in Garland County, yearly arrivals range between September 24 and October 24, and departures in the spring occur between May 3 and 20 (Deaderick 1938). Most reports in the file have involved small numbers of birds, often single individuals.

Larger numbers are sometimes seen during winter. At Conway, where other Christmas Bird Count totals have involved one or two or none of these birds, 65 Herring Gulls and 335 Ring-billed Gulls were reported in 1971. A similar number of Herring Gulls was seen at Pine Bluff on January 18, 1974. The observer, David R.

Hunter, noted that 80 percent of the flock were the brown plumaged immature birds, and that few of the remainder had acquired the full adult plumage. Herring Gulls have also been seen with fair regularity on the Christmas Count at Little Rock (reports on eight of fourteen recent Christmas Counts), with peaks of 16 and 12 birds. The 23 Herring Gulls seen on the 1979 statewide Christmas Counts were at Lake Millwood, Little Rock, and Pine Bluff. The 10 birds at Horseshoe Lake in Crittenden County on March 17 was a large late peak, as was the "small flock" that appeared at Big Lake Refuge in company with a lone Brown Pelican after a severe storm in April 1947 (Baerg 1951).

BANDING: Most of the 30 Herring Gulls recovered in the state were banded as juveniles or immatures around the Great Lakes, with distances between banding and recovery chiefly

650 to 900 miles, up to a maximum of over 1200 miles (Figure 6-53). While most birds were recovered within the first year after banding, two survived between 6.5 and 7.5 years.

GLAUCOUS GULL, *Larus hyperboreus* Gunnerus

Two well-documented records.

An immature Glaucous Gull in first winter plumage was seen at Lake Millwood in southwestern Arkansas on December 10–11, 1978. Written documentation and a photograph are on file with the Arkansas Audubon Society. Photographs of a second bird seen on December 6, 1980, also at Lake Millwood, are also on file.

BLACK-LEGGED KITTIWAKE, *Rissa tridactyla* (Linnaeus)

One record.

This gull occurs around the world on northern seas or along northern seacoasts, and occasionally on large bodies of water in the interior of North America (AOU 1983). A single kittiwake was observed at Lake Millwood in Little River County on November 24, 1985. During forty-five minutes of observation the bird was compared directly with several Bonaparte's Gulls and a Little Gull seen at the lake during that time. Written documentation and a detailed drawing submitted by Charles Mills shows that the kittiwake was in the first winter plumage, with a black ear spot, a conspicuous black mark across the lower nape, and a bold W-shaped dark pattern across the upper surface of the wing.

SABINE'S GULL, *Xema sabini* (Sabine)

Seven fall records, all from Lake Millwood.

All Arkansas records for Sabine's Gull have been obtained since 1977, with sightings occurring between September 22 and October 21. All involved one or two birds. Written documentation is on file with the Audubon Society for each of these sightings, and three are further documented with photographs. Charles Mills, who has seen each of these birds, states that one was in adult plumage (October 21, 1979), while the others were in juvenile plumage.

Subfamily Sterninae Terns

CASPIAN TERN, *Sterna caspia* Pallas

Fairly common fall transient and uncommon spring transient observed on large open bodies of water in all regions.

SPRING MIGRATION: Caspian Terns are found infrequently during the northward migration period. In the Audubon Society file there are reports between late April and early June, with a strong concentration in the last three weeks of May. There is one exceedingly early report for the northeast in March (Hanebrink 1980). Many spring reports have involved one or two birds, sometimes more. Seven were seen at the Norfork dam site in Baxter County on May 19 and five were present on the same day in a different year at Lake Fayetteville. A "flock" was seen on Bull Shoals Lake in the Sugar Loaf area in Boone County on May 30. Two records in the second half of June seem to fall in between the main period for spring and fall migration.

FALL MIGRATION: These large birds are seen regularly in the state during the southward migration. Immature birds that accompany the adults at this time are occasionally seen as they beg for and receive food from the adults. In the file there are reports between the third week of July and the third week of December, chiefly between the third week of August and mid-October, with peak numbers in late August and the first three weeks of September. There is only one record after mid-October, and this involved two birds seen at Lake Millwood during the 1977 Christmas Bird Count. While many sightings have involved a few birds or small flocks, there are also some impressively large counts. A single flock of at least 53 was seen at Lake Sequoyah in Washington County on September 16, 1983. A total of 96 were at Lake Millwood on September 19. A peak of 28 were observed along the Arkansas River at Little Rock on September 22. Some of the 43 birds seen at Lake Millwood on September 26 were immatures being fed by adults.

COMMON TERN, *Sterna hirundo* Linnaeus

Uncommon transient seen chiefly in the fall. Reports from all regions.

SPRING MIGRATION: Even though Arkansas lies in between the known breeding and wintering ranges of this species (AOU 1983), it has been seen infrequently in the state. There are relatively few reports for the northward migration period (Audubon Society file, Deaderick 1938), most of which involved one or two birds between the last week of April and the end of May. These reports are primarily from those areas of the state that have been most heavily worked in terms of bird observation: Washington, Garland, Hempstead, Crittenden, Union, and Lonoke counties.

FALL MIGRATION: There are relatively more sightings during the southward migration period, between the second week of July and the last week of October, but these also have generally involved one or a few birds. The largest report on file is from Lake Millwood in the southwest. Of an estimated 80 to 90 terns there on October 1, 1984, most were Forster's Terns, but 23 were Common Terns, and most were in first winter plumage. There are fall reports from all regions.

Certainly there is enough general similarity between this species and Forster's Tern (which is more numerous in the state by far) that observers should carefully document the appropriate field marks and vocalizations of any bird thought to be a Common Tern. Sutton (1967) once collected 30 terns of the general appearance of Common Tern in Oklahoma, but each one, when examined in hand, proved to be Forster's Tern!

FORSTER'S TERN, *Sterna forsteri* Nuttall

Fairly common transient that is much more often found in fall than in spring. There are several unusual winter records.

SPRING MIGRATION: Forster's Tern has been observed in Arkansas during the northward migration period from mid-April through May. In addition, there is at least one June record from Garland County (Deaderick 1938). Many of the spring reports have involved one or two birds in a day and rarely even as many as ten.

FALL MIGRATION: Some of the Forster's Terns seen during fall in Arkansas are still in their breeding plumage. There are records between the second week of July and mid-October, with

relatively few sightings thereafter except in the southern lowlands, where a few birds are not unusual during fall, and sometimes many more are seen, especially during August and September. Henry and Edith Halberg saw one flock of 55 at the state fish hatchery in Lonoke County on September 11, and a second flock of 15 on the same day at the Dortch Plantation near Little Rock. Large numbers have also been reported at Lake Millwood. During the fall of 1980 Charles Mills and other observers there saw 35 to 40 birds on most outings during August and September, and only one to ten on trips during July, October, and November. The 30 at Lake Millwood in July of a different year was an early peak in numbers. The latest fall reports involved one bird on the 1977 Arkadelphia Christmas Bird Count, two on the Lake Millwood count in 1980, two on the 1984 Pine Bluff count, and two on Lake Chicot (Chicot County) January 5, 1985.

LEAST TERN, *Sterna antillarum* (Lesson)

Uncommon but regular transient in all regions. Much more common in fall than spring. Irregular, local summer resident breeding on a few sandbars on the Arkansas and Mississippi rivers.

SPRING MIGRATION: Least Terns have arrived in Arkansas by the second week of May, but relatively few are seen until later in the month. Most reports involve single birds, but occasionally small flocks of four to six are seen, especially in the eastern lowlands associated with the Mississippi River. The dozen birds seen at Lonoke one year in early June may have been transients, or part of a breeding population otherwise unreported for the area. Least Terns are sometimes seen in the state in places where there are no known nesting populations.

BREEDING SEASON: In earlier years Least Terns were said to be "fairly common" near Texarkana (Howell 1911) and "present all summer" at Big Lake Refuge in 1940 and 1941 (file). Ganier (1930) published studies of Least Terns nesting on the Mississippi River at Memphis, Tennessee, adjacent to Arkansas. Deaderick (1938) found them "fairly common" at the big impoundments in Garland County, with irregular reports throughout the summer and into early September, including one flock of 20 birds. Baerg (1951) published a number of summer season records for the Arkansas River and for Arkansas and Saline counties. In the Audubon Society file there are June reports for Faulkner, Lonoke, Mississippi, Sebastian, and Union counties, and for the Arkansas River area just west of Fort Smith, Arkansas, that lies in Sequoyah County, Oklahoma.

Hardy (1957) published records of colonies "present each year on the Arkansas and White Rivers at their junctions with the Mississippi River, Desha County." The first actual observations of nests by qualified observers occurred in 1958 when Bill Beall and others reported six nests on an Arkansas River sandbar downstream from Fort Smith on June 8. The following year birds nested in the same location again, and two young were seen during the second week of July. The birds nested in the same general area in at least one subsequent year. This site disappeared after 1969 when Lock and Dam 13 was closed, flooding the sandbars used for nesting. Then on July 4, 1981, an estimated 20 birds were found nesting on an Arkansas River sandbar near Mulberry east of Fort Smith. Recent breeding has also been reported on a Mississippi River sandbar off Mississippi County in June 1980 (Ark. Nat. Heritage Comm. files) and again on July 3, 1984, when 99 chicks were banded (P. Hamel, pers. comm.). In addition, a colony with nests and young was reported and photographs made on an Arkansas River sandbar near Menifee in Conway County in June of 1984. Downing (1980) described the results of an aerial survey of the Mississippi River that reported birds nesting on sandbars above Osceola, but not below. There is also an older record that should be mentioned: the 30 birds seen in Desha County on June 12, 1935, were believed to be part of a nesting colony at Rosedale, Mississippi, just across the Mississippi River from Desha County in Arkansas.

Least Terns have been informally listed as a "threatened" breeding bird in Arkansas because their critical sandbar nesting habitat is affected by channel improvement projects that eliminate or flood sandbars required for nesting, and because the bird's nests are easily destroyed by various human activities including the use of three-wheel motorcycles or dune-buggies (James 1974). This problem was recently illustrated when three-wheel motorcyclists drove all over the colony in Mississippi County where the 99 chicks had been banded in July 1984. The Least Tern population that breeds in the interior of North America has been listed as an endangered species by the U.S. Fish and Wildlife Service.

As a result of the listing of the Least Tern, special surveys were conducted in the summer of 1985. The Arkansas and Mississippi rivers were checked in Arkansas, and partial surveys were made on the lower sections of the White, Red, and St. Francis rivers in Arkansas. These surveys resulted in the discovery of more Least Terns and more confirmed or possible nesting colonies than had ever before been found in the state. Mary C. Landin of the U.S. Army Corps of Engineers reported ten possible or confirmed nesting areas along the Mississippi River in Arkansas territorial waters, with sites in Chicot, Desha, Phillips, Lee, Crittenden, and Mississippi counties. As a result of the combined efforts of several government agencies, Arkansas River colonies were discovered in Conway, Perry, Desha, Sebastian, and Johnson counties. Agencies cooperating in these surveys included the Little Rock District of the Army Corps of Engineers, Arkansas Game and Fish Commission, and the Arkansas Natural Heritage Commission (Shepherd 1985).

FALL MIGRATION: The southward migration peak period occurs in August. In places where Least Terns do not nest, like the western Ozarks, fall transients have been observed from late July through the first week of September, with one peak of seven birds at Lake Sequoyah in Washington County on August 7. At Lonoke a peak of 15 has been reported on August 8. Observations at Lake Millwood in 1980 showed one to five birds present daily from August 21 to September 18. The largest fall report on file involved 34 birds in Arkansas County on August 30. The latest record for the state is on September 21.

BRIDLED TERN, *Sterna anaethetus* Scopoli
  One record.
  This wide-ranging oceanic species occurs

most abundantly along the Atlantic Coast of North America after storms, and it is also known to appear on a casual basis along the Gulf Coast between Florida and Texas (AOU 1983). The Arkansas record involved an adult bird observed by Charles Mills at Lake Millwood in Little River County on September 7, 1985. Mills had the bird under observation for four hours, and was able to compare it directly to Caspian, Forster's, and Black Terns. His written documentation is based upon notes made in the field, and these indicate his ability to separate this species from the similar-appearing Sooty Tern. The appearance of the Bridled Tern seems to have been related to Hurricane Elena, which brought high winds and rain to southwestern Arkansas on September 2 and 3.

SOOTY TERN, *Sterna fuscata* Linnaeus

Two records, both supported by specimens.

One Sooty Tern found dead September 4, 1950, in Van Buren County had been banded as a juvenile at the Dry Tortugas, Florida, nesting colony on June 23, 1938. This recovery followed a hurricane on the Alabama-Mississippi Gulf Coast in late August and another in Florida in early September. Another Sooty Tern, found dead in Cleveland County in September of 1961, had been banded in July of the same year, also at the Dry Tortugas. This recovery followed Hurricane Carla.

BLACK TERN, *Chlidonias niger* (Linnaeus)

Common transient on large open bodies of water in all regions. The most numerous species of tern seen in Arkansas.

SPRING MIGRATION: Black Terns nest well to the north of Arkansas, and pass regularly through the state during migration between breeding and wintering areas. They frequent rivers, lakes, sandbars, and mudflats, and impoundments, and have been seen feeding over plowed fields. There are spring reports in the Audubon Society file mainly between mid-April and mid-June. Small numbers are sometimes reported, and flocks are common. The 80 observed in Prairie County near DeVall's Bluff on April 14 was a large early flight. The largest numbers are seen usually during the last three weeks of May, at which time flights involving 100 or more birds have been reported. Flocks of 172 and 140 Black Terns were seen on May 12 over rice fields in Arkansas County, and an estimated 80 birds were seen at Lake Sequoyah in Washington County on May 19.

Even though Black Terns have been seen in all the summer months in Arkansas, there is no evidence that they have nested in the state. The perceptible gap between sightings in early and late June presumably represents a demarcation between late northward and early southward migration.

FALL MIGRATION: The period for southward migration ranges from late June to the second half of October, chiefly late July to mid-September. At Lake Millwood 10 to 30 birds were seen on most trips between July 30 and September 25, with a peak of 125 on August 21. A total of 228 Black Terns were seen at Lonoke on July 28. The 25 birds at Lake Ouachita in Garland County on August 22 were said to be eating minnows. Six flocks totalling 200 birds were seen on the Mississippi River in Crittenden County on August 13. Deaderick (1938) reported seeing "flights up to one hundred or more" on Lakes Hamilton and Catherine in Garland County. There are only a few rare reports after September, the latest of them involving a single bird at El Dorado in the third week of October.

Subfamily Rynchopinae Skimmers

BLACK SKIMMER, *Rynchops niger* Linnaeus

Three well-documented records.

This species is normally confined to coastal areas but sometimes appears inland, especially after storms. The first report for the state is undated, but involves the 1930s when a bird appeared during a storm, flew into and was caught in a tennis net, at El Dorado. The bird was mounted and placed in the collection of Dr. J. S. Rushing at El Dorado. An individual observed at Calion Lake near El Dorado on October 28, 1968, by K. Luvois Shugart and Jean Niemyer also was collected. W. G. Click, Jr., and others saw one Black Skimmer near Pine Bluff, in Jefferson County, on August 8, 1969, and written documentation was placed on file with the Audubon Society.

Family Alcidae Murrelets

MARBLED MURRELET, *Brachyramphus marmoratus* (Gmelin)

One well-documented record.

An individual identified as this species was observed on November 20 and 21, 1980, at the Denby Point use area on Lake Ouachita, Montgomery County. Photographs were taken and added to written documentation on file with the Audubon Society.

Order COLUMBIFORMES

Family Columbidae
Pigeons and Doves

ROCK DOVE, *Columbia livia* Gmelin

Common permanent resident throughout the state.

This familiar resident of urban areas is also seen far from town, with nesting and roosting activity noted in association with barns, bridges, and cliffs along rivers. Some of the populations that inhabit river cliffs, such as those along the Buffalo River in the Ozarks, occupy quite remote areas.

MOURNING DOVE, *Zenaida macroura* (Linnaeus)

Common permanent resident of forest edge and forest openings in summer, and open fields with waste grains or other seeds in late summer and winter.

BREEDING SEASON: This forest edge and open country species is common during the nesting season in farm areas, and decreases in numbers in relationship to the density of forests (therefore is absent where there are not openings in the forest). Breeding Bird Surveys show that the birds are abundant in that part of

FIGURE 6-54 Mourning Doves at Batesville in mid-October. *David Plank*

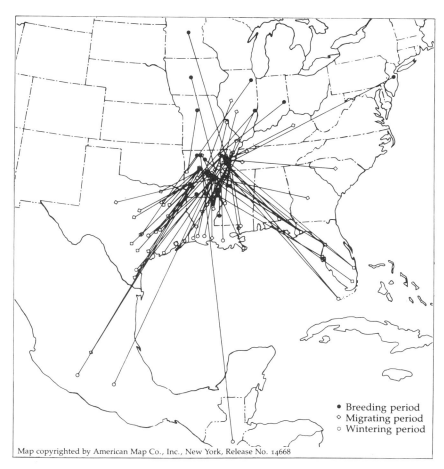

• Breeding period
◇ Migrating period
○ Wintering period

Map copyrighted by American Map Co., Inc., New York, Release No. 14668

FIGURE 6-55 Movements of the Mourning Dove based on banding records.

the state with the highest percentage of cleared land. The average annual mean number per route in each region on the surveys was 18.6 on the Coastal Plain, 48.5 on the Mississippi Alluvial Plain, and 12.6 in the highlands (including the Arkansas River Valley). The overall mean in the Mississippi region was pushed upwards by the mean of 145.1 birds on the survey in Chicot County in the extreme southeast. A summer population study in Benton County (western Ozarks) showed that there were 14 territorial males per one hundred acres of forest edge habitat (Table 3-7).

The nesting season has been observed from March to September. Some of the earliest reports involving nesting include Mourning Doves cooing as early as mid-January at the White River Refuge, and a nest of unspecified status at North Little Rock on March 2. One of the latest records on file with the Audubon Society involved two young about to fledge in Washington County on September 11. In the

Wheeler Collection there are nine clutches of eggs taken from nests between May 9 and June 3. The clutch sizes in these nests varied from one to three eggs, usually two. The nest heights varied from five to twenty-two feet above the ground, often around ten or less, with one unusual nest on the ground. According to Wheeler (1924), "They sometimes raise two and occasionally three broods in a year."

MIGRATION: Although Mourning Doves are usually observed singly or in pairs during spring and early summer, flocks predominate by mid- to late summer and through fall and winter. Large flocks numbering hundreds of individuals are sometimes seen. Banding records associated with 110 birds show that doves found in Arkansas during the breeding season fan out to the south, and migrating and wintering doves in Arkansas come from breeding populations in the midwestern states to the north (Figure 6-55). Distances between banding and recovery have varied from less than 100 miles to about

400 miles, but one bird had traveled at least 1500 miles. About half of the recoveries occurred within the first year following banding, but one bird survived eight years and seven months.

WINTER: An analysis of ten years of Christmas Bird Counts in Arkansas showed a statewide mean number of 1.5 birds per party hour. Regionally this mean varied from 0.3 to 3.1 birds per party hour on the Coastal Plain, 1.3 to 2.9 on the Mississippi Alluvial Plain, and 0.1 to 2.5 in the highlands (including the Arkansas River Valley). Generally the largest numbers are found during cold weather in the southern lowlands. Totals reported on Christmas Counts vary from year to year, but reports of 100 to 200 or more are not uncommon in those areas where there is a sufficiency of open country farm habitat. In Arkansas County the 325 birds seen along 26 miles of road on January 19 apparently had been forced to the roadway by snow and ice in the surrounding fields.

PASSENGER PIGEON, *Ectopistes migratorius* (Linnaeus)

Extinct. Once locally common to abundant in winter.

Passenger Pigeons did not nest in Arkansas, but they were very common and locally abundant in winter. Traveling in the St. Francis River region of northeastern Arkansas in 1751, Bossu (1771) saw huge numbers: "You see, in the daytime, whole clouds of turtle-doves or wood-pigeons . . ." Chronologically, the earliest records for the state involve the bones that have often been found in archeological sites (see Chapter 4). There are also a few migration dates for Arkansas (Schorger 1955, Howell 1911), and these show that the birds were present here from fall through winter into spring. They seemed to have arrived as early as October and departed by April. As late as 1883, Passenger Pigeons were still "very plentiful in winter" around Fayetteville (Howell 1911, Roberts et al. 1942). West of Fayetteville a man netted 2000 Passenger Pigeons and shipped them off to Boston (Schorger 1955), an event showing how large numbers were destroyed in a small period of time. Another such event occurred in White County where in 1879 hunters accidentally set a fire that destroyed a large pigeon roost in-

cluding many birds (Bartsch 1917). Near the White River in northeastern Arkansas, Featherstonhaugh (1835) saw "incredible quantities of wild pigeons . . . flocks of them many miles long . . . their swift motion creating a wind, and producing a rushing and startling sound . . ." Techniques that resulted in the wholesale slaughter of these flocks in large roosts included the use of guns, clubs, and nets. At Wattensas in Lonoke County millions of pigeons once roosted in blackjack oaks (Robinson 1931): "The writer has seen entire wagon loads of these birds slaughtered in one night for food." Another roost at Old Brownsville in Prairie County contained millions of birds in an area of four square miles, and here too the birds were slaughtered. This rate of slaughter helps to explain why the birds became virtually extinct by 1900.

There were some doubtful records for Arkansas as late as 1906, but the last one confirmed was in 1899: "During Christmas week 1899, a merchant in Little Rock received with some quail a male passenger pigeon that had been shipped from Cabot, Arkansas. This bird was placed on display for several days . . ." (Schorger 1955).

INCA DOVE, *Columbina inca* (Lesson)

Rare transient and winter visitor.

Inca Doves are residents of arid or semi-arid lands (including farms and parks) far south and southwest of Arkansas, but they wander casually northward (AOU 1983). The five records in the Audubon Society file are from mid-October to early May. At Saratoga in Howard County, an Inca Dove was seen on several occasions between October 26, 1968, and March 24, 1969. At Pine Bluff one was seen at a feeding station from February 24 to April 26, 1971. The same observer in Pine Bluff also saw an Inca Dove there between December 20, 1971, and March 28, 1972. A single dead bird was found headless at Fayetteville in Washington County on December 3, 1972. The most recent records involved a bird found on a willow sandbar at Murray Park in Little Rock on October 13, 1982, and one photographed at Stuttgart on May 4, 1985.

COMMON GROUND-DOVE, *Columbina passerina* (Linnaeus)

Rare and erratic transient and winter visitor.

This resident of the southern United States (and further south) wanders casually and erratically to the north. For Arkansas there are approximately 20 records involving birds that have been seen primarily in the lowlands and in the central and eastern sections of the Arkansas River Valley. There are reports in the Audubon Society file between mid-August and early May (two to four reports for the months of September, October, December, and April). Most of these have involved single birds, but four were reported in Clay County during the second week of September in 1977. The species has not been reported in the Ozark Plateaus or in the Ouachita Mountains.

Order PSITTACIFORMES

Family Psittacidae Parrots

CAROLINA PARAKEET, *Conuropsis carolinensis* (Linnaeus)

Extinct. Once locally common in the state.

FORMER STATUS: Carolina Parakeets once ranged, often in abundance, throughout the woodlands of the state, especially river bottom or swampland woods, as well as in more open areas. There are records for the state in every season and in every region (McKinley and James 1984).

When Audubon (1929) journeyed down the Mississippi River shoreline bordering Arkansas in 1820 he saw the birds frequently. His journal contains the following entries: November 30, "Parakeets numerous in the woods," December 2–3, "the woods literally filled with parakeets," and finally on December 19, he notes "immense flocks of parakeets." Other travelers who landed south of the Arkansas River in 1833 noted "the small green parrots . . . were flying in thousands about in the wood . . . Our sportsmen came running in every direction . . . carrying on their shoulders a variety of birds, among which the parrots were the most conspicuous, on account of the beauty of their plumes" (Arfwedson 1834). The modern bird enthusiast can only envy the geologist and naturalist George Featherstonhaugh (1844) who visited the Ouachita River area in Clark County during December of 1834 and wrote, "this place is the site of an ancient village of the Caddo Indians, . . . the river contains good fish, the country abounds in game . . . the sun was shining brilliantly, [and] flocks of parroquets were wheeling and screaming around." Bendire (1895) mentioned seeing large flocks in the Fort Smith area of western Arkansas throughout the year, and Widmann (1907) published a report from the year 1888: "at one time paroquets were very plentiful at Paroquet Bluff, between Newport and Batesville on the White River, but none have been seen there for at least eight years."

CAUSES OF EXTINCTION: Howell (1911) noted that Carolina Parakeets fed on "a variety of wild seeds, nuts, fruits, and berries. They were fond also of cultivated fruit and were accused of damaging corn and other grain . . ." which served as a cause for their extermination by man. This view has been challenged, and it now appears that a variety of factors contributed to their extinction, only one of them human activity (McKinley 1980). The last of these birds was seen in the state in 1885 (Howell 1911, McKinley and James 1984). Those who object to the occasional rigors of protective laws such as the federal Endangered Species Act may want to ponder the extinction of this creature.

Order CUCULIFORMES

Family Cuculidae

Subfamily Coccyzinae Cuckoos

BLACK-BILLED CUCKOO, *Coccyzus erythropthalmus* (Wilson)

Uncommon transient in all regions. Very rare summer resident in the north.

SPRING MIGRATION: Northward moving spring migrants have been observed from the fourth week of April through May. Most of these sightings have involved single birds, but occasionally two or three are seen during a day in the field. The three seen on May 14 and 15 in the St. Francis National Forest in Phillips County was a large number.

BREEDING SEASON: This species nests primarily north of the state (AOU 1983), but the birds have been found during the summer and have nested in northern Arkansas. Widmann (1907) published reports of breeding in Cleburne County (in 1888) and Carroll County (in 1906). Baerg (1951) published records of nesting in Benton County (in 1945) and in Carroll County (in 1935). In the Audubon Society file there are additional summer records in Sharp, Boone, Van Buren, Jefferson, and Craighead counties. The Craighead County record involved a bird found dead at Jonesboro on June 26. The only actual nesting details in the Audubon Society file involved Harrison in Boone County where incubation was underway in a nest ten feet high on July 6. The only summer record not in northern Arkansas involved two birds in Jefferson County on August 1 (the status of these birds is not clear).

FALL MIGRATION: Dates for the southward migration period apparently range from August until mid-October. The August dates are problematic because the birds are known to remain on occasion during summer in the northern region of the state. Most fall records have involved single birds, but in Desha County five were seen during a great flight of warblers, tanagers, and other small birds in the first week of October.

YELLOW-BILLED CUCKOO, *Coccyzus americanus* (Linnaeus)

Common migrant and summer resident in open woodlands in all regions.

SPRING MIGRATION: In the Audubon Society file there are reports of single Yellow-billed Cuckoos arriving in the extreme south as early as April 22, and scattered reports, also of single birds, thereafter through late May. The species is common in Arkansas by the second week of May. The eight at Fort Smith on May 10 was a peak. A peak of 14 was reported in a 153-acre census tract at Pine Bluff Arsenal on May 26 (Coffey 1981). Apparently the species arrives earlier (and in larger numbers) some years. On Archer Island in Chicot County (extreme southeastern Arkansas), the first Yellow-billed Cuckoo of the 1981 season was seen on April 12, and the birds were numerous on April 22.

BREEDING SEASON: Reports in the Audubon Society file show that these birds are widespread in the state during summer. Data on the Breeding Bird Surveys suggest that they are most numerous in the lowlands. The average annual mean number per route in each region reported on the surveys was 14.7 birds on the Coastal Plain, 14.0 on the Mississippi Alluvial

Plain, and 9.0 in the highlands (including the Arkansas River Valley). Eleven singing males per one hundred acres of bottomland woods were recorded on a summer population study in southern Arkansas (Table 3-3). Smaller numbers were reported on summer surveys elsewhere in the state.

The nesting season has been observed primarily from late May through September. Apparent courtship has been noticed in Washington County as early as May 6 where one bird was observed as it mounted another and fed it a caterpillar. Nest construction was observed in the same county on May 16. A female sitting on a nest ten feet high was seen in Pope County on May 27. One of the latest reports involved two young just leaving a nest in Hot Spring County on September 18 and 19. Nests fairly late in the season are apparently not uncommon. At Winslow in Washington County, Black (1935a) observed five different nests on September 11, 12, and 16, and all of the young were still in quills. In the Wheeler Collection there are seven clutches of eggs that were taken from nests between June 5 and July 17. The clutch sizes varied from two to six eggs. Heights of the nests varied from five to twenty feet above the ground, and were often fifteen feet or lower. In the file there is a record of one late season nest that was a highly unusual thirty-five to forty feet above the ground. Other nests documented in the file were usually in the range of four to ten feet high.

FALL MIGRATION: During the southward migration in fall this species is seen regularly through September to about mid-October, with records scattered thereafter until about mid-November. A peak involving 15 to 20 birds each day was reported during late August and early September in Bradley County. Also in southern Arkansas, there are several reports involving two or three birds seen on outings during the last week of October and the second week of November. The birds stop singing during September (Baerg 1930a), and they are more difficult to find thereafter. The latest report for the state involved a single bird in the first week of December.

Subfamily *Neomorphinae* Roadrunners

GREATER ROADRUNNER, *Geococcyx californianus* (Lesson)

Local permanent resident in small numbers, chiefly in western and central Arkansas. Observed in clearings associated with farms or lightly urbanized areas, also cedar glades, dry scrubby woods, and rock outcroppings.

BREEDING SEASON: This ground cuckoo of southwestern deserts and grasslands was first reported for Arkansas from Hempstead County in 1936, and by the 1940s there were records in the western quarter of the Arkansas River Valley and in the southwestern lowlands (Baerg 1950). By the 1950s, roadrunners had expanded in a belt stretching from Union County in the southern lowlands to Pulaski County in the Arkansas River Valley. There were also records for the Ozark Plateaus, but these were confined to the northwest quarter of the state. During the 1960s they advanced across the Ozarks to the Mississippi River Basin in the northeast, and in the southern half of the state there were sightings as far east as Jefferson County (James 1968c). In the 1970s, roadrunners were observed in the eastern lowlands as far south as Prairie County. One seen at Lake Georgia-Pacific on the 1978 Christmas Bird Count was the southeasternmost record for the state (Figure 6-56).

The nesting season has been reported from late March through September. The earliest such record involved a nest under construction at the edge of Morrilton in Conway County on March 26 (the young were seen on May 4). A male roadrunner called almost daily during April and May at the edge of an oak-hickory woodland in a lightly urbanized area in Washington County. The latest nesting record in the Audubon Society file involved young that fledged from a nest near Morrilton on September 22. Clutch sizes in four nests have involved three or four eggs (or young). Most nesting dates recorded in the file have involved the period during middle or late summer. This suggests "that the conditions which favor reproduction in April and May in the southwestern states occur here in July and August. Certainly it is drier in Arkansas in late summer" (James 1968c). Four nests were seen in

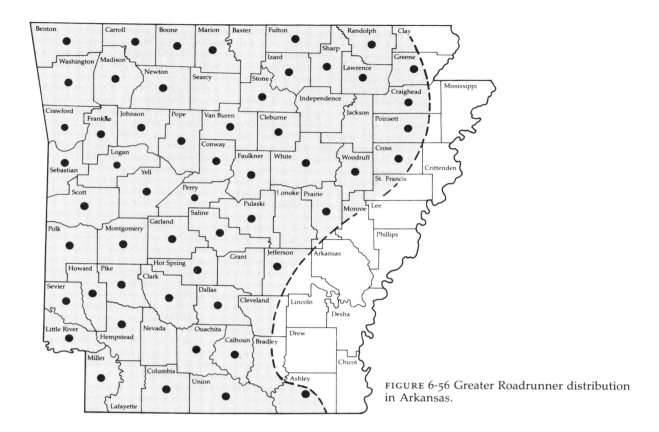

FIGURE 6-56 Greater Roadrunner distribution in Arkansas.

rural situations in central Arkansas, one between twelve to fourteen feet high in a hackberry on a mowed lawn, another was seven feet high on a post covered by a trumpet vine, a third was twelve to fourteen feet high in a pecan tree just fifty yards from a previous nest, and the last was six feet high in a clump of honeysuckle near an occupied farmhouse. A nest that was ten feet high in a cedar tree on a bluff was used two years in a row. The lowest nest was six feet high. Young in one nest were fed a snake.

WINTER: This permanent resident is reported on Christmas Bird Counts in Arkansas every year, with the numbers reported statewide varying often from between six and nine birds. On the statewide 1977 Christmas Bird Counts, for example, one or two birds were reported at Arkadelphia, the Buffalo River, Conway, Fort Smith, and Lake Millwood. On the 1980 Christmas Counts, a total of eight birds reported for the state were seen, six at Mena and two at

Arkadelphia. Lower numbers have been reported in northern Arkansas during recent years. The Missouri population of roadrunners, which is concentrated in the Ozarks bordering northern Arkansas, declined during three seasons of severe winter weather, from 1976–77 through 1978–79 (Norris and Elder 1982). This population decline may have been caused by starvation indirectly brought about by severe winter weather.

Subfamily Crotophaginae Anis

GROOVE-BILLED ANI, *Crotophaga sulcirostris* Swainson

Rare fall visitor.

This resident of scrubby open and partly open country of the southwestern United States, Mexico, and further south, wanders casually north of its permanent range (AOU

1983). All of the eight sightings in Arkansas since the 1950s are in the fall between the second half of September and late November, and most reports are from western Arkansas as far north as Fort Smith. The first state record was established when a male with a stomach full of grasshoppers was collected from a snag on the border of a brushy field in Arkansas County on September 21 (Meanley and Neff 1953a). Most reports have involved single birds, but occasionally a few more are seen: two in Sevier County on November 25, three at Fort Smith on November 17, and four on October 10 (different years).

Order STRIGIFORMES

Family *Tytonidae* Barn-Owls

COMMON BARN-OWL, *Tyto alba* (Scopoli)

Permanent resident in small numbers in all regions, especially in the eastern lowlands. Several migration records.

BREEDING SEASON: In the Audubon Society file and in the published record (Hanebrink 1980, Howell 1911, Mattocks and Shugart 1962) there are numerous reports for the breeding season essentially throughout the Mississippi Alluvial Plain and on the Coastal Plain. There are several nesting records for the Arkansas River Valley in Faulkner and Pulaski counties (file, Johnson 1979). In the highlands there is a confirmed nesting record for Garland County in the Ouachita Mountains and several additional records (file, Deaderick 1938), plus several reports in April and in summer for the western Ozarks (file, Baerg 1951, Shugart and James 1973).

Nesting activity has been reported from Feb-

FIGURE 6-57 Common Barn-Owl. *Sigrid James Bruch*

ruary through June. The earliest record of nesting involved eggs and young that were found when a tree blew over in a storm at Stuttgart in Arkansas County on February 7. Three eggs were seen in a nest at the base of a chimney near Marvel in Phillips County on March 15 (later two more eggs were found); the first egg hatched on April 11 and by May 28 five young were present in this nest. A nest on top of a bridge in Miller County had three eggs on April 5. There are several June nest records: a nest with eggs was found near St. Charles in Arkansas County on June 8. Jane Gulley, a raptor rehabilitator, obtained five birds of varying ages (from downy young to near fledgling) that were in a nest in a grain elevator at Roe in Monroe County in June. Between 1981 and 1983 Gulley received Common Barn-Owls from the following locations: Arkansas County (young associated with two nests); Pulaski County (one nest; also three young birds killed near the runway of the Little Rock airport); Garland County (injured juvenile); Monroe County (nest); Clark County (mature bird injured by shotgun pellets).

BANDING: Migration of this species into Arkansas is documented by three banding records (Stewart 1952, James 1967): a juvenile banded in summer in Wisconsin was recovered in Arkansas during spring three years later, and birds banded during summer in Pennsylvania and Ohio were recovered a few months later in southeastern and central-eastern Arkansas, respectively.

WINTER: This species is seen during most if not every winter in the state, especially in the lowlands. At Lonoke, the birds were reported on about half of the Christmas Bird Counts between the early 1960s and the early 1980s (maximum of three birds in one year). There are several Christmas Count records for Texarkana in southwestern Arkansas (one or two birds in 1966, 1972, 1976, 1980, 1981). There are winter records for the northeast (Hanebrink 1980) and there are reports in the file for Arkansas, Clark, and Prairie counties. In the Arkansas River Valley there are Christmas Count records for Fort Smith and Conway, and a winter record for Johnson County. Observers in the Ouachitas and Ozarks have not reported barn-owls in winter.

FOOD HABITS: Dissection of forty-five Common Barn-Owl pellets collected from the floor of the press box at Indian Stadium on the campus of Arkansas State University at Jonesboro (Paige, et al. 1979) showed that the birds were eating the southern bog lemming *Synaptomys cooperi* (54 percent of the pellets), followed by the cotton rat *Sigmodon hispidis,* and voles (*Microtus* spp.). A rat was in the talons of a bird hit by a car at Pine Bluff on November 26.

Family Strigidae Owls

EASTERN SCREECH-OWL, *Otus asio* (Linnaeus)

Common permanent resident in mature woodlands, including those of urban areas in all regions.

BREEDING SEASON: In the Audubon Society file there are summer reports for these birds throughout the state. Nesting activity has been reported from late February to late May. Mating has been observed as early as February 26 (Baerg 1951). The latest records that involve nesting include a young bird that fell out of a nest at Hamburg in Ashley County on May 26, and young birds being fed out of the nest at Fayetteville on May 30. In the Wheeler Collection there are seven clutches of eggs that were taken from nests between March 27 and April 30. The clutch sizes varied from three to five eggs (average 3.7). Nest heights varied from fifteen to fifty feet above the ground, often around fifteen feet. In the Audubon Society file there is a record of a nest eight feet from the ground in Miller County. At Fort Smith the birds were said to have utilized a nesting box.

WINTER: Eastern Screech-Owls are reported in small numbers on Christmas Bird Counts in all regions of the state. While normally silent during winter (and therefore more difficult to detect), screech-owls will sometimes answer an imitation of their distinctive call. This method is used to find them on the Christmas Counts. While most reports on Christmas Bird Counts usually involve five or fewer of these birds, there are several peaks of as many as 12 and 13 at Little Rock in recent years.

ADDITIONAL NOTES: In northeastern Arkansas, 84 percent of the diet of the screech-owls collected during fall and winter was insec-

FIGURE 6-58 Great Horned Owl. *David Plank*

tivorous (Hanebrink, et al. 1979). Both the gray and the red color phases have been found in the state.

GREAT HORNED OWL, *Bubo virginianus* (Gmelin)

Common permanent resident throughout the state. Inhabits both extensive, mature forests and the broken woods of farm clearings, lightly urbanized towns, and other types of openings which blend into mature forest.

BREEDING SEASON: Nesting activity has been reported between late December and April. The earliest breeding report is from Jefferson County where a pair with a com-

pleted nest were copulating on December 24, and incubation of eggs was under way by January 10. In the Wheeler Collection there is one clutch of two eggs taken from a nest forty feet above the ground on January 18 and a second clutch of three eggs taken from another nest thirty feet high on February 3. At Lake Fayetteville newly hatched young were seen in a nest on January 29. At Fort Smith, three eggs seen on March 3 had just hatched by March 20. A nest in Independence County had young just about ready to fledge in late April (Harris and Hanebrink 1980).

The Independence County record involved an old crow's nest almost forty-nine feet high in an eastern red cedar in an old fencerow associated with broken oak woods and a small meadow. Food items fed the young included numerous Common Grackles, one Blue Jay, one Northern Mockingbird, one Northern Flicker, three rabbits, and a mole (Harris and Hanebrink 1980). In northwestern Arkansas, young were reared in a nest that had been used by a Red-tailed Hawk the previous year.

WINTER: This species is regularly reported, usually in small numbers, on Christmas Bird Counts in all regions. On twelve recent Christmas Counts at Fayetteville the number varied from one to eleven, with five or more reported in nine years. On the statewide 1980 Christmas Counts the birds were reported in ten of the seventeen count areas, with a peak of five birds at Fort Smith.

SNOWY OWL, *Nyctea scandiaca* (Linnaeus)
Four records.

This owl of the tundra breeds far north of Arkansas in a vast area that includes Siberia, Alaska, Canada, Greenland, and Scandinavia (AOU 1983). During certain sporadic "flight" years it moves south of its normal wintering area and small numbers reach the southeastern United States, including Arkansas. A mounted bird found in a hardware store at Pine Bluff in 1956 was one of two seen by Charles Hunter of Moscow, Jefferson County, about ten years before. A mounted specimen in the home of James Mauldin of Quitman, Faulkner County, was taken in mid-November 1954. A bird was observed January 4, 1955, at Morrilton in Conway County, and reported by Ruth Thomas in her *Arkansas Gazette* "Country Diarist" column dated January 16, 1955. Audubon (1831–39) published a secondhand report of a bird seen during winter along the Arkansas River that could have been this species. The Pine Bluff specimen is in the University of Arkansas museum collection.

BURROWING OWL, *Athene cunicularia* (Molina)
Somewhat irregular migrant and winter resident in small numbers, chiefly on the Mississippi Alluvial Plain.

This species found in open western grasslands has been seen in Arkansas between the last week of September and the last week of March, and once as late as May 30. The first Arkansas record was in mid-February of 1937 when a bird banded in South Dakota during summer was recovered in Arkansas seven months later, 800 miles from the banding site (Cooke 1941). Two birds and three burrows were found at Lonoke on October 28, 1962, and the birds were last observed at this location on March 3, 1963. "The Lonoke birds were known to be new arrivals in the fields where they were found because these same fields had been investigated several times annually prior to autumn 1962" (James 1964). As many as three birds were observed in the same fields from October 6, 1963, to March 1, 1964. In subsequent years, single Burrowing Owls have been reported in Lonoke, Cross, Mississippi, Crittenden, Jefferson, and Craighead counties, and at Holla Bend Refuge in Pope County. The Craighead County record was from the Jonesboro airport, where Ben Coffey found them in the early 1960s. The bird in Mississippi County occupied a ten-inch highway culvert for apparently no more than one week. In January of 1983 single Burrowing Owls were observed at the Stuttgart airport in Prairie County and on the Roth Prairie in Arkansas County, and a bird was seen again at the Stuttgart airport in January of 1985. The single bird at Wapanocca Refuge in Crittenden County in late May of 1983 could not be found thereafter.

BARRED OWL, *Strix varia* Barton
Common permanent resident in all regions that is especially numerous in extensive forested swamps and river bottom woods in the lowlands. Present in forested upland ravines and river bottom woods of the highlands.

BREEDING SEASON: There are relatively few actual records of nests. The earliest such record involved a juvenile still in the "downy fluff" stage that fell from a nest in Clark County in late March (three other young were also found in this nest). At Boyle Park in Little Rock, young were seen high in a cavity of a dead limb on a tree on April 7. Five birds, among them several immatures, were seen in a canebrake in a stream bottom in Washington County on July 5. Begging young have been heard in mid-July along the Buffalo River in Newton County.

FIGURE 6-59 Barred Owl. *Max Parker*

WINTER: Small numbers of Barred Owls are reported regularly on Christmas Bird Counts in all regions of the state. Usually these reports involve fewer than six birds on a single Christmas Count. In recent years the largest numbers have often been found at Arkadelphia. On Christmas Counts between 1968 and 1983 the numbers reported there have varied from two to twelve Barred Owls, with eight or more in seven years. Smaller numbers are typically found in a highlands situation like the Fayetteville area in the western Ozarks, but even here there have been a few peak numbers on Christmas Counts involving as many as six to eight.

LONG-EARED OWL, *Asio otus* (Linnaeus)

Rare transient and winter resident in all regions.

This species found in coniferous or mixed coniferous-hardwood forests has been reported in Arkansas about a dozen times since 1962, between early November and May (Audubon Society file, Hanebrink 1980). These reports include both the lowlands and the highlands, and often involved single birds. Approximately half of the recent records have involved injured birds, or birds found killed along highways. Two birds were observed repeatedly near Pine City in Monroe County between December 23, 1980, and February 14, 1981. Four birds were seen in a dense grove of young pines east of Rogers in Benton County on April 4, 1959. Six birds were found roosting in cedars at Holla Bend Refuge on February 17, 1985, and were seen regularly there into March. Earlier in this century Long-eared Owls were considered a "fairly common winter visitant" in the Fayetteville area (Black 1933b). Before 1900 the birds were said to be breeding at Newport in Jackson County and were "resident" at Clinton in Van Buren County (Howell 1911). A bird was said to be a "permanent resident" near Texarkana (Wheeler 1924). Birds were reported during May and July in Saline County (Baerg 1951).

SHORT-EARED OWL, *Asio flammeus* (Pontoppidan)

Migrant and winter resident observed in all regions in open country such as prairies, pastures, agricultural fields, and airports. Some-times locally common, especially at a few locations on the Grand Prairie.

STATUS: Short-eared Owls have been observed from late October to late April (Audubon Society file, Hanebrink 1980), mainly from the second half of November through February. Many of these reports have involved single birds, or occasionally small flocks. The largest numbers are seen on the Grand Prairie in eastern Arkansas. During the 1950s Brooke Meanley considered them "abundant" around blackbird roosts and they were otherwise "common winter residents" in Arkansas County (file). Ben Coffey (1955a) also found them regularly at a blackbird roost on President's Island, just across the Mississippi River from Crittenden County. A party of observers counted 15 Short-eared Owls in Arkansas County on January 15, 1957, and 8 to 10 were flushed when a prairie near Stuttgart (Arkansas County) was burned on February 28, 1980. This species has also been observed on several occasions at Holla Bend Refuge in the Arkansas River Valley, at the Jonesboro airport, in the open country of the western Ozarks, on the Christmas Bird Count at Arkadelphia (one or two birds regularly since 1977), and at a few other locations in the state. In the western Ozarks of Benton County these birds were seen regularly between December 4 and March 25 during a "small invasion" that was apparently "in response to a heavy infestation of cotton rats which also attracted marsh hawks and other raptorial birds" (Baerg 1951). Single injured birds found in the western Ozarks area were taken to Joe and Vivian Stockton (raptor rehabilitators) in November 1980 and January 1982.

FOOD HABITS: An analysis of ninety pellets collected in a Short-eared Owl roost in Arkansas County (Smith and Hanebrink 1982) showed that about 50 percent of the prey items were small birds (chiefly Common Grackle, Red-winged Blackbird, Horned Lark, European Starling, and Eastern Meadowlark), and about 45 percent were small mammals (voles, harvest mice, cotton rats, and deer mice). "Results of this study are not meant to suggest short-eared owls . . . were selecting and utilizing birds over mammals as prey. To the contrary, short-eared owls appear to be opportunistic as evidenced by the wide range of prey consumed."

NORTHERN SAW-WHET OWL, *Aegolius acadicus* (Gmelin)

Rare transient and winter visitor.

The primary breeding range of this small species of owl lies north of Arkansas, but it has nested east, west, and south of the state, and winters irregularly south in a large area that encompasses Arkansas (AOU 1983). Its nocturnal habits, small size, and apparent preference for the dense vegetation of pines, mixed pine and hardwood forests, or cedar groves all suggest that it may easily go undetected. A single bird was collected in Jefferson County on November 11, 1959. One was seen in the Shores Lake area of the Ozark National Forest in Franklin County on January 30, 1967. A photographer for the *Arkansas Gazette* photographed one in Little Rock on November 7, 1969, as it perched on a street sign. An owl banded in Wisconsin on October 14, 1969, was recovered in Clay County on December 12 of the same year. An injured bird was found in Pulaski County on November 25, 1975. One was found dead in Poinsett County on November 22, 1976.

Order CAPRIMULGIFORMES

Family Caprimulgidae

Subfamily Chordeilinae Nighthawks

COMMON NIGHTHAWK, *Chordeiles minor* (Forster)

Common migrant and summer resident in open areas, including towns and cities, in all regions. Very rare or absent in heavily forested areas.

SPRING MIGRATION: Nighthawks sometimes arrive by the second week of April, but most "spring first" sightings occur in the fourth week of April and thereafter, with some migration continuing into the second half of May. There is one highly unusual early record involving a single bird seen at Conway in Faulkner County on March 19. The 50 birds at Farmington in Washington County on May 23 was a large spring flock.

BREEDING SEASON: During the nesting season nighthawks are seen as they fly or roost during the daytime, or are heard as they fly through the night sky catching insects. The daytime Breeding Bird Surveys provide little information about the abundance and distribution of these birds, but reports in the Audubon Society file show that they are well distributed in appropriate habitat in all regions of the state.

Nesting activity has been reported from the second week of May to early July. In the Wheeler Collection there is one clutch of two eggs taken from a nest on bare ground on May 12. A nighthawk was incubating two eggs at Pine Bluff Arsenal on May 30. At Mammoth Spring in Fulton County one egg was hatching on July 1. Nests have been found in gravelly places on flat ground and on flat, gravelled

building roofs in towns. Nighthawks are most common in urban areas because of the large amount of suitable nesting habitat provided by flat gravelled roofs of buildings in proximity to concentrations of nocturnal insects attracted to street lights.

FALL MIGRATION: Post-breeding season flocks have been reported as early as the second week of July, but the largest numbers are usually observed from late August into the second week of October, with a peak in September. During September, flocks numbering up to several hundred individual birds are reported, and in Lincoln County an estimated 1000 were seen on September 11, 1965. The latest sighting for the state was in early November.

Subfamily Caprimulginae Nightjars

CHUCK-WILL'S-WIDOW, *Caprimulgus carolinensis* Gmelin

Common migrant and summer resident in all regions. Inhabits open, relatively dry woodlands and forest edge associated with farmlands, and other types of forest openings. More numerous in Arkansas than the Whippoor-will, whose range it overlaps in the highlands and in a few other upland areas.

SPRING MIGRATION: The two birds heard in Union County in the extreme south on March 31 (one on March 30) were early arrivals, but there are additional scattered records of one or two birds between late March and the second week of April in all regions. The numbers reported increase markedly during the third and fourth weeks of April. The six heard near Cass in Franklin County on April 20 was a high early spring number, as were the eight at Mt. Sherman in Newton County on April 26. By late April and early May the birds have become numerous in those areas with appropriate habitat.

BREEDING SEASON: In the Audubon Society file there are summer records in every region. The birds seem to be most numerous in extensive, open river valleys, and adjoining slopes. In Van Buren County, Pleas (1890b) wrote that he found them in "open, sterile, rocky ground bordering the hillsides. . . . Of a hundred or more which I have traced out in the moonlight, every one was perched on the ground, a rock, a log, or occasionally on a low limb while singing." Results obtained on a summer population study in northeastern Arkansas showed that there were 30 singing males per one hundred acres of woods on the Crowley's Ridge uplands, and none in the adjoining bottomland woods (Tables 3-1 and 3-3).

Breeding Bird Surveys, which start at daylight, cannot provide accurate tabulations of population levels. In place of these daytime surveys, counts are sometimes conducted by driving along roads at night. Regular stops are made and the numbers of singing birds tabulated. During the past several decades Ben and Lula Coffey of Memphis have conducted these "whip-chuck" counts in Pope and Searcy counties, and elsewhere in Arkansas. On a May 1977 count in Searcy County they found 55 singing "chucks" at thirty-one stops along sixteen miles of highway, and in June 1979 in Clay County they reported 109 "chucks" on forty-seven stops along 34 miles of highway.

Nesting activity has been reported from late April through July. Eggs are laid in faint depressions among leaves on the ground. In the Wheeler Collection there are seven clutches of eggs with two eggs each collected between April 28 and June 6. There are additional nesting reports in the Audubon Society file involving eggs in the first part of July. At least five nests in the file were found in dry open woodlands where cedars are common, and the eggs were frequently placed below the cedars.

FALL MIGRATION: After these birds cease their characteristic singing between late July (Baerg 1930a) and early September (file), they are exceedingly difficult to find and hence their status in late summer and early fall is, relatively speaking, poorly known. The single bird found in Union County on October 9 is by five weeks the latest record for the state.

WHIP-POOR-WILL, *Caprimulgus vociferus* Wilson

Migrant in all regions, and summer resident in the highlands and the bordering foothills.

SPRING MIGRATION: This species has occasionally been heard as early as the last days of March, but there are many more initial reports in the first week of April and thereafter. In Arkansas County the birds were said to be common in migration along the Arkansas River by April 4. At Fayetteville in Washington County, four were heard singing on April 2. In the high elevation forests on White Rock Mountain in Franklin County, dozens were singing on April 30, with the numbers declining sharply thereafter. In Union County (in southern Arkansas where the species does not breed) the latest spring report is in the first week of May (Mattocks and Shugart 1962).

BREEDING SEASON: This northern member of the nightjar family (*Caprimulgidae*) ranges throughout the Arkansas highlands, especially the Ozark Plateaus and the Ouachita Mountains, and is found in the foothills of the Arkansas River Valley, in upland situations like Crowley's Ridge on the Mississippi Alluvial Plain, and in the foothills of the Coastal Plain bordering the Ouachitas (Figure 6-60). The ranges of this species and the similar appearing (but different sounding) Chuck-will's-widow overlap in Arkansas. At higher elevations in the Ouachitas and the Ozarks, Whip-poor-wills outnumber Chuck-will's-widows, with the case being reversed at lower elevations, especially along river valleys. Both species need openings in the forest (such as those associated with farm clearings and road rights-of-way) for their nighttime foraging, and are therefore absent from areas where the forest canopy is extensive and closed.

Rough assessments of the populations breeding in the state are made by traveling in appropriate areas during hours of darkness and stopping to listen for the distinctive calls. "Whip-chuck" counts made by Ben and Lula Coffey and others have resulted in some interesting and scientifically valuable records. In the

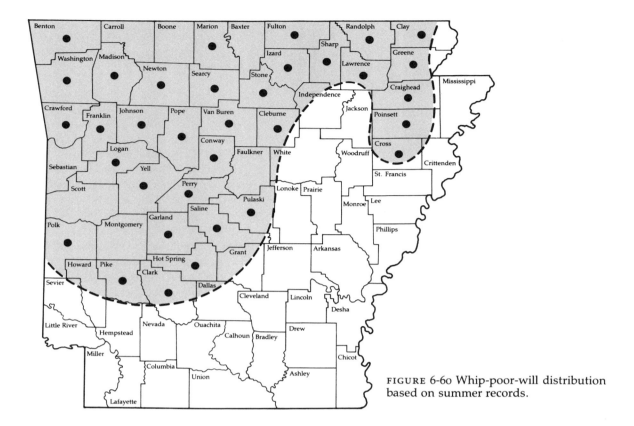

FIGURE 6-60 Whip-poor-will distribution based on summer records.

Ozarks of Pope County, the Coffeys found 50 "whips" and 21 "chucks" along twenty-three miles of highway in May of 1977. During a similar period on Crowley's Ridge in Clay County they found 10 "whips" and 109 "chucks" along thirty-four miles. In the rolling foothills of southern Hot Spring County, Max and Helen Parker heard 18 "whips" over four miles of road in May of 1983. There are also unusual summer records in the Audubon Society file for eastern Saline County in habitat that is typical of the flat pinelands of the Coastal Plain.

There are very few actual nest records for this secretive species. An adult was brooding two hatchlings on a rugged hillside near an old farm clearing above Lee Creek in Washington County on May 11. A nest with two eggs was observed in Pope County on May 19 (Wheeler 1924). Two hatchlings were seen at Camp Orr in Newton County on June 17.

FALL MIGRATION: Singing is heard during August and September (latest date September 24), but thereafter the birds are very rarely reported and their fall movements in Arkansas are poorly known. The latest record involved a bird that was hit by a train in Craighead County on October 10.

Order APODIFORMES

Family Apodidae

Subfamily Chaeturinae Swifts

CHIMNEY SWIFT, *Chaetura pelagica*
(Linnaeus)

Common migrant and summer resident in all regions. Especially numerous in urban areas where it finds chimneys for roosting and nesting.

SPRING MIGRATION: Chimney Swifts have arrived in Arkansas as early as the second week of March, and large flocks are sometimes seen late in the month: 75 at Pine Bluff on March 26, and 30 at Little Rock on March 27. Numbers increase thereafter with peaks by mid-April. At Stuttgart, 300 were "bowling over one building" on April 11, and 500 were reported at Little Rock on April 15.

BREEDING SEASON: In the Audubon Society file there are summer reports from all regions. The average annual mean number per route in each region of Chimney Swifts on the Breeding Bird Surveys was 7.1 on the Coastal Plain, 2.7 on the Mississippi Alluvial Plain, and 9.5 in the highlands (including the Arkansas River Valley). The highlands average was affected by the annual mean of 64.6 birds on the survey in Sebastian County that includes the Fort Smith area.

The nesting season has been reported from early May to early August. At Hamburg in Ashley County a nest was being constructed on May 7. In the Wheeler Collection there is one record of a clutch of four eggs taken from a nest fifteen feet down in a chimney on June 21. In Texarkana, four eggs were taken from a nest

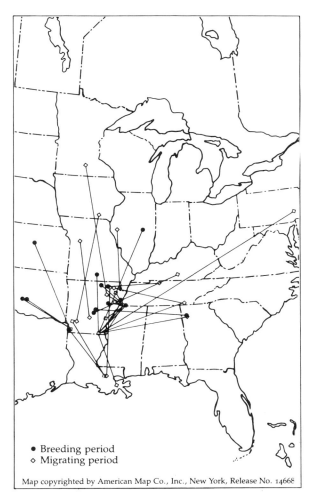

● Breeding period
◇ Migrating period

Map copyrighted by American Map Co., Inc., New York, Release No. 14668

FIGURE 6-61 Movements of the Chimney Swift based on banding records.

on June 22. At Fayetteville, young were still being fed in a nest on August 3. While chimneys furnish the usual nesting site, in former times the birds also utilized hollow trees (Pleas 1890b).

FALL ROOSTS AND MIGRATION: During fall, Chimney Swifts gather in enormous roosts that may involve hundreds or even thousands of individuals. At Pine Bluff Arsenal the swift population at a chimney one fall was comprised of three birds at mid-August, 225 at mid-September, 1250 at mid-October, and none thereafter. At Fayetteville more than 1000 birds entered a single large chimney in mid-October. At Jonesboro, an amazing 8000 were reported on October 13. There are, in addition, several records in the file involving one or a few birds into early November.

BANDING: At Memphis, Tennessee, just across the Mississippi River from Arkansas, Ben Coffey and others banded Chimney Swifts for years. Among recoveries of these banded swifts have been several from Peru (Coffey 1981). One bird banded at Memphis on September 25, 1954, was recovered on November 7 of the same year at Trujillo, Peru. Many birds originally banded at Memphis have been recovered at the same city in subsequent years. There are additional recoveries associated with Arkansas (Figure 6-61).

Subfamily Apodinae Swifts

WHITE-THROATED SWIFT, *Aeronautes saxatalis* (Woodhouse)

Two records, including one specimen.

Gregg (1935) reported a bird that was collected on the eleventh floor of an office building in Hot Springs, Garland County, on May 4, 1935. The specimen is now in the U.S. National Museum. A White-throated Swift was observed on December 19, 1981, from Big Bluff, above the Buffalo River in Newton County. The bird was seen by several experienced observers, and written documentation is on file with the Audubon Society.

Family Trochilidae Hummingbirds

GREEN VIOLET-EAR, *Colibri thalassinus* (Swainson)

One record.

This hummingbird occurs very rarely north of Mexico, having been found a few times in Texas and once in California (AOU 1983). On October 7, 1984, William B. Brazelton photographed one when it made a visit of a few seconds duration to a hummingbird feeder at Fort Smith. The photograph showed a hummingbird that was bright green with a dark violet patch behind and below the eye. The green rump graded into bluish and purplish on the tail with a dark, dusky band across the lower tail and lighter tail feather tips. The beak was nearly straight and relatively short. The bird was large, roughly half again larger than the size of the smaller Ruby-throated Hummingbird that Brazelton photographed at the same feeder. After two brief appearances the bird was not seen again.

The bird's pose was such that the chin was darkened. Thus there was the unlikely chance that the photograph showed the Sparkling Violet-ear (*C. coruscans*), which has not been found north of Colombia. Since the bird was photographed in profile, the beak was measured using a fine comparator scale laid directly on the transparency viewed through a dissecting microscope. Measurements of the beak compared to measurements of known dimensions of the hummingbird feeder were used to calculate a bill length of 16.58 mm. This was at the lower end of the bill length range for the smaller Green Violet-ear. Steven W. Cardiff at Louisiana State University measured the beaks of both species in the collection there for use in the analysis. His data showed that the range in bill measurements in the two species do not overlap. (The photographic and written documentation are on file with the Arkansas Audubon Society.)

RUBY-THROATED HUMMINGBIRD, *Archilochus colubris* (Linnaeus)

Common migrant and summer resident in all regions.

SPRING MIGRATION: These birds have arrived in the southern lowlands as early as the second week of March, but the first arrivals are not usually observed until the last of March or early April. Further north the first arrivals are not usually seen until the second week of April, and thereafter. The average arrival date for a twenty-three year period in the 19th century in Fayetteville was April 20, with dates varying between April 10 and April 28 (Smith 1844–86). The 16 birds counted in Prairie and White counties on April 14 was a peak for spring.

BREEDING SEASON: Reports in the file and on the Breeding Bird Surveys show that this species is present throughout the state in summer. The average annual mean number per route in each region reported on the Breeding Bird Surveys was 0.7 on the Coastal Plain, 1.2 on the Mississippi Alluvial Plain, and 0.5 in the highlands (including the Arkansas River Valley).

Nesting activity has been observed from late April to mid-August. The earliest nest record in the file was at Boyle Park in Little Rock on April 27, but this nest was abandoned after rain. In the Wheeler Collection there are four clutches of eggs taken from nests between May 4 and July 22. Two of these nests held two eggs each and were eight to twenty-three feet above the ground (detailed information was not available on the other two nests). In Washington County in 1982, four active nests of unspecified status were observed between June 20 and July 29. The latest nesting report in the file involved an immature bird still in the nest at Walnut Ridge in Lawrence County on August 14. Nests are usually exposed from below, but are shielded above by a canopy of leaves. They are often found in moist ravines or stream bottoms in forested areas and are frequently constructed on a horizontal limb or on the small fork of a limb. An unusual nest in Logan County on May 5 was attached to the top of a pinecone. Nest heights on file have varied from twelve to forty feet above the ground.

FALL MIGRATION: Late fall dates are presumably greatly influenced by the presence of feeding stations, but enough information independent of these feeding stations shows that the peak period for migration is in September. Near Fort Smith, 43 immatures and or females were observed as they perched on a wire between September 6 and 9. At Gunner's Pool in Stone County, 10 or more hummingbirds were feeding on jewelweed in one small area on September 20. There are scattered reports for the state into December.

RUFOUS HUMMINGBIRD, *Selasphorus rufus* (Gmelin)

One definite record, plus several additional sightings of birds in the genus *Selasphorus.*

The occurrence of this species in Arkansas has been suspected for a number of years. While it is common in the western United States, it ranges only on a casual basis into the eastern half of the country (AOU 1983). At least five birds generally fitting the description of the genus *Selasphorus* have been seen at hummingbird feeders in the state between late August and January, but positive evidence was lacking until a specimen was recovered in January 1985. According to Thomas Foti and Jane Stern, the bird was first seen at a feeder in Pine Bluff on October 25, 1984. Attempts to capture the bird alive (in order to make positive identification) were unsuccessful. However, the bird was found frozen on January 23, 1985, and identification was made at the Louisiana State University Museum of Zoology, where the specimen was deposited. The extreme difficulty in field (rather than in hand) identification of *Selasphorus* hummingbirds has been emphasized (Conway and Drennan 1979).

Order CORACIIFORMES

Family Alcedinidae Kingfishers

BELTED KINGFISHER, *Ceryle alcyon*
(Linnaeus)

Permanent resident in all regions. Common along larger streams, and the shorelines of lakes and impoundments.

BREEDING SEASON: Reports in the Audubon Society file and on Breeding Bird Surveys show that kingfishers are present regularly in small numbers during summer throughout the state. Nesting burrows have been reported from the last week of April to mid-June. A nest was seen in a dirt bank along the Buffalo River in Marion County on April 25. In the Wheeler Collection there are three clutches of six to seven eggs that were taken from nests between April 25 and June 13. Two of these nests were in banks on the Arkansas River, and the third was in a ravine bank near the Ouachita River. In Stone County, young were being fed in a burrow on May 18. In Benton County, a pair of kingfishers were excavating a cavity in a dirt bank associated with a large, deep ditch cut through an open field several hundred yards from the Illinois River in late May.

MIGRATION AND WINTER: Since kingfishers are usually seen singly or in pairs, their migratory habits are more difficult to ascertain than those of a more obviously migratory species that congregate in big flocks. Nevertheless, reports in the file indicate that they are more numerous during winter than in summer. These records may involve the presence of birds all winter in places where they are not seen in summer, or they may involve influxes in numbers. For example, one observer in Union County noted increases in numbers between September and December, with one peak involving 10 birds on October 22. The 11 seen in Garland County on November 24 also seems to have been an influx.

Kingfishers are commonly reported in impressive numbers on those Christmas Bird Counts in the state where there is a sufficiency of suitable aquatic habitat. On twelve recent counts at Fayetteville, the numbers reported have varied from 5 to 26, with 15 or more counted in half the years. There are similar reports at Conway in central Arkansas, and elsewhere in the state. On the 1979 statewide counts a total of 175 birds were reported, with numbers varying from 2 to 23 birds on counts in the twenty participating locales.

Order PICIFORMES

Family Picidae Woodpeckers

LEWIS' WOODPECKER, *Melanerpes lewis* (Gray)

One record.

A single bird was seen on Mt. Sequoyah at Fayetteville, Washington County, between June 30 and July 3, 1967. The bird was observed by numerous individuals, and documentation was placed in the Audubon Society file.

RED-HEADED WOODPECKER, *Melanerpes erythrocephalus* (Linnaeus)

Permanent resident that is common in all regions. During periodic migrations low numbers are reported in some areas in winter. Inhabits mature or overmature forests, woodlots, or similar places where there are large dead trees.

MIGRATION: While Red-headed Woodpeckers can usually be found throughout the year where they are known to nest, there are periodic migrations, and in some of these migration years the birds are uncommon or even rare in some areas during winter (see WINTER below). During mid-September of 1983, a general movement of this species was evident in the western Ozarks, with birds seen in many different places and in much higher numbers than usual. In Benton County, more than 40 birds were counted as they flew south, one or two at a time, or in small flocks. At Winslow in Washington County, small numbers of migrating birds were seen during September and early October and in the last week of April (Smith 1915). About 80 percent were immatures.

Some migrants in Arkansas have come considerable distances. Three birds banded as far away as Ohio and Indiana were recovered in Arkansas during late fall and winter. The longest time between banding and recovery was one and one-half years.

BREEDING SEASON: There are reports in the Audubon Society file for all the regions during summer. The average annual mean number per route in each region on the Breeding Bird Surveys was 3.4 on the Coastal Plain, 4.6 on the Mississippi Alluvial Plain, and 1.0 in the highlands (including the Arkansas River Valley). Peak means of 19.2 and 9.1 were reported on the surveys in Lincoln and Lafayette counties, respectively.

Nesting activity has been observed from early May to August. The earliest record in the Audubon Society file involved a male and a female at a nest on May 8 at Little Rock. In the Wheeler Collection there are five clutches of eggs taken from nests between May 11 and June 28. The clutch sizes varied from four to six eggs (averaging about five), and the heights of the nests varied from eight to sixteen feet above the ground. The latest record of nesting activity involved young being fed out of the nest on August 28. Many of the cavity trees utilized by this species are devoid, or largely devoid, of bark. A nest in one such tree on the University of Arkansas campus at Fayetteville was thirty to thirty-five feet from the ground. The removal of these old snags (or mature trees with dead limbs) from urban areas means a reduction in the numbers of these beautiful and interesting birds, as well as other species of animals (screech-owls, flying squirrels, etc.) that require snags for roosting and nesting.

WINTER: Red-headed Woodpeckers appear to be opportunistic in their migratory habits, disappearing completely (or nearly so) in years of poor acorn crops, and remaining abundant during other years (Smith 1986a). The linkage of migration to oak productivity is apparent at Fayetteville where the number of birds reported on Christmas Bird Counts seems to vary with the abundance of acorns. On twelve recent Christmas Counts there, the number of birds reported varied from 1 to 55, with sharp drops in the population occurring every three to four years, mainly when fall acorn crops were low. The numbers of birds in an area will also vary depending upon the amount of standing dead timber.

The ten-year statewide mean number of birds observed on the Christmas Bird Counts was 0.4 bird per party hour. This varied from 0.2 to 1.1 on the Coastal Plain, 0.3 to 1.2 on the Mississippi Alluvial Plain, and 0.1 to 0.5 in the highlands (including the Arkansas River Valley). Reports of 20 or more birds are fairly common on Christmas Counts in every region, and there are scattered records of more than 100, including one of 187 birds at White River Refuge.

RED-BELLIED WOODPECKER, *Melanerpes carolinus* (Linnaeus)

Common permanent resident in woodlands in all regions, especially river bottom woods. Regular visitor to feeding stations in wooded urban areas if suet or sunflower seeds are offered.

BREEDING SEASON: Breeding Bird Surveys show that this species is common and well distributed in Arkansas during summer. The average annual mean number per route in each region reported on the surveys was 5.6 on the Coastal Plain, 5.7 on the Mississippi Alluvial Plain, and 3.3 in the highlands (including the Arkansas River Valley). Peak annual means of 9.0 to 10.3 birds per survey were reported in Clark, St. Francis, and Lincoln counties.

Nesting activity has been observed from early March through May, and in one case to mid-August. The earliest nesting record involved a cavity being excavated in Ashley County on March 10. In the Wheeler Collection there are six clutches of eggs that were taken from nests between April 18 and May 8. The clutch sizes in these nests varied from three to five eggs (average of approximately four). Nest heights ranged from fourteen to seventy feet above the ground, usually twenty-three feet or lower. The latest nest record in the Audubon Society file involved a nestling about to fledge in Madison County on August 14. In the file there is one nest as low as ten feet above the ground. Wheeler (1924) states that nests are frequently found in the dead tops of living trees. Sharp competition for nesting cavities between these birds and European Starlings has been observed.

The preference of these birds for bottomland forests is indicated in summer population studies (Tables 3-1 and 3-3). In the south there were nine territorial males per one hundred acres of bottomland woods and only a "trace" in the upland woods. No preference for either type of woodland was indicated in a similar one-year study in the northeastern counties.

WINTER: Red-bellied Woodpeckers are well distributed in winter. The ten-year statewide mean of 0.7 birds per party hour on the Christmas Bird Count was exceeded in each region, and varied by region from 0.7 to 1.3 on the Coastal Plain, 0.7 to 1.4 on the Mississippi Alluvial Plain, and 0.2 to 0.8 in the highlands (including the Arkansas River Valley). Large numbers are reported in some areas of the southern lowlands. At Arkadelphia, 50 or more are usually observed during the Christmas Count, and several counts there were over 100.

Winter population studies in the state (Tables 3-2 and 3-4) showed six to fourteen birds per one hundred acres of bottomland woods and from one to five per one hundred acres in upland woods.

YELLOW-BELLIED SAPSUCKER, *Sphyrapicus varius* (Linnaeus)

Common to fairly common migrant and winter resident in all regions. Inhabits a variety of woodlands, including those found in towns.

FALL MIGRATION: Yellow-bellied Sapsuckers have arrived as early as the end of August or in early September (two birds at El Dorado on September 1), but there are few reports until the first and second weeks of October, after which they become more common. Most reports on a day's outing have usually involved only one or two birds.

WINTER: During winter sapsuckers are

present in all regions, with the largest numbers occurring in the southern lowlands, where 20 to 40 birds are typically reported on several Christmas Bird Counts there. Lower numbers (infrequently even as many as 20) are reported on Christmas Counts in the northern half of the state. The distinctive lines of holes observed in pines, cedars, maples, and other species of trees are the sap wells excavated by these birds.

A winter population study in the southern lowlands showed a population of five Yellow-bellied Sapsuckers per one hundred acres of bottomland forest, and only one per one hundred acres of upland forests (Tables 3-2 and 3-4). Smaller numbers were found elsewhere in the state.

SPRING MIGRATION: Sapsuckers are seen with fair regularity in Arkansas until about the second week of April, after which there are only scattered sightings. At Calion in Union County a highly unusual number of three were seen on May 24 and one was there ten days later (the latest report for the state).

DOWNY WOODPECKER, *Picoides pubescens* (Linnaeus)

Common permanent resident in all types of woodlands, but also leaves the forest to forage on sapling trees or tall stout plants in fields.

BREEDING SEASON: Downy Woodpeckers are well distributed in Arkansas during summer, but seem to be somewhat more numerous in the highlands than elsewhere. The average annual mean number per route in each region reported on the Breeding Bird Survey was 1.8 on the Coastal Plain, 1.5 on the Mississippi Alluvial Plain, and 2.7 in the highlands (including the Arkansas River Valley). Peak annual means of 4.6 and 5.2 birds were reported on the surveys in Garland and Newton counties, respectively.

Nesting activity has been observed from early April to early June. The extreme records for such activity include a cavity being excavated in Faulkner County on April 1, and fledglings being fed by adults in Washington County on June 4. In the Wheeler Collection there are three clutches of eggs taken from nests on April 19 and 20. These clutch sizes involved four and six eggs, and the heights of the nests were six to ten feet from the ground. Heights

of nests recorded in the Audubon Society file have ranged up to thirty-five or forty feet, but they are often much lower, often below ten feet.

Summer population studies show that this species is more numerous in the bottomland than in the upland woods (Tables 3-1 and 3-3). In the bottomland woods there was a population of up to 12 territorial males per one hundred acres in northern Arkansas, and less than half that number in the upland forests.

WINTER: During the cold months Downy Woodpeckers are frequently seen in the company of other small birds including the Tufted Titmouse, Carolina Chickadee, Golden-crowned Kinglet, and others. At this time of the year Downy Woodpeckers seem to be fairly well distributed. The ten-year statewide mean on the Christmas Bird Counts was 0.5 birds per party hour, and this mean was exceeded in at least one count area in all regions. The nearly 500 birds observed statewide on the 1980 Christmas Counts included peaks of 40 or more Downy Woodpeckers in some participating locales in all the regions.

HAIRY WOODPECKER, *Picoides villosus* (Linnaeus)

Fairly common permanent resident in mature woodlands or woodlots with dead trees. Less numerous than the similar appearing Downy Woodpecker.

BREEDING SEASON: Hairy Woodpeckers are found in small numbers in all regions during summer. Data from the Breeding Bird Survey shows very little statewide difference in abundance or distribution (the average annual mean number of birds per route in each region varied only from 0.3 to 0.4). Howell (1911) stated that Hairy Woodpeckers were nowhere common. In the Winslow, Washington County, area Smith (1915) believed they were about as numerous as Downy Woodpeckers; twenty years later, however, another observer in the same area (Black 1935a) stated that they were much less numerous, with a decline in the winter of 1925–26 and smaller numbers thereafter. Deaderick (1938) reported them to be "fairly common" in Garland County. Data in the Audubon Society file indicates that observers usually find one or two per day in appropriate habitat.

FIGURE 6-62 Red-cockaded Woodpecker. *Levi Davis*

Nesting activity has been reported from late March to late May. The earliest record involved young being fed in a nest in Arkansas County on March 30. The latest record involved young being fed in a cavity in the large dead limb of a hickory tree in Washington County on May 24. In the Wheeler Collection there are two clutches of eggs that were taken from nests on April 20 and May 4. One of these nests held four eggs. The nest heights recorded in the Audubon Society file have varied from six to forty feet, and the cavities were in snags or in the dead limbs of living trees.

WINTER: There is no noticeable population shift between summer and winter. On the 1980 statewide Christmas Bird Counts there were peak reports of 10 to 21 Hairy Woodpeckers in three count areas. Reports of 10 to 15 are not rare on Christmas Counts in all regions of the state. These numbers are far below those obtained for Downy Woodpeckers. On the 1980 statewide Christmas Counts, the grand totals for these two species were 101 Hairy Woodpeckers and 496 Downy Woodpeckers.

RED-COCKADED WOODPECKER, *Picoides borealis* (Vieillot)

Permanent resident in mature stands of loblolly pines, occasionally shortleaf pines, where the trees occur in a park-like situation relatively free from hardwood intrusion. Declining throughout its range in the southeastern United States and extirpated from much of its former Arkansas territory. An endangered species.

STATUS: In the late 19th century the species was observed in scattered stands of shortleaf pine as far north (Figure 6-63) as the Ozark Plateaus (Howell 1911, Wheeler 1924), but apparently the forest harvesting in the Ozarks resulted in its extirpation there by the turn of the century, just as heavy logging of pines has drastically reduced its numbers elsewhere. A survey from October 1977 to July 1981 (Figure 6-64) of the status of this species in Arkansas (James, et al. 1981) showed that there were an estimated 100 to 130 colonies of birds in southern Arkansas, and this probably equalled about 200 to 400 individual birds. These family colonies occurred primarily in stands of mature pines, mainly loblolly pines, that were owned by private timber companies or were public lands. The largest concentrated population on public lands was at Felsenthal National Wildlife Refuge in extreme southern Arkansas (James and Burnside 1979a), even though the number of active colonies there comprised only 10 percent of the total found in the state (James et al. 1981). Some 85 percent of the active colonies found existed on private timber company holdings primarily in the pinelands of Ashley, Drew and Bradley counties in southeastern Arkansas (Figure 6-64). Scattered colonies existed elsewhere on the Coastal Plain, in the Ouachita Mountains, and in Monroe County on the Mississippi Alluvial Plain. The four colonies in Monroe County (Burnside 1983) occupied an island of favorable habitat in an area that has otherwise been almost totally cleared for large scale agricultural production.

The decrease in the range of the Red-cockaded Woodpecker in Arkansas is evident in comparing the distributional records existing to the early 1970s, [Figure 6-63,] with those compiled in the late 1970s to early 1980s; [Figure 6-64] (Burnside 1983, James and Burnside 1979b, James et al. 1981). New colonies were discovered in Perry and Saline counties in the latter period but the bird had by then disappeared from several counties where they formerly occurred.

The populations of Red-cockaded Woodpeckers on public lands are managed under provisions of the Endangered Species Act, but private holdings are not covered by the law. Timber companies have shown a willingness to set aside small tracts of land around known nesting cavities, but these small tracts have met with mixed success. One unhappy result of the habitat problem occurred in Grant County where a paper company set aside for this species a 38-acre sanctuary which was then placed on the Arkansas Natural Areas Registry. Despite these efforts the birds disappeared by 1983. Research now shows that they must have relatively large acreages of suitable habitat as well as large, living mature pines for their roosting and nesting activities (James and Burnside 1979a, Hart 1982). Burnside (1981) found that in southern Arkansas the species occurred in mixed pine and hardwood forests that had comparatively little hardwood understory. In this forest habitat it was found that during daily

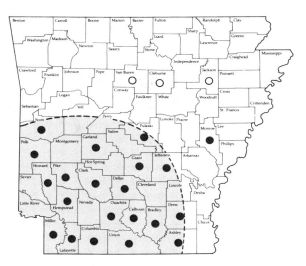

FIGURE 6-63 Distribution of Red-cockaded Woodpeckers in Arkansas showing known occurrences in the late 1800s (open circles) and occurrences in the 1900s through the early 1970s (solid circles).

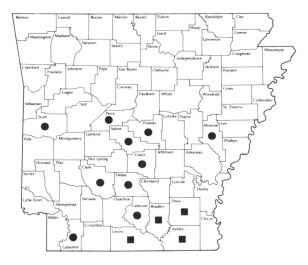

FIGURE 6-64 Distribution of Red-cockaded Woodpeckers in Arkansas in the late 1970s and early 1980s, showing counties with four or less colonies (circles) and those with over 20 colonies (squares).

foraging activity the birds definitely used the larger-sized pine trees more than any other foraging site (Hart 1982). The clans or families of these birds not only needed large living pines for cavity trees, but they also sought large mature pines for foraging within their home ranges, which varied from nearly one hundred acres to around two hundred acres depending on the quality of the habitat.

It is expected that fewer and fewer of these birds will be found in local forests. "Due to current intensified management practices on private holdings, the acreage of mature pine forests of the kind required by Red-cockaded Woodpeckers is steadily decreasing in Arkansas. Consequently, the number of these woodpeckers is expected to decline in the state by some 44% within 10 to 20 years" (James and Burnside 1979b).

BREEDING SEASON: Nesting activity has been observed during May and June from fifteen active colonies in Calhoun, Dallas, Grant, Garland, and Monroe counties. The peak period for nestlings is the second through the fourth weeks of May. Nestlings have been reported in cavities in Calhoun, Grant, and Garland counties on May 10 and 11. In Union County, fledglings have not been seen before May 26, and young have been reported in nests as late as mid-June.

NORTHERN FLICKER, *Colaptes auratus* (Linnaeus)

Permanent resident in woodlands throughout the state. Largest numbers present during migration and winter. The "yellow-shafted" form prevails, but in winter the western "red-shafted" birds are occasionally seen in the western region.

SPRING MIGRATION: Northward moving spring migrants have been reported during late February and March. Of the 20 birds counted on February 23 at Conway in Faulkner County, 18 were in one flock. At Lake Fayetteville in Washington County, a peak of 10 was reported on March 15, and the 35 seen in Union County on the same day (different year) was also a notable peak. The change in abundance is apparent in the Audubon Society file records. Most reports from April through August involve one or two birds seen during a day afield. Reports

often involve three to five (or sometimes more) from September through winter into March.

BREEDING SEASON: Flickers are present throughout the state in summer. The average annual mean number per route in each region on the Breeding Bird Survey was 2.8 on the Coastal Plain, 1.6 on the Mississippi Alluvial Plain, and 1.5 in the highlands (including the Arkansas River Valley). A peak mean of 7.9 birds was reported on the survey in Lincoln County in southeastern Arkansas. Nesting activity has been observed during April, May, and June. The earliest such report in the Audubon Society file involved flickers enlarging an old Red-bellied Woodpecker cavity in a pine snag on April 10. At Fort Smith, nests with young have been observed on May 11 and May 17. In the Wheeler Collection there is one clutch of seven eggs taken from a nest twenty feet from the ground on May 12. A nest with four eggs was found fifteen feet high in a sycamore tree on May 26 at Texarkana. A flicker was about ready to fledge from a nest in a natural cavity on the University of Arkansas campus in Fayetteville on June 7. The latest record in the file involved four eggs that did not hatch in an unusual nest constructed on open ground at El Dorado on June 14 (a photograph of this nest is on file).

FALL MIGRATION: The influx of fall transients, first noticed around the middle of September (peak in numbers during October), may continue into late November. At North Little Rock, 400 flickers had flown past observers by 8 A.M. on October 9, and flocks of 25 to 40 were seen early in the day from October 10 to 17. On Bayou Meto in Jefferson County, 47 birds (or about 10 per hour) passed through a study site on October 24.

WINTER: These birds are common throughout the state during winter. The ten-year statewide mean of 1.6 birds per party hour on Christmas Bird Counts was exceeded in some count areas in all regions, with the largest numbers in the southern lowlands. Winter population studies in the state (Tables 3-2 and 3-4) indicate up to 13 birds per one hundred acres of bottomland woods, with much smaller numbers in the upland woods.

BANDING: Banding recoveries show that nonresident flickers migrating through or wintering in eastern Arkansas breed mainly in the northern section of the midwestern United States, while those in western Arkansas in winter breed primarily in the river forests of the prairie states and provinces (Figure 6-65). Almost half of the flickers were recovered within 600 miles of the banding point, and the greatest distance was about 1500 miles. Most of the birds were recovered within a year of banding.

NOTE: The typical bird encountered in Arkansas is the eastern yellow-shafted type (AOU 1957, 1973), but there are more than a dozen reports of western red-shafted flickers, usually during winter or early spring, almost all of which were found in the western half of the state, mainly in the Ozarks. Two hybrids between the yellow-shafted and the red-shafted forms have been seen.

PILEATED WOODPECKER, *Dryocopus pileatus* (Linnaeus)

Fairly common permanent resident in mature bottomland forests throughout the state. Sometimes seen in towns where there are extensive stands of mature or overmature trees.

BREEDING SEASON: The birds are present in summer in all regions where there is sufficient habitat, with largest numbers generally found on the Coastal Plain. The average annual mean number per route in each region on the Breeding Bird Survey was 4.1 on the Coastal Plain, 1.2 on the Mississippi Alluvial Plain, and 2.6 in the highlands (including the Arkansas River Valley). Major annual means of 10.0 and 11.1 birds were reported on the surveys in Newton and Clark counties, respectively.

Nesting activity has been observed from March through June. The earliest such record involved a pair of Pileated Woodpeckers already feeding young at DeVall's Bluff in Prairie County on March 25. In the Wheeler Collection there are five clutches of eggs taken from nests between April 19 and May 9. The clutch sizes varied from three to five eggs (average about four), and the heights of the nests varied from fifteen to sixty feet (average about thirty-five feet). At Grassy Lake in Hempstead County, four eggs were found in a cavity that was two and one-half feet deep and about forty feet high in a dead cypress in the center of the lake. The latest record in the file involved adults feeding young in Pulaski County on June 21.

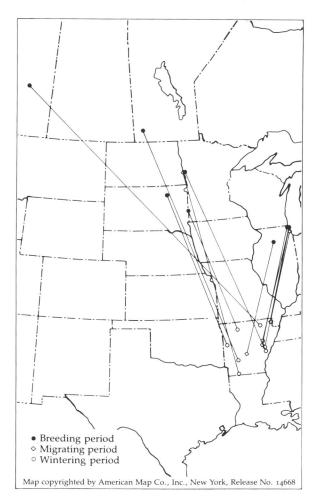

- Breeding period
- Migrating period
- Wintering period

Map copyrighted by American Map Co., Inc., New York, Release No. 14668

FIGURE 6-65 Movements of the Northern Flicker based on banding records.

Pileated Woodpeckers are often associated with two or more distinctively oval holes, either in the same or nearby trees. These cavity entrances are often seen in large old snags, or in living trees like sycamores that are sometimes hollow on the inside.

Summer population studies (Table 3-3) indicate that there are up to three territorial males per one hundred acres of forested bottomland. Small numbers have also been found in upland forests of northwestern Arkansas (Table 3-1).

WINTER: The cold weather distribution of this non-migratory species follows the same pattern that has been observed in the breeding season. The largest numbers reported on Christmas Bird Counts are in the southern lowlands, where reports of 20 to 40 are not rare in many of the count areas. In northern Arkansas the numbers are smaller, but at Fayetteville in the western Ozarks as many as 20 to 30 have been reported a few times on the Christmas Count.

IVORY-BILLED WOODPECKER,
Campephilus principalis (Linnaeus)

Extirpated from Arkansas, and nearing extinction (if it is not already extinct) throughout its range.

Within historic times this species ranged throughout the mature bottomland forests and forested swamps of the Arkansas lowlands, including both the valleys of the Arkansas and Mississippi rivers (Tanner 1942). When Audubon reached Arkansas Post on his travels down the Mississippi River in mid-December of 1820 (Audubon 1929), he was seeing these birds with relative regularity. On December 14 he was approximately one mile below the mouth of the Arkansas River, and there saw five Ivory-billed Woodpeckers that were "feeding on berries of some creeper . . . keeping up a constant cry of pet pet pet . . ." Another nineteenth-century writer (Yell 1885) stated that Ivory-billed Woodpeckers could be found in "unfrequented swamps. . . . [The species] is not rare, but is rarely met with" near Newport in Jackson County. Pindar (1924) saw the species in the valley of the St. Francis River near Marked Tree in Poinsett County in the period 1888–89: "A fine male was frequently seen in a low, wet, heavily wooded strip about two miles [from a logging camp. . . .] This was presumably the same bird as it was always seen in the same place, a territory approximately one-half by one-quarter mile in area." A female was seen in the area during the same period.

Howell (1911) published records for the Osceola (Mississippi County) area in 1887 and for the Helena (Phillips County) area where there were secondhand reports as late as 1910. As human settlement increased and the giant old growth trees upon which this species depended were logged out of the bottomlands and swamps, numbers of birds declined rapidly. The last Ivory-billed Woodpecker population remaining in the state near the mouth of the Arkansas River disappeared between 1900 and 1915 (Tanner 1942).

Order PASSERIFORMES

Family Tyrannidae

Subfamily Fluvicolinae Flycatchers

OLIVE-SIDED FLYCATCHER, *Contopus borealis* (Swainson)

Fairly common transient in small numbers during spring and fall in all regions. Observed on power lines, tall snags, and similar open perches above the forest canopy.

SPRING MIGRATION: The Olive-sided Flycatcher is generally a late springtime migrant. In the Audubon Society file there are reports between the fourth week of April and the first week of June, mainly early May to early June. For Faulkner County in central Arkansas there are four records between late April and early June (Johnson 1979). In the northeast it has been seen from late April to late May (Hanebrink 1980). Most reports for a day in the field have involved one bird. Three were seen at Little Rock on May 16. Six were seen at Lake Millwood between May 18 and 28. At Winslow in Washington County, four were seen on May 16, and a flock of five was seen one week later (Smith 1915). During spring migration there are relatively few records for eastern Arkansas.

FALL MIGRATION: In fall this species is a rather early migrant. In the file there are reports from the first week of August to the second week of October, with a cluster of sightings from the last week of August into the second half of September. Four birds were seen at Little Rock on September 13. Vernon Kleen banded three on August 29 in Poinsett County. The species has been observed in good numbers on snags in the extensive openings created by "clear cuts" in pine forest habitat (T. Haggerty, pers. comm.).

EASTERN WOOD-PEWEE, *Contopus virens* (Linnaeus)

Common migrant and summer resident in park-like forests and smaller woodlots having mature trees.

SPRING MIGRATION: Pewees have arrived as early as April 10, but few are seen until the third or fourth weeks of April, often in the last days of the month or in early May. There were three pewees at Petit Jean Mountain on April 28, and seven at Lake Fayetteville on May 20.

BREEDING SEASON: Pewees are present in all regions during summer, and may be common where there are mature, extensive deciduous or oak-pine forests. Smith (1915) stated pewees were found in "every few acres of woodland" and were "partial to the dry hillsides" in the Winslow, Washington County, area. The average annual mean number per route in each region reported on Breeding Bird Surveys was 6.7 on the Coastal Plain, 1.1 on the Mississippi Alluvial Plain, and 6.3 in the highlands (including the Arkansas River Valley). Peak numbers of 10.4 to 14.3 birds were reported on the surveys in Clark, Van Buren, and Fulton counties. Summer studies showed population levels as high as 13 territorial males (or pairs of pewees) per one hundred acres, with no appreciable difference between the bottomland or upland woods. (Tables 3-1, 3-2).

Nesting activity in Arkansas has been observed from early May through July. The extreme dates are for a nest in a tree over water at DeVall's Bluff in Prairie County on May 4, and for fledglings just out of a nest at Hamburg in Ashley County on July 28. In the Wheeler Collection there are six clutches involving two or three eggs that were taken from nests ten to thirty-two feet above the ground between May

27 and June 28. In the Audubon file there are several reports of higher nests, with one at Calion in Union County that was one hundred feet high in a black gum tree.

FALL MIGRATION: In fall few of these birds are seen after the first two weeks of October. However, there is one late report involving a single bird in Faulkner County on November 6. Most reports in fall, like those at other times of the year, involve one or a few birds. More than a dozen were seen in a single tree at Winslow on September 18 (Smith 1915).

YELLOW-BELLIED FLYCATCHER, Empidonax flaviventris (Baird and Baird)

Rare transient in all regions.

SPRING MIGRATION: There are approximately ten reports in the Audubon Society file and in published accounts (Smith 1915, Black 1935a, Baerg 1951) between the last week of April and the end of May in Union, Lonoke, Saline, Sebastian, Pulaski, Faulkner, Washington, and Benton counties. Five birds, identified by plumage and song, were in Rebsamen Park in Little Rock on May 26. A single bird at Wilton in Little River County on April 24 was heard as it gave its distinctive vocalization.

FALL MIGRATION: There are fewer than fifteen reports for the fall migration between the second week of August and the middle of October. Vernon Kleen banded one bird at Harrisburg in Poinsett County on August 10. Specimens were collected at Delight in Pike County on September 3 and 16 (Howell 1911). In recent years, single birds have been killed upon impact with a tower in Jefferson County on September 21 and 22. All the fall reports have involved single birds except for the two found at Winslow on October 13 (Black 1935a).

NOTE: Sight reports submitted for inclusion in the files of the Audubon Society should, if possible, include a notation about the vocalization of the bird seen. This is especially important in fall. Sutton (1967) states that "sight records [are not] wholly satisfactory because several flycatchers of the genus *Empidonax* are more or less yellow below in fresh fall feather . . ."

ACADIAN FLYCATCHER, Empidonax virescens (Vieillot)

Common summer resident in moist woodlands, forested stream bottoms, and forested upland ravine thickets in all regions.

SPRING MIGRATION: The five birds reported in Prairie County on April 7 is the earliest spring arrival date for the state. Except for that one date, there is little or no evidence that Acadian Flycatchers arrive before the third and fourth weeks of April, after which they are common in appropriate habitat.

BREEDING SEASON: In a study in Newton County in the western Ozarks, Smith (1977) showed that Acadian Flycatchers have highly specific moist forest habitat requirements. Reports in the Audubon Society file and on Breeding Bird Surveys show that they are found during the nesting season in all regions, with the greatest numbers on the Coastal Plain and in the highlands. The average annual mean number per route in each region reported on Breeding Bird Surveys was 3.2 for the Coastal Plain, 0.7 for the Mississippi Alluvial Plain, and 2.0 for the highlands (including the Arkansas River Valley). Peak means of 4.1 and 8.6 birds were reported on the surveys in Dallas, Grant, Saline, and Newton counties. Summer population studies (Tables 3-1 and 3-3) indicated 26 singing males per one hundred acres of bottomland forests, and 16 per one hundred acres in upland forests in southern Arkansas. Similar studies in northern Arkansas showed smaller numbers and the same preference for bottomlands.

Nesting activity has been reported from mid-May to mid-August. The extreme records involved a nest with one egg near Cass in Franklin County on May 13, and young "just able to fly" at Winslow in Washington County on August 19 (Smith 1915). In the Wheeler Collection there are records of three clutches of three eggs each taken from ten to fifteen feet high between June 3 and 20. Young either still in the nest or recently fledged have been reported on several occasions during the first half of August, suggesting that such reports at mid-August are not necessarily late or unusual. Nest heights recorded in the file have varied from three to twenty feet, with the nests usually at the end of a limb over or near water, and shielded from above by a canopy layer.

FIGURE 6-66 Acadian Flycatcher. *David Plank*

FALL MIGRATION: The last Acadian Flycatcher songs are heard between late July and late August (Baerg 1930a). After this time they are more difficult to find. Nevertheless, they have been reported with some regularity into September. The latest record in the file involved a bird caught in a mist net at Fayetteville on September 22.

ALDER FLYCATCHER, *Empidonax alnorum* Brewster

Status unclear. Infrequently reported spring transient, very rarely reported fall transient.

The status of this species in Arkansas is unclear, not only because of some difficulty in correctly identifying it in the field, but also because in earlier years the Alder Flycatcher was considered to be the same species as the Willow Flycatcher, *E. traillii* (see following species account). Now the former single taxon is considered to be two separate species (AOU 1973), which are distinguishable in the field by vocalization differences. Alder Flycatchers give the "fee-bee-o" song, while Willow Flycatchers give the "fitz-bew" song. When Jane Stern of Pine Bluff visited a known breeding area of the Willow Flycatcher (in Arkansas County) on May 25, she saw a small *Empidonax* flycatcher that gave the Alder Flycatcher vocalization. This was an acceptable record for this species. In past years, when the birds were considered to be the same species, most reports in the Audubon Society file did not include information about the vocalization, and thus cannot now be reliably assigned to either species. Since 1974 there have been only a few records submitted involving birds that gave the correct Alder Flycatcher vocalization. All of these reports are in May, and most involved single birds. In Phillips County, three were heard as they called repeatedly on May 17. At Little Rock, a party of observers studied 15 birds that were on a willow sandbar in the Arkansas River alongside Rebsamen Park on May 25. During the second half of May 1984, Alder Flycatchers were seen and heard at three lakes in the western Ozarks, including the 16 or more in a fringe of willow trees at Lake Fayetteville on May 29. Hence, it appears the species may at times be at least locally common during the northward migration through the state.

There is only one fall record in the file, and this involved a bird at Little Rock on August 16. The great reduction in vocalization that characterizes the southward migration period may account for this almost total lack of records.

WILLOW FLYCATCHER, *Empidonax traillii* (Audubon)

Migrant and summer resident, now approaching extirpation as a breeding bird in the state.

MIGRATION: The migratory status of the Willow Flycatcher is confused by the fact that in the decade prior to 1973 it was considered conspecific with the Alder Flycatcher, *E. alnorum* (AOU 1973). Most reports in the Audubon Society file, therefore, failed to distinguish between these two flycatchers. Meanley (1952) found Willow Flycatchers in a known breeding area as early as the second week of May, and in the file there are records of silent birds that could be either Willow or Alder Flycatcher as late as September, with the latest definite Willow Flycatcher sighting occurring on September 19. Most migration reports involving singing Willow Flycatchers have been recorded on the known breeding areas, including the prairies of northwestern and east central Arkansas. In recent years singing birds have been reliably reported at Mablevale and Maumelle Dam near Little Rock, on prairies in Franklin and Boone counties, and in the willow fringe of several impoundments in Washington County and in northeastern Arkansas. Many more reports of birds giving the full characteristic song (not just call note) are needed in order to fully round out the picture of migration in the state.

BREEDING SEASON AND HISTORY: The Willow Flycatcher is the only species of bird that first became known to science through its discovery in Arkansas. John James Audubon (1831–39) was the first naturalist to find and identify the bird when he collected specimens, including a female with developing eggs, on the Grand Prairie at Arkansas Post in the spring of 1822. Audubon made a watercolor in Arkansas that served as the basis for the engraving of this species in his famous Elephant Folio illustrations in *Birds of America* (1827–38).

Almost one hundred years later, the species

Willow Flycatcher   *David Plank*

FIGURE 6-67 Hawthorn nesting thicket of the Willow Flycatcher viewed across the tallgrass Konecny Prairie at Slovack, Arkansas. *Thomas L. Foti*

was still "fairly common" at Stuttgart on the Grand Prairie, where it was "living in orchards, dooryards, and about small clumps of trees on the prairie" (Howell 1911). Howell also collected a specimen in Crawford County. In the western region of the Arkansas River Valley, Wheeler (1924) found the birds nesting on the Massard Prairie in Sebastian County, and Dean Crooks found nine nests in a half mile of brushy ravine in the western Ozarks of Benton County (Baerg 1951), also prairie habitat.

Brooke Meanley (1952a) studied breeding populations at Slovak in Prairie County, not far from Stuttgart, when habitat suitable for the species was more prevalent than it is today. Nests were found in slashy thickets bordering

drainage areas of the rice fields and in islands of shrubby vegetation, such as clumps of small trees surrounded by remnants of the native prairie vegetation (Figure 6-67). Nests were commonly built in hawthorn (*Crataegus*) trees, seven to eight feet high. Some seventeen pairs of birds were found in an 18-acre tract at Slovak. The first pair was observed in the area on May 10, with finished nests by May 28, and eggs in several nests on May 31. The average clutch size was three eggs, with a maximum number of four eggs in one nest. Fledged young were still near several nests on August 10.

In 1969, observers including Thomas Foti and Jane Stern made a special effort to again study the species at Slovak. The birds arrived in early May, established their territories during the remainder of the month, nested in late May and during June, and young were fledged in late June and July. A total of eight territories was mapped in 1969. Although they obtained results similar to Meanley's, the observers in 1969 found many fewer birds.

The Willow Flycatcher is still a common breeding bird in many regions of North America, but it is disappearing rapidly from Arkansas, and has been listed there as "endangered" (James 1974). Since its breeding habitat is altered for agricultural purposes, it has no place left to nest. The only definite breeding location in the state, the Konecny Grove Natural Area at Slovak, is now preserved by the Arkansas Natural Heritage Commission. But even with this protection of the hawthorn thicket and surrounding prairie lands, the population is still dwindling. In 1982 only two or three birds were seen in the area, all in trees bordering the nearby prairies, and they have been absent from the grove since 1979. Despite intensive searches in 1983, the birds were not found in the area at all.

The only recent record outside the Konecny Grove area is from Washington County, where a singing bird was seen and heard in June of 1984 at Lake Sequoyah near Fayetteville.

LEAST FLYCATCHER, *Empidonax minimus* (Baird and Baird)

Regular transient in small numbers in open woodlands and forest edge in all regions.

SPRING MIGRATION: In the Audubon Society file there are reports for the northward migration period between mid-April and the first week of June, mainly in the last week of April and in the first three weeks of May. Spring transients call attention to themselves by frequently giving the "che-bec" vocalization. At Winslow in Washington County, the species was said to be very common between May 5 and 11 (Smith 1915). In Garland County it was "fairly common" in spring and fall migration, with spring records from April 29 and thereafter (Deaderick 1938). While the species is generally seen in only small numbers in the northeast (Hanebrink and Posey 1979), many were present at Farville in Craighead County on May 8. There are relatively few reports in the file in the lowlands of southern and south-eastern Arkansas. In the western Ozarks the birds are fairly common during spring migration. Most reports in the file have involved one or two birds seen during a day in the field, rarely even as many as four.

FALL MIGRATION: There are many fewer reports for fall than spring, no doubt in part because the birds give fewer vocalizations in fall. Reports are scattered from the end of August to the fourth week of September. A Least Flycatcher banded in Poinsett County on August 12 was early. At Winslow, birds were found in brushy edges of clearings and in orchards between September 8 and 16 (Smith 1915). In Garland County, the birds were observed after September 12 (Deaderick 1938). At Fayetteville, three were trapped in a mist net on September 20.

NOTE: Baerg (1931) published one record for June 26, and in his 1951 edition he reported that it was nesting in Benton County in 1948. No details are available on either of these reports, and there have been no summer records of this sort since.

EASTERN PHOEBE, *Sayornis phoebe* (Latham)

Permanent resident that is most numerous in the highlands and the bordering foothills in summer, and in winter most numerous in the southern lowlands. Observed primarily in forested stream bottoms and adjacent areas.

SPRING MIGRATION: While phoebes have been seen during winter in all regions, they are scarce in the northern areas and in the highlands during cold weather. An influx during the first relatively long periods of warm weather in February or early March is noticed in Faulkner County in central Arkansas by mid-February (Johnson 1979), and in the western Ozarks during the first half of March (Audubon Society file, Baerg 1930b). In extreme southern Arkansas, where the species is very scarce in summer, there are few reports after April (Mattocks and Shugart 1962).

BREEDING SEASON: Reports in the Audubon Society file and on Breeding Bird Surveys show that these birds are found in all regions in summer, but they are common and regular only in the highlands and surrounding foothills. The average annual mean number per route in each region reported on the Breeding Bird Surveys

FIGURE 6-68 Eastern Phoebe. *David Plank*

was 1.0 on the Coastal Plain, 0.3 on the Mississippi Alluvial Plain, and 2.2 in the highlands (including the Arkansas River Valley). Peak means of 3.3 to 5.6 birds were recorded on the surveys in Grant, Garland, and Cleburne counties. A few nests have been reported in the extreme south.

Nesting activity has been observed from the second week of March to early July. The extreme early and late records are of a nest being constructed under a bridge in Benton County on March 11, a half-completed nest at Winslow in Washington County on March 17, and a nest under a bridge in Randolph County on July 4 (the status of this nest was not specified in the report). In the Wheeler Collection there are five clutches of four or five eggs each that were taken between April 11 and June 3. These nests were five to ten feet high under bridges, in a culvert, and on a barn rafter. In Garland County, a nest that was used for two broods in one season was used again the next year (Deaderick 1938). Structures to which nests are attached are variable. In addition to those structures already mentioned, the birds have utilized rock ledges, old wells, building eaves and porches, all providing a shelter or roof over the nest. Sites near water are commonly used although the birds will find a building or a cave entrance suitable some distance from water. The presence of structures such as bridges and culverts has probably increased the nesting density of this species in Arkansas.

FALL MIGRATION: The arrival of fall weather and the sharp reduction in populations of flying insects largely pushes this flycatcher out of the Ozarks by mid-October, though a few may remain later, especially during years when there are long mild falls. In the south, on the other hand, the birds are most numerous from mid-October through December (Howell 1911, Mattocks and Shugart 1962).

WINTER: The fact that a few phoebes have been reported on three of twelve recent Christmas Bird Counts at Fayetteville in the northwest indicates that a very small number may remain in the northern areas of the state if the weather is unseasonably mild at that time. However, this is unusual, and the winter population is heavily concentrated further south. By comparison, at Arkadelphia on the Coastal Plain the birds are found every year on the Christmas Count. While the number there is usually fewer than 10, there are several peaks involving 25 to 34 birds. The peak numbers reported by region on the Christmas Counts were 0.2 phoebes per party hour on the Coastal Plain, 0.1 on the Mississippi Alluvial Plain, and none in the highlands (including the Arkansas River Valley). Severe winter weather adversely affects phoebe populations (James 1959).

SAY'S PHOEBE, *Sayornis saya* (Bonaparte)
One record.

An individual of this western species was seen at the Stuttgart airport, Prairie County, on December 29, 1973. Written documentation was placed in the Audubon Society file.

VERMILION FLYCATCHER, *Pyrocephalus rubinus* (Boddaert)
Rare fall and winter visitor in the southern and central-eastern lowlands.

This native of the southwestern United States and Mexico (and further south) visits Arkansas irregularly during fall and winter, and always in small numbers. It has been reported as early as the second week in October and as late as the second week in March, but most sightings involve one or two birds between the third week of November and late December. An exceptional number of two or three were observed repeatedly at Calion in Union County from November 17 to December 30 in 1961. The latest spring record involved an adult male in Union County on March 13. With the exception of the single bird at Mena in the Ouachita Mountains on October 21 (Baerg 1951), all sightings are either from the Coastal Plain in the south or on the Grand Prairie in the central-eastern lowlands.

Subfamily Tyranninae Kingbirds

GREAT CRESTED FLYCATCHER, *Myiarchus crinitus* (Linnaeus)
Common migrant and summer resident in woodlands throughout the state.

SPRING MIGRATION: Crested flycatchers have arrived on several occasions in the extreme southern counties as early as the second week of April, but there are very few reports in the Audubon Society file until the fourth week of April and thereafter. The early spring reports invariably involve one or two birds, but larger numbers are seen thereafter. The seven seen at Petit Jean Mountain in Conway County on April 28 and the six birds counted in Arkansas County between Stuttgart and the White River on April 30 were both early peaks in numbers. Two observers counted 15 at Fort Smith on May 10. At Pine Bluff Arsenal 15 were counted in a 153-acre census tract on May 17 (Coffey 1981).

BREEDING SEASON: Great Crested Flycatchers are common in summer in all regions. The average annual mean number per route in each region reported on the Breeding Bird Surveys was 5.2 on the Coastal Plain, 2.3 on the Mississippi Alluvial Plain, and 4.7 in the highlands (including the Arkansas River Valley). The peak annual mean was 13.4 birds on the survey in Clark County. This species shows a preference for bottomland woods. Summer population studies (Tables 3-1 and 3-3) in southern Arkansas showed a population of 10 singing males (or pairs) per one hundred acres of bottomland woods, and four in the upland woods. Similar results were obtained in northeastern Arkansas.

Nesting activity has been observed from early May to early July. The earliest nesting date in the file is from Little Rock where a pair was seen at a nesting box on May 1, building had started by May 9, four eggs were observed on May 18, and young were out of the nest by June 19. The latest nesting date is from Ouachita County in the south where young were being fed in a nest on July 1. In the Wheeler Collection there are five clutches of eggs collected from nests between May 24 and June 24. The clutch sizes in these nests varied from four to six eggs (average five), and the nest heights varied from three to twenty feet above the ground. Nest sites reported have included natural tree cavities and nesting boxes. At Hamburg in Ashley County the birds built their nest in an unoccupied Purple Martin house and lined it with onion peelings and a snake skin. Eggs in a nest at the same place the following year were eaten by a snake.

FALL AND WINTER: In fall few crested flycatchers are reported after the second week of September, but there are some reports involving single birds as late as the first week of October. A single bird that roosted in a shed at Little Rock between January 14 and February 26, 1975, is the only report after early October in the file.

CASSIN'S KINGBIRD, *Tyrannus vociferans* Swainson

Two sight records.

One Cassin's Kingbird was seen at Faulkner Lake in Pulaski County on June 12, 1965, and a second bird was seen at El Dorado in Union County on May 19, 1967. These two highly unusual records of a southwestern species were accepted on the basis of written documentary evidence submitted by skilled observers.

WESTERN KINGBIRD, *Tyrannus verticalis* Say

Very uncommon transient in spring and fall that is usually seen somewhere in the state every year. There is one confirmed instance of nesting, which was not successful.

Spring transients have been found primarily in the western half of the state, and usually during May. A single bird at Lake Millwood in the southwest on March 23 and 24 was unusually early. Reports for the fall season suggest that Western Kingbirds are more wide-ranging at this time. Sightings in the Audubon Society file begin with the first half of August and continue until the middle of October. During fall many records are from the southern and eastern lowlands, including the counties bordering the Mississippi River. The only confirmed instance of breeding concerned two adults and a nest at Lonoke in central-eastern Arkansas in early June of 1973. This nest was unsuccessful. All reports in the file have involved one or two birds. There is also a recent June record in 1985, for Washington County in the western Ozarks, but this bird did not remain in the area long.

EASTERN KINGBIRD, *Tyrannus tyrannus* (Linnaeus)

Common migrant and summer resident in all regions. Observed in extensive open areas with scattered tall trees.

FIGURE 6-69 Eastern Kingbird. *David Plank*

SPRING MIGRATION: Eastern Kingbirds have arrived as early as the end of March, but only small numbers reach the state until the second week of April, after which numbers steadily increase with major influxes in late April and early May. In Craighead County, 50 or more birds were observed on May 1. An influx totalling over 230 grounded birds in flocks ranging up to 20 individuals was observed in Lonoke County on May 6. In Sebastian County, 64 birds in flocks of five to seven were seen during twenty minutes after sunrise on May 14. Small flocks are seen flying overhead in early morning during daytime northward migrations.

BREEDING SEASON: This species is numerous and widespread during the breeding season. The average annual mean number per route in each region reported on Breeding Bird Surveys was 6.0 on the Coastal Plain, 3.7 on the Mississippi Alluvial Plain, and 5.2 in the highlands (including the Arkansas River Valley). Peak annual means of 10.4 to 11.9 Eastern Kingbirds were reported on the surveys in Lafayette, Cleburne, and Benton counties.

Nesting activity has been observed from mid-May to mid-August. In Union County three nests with three or four eggs each were found on May 19, and young were seen in these nests by June 2. Five recent nests in Washington County were active between the first week of June and the middle of August. Other nests with young in southern Arkansas are dated May 31, June 3, July 15–28, August 4, and August 16 (young just leaving the nest in Union County on the latter date). At Rebsamen Park in Little Rock two nests were observed forty feet above the ground in pecan and cottonwood trees on May 24. Heights of nests in the Audubon Society file have varied from fifteen to forty feet above the ground.

FALL MIGRATION: The southward migration has been observed from early August to the second week of September, with the latest departures from the state at the end of September (one record in the fourth week of October). The peak of fall migration is observed from the second half of August through the first week of September. Some of the peak counts for the period are 125 birds in willows along the Spring River at Mammoth Spring in Fulton County on August 21, and 150 to 300 or more going to roost in willows at Lake Sequoyah in Washing-

ton County on August 31, September 1, and September 6 in different years. The flock of 31 birds seen flying southward in Garland County on August 22 was also a large migratory unit.

SCISSOR-TAILED FLYCATCHER, *Tyrannus forficatus* (Gmelin)

Common migrant and summer resident in western and central Arkansas, and present in small numbers in the eastern lowlands. A few scattered winter sightings.

SPRING MIGRATION: Scissor-tailed Flycatchers have been reported in spring as early as March 21 in Miller County where they have also been observed in winter. Otherwise, there are a few scattered reports between late March and the second and third weeks of April, after which they are common in appropriate habitat throughout the western half of the state. There are no spring migration reports involving the large flocks that are characteristic of fall.

BREEDING SEASON: Although in recent years this species has expanded its range to include much of Arkansas (see below), it was apparently originally established in western Arkansas in the prairies around Fort Smith where Nuttall (1832) saw it in 1819. Bendire (1892) also reported the species occurring in Arkansas without citing a locality (Howell 1911), which could have been based upon Nuttall's record; perhaps Bendire himself saw the bird when he was stationed at Fort Smith about 1860.

Wheeler (1924) reported it nesting on the Massard Prairie region at Fort Smith, and also in Miller County in the southwestern corner of the state. By 1951 Scissor-tailed Flycatchers were observed as far east as Pulaski County in central Arkansas (Baerg 1951), and by the 1960s their range included all of the western Ozarks and several counties in eastern Arkansas. It became familiar throughout the Coastal Plain region, in north central Arkansas, and over much of the Ouachita Mountain region (James 1972), and by the mid-1970s there were May and June reports in the eastern lowlands all the way to the Mississippi River. In the northeast there have now been sightings at Big Lake Refuge, near Saffell in Lawrence County (1983 Breeding Bird Survey), and near the White River at Oil Trough in Independence County.

While the cause of this eastward spread from

FIGURE 6-70 Scissor-tailed Flycatcher. *David Plank*

Oklahoma and Texas into Arkansas cannot be known for certain, it is plausible that the bird's preference for open prairie areas with scattered tall trees is compatible with developed pastures and other agricultural lands. In 1963 members of the Audubon Society of Central Arkansas conducted a census of Scissor-tailed Flycatchers in Pulaski County between May 22 and June 6. They located ten nests and eighty-nine adults. The population was most concentrated on the grounds of three golf courses along the Arkansas River. Obviously this grassland with its scattered tall trees was suitable. The opportunity for this species to move eastward beyond the western prairie patches fringing Arkansas would not have been possible until the heavily forested areas to the east were cleared and developed for agriculture. Scissor-tailed Flycatchers not only occupy pasture grasslands, but also occur in areas dominated by extensive croplands.

The average annual mean number of birds per route in each region reported on the Breeding Bird Surveys was 4.6 on the Coastal Plain, 0.2 on the Mississippi Alluvial Plain, and 2.2 in the highlands (including the Arkansas River Valley). The population is heavily concentrated in Little River County in the southwest, where the annual mean was 16.5 birds. Peaks of 4.6 and 5.3 birds were reported on surveys on the western border of the state.

Data on approximately fifteen nesting reports in the Audubon Society file indicate that nest construction gets underway during May and June, with young out of their nests by the end of July. The earliest breeding record involved a completed nest in Lonoke County on May 8. One of the latest records is from Little Rock, where a nest was started on June 11, a clutch of four eggs was present on June 23, hatchlings were observed on July 7 and 8, and the young fledged on July 20. In the Wheeler Collection there are clutches of four and five eggs that were taken from nests twenty and twenty-five feet high on June 15 and 26. After a successful first nest, these birds nested again in Pulaski County, with the second nest underway in the second half of June. Nest heights have varied up to the height of one found approximately eighty feet above the ground on a pylon of an airport beacon in Washington County. Other reports in the file involve nests on top of power

transformers, on the crossarms of power poles, on television antennas, and in a variety of trees.

FALL MIGRATION: After the breeding season these birds congregate in communal roosts involving 20 to 25 or more birds. In Washington County, 40 to 50 were perched on wires on September 8. At Fort Smith, nearly 700 roosted in one sycamore tree on October 8. This Fort Smith tree had been used every year during the 1960s. In Miller County, 100 were seen on October 9. The birds are seen with fair regularity in the state until late October, with only scattered reports of single (occasionally two) birds to the first week of November, and very rarely thereafter.

WINTER: In the Audubon Society file there are a few rare and highly irregular reports between December and February involving single birds (once two) in Union, Miller, Clark, and Hot Spring counties.

Family Alaudidae Larks

HORNED LARK, *Eremophila alpestris* (Linnaeus)

Permanent resident primarily in extensive, flat, open pasturelands and large plowed fields in the Mississippi Alluvial Plain, and Arkansas River Valley, and in the Ozark Plateaus, where it is fairly common at least locally. Wintering flocks are observed in all regions.

BREEDING SEASON: Data on Breeding Bird Surveys show that these birds are most numerous during June on the Mississippi Alluvial Plain as far south as Lincoln County, with peak annual means per route of 9.0 to 29.4 birds on the surveys in St. Francis, Lincoln, Poinsett, Mississippi, and Woodruff counties. Smaller numbers are reported on surveys in the Ozarks. In the Audubon Society file there are summer records similar to those on Breeding Bird Surveys. Horned Larks are common in the plowed fields of the Arkansas River bottomlands around Fort Smith, and have been found elsewhere in the Arkansas River Valley. There is no summer record for Faulkner County (Johnson 1979). Recent June records for Little River County are the first for the southwestern corner of the state. The birds nest in croplands all over north-

FIGURE 6-71 Horned Larks in January at the university farm at Fayetteville. *David Plank*

eastern Arkansas (Hanebrink and Posey 1979) and are fairly common in scattered locations in the western Ozarks.

Nesting activity has been observed as early as mid-February, but more often during April and May. In the western Ozarks courtship has been observed as early as mid-February (file, Baerg 1951). In Jefferson County, a nest that was found on February 19 was destroyed by rain on February 28. Near Fort Smith a nest with four eggs was found in a cotton field in April (Wheeler 1924). There is a nesting record for May at Helena (Howell 1911). A nest with four hatchlings was found at Fayetteville in Washington County on May 14.

MIGRATION AND WINTER: Whereas reports of numbers seen per day during spring and summer usually involve only a few individuals, by late October or early November flocks may be seen in feedlots, on croplands, closely cropped pastures, and plowed fields. At the Booneville airport in Logan County, a flock of 25 or more birds was seen on October 28 in the same place where no more than a pair with young were seen in summer. Large wintering flocks, sometimes numbering more than 100 birds, are often seen in the eastern lowlands at Fort Smith in western Arkansas, and elsewhere in the state. A party of observers saw an estimated 300 Horned Larks in the clear, wet ruts of otherwise snow-covered roads at Holla Bend Refuge in Pope County on January 15. Flocks are generally seen until about the middle of February, after which only pairs remain.

Family Hirundinidae Swallows

PURPLE MARTIN, *Progne subis* (Linnaeus)

Common migrant and summer resident in all regions.

SPRING MIGRATION: Spring migrants have arrived in southern Arkansas as early as the first week of February. Analysis of forty February sightings in the file shows that thirty-four involved one or two early arriving birds that martin watchers consider harbingers of spring. At Hope in Hempstead County, arrival dates from 1963 to 1978 ranged from February 10 to March 29. While there are also some February sightings for northern Arkansas, martins are not usually seen in the Ozarks before mid-March.

BREEDING SEASON: Purple Martins nest in numbers in all the regions. The average annual mean number per route in each region reported on Breeding Bird Surveys was 17.2 on the Coastal Plain, 4.2 on the Mississippi Alluvial Plain, and 9.3 in the highlands (including the Arkansas River Valley).

In the Audubon Society file there are records of nesting activity from late March to July, mainly during April, May, and June. The earliest and latest nesting reports are from Hamburg in Ashley County: four nests were all under construction during the third and fourth weeks of March; a pair that built in a nesting box but did not lay eggs moved, re-nested, and reared young that fledged on July 20. In the Wheeler Collection there are five nests between May 5 and June 5 with clutch sizes of five or six eggs. Most nesting, of course, takes place in nesting boxes, but the birds have also nested in hollow trees (Howell 1911), under the eaves of a building, in the open ends of a pipe stand, and in nesting gourds.

FALL MIGRATION AND ROOSTS: After the nesting season Purple Martins congregate in roosts, which have been observed from June to mid-August. Such congregations may number hundreds of birds, or sometimes thousands. In Union County, a roost observed by H. H. and Luvois Shugart reached maximum numbers of 6000 to 10,000 birds in the second half of June 1965. In 1966 the same roost had 25 birds at mid-May, 1700 at mid-June, and a peak of 6000 on July 4. After July 4 the roost rapidly declined to 2000 the following day, 1200 in the last

week of July, and less than 100 in the second week of August. Only an estimated 10 percent of the birds were adult males. This roost was on the metal superstructure of a chemical plant. During roosting flights large flocks of martins were observed which seemed to be attracted to, and flew repeatedly through the large plumes of chemically-laden gases emitted by the plant.

Departure dates from nesting areas usually occur during July. At Hope in Hempstead County these departures were noted from July 1 to 20, often during the first week of the month. Martins are seen regularly through August, then irregularly during September. The latest sighting date for the state is in the first half of October.

TREE SWALLOW, *Tachycineta bicolor* (Vieillot)

Common transient in all regions that is locally abundant along the Mississippi River. Rare and irregular summer resident.

SPRING MIGRATION: Northward moving spring migrants have been reported unusually as early as the second week in February (one bird), but there are no other records until the third week of February, after which they are seen with increasing frequency until late April, with the latest regular spring record occurring in the second week of May. The largest numbers are seen near the Mississippi River. Ben Coffey saw 825 birds at Horseshoe Lake (an old oxbow of the Mississippi) in Crittenden County on February 21, 1965, and 4000 at the same place on April 28, 1935. While flocks of 20 to 50 birds are not rare, many records in the Audubon Society file have involved smaller numbers, especially in the highlands and in western Arkansas. In these areas a few Tree Swallows are often mixed in with large flocks of other swallows. The 150 at Calion near El Dorado on April 18 was a high count outside the Mississippi River region.

BREEDING SEASON: While there have been a few summer sightings off and on over the years (including two on the 1979 Arkansas Breeding Bird Survey), previous to 1980 there were only two confirmed instances of nesting. A nest with eggs was found in a stump in the middle of the St. Francis River in northeastern Arkansas in May 1894 (Howell 1911). A nest was found at Fort Chaffee near Fort Smith in 1954 (Audubon Society file). On May 25, 1980, four Tree Swallows were observed as they entered holes in cypress snags at Lake Conway in Faulkner County, and David Johnson confirmed the presence of two nests the following day. Tree Swallows were photographed with young in a nest at Big Lake Refuge on June 18, 1980. Eggs were observed in a nest at Budd Kidd Lake in Washington County on May 25, 1984. In addition, there are several other summer records (file, Callahan 1953). It appears that this species may occasionally take advantage of a favorable situation such as an impoundment with many dead trees whose natural cavities offer suitable nesting sites.

FALL MIGRATION AND WINTER: Migrants have been reported from late July through November, but mainly late August to about mid-November. In the eastern lowlands especially, peak counts in late September and October involve hundreds, sometimes thousands of birds, with smaller numbers elsewhere, particularly in the highlands and in western Arkansas. Ben Coffey saw almost 12,000 birds at Horseshoe and Porter lakes in Crittenden County on October 20, and there is one record in the file that involved even more. By contrast, the 300 at Fort Smith on September 28 was a high count for western Arkansas.

The 30 Tree Swallows seen at Lonoke during the 1980 Christmas Bird Count is the only record for this species between late November and early February.

NORTHERN ROUGH-WINGED SWALLOW, *Stelgidopteryx serripennis* (Audubon)

Common migrant and summer resident along bodies of water, especially streams and rivers, throughout the state. Locally abundant fall migrant especially in the eastern lowlands.

SPRING MIGRATION: Spring migrants have been observed in southern Arkansas as early as the first week of March, but the usual early arrival date is in the third week of March, with numbers increasing thereafter especially in the last few days of the month and in early April.

BREEDING SEASON: Reports in the Audubon Society file show that Northern Rough-winged Swallows are widespread during the nesting season. Data from the Breeding Bird Surveys show a fairly even distribution of small num-

bers in each region. A peak mean of 5.3 birds was recorded on the survey in Johnson County.

The nesting season has been recorded during May and June. On the Buffalo River in Newton County these birds were engaging in courtship and investigating solution cavity holes in a bluff just above the river on April 16. In the Wheeler Collection three nests with six or seven eggs are dated between May 17 and June 5. Two of these nests were in cavities or burrows in river banks, and the other was in the bank of a ravine near water. A nest with four eggs was observed in Miller County on May 30. In Washington County this species was still entering cavities in a dirt bank above a small stream in the first week of June. Vivian Scarlett observed nests in an Arkansas River bank at Rebsamen Park in Little Rock, in a drain pipe at Petit Jean Mountain in Conway County, and in a gravel bank at Palarm Creek in Faulkner County. All these nests were in small, loose colonies, but they also commonly nest singly. Because rough-winged swallows typically nest in cavities or burrows in banks, they are sometimes mistakenly called "bank swallows." (See the following species account for *Riparia riparia*, which typically nests in large colonies rather than small scattered colonies as in *S. serripennis*.)

FALL MIGRATION: By mid-July rough-winged swallows are gathering in post-breeding season flocks. During the second and third weeks of July one observer reported "many" flocks of about 30 birds, and some with as many as 75 individuals, all perched on wires, in eastern Arkansas. In Jefferson County, an estimated 1000 birds in groups of 200 to 300 were reported on July 18, 1956. The 500 seen in Miller County on October 1 was an exceptionally large report for western Arkansas. Flocks are generally present in the state until around mid-October, less commonly thereafter. The 300 seen in Chicot County on November 11 were late. A few individuals are occasionally seen as late as the end of November, but very rarely after that.

BANK SWALLOW, *Riparia riparia* (Linnaeus)

Regular transient throughout the state, often in small numbers, that is especially numerous in the eastern lowlands. Irregular summer resident along the Mississippi and Arkansas rivers.

SPRING MIGRATION: Bank Swallows have been reported between the fourth week of April and the fourth week of May, unusually as early as the first week of April. Most reports in the Audubon Society file involve small numbers, and there are fewer reports for spring than fall. The 80 birds at Big Lake Refuge in the northeast on May 12 was a high number. The "several hundred" seen roosting at Lake Sequoyah in Washington County on May 9 was not only an impressive count for the state, it was an extraordinary count for the highlands where small numbers are usually seen.

BREEDING SEASON: Bank Swallows and 300 nests were reported at Helena in eastern Arkansas (Howell 1911), and Wheeler (1924) stated that "the nests, sometimes 50 or 100 together, are bored out in the loess banks of Crowley's Ridge at Helena . . ." The site was apparently abandoned between 1931 and 1951 (Baerg 1931, 1951). A colony was reported on the Spring River in Lawrence County in 1931 (Baerg 1931), but no other information on this report is available. Ben Coffey (1981) found one hundred and forty-three nests in a bank of the Arkansas River in Oklahoma, just across the Garrison Avenue bridge at Fort Smith, on July 18, 1954. Most of the birds were gone by that date, but it appeared that many of the cavity nests had been used. In 1958, fifteen nests were seen in the banks of the Arkansas River near Braden's Bend (LeFlore County, Oklahoma, near Fort Smith). The closing of the navigation dam on the Arkansas River and bank stabilization projects are said to have greatly reduced suitable nesting habitat in the Fort Smith area (B. Beall, pers. comm.). An estimated 125 birds and seventy-five nest holes were observed on a Mississippi River island off Mississippi County on July 3, 1984 (P. Hamel, pers. comm.).

FALL MIGRATION: Fall migrants have been observed from the second week of July into the second week of October primarily from the last week of July into the last week of September. Sightings during migration may involve a few birds mixed in with flocks of other species of swallows, or less often involve pure flocks of Bank Swallows. Along the Mississippi River in Crittenden County, a large mixed species flock of swallows included 1800 Banks and a lesser number of Trees and Northern Rough-winged Swallows on July 27. At Lonoke, 1700 Bank Swallows were observed on August 3, and most of them were still there a week later.

CLIFF SWALLOW, *Hirundo pyrrhonota* Vieillot

Common migrant in all regions, and summer resident chiefly in the Ozarks. In recent years the nesting range has been extending southward.

SPRING MIGRATION: Cliff Swallows have been observed in Arkansas as early as the last week of March, but the usual arrival time is in the first and second weeks of April. As many as 50 birds have been seen at Norfork Dam in Baxter County on April 7. Even though some nesting activity gets underway in the state during April (see below), migrants are present during April and most of May, with a peak in early May. Over 1000 Cliff Swallows were seen at Calion Lake near El Dorado on May 2, and 300 were seen as they rested in bushes at Lake Ouachita (Montgomery County) on May 7. The last migrants have passed through regions of the state where nesting does not occur as late as the last week of May.

BREEDING SEASON: Historically, Cliff Swallows nested only in northern Arkansas. Howell (1911) considered them "rare and local" and knew of only two breeding areas, both in the Ozarks. Baerg (1951) found them along the White River and its tributaries in the western Ozarks. At one colony on the White River near War Eagle in Benton County there were about 125 to 200 of their gourd-shaped mud nests built on a low projecting rock shelf no more than six to eight feet above the ground. "During the twelve years that this swallow colony has been visited . . . the birds have shown considerable determination to build on the low shelf . . . when the shelf was under water several times in late May, the swallows merely delayed nest construction two or three weeks until the water subsided . . . Other colonies . . . observed along the White River nest 75–100 feet up and commonly some distance from water" (Baerg 1944).

Reports in the Audubon Society file for the 1950s and 1960s (Figure 6-72) showed the species nesting in seven counties in the Ozarks, and these breeding colonies were largely associated with bridges or dams. Among the sites were the Imboden bridge in Lawrence County,

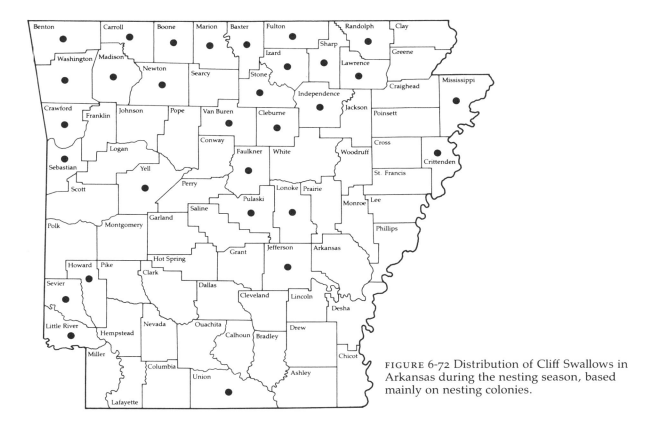

FIGURE 6-72 Distribution of Cliff Swallows in Arkansas during the nesting season, based mainly on nesting colonies.

the Sylamore Creek bridge in Stone County, Norfork Dam in Baxter County, Cotter bridge in Baxter County, the White River bridge near Eureka Springs (Carroll County), and elsewhere. Several of these colonies involved more than 100 birds, and Ben Coffey counted four hundred nests at Cotter in June 1959. Other than nests at dams or bridges, colonies were found in a ten-foot diameter culvert near Mountain View and on the White River cliffs (both in Baxter County). In the 1980s the birds continued using cliffs above the White River around Beaver Lake in the northwest and near Guion's Ferry in Stone County, and are still regularly nesting under bridges and dams throughout the Ozarks. Many of the colonies of two decades ago are still active, and new ones have been established. Others, such as the one at Imboden, seem to be used intermittently.

In addition to records for the Ozarks, there have been confirmed records of nesting in the Arkansas River Valley in Pulaski, Yell, and Faulkner counties since 1970 (Figure 6-72). The 25 birds that nested at Toad Suck Lock and Dam on the Arkansas River in May 1980 was Faulkner County's first record and a further indication that the species is moving south. In 1981, small colonies were found at the Gillham Dam and the Dierks Dam, both in Howard County in the southwest. Additional suggestions of the southward range expansion involve one or a few Cliff Swallows found in association with Barn Swallow colonies. There are recent such records from Sevier, Grant, and Little River counties, but no fully confirmed nesting records.

Nesting activity has been observed from the second half of April through July. At Lake Maumelle in Pulaski County, six nests were observed under a bridge on April 25, the earliest nesting observation in the file. Many colonies in the Ozarks are still active in late July. The presence of white excrement on the lip of the nest indicates that young have been present in the nests.

FALL MIGRATION: As judged by the pres-

FIGURE 6-73 Barn Swallow nesting colony in a culvert in early May, near Fulton in southwestern Arkansas. *David Plank*

ence of birds in regions where nesting is not known to occur, the fall migration is underway as early as mid-July, and the last migrants have usually moved south of Arkansas by the first week in October. The 125 birds seen at the state fish hatchery in Lonoke County on October 18 was a peak fall count (that did not involve birds in a nesting colony), and is the latest date in the file.

BARN SWALLOW, *Hirundo rustica* Linnaeus

Common migrant throughout the state. Summer resident in all regions, most numerous in the north. Observed near nesting sites under bridges and culverts, in old barns, and also flying low over fields and large open bodies of water.

SPRING MIGRATION: Spring arrivals have been reported unusually early in the second week of March, but most early spring arrivals involve the last days of March or first days in April, with numbers increasing thereafter. The 10 birds at Lake Fayetteville on March 26 was a large number for so early in spring. Migration also continues at the same time that part of the summer resident population in Arkansas has begun nesting (see below). Several hundred birds in a migratory flock roosted in dead weeds at Lake Fayetteville on May 9.

BREEDING SEASON: Breeding Bird Surveys show that Barn Swallows are numerous in all regions, especially in the highlands. The average annual mean number per route in each region on the surveys was 8.1 on the Coastal Plain, 7.5 on the Mississippi Alluvial Plain, and 13.5 in the highlands (including the Arkansas River Valley). Peak annual means of up to 33.4 birds were reported in extreme northern Arkansas.

During the 20th century the Barn Swallow has gradually spread southward as a nesting bird in Arkansas. In the first half of the century the bird was known to occur in summer only in the Ozark Plateaus region and was even rare and local there (Howell 1911, Wheeler 1924, Baerg 1931). However, by the 1940s it had become at least a fairly common summer resident in the western Ozarks (Baerg 1951). The records in the files of the Audubon Society show that Barn Swallows reached the Arkansas River Valley in the late 1940s. At Fort Smith, Bill Beall was aware of only one nesting in the late 1940s, but by the mid-1950s it was nesting in culverts throughout the area. By the 1950s Barn Swallows had become common summer birds in the Arkansas River Valley and were spreading eastward at that latitude to the eastern edge of the state in Prairie, Lonoke, Cross, and St. Francis counties (file, Coffey 1981). In the early 1960s they seemingly leaped over the Ouachita Mountains and became summer residents in the southwestern lowlands, becoming widespread there during the decade. The first sign of this new range expansion was the sighting of two birds in Pike County on July 5, 1959. The first nest reported for the southern edge of Arkansas was on May 13, 1962, north of Magnolia in Columbia County. This marked the swallow's final crossing of the whole state as a nesting species. Their spread southeastward seemed to lag behind the rest of the southward movement in the mid-to-late 1960s, but birds were seen near bridges in Chicot County in the extreme southeast in July 1966, and were reported in the Ouachita Mountains by the late 1960s. Possibly the widespread construction of cement culverts and bridges on highways that began in the 1950s provided new nesting sites and contributed to the range expansion. While this species is still absent from heavily forested areas, it is certainly common in summer where open country and suitable nesting sites prevail.

Nesting activity has been reported from early April to early August with a peak during May, June, and July. The earliest record involved an active nest in Poinsett County on April 4. The two active nests at Pine Bluff on August 7 provided the first breeding records for Jefferson County. Single nests occur, but more often Barn Swallows nest in small colonies. Their open mud nests are attached to supporting beams, rafters, or ledges in old, open barns and on the undersides of bridges, culverts, and porches of rural houses. Barn Swallows also nest with other species: six Cliff Swallow nests and forty-nine Barn Swallow nests were counted under a bridge over Lake Maumelle in Pulaski County on April 25. They have also been found nesting in the mouths of caves in Lawrence and Sharp counties (McDaniel and Gardner 1977).

FALL MIGRATION: Post-breeding flocks, often seen by the middle of July, frequently involve 10 to 25 birds perched on wires near the nesting area. Flocks seen in September and October are sometimes quite large, numbering up to 100 birds or more, and occasionally over 1000. These may be single species flocks, but often several species of swallows are mixed together. Fall migration is largely over by late October, but there are late reports involving one to three birds during November. Migratory flocks are particularly large in both migration seasons in the eastern lowlands.

Family *Corvidae* Jays and Crows

BLUE JAY, *Cyanocitta cristata* (Linnaeus)

Common migrant and ubiquitous permanent resident in towns and cities, forests, and forest edge. Large numbers are seen in migration.

SPRING MIGRATION: The period for northward migration seems to occur between mid-March and mid-May, with a peak usually in the second half of April when the birds are often seen in the early morning flying at low altitudes (only a few hundred feet high). Reports in the Audubon Society file show that these flocks are usually small, fewer than 30 birds, but sometimes larger numbers are seen. At Fort Smith, over 2000 were counted by Ralph Fox in two hours on April 23, 1960. The migratory period coincides with the time that resident Blue Jays are nesting (see below).

BREEDING SEASON: Breeding Bird Surveys and reports in the file show these birds are common and widespread in the state during summer. The average annual mean number of jays per route in each region on the Breeding Bird Surveys was 24.4 on the Coastal Plain (up to 40.0 in Calhoun County), 10.9 on the Mississippi Alluvial Plain, and 16.3 in the highlands (including the Arkansas River Valley).

FIGURE 6-74 Migrating Blue Jays in mid-October over the Ozarks near Batesville. *David Plank*

Nesting activity has been observed from late February to late August, primarily from mid-March through June. The earliest record was at Stuttgart in Arkansas County where jays were building a nest on February 21. The latest report involved a recently fledged bird on August 27 in Washington County. In the Wheeler Collection there are reports of nineteen nests with eggs between April 7 and June 23. The clutch sizes in these nests varied from two to five eggs (average of four), and the heights varied from six to forty feet above the ground, often between ten and fifteen. On the university campus at Fayetteville, jays have regularly nested in a small courtyard, and five nests from different years have all been at similar heights (around ten feet) in cedar trees. Among nesting materials used in each nest were plastic beverage can holders collected from the courtyard trash bin.

Summer population studies (Tables 3-1 and 3-3) indicate a population range of eight to eleven territorial males per one hundred acres of forest in the south and five to eight in the north.

FALL MIGRATION: Fall migrants have been reported from the third week in September to late October, with a few peak reports of large numbers (presumably associated with migration) during November. During the southward migration period hundreds may be seen flying overhead in various sized flocks during a day in the field, and sometimes even more. In the Arkansas River Valley at North Little Rock, migratory flights in 1973 varied from several hundred birds on September 23, to 2000 on October 1, 3000 on October 3, and a peak of 6000 on October 4. Hundreds of these birds were seen almost daily in the western Ozarks during the first two weeks of October in 1983.

Banding records associated with Arkansas also demonstrate these extensive migratory movements. The part of the jay population which comprises our winter resident and migratory birds breeds in the midwestern states to the north of Arkansas, and some birds that breed in Arkansas migrate southward (Figure 6-75). The most common distance between banding and recovery was about 500 miles and up to nearly 950 miles. Most birds were recovered within 14 months after banding, but one survived almost five years. Analysis of banding recoveries shows that the age of Blue Jays has

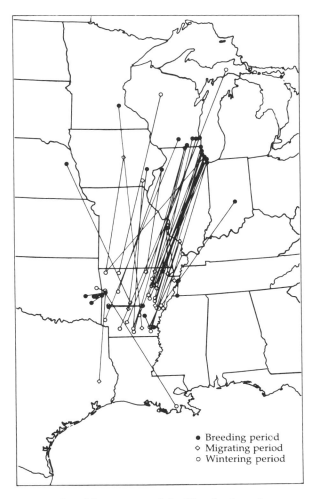

FIGURE 6-75 Movements of the Blue Jay based on banding records.

no effect on migratory versus sedentary status, and only a very small percent of the jay population migrates annually, especially in the latitudes from Kentucky southward (Wenger 1975).

WINTER: Hundreds of jays are reported on the annual Christmas Bird Counts in all regions. The statewide ten-year mean of 3.4 birds per party hour on Christmas Counts was easily exceeded in all regions. On the Coastal Plain the means varied from 2.6 to 6.8, on the Mississippi Alluvial Plain from 2.3 to 6.8, and in the highlands (including the Arkansas River Valley) from 2.9 to 4.3.

Winter population surveys (Tables 3-2 and 3-4) in southern and northern Arkansas indicated a population from 8 to 10 jays per one hundred acres of upland woods, and 11 to 15 jays in the bottomland woods. One factor affecting Blue Jay populations is the availability of acorns (Smith 1986a), an important winter food for this species. At Fayetteville 376 birds were reported on the 1978 Christmas Count, but only 17 in 1979, and then 268 in 1980. The low dip in 1979 coincided with a very poor acorn crop in the western Ozarks.

CLARK'S NUTCRACKER, *Nucifraga columbiana* (Wilson)

One record.

This species sometimes wanders outside its usual winter range (AOU 1983), a fact which presumably accounts for the lone Arkansas record. Mitchell (1894) stated that "a specimen of Clarke's Nutcracker . . . was killed at Earl, Crittenden County, Ark . . . about April 1, 1891, and sent to Memphis for identification. It came into my possession in the flesh . . ."

AMERICAN CROW, *Corvus brachyrhynchos* Brehm

Permanent resident that is common and widespread. Formerly called "Common Crow."

BREEDING SEASON: American Crows nest in all regions of Arkansas, but they are most numerous during the breeding season in open country in the highlands and on the Coastal Plain, and with generally much smaller but still significant numbers on the Mississippi Alluvial Plain. The average annual mean number per route in each region reported on Breeding Bird

Surveys was 37.9 on the Coastal Plain, 8.4 on the Mississippi Alluvial Plain, and 30.1 in the highlands (including the Arkansas River Valley). In the past this species was nowhere really abundant in the state (Howell 1911, Wheeler 1924). Presumably the large population in the state today has been encouraged by agricultural development.

Nesting activity has been reported chiefly during March and April. In the Wheeler Collection there are nine clutches of eggs taken from nests between March 11 and April 18. The clutch sizes varied from three to seven eggs (average five), and the nests fifteen to seventy-five feet (often around twenty feet) from the ground.

MIGRATION AND WINTER: During the breeding season (and through summer) American Crows are seen only in small numbers, and never in large flocks. By mid-September, however, observers find flocks of 25 to 50 or more birds in the large open fields of agricultural areas, and these are seen throughout the fall and winter. During February and March these flocks begin to break up, signaling the beginning of the breeding season.

In every region of the state hundreds of American Crows are reported on Christmas Bird Counts where there are large open fields with waste grains. Sometimes even larger numbers are seen. At Lake Millwood, 25,000 birds occupied a single roost in late December of 1975. Peak means of 4.3 up to 7.0 American Crows per party hour have been reported on Christmas Counts in all regions.

One bird banded in central Missouri in May was recovered in central-southern Arkansas the following January. Another bird banded in Ontario in May was recovered in Arkansas the following January. A third bird banded near the Arkansas River in Colorado in mid-November was recovered seven days later and 567 miles to the east near the Arkansas River in Arkansas.

FISH CROW, *Corvus ossifragus* Wilson

Local permanent resident, usually in small numbers, on or near major rivers especially in the lowlands and the Arkansas River Valley. Migrant and summer resident in the Ozarks.

SPRING: Peak numbers suggestive of the spring migration have been reported during March and April. A total of 41 Fish Crows were observed as they flew up the Arkansas River near Van Buren on March 4. Twelve birds were reported at Big Lake Refuge in northeastern Arkansas on April 24. In Faulkner County the species is numerous mainly from March to late August (Johnson 1979).

BREEDING SEASON: The majority of reports in the Audubon Society file are from the major rivers and their important tributaries including the Arkansas, Mississippi, White, Ouachita, and Red rivers. In southwestern Arkansas, Fish Crows are present all year at Grassy Lake and at Lake Millwood. Even though a population has long been known from the Arkansas River Valley, there were no acceptable records for the western Ozarks until the early 1980s. By 1984 there were summer records up and down the White River and along most of the smaller streams in the western Ozarks. Reports on the Breeding Bird Survey are spotty, with peak annual means of 1.9 to 5.6 Fish Crows on the surveys in Ashley, Dallas, and Lincoln counties, all in the southern lowlands. There are several banding records (Figure 6-76) of birds in winter on the Gulf Coast recovered along major rivers in Arkansas during the breeding season.

There are only a few nest records. A bird was carrying nesting material in Conway County on May 3. In Arkansas County, young were being fed on May 13. In Faulkner and Perry counties, hatchlings were observed in a nest one hundred and ten feet high in a sycamore tree on June 5, and eggs were observed in a nest fifty feet high on June 24 (Wheeler 1922b, Wheeler Collection).

FALL AND WINTER: Fall migrants have been reported from late August to early November. The 20 to 24 birds seen (and heard) at Lake Sequoyah in the western Ozarks in late August had declined to a single bird by September 6, and the latest record for the area is in late October. At Little Rock near the Arkansas River, 60 Fish Crows were reported on September 30, and an unusually large roost of 200 birds was reported at Murray Park in the same city in late September of a different year. The 52 birds heard calling at Lake Maumelle in Pulaski County on November 8 seemed to be a loosely knit migrating flock.

December through February sightings have mainly involved birds in the Arkansas River Valley and in the southern lowlands. The 552 reported on the Christmas Bird Count at Fort

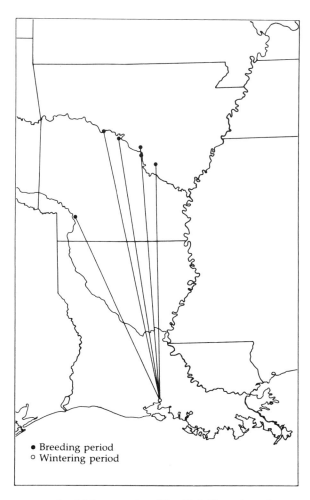

● Breeding period
○ Wintering period

FIGURE 6-76 Movements of the Fish Crow based on banding records.

Smith in 1957 was a large number for the state, but hundreds are reported elsewhere. At Lake Millwood, 360 were reported on the 1980 Christmas Count, 390 at Arkadelphia on the 1981 count, and just over 300 at El Dorado in 1978. These large numbers are not reported every year in every community where the birds are found regularly, but this is not surprising since both species of crows may range over relatively large areas, and where both are known to occur, the correct species can be identified in the field only if the calls are heard.

Family Paridae
Chickadees and Titmice

CAROLINA CHICKADEE, *Parus carolinensis* Audubon

Common permanent resident in woodlands and forest edge. Frequents home bird feeders in winter.

BREEDING SEASON: During the nesting season chickadees are most numerous on the Coastal Plain and in the highlands (including the Arkansas River Valley), and are common but less numerous on the Mississippi Alluvial Plain. The average annual mean number per count in each region reported on Breeding Bird Surveys was 7.7 on the Coastal Plain, 2.1 on the Mississippi Alluvial Plain, and 7.5 in the highlands (including the Arkansas River Valley). Peak means of 13.1 to 21.6 birds were reported on the surveys in Calhoun, Clark, Garland, and Scott counties.

Nesting activity has been observed from late February through June, with a peak of activity during April and May. A nest under construction at Stuttgart on February 21 is the earliest such report for the state. The six eggs in a gourd in Pulaski County on May 3 was a late egg date, and young being fed in a tree cavity nest in Washington County in mid-June were also relatively late. In the Wheeler Collection there are seven clutches of eggs that were collected between March 31 and April 23. Clutch sizes comprised six or seven eggs (often six), and the cavity nests were three to twelve feet above the ground, often in the range of three to five feet. Nesting sites have included rotten fence posts,

cavities in stumps or dead limbs, bird boxes, and similar places. Family groups that include adults and fledglings are commonly seen during June. The distinctive territorial song is heard as early as January or February through June, and infrequently otherwise.

Results from summer population studies (Tables 3-1 and 3-3) on the Coastal Plain indicated a population of 10 to 14 territorial male chickadees per one hundred acres of forest, and smaller numbers in the north.

WINTER: Flocks of chickadees (often mixed flocks that include chickadees and other species of small birds) can be observed in woodlands throughout the state in winter. In the Audubon Society file there are many reports involving eight to ten or more seen during a day in the field. The statewide ten-year mean on Christmas Bird Counts was 1.8 chickadees per party hour. This mean varied from 1.0 to 3.2 birds per party hour on the Coastal Plain, 0.9 to 1.8 on the Mississippi Alluvial Plain, and 1.1 to 2.5 in the highlands (including the Arkansas River Valley). On the statewide 1980 Christmas Count, ten of the participating counts reported at least 100 of these birds, and there were nearly 300 at Conway.

Winter population studies in the state (Tables 3-2 and 3-4) suggest that chickadees generally are more numerous in bottomland forest than in upland forest, though this is apparently not uniformly the case in all habitats in the state. The tendency is most strikingly evident in the western Ozarks, where there was a population of four birds per one hundred acres of uplands, and 20 per one hundred acres of bottomland.

TUFTED TITMOUSE, *Parus bicolor* Linnaeus

Common permanent resident in woodlands and forest edge. Often found at home bird feeders in winter.

BREEDING SEASON: Titmice are numerous in summer in all regions, but they are found in the lowest numbers in eastern lowlands. The average annual mean number per count in each region reported on Breeding Bird Surveys was 13.5 on the Coastal Plain, 2.9 on the Mississippi Alluvial Plain, and 10.2 in the highlands (including the Arkansas River Valley). Summer population studies (Tables 3-1 and 3-3) on the Coastal Plain indicated a population of as many

FIGURE 6-77 Tufted Titmouse. *Max Parker*

as 34 singing males per one hundred acres of bottomland forest and 20 per one hundred acres of upland forest. In the bottomlands, only Red-eyed Vireos and Carolina Wrens were more numerous. In the uplands only Red-eyed Vireos and Northern Cardinals were more numerous. Smaller titmouse numbers were recorded on population surveys in northern Arkansas than elsewhere in the state.

The chief months for nesting are April and May. In Ashley County, six nests were under construction between April 6 and 29. In the Wheeler Collection there are six clutches of eggs taken from nests between April 17 and June 1, chiefly during April. Family groups that include adults and fledglings are commonly seen during May and June. Nest sites have included natural cavities, woodpecker cavities, rotting wooden fence posts, nesting boxes, gourds, and similar items. Nesting heights in the Wheeler Collection ranged from four to twenty-three feet, often four to twelve feet above the ground.

WINTER: Titmice are found in numbers in all regions of the state during winter, and are often observed in mixed flocks that include other species of small birds. The statewide ten-year mean on Christmas Bird Counts was 2.1 birds per party hour. On the Coastal Plain this mean ranged from 0.5 to 2.1 birds per party hour, from 0.2 to 0.9 on the Mississippi Alluvial Plain, and from 0.3 to 1.5 in the high-

FIGURE 6-78 Wintering Red-breasted Nuthatch near Conway in central Arkansas in January. *David Plank*

lands (including the Arkansas River Valley). On the statewide 1980 Christmas Counts, the number reported varied from 9 to 135 birds, with 40 or more reported from half of the counts.

Winter population studies (Tables 3-2 and 3-4) suggest that this species is about twice as numerous in bottomland as in upland woods in winter, with as many as 22 birds per one hundred acres in bottomland woods.

Family *Sittidae* Nuthatches

RED-BREASTED NUTHATCH, *Sitta canadensis* Linnaeus

Fairly common and somewhat irregular or "irruptive" transient and winter resident in all regions. Observed in coniferous or mixed coniferous-deciduous forest and at home bird feeders.

MIGRATION: The earliest fall arrival date is in the last week of August, and the latest spring departure date is in the second week of May. Generally few are reported, even during "invasion" years, until mid-September and thereafter. Many reports in the Audubon Society file have involved small numbers, often one to five for one day in the field (or birds visiting home feeders). During some "invasion" years larger numbers are reported. In the Ozark National Forest in Crawford County the birds were said to be "abundant" and "literally everywhere" on November 9, 1969. Based on reports in the Audubon Society file the species characteristically is more numerous in the state during November, December, or January than in the spring.

WINTER: Observers in Arkansas have frequently noted the irregular nature of the numbers of Red-breasted Nuthatches seen from year to year. In some years, several birds or as many as four to six may be present in certain locations during most of the winter, but the following year few or none may be present. Analysis of Christmas Bird Counts for a ten-year period helped to clarify these fluctuations.

Low cycles were apparent in the years 1962, 1964, and 1970, with statewide mean numbers reported on Christmas Counts varying from zero per party hour (no birds seen), or 0.01 (very few present). Larger numbers were seen in 1968 and 1969, with means varying from 0.08 to 0.19 birds per party hour. Statewide, the ten-year mean number of birds per party hour on the Christmas Bird Counts varied from none to 0.08 on the Coastal Plain, none to 0.31 on the Mississippi Alluvial Plain, and none to 0.12 in the highlands (including the Arkansas River Valley).

In the heart of the pinelands at Lake Georgia-Pacific (Ashley County), 10 or more were reported on five of fifteen Christmas Bird Counts between 1969 and 1983, with peaks of 59 and 42 birds in two of those years. By comparison, at Fayetteville where pine forests are generally lacking, none were reported on seven of thirteen recent Christmas Counts, and the peak number of 10 was reported in one year.

WHITE-BREASTED NUTHATCH, *Sitta carolinensis* Latham

Common permanent resident in mature woods with tall deciduous trees in towns, woodlots and forests. Found throughout the state, and most numerous in the highlands.

BREEDING SEASON: In the Audubon Society file there are summer reports for all regions, especially in deciduous forests in the highlands, but also in the forested regions of the lowlands. The average annual mean number per route in each region reported on Breeding Bird Surveys was 0.3 on the Gulf Coastal Plain, 0.4 for the Mississippi Alluvial Plain, and 1.4 for the Ozark and Ouachita highlands (including the Arkansas River Valley). The peak numbers of 1.5 to 3.3 birds per survey were reported in the Ouachita Mountains and the Ozark Plateaus. Summer population studies in northwestern Arkansas (Table 3-1 and 3-3) indicated a population of two singing males per one hundred acres of upland forest, and none per one hundred acres in bottomlands.

Reports for the nesting season range from late February to the second week of May. A pair of White-breasted Nuthatches was carrying nesting materials into a cavity in the upland terrain of the university campus at Fayetteville on February 22. In the Wheeler Collection there is one clutch of six eggs that was collected from a nest twenty-four feet above the ground on April 11. On a forested hillside in Washington County, adults were carrying nesting materials into a natural tree cavity thirty to thirty-five feet high. The male was observed as he fed the female at the cavity entrance, and the female was later observed as she collected nesting materials in the forest near the tree. Young were just fledging from a nest in Prairie County at DeVall's Bluff on May 10.

WINTER: There is no apparent change in the distributional patterns for this species at any time during the year. As in the breeding season, the birds are most often found during winter in the highlands. On the 1980 statewide Christmas Bird Counts, peak totals involving 24 to 48 were reported at Fayetteville, Mena, and Hot Springs Village, all in the highlands. Smaller numbers, infrequently as many as five to eight, are reported on Christmas Counts in the lowlands. The birds are absent from regions that have been extensively deforested. Also, they are very uncommon in forest dominated by pines and in bottomland forests.

While White-breasted Nuthatches are found in both upland and bottomland woods in the highlands, they show a distinct preference for the upland woods. This preference is illustrated by winter population studies in northwestern Arkansas where there was a population of one bird per one hundred acres of bottomland woods, and three per one hundred acres of upland forest (Tables 3-2 and 3-4).

BROWN-HEADED NUTHATCH, *Sitta pusilla* Latham

Permanent resident of pine forests in the Ouachita Mountains and on the Coastal Plain.

BREEDING SEASON: Records in the Audubon Society file show that the range of this species includes the pine and pine-oak woodlands on

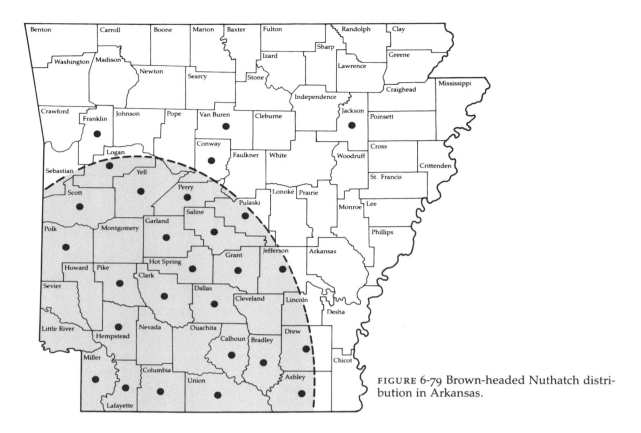

FIGURE 6-79 Brown-headed Nuthatch distribution in Arkansas.

the Coastal Plain east to eastern Drew County and northward through the pinelands of the Ouachita Mountains into the Arkansas River Valley (Figure 6-79). In the Ozarks it has been reported in a mixed pine-oak woodland north of Mulberry in Franklin County and near Shirley in Van Buren County. The prime habitat appears to be mature pine forests, but the species utilizes all types of pine areas, including "clear cuts" where snags provide nest cavities.

Nesting activity has been observed from late February to mid-June. A pair was excavating a nesting cavity near Blue Mountain Dam in Yell County on February 24, and nest activities were underway at El Dorado on the same day of a different year. At Hamburg in Ashley County, birds were building a nest on March 13 in a pine snag cavity that had been used by this species twice in the previous year. Four young fledged from this nest on April 10. At Little Rock, adults were feeding young in a nest in a rotten stump cavity four feet from the ground

in a mixed pine-oak woodland on April 1. A nest with five eggs was seven feet from the ground in a dead stump at Texarkana on April 16. At Hamburg the first egg was laid in a nest on May 20, and the four young fledged on June 14.

WINTER: This permanent resident of the pinelands is reported on Christmas Bird Counts in the Ouachitas and on the Coastal Plain. At Lake Georgia-Pacific, the numbers reported between 1969 and 1982 on the Christmas Count have varied from 33 to 305 birds, with 200 or more in eight of these years. Generally lower numbers are reported elsewhere in the pinelands, but they are found with regularity where there is appropriate habitat.

Winter population studies in Union County indicated a population of eight birds per one hundred acres of upland pine and pine-oak bottomland, and three per one hundred acres in oak-pine bottomland (Tables 3-2 and 3-4).

Family Certhiidae Creepers

BROWN CREEPER, *Certhia americana* Bonaparte

Common migrant and common to uncommon winter resident in woodlands throughout the state. Several rare summer records.

FALL MIGRATION: Brown Creepers have arrived in Arkansas as early as the first week of October, but few are seen until later in the month, with a peak in numbers during the first half of November. The single bird that wandered into a living room at Fort Smith on September 23 was unusually early.

WINTER: Brown Creepers are reported regularly on Christmas Bird Counts in all regions, but the numbers may vary considerably from year to year. At Fort Smith, creepers are reported on most Christmas Bird Counts. The average annual mean number reported between 1956 and 1983 was 4.3. In three years of this period 10 or more were counted, and in five years the number was one or zero. The ten-year statewide mean of 0.1 creepers per party hour was exceeded in at least one count in each region.

Winter population studies (Tables 3-2 and 3-4) involving both upland and bottomland woods indicated a population of from three to seven birds per one hundred acres of bottomland, and zero to two per one hundred acres of upland woods.

SPRING MIGRATION: An influx of birds during March, especially mid-March to early April, signals the main period for the northward spring migration. In Franklin County, a large influx involving 15 birds was reported on March 20. The usual departure dates for the state are in the first or second weeks of April, with only a few rare sightings after the third week.

SUMMER: While normally absent from Arkansas between late April and early October, there are three records for the species during summer: one bird in Craighead County on July 5, 1954; one in Izard County near Zion on June 24, 1972; two in cypress woods at Grassy Lake in Hempstead County on June 2, 1974. Interestingly, there is a Brown Creeper nesting record in the last century in extreme southeastern Missouri (Howell 1911).

Family Troglodytidae Wrens

ROCK WREN, *Salpinctes obsoletus* (Say)

Five records.

Arkansas is somewhat east of the usual range of this common species of the western United States (AOU 1983). Sutton (1967) states that the Rock Wren is found in Oklahoma primarily in the central and western areas, but that there are also breeding records as far east as Sequoyah County, immediately west of Fort Smith, Arkansas. In Arkansas, one bird was reported at the Narrows Dam on Lake Greeson in Pike County on May 31, 1958. One was seen among the riprap rocks on the Cove Lake Dam near Paris in Logan County on March 10, 1961. At Little Rock, there were several sightings of a Rock Wren between January 2 and March 19, 1972. A Rock Wren was observed on Archer Island in Chicot County on October 10, 1976. The most recent record, a single bird at Mountain Pine (Garland County) on October 16, 1984, was carefully documented by the observer.

CAROLINA WREN, *Thryothorus ludovicianus* (Latham)

Common permanent resident in forest edge habitat, including rural areas and lightly urbanized towns throughout the state. Especially numerous in the bottomlands.

BREEDING SEASON: Reports in the Audubon Society file show that Carolina Wrens are widely distributed during the nesting season. Data from the Breeding Bird Surveys underscore this fact. The average annual mean number per route in each region reported on the surveys was 23.8 on the Coastal Plain, 5.8 on the Mississippi Alluvial Plain, and 8.1 in the highlands (including the Arkansas River Valley). The high numbers on the Coastal Plain involved peak means of 29 to 39 birds on four of the surveys in that region. Large numbers were also reported on the surveys in Saline and Garland counties. Summer population studies (Table 3-3) in southern Arkansas indicated a population of 35 singing males per one hundred acres of bottomland woods, but only half as many in the upland woods (Table 3-1). The birds were virtually absent from the upland woods in northwestern Arkansas, but numer-

FIGURE 6-80 Carolina Wren. *David Plank*

ous in bottomlands there (Tables 3-1 and 3-3).

The nesting season has been reported from early March to late September. The two earliest breeding observations in the Audubon Society file involved a nest under construction in Ashley County on March 6, and a first egg laid in a nest in Union County on March 10. The latest reports in the file involved young still in a nest in Union County on August 12, and young just fledging from a nest at Little Rock on September 29. In the Wheeler Collection there are twelve clutches of eggs that were taken from nests between April 24 and July 5. The clutch sizes varied from four to six eggs, with an average of five.

Nests have been observed in houses, outbuildings, and under natural conditions in brush piles, tree root tangles, and similar sites. Information associated with the Wheeler Collection shows that the birds nested on a river bank, in and under stumps, on a sill in an old building, and on a shelf in a school building. Many of these nests were on the ground, but others varied in height from one and one-half to twenty feet above the ground. Several observers in Arkansas have noted this bird's habit of raising at least two broods and sometimes three in one season (file, Wheeler 1924, Black 1935a). At Winslow in Washington County, Carolina Wrens used "the same nesting site for seven consecutive summers for their first brood. Apparently during all this time a complete nest was never built, but the old one repaired . . ." (Black 1935a). Banding studies also provide information on loyalty to the hatching site: forty-six of forty-seven recoveries of these birds occurred at the banding site in Arkansas; one banded at Fort Smith in late November was captured in early January at Russellville, 78 miles east.

A nesting study at North Little Rock (Nice and Thomas 1948) showed that while the male carried more nesting material than the female, the female performed all the incubation, and was fed on the nest by the male. The incubation period required about two weeks, as did the nestling period. Both parents fed the nestlings. One bird in the study survived into its sixth year.

WINTER: This resident species, which is most numerous in summer on the Coastal Plain, is predictably most numerous in winter in the same region. The ten-year statewide mean number of birds on Christmas Bird Counts was 0.9 birds per party hour. On the Coastal Plain this mean varied from 0.5 to 3.7 birds per party hour, from 0.5 to 1.1 on the Mississippi Alluvial Plain, and from 0.2 to 0.9 in the highlands (including the Arkansas River Valley). Some of the highest numbers have been reported at Lake Georgia-Pacific in the extreme south. On Christmas Counts between 1969 and 1983 the number reported there varied from 47 to 264, with 100 or more in nine of the years.

These permanent resident birds are subject to decimation during the prolonged, severe cold of some winters, especially in the more northerly areas. This winter decimation has also been noted in the Memphis area (Coffey 1942). At Fayetteville, the winters between 1976 and 1982 varied from mild temperatures to those of severe, prolonged freezing and cold. The Carolina Wren population in this period plunged from 52 on the 1976 Christmas Count to only single birds during severe winters in the late 1970s. The population began to recover again during the mild winters of the early 1980s, up to an exceptional 69 in 1982.

BEWICK'S WREN, *Thryomanes bewickii* (Audubon)

Present in the state throughout the year. Formerly fairly common breeder in some areas, at least locally, in the Ozarks and in the Arkansas River Valley; now rare and local and infrequently reported. Winter resident or visitor that has been reported in all regions, but chiefly in the lowlands and in the Arkansas River Valley. Uncommon migrant in all regions. Seen around houses, sheds and unkempt piles of junk or tangles of vegetation in clearings in lightly developed parts of towns or rural areas.

SPRING MIGRATION: Spring migrants are observed from late February through April, but especially during March. In south central Arkansas, where it is present in winter, the latest spring sightings occurred in mid-March (Mattocks and Shugart 1962), and arrivals in the north, where the species nests, occurred at about the same time (Baerg 1951, Audubon Society file).

BREEDING SEASON: Nesting has been observed as early as the end of March and there is a record of young in one nest as late as the first week of July. In the Wheeler Collection there are eight nests with eggs collected between March 31 and June 3, mainly during April and May. The clutch sizes were six or seven eggs, and the heights of the nests ranged from two to eight feet, often four feet or higher. Wheeler (1924) indicates that the eggs were collected from nests in the Ozarks, the Arkansas River Valley and southeast to Jefferson County. The latest nesting record in the Audubon Society file involved young still in a nest in Lawrence County on July 3. Nests have been recorded in a bewildering variety of situations, including gourds, sheds, various types of outbuildings, and junk cars. "It is seldom that we find a nest . . . in the open . . . [it] prefers indoor situations, not objecting to a tomato can, a coat sleeve, or a mail box. We once found a nest built in a swinging lot gate, and they often built on porches" (Wheeler 1924).

Bewick's Wren seems in recent years to have declined in numbers. This decline has provoked concern, and the cause for the decline is not readily apparent (James 1974). At Little Rock, where nests were once commonly found, the decline was noted twenty years ago. When Bill Beall heard a bird singing during June and July of 1976 at Fort Smith, he stated, "I considered it a common summer resident here in the late 40s and early 50s [but it] became uncommon to rare here by the early 60s." While Baerg (1951) considered the species to be "fairly common" in northern Arkansas, summer records in recent years there have been relatively few and scattered.

Howell (1911) considered Bewick's Wren to be the common dooryard wren, restricted to the "hill country" of northern and western Arkansas. He thought the bird filled the same role as the House Wren, which did not then nest in the state. Howell wrote that Bewick's Wren was "much less common than the Carolina Wren." He said the former was "rare" in summer along the eastern border of the Ozarks; occurred in "small numbers" at Mammoth Spring in Fulton County, at Cotter in Baxter County, and Rich Mountain in the Ouachitas; was "fairly common" in summer at Conway and at Pettigrew in Madison County. At Winslow in Washington County, the species was an "irregular" summer resident (Black 1935a). There were no nesting

records for Garland County (Deaderick 1938).

There were only sparse records of Bewick's Wrens on the Breeding Bird Surveys in Arkansas from 1967 to 1977, and these occurred primarily in the Ozarks, and in Sebastian County in the Arkansas River Valley. The species was not found every year on any of these surveys, and when found the numbers were often single birds, rarely as many as three. Information in the Audubon Society file suggests that the birds still nest regularly in small numbers in Jefferson County where several nests have been found since 1968, and Jane Stern (pers. comm.) has said that she hears at least fragmentary reports of nesting birds there every year. A nest with young was found at Morrilton in Conway County in 1977, and singing birds have been reported from Washington and Benton counties during late spring and summer several times in the late 1970s and mid-1980s.

It appears that Bewick's Wren has never been more than fairly common at a few localities in the state. There is no indication, for example, that the species was ever as widespread as the Carolina Wren. In Fayetteville, where Bewick's Wren was "fairly common" thirty years ago, the common wren of the dooryard in the 1980s is the House Wren, a species that was first observed nesting at Fayetteville only a decade ago. Arkansas's human population has continued to grow with attendant land development, and certainly many of the places where Bewick's Wren was found in the past have now become more "citified," i.e., fewer neglected sheds and junky open lots. This apparent change in the bird's former nesting locales has provided speculation about the species' decline in Arkansas (James 1974).

FALL MIGRATION: Fall migrants are notable during October. At Winslow, the species was most numerous in the "early part of October" (Smith 1915). At Fort Smith the fall peak occurs during the last week of October. Fall arrivals in Garland County have been recorded on October 6 (Deaderick 1938). In Jefferson County, birds that nested in 1968 had departed the area by the third week of October.

WINTER: During winter Bewick's Wren has been found in every region, but most records are from the lowlands or from the Arkansas River Valley. On the 1980 Christmas Bird Counts, the 14 birds counted statewide were seen almost exclusively in the southern lowlands with a peak of five at Texarkana. While Bewick's Wren has not been of regular occurrence in the Ozarks in winter, as many as seven birds have been recorded on Christmas Counts at Fayetteville, but none have been reported on a count there since 1974. This date nearly coincides with the years in which the House Wren first arrived as a nesting bird in the towns of northwestern Arkansas and subsequently became the common urban wren there (see below).

HOUSE WREN, *Troglodytes aedon* Vieillot

Permanent resident. Migrant in all regions. Summer resident in the north, especially northwest. Fairly regular in winter in the southern lowlands. Inhabits urban yards with shrubbery during summer, and otherwise shrubby tangles in open areas and forest edge.

SPRING MIGRATION: Spring migrants are observed primarily from mid-April until mid-May. In the western Ozarks where it does not overwinter, arrivals have been reported from mid- to-late April (Audubon Society file, Baerg 1951), with the birds seen regularly in places where nesting is not known to occur as late as the second week of May. There are similar records for Faulkner County in the Arkansas River Valley (Johnson 1979). Migrants have been observed from the third week of March to the first week of May at Lake Millwood. In the western Ozarks the birds are fairly common during spring migration (file, Black 1935a), but they do not seem to be quite as common in other regions of the state (file, Hanebrink and Posey 1979).

BREEDING SEASON: Prior to the 1960s the only summer records seem to have been at Winslow in Washington County, where three pairs definitely nested in 1933 (Black 1935a) and at Lake Wedington in Washington County where Callahan (1953) listed the species as an uncommon summer resident. There were no further summer records reported until 1966, when a nest with eggs was found in a bird feeder on May 22 at Rector in Clay County. Since 1972, when they first nested in Fayetteville, House Wrens have been reported regularly in summer in Benton and Washington counties, and have become a common summer

resident in urban areas there. Birds have also been seen and heard southeast of Osceola in Mississippi County during June in the early 1980s.

Young birds have been observed in nests from mid-May to mid-August, and two broods have been reported during one season. The birds seem rather innovative in their selection of nest sites, since nests have been seen in a small bird feeder, a waxed box with a one-inch diameter entrance hole, the open end of a metal clothesline pole, and commonly in wren nesting boxes. None of these nests have been higher than six and one-half feet from the ground.

FALL MIGRATION: Fall migrants are notable from about the fourth week of September to early November. In the western Ozarks, the peak of migration has passed by mid-October, but there are some records during November and in early December. In Faulkner County peak numbers are seen from mid-October to early November (Johnson 1979). In 1982 in Washington County, migrating birds were observed from September 22 to October 10, with a peak of 11 birds seen on one day in the field October 7, and in Chicot County in the extreme southeast a party of observers saw the same number on November 27.

WINTER: Composite summaries of data from about ten recent years of Christmas Bird Counts in the state suggest that the birds are increasing in numbers in winter in the lowlands and perhaps elsewhere in Arkansas. While many Christmas Count records over the years have involved only single birds, four or five have been reported on five or more Christmas Counts in the early 1980s in the lowlands of the Coastal Plain, and at Lonoke on the Mississippi Alluvial Plain. As many as four have been found on the Christmas Count at Conway (1969), and three at Mena (1980). The species has been reported on several recent Christmas Counts at Jonesboro in the northeast, and there are a few acceptable midwinter records in the western Ozarks.

WINTER WREN, *Troglodytes troglodytes* (Linnaeus)

Fairly common to uncommon migrant and winter resident in forested bottomlands and ravines in all regions. Sometimes absent in the north after the arrival of severe winter cold.

FALL MIGRATION: Winter Wrens sometimes arrive in Arkansas from their breeding areas north of the state during the first week of October, but most "first fall" reports are in the second and third weeks of October. Most sightings recorded in the Audubon Society file have involved single birds or sometimes two found in a day in the field. An obvious fall peak in numbers is indicated by the presence of ten birds in a loose flock on the campus of the University of Arkansas at Little Rock on October 15. A single bird was heard in full song in the bottomlands along the Buffalo River in Marion County on November 25.

WINTER: This somewhat secretive or reclusive species is found in small numbers in all regions in winter. The largest numbers are reported on the Christmas Bird Counts on the Coastal Plain in the south and on the southern half of the Mississippi Alluvial Plain in the east. At Lake Georgia-Pacific, Winter Wrens have been reported in fairly large numbers, with peaks of 13 to 17 birds on the Christmas Counts in 1971, 1972, and 1973. At Lonoke, peak numbers of 9 or 10 birds have been reported on several occasions. In northern Arkansas the birds are reported in very small numbers (if they are found at all) on the Christmas Counts at Jonesboro and Fayetteville. The preference for bottomland woods is very strongly suggested in winter population studies in the state. Thus, in southern Arkansas there was a population of 12 birds per one hundred acres of bottomland forests (Table 3-4), and only two birds per one hundred acres in upland forests (Table 3-2). Smaller numbers were found in the northern regions. Occasionally Winter Wrens sing in winter in southern Arkansas.

SPRING MIGRATION: Members of the Tennessee Ornithological Society reported 10 singing birds in the wooded bottoms around Horseshoe Lake in Crittenden County on February 27. The large number of birds suggests that these birds were on the northward spring migration. The species is seen with fair regularity through March, and with less regularity to the end of April. There is also one unusually late record for May (Howell 1911).

SEDGE WREN, *Cistothorus platensis* (Latham)

Uncommon to fairly common and somewhat irregular migrant in all regions. Locally abundant upon occasion on the Mississippi Alluvial Plain. Winter resident chiefly in the southern and southeastern lowlands. Nesting has occurred locally and sporadically in rice fields on the Grand Prairie. Formerly named "Short-billed Marsh Wren," the species utilizes open marshy areas with dense vegetation of grasses or sedges, and in migration almost any large, open field, especially wet fields, with sufficient cover.

SPRING MIGRATION: The northward migration in spring seems to occur during late April and May (Audubon Society file, Mattocks and Shugart 1962, Baerg 1951, Johnson 1979, Hanebrink 1980). In years when the species is found in numbers in the state, most spring records have involved one to three birds on a day's outing. The largest number reported involved an estimated 20 on Sullivan's Island in the Arkansas River at Little Rock on May 16, 1976. Four singing birds in a harvested hay field in Randolph County in late May could not be found again in late June (B. Coffey, pers. comm.), and so presumably were migrants.

BREEDING SEASON: The only nesting records are from Arkansas, Prairie, and Jefferson counties, primarily the rice fields near Stuttgart. In 1950 in Arkansas County, Meanley (1952b) found a nest with six eggs on August 20, a nest with one fresh egg on August 29, and a third nest with five large young on September 10. These nests were all found in rice fields of the earliest maturing varieties that were furthest along in development during early August. Extensive growths of sedges and grasses (weeds) were found in the canals and fallow fields surrounding the early maturing rice fields. One sixty-acre rice field planted with the "cody" rice variety had twelve singing males in the first half of August. Meanley states that even though he was constantly in the rice fields throughout the summer of 1950, not a single Sedge Wren was heard singing until July 6, but after this date the birds became increasingly abundant, with about one third of the rice fields near Stuttgart having pairs by mid-August. He believed that the birds delayed nesting until the rice and other vegetation had obtained a suitable height, and that the birds utilized the weedy areas until then.

Other nesting records are from Prairie County where an adult was building a nest near DeVall's Bluff on June 8, 1957, and near Linwood in Jefferson County where a dummy nest that appeared to be that of a Sedge Wren was found in Johnson Grass about four feet tall on July 15, 1956.

There are records in the Audubon Society file from other regions involving singing birds during the same period in which Sedge Wrens nested in Arkansas County in 1950, but no nests or other specific evidences of breeding have been found. These records are from Benton County (file, Baerg 1951), Washington, Sebastian, and Polk counties, and doubtless other places. Even though the birds have been found during the same period in the Memphis area, and in adjacent areas of Mississippi and Arkansas, they have not been known to nest (B. Coffey, pers. comm.). Certainly there is a major break in the records in the Audubon Society file from mid-May to mid-July, suggesting (but certainly not proving) that nesting in Arkansas is sporadic, and that the fall migrants begin to pass through Arkansas during the time when some local nesting birds have been engaged in breeding activities.

FALL RECORDS: Observers in nearly every region have found Sedge Wrens singing vigorously during fall. In some places, like the cattail-lined ditches alongside fish ponds at Centerton in Benton County, no known nesting activity has apparently been associated with this singing. In other places it is not clear whether some of these singing birds are nesting or whether most are merely on migration. When biologist Brooke Meanley was in the rice fields of eastern Arkansas in 1963, he found the species very common during July and August, with singing birds in nearly every rice field throughout the region, and he presumed (pers. comm.) that these birds were nesting. Coffey (1942) recorded 40 birds in grassy fields south of Memphis on August 9, 1936, but noted that the numbers had greatly declined two weeks later. He considered the species an "erratic transient" based upon the fact that the large numbers in 1936 were never reported again, even though searches were made (pers. comm.).

Fall records for the remainder of the state span the period from July into early November, with most reports after late August. In the Memphis area, the migration period has been reported from early August through December, with very few records in midwinter (Coffey 1942, and pers. comm.). The 10 birds seen in a rice field south of Hoxie in Lawrence County on October 13 is a large fall record for the state.

WINTER: Other than records for the southern lowlands, there are winter sightings at Lonoke, and irregularly at Conway in the Arkansas River Valley. Most observations have involved single birds, but there have been two highly unusual peak reports on Christmas Bird Counts at Lonoke and at El Dorado involving 9 or 10 birds, but not in the past twenty years. On the statewide 1980 Christmas Bird Counts, only three Sedge Wrens were reported in the state, and these were at Conway and Arkadelphia.

MARSH WREN, *Cistothorus palustris* (Wilson)

Fairly regular migrant in small numbers in all regions. Local winter resident primarily in the southern lowlands. Migrants utilize all types of dense, moist, rank vegetation in open areas, especially cattails, and wintering birds are largely confined to cattails. Formerly named "Long-billed Marsh Wren."

FALL MIGRATION: Marsh Wrens have arrived in the western Ozarks as early as the second week of September, but "first fall" reports for most of the state are in the third and fourth weeks of the month, and thereafter. The three birds at Calion near El Dorado on September 29 was a large fall report, as were the 10 at Lonoke in the same county on November 16. In the western Ozarks the species is seen regularly throughout the fall until about mid-November (Audubon Society file), and until about early November in Faulkner County (Johnson 1979).

WINTER: While there are no winter records for the highlands, single birds have wintered on several occasions in Faulkner County in the Arkansas River Valley, and there is also a wintering record at Booneville in Logan County. Most winter reports are from the Coastal Plain in the south and from the Lonoke area in east-central Arkansas. The three Marsh Wrens at Arkadelphia on the 1976 Christmas Bird Count was a large number, as were the four at Lake Georgia-Pacific in 1981. As many as four to six have been reported several times on the count at Lonoke, but the usual number there, as elsewhere, is one or in some years none.

SPRING MIGRATION: Based upon the presence of birds in places where they are not known to overwinter, spring migration occurs during late April and May, usually prior to the fourth week in May. The only spring records for the western Ozarks are in the second week of May. In the northeast there is an early May record (Howell 1911). There are several reports for Faulkner County in late April and early May (Johnson 1979). An exceptionally large number of 20 was reported on Sullivan's Island in the Arkansas River near Little Rock on May 16.

Family Muscicapidae

Subfamily Sylviinae Kinglets and Gnatcatchers

GOLDEN-CROWNED KINGLET, *Regulus satrapa* Lichtenstein

Common migrant and common to uncommon winter resident in all regions. Inhabits all types of woodlands, but is most numerous in pine, or mixed-pine and hardwood forests.

FALL MIGRATION: With the exception of an unusually early fall arrival record in late September, this species is usually not present in the state until the second week of October, and is common by late October and early November. The six birds observed in Washington County in the north on October 15 was a relatively large number for early in the fall. Most records in the Audubon Society file for a day in the field have involved fewer than 10 of these birds, but larger numbers are sometimes reported. A total of 19 were seen at Hot Springs on October 31, and they were said to be "abundant" near Cass in Franklin County on November 9.

WINTER: Golden-crowned Kinglets are reported on Christmas Bird Counts throughout the state, with the largest numbers found on the Coastal Plain. The ten-year statewide mean on the Christmas Counts was 0.4 birds per party hour. Regionally, this mean varied from 0.5 to 2.0 on the Coastal Plain, 0.2 to 0.3 on the Mississippi Alluvial Plain, and 0.2 to 0.5 in the highlands. The largest means were reported at Lake Georgia-Pacific in the extreme south. On Christmas Counts there between 1969 and 1983 the numbers reported varied from 9 to 97, with 49 or more found in six of those years. At Fayetteville in the north, the numbers reported on the Christmas Count in recent years have varied from 1 to 34, often fewer than 10. Winter population studies (Tables 3-2 and 3-4) showed that Golden-crowned Kinglets were most numerous in both upland and bottomland forests in central Arkansas, with 31 birds per one hundred acres in the bottomland forest there.

SPRING MIGRATION: Spring migrants have been reported from the second half of February to early April, with the latest records in late April. The 3.5 birds per hour in a Jefferson County study area on February 20 was an increase in numbers over earlier dates. In Garland County, departure dates were February 23 to March 20 (Deaderick 1938). At Fayetteville, spring influxes have been observed during March and in early April (Baerg 1930b, Audubon Society file).

RUBY-CROWNED KINGLET, *Regulus calendula* (Linnaeus)

Common migrant in all regions. Present in winter in all regions, but uncommon to somewhat rare in the north. Inhabits all types of woodlands, but is most numerous in coniferous or mixed coniferous-deciduous woodlands.

FALL MIGRATION: Ruby-crowned Kinglets have arrived in Arkansas from their northern breeding areas as early as the second week of September, but there are relatively few reports until the third or fourth weeks of September, with peak numbers during October and thereafter. An estimated 30 birds were reported at the White River Refuge in the southeast on October 23. Relatively few of these birds are seen in the western Ozarks of northern Arkansas after late November.

WINTER: During winter Ruby-crowned Kinglets are most numerous in the southern half of the state, especially in the lowlands of the Coastal Plain and in the southeast. The ten-year statewide mean on Christmas Bird Counts was 0.8 birds per party hour. Regionally this mean varied from 0.8 to 4.3 on the Coastal

FIGURE 6-81 Ruby-crowned Kinglet. *Fred Burnside*

Plain, 0.2 to 0.9 on the Mississippi Alluvial Plain, and 0.0 to 0.7 in the highlands (with a peak at Hot Springs in the Ouachita Mountains). The largest numbers have been reported at Lake Georgia-Pacific in the extreme south. On Christmas Counts there between 1969 and 1983, the number reported has varied from 44 to 436, with 100 or more in eleven of the years. Winter population studies (Tables 3-2 and 3-4) showed a population of eight to nine birds per one hundred acres of forest in southern Arkansas, with much smaller numbers in northern Arkansas.

SPRING MIGRATION: Spring migrants are seen during March, April, and early May, with the latest record in the last week of May (three birds in Franklin County on May 26). A migration peak was reported on March 6 in Washington County. In Jefferson County, the birds were said to have become "suddenly common" on March 25, with nine birds seen in a study area there. The six reported at Fort Smith on May 10 was a large, late number.

BLUE-GRAY GNATCATCHER, *Polioptila caerulea* (Linnaeus)

Common migrant and summer resident in all regions. Rare winter visitor in the south. Numerous, inhabits a wide range of forest types including forest edge.

SPRING MIGRATION: This insectivorous species, along with several species of warblers, typically arrives in Arkansas from its wintering grounds to the south before the deciduous trees have begun to form new leaves. There is one unusually early record of a single bird seen at Mountain Home in Baxter County on March 13, but otherwise most of the "spring first" reports are in the third week, and more frequently the last week, of March. The six birds in the Lake Conway area of Faulkner County on March 25 was an early peak in numbers. Among the 16 counted at Fort Smith on March 30 was one pair already building a nest. Migrants continue to arrive in the state until at least around mid-April. A big peak involving 50 birds, was reported in Calhoun County on April 10.

BREEDING SEASON: The species is present in all regions during the breeding season, with generally low numbers in the eastern lowlands, and higher numbers in the highlands and on the Coastal Plain. The average annual mean number of gnatcatchers per route in each region reported on the Breeding Bird Surveys was 4.7 on the Coastal Plain, 1.2 on the Mississippi Alluvial Plain, and 4.7 in the highlands (including the Arkansas River Valley). Peak means of 9.9 to 13.6 birds were reported on the surveys in Izard, Grant, Clark, and Garland counties.

Nesting activity has been reported from late March to the middle of July, usually from about mid-April and thereafter. The earliest date for nesting activity is March 30 (see above). At Boyle Park in Little Rock several completed nests were observed on April 10, 11, and 12. The peak for nest building seems to occur in mid-April. A total of nine nests were found between April 16-18, 1985, during the course of a long-term research project in Washington County. Most nests were twenty to twenty-five feet high (one was at fifty feet) and eight of the nine nests had been constructed in Eastern Redcedar trees, one of the predominant species in this upland site. The latest record of nesting involved young being fed in a nest in Clark County on July 14 (the young fledged three days later). In the Wheeler Collection there are nineteen clutches of eggs taken from nests in Arkansas between April 24 and May 30, mainly by May 16. The clutch sizes varied from three to six eggs, often four or five. The nest heights varied from ten to sixty-five feet, and averaged about twenty-six feet from the ground. An uncharacteristic nest built at DeVall's Bluff in Prairie County was four feet from the ground in a Sweetgum sprout in the middle of a field. A Yellow-breasted Chat ate the eggs in this nest. Single Brown-headed Cowbird eggs were found in three of the clutches in the Wheeler Collection.

In the southern lowlands, summer populations studies indicated a population of thirteen singing males per one hundred acres of bottomland forests, and six per one hundred acres of uplands (Tables 3-1 and 3-3). A similar preference involving smaller numbers was indicated in northern Arkansas. In the western Ozarks (Table 3-7) there was a projected population of eight males per one hundred acres of dry forest, and 43 per one hundred acres in moist forest. This latter figure was inflated by the small size of the study plot and the high proportion of forest edge.

FALL MIGRATION AND WINTER: These birds are seen with fair regularity until the third or fourth weeks of September, by which time all but a few rare stragglers have moved south toward the wintering grounds. The eight birds at Pine Bluff Arsenal on September 11 was a late fall peak, as were the four at Lake Fayetteville in Washington County on September 20. Thereafter, there are only a few highly scattered reports involving single (or occasionally two) birds, mainly in the extreme south in the months of October, November, and December. During the unusually mild winter weather of December 1984, a total of nine gnatcatchers were found on four Christmas Bird Counts in the southern half of the state. There is one early January record but none for February in the state.

Subfamily Turdinae Thrushes

EASTERN BLUEBIRD, *Sialia sialis* (Linnaeus)

Common permanent resident in all regions. Observed in all seasons in the open country at the edges of towns, in farmlands, and along roadsides. Very numerous in northwestern Arkansas.

MIGRATION: Ruth Thomas conducted what is still the definitive study of the Eastern Bluebird when she resided in North Little Rock (Thomas 1946c). She found that most nesting pairs of bluebirds remained there throughout the year, but migrants were occasionally noted. Spring migrants there were seen as late as early March, and fall migrants occurred between mid-September and November. Some of these migration records involved pairs, sometimes small flocks of 6 to 12 birds, and once (on November 18) a flock of 50 birds. Flocking characteristic of the post breeding period was noticed by mid-November. Other than these, there are few migration records.

Banding records show the highly resident nature of bluebirds. Nearly all twenty-two

Arkansas-associated bluebird recoveries were encountered again at the place of banding. The single exception was a bird banded in Illinois and recovered over 400 miles south in Arkansas.

BREEDING SEASON: Bluebirds are common and widespread in Arkansas during the nesting season, and are apparently more numerous in the Ozarks than elsewhere at this time. The average annual mean number per route in each region reported by region on the Breeding Bird Survey was 3.9 on the Coastal Plain, 2.2 on the Mississippi Alluvial Plain, and 6.3 in the highlands (including the Arkansas River Valley). Peak means of 8.6 to 12.4 birds were recorded on four surveys in the Ozark Plateaus.

Nesting activity has been observed as early as mid-February. Thomas (1946c) observed one nest on February 16 at North Little Rock, but the average dates of initial nesting activity were in the first and second weeks of March, with the last brood fledged by mid-July (rarely in early August). Thomas reported three, rarely four broods in one season. The territories occupied by the breeding birds involved two to three acres, but nests were sometimes only twenty-five yards apart. About 60 percent of the eggs laid resulted in fledged young. In the Wheeler Collection there are ten clutches of eggs taken from nests between April 17 and June 30. There were four and five eggs in these nests, and the heights varied from two to ten feet above the ground. The birds nest in wooden fence posts, snags, old woodpecker cavities, and nesting boxes.

Records in the Audubon Society file for Ashley County show there were five nesting attempts there in one area from March 10 to mid-July in 1968. All five attempts involved egg laying and apparently normal incubation, but none of the eggs hatched. In 1969 four similar attempts between late March and July were also all failures.

WINTER: Bluebird populations are greatly affected by severe winter weather (James 1959). Severe prolonged cold leads to population declines, and mild weather contributes to population increases. The bluebirds in Arkansas have not escaped from this phenomenon (James 1962, 1963). They are reasonably well distributed in the state during winter, with the largest numbers apparently present in the southern

FIGURE 6-82 Eastern Bluebird. *David Plank*

lowlands. The ten-year statewide mean of 1.0 birds per party hour on Christmas Bird Counts was exceeded in some count areas in both northern and southern Arkansas, with a peak of 2.3 on the Coastal Plain, and lowest numbers overall on the Mississippi Alluvial Plain. The 175 bluebirds in the 1982 Christmas Count circle at Fayetteville was three times the recent twelve-year average for that area.

MOUNTAIN BLUEBIRD, *Sialia currucoides* (Bechstein)

One record.

This migratory bluebird of western North America has been reported on a casual basis well to the east of its breeding and winter ranges, reaching New York and Pennsylvania on rare occasions (AOU 1983). The Arkansas record can presumably be attributed to this casual eastward movement. A single immature male was first seen and identified by Max and Helen Parker on November 9, 1985, at the Lake Hamilton state fish hatchery near Hot Springs in Garland County. (Written and photographic documentation are on file with the Arkansas Audubon Society.)

TOWNSEND'S SOLITAIRE, *Myadestes townsendi* (Audubon)

One record.

An individual of this common western species was seen by a number of experienced Arkansas observers on several occasions between December 8, 1963, and January 4, 1964, near Springdale in Washington County. The species is known to range far east of its usual range on a casual basis (AOU 1983).

VEERY, *Catharus fuscescens* (Stephens)

Regular transient in small numbers during spring, chiefly on the Mississippi Alluvial Plain. Rare in the state in fall and rare at any time in the west.

SPRING MIGRATION: In the Audubon Society file there are reports between the last week of April and May 21, with a peak in numbers in the last week of April and the first week of May. At Helena it was seen "nearly every spring" from April 18 to May 19, with a peak in the first week of May (Howell 1911). In the

northeast, Veerys are said to be generally uncommon, with sightings between the last week of April and the third week of May (Hanebrink and Posey 1979, Hanebrink 1980). One observer in Craighead County stated that they were "numerous" on May 2 (file). The two Veerys seen at Little Rock on April 30 were part of a dramatic peak of migrant thrushes that included many Swainson's and Gray-cheeked Thrushes. There are five reports in the file for the western one-third of the state: one each in Franklin, Montgomery, Howard, Little River and Washington counties.

FALL MIGRATION: Veerys were said to pass through Helena during late September and early October (Howell 1911). The only recent fall records involved single birds seen at Little Rock on October 25 and in Prairie County on October 14.

GRAY-CHEEKED THRUSH, *Catharus minimus* (Lafresnaye)

Fairly common spring transient in woodlands, including shady yards, wooded parks, and mature river bottomlands, in all regions. Rarely reported during fall migration.

SPRING MIGRATION: Observations in the Audubon Society file span the period from the second week of April to late May, with a peak in numbers between the last week of April and mid-May. These reports have usually involved single birds seen or heard singing during a day in the field. A peak of nine was observed on the campus of the University of Arkansas at Little Rock on April 30. In the wooded bottomlands of the White River in Washington County, seven were observed in ones and twos on May 6. At Fayetteville, a single bird sang daily under shrubs in a yard from May 8 to 21.

FALL MIGRATION: The species is not known to sing on its southward migration through Arkansas, and this adds great difficulty to the task of finding birds at this season. The only adequately documented fall record in Arkansas involved a single bird that was netted at Pine Bluff on October 1. There are three additional sight records for fall, all single birds: at Helena in Phillips County on October 24, 1964; in Garland County on November 19 (Deaderick 1938); at Helena on October 10 (Howell 1911).

SWAINSON'S THRUSH, *Catharus ustulatus* (Nuttall)

Common spring transient in all regions. Uncommonly reported fall transient. One winter report. Observed in all types of woodlands, including yards in towns.

SPRING MIGRATION: Swainson's Thrush is often conspicuous during the northward migration because of its distinctive song, which calls attention to birds that might otherwise pass unnoticed. In the Audubon Society file there are reports between the first week of April and late May, with peak numbers between April 20 and May 20. There are numerous reports of single birds found on a day afield, and two to four are not unusual during the peak period. At Little Rock in 1978, Swainson's Thrushes were seen daily from April 16 to May 20, with a peak of 8 on April 27. Also at Little Rock, 21 were observed on the University of Arkansas campus during a big peak of thrushes on April 30. The 24 counted by two observers at Fort Smith on May 20 was a late peak. The one banding record for the state involved a bird recovered in New York in April that had been banded over 1000 miles to the southwest in Arkansas, thirteen months before.

FALL MIGRATION: There are scattered records for the southward migration period between the second week of September through October, but mainly from the last week of September to mid-October. A total of 34 Swainson's Thrushes were killed upon impact with a transmission tower in central Arkansas September 26–30, 1984. Most other fall reports have involved single birds. In terms of numbers, one of the most unusual reports in the file involved one to ten Swainson's Thrushes seen almost daily in Union County between September 25 and October 16. The birds were seen feeding on blackgum berries during this period.

WINTER: A thrush identified as this species was studied by several observers at close range on December 31, 1983, at the White River Refuge in Arkansas County. Winter season reports of Swainson's Thrush must always be viewed with caution because the expected *Catharus* thrush at this time is the following species, Hermit Thrush.

HERMIT THRUSH, *Catharus guttatus* (Pallas)

Common to uncommon transient and winter resident in all regions. Most numerous in the south in winter. Inhabits mature bottomland woods, upland ravines, and dense thickets.

FALL MIGRATION: Hermit Thrushes have arrived in Arkansas by the second week of October (two were netted in Washington County on October 11), and there are regular reports thereafter. A total of 127 Hermit Thrushes were killed upon impact with a transmission tower in central Arkansas October 24, 1984.

There are several banding reports for the state. Four Hermit Thrushes banded in late summer or fall near the shore of Lake Michigan were recovered in fall or winter in Arkansas, 425 to 675 miles south of the banding site. Only one of the four birds survived as long as a year between banding and recovery.

WINTER: Christmas Bird Counts show that Hermit Thrushes are heavily concentrated in southern Arkansas during winter. On twelve recent Christmas Counts at Fayetteville in the western Ozarks the peak number was six birds, and either single birds or none were found in eight years (the record is even sparser for Jonesboro). By comparison, in the Arkansas River Valley the birds are seen every year on Christmas Counts and often in fair numbers, with peaks of 15 to 20 in some count areas. Further south the birds are seen in even larger numbers. At El Dorado, as many as 50 to 60 Hermit Thrushes have been reported on the Christmas Count on several occasions. Cold weather can be a problem for these birds (James 1959). Even in the southern lowlands, after a severe freeze during February of 1963 several dead Hermit Thrushes were found in Union County.

Winter population studies (Tables 3-2 and 3-4) showed a population in the southern half of the state of seven birds per one hundred acres of bottomland forest and two per one hundred acres of upland forest. Much smaller numbers were found in northern Arkansas.

SPRING MIGRATION: Spring records indicating the passage of migrants are clustered from late March through the third week of April. Six birds, including a flock of four, were seen in Washington County on April 14, and six were in Arkansas County on April 13. In Jefferson

FIGURE 6-83 Hermit Thrush. *Max Parker*

FIGURE 6-84 Wood Thrush. *David Plank*

272   *Arkansas Birds*

County, the 3.6 birds per hour in a floodplain forest study area on April 20 was a seasonal peak in numbers. The single bird caught in a net in Washington County on April 26 was the latest wholly acceptable report for spring, but there is another record involving two birds as late as May 4.

WOOD THRUSH, *Hylocichla mustelina* (Gmelin)

Common migrant and summer resident in all regions. Inhabits extensive, moist, mature woodlands with small bushes or trees in the understory.

SPRING MIGRATION: Wood Thrushes sometimes arrive as early as the last of March or the first of April (there is also one earlier report in the northeast) but few are observed until mid-April and thereafter. The four birds in Prairie County near DeVall's Bluff on April 15 was a large number for the date. By late April they are common throughout the state. A flock of 15 was seen at Mallard Lake in Mississippi County on April 27. At Winslow in Washington County "it is not uncommon to see and hear as high as 100 singing males in a single afternoon around the first of May when the spring migration is at its height, their song completely dominating the forest for a few days each spring" (Black 1935a).

BREEDING SEASON: These birds are widely distributed during summer, but are more numerous on the Coastal Plain than elsewhere. The average annual mean number per route in each region reported on the Breeding Bird Survey was 8.7 on the Coastal Plain, 2.5 on the Mississippi Alluvial Plain, and 4.1 in the highlands (including the Arkansas River Valley). Peak annual means of 9.6 to 16.9 birds per survey were recorded on four surveys on the Coastal Plain, and one each in the Ouachita Mountains and the Ozark Plateaus.

Nesting activity has been observed from late April to early September, with a peak in such activity during May and June. The extreme records include a nest at North Little Rock on April 26, and a nestling being fed at the White River Refuge on September 3. In the Wheeler Collection there are nine clutches of eggs taken from nests in Arkansas between May 7 and June 14. The clutch sizes in these nests varied from three to five eggs (average about 3.5), and in addition to these eggs three Brown-headed Cowbird eggs were found in each of two nests. At Fort Smith, Black (1930b) saw a nest with one thrush and five cowbird eggs. The heights of the Wheeler nests varied from eight to twenty feet above the ground, often in the range of eight to twelve feet, and were found in tangles of vegetation, bushes, or small trees.

Summer population studies (Tables 3-1 and 3-3) in southern Arkansas indicated a population of fourteen singing male Wood Thrushes per 100 acres of bottomland woods, and six per one hundred acres in upland woods. Smaller numbers were recorded on studies in other regions.

In Arkansas the nesting habitat of the Wood Thrush tends to have less ground cover, fewer shrubs, fewer small and large trees but more moderately sized trees, and greater canopy cover than the average conditions throughout its summer range (James et al. 1984).

FALL MIGRATION: During fall Wood Thrushes are observed with fair regularity through the third week of September. The four birds near Pine Bluff Arsenal on September 8 was a fall peak. There are additional scattered records in the file to the last week of October.

AMERICAN ROBIN, *Turdus migratorius* Linnaeus

Permanent resident. Abundant migrant and winter resident in all regions. Forms large winter roosts. Most of the year found in open areas with shortgrass and scattered trees and shrubs, in winter found in cedar groves and other woodlands.

MIGRATION: Robins are especially abundant in the state between the times of their peak migration movements in mid-March and mid-to-late October (Audubon Society file, Black 1932a). It is during these times that the robins that wintered south of Arkansas are passing through the state into northern breeding areas, and later, the breeding birds are moving south into their wintering grounds. Banding records involving 73 recoveries showed that wintering and migrating birds in Arkansas were derived from breeding populations scattered all the way from the western edge of the eastern deciduous forest to the eastern edge of the midwestern states (Figure 6-85), with distances between banding and recovery varying from an average

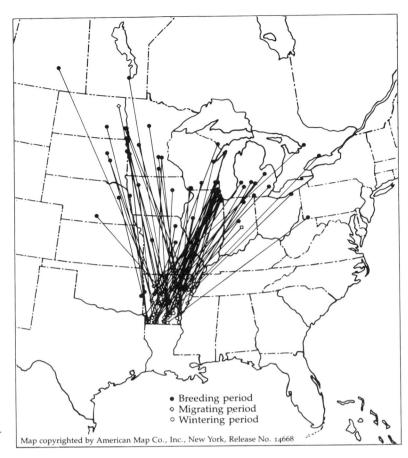

- • Breeding period
- ◦ Migrating period
- ○ Wintering period

Map copyrighted by American Map Co., Inc., New York, Release No. 14668

FIGURE 6-85 Movements of the American Robin based on banding records.

450 to 850 miles to over 1100 miles. Many birds survived three years between banding and recovery, several over four, and one six.

BREEDING SEASON: Robins are present throughout the state during summer, and are somewhat more numerous in the highlands, especially in the Ozark Plateaus, than elsewhere. The average annual mean number per route in each region reported on the Breeding Bird Survey was 5.4 on the Coastal Plain, 4.3 on the Mississippi Alluvial Plain, and 10.1 in the highlands (including the Arkansas River Valley). Peak annual means of 15.4 to 39.7 were recorded on the surveys in Sebastian, Cleburne, and Benton counties.

American Robins seem to have expanded their breeding range in Arkansas within historical times. In earlier years Howell (1911) believed their nesting was limited to northern Arkansas, and they were not nesting regularly even throughout the Ozarks (Smith 1915, Black 1935a). However, they were nesting at this time in at least some areas in the south (file, Wheeler 1924, Deaderick 1938). A nest reported at El Dorado in Union County in 1955 seems to have been the first such record for that extreme southern locality. The birds were listed as common permanent residents in south central Arkansas (Mattocks and Shugart 1962) thereafter. Presumably the nesting population of robins in the state has benefitted from the clearing of extensive forests and the subsequent creation of openings (such as yards in towns) that provide optimal nesting habitat.

Nesting activity has been observed from mid-March through late July with a peak during April, May, and June. The extreme records include an adult on a nest at El Dorado on March 14 and young still in a nest at Fort Smith on July 30. By the month of June fledglings are being fed out of nests and are universally visible in towns. In the Wheeler Collection there are two clutches of eggs (three and four eggs) that were taken from nests twenty-one and fifteen feet above the ground in April. In the Audubon Society file there are records of nests in trees, shrubs, tangles of vines, and under the eaves of buildings, with the heights varying from four to thirty-five feet, but often lower than twenty feet. Nests very early in the season, before leafing, are often in coniferous trees, and after leafing often in deciduous trees. A yard in town of only 140 by 190 feet in size may accommodate two pairs of nesting robins (Baerg 1951). The female is in charge of incubation, but both parents feed the young (Dykstra 1968).

WINTER: Robins are abundant throughout the state during winter. During the coldest weather they retreat from the open areas where they are seen in mild weather to dense vegetation that offers better cover. Communal roosts in winter may number thousands or more of these birds. Black (1932a) studied a roost near Winslow in Washington County that held over 250,000 individual robins. The first birds arrived in the area on October 22, and within days the roost had grown to thousands of birds. The roost covered a square mile of second growth trees, and the birds were observed as they fed on the berries of black gum (*Nyssa sylvatica*), fox grape (*Vitis* sp.), and other available berries. In November and December of 1965, James (1968b) visited a roost in Washington County that was estimated to contain six million robins in a 60-acre cedar tract. After a severe cold spell in early January, blackbirds began to move into the roost, displacing the robins. (Robins often roost with blackbirds, but even in the roosts begun by robins the blackbirds occupy the central areas, and the robins seem forced to the periphery.) Big roosts have also been recorded in the El Dorado area (one in 1962 was estimated at 715,000 robins). In Nevada County robins were said to have constituted 40 percent of a blackbird-starling roost estimated at 800,000 individuals in the winter of 1979–80, according to figures in the U. S. Fish and Wildlife Service annual survey of blackbird-starling roosts in the state.

Family Mimidae
Mockingbirds and Thrashers

GRAY CATBIRD, *Dumetella carolinensis* (Linnaeus)

Common migrant and summer resident in all regions. Rare winter resident chiefly in the south. Inhabits dense tangles of shrubs and vines, in towns and at the forest edge.

SPRING MIGRATION: Catbirds typically arrive in small numbers during the second or third weeks of April. An influx noted during the last week of April and the first two weeks of May results in their being common throughout the state. The four birds at Petit Jean Mountain was a peak count for April. The 23 found by two observers at Fort Chaffee near Fort Smith on May 10, 1958, was a spring peak. (There are also several March records in the Audubon Society file.)

BREEDING SEASON: There are summer records in all regions, but catbirds seem more concentrated in the highlands than elsewhere during the nesting season. The average annual mean number per route in each region reported on Breeding Bird Surveys was 0.4 on the Coastal Plain, 0.3 on the Mississippi Alluvial Plain, and 1.3 in the highlands (including the Arkansas River Valley). Peak means of 3.2 to 4.6 catbirds were found on the two surveys in the western Ozarks (the survey route involving three counties).

Nesting activity has been observed primarily during May and June. The extreme records involved two eggs in a nest on May 5 in Washington County and young still in a nest on August 9, also in Washington County. In the Wheeler Collection there are four clutches of eggs that were taken from nests in Arkansas on May 13, 15, 19, and June 19. The clutch sizes varied from three to five eggs, and the nests were nine and ten feet high. Nests on file with the Audubon Society have been in low thickets, vines, and dense trees like cedars, usually five to eight feet above the ground.

FALL MIGRATION: For fall there are fairly regular observations through September and scattered observations through October. A total of 212 catbirds were killed upon impact with a transmission tower in central Arkansas September 26–30, 1984. The latest regular observation for the western Ozarks was on October 15. The peak of migration is indicated by the unusual concentration of 35 catbirds at Rebsamen Park in Little Rock on September 14. In Jefferson County, peaks involving eight catbirds per hour were reported in the last week of September.

There are two banding records that involve fall: one bird banded in Illinois in mid-September was recovered 450 miles south in Arkansas in early October. Another bird banded in Iowa in September was recovered over 500 miles south in Arkansas during January more than a year later.

WINTER: Gray Catbirds are rare in winter but nevertheless are seen most winters in the state. These observations typically involve single birds, occasionally two, and almost always in the southern lowlands, with scattered records elsewhere. It has probably been seen during winter at El Dorado more often than elsewhere, but even there only a total of 10 birds have been reported on the Christmas Bird Counts between 1953 and 1983 (average one bird every three years). Most of the winter sightings have occurred in December, but there are also reports for January, February, and March.

NORTHERN MOCKINGBIRD, *Mimus polyglottos* (Linnaeus)

Official state bird of Arkansas. Common and highly visible permanent resident in all regions in both urban and non-urban areas where there is shrubbery, low trees, or dense fencerows (not in forests).

BREEDING SEASON: This famous mimic is present and common during the nesting season in every area of the state, though somewhat more numerous in the lowlands than in the highlands. The average annual mean number per route in each region reported on the Breeding Bird Survey was 27.6 on the Coastal Plain, 30.1 on the Mississippi Alluvial Plain, and 20.5 in the highlands (including the Arkansas River Valley). A peak mean of 70.1 birds was reported on the survey in Chicot County.

Nesting activity has been reported from late March through July. The earliest nesting reports in the Audubon Society file involved a nearly completed nest in Washington County on March 23 and four eggs in a nest in Miller County on April 12. In the Wheeler Collection there are twenty clutches of eggs taken from nests in Arkansas between April 17 and July 13. The clutch sizes varied from three to five eggs (often four) in these nests, and the heights varied from three to twenty feet above the ground, and almost always below ten feet. Two and occasionally three broods of young are reared in one year (Wheeler 1924, Baerg 1951). Nests are often constructed in low, thick, thorny shrubs or hedges. Most nests recorded in the file were in the range of four to eight feet high, but one was found at forty feet in an oak tree.

WINTER: The winter distribution of this permanent resident is similar to that of summer. The ten-year statewide mean number of 1.3 mockingbirds per party hour on Christmas Bird Counts was exceeded in all regions, with peaks of 2.0 and 2.1 on the Coastal Plain and the Mississippi Alluvial Plain. On the 1980 statewide Christmas Counts the numbers reported varied from 12 to 116 birds in the seventeen areas, with 40 or more reported on more than half of the counts.

SAGE THRASHER, *Oreoscoptes montanus* (Townsend)

One record.

An individual of this western species was photographed by Norman Lavers several miles northeast of Jonesboro, Craighead County, on November 24, 1979 (Lavers 1980). Supporting written and photographic documentation is on file with the Audubon Society.

BROWN THRASHER, *Toxostoma rufum* (Linnaeus)

Permanent resident. Common in summer, and less so in winter. Winter numbers greatest in the lowlands, especially in the south.

SPRING MIGRATION: In the western Ozarks, where thrashers are scarce in winter, spring arrivals have been noted during March (Audubon Society file, Baerg 1930b, Black 1935a). In Union County, where the birds are common all year, peak numbers have been observed also during March.

BREEDING SEASON: Nesting activity has been observed primarily between mid-April and late June. The extreme records in the Audubon Society file involved a nest under construction at Stuttgart on March 11, and new hatchlings in a nest at Hamburg in Ashley County on August 8. In the Wheeler Collection there are thirteen clutches of eggs that were taken from nests in Arkansas between April 17 and June 11. The clutch sizes in these nests varied from three to five eggs, often four eggs, and the heights of the nests varied from one to ten feet above the ground, often within the range of three to five feet. Nests have been found in thorny tangles, bushes, vines, and low trees. At DeVall's Bluff in Prairie County, young fledged from one nest on May 29 and a second nest (possibly the same pair) was found on June 10.

Thrashers are fairly well distributed in the state during June. The average annual mean number per route in each region reported on the Breeding Bird Surveys was 2.5 on the Coastal Plain, 3.8 on the Mississippi Alluvial Plain, and 3.8 in the highlands (including the Arkansas River Valley). A summer population study in Benton County in the Ozarks indicated a population of 25 territorial males per one hundred acres of habitat characterized as woody field with scattered trees including an abandoned orchard (Table 3-7).

FALL MIGRATION: Fall migrants are observed primarily during September and October. In the western Ozarks only small numbers are seen after early November (file, Baerg 1930b), with a peak of 10 at Lake Fayetteville on September 22. In Jefferson County, where the birds are common all year, the highest densities were encountered in a study area in late September. In Union County, peak numbers have been reported in October.

WINTER: The ten-year statewide mean number of thrashers found on Christmas Bird Counts was 0.4 birds per party hour. This varied by region from 0.3 to 0.8 birds per party hour on the Coastal Plain, 0.2 to 0.4 on the Mississippi Alluvial Plain, and 0.1 to 0.3 in the highlands (including the Arkansas River Valley). At Fayetteville in the north the peak number of thrashers reported on the Christmas Count was eight birds. At Little Rock in central

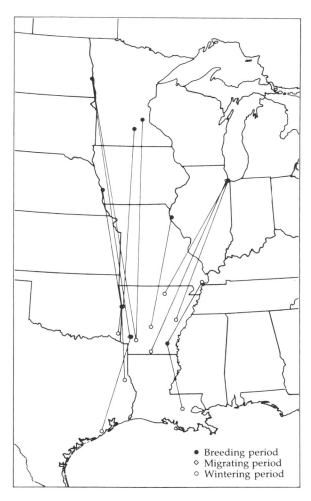

FIGURE 6-86 Movements of the Brown Thrasher based on banding records.

Arkansas there have been several peaks involving as many as 30 birds. At Lake Georgia-Pacific in the south there have been several peaks on the Christmas Count involving as many as 60 to 70 birds.

BANDING: Banded Brown Thrashers recovered in winter in Arkansas have come from breeding areas in states located essentially due north of Arkansas, and birds that nested in Arkansas were recovered in winter nearly straight south of the state (Figure 6-86). The distances between banding and recovery were scattered from 75 miles to over 900. One bird survived over four years between banding and recovery. In addition, there were 107 birds that were recovered at the original banding site in Arkansas. One injured Brown Thrasher survived several years in Ruth Thomas' yard and became the subject of her story, "Crip, Come Home" (Thomas 1952).

Family Motacillidae Pipits

WATER PIPIT, *Anthus spinoletta* (Linnaeus)

Common to fairly common migrant in all regions, at least locally. Winter resident, often in small numbers, locally in all regions. Observed on large open flats associated with drained reservoirs, along open shorelines, in shortgrass areas at airports, and on plowed fields.

FALL MIGRATION: Water Pipits have arrived from their breeding areas to the north as early as late September. Peak numbers are seen during October and November. Over 100 Water Pipits were seen at Lake Millwood on October 3 and 17. An estimated 50 were seen at the Fayetteville airport on October 7. In the Moffett, Oklahoma, bottoms just west of Fort Smith, 175 were counted on November 1. In Faulkner County the birds are seen regularly from mid-October to late November (Johnson 1979). In south central Arkansas, the peak in numbers has been reported from late October to about the middle of November (Mattocks and Shugart 1962).

WINTER: Water Pipits have been seen in all regions during winter. Most reports have involved small numbers (the seven in Benton County on January 16 was a high number for the western Ozarks in winter), but in some areas the birds are seen regularly and in impressive numbers. At Lonoke, 50 or more are often reported on the Christmas Bird Count, and almost 300 were found on one count there in the 1950s. During the 1970s more than 100 were reported on several Christmas Counts at Lonoke, Texarkana, and in the count area that includes Fort Smith, Arkansas, and Moffett, Oklahoma.

SPRING MIGRATION: The northward migration is notable during March and early April. An estimated 200 birds were seen in the Moffett bottoms on March 10, and at Lake Sequoyah in Washington County 40 birds were seen on April 9. The latest spring sighting for the state is in late May (James and James 1964).

SPRAGUE'S PIPIT, *Anthus spragueii* (Audubon)

Rarely reported migrant and winter resident that has been observed in all regions. Single birds or small loose flocks have been reported in open country, shortgrass areas such as mowed grasslands at airports, closely grazed pastures, newly sprouted crops in fields, and in stubble.

FALL MIGRATION: The earliest fall arrival record is in the first week of October, but there are few sightings until late November. When found at all, Sprague's Pipits are seen in small numbers. A useful bit of testimony about this scarcity is provided by Ben Coffey (1953) who with another observer worked eight selected fields in Crittenden County and managed to flush a total of two Sprague's Pipits. The nine birds found in the Arkansas River bottoms at Moffett, Oklahoma, near Fort Smith, Arkansas, on October 25 was a peak number, as were the 11 reported by a party of observers at the Hot Springs airport on November 24.

WINTER: These birds have been sighted with fair regularity in winter chiefly at Lonoke, Fort Smith, and Texarkana, all areas with large amounts of open country. On the Christmas Bird Count at Lonoke it was seen in numbers varying from four to nine between 1963 and 1966, and was otherwise unreported on the count between 1960 and 1972. The largest number ever reported in the state, 45 at Fort Smith in 1954, was an unusually high number. A concentrated search for the birds on the 1980 Christmas Count in the Fort Smith-Moffett area yielded an impressive total of 22.

An early, secondhand report published by Coues (1879) that this species was present in "immense numbers" at Fort Smith in winter (Baerg 1951) almost certainly involved misidentification on the part of Coues' informant.

SPRING MIGRATION: There are regular spring sightings through March and to the first half of April, but only one report as late as the third week of April. In south central Arkansas, there are scattered records from February 5 to April 9 (Mattocks and Shugart 1962). Two Sprague's Pipits seen in fields near Faulkner Lake in Pulaski County on April 4 were associated with Horned Larks.

Family Bombycillidae Waxwings

BOHEMIAN WAXWING, *Bombycilla garrulus* (Linnaeus)

Rare transient and winter visitor.

Bohemian Waxwings breed in the far northwest of North America and Eurasia no closer to Arkansas than northwestern Montana (AOU 1983). During winter it may irregularly or sporadically range as far south as central North America. The first of five Arkansas records involved a flock of 12 to 16 seen in either "April or May, 1921" at Fayetteville in the western Ozarks (Baerg 1931). Subsequently, a flock of 10 was observed as it fed on the buds of flowering dogwood at Winslow in Washington County on May 12, 1931 (Black 1932c). The species was seen at Clarksville in Johnson County on April 23, 1947 (Baerg 1951); again at Clarksville on January 27, 1960; and at Little Rock on March 16, 1962. Documentation is on file with the Arkansas Audubon Society for the two most recent sightings. In both instances the single Bohemian Waxwings were seen in association with Cedar Waxwings.

CEDAR WAXWING, *Bombycilla cedrorum* Vieillot

Common, somewhat erratic, migrant and winter resident in all regions. Observed in Arkansas in every month of the year, but only rarely at midsummer.

FALL MIGRATION: The 12 birds seen at Fayetteville on September 29 were early arrivals, since these birds do not usually arrive in the state from their breeding grounds to the north until October, and often not until the fourth week of that month. Thereafter, Cedar Waxwings are seen with fair regularity, with peak numbers (like the 85 at Pine Bluff on November 15) after mid-November. Cedar Waxwings wander unpredictably in search of berry crops, either wild berries or those on ornamental trees and shrubs in town. Flocks numbering 10 to 30 individuals are common, and much larger numbers may sometimes gather where there is an especially large food crop.

WINTER: The pattern of distribution and abundance observed in fall after mid-November carries on through the winter. On one Christmas Bird Count at Conway, one flock of 500 and a second flock of 200 birds were observed as they fed on cedar berries along the Arkansas River. On the thirty Christmas Counts held at El Dorado since 1953, 100 or more have been reported in ten years, and there is one peak count of 334. On the statewide 1980 Christmas Counts, 100 to nearly 500 Cedar Waxwings were reported in about half of the seventeen participating locales, with the highest numbers generally on the Coastal Plain.

SPRING MIGRATION AND SUMMER: The birds are present throughout spring, and commonly remain in the state until late May and early June. Certainly late ripening berries slow the pace of their northward migration. Mulberries, ripening in late spring and early summer, attract flocks of Cedar Waxwings. In addition to these late migrants, there are several midsummer records, including several instances of nesting. In 1969 Ben Coffey saw two family groups, including young being fed, at Pruitt in Newton County (Ozarks) on July 10 (file). The following day he saw two adults and two immatures at Eureka Springs, also in the Ozarks. The most recent summer reports that may have involved nesting occurred in 1985, when three

FIGURE 6-87 Cedar Waxwing. *Sigrid James Bruch*

FIGURE 6-88 Loggerhead Shrike near Harrison in northern Arkansas in mid-January. *David Plank*

separate flocks were observed in the western Arkansas Ozarks during August. The most intriguing of these reports was from Jasper in Newton County where eight of ten birds seen on August 17 were in the immature plumage. In former times breeding was reported at Clinton in Van Buren County (Howell 1911). There are several additional summer records, especially from El Dorado, where 16 were seen on June 27, 1962, and 15 in cherry trees on July 23, 1966.

Family Laniidae Shrikes

LOGGERHEAD SHRIKE, *Lanius ludovicianus* Linnaeus

Fairly common permanent resident in small numbers in all regions. Most numerous in winter. Observed in open country where it perches on wires or in small trees and shrubs.

BREEDING SEASON: Reports in the Audubon Society file and on Breeding Bird Surveys show that shrikes are present in small numbers in all regions during summer. The average annual mean number per route in each region on Breeding Bird Surveys was 3.1 on the Coastal Plain, and 1.9 on both the Mississippi Alluvial Plain and in the highlands (including the Arkansas River Valley). Peak means of 5.2 to 6.2 birds were reported on the surveys in Little River, Chicot, and Cleburne counties. Numbers recorded on Breeding Bird Surveys have steadily declined in Arkansas in the past fifteen years (Shepherd 1983). The total of 75 to 100 birds observed statewide on surveys in the 1960s decreased to 30 to 40 in the early 1980s. During the same period the average number found per survey route declined from three or four down to one or two.

Nesting activity has been reported from mid-March to July, with the chief period during April, May, and June. The earliest report involved an all but complete nest in Benton County on March 20. Young were seen in this nest on April 26, and three short-tailed fledglings were nearby on May 8. In the Wheeler Collection there are clutches of five and six eggs taken from two nests that were sixteen and twenty-five feet high on May 7 and July 6. In Benton County, shrikes nested in the same small thicket adjoining a large open field in 1979, 1980, and 1981. Nests in the file have usually been found in a thorny tree or shrub, often about five to ten feet above the ground (once as low as two feet, and unusually as high as the nests in the Wheeler Collection), and always in open areas.

MIGRATION AND WINTER: Shrikes are most numerous in Arkansas from late September or October through winter to March. One bird banded in Iowa in May was recovered over 400 miles south in Arkansas the following January. Another shrike banded in North Dakota in summer was recovered nearly 900 miles south in Arkansas three winters later.

During winter shrikes are generally more numerous in the cleared lands of the lowlands of southern and eastern Arkansas than elsewhere, but they are present regularly in all regions where there is appropriate habitat. Analysis of Christmas Bird Counts in the state during the 1960s showed that the mean numbers by region varied from 0.3 to 1.8 birds per party hour on the Coastal Plain, 0.9 to 1.1 on the Mississippi Alluvial Plain, and 0.5 to 1.1 in the highlands (including the Arkansas River Valley). The number of birds reported on Christmas Counts at

Jonesboro between 1967 and 1979 varied from 12 to 48, with 34 or more in eight of these years, and peaks of 48 in both 1972 and 1979 (Hanebrink 1980). On the 1980 statewide Christmas Counts, peaks of 22 to 50 birds were reported in six participating locales, four of which were on the Coastal Plain.

Family *Sturnidae* Starlings

EUROPEAN STARLING, *Sturnus vulgaris* Linnaeus

Abundant permanent resident. Especially numerous in winter in agricultural areas where the birds benefit from waste foods. Least numerous in heavily forested areas.

HISTORY: This Old World species was introduced into the United States at New York City in 1890 (AOU 1983) and subsequently spread throughout most of North America. The 3000 European Starlings observed during December in 1925 on Big Island at the confluence of the Arkansas, White, and Mississippi rivers in eastern Arkansas (Vaiden 1940) was the first record for this state. The next sighting was at the western end of the Arkansas River in Arkansas at Fort Smith where starlings were first seen in the winter of 1928–29 (Black 1932b) and returned the following two winters. Then a bird was collected at Fayetteville on January 25, 1930, also in northwestern Arkansas (Baerg 1930c, 1933).

The flocking behavior and the occurrence only in winter of these early starlings indicated that they were wandering or seasonal migrations into the state. This is supported by the fact that some of the first starlings to appear in Fort Smith were banded and two were later recovered in Illinois (Black 1932b). The first starling nesting reported in the state was observed at Rogers in extreme northwestern Arkansas in May and June 1938 (Crooks 1939), and by about 1950 it had become firmly established as a breeding bird in the state even though still rather uncommon in summer (Baerg 1951). Presently the European Starling is common throughout the state in all seasons.

BREEDING SEASON: The current abundance of starlings in summer in Arkansas is documented by the large numbers found on the

Breeding Bird Survey. The average annual mean number per route in each region reported on the survey was 7.4 birds on the Coastal Plain, 28.3 on the Mississippi Alluvial Plain, and 27.9 in the highlands.

Nesting activity has been reported from March through August, with many young out of the nest by mid-May. Starlings utilize all sorts of cavities including the eaves of buildings, old Purple Martin nesting boxes, cavities initially excavated by woodpeckers, and natural cavities in trees. Starlings engage in aggressive activities with native birds. In Washington County they were observed as they carried nesting materials into a newly excavated Red-bellied Woodpecker cavity on March 30. On April 6, starlings contended with Carolina Chickadees for a cavity having an entrance too small for the starlings. Undaunted, the starlings began to enlarge the entrance. While starlings are correctly charged with usurping the nesting places of native species, they also utilize cavities that are not usually used by the native species, and so are not always villainous in their nesting behavior.

MIGRATION AND WINTER: There are 117 banding recoveries of starlings associated with Arkansas (Figure 6-89). These recoveries involved birds present in Arkansas during winter, but were north and east of the state during other times of the year. Distances of 350 to 850 miles were recorded between banding and recovery for 86 of the 117 birds, with the longest distance being nearly 1400 miles. All but 15 were recovered within two years after banding, but one survived over six years.

Huge numbers of migrants pour into the state every winter. Large roosts begin to form in late summer and fall, reach their maximum numbers at midwinter, and break up with the approach of warm weather in late winter and early spring. The blackbird-starling winter roost survey conducted by the U. S. Fish and Wildlife Service in 1980 showed that there were forty-eight major roosts involving over 48 million blackbirds and starlings throughout Arkansas (Figure 6-90). The largest roosts, each numbering two to five million birds, were in the lowlands, but large roosts also were reported in favorable agricultural lands throughout the state. In the very largest of these roosts, starlings usually form a relatively small percentage

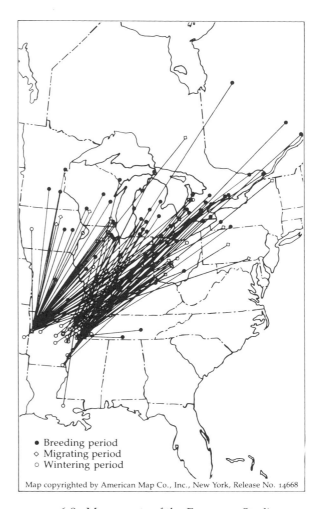

• Breeding period
◇ Migrating period
○ Wintering period

Map copyrighted by American Map Co., Inc., New York, Release No. 14668

FIGURE 6-89 Movements of the European Starling based on banding records.

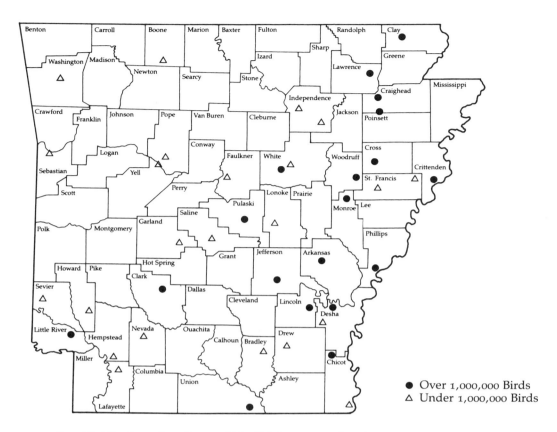

● Over 1,000,000 Birds
△ Under 1,000,000 Birds

FIGURE 6-90 Distribution of starling and blackbird communal night roosts in Arkansas during the winter of 1980.

of the birds present, often 10 or 20 percent of the total. In Monroe County, starlings constituted about 10 percent of a roost containing 3.5 million birds during the winter of 1979–80, but they formed 90 percent of a roost on the Pope-Yell County line that contained 400,000 birds in the same winter.

Family Vireonidae Vireos

WHITE-EYED VIREO, *Vireo griseus* (Boddaert)

Common migrant and summer resident throughout the state. Inhabits moist dense thickets at forest edge in bottomlands. Several winter records.

SPRING MIGRATION: White-eyed Vireos frequently arrive in southern Arkansas during the third and fourth weeks of March, and there is one record in the Audubon Society file involv-

ing as many as four birds in Columbia County on March 30. (Several observations earlier than the third week of March might have involved either early spring migrants, or overwintering individuals.) A migration peak is evident by the second week in April. A party of observers counted 30 in the Ouachita River bottoms in Calhoun County on April 10, and six per hour were counted in a Jefferson County study area on April 12. The species becomes generally common throughout the state by the second half of April.

BREEDING SEASON: The average annual mean number per route in each region reported on the Breeding Bird Survey was 13.2 on the Coastal Plain, 0.9 on the Mississippi Alluvial Plain, and 5.2 in the highlands (including the Arkansas River Valley). Peak annual means of 21.6 and 20.6 were reported on the surveys in Ashley and Dallas counties. The preference of this bird for bottomland habitat is suggested by a summer population study in southern Arkansas where there was a projected population of eighteen singing males per one hundred acres of stream bottomland and only two per one hundred acres in a similar size upland forest (Tables 3-1 and 3-3).

Nesting activity has been observed from the second week of April through July. A nest under construction in Calhoun County on April 10 was the earliest record of breeding activity. The latest such records included a nest with eggs in Columbia County on July 1, and fledglings being fed out of the nest in Washington County on August 8. In the Wheeler Collection there are ten clutches of eggs that were taken from nests between May 13 and June 26. The clutch sizes varied from one to four eggs (usually three), and there was in addition one Brown-headed Cowbird egg in each of three nests. The heights of these nests varied from four to twelve feet from the ground, usually between five and eight feet. In addition to the Wheeler Collection nests, in the file there are three reports in which the birds abandoned nests that were parasitized by cowbirds.

FALL AND WINTER: During fall most White-eyed Vireos have passed through Arkansas by late September or early October. Late peak records have included eight at Horseshoe Lake in Crittenden County on September 23, and in Union County 10 were seen on October 6. Reports after early October are highly scattered and usually involve one or two birds. An unusually high number of four were reported in Grant County on November 22. There have been reports of single birds on the Christmas Bird Counts at Little Rock, Lake Georgia-Pacific, and the White River Refuge, plus two birds seen in Union County on February 27.

BELL'S VIREO, *Vireo bellii* Audubon

Migrant throughout the state. Local summer resident in small numbers in all regions, but chiefly in the north. Inhabits thickets in open country.

SPRING MIGRATION: Bell's Vireo has arrived in Arkansas as early as the second week of April, but usually not until after mid-April, with a migratory peak during the first two weeks of May. In the western Ozarks there are arrival records as early as April 8, but often the birds are not found until the last week of April or the first week of May (Baerg 1930b). The species was said to be "common on prairie" in Arkansas County, with 45 birds counted between May 1 and 15, 1962. A peak of 10 was reported in Sebastian County on May 10.

BREEDING SEASON: Bell's Vireo has been found during the breeding season in all regions, but the summer sightings on file with the Audubon Society have been concentrated in the northern areas, especially in the Ozark Plateaus and in the Arkansas River Valley. The average annual mean number per count in each region reported on the Breeding Bird Survey was 0.2 on the Coastal Plain, 0.3 on the Mississippi Alluvial Plain, and 1.7 in the highlands (including the Arkansas River Valley). Peak means of 1.4 to 5.2 were reported on the surveys in Sebastian, Johnson, and Benton counties. In the northeastern counties it is said to be uncommon (Hanebrink and Posey 1979), but occurs there locally on a regular basis. Among several summer reports from Jefferson County in the southeast is one that involves plum thickets on sandy soil along the Arkansas River where Bell's Vireo nests regularly. The species has also nested at DeVall's Bluff in Prairie County and in Union County and elsewhere in the lowlands.

Nesting activity has been observed from the second week of May to late July. The earliest record is from DeVall's Bluff in Prairie County where incubation was already underway on May 10. Among the latest records in the file, several are for pairs of young being fed out of the nest at El Dorado on July 16, and a downy young fledgling was being fed at Fayetteville on July 26. In the Wheeler Collection there are four clutches of eggs (four eggs in each nest) that were taken from nests between May 27 and June 30. These nests were one to four feet from the ground. Brown-headed Cowbird egg parasitism has been frequently reported in Arkansas nests of this vireo. The most extreme case was in Benton County where Dean Crooks observed the birds build and abandon in succession three nests after each was parasitized by cowbirds (Baerg 1951). In the fourth nest they finally succeeded in rearing four young. Bell's Vireo inhabits bushes or thickets in open country, such as prairies and overgrown pastures, especially where the vegetation is along a stream, pond, or other source of moisture. In such places several pairs may be found during summer in relatively close proximity. Three pairs were found in a small area at Russellville. Four singing birds were found in a dense fence-row a quarter of a mile long east of the Fayetteville airport during June. As many as nine birds have been found on the Breeding Bird Survey route in Benton County in the extreme northwest.

FALL MIGRATION: Bell's Vireo has been reported in Arkansas as late as the end of September, but there are few reports after the second week. In the Fayetteville area the last dates ranged between August 7 and September 6, mainly during the first week of September (Baerg 1930b). A peak of 10 was reported at the state fish hatchery in Lonoke County on August 25. The fall migration is especially notable because the birds often sing in migration.

SOLITARY VIREO, *Vireo solitarius* (Wilson)

Fairly common migrant in woodlands throughout the state. Rare in winter primarily in the southern lowlands.

SPRING MIGRATION: In the Audubon Society file there are sightings for the northward migration period mainly between the last week of April and the third week of May (latest report, first week of June). There are several March records, mainly in the south, where the species is known to remain during winter. However, the fact that there are relatively few reports during January and February suggests that these birds may move into the extreme southern region of the state during March, and into the northern half of the state significantly later (there are no reports for the western Ozarks until April 21). Solitary Vireos are usually seen in small numbers. The eight seen at Fort Smith on May 10 was a peak.

FALL AND WINTER: The main period for fall migration seems to occur from mid-September to the last week of October or early November (earliest arrival date is in the first week of September). A strong cold front in early fall can be expected to produce a few of these birds. Such was the case when seven were seen at Lake Fayetteville on October 7. The latest reports for the western Ozarks, where they have not been known to overwinter, is on October 28, and for Garland County on November 1 (Deaderick 1938). Sightings after early November have generally been in the southern lowlands and to a

much lesser extent in the central Arkansas River Valley, and have involved one or two birds. It has been found with the greatest regularity in winter on the Christmas Bird Count at Lake Georgia-Pacific (peak of seven in 1979) and at El Dorado (peak of three in 1975). Very few have been seen in January and February.

YELLOW-THROATED VIREO, *Vireo flavifrons* Vieillot

Fairly common migrant and summer resident in extensive tracts of mature forest in most regions, with the largest numbers on the Coastal Plain.

SPRING MIGRATION: Yellow-throated Vireos have arrived in southern Arkansas as early as the third week of March, but they are most numerous during the last week of March and during the first two weeks of April (Mattocks and Shugart 1962, Audubon Society file). In Garland County there were arrivals during the last week of March (Deaderick 1938), and in the western Ozarks there are no reports earlier than April 7, with some first arrivals as late as the third and fourth weeks of April (Smith 1915, Baerg 1930b, Black 1935a). A party of observers found nine in the Ouachita River bottoms near El Dorado on April 10, and a peak of six birds per hour was reported in a study area in Jefferson County on April 12.

BREEDING SEASON: There are summer reports for all regions on file. The average annual mean number per route in each region reported on the Breeding Bird Survey was 2.2 on the Coastal Plain, 0.1 on the Mississippi Alluvial Plain, and 0.6 in the highlands (including the Arkansas River Valley). Howell (1911) stated that the species was a "common summer resident in . . . upland timber tracts in company with the red-eye." Due to extensive deforestation of eastern Arkansas (Holder 1970), the species now seems to occur there locally where suitable habitat remains. Records in the file show that they have nested regularly at DeVall's Bluff in Prairie County and are occasional nesters in Lonoke County. A recent summer population study at the White River Refuge showed this species was present there in very small numbers (Christman 1983a, b). However, it has not been found during summer in recent years in the northeastern counties (Hanebrink and Posey 1979). The birds have nested regu-

FIGURE 6-91 Warbling Vireo in mid-June, forty miles downstream from Pine Bluff, along the Arkansas River on the Mississippi Alluvial Plain. *David Plank*

larly at Boyle Park in Little Rock and are found regularly in the most heavily forested regions of the Ozarks, especially in the Ozark National Forest, Buffalo National River, and other places where the forest is extensive. It was "fairly common" in summer at Winslow in Washington County (Black 1935a). Summer population studies in the state (Tables 3-1 and 3-3) showed a population in southern Arkansas of thirteen singing males per one hundred acres of bottomland forests and seven per one hundred acres in upland forests; a similar study in northwestern Arkansas showed four singing males per one hundred acres of upland forests and five in the bottomland forest.

Nesting activity has been observed from mid-April to late August, chiefly during April, May, and June. The earliest record involved nest construction at Boyle Park in Little Rock on April 16 (incubation on April 22). In the Wheeler Collection there are five clutches of eggs that were taken from nests between May 11 and June 6. There were three and four vireo eggs in these nests, and there was additionally a Brown-headed Cowbird egg in one nest. The latest record in the file involved young being fed out of the nest in Ouachita County on August 24. Nests observed by Vivian Scarlett at Boyle Park, Lake Nimrod (Yell County), and DeVall's Bluff were high, usually about twenty feet higher than Red-eyed Vireo nests.

FALL MIGRATION: Yellow-throated Vireos have been seen in the state with some regularity until the middle of September with scattered sightings thereafter to about mid-October. The 12 observed in Union and Ouachita counties on August 27 was a fall peak. Other than these reports, there is also one late in October, and a highly unusual one in December.

WARBLING VIREO, *Vireo gilvus* (Vieillot)

Fairly common migrant in all regions. Summer resident chiefly in the eastern lowlands, local and in small numbers elsewhere. Observed in open woodlands in migration, and among open woodlands along bodies of water during summer.

SPRING MIGRATION: Warbling Vireos have

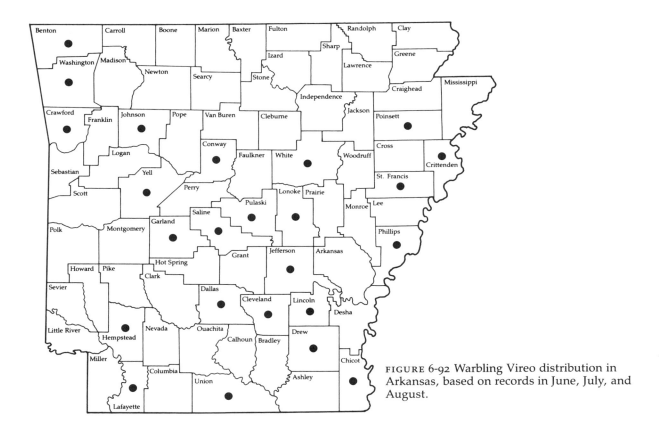

FIGURE 6-92 Warbling Vireo distribution in Arkansas, based on records in June, July, and August.

arrived in Arkansas by late March (Howell 1911), but few are usually seen until about the third week of April and thereafter, with migrants observed as late as the third week of May. Among several April 1 arrival records one is from Winslow in Washington County where the birds were present in small numbers until April 18, and became "common" thereafter (Black 1935a). The 10 birds in Prairie County on April 7 was a large number so early in the spring. A peak of 30 was reported in Pulaski County on April 25, and 19 were counted near the Rebsamen Park Golf Course and along the Arkansas River at Little Rock on May 17.

BREEDING SEASON: In summer Warbling Vireos appear to be locally common in the state, and most widespread in the eastern lowlands (Figure 6-92). The average annual mean number per route in each region reported on the Breeding Bird Survey was 0.5 on the Coastal Plain, 2.5 on the Mississippi Alluvial Plain, and 0.3 in the highlands (including the Arkansas River

Valley). Peak annual means of 1.2 and 4.8 were recorded on the surveys in St. Francis and Lincoln counties. The birds were said to be common summer residents at Helena (Howell 1911), and Baerg (1951) mentioned summer records from Little Rock, Lake Village, Van Buren, and Rogers. In the Audubon Society file there are summer records in Union County in south central Arkansas, and in several eastern counties, including Jefferson, Lonoke, White, Crittenden, Poinsett, and Cleveland, in addition to those already mentioned. As many as nine birds have been reported on the Breeding Bird Survey in Lincoln County, which includes the Arkansas River bottomlands. An estimated 10 birds were found in low swampy woods along the Arkansas River at Little Rock on June 5. Twenty birds (fourteen singing) were found near Pine Bluff on July 14. The species has been found in summer in recent years in the forested edges of several impoundments and rivers in the western Ozarks, and in the scattered tall trees at the Centerton fish hatchery in

Benton County. Hanebrink and Posey (1979) listed it as "very rare" in summer in the northeast.

Nesting activity has been observed during May and June. The earliest such record involved a female on a nest and a male singing nearby at Rebsamen Park Golf Course in Little Rock on May 15. The latest such records are from the state fish hatchery in Lonoke County, where a bird was singing while on the nest on June 7, and from Cleveland County where nesting was observed on June 9. Heights of nests found in Yell, Lonoke, Pulaski, and Conway counties have varied from twenty to fifty feet above the ground.

FALL MIGRATION: There are only scattered reports after the breeding season. At Winslow the species departed by the second week of September (Smith 1915, Black 1935a). In the file there are reports, usually of single birds, until the end of October.

PHILADELPHIA VIREO, *Vireo philadelphicus* (Cassin)

Transient in small numbers throughout the state. Found in woodland habitat, especially riparian woods.

SPRING MIGRATION: In the Audubon Society file there are reports of sightings from the last week of April through May, unusually as early as the first week of April. For Faulkner County there are reports between April 30 and May 22 (Johnson 1979). In the northeastern counties Philadelphia Vireos have been seen primarily from the last week of April to the end of May, and there is one additional report in June (Hanebrink 1980). Most observers during spring or fall report single birds, or sometimes as many as three, during a day when the birds are found. A party of observers counted eight in Craighead County on May 20.

FALL MIGRATION: There are fewer records for fall than spring, and these have involved observations from the second week of September through October, and primarily from the fourth week of September to mid-October. At Rebsamen Park in Little Rock, Gary Graves and others saw one to eight Philadelphia Vireos daily between September 19 and 29, 1975. These observations were made as part of an informal study to determine the status of these birds during migration through the state (information

about this study is on file). A total of 134 Philadelphia Vireos were killed upon impact with a transmission tower in central Arkansas, September 26–30, 1984.

RED-EYED VIREO, *Vireo olivaceus* (Linnaeus)

Common migrant and summer resident in extensive tracts of moist mature forest in all regions.

SPRING MIGRATION: Red-eyed Vireos have arrived in southern and central Arkansas as early as March 23 and 24, and many were seen by a party of observers at Lake Georgia-Pacific on April 3. However, they become generally more widespread during the second and third weeks of April, and migration seems to continue well into the second half of May. A total of 112 were counted in the Ouachita River bottoms near Calion Lake on April 10, 1965. At Fort Smith two observers counted 58 on May 10. The 18 birds in a regularly censused forest tract at Pine Bluff Arsenal on May 19 was a peak in numbers.

BREEDING SEASON: Red-eyed Vireos nest in appropriate habitat wherever this occurs in Arkansas, but the largest numbers have been observed in the Coastal Plain and highland regions, with generally much smaller numbers in the eastern lowlands. The average annual mean number per route in each region reported on the Breeding Bird Survey was 9.7 on the Coastal Plain, 0.7 on the Mississippi Alluvial Plain, and 6.3 in the highlands (including the Arkansas River Valley). Peak annual means in excess of 27.0 were recorded on the surveys in Dallas and Newton counties. In a study in the upper part of Buffalo National River this species was the most numerous bird inhabiting the oak-hickory forest (Hunter et al. 1980). Summer population studies in southern Arkansas (Tables 3-1 and 3-3) showed a population of seventy-eight singing males per one hundred acres of forested stream bottomland, and thirty-five per one hundred acres of upland forests. A summer population study in northwestern Arkansas (Table 3-7) showed a population of four territorial males per one hundred acres of dry mature forest, and fifty per one hundred acres in the moist mature forest. In both of these studies the Red-eyed Vireos were much more numerous than the other species found.

Nesting activity has been observed in May, June, and July. The earliest such record involved several nests that were almost completed in the Winslow (Washington County) area on May 8 (Smith 1915). Near Mena in Polk County a nest with four eggs was found on May 25. On June 4 a nest six feet high in an oak sapling held two young in the Ozark National Forest near Fayetteville. On June 28 a female was observed as she built a nest ten feet from the ground at Little Rock. In the Wheeler Collection there is one clutch of three vireo eggs and one Brown-headed Cowbird egg that was taken from a nest ten feet high on July 3. Young were being fed out of the nest at El Dorado on July 4 (Howell 1911). At Lost Valley in Newton County young were being fed out of the nest on July 25.

FALL MIGRATION: The southward migration period seems to range from mid-to-late August until late September or early October. In Garland County and in the Fayetteville (Washington County) areas, departures were reported from the latter part of August to about mid-September (Deaderick 1938, Baerg 1930b). A total of 168 Red-eyed Vireos were killed upon impact with a transmission tower in central Arkansas September 26–30, 1984. The latest migration record for the state is in mid-October.

Family Emberizidae

Subfamily Parulinae Warblers

BACHMAN'S WARBLER, *Vermivora bachmanii* (Audubon)

Extirpated from the state and possibly extinct. Formerly present in the northeastern lowlands during the breeding season, but there have been no unquestionable records in over seventy years in Arkansas.

Bachman's Warbler was first observed in Arkansas in the St. Francis River bottoms of Greene County in May 1896 (Widmann 1896). A nest with eggs was found across the river in Dunkin County, Missouri, during the following year (Widmann 1897). According to Howell (1911), "the bird is a moderately common breeder in the Sunken Lands of northeastern Arkansas. I saw one at Turrell April 28, 1910, and on May 10 collected two specimens at the same place in heavy timber with a dense undergrowth of cane. One was seen May 4 in the cypresses at Walker Lake. On the St. Francis River, 12 miles above Bertig, I found the birds rather numerous in 1909 (April 25–28) on the Missouri side of the river. . . ." With the exception of these, the only report involved a bird at Winslow, Washington County, on May 5, 1914 (Smith 1915, Black 1935a, Baerg 1951). The bird was collected, but attempts to locate this specimen and verify the identification were unsuccessful.

BLUE-WINGED WARBLER, *Vermivora pinus* (Linnaeus)

Migrant in all regions. Local summer resident in small numbers in the Ozarks. Inhabits brushy fields with sapling trees and other second growth.

SPRING MIGRATION: The species is found during the northward migration period in all regions during April. The earliest arrival date is April 1, and involved a single bird in Cleveland County. Otherwise, most birds are observed from the second week of April and thereafter, and almost all involved single individuals. In the Fayetteville area where the species has nested, there are no arrival dates prior to April 10, and few are seen before the middle of the month (Audubon Society file, Baerg 1931). In earlier times at Winslow in Washington County it was "one of the commonest warblers of the spring migration," strongly associated with Sweetgum trees (Smith 1915).

BREEDING SEASON: The Arkansas Ozarks lie at the southwestern limit of the breeding range of this species (AOU 1983). Here (Figure 6-94), they may be locally common on abandoned farms where early successional or second growth old fields include dense tall saplings or unkempt orchards (James 1974). In the file there are summer records for the Boy Scout camp near Hardy in Sharp County, at Blanchard Springs in Stone County, near Sandgap (Pelsor) in the Ozark National Forest (Pope County), near Cherry Bend in Franklin County, Mt. Judea in Newton County, in the Wedington unit of the Ozark National Forest (Washington and Benton counties), and at Pea Ridge Na-

FIGURE 6-93 Blue-winged Warbler in late April, near Compton in the northwestern Arkansas Ozarks. *David Plank*

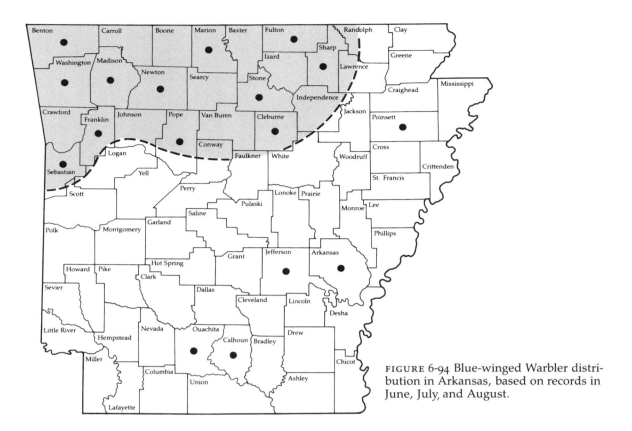

FIGURE 6-94 Blue-winged Warbler distribution in Arkansas, based on records in June, July, and August.

tional Military Park in Benton County. There are also other summer records for Washington County (Smith 1915, Baerg 1931). In addition to the above records, the birds have been found on Breeding Bird Surveys in several other counties in the Ozark region, and in Sebastian County immediately south of the Ozarks.

There are two confirmed breeding records. A nest with five eggs was found on the ground in Pope County on May 8, 1922 (Wheeler 1924). An adult with fledglings was seen in an old field associated with an abandoned farm along Lee Creek in Washington County on June 7, 1980.

FALL MIGRATION: Fall migrants have been observed from early August to mid-September (Audubon Society file, Johnson 1979, Mattocks and Shugart 1962). In recent years the latest fall record was a single bird in Union County on October 10. At Winslow in Washington County, 20 Blue-winged Warblers were observed "in a

single maple tree" during a wave of warblers on October 14 (Black 1935a).

GOLDEN-WINGED WARBLER, *Vermivora chrysoptera* (Linnaeus)

Very uncommon transient in small numbers chiefly in the central and eastern regions of the state. Rare in the west in spring and unreported there in fall. Several observations of the hybrid "Brewster's Warbler."

SPRING MIGRATION: In the Audubon Society file there are sightings of Golden-winged Warblers between the third week of April and the fourth week of May, primarily from the last week of April to the second week of May. These sightings have involved single birds except in two instances: two were seen at El Dorado on April 22, and three by a party of observers at the Ozark Boys' Camp in Montgomery County on May 6. For western Arkansas there are about five spring records (file, Smith 1915) in Sebastian and Washington counties. In the north-eastern counties the species has been seen as early as about the second week of April and as late as about the fourth week of May (Hanebrink 1980).

FALL MIGRATION: There are ten reports in the file between the first week of September and the second week of October. These sightings have occurred in Lonoke, Jefferson, Craighead, St. Francis, and Pulaski counties, and all involved single birds.

HYBRID: "Brewster's Warbler" is one type of hybrid between the Golden-winged and the Blue-winged Warbler. This form has been seen at least twice in the state: in Benton County on May 14, 1961, and in Washington County on May 5, 1983.

TENNESSEE WARBLER, *Vermivora peregrina* (Wilson)

Common transient and in woodlands throughout the state.

SPRING MIGRATION: Tennessee Warblers are among the most prominent members of the mixed flocks of small passerines that seem literally to flood the trees of towns and forests during peak migration periods. Northward moving Tennessee Warblers are seen and heard during April and May, mainly during the last ten days of April to the second week of May. Single birds are observed, but there are many reports in the Audubon Society file that involve five or more Tennessee Warblers in a day. At Little Rock in 1979, 10 or more were found on every field trip between April 28 and May 12. At Mammoth Spring in Fulton County, 27 were reported in one and one-half hours on May 4, and 30 were at Little Rock on May 6.

FALL MIGRATION: Reports for the southward fall migration period are far fewer than in spring, and involve smaller numbers. There are reports during September and October, mainly from mid-September to mid-October. Though many of these reports involve single birds, there are several of three in a day.

ORANGE-CROWNED WARBLER, *Vermivora celata* (Say)

Fairly common migrant in all regions. Winter visitor or resident in small numbers chiefly in the southern lowlands. Observed in open areas or in forest edge in shrubs, tangles of vegetation, or small trees.

FALL MIGRATION: Orange-crowned Warblers have arrived as early as the first two weeks of September (Audubon Society file, Deaderick 1938), but reports are generally few until the first week of October. A total of 26 birds were killed upon impact with a transmission tower in central Arkansas, October 24, 1984. Fall sightings usually involve single birds during October and early November. The six birds in a loose flock at Budd Kidd Lake in Washington County on November 5 was a relatively high count. After early November the species is seen primarily in the southern half of the state.

WINTER: During winter Orange-crowned Warblers are seen with fair regularity on the lowlands of the Coastal Plain and in the southeast, and with less regularity in the Arkansas River Valley (especially the central area between Conway and Little Rock). While the usual report on the Christmas Bird Counts in the southern lowlands involves a single bird, reports of as many as three are not rare, and there are reports of as many as five or six. On the 1981 Christmas Count, a total of 18 were seen statewide, with peaks of three to six birds at Arkadelphia, Conway, and Texarkana. During the mild winter of 1982–83, single birds were also reported on the Christmas Counts at Fayetteville and Siloam Springs in the western Ozarks.

SPRING MIGRATION: Most records for spring involve April and May, mainly mid-April to mid-May. Early dates of spring arrival are suggested by the sudden presence of birds in the north where wintering rarely occurs. In Washington County, reports for the spring migration in 1981 and 1982 ranged from the last week of April into the second week of May. The latest spring date for the state involved a bird "in good song" in Washington County on May 22 (Baerg 1951). A peak number of five birds, all singing, was reported in Washington County on April 28.

NASHVILLE WARBLER, *Vermivora ruficapilla* (Wilson)

Common transient in woodlands throughout the state.

SPRING MIGRATION: Nashville Warblers have

been reported during spring in Arkansas from late March through late May, and with regularity between the third week of April and the second week of May. Most reports have involved one to three birds seen during a day in the field, but larger numbers are common. Eight were seen at Petit Jean Mountain on April 28, and at Fayetteville 10 were seen on May 2. They commonly sing during spring migration.

FALL MIGRATION: In the Audubon Society file there are sightings between late August and the second week of November, but few before the last week of September and after the last week of October. The numbers reported from late September to late October are similar to the large numbers seen in spring. At Lake Fayetteville, seven were seen on October 2. Also in the Fayetteville area, five to twenty birds were seen between October 2 and 16 of a different year (the peak number of 20 involved one flock).

NORTHERN PARULA, *Parula americana* (Linnaeus)

Common migrant in woodlands throughout the state. Fairly common summer resident in extensive moist forests, especially those of river bottoms, in most regions. One winter record.

SPRING MIGRATION: Parulas have arrived in Arkansas as early as the second week of March, but few are generally seen until the third and fourth weeks of the month, and migration continues at least until the second week of April. These birds arrive when the deciduous trees are still leafless. Parulas were said to be common at Cypress Bayou in Arkansas County on March 14. Seven birds were seen at the Ouachita River bottoms in Calhoun County on March 24, and a party of observers counted 25 in the same area (different year) on April 10.

BREEDING SEASON: Parulas are common in most areas of the state in summer, but are generally least common in the eastern lowlands (file, Hanebrink and Posey 1979). The average annual mean number per route in each region reported on the Breeding Bird Surveys was 1.1 on the Coastal Plain, 0.6 on the Mississippi Alluvial Plain, and 1.5 in the highlands (including the Arkansas River Valley). Summer population studies conducted in the state (Tables 3-1 and 3-3) indicated a population of 13 singing males per one hundred acres of forested stream bottomland in southern Arkansas. Smaller num-

bers were found in a moist upland forest in northwestern Arkansas.

Nesting activity has been observed between the second week of April and the end of June. Unspecified nesting activity was observed in Calhoun County on April 10. In Madison County a nest was being constructed on April 28. Young were being fed in a nest in Union County on May 6. In the Wheeler Collection there are two clutches of eggs that were taken from nests on May 20 and June 29. One nest had three eggs and was twenty feet from the ground, and the other had four eggs and was four feet from the ground. In Benton County, Dean Crooks found a nest described as "a very flimsy structure, made of lichens, placed in some leaves of hickory tied together with caterpillar silk" (Baerg 1951). At DeVall's Bluff in Prairie County, Vivian Scarlett found nests made wholly of Spanish moss and placed in vines. One of these nests was seven feet, the other three feet, from the ground. There are several later nesting records including short-tailed young being fed out of a nest in Washington County on July 8, and a family group of three birds in Fulton County on August 14.

FALL MIGRATION AND WINTER: Parulas are fairly common through September, with several observations as late as the third week of October (only one later). The nine birds seen in a census area near Pine Bluff on August 31 were presumably migrants since the species was not known to breed in the immediate area. In Faulkner County parulas are of regular occurrence until the second week of October (Johnson 1979). The latest record for the western Ozarks is on October 16. The three birds in Calhoun County on October 8 was a relatively large number so late in the season. An adult Northern Parula collected near Little Mud Lake in Calhoun County on January 2, 1967, is the only known record after October.

YELLOW WARBLER, *Dendroica petechia* (Linnaeus)

Fairly common migrant in all regions. Local summer resident in small numbers in the Ozarks. Inhabits open areas, including the fringe of trees bordering bodies of water, and the scattered trees and shrubs in lightly urbanized towns.

SPRING MIGRATION: Northward-moving

FIGURE 6-95 Yellow Warbler in mid-June, along the Buffalo River in southern Marion County in the Ozarks.
David Plank

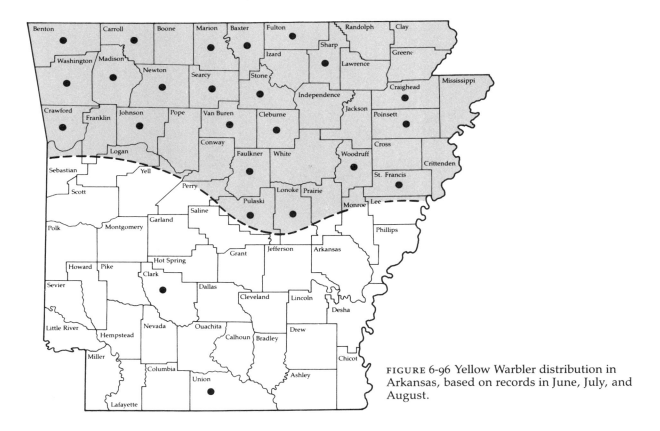

FIGURE 6-96 Yellow Warbler distribution in Arkansas, based on records in June, July, and August.

spring migrants sometimes arrive by the middle of April, but usually later, with most sightings from the last week of April and during the first two weeks of May. Two Yellow Warblers were seen on Archer Island in Chicot County on April 14. There are sightings as late as the last week of May in southern Arkansas where the species does not breed. Most reports in the Audubon Society file have involved one or two birds seen during a day in the field, but there are several larger peak records. At Fort Smith, 17 were observed on May 10. At Mammoth Spring in Fulton County, 7 were reported on May 13. A late spring peak is indicated by the presence of 5 at Calion in Union County on May 25.

BREEDING SEASON: The species was reportedly uncommon in summer in Benton and Washington counties (Baerg 1951) and a "common summer resident" at Winslow in Washington County (Black 1935a). The confirmed nesting record for Faulkner County in the Arkansas River Valley (Wheeler 1924) is the

only breeding record outside of the Ozarks. There are June and July records in the Audubon Society file and on Breeding Bird Surveys for counties throughout the Ozarks (Figure 6-96). Baerg (1951) described the summer habitat as "clumps of young persimmon trees, in willow bushes around ponds and streams, in orchards, and in similar situations." James (1974) reported that the birds favored relatively open areas dominated by willows and cottonwoods fringing open water of gravel bars along streams and the scattered trees and shrubs of rural areas and small towns. Since river habitat is often inundated when streams are dammed to create reservoirs, the Yellow Warbler was included on the unofficial list of threatened or endangered species in Arkansas. In the Ozarks, Yellow Warblers have been found with some regularity at Mt. Judea in Newton County, at Buffalo Point on the Buffalo National River in Marion County, in Stone County where Sylamore Creek meets the White River, and in the swampy sections of impoundments where there is a well-developed fringe of willow trees.

While the birds have been found with regularity in summer in the Ozarks, there is only one actual observation of a nest. In Faulkner County, four eggs were collected from a nest twelve feet high in a peach tree on May 31, 1921 (Wheeler 1924).

FALL MIGRATION: Fall migrants are seen as early as the second week of August (file, Baerg 1951), but more often after the middle of the month, with fairly regular sightings thereafter until the middle of September (file, Black 1935a). The latest sighting involved a single bird at Calion in Union County on October 1. The 16 birds at Lonoke in Lonoke County on September 8 was an unusually large peak in numbers.

CHESTNUT-SIDED WARBLER, *Dendroica pensylvanica* (Linnaeus)

Fairly common spring transient in open woodlands and forest edge throughout the state. Much less common fall transient seen chiefly in the eastern half of Arkansas.

SPRING MIGRATION: In the Audubon Society file there are observations for the northward migration period between the third week of April and the first week of June, mainly from the last week of April to the fourth week of May. Most reports for a day in the field involve one to three birds. Several peak counts include five at West Memphis on April 28 and 8 in Jefferson County on May 6 (file); 12 near Pine Bluff in a 153-acre census tract on May 11 (Coffey 1981). The species is of regular occurrence in Faulkner County from late April to mid-May (Johnson 1979); from mid-April through the first three weeks of May in the northeast (Hanebrink 1980); common in south central Arkansas in the last week of April and the first two weeks of May (Mattocks and Shugart 1962).

FALL MIGRATION: The relatively few sightings on file for fall migration all involved single birds seen from the end of August into the second week of October. All but one of these reports is from Jefferson, Union, Arkansas, Lonoke, and Poinsett counties. A total of 19 Chestnut-sided Warblers were killed upon impact with a transmission tower in central Arkansas September 26–30, 1984.

MAGNOLIA WARBLER, *Dendroica magnolia* (Wilson)

Fairly common spring transient in woodlands throughout the state, and uncommon fall transient. Found in lower, thick vegetation rather than in high tops of trees.

SPRING MIGRATION: In the Audubon Society file there are sightings for spring between the fourth week of April and the first week of June, with a peak during the first two weeks of May. Many reports for a day in the field have involved sightings of one or sometimes three birds. Two observers at Fort Smith saw five on May 10, and four were reported near Pine Bluff on May 6. At the latter location, nine were found in a 153-acre census tract on May 11 (Coffey 1981).

FALL MIGRATION: Southward-moving fall migrants have been reported from the second week of September into the fourth week of October, chiefly mid-September to mid-October, and mainly in the eastern half of the state. In northeastern Arkansas the species is a fairly common transient seen during most of September (Hanebrink and Posey 1979, Hanebrink 1980). For the western Ozarks there are only three fall reports between September 16 and 24. There was one older record in Garland County (Deaderick 1938) and one in Faulkner County (Johnson 1979). The fall peak in numbers involved six birds at Menard Bayou in Arkansas County on September 13.

CAPE MAY WARBLER, *Dendroica tigrina* (Gmelin)

Rare transient. In addition, there are two winter records.

SPRING MIGRATION: In the Audubon Society file there are scattered observations during April and May, and these are relatively concentrated between late April and the third week of May. Baerg (1951) published three records from Pulaski County for April 28, 30, and May 1. Five of the nine observations in the file between April 25 and May 22 involved the eastern half of the state, and in addition there are several more sightings during the first three weeks of May for the northeastern counties (Hanebrink, pers. comm.). While most of the sparse number of reports have involved single birds, two were seen near the Little Buffalo

River at Jasper in Newton County on May 22, and three were seen near the Knob community in Clay County on May 12.

FALL AND WINTER: There are four fall reports that involved single birds in Arkansas, Hot Spring, Little River and Washington counties between the second week of October and late November. In addition to these three observations, a single male Cape May Warbler was observed between January and April of 1965 at a bird feeder in Conway County, and was photographed. Another bird was seen at a feeder in late November and early December of 1981 at Gentry in Benton County.

BLACK-THROATED BLUE WARBLER, *Dendroica caerulescens* (Gmelin)

Rare and irregular transient in the eastern half of the state.

Howell (1911) was aware of only one record of this species, a single bird at Helena on April 7. Subsequently there have been no more than three additional spring sightings, all in the last two weeks of May. Single birds were seen in Arkansas and Union counties on May 15 and 17 respectively, and two were seen in Union County on May 22. There are five additional records in the Audubon Society file during fall involving single birds between the third week of September and the third week of October. These reports were from Calhoun, Union, and Craighead counties, plus single birds killed upon impact with a tower in central Arkansas on September 22 and October 6.

YELLOW-RUMPED WARBLER, *Dendroica coronata* (Linnaeus)

Common migrant and common to uncommon winter resident in woodlands in all regions. In winter most numerous in the southern lowlands. Formerly called "Myrtle Warbler."

FALL MIGRATION: Yellow-rumped Warblers have arrived in Arkansas as early as the third week of September (several birds at Wapannocca Refuge in Crittenden County), but there are only scattered reports thereafter until the first and second weeks of October, when most initial sightings occur. After mid-October the species becomes generally common in the state. The five at Saddle in Fulton County on October 3 was a large early number, as were the 60 at

Lake Fayetteville on October 13. The species is common throughout the state during late October and November to early December, after which smaller numbers are usually seen in the north. During the peak of fall migration flocks of 10 to 25 birds are fairly common and as many as 100 have been seen during a day in the eastern lowlands in late October.

WINTER: The usual scarcity of these birds in northern Arkansas during winter is strongly suggested by results from the Christmas Bird Counts. On twelve recent counts at Fayetteville the number reported varied from 0 to 54 birds, with seven or fewer in half those years. At Jonesboro the peak number observed in the past thirteen years was 16 on one count, and they were unreported in six years. This contrasts with the Arkansas River Valley, where the species is seen every winter, and the Coastal Plain in the south where reports of hundreds are not unusual on Christmas Counts. At Little Rock, more than 100 have been reported on seven of ten recent Christmas Counts, and 472 were found there on the 1982 count. More than 1300 Yellow-rumped Warblers were reported on a Christmas Count at Magnolia in the early 1970s, apparently the largest such record for the state.

A Yellow-rumped Warbler recovered in Arkansas in winter had been banded in North Dakota in the fall, 1000 miles away. Another bird banded in Arkansas was recaptured in the same place a year later.

Winter population studies in the state (Tables 3-2 and 3-4) showed that Yellow-rumped Warblers were most widespread in bottomland forest, but in southern Arkansas similar numbers were found in both upland and bottomland forests.

SPRING MIGRATION: The northward migration seems to be performed primarily between the second week of March and late April, with small numbers lingering into the first half of May (latest report: two birds in Craighead County on May 20). The spring peak seems to occur between mid-March and mid-April. In Jefferson County, 6.5 birds per hour passed through a study area on March 26. An estimated 300 were observed in Union County on March 18, and 125 were seen at Bois D'Arc Wildlife Management Area in Hempstead County on March 20. Many of the hundreds

FIGURE 6-97 Yellow-rumped Warbler in April, near Boxley in the Ozarks. *David Plank*

seen on Archer Island in Chicot County on April 13 and 14 were in breeding plumage.

NOTE: Although the Arkansas population is assignable to what was known as the "Myrtle Warbler" (AOU 1973), birds assignable to "Audubon's Warbler" have been identified twice: one at El Dorado on October 6, 1965, and the other at Fort Smith on April 10, 1972.

BLACK-THROATED GREEN WARBLER, *Dendroica virens* (Gmelin)

Fairly common to common transient in open woodlands and forest edge throughout the state. More often observed in spring than in fall.

SPRING MIGRATION: In the Audubon Society file there are observations for spring be-
tween the fourth week of March and late May, chiefly the first week of April to mid-May. An apparent peak in migration occurs during the final two weeks of April and the first week of May. Most reports for spring or fall in Arkansas have involved one or two birds seen during a day, or occasionally as many as four. On May 4, seven birds were seen at Mammoth Spring in Fulton County and 4.7 birds per hour moved through a study area near Pine Bluff on April 23.

FALL MIGRATION: Most sightings for fall occur between mid-September and mid-October, but there are reports as early as the first week of August and as late as the third week of November. The 10 birds in Washington County on October 2 was a peak in numbers, as were the seven near Pine Bluff on October 5. In recent years single birds have been killed upon impact with transmission towers in central Arkansas on September 22 and October 6. One bird banded in Massachusetts in May was recovered over 1100 miles to the southwest in Arkansas five months later.

BLACKBURNIAN WARBLER, *Dendroica fusca* (Müller)

Uncommon to fairly common transient usually observed in mature trees in all regions, but chiefly in central and eastern Arkansas. More records for spring than fall.

SPRING MIGRATION: In the Audubon Society file there are spring reports between early April and the first week of June, mainly late April to mid-May. Most reports for spring or fall have involved one or occasionally two birds seen per day in the field. Two or more were found in the Fayetteville area during a wave of migration on April 30. Eight were seen in one tree at Malvern in Hot Spring County on May 7.

FALL MIGRATION: There are approximately ten reports on file between the first week of September and the second week of October. There are no fall reports for the Ozarks or the Ouachitas, and apparently very few anywhere in the western one third of the state. The seven birds reported on the campus of the University of Arkansas at Little Rock on September 22 was an unusually large concentration.

YELLOW-THROATED WARBLER, *Dendroica dominica* (Linnaeus)

Fairly common migrant and summer resident in all regions. Mainly inhabits forested river bottoms possessing large trees, and to a lesser extent upland forests of pine or oak-pine. Several winter records.

SPRING MIGRATION: Yellow-throated Warblers have arrived in the southern counties as early as the second week of March, and there are several reports of large numbers before April: six birds counted by a party of observers in the Ouachita River bottoms in Union County on March 22, and 12 at Grassy Lake in Hempstead County on March 24. The species therefore seems to be common in southern Arkansas by the last week of March, often arriving in the north by the end of the month, and present in

appropriate habitat throughout the state by early April. This species, like the Northern Parula, Louisiana Waterthrush, and the Black-and-white Warbler, characteristically arrives in Arkansas when the deciduous trees are still leafless from winter.

BREEDING SEASON: In the Audubon Society file there are summer records for all regions. Data associated with the Breeding Bird Surveys are somewhat spotty because these surveys do not, in large measure, cover riparian habitats where these birds are often found. Nevertheless, there are reports for each region, with annual means of as high as 1.9 to 2.0 birds on the surveys in Garland and Dallas counties.

Nesting activity has been observed between late April and late June. A completed nest sixty feet high in a Sweetgum tree was found at Boyle Park in Little Rock on April 26. An adult was seen carrying food in Washington County on May 31. An adult accompanied by fledglings was observed on Lee Creek in Washington County on June 7. An adult was feeding a downy fledgling at Steele Creek in Newton County on June 17. Young were being fed out of the nest in Union County at Calion on June 26.

The preference of this species for stream bottomland forests is illustrated by summer population studies (Tables 3-1 and 3-3). On the Coastal Plain there was a population of nine singing males per one hundred acres of bottomland forest, and two per one hundred acres of upland mixed pine-hardwood forest. In the western Ozarks the population was five per one hundred acres of forested bottomlands, and zero in the uplands.

FALL MIGRATION: In the Audubon Society file there is a sharp drop in the number of reports after early July, presumably because they are harder to find after the cessation of territorial singing. In south central Arkansas the birds have been found commonly until mid-August, and much smaller numbers thereafter (Mattocks and Shugart 1962). Smith (1915) found several Yellow-throated Warblers associated with Northern Parulas at Winslow in Washington County on September 16. There are several reports in the south during October. The latest fall date involved two birds at Lake Georgia-Pacific in Ashley County on October 21.

WINTER: Five or more of these birds were seen on the grounds of the oil refinery at El

Dorado on January 24, 1966. The only other winter report in the file involved a single bird at Lake Hamilton in Garland County on January 22, 1975.

PINE WARBLER, *Dendroica pinus* (Wilson)

Common permanent resident in pine forests (also mixed pine-hardwood), mainly in the Ouachita Mountains and on the Coastal Plain, with additional records in all regions.

MIGRATION: Even though Pine Warblers are present throughout the year in the principal areas where they nest, migratory activity has been recorded. One bird banded in central Arkansas in winter was recovered over two hundred miles east in Mississippi the following winter (twelve other recoveries occurred at the banding site). While no Pine Warblers could be found during midwinter at Lake Wedington in Washington County, several singing birds were observed there during the third week of February. In Jefferson County, peak numbers in spring were observed in late March.

Flocking characteristic of fall has been reported in Jefferson County as early as the first week of July. In Garland County "flock movement [was] noted especially during September and October" (Deaderick 1938). At Winslow in Washington County, two Pine Warblers were associated with a "migratory wave" on September 29 (Smith 1915). The fall peak in Union County was noted during the second week of October.

BREEDING SEASON: Pine Warblers have been found during summer principally in the Ouachita Mountains and on the Coastal Plain where the largest expanses of pines are found in the state. They have also been found in the scattered pine forests on the Mississippi Alluvial Plain and in the Ozarks. The average annual mean number per route in each region reported on the Breeding Bird Surveys was 7.6 on the Coastal Plain, 0.1 on the Mississippi Alluvial Plain, and 4.0 in the highlands (including the Arkansas River Valley). Peak annual means ranging from 10.6 to 19.1 birds were recorded on three survey routes in the Coastal Plain and on two routes in the Ouachita Mountains. Summer population studies (Tables 3-1 and 3-3) showed a population on the Coastal Plain of 19 singing males per one hundred acres of upland

pine, pine-oak woodland, and nine per one hundred acres in oak-pine stream bottomland.

Nesting activity has been observed from late March to early July. The earliest such record in the Audubon Society file involved a nest under construction in Calhoun County on March 26, and another nest, presumably completed, thirty feet above the ground in a pine tree at Little Rock on March 28. In the Wheeler Collection there are ten clutches of eggs taken from nests in Arkansas between April 10 and July 1 (mainly in April). There were either three or four eggs (usually four) in these nests, and one nest held three Pine Warbler eggs and one Brown-headed Cowbird egg. The heights of these nests varied from sixteen to forty feet from the ground, and were often around thirty feet high.

WINTER: The ten-year mean number of Pine Warblers reported on Christmas Bird Counts in the main pine regions of the state was 0.4 birds per party hour, and this mean was exceeded in four count areas in the south, up to a peak of 2.1 at Lake Georgia-Pacific. The number of Pine Warblers on the Christmas Count at Lake Georgia-Pacific between 1969 and 1982 has varied from 22 to 223 birds, with 100 or more reported in six years. In the Ozarks, where mature pine stands are highly scattered, Pine Warblers may still be common in appropriate habitat. In the Ozark National Forest in Franklin County, 19 singing birds were reported on January 30 around Shores Lake.

Winter population studies (Tables 3-2 and 3-4) indicated a projected population on the Coastal Plain of nine birds per one hundred acres of upland woods, and three per one hundred acres in the bottomland woods.

PRAIRIE WARBLER, *Dendroica discolor* (Vieillot)

Fairly common to common migrant and summer resident in appropriate habitat primarily in the highlands and on the Coastal Plain, and to a much lesser extent on the Mississippi Alluvial Plain. Observed in dry old fields with scattered saplings, small trees, also on prairies with cedars, and in cutover pinelands.

SPRING MIGRATION: Prairie Warblers have arrived as early as April 5 (Baerg 1930b), but few are seen until the second week of April,

FIGURE 6-98 Prairie Warbler in early May, in southern Marion County in the Ozarks. *David Plank*

and the species is not common until the last week of April or early May. One observer found "many" at Cass in Franklin County on April 23. In Washington County, a peak of 3.3 birds per hour was reported in a study area on May 1, and a total of six were seen near Camp Ozark in Montgomery County on May 3.

BREEDING SEASON: Prairie Warblers have been found during summer in all of the regions. The few reports for the eastern lowlands are primarily on Crowley's Ridge, an upland area. The average annual mean number per route in each region reported on the Breeding Bird Survey was 2.8 on the Coastal Plain, 0.2 on the Mississippi Alluvial Plain, and 2.8 in the highlands (including the Arkansas River Valley). Peak annual means of 7.1 and 9.0 were reported on the surveys in Clark and Fulton counties. A study in the western Ozarks (Table 3-7) showed a population of from 21 to 28 territorial males per one hundred acres of habitats characterized as broomsedge fields to forest edge, with the peak numbers in abandoned fields with clumps of small trees, a habitat similar to the cutover pinelands of the Coastal Plain.

Nesting activity has been observed from the second week of May to early July. In the Wheeler Collection there are twelve clutches of eggs taken from nests between May 13 (the earliest known date for the state) and June 1. The clutch sizes in these nests varied from three to five eggs (average about four), and single Brown-headed Cowbird eggs were found in four nests. The latest records in the Audubon Society file involved a nest with eggs in Miller County on July 1, and young being fed out of a nest in Sharp County on July 3.

FALL MIGRATION: Smith (1915) believed that this species departed "very early" with latest dates in the Winslow area of Washington County in July. Sightings on file are fairly concentrated until about mid-July, then scattered to early September. In the western Ozarks the latest departure date is on September 13 (Baerg 1930b). In Faulkner County there is a sighting as late as September 18 (Johnson 1979), and in the northeast, Hanebrink (1980) indicates the birds are seen through approximately the first three weeks of September.

PALM WARBLER, *Dendroica palmarum*
(Gmelin)

Generally very uncommon to somewhat rare transient that is sometimes at least locally common in the northeastern lowlands. Several December records. Observed in open fields and other open country where there is brush and similar vegetation.

SPRING MIGRATION: In the Audubon Society file there are spring observations during April and May, mainly the last week of April and the first week of May. The most impressive reports are from the Mississippi River region. In Crittenden County, five birds were seen on April 28. The species was said to be numerous in Craighead County from April 21 to 27 in 1977, and on April 24 in 1978, and a total of 13 were seen there in 1980 between April 29 and May 6. In the Ozarks, where the species is generally rare, reports were relatively numerous in spring 1984, including a peak of four birds in Benton County on May 8.

FALL AND WINTER: There are far fewer records of Palm Warblers for fall than spring, and these few sightings were in September and October, chiefly from late September and thereafter. In Pulaski County one bird struck a tower on October 2. The two birds at Little Rock on September 30 were seen on a large willow-covered sandbar of the Arkansas River. For the northeastern counties there is only one fall record (Hanebrink 1980). There is one record for the western Arkansas Ozarks in fall, a single bird seen at Lake Fayetteville, October 15, 1985.

There are four reports in the file between late November and late December. Three of these observations involved single birds at Lonoke, Malvern, and Arkadelphia (the latter bird was at the city oxidation ponds). The four birds at Lonoke on December 26, 1965, represent the only late report that involved more than a single bird (one was also seen at Lonoke on the 1974 Christmas Bird Count).

BAY-BREASTED WARBLER, *Dendroica castanea* (Wilson)

Uncommon to fairly common transient in woodlands in all regions, and most numerous in the eastern half of the state.

SPRING MIGRATION: In the Audubon Society file there are spring reports from mid-April to the fourth week of May, but chiefly from late April to the third week of May. This species was listed as common from late April to mid-May in south central Arkansas (Mattocks and Shugart 1962) and common in the northeastern counties from mid-April to the third week of May (Hanebrink and Posey 1979, Hanebrink 1980). Many reports in the file have involved one or two birds seen during a day in both spring and fall, but larger numbers are sometimes reported. Eight were seen in Union County on May 4, and there is a similar report for North Little Rock on May 12. Several observers counted 20 or more Bay-breasted Warblers just north of Helena near the Mississippi River on May 14. Near Pine Bluff, 47 were seen in a 153-acre census tract on May 11 (Coffey 1981).

FALL MIGRATION: There are reports of fall migrants between the second week of September and the first week of November, chiefly between the last week of September and the second week of October. There have been peak reports of 10 or 15 birds in a day during the first week of October in Arkansas, Crittenden, Jefferson, and Craighead counties. A total of 29 immature birds were killed when they flew against a tower in Jefferson County on October 9, 1981. The four birds caught in a net at Fayetteville on September 24 comprise one of the larger reports for the western Ozarks.

BLACKPOLL WARBLER, *Dendroica striata*
(Forster)

Fairly common spring transient in woodlands throughout the state. The few fall reports are questionable.

SPRING MIGRATION: Spring transients are seen primarily from the last week of April and during the first three weeks of May, but there are some additional early spring sightings in the second week of April (Audubon Society file, Hanebrink 1980) and some as late as the last week of May (Black 1935a). Most sightings for a day in the field have involved one or two birds, but more are seen on occasion, especially during May: eight at Fayetteville on May 3; five at Mammoth Spring (Fulton County) on May 4; four "plus" at El Dorado on May 7; and seven at Fort Smith on May 10. There have been two very large reports during recent years, both in the Mississippi River region near Helena: 20 or more on May 16, 1980, and 25 on May 8 and 9, 1982. At Winslow in Washington County the species was said to be "an irregular spring migrant, common when occurring at all" (Black 1935a), a situation that is true fifty years later. During a peak year in 1928 the birds were seen regularly at Winslow from April 29 to May 25.

FALL MIGRATION: There are three fall records on file and one listed by Hanebrink (1980). Of these four reports, one is in September, three in October. However, all of these records must be considered questionable. Full details of the sightings in the file were not submitted, except for the statement with one of them that the bird "had appropriate leg color, as well as other features noted." The Blackpoll Warbler, which is well known to migrate northward in spring across the eastern United States, but southward in fall only along the Atlantic Coast, can easily be confused in fall with the Bay-breasted Warbler, which is a regular fall migrant in Arkansas. Lowery (1974) also had difficulty dealing with this bird identification problem in noting the regularity of fall sightings of Blackpoll Warblers in Louisiana, actually accepting the validity of only one record, which was a collected specimen.

CERULEAN WARBLER, *Dendroica cerulea* (Wilson)

Migrant and summer resident in those regions of the state having extensive tracts of tall mature deciduous forests.

SPRING MIGRANTS: Cerulean Warblers have arrived in the southern counties as early as the last few days of March, but there are only scattered sightings involving single birds until the third and fourth weeks of April, after which the species becomes generally widespread. In the northeast, where there are very few summer records, Cerulean Warblers have been reported from the second week of April to the second week of May (Hanebrink 1980). Many reports in the Audubon Society file have involved single birds. In Marion County, one observer found "many" Cerulean Warblers on April 26 along the Buffalo River, and eight were counted in the forested highlands in northern Franklin County on April 28.

BREEDING SEASON: Most of the summer records in the file involve the Ozark Plateaus, Ouachita Mountains, and the Coastal Plain. In the northeastern lowlands there is one summer record (at Lake City in Craighead County). Further south in the region, however, it has been found to be a "common breeder in the floodplain forest" of Arkansas County (1952), and in Prairie County almost three birds per hour were reported in both mature and immature forest (1955). In earlier times, before the extensive deforestation of the Mississippi region (Holder 1970), Howell (1911) recorded, "its distribution is apparently limited only by the occurrence of heavy deciduous woodland, for the bird is equally common in the river bottoms of the Mississippi and on the slopes of the mountains." In the rugged Ozarks of Newton County it was said to be "rather numerous in both miscellaneous upland and bottomland woods" (file). Reports on the Breeding Bird Surveys are sparse, with records only on a few surveys of the Coastal Plain, Ouachita Mountains, and the Ozark Plateaus, and no annual means higher than 1.3 birds on a single survey. The birds breed in the Saline River bottoms of Grant County in the Coastal Plain, and Black (1935a) noted that they were "fairly common as a summer resident . . . where the large, dark ravines are found" in the Winslow area of Washington County. A summer population study (Table 3-1) conducted in northern Franklin County in the Ozarks of northwestern Arkansas indicated a population of 13 singing males per one hundred acres of upland forest.

Very little is actually known about nesting activity in the state. At DeVall's Bluff in Prairie County, Virginia Springer (file) saw a female carrying nesting material on May 9, and later saw adults with four fledglings.

FALL MIGRATION: Cerulean Warblers have been seen with fair regularity in Arkansas through July, but thereafter their status is poorly known. Smith (1915) believed that they left the Winslow area "soon after the middle of August." In the Audubon file there are only five reports during August and September, and the latest of them involved a single bird in Chicot County in the second week of September.

BLACK-AND-WHITE WARBLER, *Mniotilta varia* (Linnaeus)

Common migrant in woodlands throughout the state. Common summer resident in extensive tracts of mature upland forests in most regions.

SPRING MIGRATION: The distinctive song of these birds is first heard when the deciduous woodlands still have the leafless appearance of winter, and only serviceberries (*Amelanchier arborea*) are in bloom. Spring arrivals have been reported in southern Arkansas unusually as early as the first week of March, but they do not usually reach the state until the third week of the month, and first arrivals in the north often occur in the latter part of March or in early April. A day's total of approximately 100 birds observed in Cleveland County on March 25, 1967, marked a peak movement. The main peak in the migration seems to have passed by mid-April, but some records suggest that migration may continue into early May, at which time some birds in Arkansas have begun to nest.

BREEDING SEASON: This species has been found regularly during summer through the highlands and on the Coastal Plain, but there are few reports on the Mississippi Alluvial Plain. The pattern of distribution is apparent also on the Breeding Bird Surveys where the average annual mean number of birds per route in each region was 1.6 on the Coastal Plain, 0.1 on the Mississippi Alluvial Plain, and 2.0 in the highlands (including the Arkansas River Valley). Peak annual means of 3.8 to 6.4 were reported on surveys in Clark, Garland, Scott, and Newton counties.

Nesting activity has been observed from late March to early July. The earliest breeding observation involved a nest with eggs in Pope County on March 26 (Wheeler 1924). A female was observed as she carried nesting material on April 14–15 at Boyle Park in Little Rock. This nest was finished on April 20, held four eggs on April 26, the young hatched on May 10, and the parents were feeding fledglings by May 18. In the Wheeler Collection there are five clutches of eggs that were taken from ground nests between April 30 and May 27. The clutch sizes varied from three to five eggs (average about 4.5), and in two nests there were also two Brown-headed Cowbird eggs. The latest nest-

ing report involved short-tailed, downy young being fed out of the nest at Lost Valley in Newton County on July 7.

Summer population studies in the western Ozarks (Table 3-7) showed a population of 14 territorial males per one hundred acres of dry mature forest, and 29 per one hundred acres of moist mature forest. Another study (Tables 3-1 and 3-3), also in the Ozarks of northwestern Arkansas, indicated a population of 10 singing males per one hundred acres of upland forests, and none in the bottomland forest. Smaller numbers were reported on other studies in Arkansas. The species seems to require a minimum of 750 acres of continuous forest for maintenance of a viable breeding population (Robbins 1979).

FALL MIGRATION: This species has been seen in the state until late October, but most birds have departed by the first week of that month. A migratory peak is indicated by the record of 44 birds killed upon impact with a transmission tower in central Arkansas, September 26–30, 1984.

AMERICAN REDSTART, *Setophaga ruticilla* (Linnaeus)

Common migrant in woodlands in all regions. Summer resident usually in small numbers in forested bottomlands, and in moist upland forests in the highlands.

SPRING MIGRATION: Redstarts have arrived in the southern counties usually as early as the last week of March, and as many as three have been counted in the Ouachita River bottoms as early as April 10. However, most observations occur in the third and fourth weeks of April and thereafter, with migration seeming to continue until about the second week of May. Many singing redstarts were heard at Cass in Franklin County on April 23, and they were said to be abundant in the Arkansas River bottoms in Arkansas County on April 27. As many as 17 or 18 have been reported in a day several times as late as May 12 (Sebastian and Crittenden counties).

BREEDING SEASON: In the Audubon Society file there are summer reports for all regions. Only small numbers have been reported on the Breeding Bird Surveys, with the average annual mean number per route in each region being

0.8 on the Coastal Plain, 0.3 on the Mississippi Alluvial Plain, and 0.7 in the highlands (including the Arkansas River Valley). Peak annual means of 1.4 to 2.9 were reported on the surveys in Dallas and Grant counties on the Coastal Plain, and on one survey route in northwestern Arkansas. In the northeast, redstarts are said to be "uncommon" in summer (Hanebrink and Posey 1979). In the 1950s they were considered a "common breeder in the heavily timbered bottom lands of the eastern part of the state" (file). They are found regularly in the Ozarks along the Illinois, White, and Buffalo rivers, and sometimes in the moist forests of the higher Ozark uplands.

Summer population studies (Tables 3-1 and 3-3) showed that redstarts occur regularly in bottomland forests with population densities as high as 19 males per one hundred acres. Lowest numbers were recorded in northeastern Arkansas.

Nesting activity has been observed from the second week of May to the second week of June. A nest under construction at DeVall's Bluff in Prairie County on May 9 was the earliest such record in the file. A nest in Pope County on May 13 was only four feet from the ground (Wheeler 1924). Three young left a nest at DeVall's Bluff on June 8. The latest breeding observation involved a nest that was under construction in Ouachita County on June 11. Several nests were reported "high in trees" (file).

FALL MIGRATION: By late summer, redstarts are seen in such places as town woodlots, where they are not known to nest. In Jefferson County, the 2.7 birds per hour in a study area on August 24 was a fall peak in numbers. They are seen in the state through much of September. The four in St. Francis County on September 24 were part of a wave of migrant warblers. The latest regular sighting on file is in the second week of October.

PROTHONOTARY WARBLER, *Protonotaria citrea* (Boddaert)

Common migrant and summer resident in forested swamps and extensive forested stream bottoms, sloughs, and overflow areas in all regions.

SPRING MIGRATION: These brilliantly colored birds have arrived as early as March 21 (two birds at El Dorado) and March 23 (three at DeVall's Bluff), but the usual arrival dates in southern Arkansas are in the first or second weeks of April. The earliest record in the western Ozarks is for April 5, but there are generally few reported there until the third and fourth weeks of the month. The 21 birds seen in the Ouachita River bottoms in the south on April 10 was a very large spring count, but as many as 23 birds (including one flock of 10) have been reported on May 14 at Grassy Lake in Hempstead County.

BREEDING SEASON: The largest numbers in summer are found on the Mississippi Alluvial Plain. In the Ozarks the birds are fairly common locally in the larger forested stream bottoms. The average annual mean number per count in each region on the Breeding Bird Survey was 1.5 on the Coastal Plain, 4.0 on the Mississippi Alluvial Plain, and 0.7 in the highlands (including the Arkansas River Valley). The annual mean in the Mississippi region was pushed upwards by the 20.5 recorded on the survey route in Lincoln County.

Nesting activity has been observed from the second week of April to late July, with most such reports in May, June, and early July. Some of the earliest nesting activity observed has involved males carrying green moss into nesting cavities. There is one such record from Hamburg in Ashley County on April 10 and another from Washington County on April 19, but in neither case did the nest seem to progress beyond this stage. New young were seen in a nest in Hempstead County on May 14 and five young were seen in a nest at El Dorado on May 27. In the Wheeler Collection there are three clutches of eggs (four and five eggs) that were taken from nests either two or three feet above the ground on May 27, June 6, and June 9. The latest nesting activity in the file involved young just fledging from a cup in a cola machine at DeVall's Bluff on July 29. The typical nesting site in Arkansas has been a cavity in a snag over or near water, usually fairly low, with the cavity entrance under ten feet in height. Other sites have included a hanging gourd, a hat, a fence post, etc.

Summer population studies (Table 3-3) on the Coastal Plain indicated a population of 14 singing males per one hundred acres of forested stream bottomlands. Smaller numbers were

FIGURE 6-99 Prothonotary Warbler. *Howard Stern*

found in bottomlands elsewhere in the state.

FALL MIGRATION: The fall status of this species is not well known. Three birds were seen at DeVall's Bluff on August 23, and thereafter in the Audubon Society file there are only sightings of single birds, with the last ones just after mid-September. Late records for Faulkner County are in the last week of August (Johnson 1979).

WORM-EATING WARBLER, *Helmintheros vermivorus* (Gmelin)

Migrant in appropriate habitat in all regions. Fairly common summer resident chiefly on the Coastal Plain and in the highlands. Inhabits moist mature extensive forests with ample understory, ravines and hillsides of the highlands, and similar forests in lowlands.

SPRING MIGRATION: Worm-eating Warblers have arrived in the southern lowlands unusually as early as the last week of March, but the usual time is the first and second week of April, with as many as four birds seen in Columbia County by April 8. The earliest records for the western Ozarks are for the third and fourth weeks of April, with a peak of five birds in northern Franklin County on April 28. In the northeastern counties the birds have been seen from approximately the second week of April to mid-May, but not thereafter (Hanebrink 1980).

BREEDING SEASON: Records in the Audubon Society file, on the Breeding Bird Surveys, and in published literature (Smith 1915, Baerg 1951, Johnson 1979), show that Worm-eating Warblers are present regularly during summer in the Ozarks and on the Coastal Plain, but are rather rare in the eastern lowlands and are infrequently reported in the Arkansas River Valley. There is only sparse data on the Breeding Bird Surveys, with average annual means per route in each region of 1.5 birds on the Coastal Plain, none on the Mississippi Alluvial Plain, and 0.5 in the highlands. Peak annual means of 1.0 to 2.9 were reported on the surveys in Ashley, Dallas, Clark, and Newton counties. Apparently the only summer record from the northeast involved a bird banded in August on Crowley's Ridge in Poinsett County. In the Ozarks the birds are locally common on moist, shady, rocky slopes and in upland ravines. Smith (1915) reported that three or four pairs

nested at the bottom and on the slopes of one ravine at Winslow in Washington County. It has also been found in summer in dense stands of young pines in the Ouachitas (T. Haggerty, pers. comm.). Summer population studies (Table 3-1) in the western Ozarks indicated a population of four singing males per one hundred acres of upland forests.

Certainly one of the more important habitat requirements for this species is extensive forest. Robbins (1979) found the critical size requirement for a viable breeding population was more than 750 acres in his Maryland study areas.

The six nesting records in the file all involved adults feeding young out of the nest between the second week of June and the second week of August in Saline, Union, Perry, Arkansas, and Franklin counties.

FALL MIGRATION: The latest record for the state involved a single bird in Ashley County in the first week of October. There are scattered sightings during September, especially in the first half of the month. Birds that nested at Winslow departed by September 14 (Smith 1915). One observer saw 10 in Pulaski County on September 22. One of the few sightings for Faulkner County is just after mid-September (Johnson 1979).

SWAINSON'S WARBLER, *Limnothlypis swainsonii* (Audubon)

Migrant and summer resident in all regions. Fairly common locally in the larger forested stream bottomlands where there is a dense understory of vegetation including canebrakes, especially in the southeastern lowlands. Local, rare or uncommon elsewhere, sometimes found in uplands.

SPRING MIGRATION: Swainson's Warbler has arrived in Arkansas as early as the third week of March, but in areas like Boyle Park in Little Rock that have been checked for this species regularly, the birds are first heard in the third week of April. A peak number of five birds was reported at Harris Brake in Perry County on April 19.

BREEDING SEASON: The largest summer populations (Figure 6-101) have been found in those regions with the greatest amount of forested stream bottomland. Meanley (1971b) found Swainson's Warbler "locally common" on

David Plank 1981

FIGURE 6-100 Swainson's Warbler in mid-June, along the Buffalo River in southern Marion County in the Ozarks. *David Plank*

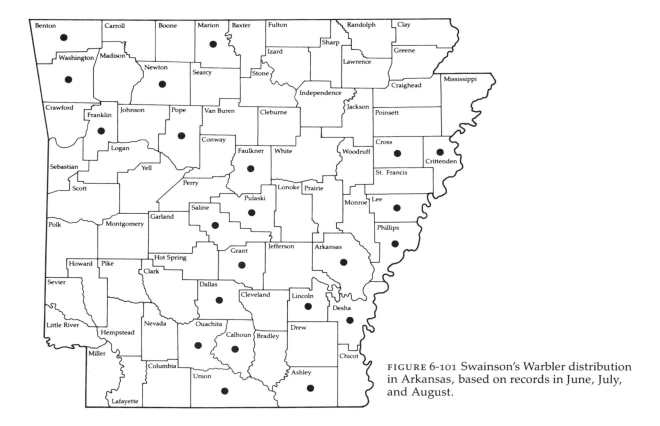

FIGURE 6-101 Swainson's Warbler distribution in Arkansas, based on records in June, July, and August.

the batture (land between the river and the levee) of the lower Arkansas River from the mouth of Bayou Meto to Pendleton in Arkansas County. Construction of at least one nest found by Meanley apparently commenced as early as the third week of April, but the usual time was in the first week of May. The nests found were in the "predominant understory vegetation," including cane, greenbriar, poison ivy, Virginia creeper, and low shrubs. "In a canebrake the nest is rarely located in the densest part of the stand, but is usually nearer the edge where the stand is thinner and the cane poles are smaller." Meanley's five Arkansas nests were at an average of four feet above the ground, and three had suffered cowbird egg parasitism.

Research in 1980 at White River Refuge showed Swainson's Warbler to be fairly common over much of the refuge, and always present in areas with cane. A walk along a road in an area with cane resulted in hearing two to four singing males per five hundred meters of road. The

birds were much less common in areas where no cane was present (Ark. Nat. Her. Comm.).

There are reports of impressive numbers in other areas of Arkansas. Helen and Max Parker report that at least half a dozen singing males can be heard "in wet hardwood timber stands with dense understories" in the Saline River bottoms of Grant County. These birds are not necessarily associated with canebrakes. They have been found in several places in summer in Union County. Singing birds have been found in the early 1980s along the Mulberry River bottoms east of Cass in Franklin County, and on July 29, 1983, four adults feeding fledglings were seen at this location. Birds have also been found in summer in the northwest on the White River, and several times at Buffalo Point on the Buffalo National River in Marion County. While there have generally been few records from northeastern Arkansas, singing birds were reportedly at Village Creek State Park in Cross County in July 1980. There have been additional summer records since 1979 in Dallas, Lee, Desha (Snow Lake), Pulaski (Pinnacle Mountain area), Grant, and Phillips counties (Ark. Nat. Her. Comm.).

Swainson's Warbler is not strictly limited to bottomlands. Sometimes it inhabits moist upland forests with a dense understory just as it does in the Appalachian Mountains. Wheeler (1924) described a nest found in a typical upland situation above Big Piney Creek in Pope County on May 24. This nest was in cane sometimes found in moist upland forests in the Ozarks. A territorial male was observed daily in a moist upland thicket in hills outside Fayetteville during May and June in 1966.

FALL MIGRATION: Meanley (1971b) found that the breeding population in the southeast remained until about mid-September. Interestingly, while the birds sang most vigorously during April and May, sporadic singing was heard also from mid-August until mid-September. The latest data in the Audubon Society file in-

volved a single bird in Desha County during the first days of October.

OVENBIRD, *Seiurus aurocapillus* (Linnaeus)

Common migrant in extensive upland and lowland woods throughout the state. Common summer resident in very extensive forests at higher elevations in the Ozarks and the Ouachitas, and to a lesser extent in the foothills bordering the lowlands.

SPRING MIGRATION: Ovenbirds have been found on several occasions in the western Ozarks as early as April 7 (Audubon Society file, Black 1935a), but few are reported generally until two weeks later. The species becomes common by the last week of April and thereafter. In the high Ozarks area of northern Franklin County, 15 Ovenbirds were seen on April 21, and 23 were there on April 28. Ovenbirds are also seen in the lowlands during spring. At Mallard Lake in Mississippi County

FIGURE 6-102 Ovenbird in early May, near Winslow in the western Arkansas Ozarks. *David Plank*

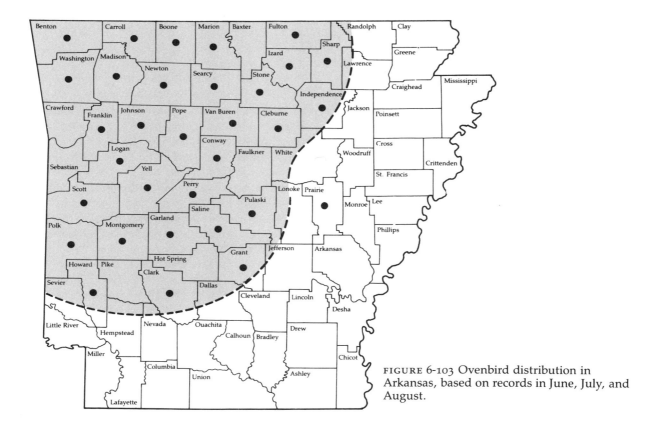

FIGURE 6-103 Ovenbird distribution in Arkansas, based on records in June, July, and August.

there were 15 Ovenbirds on April 27, and 18 were seen at another place in Mississippi County on May 5 (different year). Migrants are apparently seen, at least sometimes, well into the month of May (Mattocks and Shugart 1962, Johnson 1979) at the same time some Arkansas summer resident birds are nesting.

BREEDING SEASON: Summer distribution of Ovenbirds in Arkansas shows a strong association with the highlands (Figure 6-103). The average annual mean number per route in each region was 0.3 on the Coastal Plain, none on the Mississippi Alluvial Plain, and 3.6 in the highlands. The Coastal Plain reports were from Clark and Grant counties, which border the Ouachitas. Peak annual means were recorded in Scott County (4.9), the survey area where three counties join in northwestern Arkansas: Carroll-Boone-Newton (7.2), and Newton County (22.0). The survey in Newton County has a higher elevation than any other Breeding Bird Survey in Arkansas. In the Audubon

Society file there is also a nesting record for DeVall's Bluff in Prairie County, which is an exceptional low-elevation breeding area for Ovenbirds in Arkansas.

The Ovenbird's preference for high elevations in Arkansas in summer is documented by several investigations. On Magazine Mountain, the highest point in the state, "so far as song is concerned, this is the dominant species on the mountain. More than 10 pair nest in a small area there" and they were found on only the upper half of the mountain (Baerg 1927). Ben Coffey undertook a similar investigation there, and found five birds at the 2400 foot level, and 14 above that level (file). At Winslow in Washington County, Black (1935a) found that Ovenbirds were "one of the most common warblers as a summer resident" above 1400 feet. Summer population studies (Table 3-1) in the western Ozarks indicated a population of 33 singing males per one hundred acres in upland forest.

Ovenbirds require large tracts of forest. Robbins (1979) found that a fully viable breeding population of Ovenbirds required at least 6550 acres of unbroken forest in his Maryland study areas.

Nesting activity has been reported from the second or third week of April to the second week of June. The earliest breeding observation involved a pair of Ovenbirds that were seen feeding together at Boyle Park in Little Rock on April 13. A bird was seen carrying nesting material, and a nearly completed nest was found on the ground on a hillside on April 21. Five eggs (including one Brown-headed Cowbird egg) were seen in the nest on April 29 (the eggs disappeared after May 2). In the Wheeler Collection there are five clutches of eggs that were taken from ground nests between May 6 and 24. Two of these nests held four Ovenbird eggs (and one also held a cowbird egg), and the other three had five eggs each. The latest breeding report involved a nest with three eggs in Newton County on June 12.

FALL MIGRATION: Fall migrants have been observed from the last week of August to mid-October. In Jefferson County, where Ovenbirds do not nest, there were reports one year on August 23, September 26, and October 3. A total of 199 Ovenbirds were killed upon impact with a transmission tower in central Arkansas, September 26–30, 1984. At Winslow, where the species nests commonly, departures occurred about mid-September (Black 1935a). One of two Ovenbirds seen by Luvois Shugart and Jimmie Brown in Union County on October 8 was collected.

NORTHERN WATERTHRUSH, *Seiurus noveboracensis* (Gmelin)

Fairly common transient in all regions. Observed in open, low-lying woods or thickets along major bodies of water, including rivers and lakes.

SPRING MIGRATION: In the Audubon Society file there are reports for the northward migration period from March 22 (Union County) to May 21, chiefly between mid-April and mid-May. At Big Lake Refuge there were twenty of these birds on April 24, and at least eight were seen in a small area along the White River in Washington County on May 2. A specimen was collected at Petit Jean Mountain on May 12.

Most reports in the file have involved single birds seen during a day in the field in both spring and fall.

FALL MIGRATION: Observations on file span the period between the second week of July and the fourth week of September, mainly from mid-August and thereafter. Tom Imhoff (file) reported a single bird near Pine Bluff that sang what he described as "snatches" of the proper song on July 13, and two birds were found in the same place the following day. A Northern Waterthrush was banded at Harrisburg in Poinsett County on August 12. Six birds were killed upon impact with a tower in Jefferson County on September 22. There is also one highly unusual report of a single bird that was seen at very close range by a skilled observer in Union County on December 9.

LOUISIANA WATERTHRUSH, *Seiurus motacilla* (Vieillot)

Common migrant in all regions. Summer resident chiefly in the highlands and on the Coastal Plain. Observed or heard along upland streams in extensively forested areas.

SPRING MIGRATION: Louisiana Waterthrushes have arrived in Arkansas as early as mid-March (one bird in Greene County), but most reports of first arrival involve the third and fourth weeks of the month. This is another warbler that arrives when the deciduous trees are still leafless from winter. Six birds were found in Marion County on March 26, and five at DeVall's Bluff in Prairie County on April 5. Migrants are seen at least until the second week of April (Deaderick 1938), and apparently into May (Hanebrink 1980).

BREEDING SEASON: In the Audubon Society file there are summer reports for all the regions, especially in the Ozarks, and there is additional data that show these birds are present regularly on the Coastal Plain. There is only sparse data on the Breeding Bird Surveys, which sample only a small percentage of the summer habitat favored by these birds: forested stream bottoms and upland ravines with creeks flowing through them. The average annual mean number per route in each region reported on the Breeding Bird Survey was 0.4 on the Coastal Plain, none on the Mississippi Alluvial Plain, and 0.4 in the highlands (which includes the

Arkansas River Valley). The species was said to be "common along all the hill streams of any size" in the Winslow area, Washington County (Black 1935a). It was a "fairly common summer resident" in Garland County (Deaderick 1938), but was not listed as a summer resident in the northeast in either the Ozarks or the lowland counties (Hanebrink and Posey 1979). The species was present during the breeding season in Prairie County where there were 1.7 birds per hour in a study area on May 22. There is a nesting record for Faulkner County (Johnson 1979), but apparently no nesting record for the Fort Smith area in the western Arkansas River Valley (file). Summer population studies (Table 3-3) in southern Arkansas showed a population of 14 singing males per one hundred acres of forested stream bottomland. Smaller numbers were recorded elsewhere.

Nesting activity has been observed from late April to early June. In Union County there were five eggs in a nest on April 28, and this is the earliest such record for the state. Most of the nesting reports in the file involved the month of May. Additionally, in the Wheeler Collection there are three clutches of four and five eggs that were taken from nests on May 1, 18, and 19. The latest nesting record on file involved new hatchlings on June 6 along Blackburn Creek in Washington County (the call notes of the adults associated with this nest could easily be heard above the roar of a fast-flowing mountain stream). Nests found in Arkansas have been on the ground, often on a stream bank, either in plain sight or well concealed by roots, leaves, ferns, or other vegetation, and always alongside running water in forest habitat.

FALL MIGRATION: Louisiana Waterthrushes are seen by mid-July in some places where they do not nest. In Garland County the latest records were between July 21 and August 23 (Deaderick 1938). In the Fayetteville area the latest records ranged between September 4 and October 4 (Baerg 1930b). The latest record for the state is in the second week of October.

KENTUCKY WARBLER, *Oporornis formosus* (Wilson)

Migrant in all regions. Common summer resident chiefly in the highlands and on the Coastal Plain. Inhabits moist shrubby forest understory and forest edge.

SPRING MIGRATION: Kentucky Warblers have arrived in the southern counties as early as the last week of March and the first week of April, but few are seen until mid-April and thereafter, with migration apparently continuing until at least the second week of May (Audubon Society file, Deaderick 1938).

BREEDING SEASON: This species has been found during summer in all regions. Howell (1911) noted that "it is a lover of damp, river bottom woods, but it is found also in ravines and along streams well up on the mountains." In the high elevations at Winslow in Washington County, Black (1935a) stated that it "frequents the cut-over hillsides, especially north slopes, where it is sometimes the predominating bird." Deaderick (1938) considered it an uncommon summer resident in Garland County. In the northeast, Kentucky Warblers are common in summer in the Ozark counties, and uncommon in summer in the lowland counties (Hanebrink and Posey 1979). In Arkansas County the species is considered a "common breeder" (file). Summer population studies (Tables 3-1 and 3-3) in southern Arkansas showed a population of 26 singing males per one hundred acres of forested stream bottomland and 16 per one hundred acres in upland woods. Smaller numbers were recorded on studies elsewhere in the state.

The average annual mean number per route in each region on the Breeding Bird Survey was 8.1 on the Coastal Plain, 0.1 on the Mississippi Alluvial Plain, and 4.2 in the highlands (including the Arkansas River Valley). An annual mean of 18.8 was reported on the survey in Dallas County in southern Arkansas.

Nesting activity has been observed during May and June. In the Wheeler Collection there are three clutches of four and five eggs that were taken from nests between May 5 and May 23. Each of these nests was on the ground. At DeVall's Bluff in Prairie County a nest with eggs was collected on May 17, and the (possibly same) birds commenced to nest again one week later about one hundred yards away. There are reports of young being fed out of the nest in both Garland and Washington counties on June 20. All nests on file were in forests or at the forest edge, positioned on the ground under thickets or other low concealing vegetation.

FALL MIGRATION: This species has been found with regularity in the state through the month of August, and then irregularly during September. A single bird was caught in a mist net at Fayetteville on September 20. A total of 23 were killed upon impact with a transmission tower in central Arkansas, September 26–30, 1984. The latest report involved two birds at El Dorado on October 6.

CONNECTICUT WARBLER, *Oporornis agilis* (Wilson)

Very rare spring transient.

This species usually migrates well to the east of Arkansas (AOU 1983). Each of the eleven reports for Arkansas have involved single birds, mainly in the eastern half of the state, occurring between the third week of April and the fourth week of May (Audubon Society file, Deaderick 1938, Baerg 1951). The counties where these birds have been reported, and the number of records for each county, are as follows: Craighead, one; Pulaski, three; Arkansas, three; Union, two; Garland, one; Washington, one. There are no adequately documented fall sightings.

MOURNING WARBLER, *Oporornis philadelphia* (Wilson)

Fairly common spring transient in small numbers observed in woodlands and forest edge in all regions. Uncommon fall transient. Observed in undergrowth including shrubs, vines, and other low vegetation.

SPRING MIGRATION: In the Audubon Society file there are sightings between the third week of April and early June, primarily during the second, third, and fourth weeks of May. Most sightings have involved single birds in a day in the field, but there are a few reports of larger numbers. At DeVall's Bluff in Prairie County, five were seen on May 22, and three have been seen in different years on either May 15 or 16 in the Mississippi River region in Phillips County north of Helena.

FALL MIGRATION: There are relatively few fall sightings in the file, and these involve the period between the last week of August and

the second week of October, mainly in September. All were single birds. One was banded at Harrisburg in Poinsett County on August 26. Mourning Warblers were trapped in mist nets on September 12 and 22 of different years at Fayetteville. A total of eight were killed upon impact with a transmission tower in central Arkansas, September 26–30, 1984.

COMMON YELLOWTHROAT, *Geothlypis trichas* (Linnaeus)

Common migrant and summer resident throughout the state. Irregular winter resident in small numbers chiefly in the southern lowlands. Inhabits moist thickets in open areas.

SPRING MIGRATION: While some yellowthroats are seen during winter in the state, spring migrants commonly arrive by the second week of April, and are widespread by the third or final weeks of the month. (Some March records in the south might involve early spring arrivals or they could be overwintering birds.) The 65 birds found by a party of observers in Calhoun County near Calion on April 10 was a major influx. Eight birds were seen at Lake Fayetteville on April 28.

BREEDING SEASON: The species is widespread during summer, and most numerous in the lowlands of both the southern and especially eastern regions. The average annual mean number per route in each region reported on the Breeding Bird Survey was 9.6 on the Coastal Plain, 12.9 on the Mississippi Alluvial Plain, and 4.2 in the highlands (including the Arkansas River Valley). Peak annual means of 16.4 to 20.6 were reported on three surveys in the Mississippi region.

Breeding activity has been observed from early May to mid-August, but not often after mid-July. The earliest record on file involved a nest on the ground at Little Rock on May 5 that was later destroyed by rain. Howell (1911) found a nest in Crittenden County that had five eggs on May 7. In the Wheeler Collection there are five clutches of eggs that were taken from nests between May 19 and June 8. Four of these nests held four yellowthroat eggs, another held three, and additionally there were either one or two Brown-headed Cowbird eggs in three of the nests. The heights of these nests varied from two that were on the ground in thick grass or weeds to as high as three feet from the ground. Two of the latest records in the file involve a female incubating eggs in Ouachita County on June 24, and recently fledged young being fed out of a nest in Washington County on August 16.

FALL AND WINTER: Yellowthroats are still numerous in the state during September, but the numbers decline sharply by early October, with the last regular sightings by around mid-month. A total of 57 were killed upon impact with a transmission tower in central Arkansas, September 26–30, 1984. After early October almost all the sightings involve single birds in the southern lowlands, and most were seen during December but also some occurred during January and February. There are a number of records from Christmas Bird Counts in the southern part of the state.

HOODED WARBLER, *Wilsonia citrina* (Boddaert)

Fairly common migrant and locally common summer resident in most regions. Inhabits extensive tracts of mature forest with moist thickets or ravines.

SPRING MIGRATION: Hooded Warblers have arrived in the extreme southern counties as early as the third week of March, but the usual arrival time there is about the first week of April, and not until the second and third weeks of the month in the north. Ten birds in the Ouachita River bottoms of Calhoun County on April 10 was a spring peak, as were the 5.0 birds per hour in a Jefferson County study area on April 12.

BREEDING SEASON: The summer population in Arkansas is concentrated in the Coastal Plain and in the highlands, with small numbers in the Mississippi region. Breeding Hooded Warblers characteristically occupy the more luxuriant parts of mature forest tracts in both bottomland and upland reliefs. Howell (1911) observed the species in drier situations, like brushy forest tracts on mountain sides, including the summit of Rich Mountain. Baerg (1927) reported a similar situation on Magazine Mountain. The average annual mean number per route in each region on the Breeding Bird Survey was 4.1 on the Coastal Plain, 0.3 on the Mississippi Alluvial Plain, and 1.6 in the highlands (including the Arkansas River Valley). Peak annual means of 5.0 and 9.4 were reported on the surveys in Dallas, Grant, and Newton counties. These birds were formerly said to be common in the sunken lands of northeastern Arkansas (Howell 1911), but apparently are now absent in the breeding season (Hanebrink and Posey 1979). Summer population studies (Tables 3-1 and 3-3) showed a population of 23 singing males per one hundred acres of forested stream bottomland in southern Arkansas, and only two per one hundred acres of upland forests there. In northwestern Arkansas there were eight per one hundred acres of upland forests, and none in the bottomlands.

Nesting activity has been observed between May and September. The earliest such observation in the Audubon Society file involved an unfinished nest on May 5 in Franklin County at the Redding campground in the Ozark National Forest. There is a similar report at Winslow in Washington County (Smith 1915). Some of the latest reports in the file include a nest with three eggs in Union County on August 1, and adults feeding young out of the nest in Jefferson County on September 14. There was one Brown-headed Cowbird egg in a nest at El Dorado on May 21. The only nest in the Wheeler Collection was on May 11 and the clutch size was four eggs. The nests are usually near the ground. The Franklin County nest was in the densely forested overflow channel of the Mulberry River, and was three feet high in a small shrub.

FALL MIGRATION: Even though some nesting activity has been observed in the state during September, migrants are also seen during that month. Records of migrants may involve Hooded Warblers found in places where breeding is not known to occur, or it may involve seasonal peaks in numbers. In Faulkner County, the birds were common from about the second week of September to early October (Johnson 1979). One of only two recent records for the northeastern counties was in September (Hanebrink 1980). In Garland County the latest sighting was on September 10 (Deaderick 1938). There are no records for the state after the second week of October.

WILSON'S WARBLER, *Wilsonia pusilla*
(Wilson)

Fairly common transient in all regions. Observed in low trees, shrubs, and thickets in both open fields or fencerows and in open woodlands.

SPRING MIGRATION: In the Audubon Society file there are spring reports between the second week of April and early June, with a peak during the second and third weeks of May. Many reports for a day afield in spring or fall have involved one or two Wilson's Warblers, sometimes more. Six were seen in the vicinity of the Rebsamen Park Golf Course in Little Rock on May 13, and a very high number of 47 was found by two observers at Fort Smith on May 10.

FALL MIGRATION: During the southward migration period Wilson's Warbler has been observed from the third week of August to the third week of October, with a peak during September. Five were seen at Lake Fayetteville on September 5, and a party of observers counted 12 in Union County on September 3. There is also one highly unusual report of a single bird at Lonoke on December 22.

CANADA WARBLER, *Wilsonia canadensis*
(Linnaeus)

Uncommon transient in small numbers in woodlands throughout the state.

SPRING MIGRATION: Combining the information in the Audubon Society file with the findings of Johnson (1979) and Hanebrink (1980), it is evident that except for a few records in the latter part of April the spring migration of this species through Arkansas is confined to May and occurs throughout that month. It is nearly always uncommon or even rare, so that the total number of sightings reported over the years has not been great. When it is found, most reports have involved one or two birds, but six were found by a party of observers at Boyle Park in Little Rock on May 11, and eight were seen by two observers at Helena in Phillips County on May 15. There are more sightings in the file for spring than fall. While sightings are fairly well distributed in the regions of the state, there is a concentration in the south.

FALL MIGRATION: Reports for the southward migration period are few, and these are scat-

tered from the last week of August to the last week of September. Most have involved single birds, but a party of observers found 10 at Calion in Union County on September 13, and 14 were killed upon impact with a transmission tower in central Arkansas, September 26–30, 1984. Most fall reports have involved the eastern half of the state.

YELLOW-BREASTED CHAT, *Icteria virens*
(Linnaeus)

Common migrant and summer resident throughout the state. Inhabits open country thickets and the scrubby, tangly regenerative growth in forest clear-cut areas.

SPRING MIGRATION: Chats have arrived as early as the first week of April in southern Arkansas, but few are generally seen until the third and fourth weeks of the month, and migration continues until early May. Twelve birds were seen at West Memphis in Crittenden County on April 28. In Washington County, a peak of 5.1 birds per hour was reported in a study area on May 1 (down slightly to 4.0 on May 8). Five chats were killed upon impact with a tower in Jefferson County on May 2.

BREEDING SEASON: Chats are very common during summer, especially in the southern lowlands. The average annual mean number per route in each region reported on the Breeding Bird Survey was 20.6 on the Coastal Plain, 12.4 on the Mississippi Alluvial Plain, and 11.2 in the highlands (including the Arkansas River Valley). Peak annual means of 31.4 and 27.9 were reported on the surveys in Calhoun and Chicot counties in the southeastern lowlands. A study in the western Ozarks (Table 3-7) showed a population of 50 territorial males per one hundred acres of habitat characterized as late stage densely overgrown old field. Chats are impressively numerous in second growth where pine forests have been clear-cut.

Nesting activity has been observed from early May through July, chiefly through June. The earliest record in the Audubon Society file involved a nest with one egg (presumably an incomplete clutch) in Washington County on May 11. In the Wheeler Collection there are ten clutches of eggs that were taken from nests between May 14 and July 15, chiefly by the first week of June. The clutch size in these nests involved three or four eggs (usually four) and one or two Brown-headed Cowbird eggs were found in five nests. The heights of nests in the Wheeler Collection varied from two to seven feet from the ground (average slightly over four feet). Chat nests are usually in low thickets, tangles of thorny vines, or in vine-covered shrubs or small trees.

FALL MIGRATION: Chats cease singing between late July and late August (Baerg 1930a), and are infrequently reported thereafter. For the western Ozarks there are no reports after late August. In Garland County the last records were between August 1 and September 5 (Deaderick 1938). A migration peak is suggested in the deaths of 17 chats killed upon impact with a transmission tower in central Arkansas, September 26–30, 1984. There are a few highly scattered sightings in October and November, plus one highly unusual winter record from Fort Smith.

Subfamily Thraupinae Tanagers

SUMMER TANAGER, *Piranga rubra* (Linnaeus)

Common migrant and summer resident in open mature woodlands in all regions. More common at lower elevations than the Scarlet Tanager. Rare in winter.

SPRING MIGRATION: Spring migrants sometimes reach southern Arkansas during the first week of April, but there are only scattered records until the last week of the month. In Washington County in the Ozarks, arrivals were reported between April 20 and 27 (Baerg 1930b). The five birds at Lake Fayetteville and the 10 at Petit Jean Mountain, both on April 28, were relatively large numbers. A spring peak of 11 Summer Tanagers was reported from a 153-acre census tract near Pine Bluff on May 11 (Coffey 1981).

BREEDING SEASON: Results from Breeding Bird Surveys show the largest numbers present during June in the Coastal Plain and in the highlands (especially the Ouachita Mountains), and low numbers in the Mississippi Alluvial Plain. Annual means of 8.8 to 11.9 Summer Tanagers were reported on the surveys in Ashley, Dallas, and Clark counties on the Coastal

Plain; Garland and Scott counties in the Ouachitas; and Fulton County in the Ozarks.

Nesting activity has been reported from the second week of May to mid-August, and once as late as mid-September. The earliest nest had eggs on May 10 in Ashley County. One of the latest records was from Washington County, where young were still in a nest on August 13. The latest record in the file involved a juvenile being fed out of the nest in Jefferson County on September 13. In the Wheeler Collection there are ten nests with eggs dated from May 21 to June 27. The nest heights ranged from eight to twenty feet above the ground, and the number of Summer Tanager eggs in the nests varied from two to five (average 3.5); six of the nests also held one Brown-headed Cowbird egg. Additional breeding records in the file involve nest heights up to thirty-five feet. Nests were found in both pine and deciduous trees.

Summer population studies (Tables 3-1 and 3-3) in the state have shown that when Summer Tanagers are present in study areas the population of territorial males per one hundred acres of upland and lowland woods may be as high as 12 birds. In Benton County in the western Ozarks, peak numbers of 9 to 14 territorial males per one hundred acres were found in habitats ranging from the forest edge to the intermediate zone between dry and moist forests (Table 3-7).

FALL AND WINTER: Summer Tanagers are common in the state during September, and are reported with regularity to the second week of October. The 11 birds seen in Washington County on September 8 was a fall peak, as were the five near Pine Bluff on October 2. Stragglers may sometimes remain in the state longer. In the file there are reports involving at least ten Summer Tanager records between December and February. These reports have come primarily from central and southern Arkansas, but there are also two records for the northwest. Each report has involved a single bird, most of which seem to have survived winters in Arkansas by coming to home feeders. Photographs of several of these birds are on file with the Audubon Society. One of the longest stays involved a bird at Little Rock from November 10, 1967, until April 7, 1968.

FIGURE 6-104 Scarlet Tanagers in early May, east of Brentwood in the Boston Mountains section of the Ozarks.
David Plank

SCARLET TANAGER, *Piranga olivacea* (Gmelin)

Common migrant in extensive woodlands in all regions. Common summer resident in extensive upland woods, chiefly in the Ozarks and the Ouachitas, and in smaller numbers elsewhere. Favors higher elevations.

SPRING MIGRATION: Scarlet Tanagers have been seen as early as the first week of April in southern and central Arkansas, but most are found after mid-month, with migration continuing into the second week of May. In the heavily forested Boston Mountain region of the Ozarks near Winslow (Washington County) where this species is common in summer, the males arrived on April 12, and the females one week later (Black 1935a). In Garland County in the Ouachitas, arrivals were noted April 27–28 (Deaderick 1938).

BREEDING SEASON: During the period from 1967 to 1977, Scarlet Tanagers were found on Breeding Bird Surveys in all regions. On the Coastal Plain there were reports in Dallas and Clark counties; in St. Francis, Poinsett, and Woodruff counties of the Mississippi Alluvial Plain; and in nine counties of the highlands. By far the largest number, up to 10 and 20 birds, were found in the Ozarks on surveys in Van Buren and Newton counties, and on the Compton survey (junction of Carroll-Boone-Newton counties). Reports in the Audubon Society file reflect a similar pattern of abundance and distribution in the state (Figure 6-105), with additional summer records in Union, Grant, Hot

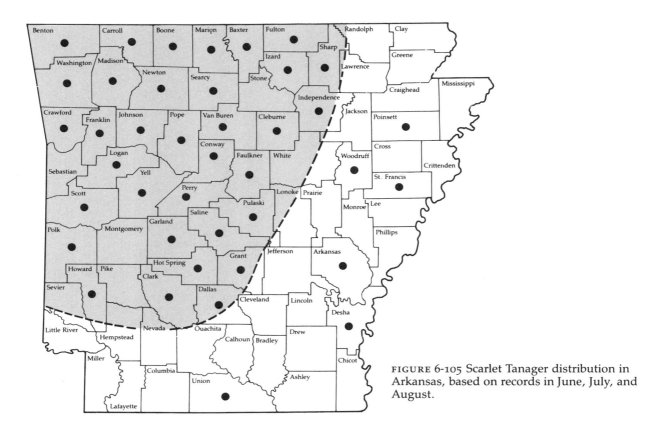

FIGURE 6-105 Scarlet Tanager distribution in Arkansas, based on records in June, July, and August.

Spring, and Howard counties on the Coastal Plain; Arkansas County on the Mississippi Alluvial Plain; and several records in the Arkansas River Valley.

Nesting activity has been reported during May, June, and July. At Petit Jean Mountain in Conway County, a pair was observed as they built a nest on May 6. In the Wheeler Collection, there are two nests with eggs dated May 17 and June 18. One of the nests was twenty feet high and held four eggs. The other was twenty-five feet high, and held four Scarlet Tanager eggs and one Brown-headed Cowbird egg. An adult male was seen feeding a fledgling in Dallas County on June 8. A nest was seen on a limb of an oak tree about thirty feet high on June 12 in Newton County. A male was observed in Grant County as it carried food on July 11.

The Scarlet Tanager's preference for higher elevations is well-documented in Arkansas. On Rich Mountain in Polk County, Ben Coffey found 11 birds at the 2000 foot level on May 30, and 18 birds at the 2300 foot level on Magazine Mountain on June 22 (file). Baerg (1927) counted this species on Magazine Mountain during June and found them second in numbers only to Ovenbirds. On top of the mountain, at 2800 feet, he found eight to ten pairs, and several more were seen 300 to 400 feet down the slope. Summer population studies (Table 3-1) in the Ozarks showed a population of two singing males per one hundred acres of upland forest.

FALL MIGRATION: Departures usually occurred from mid-August to early September at Winslow (Black 1935a). Fall sightings, except at high elevations, are uncommon, and thus the fall migration is not well known for Arkansas. There are scattered records from late September to the second week of October. The three birds seen in Union County on September 26 were a large number so late in the season.

WESTERN TANAGER, *Piranga ludoviciana* (Wilson)

Three records.

Baerg (1951) published a record of one Western Tanager at Hot Springs on April 8, 1945. One male and one female were seen in Clark County near Arkadelphia on September 1–3, 1971, and documentation associated with this sighting is on file with the Arkansas Audubon Society. A single male was seen at Village Creek State Park in Cross County on May 14, 1978.

Subfamily Cardinalinae Grosbeaks and Buntings

NORTHERN CARDINAL, *Cardinalis cardinalis* (Linnaeus)

Common permanent resident. Observed in open woodlands and at the forest edge, in thickets and fencerows in fields, and in yards with bushes. A common bird at home bird feeders in winter.

BREEDING SEASON: Data from the Breeding Bird Survey show that cardinals are most numerous in summer in the lowlands. The average annual mean number per route in each region on the surveys was 45.9 birds on the Coastal Plain, 43.9 on the Mississippi Alluvial

FIGURE 6-106 Northern Cardinal. *Thase Daniel*

Plain, and 24.0 in the highlands (including the Arkansas River Valley). Only a few species were found in larger numbers on the surveys.

Nesting activity has been observed from late March to mid-September. Extreme records include a nest under construction at Winslow in Washington County in late March (Smith 1915), and young about ready to leave a nest in Craighead County on September 15. In the Wheeler Collection eleven nests with eggs are dated from April 2 to June 12. The clutch sizes in these nests were three or four eggs (often three), with the nest heights ranging from one to ten feet above the ground, often no higher than four feet. In the Audubon Society file there is one record of a nest twelve feet high. Cowbird egg parasitism has been noted in cardinal nests in Arkansas.

Summer population studies (Tables 3-1 and 3-3) in woodlands in the state showed a population of as many as 36 territorial males per one hundred acres. In the western Ozarks, however, there were 61 males per one hundred acres of forest edge (Table 3-7), strongly demonstrating the species' preference for this habitat.

WINTER: From early spring through summer, cardinals are usually seen in pairs, or after the young have fledged, in small family groups. By late fall and during winter, flocks numbering a dozen individuals or more are sometimes seen. The birds are found in large numbers on Christmas Bird Counts, with hundreds annually reported in both northern and southern Arkansas. As in summer, the largest numbers are found in the lowlands. At Fayetteville the number of cardinals reported on the Christmas Count has ranged from over 100 to just over 300. At Arkadelphia on the Coastal Plain in southern Arkansas, reports of 400 have been fairly common on the Christmas Count, and nearly 700 were seen one year. The ten-year statewide mean on Christmas Counts was 5.1 birds per party hour. On the Coastal Plain the means ranged from 4.5 to 8.2; on the Mississippi Alluvial Plain from 4.0 to 7.3; and in the highlands (including the Arkansas River Valley) from 3.6 to 5.6.

ROSE-BREASTED GROSBEAK, *Pheucticus ludovicianus* (Linnaeus)

Fairly common transient in woodlands, including those of towns, in all regions. More often reported in spring than fall. There are several extra-seasonal records for summer and winter.

SPRING MIGRATION: Reports for the northward spring migration span the period from the second week of April to the fourth week of May, mainly fourth week of April to mid-May. Observers usually report no more than one to three birds in a day. Nine were found in two hours in Washington County on May 8, and 18 in one and one-half hours in Fulton County on May 4.

FALL MIGRATION: Fall transients have been reported from late August through October, mainly from the fourth week of September to the third week of October. Ten were reportedly in Cross County on September 23. A party of observers counted 29 at Little Rock on October 4. A total of 36 were killed upon impact with a transmission tower in central Arkansas, September 26–30, 1984.

EXTRA-SEASON REPORTS: A single male was observed at a feeder in Cherokee Village (Sharp County) on March 1, 1976. Also in Sharp County, a male at a distance of fifteen yards was viewed without binoculars on July 10, 1938. A single female was seen in Newton County on June 12, 1979. Another single bird was reported on the Christmas Bird Count at Little Rock in 1960. A male was observed at the White River Refuge on December 30, 1969.

BLACK-HEADED GROSBEAK, *Pheucticus melanocephalus* (Swainson)

Rare transient and winter visitor.

This common species of the western United States has been observed in Arkansas fewer than twenty times, with sightings spanning the period from late September to mid-May, mainly during January, February, and March. Most sightings have been reported in the southwest quarter of the state, either in the lowlands or in the Arkansas River Valley. There are also two reports from the Ozarks. The species has been observed to linger on several occasions. Two birds were observed frequently at El Dorado from February 23 to April 27, 1969. One was seen at El Dorado from March 2 to 21, 1957. One was present at Conway in Faulkner County from March 23 to April 15, 1972. The three birds at Little Rock on December 28, 1956, is the largest single record. The species has been reported primarily from Pulaski and Union counties (five and four records respectively), plus single records in Saline, Conway, Logan, Columbia, Miller, Howard, Cleveland, Newton, and Cleburne counties. Several of these sightings have been supported by written and or photographic documentation.

BLUE GROSBEAK, *Guiraca caerulea* (Linnaeus)

Common migrant and summer resident in the highlands and in the uplands of the Coastal Plain; much less numerous in the Mississippi Alluvial Plain and the Arkansas River Valley. Inhabits bushy, overgrown fields with tangles, thickets, small trees, and forest edge associated with open fields.

SPRING MIGRATION: Blue Grosbeaks have been reported in Union County in the extreme south as early as the second week of April, but the usual arrival time for Arkansas is in the third or fourth week of the month and thereafter. The eight birds counted at Petit Jean Mountain in Conway County on April 29 was a peak number. Most reports on file for April have involved single birds. Baerg (1930b) reported most arrivals in the Fayetteville area either in the last days of April or in the first week of May.

BREEDING SEASON: Reports in the Audubon Society file and on Breeding Bird Surveys show that Blue Grosbeaks are present in June in all regions, but the largest numbers are seen in upland areas, especially in the Ozarks. On the Breeding Bird Surveys average annual means ranging from 5.1 to 13.4 Blue Grosbeaks were reported on the following surveys: Lafayette and Little River counties on the Coastal Plain; Saline and Garland counties in the Ouachitas; Van Buren, Izard, and Benton counties, and the Fulton route (junction of Boone-Newton-Carroll counties) in the Ozarks. The species' choice of uplands over lowlands is well illustrated in the northeastern counties where it has never been recorded on the survey in Mississippi County (on the Mississippi Alluvial Plain),

but has been recorded regularly on the survey in Randolph County, which is in the Ozark foothills.

Nesting activity has been observed from the second half of May into the second half of August. Extreme records include nest construction just beginning at DeVall's Bluff in Prairie County on May 20, and a nest with three hatchlings in Washington County on August 17. In the Wheeler Collection there are three nests dated from May 31 to June 16. The clutch size in two Wheeler nests was four eggs, and in the third nest there was one Blue Grosbeak and two Brown-headed Cowbird eggs. The Wheeler nests were four to eight feet high, and one in the Audubon file was three feet high. Wheeler (1924) reports that a snakeskin was found in one nest.

In the western Ozarks of Benton County, a population of three territorial males occupied one hundred acres of abandoned pastures characterized by open broomsedge fields and clumps of small trees (Table 3-7).

FALL MIGRATION: Blue Grosbeaks are infrequently reported after the cessation of singing, often during August (Baerg 1930a). The latest report in the file is in the second week of October. Most of these fall sightings involved a single bird, but in Union County 100 birds were found at Calion on October 3, and as many as 15 were there six days later in the same area.

LAZULI BUNTING, *Passerina amoena* (Say)

One record.

There is written documentation in the Audubon Society file concerning a male Lazuli Bunting seen by experienced observers at a bird feeder in Little Rock on March 15, 1980. The bird was said to have been visiting the feeder for several months.

INDIGO BUNTING, *Passerina cyanea* (Linnaeus)

Common migrant and summer resident in all regions. One of the commonest native birds in Arkansas. Usually observed at the forest edge, in shrubby fields with scattered trees, or in openings in extensive forests.

SPRING MIGRATION: The seven birds (both sexes) reported in Union County on March 21 marked the earliest arrival date for the state. However, few are usually seen until the second week of April, with numbers increasing thereafter during the third and fourth weeks of the month and in early May. On Archer Island in Chicot County, several hundred were observed in different flocks on April 18. In Jefferson County, a peak of 30 was reported on May 3.

BREEDING SEASON: These birds are numerous in all regions in summer. The average annual mean number per route reported on Breeding Bird Surveys showed very little variation from region to region, ranging between 22.5 and 26.1. A study supported by the National Science Foundation at the Buffalo National River found that Indigo Buntings were the commonest breeding bird (Hunter et al. 1980). In the northeast, Indigo Buntings were one of the commonest species found on the Breeding Bird Surveys, ranking twelfth among all birds found (Hanebrink 1980).

Nesting activity has been observed from the second week of May to mid-August. Extreme records include a nest under construction on May 8 at DeVall's Bluff in Prairie County, and two young still in a nest in Union County on August 10. In the Wheeler Collection six nests with eggs are dated from May 17 to June 20. The clutch sizes in these nests were usually four eggs, but in two nests there were eggs of three Indigo Buntings and one Brown-headed Cowbird. The Wheeler nests ranged in heights from one to six feet. Nests on file were found in saplings, shrubs, a honeysuckle thicket, and an upper fork of a *Cannabis sativa* plant in the middle of a corn field.

Jane Fitzgerald studied the Indigo Bunting in the western Ozarks in 1984 and 1985. There were Brown-headed Cowbird eggs in seven of nine nests she found. Another study in Benton County showed a population of 25 territorial males per one hundred acres of forest edge vegetation (Table 3-7).

FALL MIGRATION: Fall migration is notably heavy from mid-September into late October, with the latest records for the state in early November. In Washington County a flock of 10 birds associated with Dickcissels was observed on September 18, and 48 Indigo Buntings were seen in the same place on October 3. In Union County, 25 birds were reported on October 27, and five in the same county on November 2.

PAINTED BUNTING, *Passerina ciris* (Linnaeus)

Fairly common migrant and summer resident in all regions. Especially numerous in the eastern lowlands. Typical habitat is open country, particularly shrubby old fields with at least some taller trees in a grove, fencerow, the forest edge, or lightly developed places in towns.

SPRING MIGRATION: The earliest spring arrival date for Arkansas is the second week of April, and the three birds seen in Union County on April 17 were also relatively early. The frequency of sightings in the Audubon Society file increases thereafter, especially in the final week of April and during early May. Almost all of these sightings have involved one or two birds seen during one day. In Union County, six were found during the second week of May. A total of 36 birds were counted during the first two weeks of May on the Grand Prairie in eastern Arkansas.

BREEDING SEASON: Based upon information in the file and on the Breeding Bird Surveys, Painted Buntings are most numerous during summer in the southeastern lowlands and secondarily in the Arkansas River Valley. Average annual mean numbers per route in each region on Breeding Bird Surveys were 0.5 birds on the Coastal Plain, 2.4 on the Mississippi Alluvial Plain, and 0.9 in the highlands (including the Arkansas River Valley). An extraordinary number, comprising as many as 28 birds in a single year, have been reported on the survey in Chicot County in the extreme southeast. In nearby Desha County, one observer (file) stated that Painted Buntings were "abundant in rows of tall trees and shrubby land near the Mississippi River and inland." Overall, the lowest numbers seem to occur in the heavily forested regions in the highlands.

Information in the file about the nesting of this species covers the period from early June to mid-July. On June 6 a partly constructed nest was found in the thicket of an uncut grassy area of a Little Rock golf course. In the same city, a female was incubating four eggs in a ragweed clump almost under a thorn tree on June 15. At a third nest in Little Rock, young had just fledged on June 24. The latest report in the file, on July 16, involved three fledglings at El Dorado.

Several records in the file and in the pub-

FIGURE 6-107 Painted Bunting in late June, along the Arkansas River near Arkansas Post on the Mississippi Alluvial Plain. *David Plank*

lished literature (Howell 1911, Baerg 1951) indicate that Painted Buntings are common locally in appropriate habitat. At Clarksville in Johnson County, three pairs have been found in close proximity in the breeding season. There are similar reports involving several pairs in close proximity at Little Rock, Russellville, Fort Smith (all in the Arkansas River region), and at El Dorado and Fayetteville. Near Stuttgart, 10 males were seen in edge and brushy field habitat. There are numerous June and July records for this species in the northeast, especially at Jonesboro where the birds have been found in clear-

ings associated with railroad rights-of-way (E. Hanebrink, pers. comm.).

The large population recorded in the past in Chicot County (see above) has been steadily declining since 22 birds were reported there on the 1968 Breeding Bird Survey. By 1971 only 12 were reported on the survey, and this had declined to three by 1975. Parallel to this decline, there has been an increase of Indigo Buntings, so that on recent surveys Painted Buntings ranged in numbers from zero to five, while Indigo Buntings ranged from 10 to 14, up from three in 1968. H. H. Shugart, a longtime partici-

FIGURE 6-108 Dickcissels in early May, on the Grand Prairie near Slovak. *David Plank*

pant in Breeding Bird Surveys in southern Arkansas, has attributed these population changes to more and more clearing for planting.

FALL MIGRATION: Reports of Painted Buntings after July are sparse. In part this is attributable to the cessation of singing, after which this secretive species is much harder to locate. There are a few scattered sightings through the fourth week of September. The latest record involved a male found dead in Hempstead County on November 13.

DICKCISSEL, *Spiza americana* (Gmelin)

Common migrant and summer resident in extensive, open, overgrown fields with dense grassy and other herbaceous vegetation. Present in all regions, and most numerous in the eastern lowlands. Several winter records.

SPRING MIGRATION: Spring migrants have arrived as early as the second and third weeks of April, but the main influx occurs late in the month and during early May. At Holla Bend Refuge in Pope County, flocks of 43, 13, and 20 were observed on May 3. In Clark County, 100 birds were reported on May 2.

BREEDING SEASON: Reports in the Audubon Society file and on the statewide Breeding Bird Survey show that Dickcissels are present during the nesting season in all regions, and are in fact rather numerous, especially in the eastern lowlands. The average annual mean number per route in each region on Breeding Bird Surveys was 7.7 on the Coastal Plain, 37.8 on the Mississippi Alluvial Plain, and 3.4 in the highlands (including the Arkansas River Valley). Peak numbers ranging from 40.0 to 89.2 were reported on surveys in Mississippi, Prairie,

Lincoln, Poinsett, and Woodruff counties, all in the east.

Meanley (1963) studied the ecology and habits of these birds on the Grand Prairie. He found that it is "essentially a bird of the briar patches . . . [and its] optimum nesting habitat . . . consists of briar patches along roadsides bordering mature oat fields." Nest construction was observed as early as May 5, and four nests had complete clutches of eggs by May 15. Young fledged from the latest nest on July 22. Clutch size in thirteen nests ranged from three to five eggs (often four). The nests were three inches to four feet above the ground, with an average height of approximately three feet in twenty nests. The nests were found predominantly in briar (*Rubus* sp.), with other nests in shrubs, small trees, and even clumps of grass. "The average density along roadside borders was approximately one territorial male (or pair) per 7 acres, compared with one male (or pair) per 20 acres out in open fields" (Meanley, 1963).

In the Audubon Society file there is one record somewhat later than Meanley's findings reporting a recently fledged, short-tailed young bird being fed out of the nest by adults in Washington County on August 21. Four nests with eggs in the Wheeler Collection were dated June 2, 5, and 7, and July 20. Clutch sizes were similar to Meanley's findings, and one nest had been parasitized by the Brown-headed Cowbird.

In a study in the western Ozarks of Benton County, there was a population of 21 territorial males per one hundred acres of habitat characterized as an open field where the vegetation was generally less than four and one-half feet high, and where there were no trees or other tall plants (Table 3-7).

FALL MIGRATION: Flocking was observed on the Grand Prairie shortly after the breeding season (Meanley 1963). One flock of 30 birds was seen on July 24, and a flock of 500 was observed feeding in rice fields on September 6. The latest regular report for the western Ozarks involved two birds in the second week of October. Overall, there are only a few scattered reports for Arkansas after mid-September.

WINTER: A few Dickcissels are seen most winters somewhere in the lowland regions, especially in the Grand Prairie, and occasionally elsewhere. Winter reports usually involve one or two birds. At Stuttgart in Arkansas County,

four were seen on February 14. Frequently these isolated wintering Dickcissels accompany flocks of House Sparrows or are observed at home bird feeders.

Subfamily Emberizinae
New World Sparrows

GREEN-TAILED TOWHEE, *Pipilo chlorurus* (Audubon)

One record.

This common species of western North America occurs on a casual basis much further to the east, sometimes reaching states east of Arkansas (AOU 1983). The Arkansas record was submitted by Arnold Hoiberg, who observed a bird at close range on November 8, 1952, at El Dorado in Union County.

RUFOUS-SIDED TOWHEE, *Pipilo erythrophthalmus* (Linnaeus)

Permanent resident in all regions. Nests principally in the northern highlands, but is present locally in small numbers in the other regions. During winter uncommon in the Ozarks, but fairly common to common elsewhere, especially in the lowlands. The western spotted forms are a rare winter visitor.

MIGRATION: The northward migration in spring is performed between mid-February and late April. In the western Ozarks, where the species is scarce in winter, influxes are noted in the second half of February and in the first half of March. In Jefferson County, the 4.4 towhees per hour on February 27 represented a migratory peak, as did the 5.7 per hour in Washington County on April 24. Most of the winter population present in the southern lowlands departs by mid-to-late April (Audubon Society file, Mattocks and Shugart 1962).

During fall, towhees begin to become common in southern Arkansas during the first half of September, and are widespread during October and thereafter. In the western Ozarks, the birds are uncommon and of only local occurrence after mid-November. A bird banded in Ohio was recovered 662 miles south in Arkansas the following spring.

BREEDING SEASON: Historically, towhees

FIGURE 6-109 Rufous-sided Towhee. *David Plank*

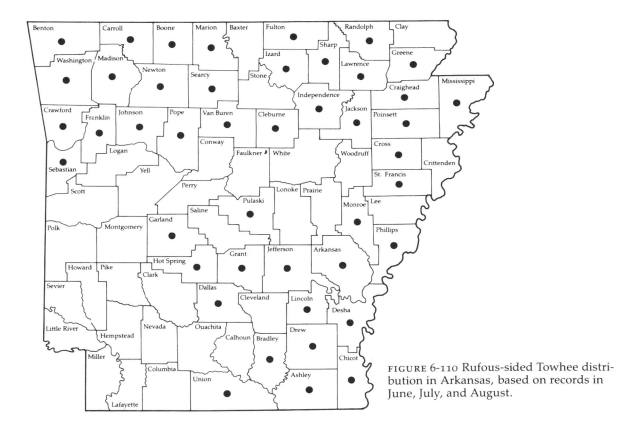

FIGURE 6-110 Rufous-sided Towhee distribution in Arkansas, based on records in June, July, and August.

nested commonly in Arkansas only in the western Ozarks (Howell 1911, Wheeler 1924, Coffey 1941, Baerg 1951). The first record for the eastern Ozarks was found by Ben Coffey in Sharp County in 1955, but the birds were not seen there again in summer until 1981. During the 1950s and 1960s he found towhees regularly on the uplands of Crowley's Ridge (northeastern counties) from the Missouri line south to Helena, Arkansas, and he also found them in the Black River area as far south as Newport in Jackson County. It is not clear if these birds were part of a range extension, or had been overlooked previously (B. Coffey, pers. comm.). The files of the Audubon Society and information from Breeding Bird Surveys show that the summer population is still heavily concentrated in the uplands of northern Arkansas. As many as seven or eight birds have been reported on the Poinsett County survey (on Crowley's Ridge) and 10 or more birds, up to a peak of 30, have been found on several surveys in the Ozarks.

Towhees have also been found during summer in other regions (Figure 6-110).

In 1956 a towhee was reported during summer in Union County in the extreme south. In 1967, adults and an immature bird were seen in Ashley County in the southeast, and a nest was found the following year. In 1968 there were sightings in Monroe and Phillips counties, and since 1969 the birds have been found in six additional counties in the southern lowlands. In the early 1980s the birds were quite common in southern Hot Spring County in the Ouachita foothills. Information from the Breeding Bird Survey in Dallas County shows that in 1981 a total of two individuals were recorded at two locations, and in 1982 a total of four individuals were recorded at three locations there.

The birds that nest in the Ozarks are assigned to the northern race of towhees, *P. e. erythrophthalmus*, that reaches its southern limit in northern Arkansas (AOU 1957). The recent records in southern and eastern Arkansas might involve a range extension of the race *P. e. canaster* that summers in northeastern Louisiana, northwestern Mississippi, and in southwestern Tennessee, but this supposition awaits confirmation from the examination of specimens.

Nesting activity has been reported from mid-April to the third week of August. In Washington County, a nest with two towhee eggs and one Brown-headed Cowbird egg was found on April 19. The latest record of nesting is also from Washington County, and involved nestlings on August 17. In the Wheeler Collection six nests with eggs are dated from April 29 to June 21. The nests contained two or four towhee eggs, and five of the nests were parasitized by cowbirds. Two of the Wheeler nests were on the ground, and the other four ranged in height from twenty-two inches to ten feet. Wheeler (1924) reported that the higher nests are constructed later in the season.

WINTER: Analysis of Christmas Bird Counts showed a statewide mean of 0.5 towhees per party hour. This mean was exceeded in some places in the lowlands, with peaks of more than 1.0 per party hour in the extreme south. By contrast, Fayetteville in the Ozarks reported only 0.2 per party hour. At Lake Georgia-Pacific more than 100 birds have been reported on several Christmas Counts, and over 250 in 1974. By comparison, the largest number ever found at Fayetteville was 24 (in 1981). Winter population studies in southern Arkansas (Tables 3-2 and 3-4) show a population in bottomland woods of up to as many as 27 per one hundred acres, but virtually none in upland woods.

There have been nearly two dozen sightings of the western spotted forms of this towhee, usually in winter, but also in late fall and in early spring. Some of these spotted towhees have been seen at home feeders.

BACHMAN'S SPARROW, *Aimophila aestivalis* (Lichtenstein)

Locally common summer resident in young pine plantations in the Ouachitas and on the Coastal Plain. Uncommon or absent in other regions.

MIGRATION: During spring migration Bachman's Sparrow has been found in Arkansas as early as mid-March, but arrivals are usually not reported until the second week of April and thereafter. During spring the species has been seen throughout much of the Coastal Plain, the eastern Ouachita Mountains, in the Arkansas River Valley, and in the eastern Ozarks.

Reports for late summer and fall, especially after the birds stop singing, are highly scattered. Five were counted in Hot Spring County as late as September 23, with some birds still singing. Thereafter there are scattered records to the second week in November.

BREEDING SEASON: Bachman's Sparrow has been found most regularly during summer in recent years in the extensive pine region of the central and eastern Ouachitas and in the northern section of the Coastal Plain (Figure 6-111). There are additional summer records in the Arkansas River Valley and in the scattered stands of pines in the eastern half of the Ozarks. There have been no summer reports from the Mississippi Alluvial Plain or the western Ozarks.

Wheeler (1924) found nesting birds in Sebastian, Pope, Faulkner, and Lawrence counties. The twelve nests with eggs in the Wheeler Collection are dated from May 6 to July 21, with eight of these clutches complete by June 12. The clutch size in each nest was four or five eggs, and all the nests were found in old fields, on the ground, and concealed under heavy vegetation including weeds, grasses, green briar, ragweed, etc.

In 1971 near the Faith community in Jefferson County, Jane Stern found a large summer population of Bachman's Sparrows in a young pine plantation in a clear-cut area characterized by a heavy tangle of vegetation including young pines, hardwood sprouts, and weeds averaging four to six feet in height. In 1982, Max and Helen Parker reported 25 singing birds in northern Hot Spring, northern Garland, and Dallas counties during May, June, and July. The birds were primarily in pine plantations one to three years in age that were planted following forest clear-cutting, but two birds were in open pine woods.

Between 1983 and 1985 Tom Haggerty from the University of Arkansas studied Bachman's Sparrow in Hot Spring County near Malvern. He counted as many as seven singing birds in a two-year-old, 35-acre pine plantation, and somewhat lower numbers on other tracts. Of the sixteen nests he observed in 1983, the clutch sizes ranged from three to five eggs (often four), and the average number of nestlings was 3.5.

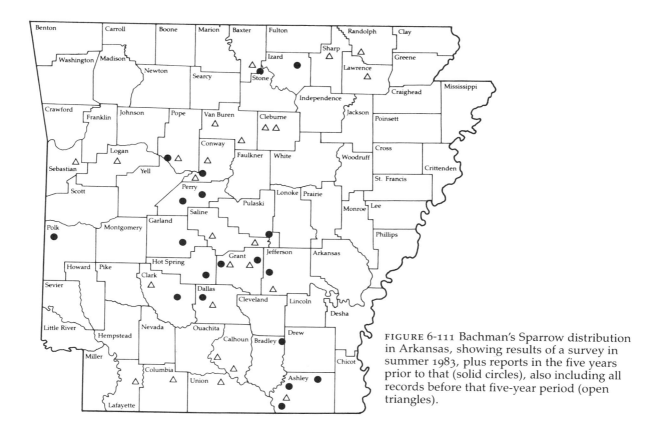

FIGURE 6-111 Bachman's Sparrow distribution in Arkansas, showing results of a survey in summer 1983, plus reports in the five years prior to that (solid circles), also including all records before that five-year period (open triangles).

During the 1984 field season he was still finding both eggs and recently hatched young as late as the first week of September. One pair of banded birds made five nesting attempts during the 1984 season. A few of the birds he banded returned inland two years following banding.

In the Audubon Society file there are a number of older records in the eastern Ozarks in Van Buren, Cleburne, Baxter, Sharp, and western Randolph counties. In a survey in 1983 Kimberly Smith of the University of Arkansas found Bachman's Sparrow in Baxter and Izard counties, where the species was present in old pine areas where fires had recently occurred, clearing the understory, and where broomsedge (*Andropogon virginicus*) was present in open areas among the trees. The birds were not found in some areas in the eastern Ozarks where apparently suitable habitat existed. Similar checks of one- to three-year-old pine plantations in Grant and Jefferson counties on the

Coastal Plain during the same period resulted in finding at least a few birds.

RUFOUS-CROWNED SPARROW, *Aimophila ruficeps* (Cassin)

Rare and local permanent resident in small numbers on a rocky clifftop scrubland on Magazine Mountain in Logan County. Very rare elsewhere in Arkansas.

This species was first discovered in Arkansas on Magazine Mountain in 1972. William Shepherd and a party of observers eventually located nine individuals, among which was at least one juvenile. The location is the highest point in Arkansas, and is in the Ozark National Forest. The site is characterized by open oak and cedar scrubland atop a rocky, precipitous cliff having a southern exposure. While not every person who visits the Magazine Mountain site can find Rufous-crowned Sparrows, Shepherd has consistently been able to find at

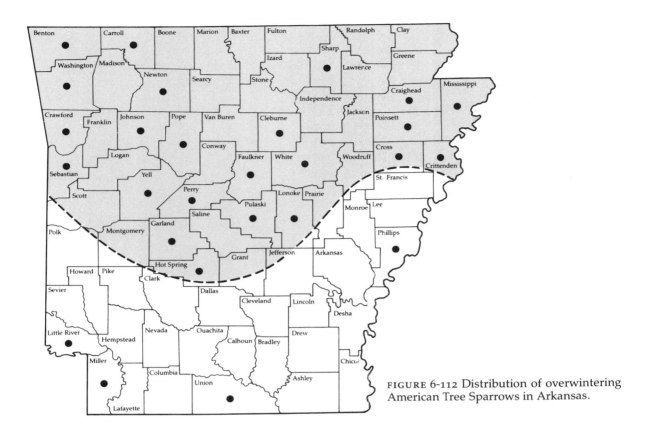

FIGURE 6-112 Distribution of overwintering American Tree Sparrows in Arkansas.

least single individuals since 1972. The birds are present in each season of the year, but there are only a few winter sightings. During a thorough census in the summer of 1983, three territories were located, in two of which fledged young were being fed by adult birds. After the severe winter weather of 1983–84, only single birds could be found during May and June, but on May 7, 1985, Shepherd located two pairs of birds, both apparently feeding young.

There are only a few other records for the state. A single bird was found a short distance northwest of Magazine Mountain in Franklin County south of the Arkansas River on June 1, 1974. One bird was observed by Tom Haggerty on August 20, 1983, in a burned forest clearing several miles southeast of Magazine Mountain in western Perry County. Two birds were observed November 16, 1985, on Mount Nebo in Yell County in habitat characterized by Shepherd as being a "shrubby steep hillside with many dead trunks of small trees killed by a fire

a few years ago—below a rocky ledge that marks the edge of the mountain's top."

AMERICAN TREE SPARROW, *Spizella arborea* (Wilson)

Fairly common to locally abundant migrant and winter resident in northern Arkansas, especially in the northwest, with scattered records over most of the state. Observed in brushy fields and occasionally in yards at bird feeders.

MIGRATION: Fall flocks of tree sparrows have arrived as early as the second week of October, but there are relatively few sightings until December. Influxes are usually associated with severe cold weather. The 30 birds in Crittenden County on October 11 were early, and the 150 at Horseshoe Lake in the same county on October 30 was a large number so early in the season. One tree sparrow banded in Illinois in fall was recovered in Arkansas during winter of the same year 555 miles south.

A concentration of sightings during February and March suggests that the spring migration occurs as soon as the severe cold weather passes. Two flocks totalling over 200 birds were seen at Mountainburg in Crawford County on February 28. The 10 birds seen on a field trip in Washington County on March 7 was a high number for so late in the season. The latest record is in the first week of April (Baerg 1931).

WINTER: Most records for the state are from this season, mainly from northern Arkansas (Figure 6-112), mid-December through February. At Fayetteville in the western Ozarks the birds have been found on ten of twelve recent Christmas Bird Counts, in numbers ranging from one to twenty-five, often around five. During some winters unusually large numbers of tree sparrows enter the state, and in these years they are reported in areas where they are not usually seen. During January and February of 1977 and 1979, the birds ranged as far east as the center of the state in Pulaski County, and down into the extreme south in Union and Little River counties. At Hot Springs Village in Garland County they arrived on January 27, 1979, and became the most numerous sparrows during the snowy season, departing for the most part by mid-to-late February. As many as 30 birds were seen in extreme southwestern Arkansas in February 1979, and in the same period flocks of 50, 50, 70, 80, and 90 were reported in Newton County in northwestern Arkansas. Presumably 1953 was also one of these big peak years since 420 tree sparrows were seen in one field near Fort Smith on December 23.

CHIPPING SPARROW, *Spizella passerina* (Bechstein)

Permanent resident. Common summer resident in all regions, especially the highlands. Winter resident chiefly in central Arkansas and in the southern lowlands. Inhabits lightly developed or undeveloped parkland including pastures with scattered trees and shrubs, urban lawns, picnic and camping areas in parks, and golf courses.

MIGRATION: Spring migrants are seen from about mid-March to mid-May. In the western Ozarks, where the species is rare in winter, spring arrivals are often noted around mid-to-late March (Audubon Society file, Baerg 1930b,

Black 1935a). In Faulkner County, the species is most numerous from mid-March to mid-May. The 30 birds at Grassy Lake in Hempstead County on March 24 was a very large number.

The fall migration occurs mainly during October and November. In the western Ozarks there are few reports after late October (file, Baerg 1931, Black 1935a). In Faulkner County, the species is regular from late October to late November (Johnson 1979).

BREEDING SEASON: Chipping Sparrows are present throughout the state during the nesting season. The mean number reported on the Breeding Bird Surveys in the highlands was more than twice that on the Coastal Plain and four times that on the Mississippi Alluvial Plain. The largest numbers, yearly means ranging from 7.6 to 17.7 Chipping Sparrows, were found on the surveys in Garland, Cleburne, and Fulton counties, and on the Compton survey (junction of Boone-Carroll-Newton counties) in the western Ozarks.

Breeding activity has been observed from the second week of April to early September, with most young out of the nest by mid-July. The extreme breeding records include a nest under construction in Ashley County on April 10, and begging young just out of the nest in Washington County on September 4. In the Wheeler Collection, six nests with four or five eggs are dated from April 23 to May 21. In Ashley County, birds in a May nest fledged in early June; a second nest was constructed in the same tree in mid-June, and the young flew from that nest in mid-July. Nests in the file have varied from seven to forty feet high. The six nests in the Wheeler Collection were three to twenty-five feet high. Nests (from both sources) were observed in thorny bushes, cedars, and both hardwood and pine trees.

WINTER: Chipping Sparrows are rare and irregular in northern Arkansas in winter, but there are reports in the Arkansas River Valley and in the Ouachitas, and the birds are common in winter in the southern lowlands. The statewide ten-year mean on Christmas Bird Counts was 0.1 birds per party hour. This mean was exceeded in much of the Coastal Plain (peak of 0.6 at Lake Georgia-Pacific), and at Conway and Little Rock in the Arkansas River Valley. On Christmas Counts at Conway, the number found has varied from 1 to 20, often

4 to 13. At Arkadelphia the numbers have varied from 1 to 99, with 40 or more seen on many counts in the past decade. Between 1953 and 1982 at El Dorado, Chipping Sparrows were seen in numbers varying from 0 to 78, with 25 or more in eight of those years.

CLAY-COLORED SPARROW, *Spizella pallida* (Swainson)

Uncommon to somewhat rare transient, with a preponderance of sightings in the western part of the state.

SPRING MIGRATION: During migration this predominantly western species regularly reaches the Mississippi Valley (AOU 1983), and as might be expected there are relatively more reports for western than eastern Arkansas. Most spring reports involve the period from the last week of April to the second week of May, but there is a record in the file as early as the second week of March. There are more reports for spring than fall, and almost all of them in either season have involved only one or two birds observed in a shrubby field or in thickets. A flock of 12 seen in Washington County on April 28 was very unusual. During spring of 1984 efforts by several observers in the western Ozarks turned up seven records between April 28 and May 9. Some of these birds were seen in urban areas rather than in shrubby fields. In the file there are also spring reports from Union, Conway, Clark, Craighead, and Lonoke counties.

FALL MIGRATION: Five reports in the file range chiefly from early September to mid-October. A specimen was collected in Union County on September 11, 1960. In northeastern Arkansas there is a November record (Hanebrink 1980), and a bird was reported in Clark County on December 17. In addition to the fall location already mentioned, there are records from Pope, Howard, and Pulaski counties. Examination of museum specimens makes clear the necessity for taking great care in identifying this species. Some individuals bear a strong resemblance to immature Chipping Sparrows especially in the field when birds are often seen briefly and under suboptimal conditions.

FIELD SPARROW, *Spizella pusilla* (Wilson)

Common permanent resident in all regions.

SPRING MIGRATION: Spring migrants have been reported during February, March, and the first few weeks of April. In Washington County, where winter numbers are generally low, a big peak of 105 on February 5 seems to have been an influx. In Union County, peaks have been reported during March, with only small numbers after mid-April (file, Mattocks and Shugart 1962). Migration is strongly suggested by the presence of these birds in places where they are not usually found. At Fayetteville, the presence of flocks in a small woodlot in the middle of town during March and early April was a strong suggestion that the birds were migrating.

BREEDING SEASON: Breeding Bird Surveys show that Field Sparrows are common in all regions during the nesting season, but the population is most heavily concentrated in the Ozarks. While no survey outside the Ozarks reported annual means of over 6.9 birds, surveys in the Ozarks ranged primarily from 11.6 to 31.0. Fewer than 1.0 were reported on three of the surveys in the Mississippi Alluvial Plain. A breeding population study in Benton County (Table 3-7) indicated a population of 19 to 69 territorial males per one hundred acres in a variety of old field habitats, with peak numbers occurring in overgrown broomsedge fields with clumps of small trees.

Nesting activity has been reported from the second half of April through July. The earliest nest had one egg at Petit Jean Mountain in Perry County on April 21. The latest nest was in Faulkner County and had eggs on July 30 (Wheeler 1924). In the Wheeler Collection there are seventeen nests with three to four eggs from April 26 to July 24. The nests were either on the ground or in low sprouts, bushes, or tangles of vines, often three feet above the ground or lower, but once as high as twelve feet. Cowbird egg parasitism has been reported in several nests.

FALL MIGRATION: The pattern seen in spring is reversed during fall. Field Sparrows are then observed in numbers in the southern lowlands during October, with big flocks arriving during late November. In the Fayetteville woodlot, where the birds are absent in summer and winter, they are seen during October and November.

WINTER: Large flocks characteristic of the winter season have been reported from late November through March. The ten-year statewide mean on Christmas Bird Counts of 2.3 birds per party hour was exceeded on some counts in each region. Peak means of 3.8 up to 5.8 birds per party hour were reported in the Arkansas River Valley and in the lowlands. It is not unusual for 100 or more Field Sparrows to be reported on Christmas Counts in all regions, and as many as 300 to 500 have been reported in count locales in the lowlands and in the Arkansas River Valley.

One Field Sparrow banded in Indiana in summer was recovered the following winter in southwestern Arkansas, at least 700 miles away.

VESPER SPARROW, *Pooecetes gramineus* (Gmelin)

Fairly common transient in small numbers in all regions. Winter resident that has been reported in all regions, but chiefly in the southern lowlands and secondarily in the Arkansas River Valley. Observed in weedy borders of open fields, pastures, roadsides, and sometimes forest edge.

FALL MIGRATION: Fall migrants have arrived by mid-October, but most first arrivals are reported during the third and fourth weeks of the month. The 12 birds at Lake Millwood on October 26 were considered a high number indicative of a migratory influx. The seven at Farmington in Washington County on October 20 was a large early number for the western Ozarks.

WINTER: Vesper Sparrows have been found only three times in twelve recent Christmas Bird Counts at Fayetteville, and the peak number was three birds. Further south, especially in the lowlands, the birds are more regular and numerous. At Arkadelphia at least one to six birds are seen most years on the Christmas Count, and 21 were reported in 1975. Probably the best place to find this species during winter is in the Lonoke area, where they are reported almost every year on the Christmas Count, with several peaks of as many as 50 to over 100. On the 1980 statewide Christmas Counts, a total of 50 birds were reported, with 10 or more of these 50 on the counts at Conway, Lonoke, and at Village Creek State Park in Cross County.

SPRING MIGRATION: Spring transients have been reported primarily during March and April, especially during the second half of March and the first half of April. Spring arrival dates at Fayetteville ranged between March 14 and 28 (Baerg 1930b). The 10 birds at Calion in Union County on March 22 was a large number. At Winslow in Washington County, an influx estimated at 25 birds was observed on March 25 (Smith 1915). In Faulkner County, Vesper Sparrows are of regular occurrence between late March and the last week of April (Johnson 1979).

LARK SPARROW, *Chondestes grammacus* (Say)

Locally common migrant and summer resident in all regions except very uncommon in the Mississippi Alluvial Plain, and in bottomlands generally. Rare in winter. Observed in open country, including plowed fields, grasslands, or along dirt roads.

SPRING MIGRATION: There are several reports in the Audubon Society file involving single birds in March (usually the last week), but small flocks are not seen until the second week of April and thereafter. The 16 birds seen in Washington County on April 10 comprised one of the largest spring reports in the file.

BREEDING SEASON: Most reports in the file for Lark Sparrows in summer are from the Ozarks and on the Coastal Plain, but there are records for all regions. Breeding Bird Surveys show that Lark Sparrows breed in similar numbers in the highlands and on the Coastal Plain, but are far less numerous on the Mississippi Alluvial Plain. The largest numbers, involving annual means ranging from 1.6 to 2.9 Lark Sparrows, were reported on surveys in Lafayette County on the Coastal Plain, Garland County in the Ouachitas, and Cleburne and Izard counties in the eastern Ozarks.

Breeding activity has been observed from late April to early July. The earliest record involves copulation and the gathering of nesting material at Petit Jean Mountain in Conway County on April 29. One of the latest nests reported involved young fledging from a nest in Clark County on July 9. In the Wheeler Collection there are fifteen nests with eggs dated from April 30 to July 1. The clutch sizes ranged from three to five eggs, often four, and the nests were usually on the ground, but once as high as sixteen feet above the ground. In the Audubon Society file there is also one record of a nest in a low bush, and another 48 feet high in a pine tree. Wheeler (1924), describing the Lark Sparrow, wrote that "his home is on the farm and quite frequently he builds his nest in cultivated fields, but he promenades on the dusty roads . . ." William Shepherd has found Lark Sparrows in the breeding season only where sand or broken rock is exposed.

FALL MIGRATION: Fall reports are scattered after July, especially in the northern half of the state. The 30 observed at Hardy in Sharp County on July 3 was a large report, as were the 11 or more in Logan County near Boone-ville on August 28. Reports from September and thereafter involve only single birds, and these are seen primarily in the southern and southeastern lowlands. In Garland County the departure dates ranged between August 6 and September 29 (Deaderick 1938).

WINTER: There are a few records of Lark Sparrows in the southern half of the state during December and January. Usually these have been single birds. However, there were 18 seen at Texarkana on January 18, 1967, and there are several additional January records of small numbers in that area.

SAVANNAH SPARROW, *Passerculus sandwichensis* (Gmelin)

Common migrant and winter resident in all regions that is sometimes locally abundant. Inhabits open country including prairies, airports, pastures with native grasses, and weedy margins of ponds, ditches, and the like.

FALL MIGRATION: Savannah Sparrows sometimes arrive as early as the second week of September, but they are not usually widespread until early or mid-October. Large numbers are present by late October and early November. At Stuttgart they were said to be abundant on September 29. In Faulkner County, an estimated 50 were seen at Conway on October 24. In Washington County, a fall peak of 6.7 per hour was reported on October 30. A total of 34 died upon impact with a transmission tower in central Arkansas, October 24, 1984.

WINTER: The species is found regularly on Christmas Bird Counts in all regions where there is appropriate habitat, and the largest numbers are found in the southern lowlands. The ten-year statewide mean on Christmas Counts was 0.9 Savannah Sparrows per party hour, and this mean was easily exceeded in the southern lowlands where means at Arkadelphia, Texarkana, Lonoke and the White River Refuge ranged from 1.2 to 2.9 birds per party hour. By comparison, the mean at Fayetteville, where the birds are found regularly in winter, was only 0.2. At Lonoke, more than 100 to nearly 400 birds have been reported on Christmas Counts, with a low count one year of 47.

SPRING AND SUMMER: Savannah Sparrows are present regularly until mid-May, with a few records as late as the end of the month. In Union County, where 15 birds were seen regularly in one place from late February to early May, an influx involving 100 birds was reported at mid-March. In Washington County, a peak of 7.6 birds per hour was observed on April 10. Baerg (1951) reported Savannah Sparrows nesting on the Main Experiment Station of the University of Arkansas in Fayetteville on May 17, 1934, and June 17, 1940. No further details were published. While Savannah Sparrows are sometimes seen in the state as late as the end of May, there have been no summer reports since 1940.

GRASSHOPPER SPARROW, *Ammodramus savannarum* (Gmelin)

Migrant and local summer resident in all regions. Usually found in small numbers. Inhabits open grasslands, including shortgrass hayfields, mowed fields at airports, and fields associated with river levees.

SPRING MIGRATION: Grasshopper Sparrows usually arrive in Arkansas after mid-April, especially from the fourth week of April and thereafter. There are also a few, highly unusual records of arrivals during March (Audubon Society file, Smith 1915). The 20 to 30 singing birds counted in a fallow field in Pulaski County on April 27 was a peak number. In Franklin County in the Arkansas River Valley, four or more were heard singing on natural prairie habitat on April 30. During migration Grasshopper Sparrows seem to occupy more habitats than they do during the breeding season. During early May in Washington County, singing birds were found in a large pasture planted with fescue and also in an adjoining broom-sedge old field associated with the Fayetteville airport. After heavy spring rains, the fescue grass grew rapidly to almost two feet tall, whereas the growth of grasses at the airport field was much slower. After these rains, Grasshopper Sparrows could be found only in the short-grasses at the airport.

BREEDING SEASON: Grasshopper Sparrows have been found in summer at widely scattered places in most regions, with most observations occurring on the Mississippi Alluvial Plain and in the western Ozarks. There are no summer records for the Ouachita Mountains. On the Mississippi Alluvial Plain, a population numbering thirteen pairs was studied at the Jonesboro airport in Craighead County (Bruce 1967). In Desha County, as many as six pairs have been recorded along 1.5 miles of Arkansas River levee grasslands most years since 1967, but the birds were absent there during four summers from 1967 to 1982. In Phillips County, nine or ten birds have been found on the Mississippi River levee during mid-May in recent years, but there is no information about whether or not these birds were nesting. In the western Ozarks, they were said to be common in fields near Rogers in Benton County where nests were found (Baerg 1951). Recently Grasshopper Sparrows have been found in summer on over-grown pastures in the Wedington unit of the Ozark National Forest, and at the Fayetteville airport, both in Washington County, and on Baker Prairie in Boone County, and elsewhere.

Other than the counties already mentioned, there are summer records in Newton, Madison, and Fulton counties in the Ozarks; Sebastian County in the Arkansas River Valley; Clark and Little River counties on the Coastal Plain; Mississippi, Lawrence, Crittenden, Arkansas, St. Francis, and Lincoln counties on the Mississippi Alluvial Plain. These records are derived from Breeding Bird Surveys and the Audubon Society file.

Nesting activity has been observed during May, June, and July. Near Rogers in Benton County, Dean Crooks found a nest with four young in May, and another in July, but no other information about these nests is available (Baerg 1951). At the Jonesboro airport in Craighead

County, one nest on the ground contained four eggs on June 17, and the young had fledged by June 26; two eggs and two hatchlings were seen in a second nest on June 26. Both nests were found on a "cultivated grassland" maintained six to eight inches in height (Bruce 1967).

FALL MIGRATION: Very little is known about this species after singing ceases in July. There are highly scattered reports from August through November (Audubon Society file, Mattocks and Shugart 1962), and a documented sighting of a single bird at Lonoke on December 26. Migration is indicated by the nine birds that perished when they flew into a transmission tower in central Arkansas on October 24, 1984.

HENSLOW'S SPARROW, *Ammodramus henslowii* (Audubon)

Rare and irregular transient and winter visitor usually observed in the lowlands. All reports have involved single individuals.

Sightings recorded in the Audubon Society file and in Baerg (1951) are scattered, chiefly from mid-October to early March, with additional records in April and May. The birds have been seen in Union, Clark, and Little River counties on the Coastal Plain; in Arkansas, Lonoke, and Craighead counties on the Mississippi Alluvial Plain; Pulaski County in the Arkansas River Valley; and Baxter County in the Ozarks. One bird was seen repeatedly at El Dorado between December 29, 1950, and March 3, 1951. At Mountain Home in Baxter County, one bird was seen often as it fed on the ground with juncos from December 30, 1976, into February, 1977. There have been only three reports between 1974 and 1983.

LE CONTE'S SPARROW, *Ammodramus leconteii* (Audubon)

Fairly common migrant and winter resident, usually in small numbers, in all regions. Typical habitat includes large, open, grassy fields or low-lying, wet flats with rank vegetation.

FALL MIGRATION: Arrivals have been reported as early as the first week of October, but few are seen until the third or fourth weeks of the month, after which Le Conte's Sparrow is of regular occurrence, at least locally. Many reports in the Audubon Society file have involved

FIGURE 6-113 Le Conte's Sparrow in late January, near Clarendon on the Mississippi Alluvial Plain of eastern Arkansas. *David Plank*

one or two birds seen on a day's outing. The four at Booker in Crittenden County on October 21 was a large early number, but at the Hope airfield in Hempstead County, 116 birds in flocks of 8 to 37 were reported on November 30, and three observers counted 66 at Fort Chaffee in Sebastian County on November 30 of a different year.

WINTER: Le Conte's Sparrow has been reported on Christmas Bird Counts in both northern and southern Arkansas, but the birds are numerous only in a few places where there is a large amount of suitable habitat, principally in the southern and southeastern lowlands. The 107 birds on the 1971 Christmas Count at Slovak (Prairie County) and 64 at Lake Millwood in 1974 were both the largest number reported on any Christmas Count in the United States in those years. As many as 70 have been found on the count at Lonoke, but the usual number is 25

or fewer. Lonoke also led the Christmas Counts in numbers of Le Conte's Sparrow several years. At Fayetteville in the western Ozarks, the species is seen during winter some years but usually in very small numbers. Ben Coffey (1981) found them in "half erect, partly matted grass [*Panicum* sp.]" and in rice stubble; also, on airfield grasslands and similar pastures "the sparrows are in the unmowed areas,—weedy, and sometimes only Johnson grass or perhaps sedge [*Andropogon*]; however, occasionally in the open with no cover but well concealed from sight."

SPRING MIGRATION: Le Conte's Sparrow is often last reported in mid-to-late April, but there are also several unusual reports during May. The spring peak in numbers seems to occur by around mid-March. At Fort Chaffee it was said to be very numerous on March 14, with flocks of 8 and 10 birds seen. At North Little Rock in Pulaski County, an estimated 20 were present on March 17. Smaller numbers are usually reported thereafter, but there are records of five at Pine Bluff Arsenal on April 1, and as many as three late in April in Conway County.

SHARP-TAILED SPARROW, *Ammodramus caudacutus* (Gmelin)

Somewhat rare transient in all regions that is sometimes fairly common locally in prime habitat. Observed in marshy, low-lying open country including wet meadows, rice fields, and other rank vegetation in marsh-like situations. More sightings in fall than spring.

SPRING MIGRATION: Most spring sightings have been in May. Howell (1911) found "several in the valley" at Mena in Polk County on May 14, and he collected a specimen. Baerg (1951) published single records for Arkansas and Pulaski counties, both seen during May. At Calion in Union County, four were seen on May 16, the largest number reported for spring in the state. There is, in addition, one highly unusual sight record involving three birds, thought to be this species, observed in broom-sedge and low grass along a creek at Fort Chaffee near Fort Smith on February 13.

FALL MIGRATION: Fall sightings range from the third week of September through October, chiefly in October. While most records have involved single birds, seven were seen on October 3, and ten on October 16, both times in Lonoke County. The largest report in the file involved 18 birds in the drier portions of a cattail marsh on Sullivan's Island in the Arkansas River near Little Rock on October 14. Only a single bird could be found there three days later. There is also one record for the northeast (Hanebrink 1980), two records for the western Ozarks in Benton County (both in October), plus additional sightings from Faulkner, Ouachita, Prairie, and Union counties. Upon impact with a transmission tower in central Arkansas, three were killed September 26–30, and four on October 24, 1984.

FOX SPARROW, *Passerella iliaca* (Merrem)

Fairly common to common transient in all regions. Winter resident in all regions, with the largest numbers in the southern lowlands. In-habits brushy bottoms in close proximity to forests, especially bottomland forests.

FALL MIGRATION: Fox Sparrows arrive in the north as early as the second week of October, but the major influxes seem to follow behind those of other common wintering sparrows, with no really large numbers of Fox Sparrows until mid-November, after which observers can find small flocks of 10 individuals or more. In Chicot County, a party of observers reported 21 birds, some of them singing, on November 27. A Fox Sparrow banded in Illinois during the fall was recovered 500 miles away the following spring in Arkansas.

WINTER: The ten-year statewide mean of 0.3 Fox Sparrows per party hour on Christmas Bird Counts was exceeded in much of the Coastal Plain with ranges of 0.2 to 0.8 at several locations in the Arkansas River Valley and at Lonoke. The numbers of Fox Sparrows reported on the Christmas Count between the early 1950s and the early 1980s have shown considerable fluctuation at El Dorado on the Coastal Plain, from as few as 10 birds in 1954 to over 200 in 1975, with the usual number in the range of 25 to 50 birds. At Fayetteville in the northern highlands the usual report has been fewer than 10 on the Christmas Count (one peak of 55 in 1981).

SPRING MIGRATION: In spring, Fox Sparrows are seen regularly during most of March, but numbers decline sharply during late March and early April, and there are few reports after mid-April. In Union County, peaks of up to 50 Fox Sparrows in a day have been reported as late as February. The 31 seen in Washington County on February 26, including a flock of 10, was a peak, as were the seven in the same county on April 4.

SONG SPARROW, *Melospiza melodia* (Wilson)

Common migrant and winter resident in all regions. Observed in open country, often in low-lying moist fields with dense grasses and weeds, as well as in the weedy margins of ditches and ponds.

FALL MIGRATION: Song Sparrows have arrived as early as the end of September, but the usual early arrival date is in the second week of October. No more than scattered individuals are seen until the third week of October, and large numbers arrive along with the first major cold fronts in the last week of October and in early November. The 15 birds at Lonoke on October 18 was a large count for so early in the season. The 75 seen in Union County on November 7 was also a large number, but not really that atypical of the big peaks in numbers during the month of November. In Washington County the peak was measured at 16.5 birds per hour on November 22. Certainly one of the pleasures of fall birding is hearing these birds sing, as they often do upon arrival in Arkansas from their breeding grounds in the north. There is one banding record that illustrates the long distances they travel. A Song Sparrow banded in fall in Massachusetts was recovered over two years later and almost 1200 miles away in Arkansas.

WINTER: While there is no shortage of Song Sparrows in any region during winter, the largest numbers are present in the southern lowlands. The statewide ten-year mean on Christmas Bird Counts was 1.8 birds per party hour, and this was exceeded throughout most of the Coastal Plain and at Lonoke. Peaks involving 100 or more birds have been recorded on Christmas Counts in all regions. At Lonoke, 500 to over 1100 have been observed on several Christmas Counts, and the number counted there has rarely dropped even as low as 200.

SPRING MIGRATION: Large numbers characteristic of winter and early spring are seen as late as about mid-March, but the numbers decline thereafter, with only a few scattered records after late April, and the latest report in the file is in mid-May. A peak of 44 was reported in Washington County on March 4. The 31 birds seen in the same county on March 11 was also a high number for spring. Despite the close proximity of its breeding range in Missouri (Clawson 1982) there has been no evidence for the past five decades that Song Sparrows have summered or nested in Arkansas. Formerly the species was thought to nest rarely in part of northern Arkansas (Black 1935a, AOU 1957).

LINCOLN'S SPARROW, *Melospiza lincolnii* (Audubon)

Common migrant, especially in central and western Arkansas. Winter resident in all re-gions but most numerous and regular in the southern lowlands. Observed in migration in open grassy areas and thickets as well as forest edge; in winter often in tangles and other types of thickets where there is dense wet vegetation.

FALL MIGRATION: In the northwestern counties Lincoln's Sparrow has been observed as early as the fourth week of September, including one record of three birds in Washington County on September 27, but the species is not seen elsewhere until the first week of October and thereafter, after which it is seen regularly, especially in the central and western regions. While there are many reports in the Audubon Society file involving single birds, three to five observed on a day in the field is not unusual in the northwest. The 27 at Lake Fayetteville on October 2, however, was a large number.

WINTER: The birds are not nearly as common after fall migration, but they are found with fair regularity on Christmas Bird Counts in all regions. At Fayetteville, where they are comparatively numerous in migration, they are much harder to find in winter. This is reflected in the Christmas Bird Count, where the peak record was six birds, and in many other years four or fewer or none were seen. Larger numbers, involving peaks of 15 birds (and unusually as many as 30), have been reported on several Christmas Counts in the Arkansas River Valley and in the southern lowlands. At Arkadelphia peaks of 35 and 38 have been reported on fifteen recent Christmas Counts, but the usual number counted there has been 10 or fewer.

SPRING MIGRATION: Most Lincoln's Sparrows have passed through the state on the northward migration by mid-May, but there is one record as late as the last week of the month, and a very unusual record in Clark County in the first week of June. In Faulkner County, the birds are seen during spring primarily from late March to the fourth week of May (Johnson 1979). At Rebsamen Park in Little Rock, 40 were seen during a four hour walk around the edge of the golf course on April 25, and the species was said to have been abundant at Mablevale in Pulaski County on April 26 of another year. The eight birds in Washington County on May 3 was a high late count.

FIGURE 6-114 Lincoln's Sparrow. *David Plank*

SWAMP SPARROW, *Melospiza georgiana* (Latham)

Common migrant and winter resident in all regions. Inhabits marshy places including open wet low-lying fields as well as natural or artificial marsh.

FALL MIGRATION: Swamp Sparrows have arrived as early as the third and fourth weeks of September on the Grand Prairie, but few are generally seen in the state until the second week of October, with major influxes associated with cold fronts in late October and early November. The 35 seen at West Memphis in Crittenden County on October 19 comprised a large early report, but within two weeks even larger numbers can be found elsewhere in the state in appropriate habitat. At Farville in Craighead County, 40 to 50 Swamp Sparrows were found on November 3 in an area normally inhabited by five or six. During these large influxes, Swamp and Song Sparrows, as well as other sparrow species, are often crowded into the same places.

WINTER: While this species is much more numerous in the southern lowlands than elsewhere in the state during winter months, it is common everywhere in appropriate habitat. At Fayetteville in the western Ozarks, 10 or more are observed on most Christmas Bird Counts. In the lowlands, especially in the southern counties, hundreds may be seen on some Christmas Counts. At El Dorado the usual Christmas Count total involves around 35, but 200 or more have been reported four times. At Conway the usual number is fewer than 20, but there was a peak of 42 in 1980. Statewide, the ten-year mean on Christmas Counts was 0.7 birds per party hour, and this was exceeded at El Dorado, Lake Georgia-Pacific, and at Lonoke, where the means varied from 1.6 to 2.7 birds per party hour.

SPRING MIGRATION: Swamp Sparrows are still numerous in early March, but the numbers decline sharply late in the month, and most reports in April and early May involve one or two birds. There are two unusual late records in the second week of May, each involving a single Swamp Sparrow. In Jefferson County, the spring peak was measured at 18.7 birds per hour on March 6, and this peak had fallen to 3.3 birds per hour on March 20. The four birds at Conway in Faulkner County on April 16 was a high number for such a late date in spring.

WHITE-THROATED SPARROW, *Zonotrichia albicollis* (Gmelin)

Very common migrant and winter resident in all regions. Scattered reports in summer. Usually seen in or close to undergrowth, bushes, brush piles, or tangles of honeysuckle and other dense cover in forest edge habitat. Commonly visits home bird feeders in winter.

FALL MIGRATION: White-throated Sparrows occasionally arrive in early October, but reports of even small flocks are unusual before mid-month, after which there is a steady increase in numbers with peaks occurring during major influxes in late October and early November. In Union County, hundreds were seen during a peak reported on November 1. In Washington County, a peak involving more than 20 birds per hour in a study area was reported on November 8. A fairly typical report for fall (and winter and spring as well) included 33 birds seen during two hours of observation in Chicot County on November 27.

WINTER: Based on data from the Christmas Bird Counts, of all wintering native sparrows in Arkansas, only juncos are observed in larger numbers, and even this difference may be illusionary since juncos often feed in the open and are therefore more easily seen. The ten-year statewide mean on Christmas Counts was 7.5 White-throated Sparrows per party hour, and this was exceeded primarily in the southern lowlands. On the Coastal Plain the means ranged from 5.2 to 14.1; on the Mississippi Alluvial Plain, 3.3 to 18.8; in the highlands (including the Arkansas River Valley), 2.0 to 8.8. In the north there is one unusually high peak on a Christmas Count involving over 400 birds (at Jonesboro in 1978). More than 1400 have been reported on several occasions on Christmas Counts in Arkansas.

The preference of this species for bottomland woods is shown by the results of winter population studies (Tables 3-2 and 3-4). White-throated Sparrows were found to be abundant in association with bottomland woods and virtually absent in upland woods.

SPRING MIGRATION AND SUMMER: Large numbers of birds are seen from February to mid-April, but thereafter a sharp decline is observed, with small numbers remaining until the second week of May. In the Audubon Society file there are a few scattered reports during summer in Jefferson, Polk, Union, and John-

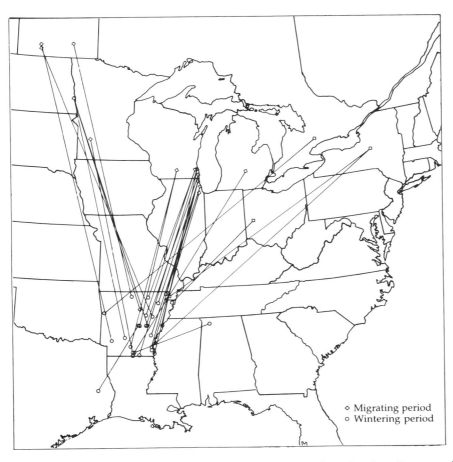

FIGURE 6-115 Movements of the White-throated Sparrow based on banding records.

son counties, plus an older record in Benton County (Baerg 1951). All involved single birds, and at least one bird apparently had an injured wing.

BANDING: A total of 28 Arkansas-associated banding recoveries show that White-throated Sparrows wintering in eastern Arkansas migrate mainly from the northern midwestern states, while wintering populations found in western Arkansas are derived from the edge of the northern prairies (Figure 6-115). The most common distance between banding and recovery was about 700 miles, but others ranged up to over 1100 miles. Most birds were recovered within a year after banding, but one lived over three years.

A different banding study, conducted by Ruth Thomas of Morrilton, showed that White-throated Sparrows return to the same areas year after year. One bird returned to the same

back yard six years in succession, and many returned two to four years in succession (Baerg 1951).

WHITE-CROWNED SPARROW, *Zonotrichia leucophrys* (Forster)

Common migrant and winter resident in all regions. Seen in old field thickets and bushy fencerows in open country.

FALL MIGRATION: White-crowned Sparrows have arrived in the northern counties as early as the first week of October, but flocks normally are not seen until the third or fourth weeks of the month and thereafter. More than 40 birds, some of them singing, were observed along a dense fencerow in Benton County on November 1. In Jefferson County, it was said to be exceedingly abundant after the passage of a cold front on November 6.

FIGURE 6-116 White-crowned Sparrow. *Max Parker*

WINTER: The largest numbers during winter are usually reported in the south, but birds are present in numbers in all regions. At Fayetteville, the numbers reported on twelve recent Christmas Bird Counts varied from 8 to 152, with three records of over 100. Many reports on Christmas Counts at Lonoke have involved over 200, with a peak of over 500. The ten-year statewide mean on Christmas Counts was 1.1 birds per party hour: on the Coastal Plain the means varied from 0.0 to 3.9; on the Mississippi Alluvial Plain from 0.7 to 3.5; in the highlands (including the Arkansas River Valley) from 0.0 to 0.6.

Banding records (Figure 6-117) involving 10 birds showed that White-crowned Sparrows found during winter in Arkansas are derived from breeding populations that migrate through the northeastern United States, with distances between banding and recovery varying from over 1000 to a maximum of 1300 miles. While most birds were recovered within the first year following banding, one bird survived over six years.

SPRING MIGRATION: During spring the last birds have generally moved through the state by the second week of May, but there are a few unusual reports in the Audubon Society file as late as the end of the month. In southern Arkansas, the 20 birds at Portland in Ashley County on April 22 was a large late count, as were the 30 in Newton County (northern Arkansas) on May 6.

HARRIS' SPARROW, *Zonotrichia querula* (Nuttall)

Uncommon but regular migrant and winter resident in small numbers in western and central Arkansas; irregular and usually somewhat rare in the east. Often associated with White-

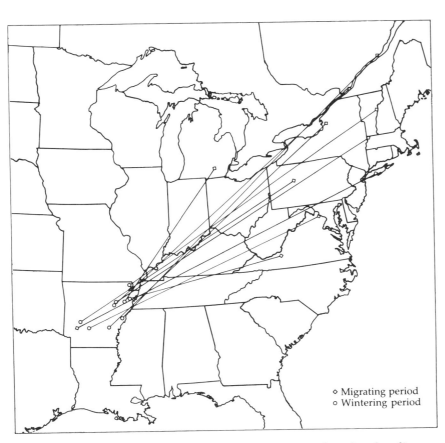

FIGURE 6-117 Movements of the White-crowned Sparrow based on banding records.

FIGURE 6-118 Harris' Sparrows in January, at Fayetteville in the northwestern Ozarks. *David Plank*

crowned Sparrows in open fields with thickets or overgrown fencerows.

FALL MIGRATION: Fall-arriving Harris' Sparrows have been observed in the northwestern counties as early as the third week of October, but few are seen before late October and the usual arrival date is in the second week of November. Relatively large numbers are seen thereafter. In the Fayetteville area the arrival dates range between October 25 and November 16 (Baerg 1930b). During fall peaks observers find 10 birds or more in a day's outing. At Fort Smith, 67 were reported on November 26. In Washington County, 29 birds per hour were counted in a study area on November 22, and 40 per hour on December 15. These large numbers are mainly based upon reports in the Audubon Society file from the 1950s. Such high numbers have not been reported for many years. Few of the recent reports have involved as many as 8 or 10 in a day.

WINTER: The ten-year statewide mean on Christmas Bird Counts (in the 1960s and early 1970s) was 0.1 birds per party hour, and this was exceeded only in the northwest with a peak of 0.7. For the lowlands, the peak was 0.1. Ben Coffey (1956a), and others who have searched for this species in eastern Arkansas, state that they were usually able to find it, but only with "intensive birding," and not every year. On twelve recent Christmas Counts at Fayetteville, Harris' Sparrow was reported ten times, usually fewer than 10 birds, but once as many as 29 (1971). At Conway in central Arkansas, the species was reported on nine of sixteen recent Christmas Counts, with a peak of six (1969). It has also been reported with regularity at Fort Smith. A total of 95 were observed there on the 1955 Christmas Count, but the usual number has been 10 or fewer.

SPRING MIGRATION: Harris' Sparrow is last seen in the state during the first week of May, but it seems that migratory movements suggestive of the northward migration are underway as early as late February and thereafter. There are several reports for the southern lowlands that seem to involve migrants. An unusual flock of 20 was observed in Miller County on February 24. The 12 seen in Chicot County on April 15 were not observed thereafter. The 30 found in Desha County on April 24 were unusual for that area, and it was a late report

of high numbers. As many as 10 have been reported in the first week of May in Washington County.

DARK-EYED JUNCO, *Junco hyemalis* (Linnaeus)

Very common migrant and winter resident in all regions. Observed in larger numbers than the other wintering sparrows. A few rare summer reports. Both "Gray-headed" and "Oregon" forms of juncos have been reported. Found in open forest edge, in open woodlands, on parks and urban lawns where there are scattered trees and shrubs. Commonly frequents home bird feeders in winter.

FALL MIGRATION: Juncos have arrived as early as October 1, but there are no reports involving more than one or two birds before mid-October, and no flocks of substantial size before the fourth week of the month. Big flocks begin to arrive when there are major cold fronts and frost, usually during late October and early November, after which the numbers increase. In Crittenden County, 30 were seen at Horseshoe Lake on October 30, and a flock of 50 was reported at Lake Fayetteville on November 6.

WINTER: Juncos are numerous and well distributed during the coldest months. The ten-year statewide mean on Christmas Bird Counts was 10.3 birds per party hour, and this mean was exceeded on some counts in each region, and there was also an unusually high peak mean of 23.3 at Magnolia in the southern lowlands. The number of juncos reported statewide on the 1980 Christmas Counts varied from a low of only 60 birds on one count to nearly 3000 on another. Half of the seventeen participating locales reported over 600 birds, and 900 or more were observed at Arkadelphia, Fayetteville, Conway, and Hot Springs Village (Garland County).

SPRING MIGRATION AND SUMMER: Large flocks associated with the northward migration period are seen from mid-February into the fourth week of March, after which the numbers decline sharply. A peak of 300 birds was reported in Union County on February 12 and 22. Many of the 90 or more juncos in a single flock in Washington County on February 26 were singing. All reports in the file after the second week of April have involved single birds.

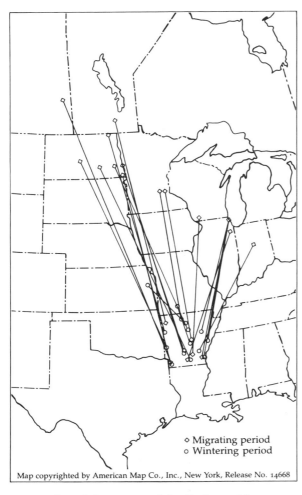

FIGURE 6-119 Movements of the Dark-eyed Junco based on banding records.

Stragglers are occasionally seen as late as the second week of May, after which there are only a few reports during June and July, none of them involving nesting birds.

BANDING: Information derived from nineteen recoveries of juncos banded at least 525 to over 1300 miles from Arkansas suggest that populations observed in the eastern and western regions of the state come from different breeding areas to the northeast and the northwest, respectively (Figure 6-119). Most of the 19 birds were recovered within three years following banding, but one survived over five years. A different banding study, conducted by Ruth Thomas of Morrilton, showed that juncos sometimes return in winter to the same area year after year, with records of returns as many as four years in succession (Baerg 1951).

NOTE: Although the Arkansas population is assigned to what was formerly known as the Slate-colored Junco (AOU 1957, 1973), Oregon Junco forms are occasionally encountered, mainly in winter but also during migration. One Gray-headed Junco was photographed at a bird feeder in Little Rock where it remained from February 22 to March 2, 1963.

LAPLAND LONGSPUR, *Calcarius lapponicus* (Linnaeus)

Migrant and winter resident, often in small numbers, in all regions. Sometimes locally common to abundant, especially at a few places in the eastern lowlands. Inhabits open, sparsely vegetated grasslands, including prairies, airfields, and pastures, and is also seen on plowed fields. It is the most numerous of the longspurs in Arkansas.

FALL MIGRATION: Lapland Longspurs have arrived as early as the first week of November, but there are no reports of flocks until the second week, with numbers increasing thereafter, especially by late in the month. The 40 near Booker in Crittenden County on November 12 was a large early report. At the old army airfield in Prairie County near Stuttgart, 3000 Lapland Longspurs were seen on November 23, 1967, and 1700 were counted in flocks of 300, 500, 200, 500, and 200 on November 29, 1959. Reports from other regions, including other areas in southeastern Arkansas, have often involved none or only a few of these birds on a day's outing even in apparently suitable habitat.

WINTER: These birds have been found in all regions between December and February. Many reports are like those from the western Ozarks, where two to five birds are sometimes seen in association with large flocks of Horned Larks. The largest winter numbers have been reported in Sebastian County and on the Mississippi Alluvial Plain. The following reports in the Audubon Society file illustrate some of the big peaks since the 1950s: 6190 at Lonoke on December 24; 3000 at the Fort Chaffee (Sebastian County) golf course and vicinity December 25–30; 1300 at Booker in Crittenden County on December 17; 2500 at the old army airfield near Stuttgart on December 18; 4096 at Slovak in Prairie County on December 18. The 50 in Benton County on December 15 was a peak for the Ozarks.

SPRING MIGRATION: Northward migration seems to occur during February or early March. In the areas where Lapland Longspurs winter regularly they can often be found through February, but by the end of the month the vast majority has moved north, and there are only highly scattered sightings in the Audubon Society file after early March. The estimated 300 at the Stuttgart airport on March 3 was a large number for the date. The latest record is in the fourth week of March.

SMITH'S LONGSPUR, *Calcarius pictus* (Swainson)

Migrant and winter resident, usually in small numbers, in all regions. Sometimes it is locally fairly common in open country with short sparse grasses such as those found at airports.

FALL MIGRATION: Smith's Longspur arrives in the first week of November. The 15 at Fort Smith on November 7 were early arrivals. Few are seen until the fourth week of the month and thereafter. The 155 at Fort Smith on November 26, 1955, and the 110 at the Hot Springs airport on November 27 the same year were both very large numbers. Generally it is scarce and hard to find and is seen in small numbers, seldom as many as 30, even in prime areas. There are four reports for the Ozarks region (Audubon Society file, Howell 1911).

WINTER: Smith's Longspur breeds on the tundra in northern Canada and Alaska, and winters primarily to the west of Arkansas (AOU 1983). The low numbers seen in Arkansas can therefore be attributed in part to the state being on the eastern edge of the winter range. "Like the Sprague's Pipit, this species has followed man's artificial short-grass 'prairies' eastward" (James 1960). Coffey (1954), who found these birds on several occasions in Arkansas, noted their preference for *Aristida* or three-awn grasses, and this preference has been confirmed by other observers frequently since then.

Winter reports are primarily from Fort Smith in the extreme west (especially in past years) and from the Mississippi Alluvial Plain, especially on the Grand Prairie. Smith's Longspur was found annually on the Christmas Bird Count at Fort Smith 1955 to 1961 (peak of 109 in 1956), but was unrecorded there from the early 1960s to early 1980s. At Jonesboro, the birds have been found on five of thirteen recent Christmas Counts, with one peak of 24 (Hanebrink 1980). At Lonoke the birds have been reported on seven Christmas Counts between 1952 and 1982 (peak of 30 in 1965). Some other peak reports for the state include: 30 at Conway in Faulkner County on January 6; at the Little Rock Municipal airport 28 were observed on December 26; at Grider Field in Pine Bluff 35 were reported on February 11; and 25 were seen at the old Stuttgart army airfield on January 26. There are also several recent winter reports from Smith's Field, the municipal airport at Siloam Springs, Benton County, in northwestern Arkansas.

In the past this species was commonly found on the expansive *Aristida* grasslands associated with municipal airports. In most cases today security provisions including fencing prohibits access to these areas. This may explain, in part, the decline in records of Smith's Longspurs reported in recent years.

SPRING MIGRATION: In those areas where the birds are found with at least fair regularity during winter they may remain through February, with the last regular occurring reports around mid-March. There are also two records for April, but neither involved flocks. A total of 52 were seen at the Jonesboro airport on February 26 and 13 on March 13, a high number for so late in the season.

CHESTNUT-COLLARED LONGSPUR, *Calcarius ornatus* (Townsend)

Rare transient and winter visitor.

The breeding range and the primary winter range for this species lies west of Arkansas (AOU 1983). There are only five reports for the state. Six Chestnut-collared Longspurs were associated with Lapland Longspurs on the golf course at Fort Chaffee near Fort Smith on December 25 to 30, 1953. A specimen was collected from among 20 birds seen near the Fort Smith airport on December 29, 1956. Three birds were seen at Lonoke on January 26, 1957, and one in the same area on September 5, 1970. A single bird was found at the University of Arkansas farm in Fayetteville on April 15, 1983.

SNOW BUNTING, *Plectrophenax nivalis* (Linnaeus)

Two records.

A Snow Bunting was collected in Union County on November 6, 1959, after an extremely cold period that week. The specimen is in the University of Arkansas museum collection. A second bird was seen repeatedly at Burns Fish Farm west of Jonesboro between October 23 and November 5, 1967. A documentation form is on file with the Audubon Society involving the latter sighting.

Subfamily Icterinae Blackbirds and Orioles

BOBOLINK, *Dolichonyx oryzivorus* (Linnaeus)

Spring transient in all regions. Fall transient in the rice fields of the Grand Prairie. Much more common and widespread in spring than fall. Observed in large open fields of grain or tall grasses.

SPRING MIGRATION: During spring Bobolinks have been observed between the first week of April and late May, chiefly from late April to the third week of May. Roughly one third of the reports in the Audubon Society file involved single birds, but small flocks of about a dozen are seen, and occasionally even more. The 150 at Holla Bend Refuge in Pope County on May 7 was a high count. In the western

Ozarks, Bobolinks have been seen most consistently in alfalfa fields near Harrison, and not often elsewhere.

FALL MIGRATION: During the southward migration period Bobolinks have been seen from mid-August to late October, mainly during the first three weeks of September. Other than fall records for rice field areas in the Grand Prairie, there are only four reports elsewhere in the state. These were one to four birds from Union, Pulaski, and Washington counties, and 60 in Crittenden County. The 520 birds in Chicot County on September 18, 1961, is the highest number in the file. When veteran observers Ben and Lula Coffey saw the 60 Bobolinks in Crittenden County on September 11, 1970, they commented that this was only their second fall record for the species in 42 years! Certainly in their winter plumage Bobolinks look much like ripening grain or even fall grasses.

Meanley and Neff (1953b) observed Bobolinks almost daily in the Arkansas rice fields of the Grand Prairie during September. The peak numbers were seen at mid-month, with 435 birds on September 15, and as many as 100 seen in a single field over a twenty-five day period. They collected thirty birds for stomach analysis and found that "although Bobolinks may be seen in rice fields during any day throughout September, the few individuals involved inflict little damage to the crop."

RED-WINGED BLACKBIRD, *Agelaius phoeniceus* (Linnaeus)

Abundant permanent resident. During spring and summer the birds are associated with open wet areas. Found in winter in feedlots, open fields, and yards in towns.

BREEDING SEASON: The average annual mean number per route of Red-winged Blackbirds reported on the Breeding Bird Survey was 18.2 on the Coastal Plain, 272.1 on the Mississippi Alluvial Plain, and 23.2 in the highlands (including the Arkansas River Valley). The huge population in the Mississippi region is concentrated on the Grand Prairie and associated areas that are characterized by extensive production of rice and where flooded fields and wet ditches provide optimum breeding habitat. The peak annual means ranging from 321.5 to 662 birds were reported on the surveys in

Chicot, Prairie-Lonoke, Lincoln, and Poinsett counties.

Meanley (1971a) studied breeding populations on the Grand Prairie. Territories were established during March, April, and May. The chief period for nesting was between May and July. His earliest record for nest building was April 7, and the latest (involving a six-day-old nestling) was on August 23. There were 20 territorial males per one hundred acres of roadside ditches, and 10 males per one hundred acres in the rice fields. He found that nest height was a critical factor in nest success and indicated that "in one study on the Grand Prairie where all 100 nests were two feet or more above the ground, the average clutch size was 3.2 eggs, and an average of two young birds per nest survived. . . . By contrast, in another study where nests were less than two feet above the ground, one or more young survived in only 10 of 100 nests. Snakes, especially the blacksnake (*Coluber constrictor*) and the king snake (*Lampropeltis getulus*), are responsible for most of the predation in Arkansas redwing nests."

Nests placed in a large variety of low vegetation including rushes, cattails, buttonbush, and willows, have been found in Arkansas. The nesting site is typically wet, open, and marshlike. These requirements are fulfilled in wet ditches, agricultural fields, along the borders of ponds, streams, and other bodies of water. The birds nest in loose colonies in favorable habitat.

MIGRATION AND WINTER: After the nesting season Red-winged Blackbirds gather in flocks that on the Grand Prairie may number thousands of individuals as early as late July. As fall advances the Arkansas summer resident population is swelled by transients, and at least some of the Arkansas breeding population migrates south. By Christmas enormous roosts containing several hundred thousand to several million Red-winged and other blackbirds (plus starlings and sometimes robins) can be found in all regions, though the principal ones are in the lowlands (Figure 6-90). The huge winter roosts begin to break up with the first warm weather during February. By the end of March or in early April the population is once again reduced to the summer resident level.

In the 1960s a huge blackbird roost (including starlings) existed at North Little Rock that was counted annually on the Little Rock Christmas

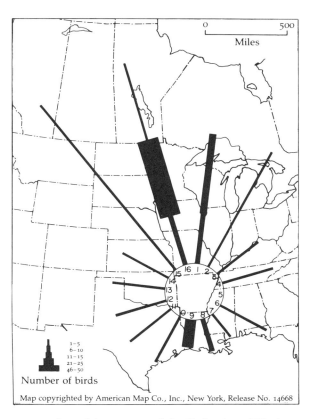

FIGURE 6-120 Movements of the Red-winged Blackbird based on banding records.

Bird Count (Halberg 1971). The roost sometimes contained nearly 40 million birds. In 1965 there were 21 million Red-winged Blackbirds on this roost, the most abundant species, out of a total of 36 million birds. The method of counting the population was described by Halberg (1971).

Recoveries of birds banded in Arkansas support the contention that the northern midwestern states are the major breeding area for the Red-winged Blackbirds that winter in Arkansas (Figure 6-120). In addition, many birds breeding or migrating through Arkansas overwinter on the Gulf Coast. Over 95 percent of the 146 recoveries of banded birds were initially banded in Arkansas, with the distance between banding and recovery often 300 to 800 miles, the longest distance being nearly 1500 miles. A considerable number of birds survived two or three years. Six survived over six years, and one over eight years.

CROP DAMAGE: Much study has involved the problem of damage caused by blackbirds to the state's agricultural crops. The results may be somewhat surprising (Neff and Meanley 1957a). The enormous winter roosts do not occur until after the rice harvest. It seems therefore that roosting birds mainly take waste grain. Nevertheless, real damage does occur during summer, caused by the much reduced but still numerous summer resident population. This study in the twelve counties of Arkansas rice country showed that losses to these birds totalled less, on average, than losses during the harvesting of the crop itself. While causing serious damage to some farms, this species also provides an important service by gleaning the undesirable "red rice," plus eating insects and weed seeds that also pose threats to the rice industry.

The U. S. Department of Agriculture provides assistance to farmers through its Animal Damage Control Program. This assistance relates to projects dealing with bird roosts and depredation on crops and on livestock feeding operations.

EASTERN MEADOWLARK, *Sturnella magna* (Linnaeus)

Very common permanent resident in open country.

SPRING AND FALL: The migratory movements of Eastern Meadowlarks are not as evident as they are in some other species of birds, but the presence or absence of large flocks is highly suggestive of the demarcation between the breeding and the nonbreeding seasons. While observers can often find 10 to 20 individual meadowlarks during a day's outing in appropriate habitat in all seasons, large flocks suggestive of fall and winter are sometimes seen as early as September (and thereafter), and the breakup of these flocks, which occurs by early March (and thereafter), is suggestive of the onset of breeding in spring and summer. In Scott County, 128 birds were observed in flocks of up to 50 birds on November 27. In Union County, flocks with up to 30 individuals were seen by Arnold Hoiberg between late October and early March.

In the northeastern counties a study showed significant population shifts between summer and winter which are indicative of migration, whereas the breeding population largely involved the southern form of the Eastern Meadowlark, *S. m. argutula*, the overwintering population was largely the northern form, *S. m. magna* (Lowery and Hanebrink 1967).

One Eastern Meadowlark banded in Arkansas in winter was recovered 350 miles north in Iowa in May of the same year.

BREEDING SEASON: Reports in the Audubon Society file show that these birds are present and numerous in all regions during the nesting season. The average annual mean number per route in each region reported on Breeding Bird Surveys was 39.6 on the Coastal Plain, 65.6 on the Mississippi Alluvial Plain, and 37.5 in the highlands (including the Arkansas River Valley). Unusually large means of 79.9 to 265.9 were reported on the surveys in Little River, Chicot, and Lincoln counties in the lowlands, and Benton County in the western Ozarks.

Nesting activity has been reported in late April, May, and June. The fourteen nests in the Wheeler Collection are dated from April 27 to June 18, with clutch sizes varying from four to six eggs. All the nests were on the ground. A summer population study in Benton County (Table 3-7) indicated a population of as many as 59 territorial males per one hundred acres in mowed hayfields.

WINTER: The ten-year statewide mean number of Eastern Meadowlarks on Christmas Bird Counts was 6.6 birds per party hour. This mean was exceeded on some Christmas Counts in each of the regions. On the Coastal Plain these means varied from 2.1 to 10.6 birds per party hour; on the Mississippi Alluvial Plain, 8.6 to 9.0; in the highlands (including the Arkansas River Valley), 1.0 to 13.3. On the statewide 1980 Christmas Counts, the totals reported varied from 32 to 621 birds, and sixteen of the twenty participating locales reported at least 140 birds. The 1280 at Lonoke on the 1963 count was one of the highest numbers ever reported in the state. At Conway, 1100 were reported in 1972.

WESTERN MEADOWLARK, *Sturnella neglecta* Audubon

Uncommon but regular migrant and winter resident in small numbers in all regions.

FALL MIGRATION: Western Meadowlarks have arrived as early as the third week of October, but few are heard before the last week of October and thereafter, with peak numbers occurring during November. Eastern and Western Meadowlarks can be separated in the field on the basis of the distinctive call notes or song. Two Western Meadowlarks at Crawfordsville in Crittenden County on October 18 were singing. In Garland County, there is an unusually large report involving 30 Western Meadowlarks in "full song" on November 13 (Deaderick 1938).

WINTER: Western Meadowlarks are found every winter in small numbers. When compared to the numbers of Eastern Meadowlarks, however, these reports of Western Meadowlarks seem few indeed. At Lonoke, a total of 22 Western Meadowlarks were reported on the same thirteen Christmas Bird Counts on which over 8000 Eastern Meadowlarks were found. Certainly the fact that singing is at a low ebb in winter makes it difficult to determine just how many Western Meadowlarks migrate into Arkansas and spend the winter. The 28 in flocks of 2, 15, and 11 at Lake Fayetteville in Washington County on January 12 were high numbers for the state. In northeastern Arkansas nine Western Meadowlarks were identified in a study, and all were associated with feedlots on the Crowley's Ridge uplands, rather than in the surrounding lowlands (Lowery and Hanebrink

1967). This species is also found in or near feedlots in the northwest and on the Grand Prairie. In winter the feedlot habitat seems to be favored by a higher proportion of Western Meadowlarks than by their eastern counterparts.

SPRING MIGRATION: During spring the birds are reported with some regularity in March, but there are only scattered records thereafter in April and very rarely in May. The latest report involved a singing bird at Jonesboro on May 21 (Lowery and Hanebrink 1967).

BANDING: A Western Meadowlark banded in Nebraska in winter was recovered over 500 miles south in northwestern Arkansas during the following fall. Another bird, also recovered in northwestern Arkansas in fall, had been banded in summer almost 1300 miles north in Saskatchewan. A bird recovered in southeastern Arkansas in winter had been banded during summer the previous year over 600 miles north in Wisconsin.

YELLOW-HEADED BLACKBIRD, *Xanthocephalus xanthocephalus* (Bonaparte)

Uncommon but regular transient, especially in western Arkansas. Rare winter visitor. Reports in all regions, with peak counts in the west.

SPRING MIGRATION: There are many more reports for the northward migration period than for the one southward. Most spring reports involve the period from mid-April to mid-May, but there are earlier records, and several during June (see below for summer records). The usual record has involved four or fewer birds, but there are several higher peak counts in the west: 15 in bottomland fields near the Arkansas River west of Fort Smith on May 1, and 41 birds, many of them in bright male plumage, in a pasture in Benton County on April 15, 1984. The species appears to occur with fair regularity in spring in at least the northwestern counties.

FALL MIGRATION: The scattered fall observations are mainly within the period of late August to mid-October, and have almost uniformly involved single birds. It was unusual, therefore, to find four in a flock of 1000 Red-winged Blackbirds at Lonoke on September 5. There is also a report of a bird at a home bird feeder in late November.

ADDITIONAL RECORDS: There are three reports in the file involving single birds for December, January, and February in Miller, Washington, and Faulkner counties. These are the only winter records. A nesting pair was reported in Benton County on May 3, 1947 (Baerg 1951), but no further information is available. A single bird was reported at the Claypool Reservoir area in Poinsett County on June 13, 1977.

RUSTY BLACKBIRD, *Euphagus carolinus* (Müller)

Common migrant and winter resident in all regions. Observed in low-lying fields, wet woodlands, and swampy margins. Forms a small component of the large winter blackbird roosts.

FALL MIGRATION: There are several unusually early fall arrival reports in the Audubon Society file spanning from the last week of September to mid-October, including one of 20 birds at Booker in Crittenden County on October 6. Otherwise, Rusty Blackbirds are usually observed from early to mid-November and thereafter (file, Deaderick 1938, Johnson 1979, Hanebrink 1980). In Craighead County, 80 were seen on mudflats on November 18.

WINTER: Rusty Blackbirds can be found during winter in all regions where there is appropriate habitat. Small numbers, often fewer than 100, are reported on Christmas Bird Counts in all regions. While they generally form only a small percentage of the blackbirds and starlings present in the state in winter, they are sometimes seen in huge numbers. At El Dorado, a roost estimated at 400,000 Rusty Blackbirds was reported on the 1964 Christmas Count. Birds have been reported on most recent Christmas Counts at Fayetteville. Usually fewer than 50 are observed there, but more than 1000 were reported on two of these counts. At Lonoke the usual number on the Christmas Count is 500 or fewer, but there are two records involving more than 10,000.

SPRING MIGRATION: The numbers of Rusty Blackbirds decline sharply after the breakup of winter roosts, with relatively few seen after mid-April. The 60 in a roost in Washington County on March 8 was a high number for that time of the year, as were the 11 in Union County on April 20. The latest report is in early May (Hanebrink 1980).

BREWER'S BLACKBIRD, *Euphagus cyanocephalus* (Wagler)

Migrant and winter resident that is sometimes locally abundant in all regions, especially in the open areas of the eastern lowlands. Forms a small percentage of the winter population of blackbirds and starlings in the state.

FALL MIGRATION: Brewer's Blackbird has arrived as early as the first week of October, but there are generally few reports until early November, and no large concentrations until the second week of November and thereafter (Audubon Society file, Neff and Meanley 1957b). The September record in the northeast (Hanebrink 1980) is unusual. While there are some reports on file involving only small numbers in a day, when the species is seen at all there is usually at least a small flock. In Yell County, a flock of 800 was reported on November 29. At the Stuttgart airport, flocks of 80, 50, 9, 12, and 10 were seen on November 29. Neff and Meanley (1957b) found flocks of 2000 on the Grand Prairie during fall. Brewer's Blackbird appears to be of somewhat irregular occurrence, at least in the western Ozarks.

WINTER: In the rice country of eastern Arkansas Brewer's Blackbird feeds in "plowed fields, fallow land, stubble, and on newly-planted grain fields, and occasionally about cattle feed lots, hog pens, and straw stacks. . . . The food of Brewer's Blackbird during its winter sojourn on the Grand Prairie is . . . largely made up of waste grain that has little or no value to the farmer" (Neff and Meanley 1957b). Coffey (1981) found that flocks of Brewer's Blackbirds usually "move alone," or may sometimes be found at "the edge of a larger flock of Grackles or Cowbirds."

It is of erratic occurrence on Christmas Bird Counts in all regions. The general similarity in appearance of Brewer's and Rusty Blackbird makes some records of either species questionable. Hundreds have been reported on some counts in each of the regions, with the highest numbers found in the open country of eastern Arkansas (14,000 at Lonoke in 1966). Neff and Meanley (1957b) reported that "fully 10,000 birds wintered within a radius of 25 miles of

Stuttgart and there was little or no visible fluctuation in their numbers during Meanley's four winters of observation."

SPRING MIGRATION: Brewer's Blackbird is present throughout February and probably common until late March (Audubon Society file, Meanley and Neff 1957b), but declines thereafter. There are few reports after the second week of April, and none after the end of the month. A total of 30 birds including males and females were observed feeding in a freshly plowed field in Yell County on March 11. The 40 seen on April 6 in Lawrence County south of Imboden was a high number late in the season.

BANDING: One Brewer's Blackbird banded in Iowa during summer was recovered almost 600 miles south in Arkansas the following spring. Two birds banded during fall in Minnesota were recovered in winter the next year in Arkansas, approximately 800 miles south of the banding site.

GREAT-TAILED GRACKLE, *Quiscalus mexicanus* (Gmelin)

Permanent resident in the southwest, and recent summer resident in small numbers in the northwest.

BREEDING: The male and female birds observed near the Spirit Lake oil field in Lafayette County on April 25, 1969, were the first records for this species for Arkansas. The first positive summer records were obtained nearby on June 3, 1976, near Ashdown in Little River County. Charles Mills and others have found five nests since 1977, with two or three of them definitely successful. Recently fledged young were noted in Miller County in 1977 and in Little River County in 1982. Nest placement has shown considerable variation. Three nests were observed approximately eighteen inches above water in a stand of cattails, another was forty feet high in a pine tree, and the fifth was in a shallow cavity created by the loss of a large limb in a willow tree. Other populations of Great-tailed Grackles have spread into northern Oklahoma (Sutton 1967). This species is usually associated with heron nesting colonies, and during summer of 1982 an estimated 30 birds were reported in a heronry near the Arkansas River at Van Buren in Crawford County, not

far from the Oklahoma populations, and the species was present in the area again in 1985. Other recent evidence of the spread of Great-tailed Grackles is from Benton County where one male and two females were seen in spring 1984, and a nest with two eggs was found in cattails on June 3. This nest, however, was abandoned, and the birds were not seen after late June. Three birds were present in the breeding season in the same area in 1985.

WINTER: Great-tailed Grackles have been found with regularity on the Christmas Bird Count at Texarkana since the mid-1970s, with a peak count of 72 birds in 1979. There are also winter records for Little River and Howard counties.

COMMON GRACKLE, *Quiscalus quiscula* (Linnaeus)

Abundant permanent resident. Numerous in every season, especially during winter. Inhabits both woodlands and open country.

BREEDING SEASON: The average annual mean number per route in each region of Common Grackles on the Breeding Bird Survey was 19.8 on the Coastal Plain, 79.4 on the Mississippi Alluvial Plain, and 20.7 in the highlands (including the Arkansas River Valley). Peak means in eastern Arkansas ranged from 103.6 to 196.5 birds in Chicot, Lincoln, and Mississippi counties.

Data from nests on file and in the Wheeler Collection indicate a nesting season from late March through June. In the Wheeler Collection there are fifteen nests with eggs from May 8 to June 5. The clutch sizes varied from two to six eggs, often four or five. The heights of the nests varied from six to fifty feet, often in the range of ten to twenty-five feet. According to Wheeler (1924), the birds usually nest "in trees whose foliage is generally dense. . . . They build in the vicinity of water, using much mud in the construction of their nests. . . . They are communistic in their nesting, many pairs resorting to the same retreat."

Nesting activity in the rice country of eastern Arkansas, where the species is most heavily concentrated, was studied by Meanley (1971a). "In late March, native grackles disperse from communal winter roosts to the prairies and delta lands to nest. For some days after the

FIGURE 6-121 Common Grackles going to a winter night roost on the Grand Prairie part of the Mississippi Alluvial Plain near Lonoke. *David Plank*

first local birds begin to move to their nesting grounds, northern grackles are still in the area, but virtually all have departed northward by early April. Grackles in the ricelands usually nest in colonies in shade trees of the towns, in cedar trees about old farmsteads, and in wood-lots or oak groves out on the prairie. Nesting begins in late March, reaches its peak in May, and is virtually over by June. . . . An average of 2.8 young per nest reached flight stage in one colony of 45 nests. In another colony, one or more young survived to flight stages in 38 of 42 nests."

MIGRATION: The big influx of migrants into the state from breeding areas to the north awaits the first cold weather of fall, usually in late Oc-tober or early November, and the return spring migration begins in late February and con-tinues through March or early April, after which only breeding birds remain.

Recoveries of more than 2000 grackles associ-ated with Arkansas showed that birds migrat-ing through or wintering in Arkansas were derived from breeding populations to the north, mainly the northern midwest (Figure 6-122). Birds making the northward spring migration through Arkansas wintered on the Gulf Coast. The distance traveled between banding and re-covery was over 700 miles for many birds, and the greatest straight line distance was nearly 2000 miles. Most were recovered within the first year after banding, but a considerable number reached two to three, and even up to seven years; six survived eight years, four more than nine years, and one just shy of twelve years.

WINTER: By mid-October or early November large flocks of these birds are common in the state, and these numbers build into enormous roosts. In Union County, 1.6 million grackles were reported in late December of 1965. Large roosts involving thousands of these birds are reported on the annual surveys conducted by the U. S. Fish and Wildlife Service. Common

Grackles constituted 55 percent of a total of three million blackbirds and starlings in a Clark County roost during the winter of 1979–80 (Figure 6-90). A study of the relative abundance of major blackbird-starling roosts on the Grand Prairie between 1960 and 1965 showed that grackles constituted 22 percent of the birds present (Meanley 1971a).

During the 1960s there was a huge blackbird roost (including starlings) at North Little Rock that was counted annually on the Little Rock Christmas Bird Count (Halberg 1971). This roost sometimes contained nearly 40 million birds. In 1965 the Common Grackle constituted 14 million birds out of a total of 36 million on the roost. The method of counting this population was described by Halberg (1971).

BROWN-HEADED COWBIRD, *Molothrus ater* (Boddaert)

Abundant permanent resident. Especially conspicuous from late summer through winter to early spring when enormous flocks feed in open areas, often associated with other blackbirds and starlings.

BREEDING SEASON: The average annual mean number per route in each region reported on the Breeding Bird Survey was 14.3 on the Coastal Plain, 20.9 on the Mississippi Alluvial Plain, and 10.7 in the highlands (including the Arkansas River Valley). Numbers in the Mississippi River region were generally higher, with a peak of 108.5 birds on the survey in Lincoln County.

Cowbirds lay their eggs in the nests of other species, leaving them for the foster parents to

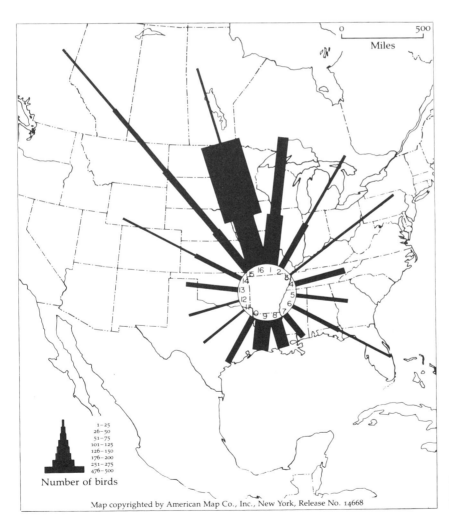

0   500
Miles

1–25
26–50
51–75
101–125
126–150
176–200
251–275
476–500

Number of birds

Map copyrighted by American Map Co., Inc., New York, Release No. 14668

FIGURE 6-122 Movements of the Common Grackle based on banding records.

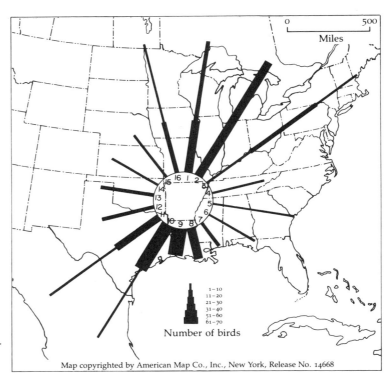

FIGURE 6-123 Movements of the Brown-headed Cowbird based on banding records.

raise. The subsequently parasitized species are similar in size or somewhat smaller than cowbirds. Information in the Audubon Society file and in the Wheeler Collection shows that cowbirds have laid their eggs between the last week of April and the second week of July. The following species are known to have been parasitized by cowbirds in Arkansas (if more than one nest is involved, the number is given in parenthesis): Willow Flycatcher, Carolina Wren, Blue-gray Gnatcatcher (3), Wood Thrush (3), White-eyed Vireo (4), Yellow-throated Vireo, Red-eyed Vireo, Black-and-white Warbler, Pine Warbler, Prairie Warbler (4), Ovenbird, Kentucky Warbler, Common Yellowthroat (2), Hooded Warbler, Yellow-breasted Chat (6), Summer Tanager (6), Scarlet Tanager, Blue Grosbeak, Indigo Bunting (9), Dickcissel, Rufous-sided Towhee (5), Field Sparrow (2), Red-winged Blackbird, and Orchard Oriole (2). Cowbirds generally lay one egg in each nest, but two eggs were laid in nests belonging to the Black-and-white Warbler, Common Yellowthroat, Yellow-breasted Chat, and Summer Tanager. Three eggs were laid in two Wood Thrush nests, and five in the other.

Summer population studies (Tables 3-1 and 3-3) indicated a population of four territorial males per one hundred acres of immature oak-pine forest in central Arkansas; eight males in the upland forest and two in the lowland forest in the northeast; 19 males in bottomland forest in the northwest; and a trace in the uplands.

MIGRATION AND WINTER: By the second half of June small flocks begin to appear in the rice country and other areas of the state where there are ample food crops. These flocks increase continually as summer resident birds are augmented by migrants. Banding of cowbirds in northeastern Arkansas has shown that many birds banded during September and October are still present in the same area in December, while others have migrated south into Mississippi and Louisiana by that time (Meanley 1971a). Data from 388 Arkansas-associated banding recoveries show that cowbirds arriving in Arkansas from northern breeding areas tend to pass through the state and move on to wintering grounds along the Gulf Coast (Figure 6-123). The pattern of movement shows a somewhat northeast to southwest trend. Distances between banding and recovery commonly range up to 425 miles, with a maximum distance of just over 1200 miles. The majority of birds recovered were within two years following banding, but 48 survived two to three years, and seven survived from four to six years.

Banding activity in Drew and Arkansas counties involving over 13,000 cowbirds showed that during February and March the birds move north and northeast of Arkansas into breeding areas extending beyond the Great Lakes (Baerg 1951).

Results from the U. S. Fish and Wildlife Service's winter blackbird-starling roost survey 1979–80 (Figure 6-90) showed the largest single concentration of cowbirds was in Clark County, where they totalled 10 percent of a mixed roost estimated at three million birds. In Arkansas County cowbirds formed about 5 percent of a mixed roost estimated at five million birds. Smaller, but still considerable numbers of cowbirds occur in appropriate habitat in winter throughout the state where they commonly roost overnight in communal sites involving several species of blackbirds, starlings, and sometimes robins.

ORCHARD ORIOLE, *Icterus spurius* (Linnaeus)

Common migrant and summer resident in all regions. Inhabits open woodlands including those with scattered trees (orchard-like) in rural or lightly urbanized areas, and at the forest edge.

SPRING MIGRATION: Orchard Orioles have arrived unusually as early as the end of March in Crittenden County. In Chicot County in the extreme southeast there were so many Orchard Orioles on April 15 the observer said she could not "get out of the sound of them." Between 1937 and 1945 at North Little Rock in Pulaski County, male Orchard Orioles appeared regularly between April 10 and 16 (Thomas 1946d). The big influx is noticed toward the latter part of April. In Ashley County, 40 were seen on April 22. A mixed flock of Northern and Orchard Orioles numbering 125 birds was seen along the Arkansas River in Jefferson and Lincoln counties on May 1.

BREEDING SEASON: These birds are common in all regions in summer, especially in the southern half of the state. The average annual mean

number per route in each region reported on the Breeding Bird Survey was 16.2 on the Coastal Plain, 8.7 on the Mississippi Alluvial Plain, and 6.7 in the highlands (including the Arkansas River Valley). Peak means ranging from 15.2 to 35.8 were reported on the surveys in Ashley, Calhoun, Little River, and Grant counties (all on the Coastal Plain), Chicot and Lincoln counties (Mississippi Alluvial Plain), and Saline and Garland counties (Ouachitas).

Breeding activity has been reported during May, June, and July. The earliest and latest records include unspecified nesting activity underway in Arkansas County on May 7, and young just fledging from a nest at Hamburg in Ashley County on July 18. In the Wheeler Collection sixteen nests with eggs are dated from May 20 to July 4. Clutch sizes in these nests varied from two to five eggs, often four, and the nest heights varied from seven to twenty-five feet. Thomas (1946d) found seven nests in a 2.5 acre area at North Little Rock in Pulaski County. She characterized this habitat as a ridge in low, thinly wooded hills with stunted oak trees.

BANDING: Thomas (1946d) banded this species during the nine summers between 1937 and 1945. In the years following the initial year of banding, she recovered 9 of 26 mature males, 4 of 27 females, and 8 of 127 juveniles. Of 14 males banded as yearlings in the eight years up to 1945, none returned (or were recaptured) in later years, suggesting to her "that with few exceptions males do not return to the first-year breeding area, but in their second season seek a new area. . . ." Two males and one female were at least seven years old at the time of their last recapture, and three were four years old.

There is also one other banding record associated with Arkansas. A bird recovered in northwestern Arkansas in July had been banded over 1300 miles south on the coast of Honduras in March, more than one year previously.

FALL: There are very few records for Arkansas after August. The six birds at Pine Bluff Arsenal on August 17 was a large number for that time of the year. The three seen in a wooded area near Conway on September 20 not only comprised a large number for September, but also formed the latest record for the state.

FIGURE 6-124 Male and female Northern Orioles in mid-June, along Bayou Meto near Gillett in eastern Arkansas. *David Plank*

NORTHERN ORIOLE, *Icterus galbula*
(Linnaeus)

Common migrant in woodlands and open fields or forest edge throughout the state. Locally common summer resident in all regions, especially in the larger river valleys of the lowlands and of the Arkansas River Valley; uncommon in summer in the highlands. Inhabits open woodlands with tall spreading trees. A few rare winter records. Formerly called "Baltimore Oriole."

SPRING MIGRATION: Northern Orioles have arrived in the southern counties as early as the first week of April, and there are reports for the Arkansas River Valley as early as mid-April. At Little Rock, counts as high as 24 birds have been made by April 25. Observers who covered 7.5 miles of Arkansas River levee in Jefferson and Lincoln counties on May 1 counted 125 birds in a mixed flock of Northern and Orchard Orioles. More than 100 Northern Orioles were observed in the Harrison area on May 5, after the arrival of a strong cold front which slowed the pace of the northward migration.

BREEDING SEASON: Reports in the Audubon Society file and on the Breeding Bird Surveys show that these birds have been found during the nesting season in all regions (Figure 6-125). However, the largest numbers are present in the Mississippi River region, especially in St. Francis, Lincoln, and Mississippi counties where the average annual mean number per route of birds on the Breeding Bird Survey varied from 11.6 to 17.0. The species is also reported regularly but generally in smaller numbers on surveys in the Arkansas River Valley and in the southwestern lowlands of the Coastal Plain. Northern Orioles are uncommon during summer in the Ozark Plateaus and in the Ouachita Mountains.

Nesting activity has been observed from late April to early August, mainly during May and June. Extreme records include a female constructing a nest in Lee County on April 26, and

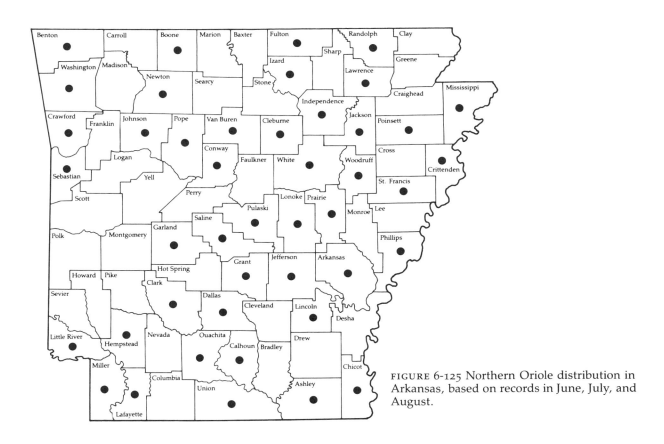

FIGURE 6-125 Northern Oriole distribution in Arkansas, based on records in June, July, and August.

two nests (status unspecified) in early August at Harrison in Boone County. Vivian Scarlett found eleven nests at the golf course in Rebsamen Park in Little Rock during May. Six of these nests were in a row of elm trees less than two blocks long, and two nests were found in one tree. A colony has been present for several years in tall cottonwood trees near the Arkansas River at Fort Smith. Nest heights in the Audubon Society file varied from 15 to 40 feet above the ground.

Deaderick (1938) had no summer records for Garland County in the Ouachitas. Black (1935a) knew of no summer records in the Winslow area in Washington County. However, the birds have nested in Benton County in the western Ozarks (Baerg 1951). There are also very few nesting records in the Audubon Society file for Washington and Boone counties. A male Northern Oriole was seen near a nest at Fayetteville on June 16, and a cowbird was found dead at the nest, its wing wrapped in nylon fishing line that had been used in construction of the nest.

FALL AND WINTER: The last regular sightings usually occur in the second and third weeks of September, and occasionally in early October. Most reports thereafter have involved a few rare wintering birds. Fall peak reports have been much lower than those at spring: five birds in Washington County on September 13, and five at Texarkana in Miller County on September 24.

There are several well-documented instances of overwintering, usually single birds at bird feeders either in the southern lowlands or in the Arkansas River Valley. At Hamburg in Ashley County two birds were observed at a feeder from mid-November 1957 through March the following year. Although the Arkansas population is assigned to what was known as the "Baltimore Oriole" (AOU 1957, 1973), there are two wintering occurrences of the "Bullock's Oriole," both at bird feeders at El Dorado: one February 13 to March 16, 1963, and the other from January 15 to February 20, 1965.

Family Fringillidae Finches

PINE GROSBEAK, *Pinicola enucleator* (Linnaeus)

Three records.

Normally Pine Grosbeaks winter to the north and west of Arkansas, and only sporadically do they move further south (AOU 1983). The first record involved a single male that was photographed near a bird feeder at Salesville, near Mountain Home in Baxter County in early January of 1978. The second record involved three birds near Mena in Polk County in 1980. According to documentation filed with this sighting, these were "large birds with olive green plumage on females, to reddish on male, with white wingbars and heavy black bill, fairly long notched tail." The birds were seen between July 15 and August 24 by a number of observers. Since the sporadic invasions of this species and other finches (such as the Evening Grosbeak) occur during winter, one can only wonder about these birds in Arkansas in summer. The third record involved a single male in Garland County on March 14, 1981.

PURPLE FINCH, *Carpodacus purpureus* (Gmelin)

Common migrant and winter resident in all regions. Numbers show considerable variation from year to year. One breeding record. Common at bird feeders in winter.

FALL MIGRATION: Purple Finches have arrived as early as the first week of October, but few are seen until the last week of the month, with fair numbers arriving in the state at the time of the big cold fronts of November, often by the second week. Among the approximately 20 birds found in Washington County on November 19 was one that had been banded two months before in Manitoba, Canada.

Banding information shows that Purple Finches in Arkansas come from populations breeding to the north and especially toward the northeast of the state (Figure 6-127). Most banding recoveries associated with Arkansas document travel distances amounting to over 1000 miles, and one bird went almost 1400 miles. A majority of the banded birds were recovered within two years following banding, and one had survived almost eight years.

FIGURE 6-126 Purple Finch. *Charles Mills*

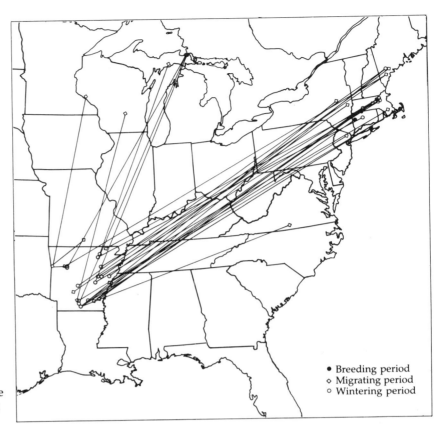

FIGURE 6-127 Movements of the
Purple Finch based on banding
records.

● Breeding period
◇ Migrating period
○ Wintering period

WINTER: The numbers of Purple Finches
found in the state during winter show considerable fluctuation from year to year. On the
Christmas Bird Counts at Lake Georgia-Pacific
(extreme southern Arkansas) between 1969 and
1983, 10 or fewer Purple Finches were reported
six years, and 100 or more (up to over 200) in
three years. This is an example of the irregular
fluctuations of numbers associated with several
species of winter finches (including Pine Siskins, Evening Grosbeaks, and Red Crossbills)
in Arkansas. Winter flocks of Purple Finches
can sometimes be quite large. In Washington
County 75 to 100 birds were reported in one
place on January 26. Over 400 were reported on
the Christmas Bird Count at Hot Springs in
1969. On the statewide 1980 Christmas Count
the birds were fairly numerous, with reports
varying from 9 to 82 birds, and 50 or more on
about half of the 17 counts.

In the winter of 1966–67, Purple Finches that
had been banded during two previous winters
were retrapped in the same place, suggesting
that they return to the same places in successive winters. Of the more than 2000 birds
banded in the winter of 1966–67, 23 percent
were in the adult male plumage (Audubon Society file).

SPRING MIGRATION: Influxes presumably associated with northward migration are evident
during March and April, with only scattered
reports as late as the first week of May. Migratory waves involving 50 to 150 birds were reported in Johnson County between late March
and mid-April. Big flocks are seen as they crowd
around feeders. Tree buds and early tree flow-
ers in spring provide food on the northward
migration.

BREEDING SEASON: There is one old record
of nesting of Purple Finches at Winslow (Washington County) in the western Ozarks (Black
1929b), but this is certainly far south of its normal breeding range (AOU 1983). There have
never been any other such records of this species in the state.

HOUSE FINCH, *Carpodacus mexicanus* (Müller)

Rare visitor that has been seen in the state in all seasons of the year and has recently nested for the first time.

Originally indigenous to western North America, the House Finch was inadvertently introduced into the eastern United States forty years ago and has since steadily expanded its range (AOU 1983). Arkansas lies between these two populations. The first record for Arkansas was a single bird that visited bird feeders in El Dorado, January 22 to March 14, 1971. A single bird was observed at Wilton in Little River County on February 17, 1979. A male and a female House Finch were photographed in Desha County from December 31, 1980, to January 6, 1981. A single bird was present at feeders in Stuttgart in 1982. Another single bird was captured at Little Rock on July 21, 1983, and an individual was photographed on December 17, 1983, during the Christmas Count week at Jonesboro.

On May 21, 1985, an adult male and female appeared at a feeder in Jonesboro and were seen on a daily basis thereafter by Mrs. Cathryn Steele and others. On August 11 the adults brought an immature bird to the feeder and by August 23 there were two males and five females or immatures visiting the feeder. Mrs. Steele provided written and photographic documentation to support this record. This material is on file with the Arkansas Audubon Society. It is expected that House Finches will become more numerous in Arkansas in the future.

RED CROSSBILL, *Loxia curvirostra* Linnaeus

Somewhat rare and irregular winter visitor in all regions. Especially rare in the northwest, and locally common some years in the south. Occasionally observed during summer.

Although the usual range of this species in North America lies north and west of Arkansas (AOU 1983), during invasion years they occasionally appear in the state, especially in areas with extensive pines, and only rarely in hardwood forests. Reports in the Audubon Society file span the period from the first week of September through winter into the second week of May, and rarely thereafter. Among late records

are five birds seen in Ashley County on May 22, 1978, three birds in Saline County on June 18, 1974, and 15–20 (including some juveniles) in Cleveland County on May 4, 1985. Between June 8 and July 23, 1985, Tom Haggerty saw several birds in Hot Spring County, and on July 23 he saw an adult male feeding a heavily streaked juvenile. It is possible that these crossbills nested in Arkansas in 1985, but no nests were actually observed.

Red Crossbills were found on the campus of Arkansas State University in Jonesboro from September to May in 1969–70, with reports of single birds and as many as 15 to 18 there (peak on March 12). In the following two winters they were largely absent from the state, but there were reports from Lake Georgia-Pacific in the heart of the Arkansas pinelands. The winter of 1972–73 featured a large invasion recorded from September through April, with several flocks that consisted of more than 25 birds. A flock estimated at more than 100 birds was observed at Lake Georgia-Pacific on February 12, 1973. The birds have been reported with the greatest regularity on Christmas Bird Counts at Lake Georgia-Pacific. Between 1969 and 1983 they were found on eight Christmas Counts there (1971 to 1979), with peak numbers of 54 and 75 birds in 1973 and 1974, respectively. Interestingly, these records at Lake Georgia-Pacific have included some non-invasion years when the species was otherwise absent or largely absent from the state.

WHITE-WINGED CROSSBILL, *Loxia leucoptera* Gmelin

Rare transient and winter visitor.

In North America this species nests in coniferous forest and mixed coniferous-deciduous woodland far north of Arkansas in Canada and Alaska, and winters irregularly and sporadically further south into the central United States (AOU 1983), but rarely as far south as Arkansas. The single bird at Little Rock in March of 1947 (Baerg 1951) was the first of five reports for the state. Subsequently, there have been four sightings, and documentation for each is on file with the Audubon Society. A single bird was reported in Ouachita County on January 3, 1969, and a single female was seen at Little Rock on March 10, 1970. The only report in the file involving more than a single bird was at Lake Georgia-Pacific in Ashley County where 15 were seen on February 12, 1973. According to documentation submitted by Louvois and H. H. Shugart, broad white wingbars were seen on all of the birds, the crossed bill was in evidence, and the pink color on the head and neck of the male was described. The birds were feeding on cones in the crowns of shortleaf pine trees. The most recent record involved a single female seen at a bird feeder in Benton County on April 4, 1982.

COMMON REDPOLL, *Carduelis flammea* (Linnaeus)

Rare transient and winter visitor.

Common Redpolls normally winter far north of Arkansas (AOU 1983), but occasionally a few reach the state. There is one undocumented report in the Audubon Society file involving a flock estimated to contain 35 to 40 of these birds at Natural Dam in Crawford County on March 6, 1955. Documentation was submitted on three birds thought to be of this species, south of Hazen in Prairie County on November 2, 1959. Documentation was provided for a single bird among goldfinches feeding on a patio at Little Rock on February 5, 1978. One was photographed at a home bird feeder at Harrison in Boone County between January 25 and February 1, 1982. There was a well-documented report of four males in Carroll County on February 5, 1985. Also, a female bird was photographed at a feeder in Benton County, March 3–17 the same year.

PINE SISKIN, *Carduelis pinus* (Wilson)

Migrant and winter resident in all regions that is especially numerous during invasion years, otherwise uncommon. Most numerous in the coniferous regions of the Ouachita Mountains and the Coastal Plain. Frequently visits bird feeders.

FALL MIGRATION: Pine Siskins have arrived as early as the last of September, when a flock of nineteen was seen by William Shepherd as they fed on weed seeds at Magazine Mountain in Logan County. Otherwise, flocks are rarely seen before mid-October with numbers increasing thereafter. Over 100 were seen on November 4 in Union County, and four Sweetgum trees were said to be full of them. A single bird, whose presence was documented at Magazine Mountain on August 6, provides an unusual extra-seasonal record.

WINTER: Pine Siskins seem to winter in Arkansas in a cycle of high numbers about every other year. They were common in the winter of 1963–64, largely absent in fall of 1964, numerous in the fall of 1965, rare during winter of 1967–68, and numerous again in the winter of 1969–70. Though the species was largely absent in the winter of 1967–68, a flock of a dozen birds was observed regularly at Hamburg in Ashley County between late November and late March, with one peak of 100 in November.

This cycle of abundance and scarcity is illustrated on the Christmas Bird Count at El Dorado. Between 1969 and 1983, Pine Siskins were absent on six counts, fewer than 10 were seen on three additional counts, and 100 or more (up to 265 in 1981) were reported on three counts. Pine Siskins were scarce in the winter of 1979–80, with a total of 12 birds reported statewide on the Christmas Bird Counts, all at Magnolia. The following year was one of abundance, with siskins found throughout the state, and over 260 reported on the Christmas Counts at El Dorado and Hot Springs Village (Garland County).

SPRING MIGRATION: During major invasion years siskins are present all over the state, with large flocks observed during April and spilling over to mid-May. The numbers can be spectacular. In downtown Little Rock, 275 siskins along with hundreds of goldfinches were observed as they fed on lawns and in budding trees on April 25. Late records involving single birds have been recorded as late as early June.

LESSER GOLDFINCH, *Carduelis psaltria* (Say)

One record.

A single Lesser Goldfinch in the company of American Goldfinches was observed at close range by several ornithologists in March 1984 at a home bird feeder near Gravette, Benton County. The bird had been present since the summer of 1983, and was still making periodic visits to the feeder into the spring of 1985. This bird exhibited the adult male green-backed plumage.

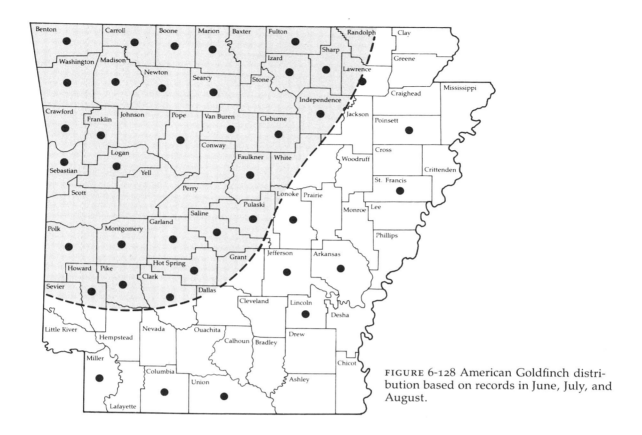

FIGURE 6-128 American Goldfinch distribution based on records in June, July, and August.

AMERICAN GOLDFINCH, *Carduelis tristis* (Linnaeus)

Permanent resident. Common summer resident primarily in the highlands and secondarily in uplands of other regions. Common throughout the state during migration and winter. Inhabits open country where there are bushy or weedy old fields, saplings, or small groves of trees. Common at bird feeders in winter.

SPRING MIGRATION: Even in those parts of the state where this species nests, reports for a day in the field usually involve only a few goldfinches, thus migratory movements are very noticeable, ranging from sightings of small flocks of 10 or 20 birds, up to peaks involving ten times that number. Spring migrants have been seen as early as late March (Deaderick 1938), but are observed primarily between April and mid-May. More than 100 birds are seen on some outings during this period. Edith Halberg reported that during April along the Arkansas River at Little Rock "the chorus of

goldfinches drowns out all the other bird song." Also at Little Rock, 300 goldfinches with Pine Siskins were observed on April 25. One observer in Faulkner County saw 250 goldfinches on May 1. In southern Arkansas the last goldfinches have passed through by late April or early May, and the late dates for Faulkner County are in mid-May (Johnson 1979).

BREEDING SEASON: Goldfinches are present in summer in all regions (Figure 6-128), with significant populations only in the Ozarks and in the Ouachitas, and smaller numbers on Crowley's Ridge in the northern Mississippi Alluvial Plain, and in the foothills of the northern Coastal Plain. Peak average annual means per route on the Breeding Bird Surveys varied from 1.6 to 5.2 on the surveys in Garland County in the Ouachitas, and on six survey routes in the Ozarks.

Nesting activity has been recorded from late July to mid-September. Extreme records are for a nest with eggs in Lincoln County on July 23, and young still in a nest in Washington County on September 10. Four recent nests observed in Washington County were five to twenty feet high in saplings (two nests), in a mature tree, and in a stout weed.

In the western Ozarks of Benton County (Table 3-7) there was a population of 25 territorial males per one hundred acres of open fields having small woody plants such as sassafras, red cedar, and black oak.

FALL AND WINTER: Flocking characteristics of the post-breeding period are evident in the Ozark Plateaus by mid-to-late September, and the first migrants begin to arrive in the southern lowlands during October. Peak numbers seen in spring may again be evident in fall, especially in November. One observer in Perry County saw 215 birds in flocks of 25, 100, 70, and 20 during three hours on November 28. They are very common in the state in winter, with 100 or 200 reported on some Christmas Bird Counts in every region on a fairly regular basis. On the 1980 Christmas Counts, 130 to 390 birds were reported on some counts in every region, and the lowest numbers were in the range of 25 to 75 birds. The ten-year statewide mean number of goldfinches on Christmas Counts was 2.8 birds per party hour. On the Coastal Plain this varied from 2.6 to 6.3; on the Mississippi Alluvial Plain, 1.0 to 2.4; in the highlands (including the Arkansas River Valley), 2.0 to 4.6.

BANDING: Out of a total of 499 recoveries in Arkansas, 493 banded goldfinches were recovered at the place of banding, mainly not in the same year but in years subsequent to banding. This shows that goldfinches return annually to the same sites. Two of the remaining six birds were recovered to the north in Missouri and Saskatchewan. The Saskatchewan site was 1265 miles from the place of banding and involved a bird banded in spring and recovered in summer three years later. Two other birds were recovered in Arkansas less than 100 miles from the banding site, and one of them was recovered in spring three years later. A fifth bird that was banded in Arkansas was recovered in Oklahoma four years later. The sixth bird was banded in Massachusetts in spring and recovered the next winter 1215 miles to the southwest in Arkansas.

EVENING GROSBEAK, *Coccothraustes vespertinus* (Cooper)

Sporadic migrant and winter resident in all regions. Absent some years, and numerous in other years when unpredictable flights or invasions occur. Crowds around home bird feeders during invasion years.

MIGRATION AND WINTER: During invasion years this species moves far south of its normal range north of Arkansas in the northern United States and southern Canada. During the years when the birds are present, observers may report only single birds, but usually flocks of varying sizes are seen. They have been found primarily between early November and the first week of May, and once in early June. Although the birds are observed throughout the state, they show a strong preference for mixed pine and hardwood forests, which in Arkansas are most similar to the northern coniferous forests where they nest.

The first record for Arkansas was at Rogers in February 1942 (Baerg 1951). The birds were next reported at Mountain Home in December 1961, and had spread throughout the state by late January 1962. Reports of this invasion came from twenty-seven cities in all regions of Arkansas, with birds frequently stopping at home bird feeders. The average flock size was about 25 birds, with the largest flock numbering approximately 100. A statewide count showed at least 900 Evening Grosbeaks were present in the 1961–62 invasion.

A sampling of data from invasions since 1961–62 includes a large report in 1968–69 (James 1969), which involved over 5500 birds tallied among seventy-five Arkansas cities and towns. The average flock size was 40, with several flocks numbering up to 200 individuals. The invasion of 1975–76 was observed mainly during March and April 1976; that of 1977–78 mainly at midwinter. The most recent invasion, a small one that began in late December 1984, was observed in all regions.

BANDING: The northern rather than western origin of Evening Grosbeaks reaching Arkansas is suggested by banding recoveries. Three birds recovered in Arkansas during the invasion of 1961–62 had been banded 900 to 1200 miles north in Connecticut, Massachusetts, and Ontario. These birds survived three to six years

FIGURE 6-129 Evening Grosbeak. *David Plank*

between banding and recovery. Seven banding records associated with the 1968–69 invasion involved birds that survived not less than two and one-half years between banding and recovery, up to a maximum of almost seven years. These birds were banded in the states of Maine, Massachusetts, New York, New Hampshire, and Connecticut, and recovered at scattered locations in Arkansas. Additionally, a bird banded at Conway on January 11, 1969, was recovered on February 8, 1970, in Pennsylvania.

The northern origin of these birds that reached Arkansas is further supported by the fact that there are nine specimens in the University of Arkansas museum collection, of which six have been identified to subspecies, all assignable to the northern form *C. v. vespertinus.*

Family Passeridae Old World Sparrows

HOUSE SPARROW, *Passer domesticus* (Linnaeus)

Abundant permanent resident.

This native bird of Europe and Asia was introduced into the United States more than a century ago. In Arkansas, the House Sparrow "is said to have been introduced at Hot Springs between 1876 and 1880, but prior to this (in 1871) it had been introduced into Memphis, Tenn., and doubtless first into Arkansas from that point" (Howell 1911). Today these gregarious birds live in colonies throughout the state, mainly in urban and farmyard areas. It commonly visits home bird feeders in urban environments.

In Garland County, House Sparrows have been observed carrying nesting materials in every month of the year and copulating in January (Deaderick 1938). The favored nesting sites are old houses, barns, sheds, garages, and almost any structure with a loose eave or supporting thick vine where the large bulky nests can be concealed and where there is an ample food supply nearby. The birds also utilize deteriorating nests of Cliff Swallows, woodpecker cavities, and nesting boxes intended for other species. In Fulton County a large pine tree supported over thirty of their nests. The bulky nests of dried grasses are sometimes positioned in the open on the branches of deciduous trees.

REFERENCE MATERIAL

David Plank 1981

Appendix: Specimens of Arkansas Birds

In the process of gathering material for this book, catalogue searches were conducted in North American museums during the early 1960s for specimens of birds collected in Arkansas. Some, but not extensive, use was made of these specimens in preparing the species accounts. For many years now there has been essentially no collecting of birds in Arkansas, which reflects a trend occurring in states throughout the country. Future investigators, however, may have a need to study specimens of Arkansas birds. To assist them in this activity the specimens scattered through various museums are listed in this appendix. Based on the results of inquiries to many museums in the United States and Canada the list is considered to include the bulk of specimens that have been collected in Arkansas. (Most are bird skins, but many specimens at the University of Kansas are skeletal material.) Acronyms used and the identity of the museums are as follows:

AMNH   American Museum of Natural History, New York, New York.

FMNH   Field Museum of Natural History, Chicago, Illinois.

KU   University of Kansas Museum of Natural History, Lawrence, Kansas.

LSUMZ   Louisiana State University Museum of Zoology, Baton Rouge, Louisiana.

MCZ   Museum of Comparative Zoology, Harvard University, Cambridge, Massachusetts.

ROM   Royal Ontario Museum, Toronto, Canada.

UMMZ   University of Michigan Museum of Zoology, Ann Arbor, Michigan.

USNM   National Museum of Natural History, Smithsonian Institution, Washington, D.C.

The number in parentheses (n) following each species indicates the number of Arkansas skins existing in 1985 in the collection at the Department of Zoology at the University of Arkansas (UADZ). Containing only Arkansas specimens, the collection has been transferred to the university museum, University of Arkansas, Fayetteville. When there are two numbers in the parentheses following a species. the second number refers to the number of skeletal specimens from Arkansas that are in the collection of the Department of Biology, University of Arkansas at Little Rock. (Some specimens mentioned in the species accounts are not included here because they were lost in a series of freezer failures at the University of Arkansas, Fayetteville.)

The user of this list should be cautioned that it was compiled solely from searching museum catalogues. Only in the case of a few interesting entries were actual specimens inspected, and for some of these the skins were mis-identified. Therefore, the user should expect some errors in species identifications when seeking the bird skins indicated by catalogue numbers.

ORDER GAVIIFORMES

Family Gaviidae

Gavia stellata (1)
Gavia immer (2)

ORDER PODICIPEDIFORMES

Family Podicipedidae

Podilymbus podiceps (4):FMNH 156073, 156074; KU 21300; MCZ 41950, 41951, 41952.
Podiceps auritus (1)
Podiceps nigricollis (2)

ORDER PELECANIFORMES

Family Pelecanidae

Pelecanus erythrorhynchos (2): FMNH 156155; MCZ 42970
Pelecanus occidentalis (1)

Family Phalacrocoracidae

Phalacrocorax auritus (2): FMNH 160054; MCZ 42913, 42914, 42915, 42916; USNM 207971, 207972, 207981, 207982, 207983, 207993.

Family Anhingidae

Anhinga anhinga (1): USNM 207971

ORDER CICONIIFORMES

Family Ardeidae

Botaurus lentiginosus (2): AMNH 350000; FMNH 160095; MCZ 42533
Ixobrychus exilis: MCZ 42586
Ardea herodias (4): FMNH 156255, 160068; KU 19903; USNM 228024
Casmerodius albus (2): FMNH 160081; ROM 81778; USNM 228024
Egretta thula: KU 19117
Egretta caerulea (2): AMNH 349812, 349813; ROM 82063; USNM 208026, 208028, 208029, 208044
Butorides striatus (2): FMNH 156272, 156275, 160079; USNM 12599
Nycticorax violaceus: USNM 208047

Family Threskiornithidae

Eudocimus albus (1)
Plegadis sp. (1)

ORDER ANSERIFORMES

Family Anatidae

Dendrocygna bicolor: USNM 420637
Aix sponsa (3): FMNH 11074, 74423; MCZ 42757, 42758, 42759, 42760, 42761, 42762; USNM 231512
Anas crecca (3): MCZ 42824, 42825
Anas rubripes (1): MCZ 42870; USNM 239824, 207988
Anas platyrhynchos (7): FMNH 160135; MCZ 42850, 42851, 42852, 42853, 42854; USNM 207995, 239825, 239826
Anas acuta (3): FMNH 160144; MCZ 42779
Anas discors (2)
Anas clypeata (2): MCZ 42789, 42790, 42801, 42802
Anas strepera (2): MCZ 42878, 42879, 42880; USNM 240760
Anas americana: MCZ 42840, 42841
Aythya valisineria: USNM 207955, USNM 207967
Aythya americana: USNM 208025
Aythya collaris: MCZ 42751, 42752, 42753, 42754; USNM 207952, 207953, 208026, 208041, 208043, 240755, 240756, 240758

Aythya affinis (3): FMNH 156563, 156569, 160157; MCZ 42743; USNM 207969, 240757; 240759
Clangula hyemalis (1)
Bucephala albeola (1): MCZ 42703, 42704, 42891, 42892, 42893; USNM 207963
Lophodytes cucullatus (1)
Mergus serrator (2)
Oxyura jamaicensis (1): MCZ 42643; USNM 207965

ORDER FALCONIFORMES

Family Cathartidae

Coragyps atratus (1): MCZ 42975
Cathartes aura: AMNH 351991, 351992; FMNH 106500; KU 19902, 21255; MCZ 42984

Family Accipitridae

Pandion haliaetus (1): KU 22836
Ictinia mississippiensis (1)
Haliaeetus leucocephalus: MCZ 43096
Circus cyaneus: FMNH 156980, 160283, 160284, 39848; UMMZ 60697, 60698, 62050, 62055; USNM 414329, 414330
Accipter sp., USNM 228008
Accipiter striatus (3): AMNH 352210, 352211, 352226, 352227, 352228, 352229; FMNH 156806, 160232, 160233, 160234, 160235
Accipiter cooperii (3): AMNH 352247, 352248, 352249, 352250, 352251, 352252, 352253, 352254; FMNH 156801, 156802, 160224, 160225, KU 19484, 19698; UMMZ 62410; USNM 228008, 414229, 414230
Accipiter gentilis: FMNH 160218
Buteo lineatus (3): AMNH 352513, 352514, 352515; FMNH 74686; MCZ 43062; ROM 83761, 83763, 83764; USNM 11993, 228004, 228005, 229689, 231523, 231524, 414274, 414279, 414280, 414281, 414284, 208004, 208197, 208198, 228025, 229689, 414293, 419839
Buteo platypterus (1): AMNH 352615, 352573, 352574, 352575, 352576, 352577, 352578, 352579, 352580, 352581, 352582; FMNH 74698, 156929, 156933, 160275, 160276; KU 19747, 20401, 20804; UMMZ 62263, 62466; USNM 414289, 414290, 414291, 414292
Buteo jamaicensis (6): AMNH 352434, 352435, 352440; FMNH 156836, 156837, 156838, 156839, 156840, 156852, 156883, 156884, 160248, 160249; KU 19899, 21265; MCZ 252580, 252581; ROM 83442, 83445, 83446, 83447, 83449, 86066, 86067, 86091, 86092; UMMZ 60602, 60657, 60658, 60661, 60662, 60663, 60664, 60665, 60666, 60670, 60671, 60672, 60673, 60675, 60676, 60677, 60678, 60679, 60680, 60681, 60682, 60683, 60684, 60685, 60686, 60687, 60688, 60690, 60691, 60692, 60693, 60694, 60701, 61961,

61962, 61963, 61964, 61965, 61966, 61968, 61969,
61970, 61971, 61972, 61973, 61974, 61975, 61976,
61977, 61978, 61979, 61980, 61981, 61982, 61995,
61996, 62089, 62090, 62091, 62092, 62093, 62094,
62095, 62096, 62097, 62098, 62099, 62100, 62101,
62102, 62103, 62104, 62105, 62106, 62107, 62108,
62109, 62110, 62111, 62112, 62113, 62114, 62115,
62116, 62126, 62127, 62128, 62129, 62130, 62131,
62132, 62133, 62134, 62135, 62136, 62137, 62138,
62139, 62140, 62141, 62142, 62143, 62144, 62145,
62146, 62147, 62148, 62149, 62150, 62151, 62152,
62153, 62154, 62155, 62156, 62157, 62158, 62159,
62160, 62161, 62162, 62163, 62164, 62165, 62166,
62167, 62168, 62169, 62170, 62171, 62172, 62173,
62174, 62175, 62176, 62177, 62178, 62179, 62180,
62181, 62182, 62464, 62465, 66699, 67145, 67146,
67147, 67148, 67149, 68240, 68241, 68242, 68243,
68244, 68245, 68460, 71869, 71917, 89950, 107224,
107225, 121590, 121591, 121592, 121615, 121622,
121623, 121624, 121625, 121626, 121627, 121628,
121629, 121648, 121649, 121650, 121651, 121652,
121653, 121654, 121655, 121656, 121657, 121658,
121659, 121660, 121661, 121662; USNM 231525,
335308, 414250, 414288, 414260, 419838
Aquila chrysaetos: FMNH 160279; UMMZ 61949

Family *Falconidae*

Falco sparverius (4): AMNH 353016, 353017, 363018,
353019, 353020, 353021, 353022, 353023, 353024,
353025, 353026, 353027, 353028, 353029, 353030,
353031, 353032; FMNH 39850, 157079, 160321,
160322; UMMZ 69188; USNM 141154, 141155,
414354, 414356, 414357, 419332, 157079
Falco columbarius (1): FMNH 160312; KU 20696

ORDER GALLIFORMES

Family *Phasianidae*

Meleagris gallopavo (1): USNM 208090, 208091, 421478
Colinus virginianus (7): AMNH 353717, 353718,
353719, 353720, 353721, 353722, 353723, 353724,
353725; FMNH 4655, 4656, 4657, 4658, 39817,
39818, 39819, 39820, 39821, 39822, 39823, 39824,
39825, 157385, 160395, 160396; KU 18519, 19628,
19856; UMMZ 122775, 122776, 122777, 122778,
122779, 122780, 122781, 122782, 122783; USNM
140961, 229708, 229709, 414442, 414443, 418256,
419846, 419338, 419339

ORDER GRUIFORMES

Family *Rallidae*

Coturnicops noveboracensis (1): USNM 12641
Rallus elegans (4): USNM 419491, 420023, 420501,
421048, 421294, 428647, 428648, 428649, 428650
Rallus limicola (1)
Porzana carolina (7): FMNH 157468, 160410, 160411;
MCZ 41916, 41917, 41918, 41919
Porphyrula martinica (1)
Gallinula chloropus (1): USNM 419492
Fulica americana (5): FMNH 157512, 157513, 160412,
160413, 160414; KU 22967; MCZ 41976, 41977,
41978, 41979, 41980; USNM 414641

ORDER CHARADRIIFORMES

Family *Charadriidae*

Pluvialis squatarola (2): USNM 141031, 141032
Pluvialis dominica (4): USNM 419167, 419168, 419840,
419841, 420024, 420025
Charadrius semipalmutas (1): USNM 418737
Charadrius melodus (1)
Charadrius vociferus (3): FMNH 160451; KU 25283,
39058; MCZ 42236, 42237

Family *Recurvirostridae*

Recurvirostra americana (1)

Family *Scolopacidae*

Tringa melanoleuca (2)
Tringa flavipes (3): FMNH 160488, 160489; KU 20702
Tringa solitaria (3): FMNH 157842, 157846
Catoptrophorus semipalmatus (3)
Actitis macularia (4): USNM 141030
Bartramia longicauda (1)
Calidris alba (2)
Calidris pusilla (4): USNM 419359
Calidris mauri (2)
Calidris minutilla (3): USNM 140990
Calidris fuscicollis (1)
Calidris bairdii (1)
Calidris melantos (3): FMNH 160584, 160585
Calidris alpina (5)
Calidris himantopus (3)
Tryngites subruficollis (2)
Limnodromus griseus (2)
Limnodromus scolopaceus (5)
Gallinago gallinago (3): MCZ 42353, 42354
Scolopax minor (2): FMNH 39771, 39772
Phalaropus tricolor (2)

Family Laridae

Larus pipixcan (1)
Larus philadelphia (1)
Larus delawarensis (2): FMNH 158455
Larus argentatus (1)
Sterna caspia (3)
Sterna hirundo (4)
Sterna forsteri (2)
Sterna antillarum (3)
Chlidonias niger (3)

ORDER COLUMBIFORMES

Family Columbidae

Zenaida macroura (7): AMNH 46053; KU 25343, 25344;
USNM 415779, 415780, 419798, 421296, 421297,
421298, 421299, 421352, 421353, 467109, 467719

ORDER PSITTACIFORMES

Family Psittacidae

Conuropsis carolinensis: USNM 3890, 23701

ORDER CUCULIFORMES

Family Cuculidae

Coccyzus erythropthalmus (2): AMNH 360174
Coccyzus americanus (5): AMNH 360070, 360071,
360072, 360073, 360074, 360075; FMNH 160790; KU
19559, 19745, 19746
Geococcyx californianus (1)
Crotophaga sulcirostris (1): USNM 420636

ORDER STRIGIFORMES

Family Tytonidae

Tyto alba (3): AMNH 360312

Family Strigidae

Otus asio (7): AMNH 360176, 360377, 360378, 360379,
360380, 360381, 360382, 360383, 360384, 360385;
FMNH 159347, 159348, 159359, 159360, 160817;
UMMZ 60700, 61984, 125525, 125576, 125577,
125578, 125579, 125580, 125581, 125582, 125583,
125584, 125585, 125586, 125587, 125588, 125589,
125590, 125591, 125592, 125593, 125594, 125595,
125596, 125597, 125598, 125599, 125600, 125601,
125602; USNM 208179, 208186, 208187, 229692,
231496, 231497, 415860, 415861, 415862, 421049,
421050
Bubo virginianus (1): AMNH 360508, 360509, 360510,
360511, 360512, 360513, 360514, 360515; FMNH
159488, 159489, 159490, 159491; MCZ 252248,
252249, 252250; UMMZ 60696, 61948, 62983,
125902, 125903; USNM 141215, 415876, 415877
Nyctea scandiaca (1)
Strix varia (7): AMNH 360825, 360826, 360827,
360828, 360829, 360830; FMNH 159596, 159597,
159598, 159599, 160907, 160908, 160909; KU 19304,
19389; UMMZ 59973, 60699, 61946, 61947, 62560,
62980, 125997, 125998, 125999, 126000, 126001,
126002, 126003, 126004, 126005; USNM 208166,
208167, 208168, 229691, 415906, 415907, 420633
Asio otus (2): FMNH 159620, 160911; UMMZ 61983,
62544, 62545
Asio flammeus (1): FMNH 160919
Aegolius acadicus (1)

ORDER CAPRIMULGIFORMES

Family Caprimulgidae

Chordeiles minor (2): FMNH 159731, 159745, 159753;
KU 19385; USNM 228070, 419336
Caprimulgus carolinensis (3): AMNH 361012, 361013;
FMNH 160978; KU 19339, 19496, 19526, 21176;
UMMZ 126191; USNM 415935, 415936
Caprimulgus vociferus (1): AMNH 361050

ORDER APODIFORMES

Family Apodidae

Chaetura pelagica (4): AMNH 361350; FMNH 159756,
160986; KU 19596
Aeronautes saxatalis: USNM 335155

Family Trochilidae

Archilochus colubris (2): FMNH 159832
Selasphorus rufus: LSUMZ 121495

ORDER CORACIIFORMES

Family Alcedinidae

Ceryle alcyon (2): FMNH 161065; KU 22863, 19730;
USNM 142332

ORDER PICIFORMES

Family Picidae

Melanerpes erythrocephalus (4): AMNH 362600,
362602, 362603, 362604, 362605, 362606; FMNH
70254, 159939, 159940, 161111; KU 19797, 25413,
25414; ROM 82123; USNM 228133
Melanerpes carolinus (7): AMNH 362477, 362478,

362479, 362480, 362481, 362483, 362484, 362485, 362486, 362487, 362488; FMNH 39884, 70265, 161114; KU 22348; MCZ 253172, 43459; ROM 83274, 83275, 83276; USNM 142302, 339005, 379929, 418262

Sphyrapicus varius (3): AMNH 362891, 362892, 362893, 362894, 362895; FMNH 161282, 173313, 173314, 173315; KU 19422, 19638, 25440, 25441, 25442, 25443, 25444, 25445, 25446, 25447, 25448; USNM 229903

Picoides pubescens (14): AMNH 363293, 363294; FMNH 70350, 70351, 161222, 161228, 161229, 173194; KU 18522, 18523, 19521, 19622, 19808, 25478, 25479, 25480, 25481; LSUMZ 8627, 13398; MCZ 43304, 43305; USNM 140718, 228156, 228157, 228158, 229806, 229807, 229813, 416079, 416297

Picoides villosus (2): AMNH 363059, 363060, 363061, 363062, 363063, 363064, 363065, 363066, 363067, 363295, 363296, 363297, 363298, 363299, 363300; KU 19375, 19376, 20128, 20129, 20130, 20131; LSUMZ 13396; MCZ 43270; UMMZ 127091; USNM 228155, 419356, 419357

Picoides borealis: KU 25484, 25485; USNM 416311

Colaptes auratus (5): AMNH 362058, 362059, 362060, 362061, 362062; FMNH 70310, 159965, 159966, 161074; KU 19812, 19813, 22970, 39096; MCZ 43484, 43485; UMMZ 92181; USNM 228034, 228035, 229699, 229700, 229898

Dryocopus pileatus (3): AMNH 362386, 362387, 362388, 362389; FMNH 39902, 161148, 173068, 173069; KU 18518, 19336, 19337, 19338, 19518, 19483, 19558, 19705, 19706, 20354, 22969; LSUMZ 9631; MCZ 43409, 43410; UMMZ 61985, 61986, 65945, 69979, 126612, 126613, 126614, 126615, 126616, 126617, 126618, 126619; USNM 12087, 12088, 228129, 231518, 231519

Campephilus principalis: FMNH 103080, 103081; USNM 12271

ORDER PASSERIFORMES

Family Tyrannidae

Contopus borealis: USNM 228297

Contopus virens (3): AMNH 370263, 370264, 370265, 370266, 370267, 370268; FMNH 70454; KU 22415, 19486, 19760

Empidonax sp.: USNM 228337, 228338, 228339, 228340

Empidonax flaviventris: AMNH 369722

Empidonax virescens (6): AMNH 369762, 369763, 369764, 369765, 369766, 369767, 369768, 369769; FMNH 70483, 70484; USNM 420642

Empidonax traillii (1): ROM 80275; USNM 418678, 418679, 418680, 420634

Empidonax minimus (2): AMNH 369927, 369928, 369929; FMNH 70485

Sayornis phoebe (4): AMNH 369513, 369514, 369515, 369516; KU 19630, 19783; MCZ 43634

Pyrocephalus rubinus: Cornell University 12619; USNM 419030, 419161, 419162

Myiarchus crinitus (3): AMNH 369262; USNM 420510

Tyrannus verticalis (1)

Tyrannus tyrannus (1): FMNH 161371

Family Alaudidae

Eremophila alpestris (6): FMNH 161546, 173820; USNM 230055, 230056, 230057, 230058, 230059, 419842, 419843, 419844

Family Hirundinidae

Progne subis: FMNH 161618, 173949, 173950

Trachycineta bicolor: USNM 419360

Stelgidopteryx serripennis (1)

Hirundo pyrrhonota (1)

Hirundo rustica: USNM 12128, 12130, 419334

Family Corvidae

Cyanocitta cristata (13): FMNH 70583, 161722, 161723, 161724, 161725, 174302, 174303, 174304, 174305, 174306; KU 19827, 19828, 19830, 25597, 25598; MCZ 43783; USNM 239797, 239798, 418257, 419186

Corvus brachyrhynchos: FMNH 174149, 174150, 174154; KU 20357, 20358, 20359; MCZ 43915, 43916, 43917

Family Paridae

Parus carolinensis (28): AMNH 372895, 373023, 373024, 373025, 373026, 373027, 373028, 373029, 373030, 373031, 373032, 373033, 373034; FMNH 69982, 69983, 161753, 161754, 174588, 174589; KU 19725, 19728, 25672, 25673, 25674, 25675, 25676, 25677, 22964; LSUMZ 13507; MCZ 47021, 47022; UMMZ 129737; USNM 228254, 228255, 228256, 228257, 228258, 229886, 229887, 229888, 229889, 229890, 229891, 229892, 229893, 229894, 229895, 269132, 419358, 420508

Parus bicolor (7): AMNH 373376, 373377, 373378, 373379, 373380, 373381, 373382, 373383; FMNH 69921, 74844; KU 19494, 20343, 21956, 22383, 22864, 23032, 25745, 25746, 25747, 25748, 25749, 25750, 25751; MCZ 45797, 45798, 45799; USNM 229984

Family Sittidae

Sitta canadensis (1)

Sitta carolinensis (18): AMNH 373773, 373774, 373775, 373776, 373777, 373778, 373779; FMNH 161913, 174816; KU 19489, 19738, 25771, 25772, 25773,

25774, 25775, 25776; LSUMZ 13514; MCZ 45744, 45745; UMMZ 160338, 160339; USNM 229988, 420638
Sitta pusilla (1)

Family Certhiidae

Certhia americana (4): AMNH 374178, 374179, 374180; KU 19583, 19712, 25818, 25819, 25820, 25821; MCZ 45730; USNM 229869

Family Troglodytidae

Thryothorus ludovicianus (5): AMNH 374843, 374844, 374845, 374846, 374847, 374848, 374849, 374850, 374851; Cornell University 12990, 13000; FMNH 69761, 69762, 175063, 175064; KU 18521, 19721, 19722, 21173, 21982, 25846, 25847, 25848, 25849, 25850, 25851, 25852, 25853, 25854; MCZ 45677, 45678, 257612, 257613, 257614, 257615, 257616, 257617, 257618, 257619; UMMZ 69601, 71817, 160997; USNM 229867, 394789, 394790, 418259
Thryomanes sp.: USNM 228582
Thryomanes bewickii (2): AMNH 374766; FMNH 175089; KU 19566, 25855; USNM 419849
Troglodytes aedon (2): USNM 230906, 419854
Troglodytes troglodytes (2): AMNH 374580; KU 25842, 25843, 25844, 25845; MCZ 45705, 45706; USNM 229868, 420233
Cistothorus platensis (1): USNM 418258, 419196
Cistothorus palustris: USNM 419160, 419851, 419852, 419853

Family Muscicapidae

Regulus satrapa (1): AMNH 377610; FMNH 175743; KU 19791, 19792; MCZ 47260, 47261, 47262; UMMZ 69603; USNM 418757
Regulus calendula (2): AMNH 377757, 377758, 377759; FMNH 70036, 162378, 175776; KU 26168, 26169, 26170, 26171, 26172, 26173, 26174, 26175, 26176
Polioptila caerulea (6): AMNH 377492, 377493, 377494, 377495, 377496; KU 19468, 26130, 26131, 26132, 26133, 26134, 26135, 26136, 26137, 26138, 26139, 26140, 26141; ROM 82814
Sialia sialis (5): AMNH 377055, 377056, 377057, 377058, 377059, 377060, 377061, 377062, 377063, 377064, 377065, 377066, 377067, 377068; FMNH 48374, 162289, 162290, 175625; KU 19754, 19755, 19756, 19757, 26047, 26048, 26049, 26050, 26051, 26052, 26053, 26054, 26055; MCZ 45914, 45915; USNM 419333, 419850
Catharus minimus (3): AMNH 376894, 376895; FMNH 175607
Catharus ustulatus (6, 5): AMNH 376722, 376723, 376724, 376725, 376726, 376727; FMNH 70081, 70082, 162272; USNM 12199
Catharus guttatus (6): AMNH 376468, 376629; FMNH

175540; KU 18529, 18530; MCZ 45869, 45870; USNM 230118
Hylocichla mustelina (3, 5): AMNH 376273, 376274, 376275, 376276, 376277; KU 21873, 21874, 21875
Turdus migratorius (40): FMNH 162185, 162186, 162187, 175368, 175369, 175370, 175389, 175390, 175391, 175392, 175393; MCZ 45887; USNM 229035, 229036, 230013, 230014, 419795, 420230

Family Mimidae

Dumatella carolinensis (5, 20): KU 19498, 19573; USNM 420509
Mimus polyglottos (5): AMNH 375284, 375285, 375286, 375287, 375288, 375289; FMNH 40141, 162170, 162171, 162172, 175334; KU 19487, 22543, 25885, 25886; UMMZ 161313, 161314, 161315, 161316, 161317; USNM 229985, 419335
Toxostoma rufum (15, 5): AMNH 375668; FMNH 175257; USNM 228365, 419337

Family Motacillidae

Anthus spinoletta: USNM 229857
Anthus spragueii (2): KU 26194, 26195, 26196, 26197; USNM 409182

Family Bombycillidae

Bombycilla cedrorum (17): AMNH 378403; FMNH 162418, 162419, 162420, 175872; KU 18520, 26204

Family Laniidae

Lanius ludovicianus (14): AMNH 378549, 378550, 378551, 378552, 378553, 758790; FMNH 162470, 162471; KU 26234; MCZ 45088; USNM 228192, 228193, 228194, 228195, 228196, 228197, 228198, 228199, 230076, 230077, 230078, 230079, 418732, 438637

Family Sturnidae

Sturnus vulgaris (8): KU 20336

Family Vireonidae

Vireo sp.: USNM 228553, 228556
Vireo griseus (8): AMNH 378746, 378747, 378748, 378749, 378750, 378751, 378752, 378753, 378754, 378755; FMNH 5327, 69356, 162549; KU 19495, 20303; USNM 418263
Vireo bellii: USNM 419344
Vireo solitarius (2): FMNH 69335
Vireo flavifrons (5): AMNH 379008, 379009, 379010, 379011, 379012, 379013, 379014; KU 19350, 22707
Vireo gilvus (2): USNM 420506, 419189
Vireo philadelphicus (2, 20)

Vireo olivaceus (3, 20): AMNH 379258, 379259, 379260, 379261, 379262, 379263, 379264; FMNH 74896, 162595; KU 19750, 20115, 21194, 21214; USNM 137843

Family Emberizidae

Vermivora bachmanii: USMN 228503, 228504
Vermivora pinus (1): AMNH 380039, 380040; FMNH 69380, 151933
Vermivora peregrina (4)
Vermivora celata (4)
Vermivora ruficapilla (2): AMNH 380392; FMNH 69405, 162643; USNM 137625, 230905
Parula americana (15): AMNH 380592, 380593, 380594, 380595, 380596, 380597, 380598, 380599, 380600, 380601, 380602, 380603, 380604, 380605, 380606, 380607, 380608, 380609, 380610, 380611, 380612, 380613; FMNH 118881, 176026, 5293; KU 19623; USNM 228505, 228506, 228507, 228508, 228509
Dendroica sp.: USNM 228459
Dendroica petechia: KU 19765
Dendroica pensylvanica (3)
Dendroica magnolia (4): AMNH 381075
Dendroica coronata (13): AMNH 381723; FMNH 162701, 162702, 162703; KU 26299, 26300, 26301, 26302, 26303, 26304
Dendroica virens (3): AMNH 382122, 382123; MCZ 45391; USNM 418756
Dendroica fusca (1)
Dendroica dominica (1)
Dendroica pinus (6): AMNH 383042, 383043; KU 19344, 19345, 19663, 19664
Dendroica discolor (3): AMNH 383206; ROM 82030
Dendroica palmarum: AMNH 383318
Dendroica castanea (1)
Dendroica striata (1)
Dendroica cerulea (3): AMNH 382437, 382438, 382439, 382440, 382441, 382442, 382443, 382444, 382445, 382446; KU 19346, 21852; USNM 420512
Mniotilta varia (5): AMNH 379689, 379690, 379691, 379692, 379693, 379694, 379695, 379696; FMNH 162615; KU 19491, 19715, 21086, 21853
Setophaga ruticilla (2): AMNH 384936, 384937, 384938, 384939, 384940, 384941, 384942, 384943; FMNH 74987; KU 19655, 21150, 21163, 21165; USNM 420513
Protonotaria citrea (3)
Limnothlypis swainsonii (1): USNM 420511
Seiurus sp.: USNM 228516
Seiurus aurocapillus (2, 20): AMNH 383466, 383467, 383468, 383469, 383470, 383471, 383472, 383473; FMNH 69602, 162785; KU 21161, 23405; ROM 82514, 82515
Seiurus noveboracensis (2, 5): USNM 420635
Seiurus motacilla (2): AMNH 383763, 383764, 383765, 383766, 383767, 383768, 383769, 383770, 383771, 383772, 383773, 383774; FMNH 69603; KU 19566, 20195, 21164
Oporornis formosus (5): AMNH 383814, 383815, 383816, 383817, 383818, 383819, 383820, 383821, 383822, 383823, 383824, 383825, 383826, 383828, 383829, 759963; FMNH 176433; KU 19342, 19343, 19681, 19682, 20473, 20612, 21212
Oporornis philadelphia (1): FMNH 176452
Geothlypis trichas (4, 7): FMNH 162803; KU 20774, 21180; USNM 228474, 228475, 228476, 228477, 228478, 228479, 228480; USNM 367706, 420507
Wilsonia citrina (3): AMNH 383827, 383830, 384552, 384553, 384554, 384555, 384556, 384557, 384558, 384559, 384560, 384561, 384562; FMNH 5115, 69668, 69669; KU 21120, 21849
Wilsonia pusilla (2)
Icteria virens (5): AMNH 384432, 384433, 384434, 384495, 384496; FMNH 176563; KU 19341, 19482, 22494
Piranga rubra (5): AMNH 364191, 364192, 364193, 364194; FMNH 5021, 71928, 177153; KU 19352, 24091
Piranga olivacea (1): AMNH 364012, 364013, 364014, 364015, 364016, 364017, 364018, 364019; FMNH 71986, 163203, 177190; KU 19351, 19497
Cardinalis cardinalis (8): AMNH 364331, 364332, 364333, 364334, 364335, 364336, 364337, 364338, 364339, 364340, 364341, 364342, 364343, 364484, 364485; FMNH 40075, 71844, 71845; KU 19794, 26581, 26582, 26583, 26584, 26585, 26586; LSUMZ 8197; MCZ 44814, 44815; UMMZ 69624, 85016, 85017; USNM 229839, 229840, 229841
Pheucticus ludovicianus (2, 10): FMNH 71873
Guiraca caerulea (5)
Passerina cyanea (8): FMNH 5341, 71342; KU 19821, 19824; USNM 228874
Passerina ciris (4): USNM 420514
Spiza americana (3, 5): USNM 378216
Pipilo erythrophthalmus (11): AMNH 367876, 367877, 367878, 367879, 367880; FMNH 163538; MCZ 44776, 44777; USNM 229838, 421047
Spizella sp.: USNM 228764, 228765
Spizella arborea (1): AMNH 403253
Spizella passerina (3): AMNH 403424, 403570; FMNH 71593; KU 19377, 19585, 21168; LSUMZ 14072; USNM 138698
Spizella pallida (2)
Spizella pusilla (10): AMNH 403881, 403882, 403883, 403904, 403905, 403906, 403907, 403908, 403909, 403910, 403911; FMNH 71635; KU 18524, 19845, 19846, 20272, 21202, 21204, 21921, 26981, 26982, 26983, 26984, 26985, 26986, 26987, 26988; MCZ 44639, 44640, 44641; UMMZ 74838; USNM 229963, 229964, 230090, 367890, 419165
Pooecetes gramineus (1): AMNH 401193
Chondestes grammacus (4): AMNH 401464; FMNH 53805; USNM 228638, 228639
Passerculus sandwichensis (9): AMNH 399543, 399544,

399545; MCZ 44441, 44442, 44443, 44444; USNM 419187

Ammodramus savannarum (3): USNM 230907, 231491, 231492

Ammodramus leconteii (2): AMNH 401126, 401127; USNM 230035, 230036, 231493, 442309, 442310, 442311, 442312, 442313

Ammodramus caudacutus: USNM 228633

Passerella iliaca (7): AMNH 404634, 404635, 404636, 404637; KU 27126, 27127, 27128, 27129, 27130, 27131, 27132; MCZ 44757, 44758; USNM 230127, 421053

Melospiza melodia (13): AMNH 405581, 405582, 405583, 405601, 405602; FMNH 155372, 155373, 155374; KU 18528, 19909, 27170, 27171, 27172, 27173, 27174, 27175, 27176, 27177, 27178, 27179, 27180, 27181, 27182, 27183; LSUMZ 14098; MCZ 44706, 44707, 44708; USNM 407853, 407855, 407860, 407863, 407868, 407959, 420232

Melospiza lincolnii (5): AMNH 405000, 405001, 405002, 405003, 405004; FMNH 71133; KU 27143, 27144, 27145, 27146, 27147; USNM 230106, 419164

Melospiza georgiana (8): AMNH 405160, 405161, 405162; KU 27154, 27155, 27156, 27157, 27158, 27159, 27160; MCZ 44743, 44744, 44745, 44746; USNM 230107

Zonotrichia albicollis (17): AMNH 404594, 404595, 404596, 404597, 404598, 404599, 404600, 404601, 404602, 404603, 404604, 404605, 404606, 404607, 404608; FMNH 71269, 71270, 71296; KU 19766, 27076, 27077, 27078, 27079, 27080, 27081, 27082, 27083, 27084, 27085, 27086, 27087, 27088, 27089, 27090, 27091, 27092, 27093, 27094, 27095, 27096, 27097, 27098, 27099, 27100, 27101, 27102, 27103, 27104, 27105; MCZ 44574, 44575; USNM 394920, 421052

Zonotrichia leucophrys (6): KU 26922, 26923; USNM 229952, 229953, 229954, 229955, 229956, 421051

Zonotrichia querula (6): USNM 230119, 421295

Zonotrichia albicollis × *Junco hyemalis* (1)

Junco hyemalis (14): AMNH 401987, 401988, 401989, 401990, 401991, 401992, 401993, 401994, 401995, 401996, 401997, 401998, 401999, 402000, 402001, 402002, 402003, 402004, 402005, 402006; FMNH 178489; KU 18526, 18527, 18531, 19817, 19818, 20604, 21349, 26848, 26849, 26850, 26851, 26852, 26853, 26854, 26855, 26856, 26857, 26858, 26859, 26860, 26861, 26862, 26863, 26864, 26865, 26866, 26867, 26868, 26869, 26870, 26871, 26872, 26873; MCZ 44656, 44657; USNM 419188, 420231

Calcarius lapponicus: USNM 419847

Calcarius ornatus (1)

Plectrophenax nivalis (1)

Dolichonyx oryzivorus (2)

Agelaius phoeniceus (19): AMNH 385971; FMNH 163147, 163148, 177053, 177054, 177055; KU 26541,

26542, 26543, 26544, 26545, 26546, 26547; MCZ 44030; USNM 208132, 208133, 208134, 199177, 230051, 230052, 230053, 230054, 269035, 269036, 269037, 269038, 299176, 418723, 418724, 418725, 418726, 418727, 418728, 418729, 418730, 418731, 418758, 418759, 418760, 419063, 419064, 419065, 419156, 419157, 419158, 419169, 419170, 419176, 419177, 419178, 419179, 419180, 419181, 419182, 419183, 419184, 419185, 419340, 419341, 419342, 419343, 419352, 419353, 419354, 419355, 419797, 420026, 420227, 420228, 420502, 420503, 421046

Sturnella magna (25): AMNH 385441; FMNH 163173, 163174, 163175, 163176, 163177, 163178, 163179, 163180, 163181, 177104, 177105, 177108, 177109, 177110, 177111; KU 19855, 21306, 21307; MCZ 44060; USNM 208102, 208104, 208105, 229991, 229992, 418260, 419351, 419361, 419362

Sturnella neglecta (3): USNM 419845

Xanthocephalus xanthocephalus (2)

Euphagus carolinus (12): AMNH 386682, 386683, 386684; FMNH 162878, 176718, 176719; KU 26563, 26564, 26565; MCZ 44149; USNM 230108

Euphagus cyanocephalus (5): AMNH 386743; USNM 419166, 421054, 421055

Quiscalus quiscula (20): AMNH 322551, 322552, 322553, 322554, 322555, 322556, 322557; FMNH 162874, 162875, 176689, 176690, 176691; MCZ 44184, 44185; ROM 85276, 85282, 85284; USNM 228037, 228038, 228045, 269032, 269033, 269034, 418261, 419796, 420504, 420505

Molothrus ater (14): FMNH 162855, 162856, 162857, 162858, 162859, 162860, 176670, 176671; USNM 269039, 269040, 418755

Icterus spurius: FMNH 176770; KU 21162; ROM 82042

Icterus galbula (3): FMNH 162905

Family Fringillidae

Carpodacus purpureus (23): AMNH 365479, 365480, 365481, 365482, 365483, 365484, 365485; FMNH 70841, 177456; KU 18525, 26601, 26602, 26603, 26604; MCZ 44230; USNM 229920, 229921, 419848

Cardeulis pinus (2): KU 26635

Cardeulis tristis (5): AMNH 367078, 367079, 367080, 367081, 367082; FMNH 4848, 70992, 163410, 177703; KU 19802, 20332, 26644, 26645, 26646, 26647, 26648, 26649, 26650; MCZ 44328; UMMZ 92560; USNM 419159, 420229

Coccothraustes vespertinus (9)

Family Passeridae

Passer domesticus (6): FMNH 162848, 177231; KU 19490; MCZ 44921, 69472, 69473, 69474, 69475, 69476, 69477, 69478, 69479, 69480, 69481, 69482, 69483, 69484, 69485, 69486

Bibliography

This bibliography provides a complete list of written works concerning the birds of Arkansas. It substantially extends two earlier bibliographies of Arkansas birds (Howell 1924, Deaderick 1940b) by including complete literature searches through 1979 with many titles to 1986 added. Some basic standard works that commonly describe birds occurring in Arkansas and elsewhere have not been included, such as the volumes by A. C. Bent devoted to the life histories of North American birds and Robert Ridgeway's series describing birds of North and Middle America, both published as various bulletins by the U. S. National Museum. The more recent volumes by R. S. Palmer comprising a *Handbook of North American Birds* (Yale University Press) are also omitted along with other such basic references that have a broad scope in application.

The bibliography is a complete listing whether or not titles were actually cited in the text. A number of cited works are also included that do not specifically refer to birds in Arkansas, some not even mentioning birds. These are marked in the bibliography with an asterisk (*), and are included as cognate references to complement discussions of Arkansas birds and such subjects as climate, physiography, and vegetation within the state. Articles in the ornithological literature that mention the recovery of banded birds associated with Arkansas are included. Theses and dissertations comprising studies of birds in Arkansas produced by graduate students at Arkansas institutions are also listed, and are available in the libraries of the institutions concerned. Some were laboratory studies. A number of final reports for federal and state supported research grants relating to birds in Arkansas are listed too, and many of these are available in the university libraries in Arkansas. Breeding Bird Censuses and Winter Bird Population Studies conducted in Arkansas and published in the pages of *Aubudon Field Notes* and *American Birds* by the National Audubon Society are listed in the bibliography. However, the numerous Christmas Bird Counts conducted in Arkansas and published in the same two journals are not listed except for some early counts that have special historical significance, nor are the Arkansas references in *The Changing Seasons* sections of these two journals cited.

The authors would welcome information on written studies concerning Arkansas birds that may have been inadvertently omitted from this bibliography for the period prior to 1980.

Abbott, R. T. 1973. American molocologists. Amer. Molocol. Falls Church, Va. 494 p.

Alexander, N., and J. Kirby. 1943. A game survey of Hempstead County. Prelim. Rpt., Pittman-Robertson Project, Ark. Game & Fish Comm. 11-R, 22 p.

Aldrich, J. W. 1951. A review of the races of the Traill's flycatcher. Wilson Bull. 63:193–194.

Allen, R. P. 1952. The whooping crane. Res. Rpt. No. 3, Natl. Audubon Soc. N.Y., 246 p.

Allred, B. W., and H. C. Mitchell. 1955. Major plant types of Arkansas, Louisiana, Oklahoma and Texas and their relation to climate and soils. Texas J. Science 7:7–19.

American Ornithologists' Union. 1957. Check-list of North American Birds, 5th ed. Amer. Ornith. Union, 691 p.

American Ornithologists' Union. 1973. Thirty-second supplement to the American Ornithologists' Union Check-list of North American Birds. Auk 90:411–419.

American Ornithologists' Union. 1983. Check-list of North American Birds, 6th ed. Amer. Ornith. Union, 877 p.

*Ames, P. L., and G. I. Mersereau. 1964. Some factors in the decline of the Osprey in Connecticut. Auk 81:173–185.

*Anderson, J. A. 1935. Centennial history of Arkansas Methodism. L. B. Smith Printing Co., Benton, Ark., p. 202, 274.

Anon. n.d. Birds of Devil's Den State Park. Devil's Den State Park, West Fork, Ark.

*Anon. 1950. Instructions for making bird population studies. Audubon Field Notes 4:183–187.

Anon. 1967. Birds of the White River National Wildlife Refuge. U.S. Fish Wildl. Serv., Refuge Leaflet 103-R-2, 4 p.

*Anon. 1973. Ruth Harris Thomas. Obituary. Ark. Audubon Newsletter 18(1):2.

Anon. 1976. Puddle ducks: from Canadian prairies to Arkansas rice fields. Ark. Game & Fish 9(1): 6–8.

Arfwedson, C. D. 1834. The United States and Canada, in 1832, 1833, and 1834. R. Bentley, London. 2 vols.

Arkansas Agricultural Extension Service. 1964. Arkansas state summary on blackbird damage (1963). Univ. Ark. Agric. Ext. Serv., 6 p.

*Arkansas State Game and Fish Commission. 1948. Wildlife and cover map of Arkansas. Ark. State Game & Fish Comm., Little Rock.

*Arkansas Game and Fish Commission. 1979. Wildlife management areas guide. Ark. Game & Fish Comm., Little Rock, 25 p.

*Arkansas Game and Fish Commission. 1982. Public owned fishing lakes. Ark. Game & Fish Comm., Little Rock, 29 p.

*Armstrong, M. R. 1975. Ruth Armstrong greets charter members at AAS twentieth anniversary. Ark. Audubon Newsletter 20(2):2–3.

Armstrong, M. R., and B. W. Beall. 1962. Arrival and departure dates of Arkansas birds. Mimeographed list for the Fort Smith, Arkansas, and Moffett, Oklahoma, areas. 6 p.

Audubon, J. J. 1827–1838. The Birds of America. 4 vols. Published by the author.

Audubon, J. J. 1831–1839. Ornithological Biography. 5 vols. A. & C. Black, Edinburgh.

Audubon, J. J. 1929. Journal of John James Audubon made during his trip to New Orleans in 1820–1821. H. Corning, editor. The Club of Odd Volumes, Boston, p. 40–83.

Bacon, W. J. 1907. A camp hunt in Arkansas. Amer. Field 67:362.

Baerg, W. J. 1926. Trying to tame a Great Horned Owl. Auk 43:214–217.

Baerg, W. J. 1927. Summer Birds on Mt. Magazine, Logan Co., Arkansas. Auk 44:545–548.

Baerg, W. J. 1930a. The song period of birds of Northwest Arkansas. Auk 47:32–40.

Baerg, W. J. 1930b. Bird Migration Records in Northwest Arkansas. Wilson Bull. 42:45–50.

Baerg, W. J. 1930c. Starling in Arkansas. Auk 47:256.

Baerg, W. J. 1931. Birds of Arkansas. Univ. Ark. Agric. Exp. Sta., Bull. No. 258, 197 p.

Baerg, W. J. 1933. Record of the starling in Arkansas: a correction. Wilson Bull. 45:29.

*Baerg, W. J. 1937. Elementary ornithology (mimeographed), 62 p.

*Baerg, W. J. 1941. Elementary ornithology (Rev. Edition). Russellville Printing Co., Russellville, Ark., 68 p.

Baerg, W. J. 1944. Ticks and other parasites attacking northern Cliff Swallows. Auk 61:413–414.

Baerg, W. J. 1950. Occurrence of the Road-runner in Arkansas. Condor 52:165.

Baerg, W. J. 1951. Birds of Arkansas. Univ. Ark. Agric. Exp. Sta., Bull. No. 258 (rev.), 188 p.

*Baerg, W. J. 1984. Dr. William J. Baerg, entomologist extraordinary. Flashback 34(2):1–18 (Washington Co. Historical Soc., Ark.).

Baerg, W. J., and L. O. Warren. 1949. The Bobwhite quail in Arkansas. Univ. Ark. Agric. Exp. Sta., Bull. No. 488, 46 p.

Ballam, J. M. 1981. The use of soaring by the Red-tailed Hawk (*Buteo jamaicensis*). M.S. thesis, Univ. Ark., Fayetteville, 33 p.

Ballam, J. M. 1984. The use of soaring by the Red-tailed Hawk (*Buteo jamaicensis*). Auk 101:519–524.

Barkley, S. 1979. The state of the eagle. Ark. Game & Fish 10(4):5–6.

Barkley, S. 1984. Eagle restoration. Ark. Game & Fish 15(1):8–9.

*Barrows, W. B. 1889. The English Sparrow (*Passer domesticus*) in North America. U.S. Dept. Agric., Div. Econ. Ornith. and Mamm., Bull. No. 1, 405 p.

Bartsch, P. 1917. Destruction of Passenger Pigeons in Arkansas. Auk 34:87.

Bates, T. L., R. Davis, R. Ashcraft, and A. Lano. 1921. Bird-Lore's twenty-first Christmas census. Fayetteville, Ark. Bird-Lore 23:28.

Baugh, S. T., L. Baugh, and T. Baugh. 1931. Bird-Lore's thirty-first Christmas census. Little Rock, Ark. Bird-Lore 33(1):69.

*Beilmann, A. P., and L. G. Brenner. 1951. The recent intrusion of forest in the Ozarks. Ann. Missouri Botan. Garden 38:261–282.

Bellrose, F. G. 1958. The orientation of displaced waterfowl in migration. Wilson Bull. 70:20–40.

Bellrose, F. C. 1968. Waterfowl migration corridors east of the Rocky Mountains in the United States. Ill. Natural Hist. Survey, Biol. Notes No. 61., p. 1–24.

Bendire, C. E. 1892. Life histories of North American birds with special reference to their breeding habits and eggs, with twelve lithographic plates. Smithsonian Inst., U.S. Nat. Museum, Spec. Bull. No. 1, 445 p.

Bendire, C. E. 1895. Life histories of North American birds. U.S. Natl. Mus., Spec. Bull. No. 2, 518 p.

Bennitt, R. 1932. Check-list of the birds of Missouri. Univ. Missouri Studies 7(3):1–81.

Bierly, M. L. 1980. Bird finding in Tennessee. Published by the author, 3825 Bedford Ave., Nashville, Tennessee 37215.

Bigger, R. E. 1968. A comparison of breeding bird populations in upland and delta areas of northeastern Arkansas. M.S. paper, Ark. State Univ., Jonesboro, 54 p.

Black, J. D. 1922. Arkansas birds. Oologist 39:11–13.

Black, J. D. 1925. The Blue-headed Vireo. Oologist 42:120–121.

Black, J. D. 1928a. The Sycamore Warbler in Arkansas. Wilson Bull. 40:251–252.

Black, J. D. 1928b. A two-day field study from the window of a car. Oologist 45:98–99.

Black, J. D. 1928c. A swift tragedy. Oologist 45:165–166.

Black, J. D. 1929a. The Bald Eagle in Arkansas. Wilson Bull. 41:41.

Black, J. D. 1929b. Nesting of the Purple Finch in Arkansas. Wilson Bull. 41:190–91.

Black, J. D. 1930a. The way of the wicked—Cooper's Hawk. Oologist 47:18.

Black, J. D. 1930b. A much imposed upon Wood Thrush. Oologist 47:80, 147.

Black, J. D. 1931. Pectoral Sandpiper at Winslow. Wilson Bull. 43:223.

Black, J. D. 1932a. A winter Robin roost in Arkansas. Wilson Bull. 44:13–19.

Black, J. D. 1932b. The record of the Starling in Arkansas. Wilson Bull. 44:235.

Black, J. D. 1932c. The Bohemian Waxwing in Arkansas. Wilson Bull. 44:240.

Black, J. D. 1933a. Snowy Egret in Arkansas. Auk 50:206.

Black, J. D. 1933b. Long-eared and Short-eared Owls in Arkansas. Auk 50:436.

Black, J. D. 1935a. Birds of the Winslow, Arkansas, region. Amer. Midland Naturalist 16:154–176.

Black, J. D. 1935b. The southern crow in Arkansas. Auk 52:90.

Bock, C. E., and L. W. Lepthien. 1976. A Christmas count analysis of the Fringillidae. Bird-Banding 47:263–271.

Bogan, A. E. 1974. A preliminary faunal sample from the Knappenberger site. Ark. Archeol. 15:73–75.

Booth, T., F. Burnside, J. Burnside, and P. R. Dorris. 1976. A continuation of Mourning Dove studies in Clark County, Arkansas, with emphasis on cyclical behavior patterns. Ark. Acad. Sci. Proc. 30:19–21.

Booth, T., P. R. Dorris, W. N. Hunter, and B. Mays. 1975. Preliminary dove banding studies in Clark County, Arkansas. Ark. Acad. Sci. Proc. 29:22–23.

Bossu, J. B. 1771. Travels through that part of North America formerly called Louisiana. London, Printed for T. Davies, p. 93–113.

Bowden, G. W. C. 1902. A duck hunt in Arkansas. Amer. Field 57:166–167.

Boyce, J. G. 1925. Bird-Lore's twenty-fifth Christmas census. Texarkana, Ark. Bird-Lore 27:54.

Bray, O. E., W. C. Royall, Jr., J. L. Guarino, and J. W. De Grazio. 1973. Migration and seasonal distribution of Common Grackles banded in North and South Dakota. Bird-Banding 44:1–12.

Brewster, W. 1902. An undescribed form of the Black Duck (Anas obscura). Auk 19:183–188.

Briggs, R. L. 1978. Wood ducks gathering acorns. N. Amer. Bird Bander 3:102.

Brown, J. R. 1966. Nightly unrest in the White-throated Sparrow Zonotrichia albicollis (Gmelin), in response to varying nighttime light intensities. M.S. thesis, Univ. Ark., Fayetteville, 72 p.

Bruce, J. W. 1967. An ecological and behavioral study of the Grasshopper Sparrow. M.S. paper, Ark. State Univ., Jonesboro, 30 p.

Buercklin, F. A. 1967. The effects of DDT in the diet on discrimination in the Bobwhite, Colinus virginianus (Linnaeus), during continuous feeding and food deprivation. M.S. thesis, Univ. Ark., Fayetteville, 46 p.

Bump, G., R. W. Darrow, F. C. Edminster, and W. F. Crissey. 1947. The Ruffed Grouse, life history, propagation, management. N.Y. State Consv. Dept., Albany, 915 p.

Burnside, F. L. 1981. The Red-cockaded Woodpecker in Arkansas: its distribution, abundance and habitat characteristics. M.S. thesis, Univ. Ark., Fayetteville, 23 p.

Burnside, F. L. 1983. The status and distribution of the Red-cockaded Woodpecker in Arkansas. Amer. Birds 37:142–145.

Butsch, E. A. 1971. Vertebrate faunal remains from the Roland Mound site, #AR30, Arkansas County, Arkansas, p. 91 in J. A. Scholtz. Investigations at the Roland Mound site, 3AR30, Arkansas County, Arkansas 1966. Report sub. to Nat. Park Serv. by Univ. Ark. Mus., Fayetteville.

*Cabot, S. 1847 (1848). (Announcement of donation from Major Townsend of two specimens of birds from Arkansas.) Proc. Boston Soc. Natural Hist. 2:259.

*Cade, T. J. 1955. Variation of the common Rough-legged Hawk in North America. Condor 57:313–346.

Callahan, P. S. 1953. A study of the bird population of the Lake Wedington area. M.S. thesis, Univ. Ark., Fayetteville, 52 p.

Callahan, P. S., and H. Young. 1955. Observations on the avifauna of an Ozark plateau. Auk 72:267–278.

Carr, H. A. 1982. Preliminary analysis of the faunal remains, p. 91 in J. H. House, Powell Canal: Baytown Period occupation on Bayou Macon in southeast Arkansas, Ark. Archeol. Surv. Research Ser. No. 19.

Cavaness, S. 1911. Bird-Lore's eleventh bird census. Bird-Lore 13:41.

Chafin, B. T. 1923. Our winter guests. Bird-Lore 25:375–379.

Chapin, Mrs. J. T., S. Cavaness, and V. Cavaness. 1923. Christmas bird census. Bird-Lore 25:39.

Chapman, F. M. 1914. The warblers of North America. D. Appleton & Co., New York, 306 p.

Chapman, F. M. 1932. Handbook of birds of eastern North America. D. Appleton & Co., New York, 581 p.

Christman, S. P. 1983a. Mississippi delta bottomland hardwoods (managed). Amer. Birds 37:67.

Christman, S. P. 1983b. Mississippi delta bottomland hardwoods (unmanaged). Amer. Birds 37:67.

Christman, S. P. 1984. Plot mapping: estimating densities of breeding bird territories by combining spot mapping and transect techniques. Condor 86:237–241.

*Clawson, R. L. 1982. The status, distribution, and habitat preferences of the birds of Missouri. Missouri Dept. Consv., Terrestrial Series No. 11, 80 p.

Cleland, C. E. 1965. Faunal remains from bluff shelters in northwest Arkansas. Ark. Archeol. 6(2–3):39–63.

Coffey, B. B., Jr. 1930. Bird-Lore's thirtieth Christmas census. Mammoth Spring, Ark. Bird-Lore 32:58.

Coffey, B. B., Jr. 1938. Blackbird banding in the mid-south—1. Migrant 9:59–63, 73–76.

Coffey, B. B., Jr. 1941. Summer range of mid-south towhees. Migrant 12:51–57.

Coffey, B. B., Jr. 1942. The wrens of Tennessee. Migrant 13:11–13.

Coffey, B. B., Jr. 1943a. Post-juvenal migration of herons. Bird-Banding 14:34–39.

Coffey, B. B., Jr. 1943b. Purple Gallinule in Arkansas and in Memphis area. Migrant 14:54.

Coffey, B. B., Jr. 1947. Franklin's Gull at Memphis. Migrant 18:60–61.

Coffey, B. B., Jr. 1953. Sprague's Pipit in the mid-south. Migrant 24:28–29.

Coffey, B. B., Jr. 1954. Smith's Longspur in the mid-south. Migrant 25:46–48.

Coffey, B. B., Jr. 1955a. The Short-eared Owl in the mid-south. Migrant 26:24–25.

Coffey, B. B., Jr. 1955b. Notes on the Blue Grosbeak in the mid-south. Migrant 26:41–42.

Coffey, B. B., Jr. 1956a. Harris's Sparrows in the mid-south. Migrant 27:37–39.

Coffey, B. B., Jr. 1956b. Whip-poor-will in the mid-south in summer. Migrant 27:63–64.

Coffey, B. B., Jr. 1962. Mid-south Whip-poor-will distribution runs—1962. Migrant 33:55.

Coffey, B. B., Jr. 1963. Mid-South Whip-poor-will distribution runs, 1963. Migrant 34:92.

Coffey, B. B., Jr. 1964. Cliff Swallow colonies—1963 notes. Migrant 35:52.

Coffey, B. B., Jr. 1981. Mid-south bird notes, p. 1–111 in J. A. Jackson (ed.), the "Mid-South Bird Notes" of Ben B. Coffey, Jr., Mississippi Ornith. Soc., Spec. Publ. No. 1.

Collins, K. W. 1960. Winter and breeding season populations of upland and bottom land forest birds in Northeast Arkansas. M.S. thesis, Univ. Ark., Fayetteville, 68 p.

*Conway, A. E., and S. R. Drennan. 1979. Rufous Hummingbirds in eastern North America. Amer. Birds 33:130–132.

Cooke, M. T. 1937a. Some longevity records of wild birds. Bird-Banding 8:52–65.

Cooke, M. T. 1937b. Some returns of banded birds. Bird-Banding 8:144–155.

Cooke, M. T. 1938a. Returns of banded birds: recoveries of banded marsh birds. Bird-Banding 9:80–87.

Cooke, M. T. 1938b. Some interesting recoveries of banded birds. Bird-Banding 9:184–190.

Cooke, M. T. 1941. Returns from banded birds: recoveries of some birds of prey. Bird-Banding 12:150–160.

Cooke, M. T. 1942. Returns from banded birds: some longevity records of wild birds. Bird-Banding 13:34–37, 70–74, 110–119, 176–181.

Cooke, M. T. 1943. Returns from banded birds: some miscellaneous recoveries of interest. Bird-Banding 14:67–74.

Cooke, M. T. 1945. Returns from banded birds: some interesting recoveries. Bird-Banding 16:15–21.

Cooke, M. T. 1946a. Returns from banded birds: some recent records of interest. Bird-Banding 17:63–71.

Cooke, M. T. 1946b. Bobwhites that traveled. Bird-Banding 17:74.

Cooke, M. T. 1950a. Returns from banded birds. Bird-Banding 21:11–18.

Cooke, M. T. 1950b. Returns from banded birds. Bird-Banding 21:145–148.

Cooke, W. W. 1883. Mississippi Valley migration. Ornith. & Oology 8(5):33–34.

Cooke, W. W. 1888. Report on bird migration in the Mississippi Valley in the years 1884 and 1885. U.S. Dept. Agric., Div. Econ. Ornith. Bull. No. 2, 313 p.

Cooke, W. W. 1903-1906. The migration of warblers. Bird-Lore 5:189; 6:22, 23; 7:33, 135, 203, 278; 8:168.

Cooke, W. W. 1904. Distribution and migration of North American warblers. Biol. Surv. Bull. No. 18, 142 p.

Cooke, W. W. 1907. The migration of thrushes. Bird-Lore 9:32, 34.

Cooke, W. W. 1908-1909. The migration of flycatchers. Bird-Lore 10:115, 169; 11:12.

Cooke, W. W. 1909. The migration of vireos. Bird-
Lore 11:79, 80, 81, 118, 166.

Cooke, W. W. 1909-1914. The migration of North
American sparrows. Bird-Lore 11:257; 12:15;
13:15, 200, 249; 14:45, 98, 99, 103, 104, 160, 161,
288; 15:107; 16:440, 441.

Cooke, W. W. 1910. Distribution and migration of
North American shorebirds. U.S. Dept. Agric.,
Biol. Surv. Bull. No. 35, 100 p.

Cooke, W. W. 1915a. The migration of North American kinglets. Bird-Lore 17:118–125.

Cooke, W. W. 1915b. The migration of North American birds: Brown Creeper and gnatcatchers. Bird-
Lore 17:199–203.

Cooke, W. W. 1915c. The migration of North American birds: the nuthatches. Bird-Lore 17:443–445.

Cooley, R. A. 1942. A new species of tick from
Arkansas. Public Health Reports 57:1869–1872.

Coues, E. 1877. Winter birds of Arkansas. Amer.
Naturalist 11:307–308.

Coues, E. 1879. Southward range of Centrophanes lap-
ponica. Bull. Nuttall Ornith. Club 4:238.

*Coues, E. 1882. The Coues check list of North
American birds. 2nd ed. Estes & Lauriat, Boston,
165 p.

Cramer, Z. 1966. The navigator. 8th ed. Univ. Microfilms, Ann Arbor, Mich., 360 p.

Crooks, F. D. 1939. Starlings nesting near Rogers,
Arkansas. Auk 56:477.

Cypert, E., and B. S. Webster. 1948. Yield and use
by wildlife of acorns of water and willow oaks.
J. Wildl. Mgmt. 12:227–231.

Daniel, Thase. 1984. Wing on the southwind. Ox-
moor House, Birmingham, Alabama, 157 p.

Davis, K. B. 1965. The effects of lethal and sublethal
doses of DDT on the learning ability, group behavior, and liver glycogen storage in the Bobwhite,
Colinus virginianus (Linnaeus). M.S. thesis, Univ.
Ark., Fayetteville, 54 p.

Deaderick, W. H. 1935. Some notes from Arkansas.
Auk 52:324.

Deaderick, W. H. 1936a. Some notes from Arkansas.
Auk 53:349–350.

Deaderick, W. H. 1936b. Some notes from Arkansas.
Auk 53:455–456.

Deaderick, W. H. 1937. The Willet in Arkansas. Auk
54:204.

Deaderick, W. H. 1938. A preliminary list of the birds
of Hot Springs National Park and vicinity. Wilson
Bull. 50:257–273.

*Deaderick, W. H. 1940a. Obituary: Louise McGowan
Stephenson. Auk 57:446–448.

Deaderick, W. H. 1940b. Annotated bibliography of
Arkansas ornithology. Amer. Midland Naturalist
24:490–496.

Deaderick, W. H. 1941. A history of Arkansas Ornithology. Amer. Midland. Naturalist 26:207–217.

Deane, R. 1895. Additional records of the Passenger
Pigeon in Illinois and Indiana. Auk 12:298–300.

Dickinson, J. C., Jr. 1951. A twelve-year-old Sooty
Tern in Arkansas. Bird-Banding 22:79.

Dolbeer, R. A. 1978. Movement and migration patterns of Red-winged Blackbirds: a continental
overview. Bird-Banding 49:17–34.

Donaldson, D. 1968. Honkers avoiding Arkansas,
but why? Ark. Game & Fish 2(1):23–26.

Dorsey, J. O. 1891–1894. Papers relating to Quapaw
oral tradition, 4800 Dorsey Papers, Quapaw
(3-2-4), No. 275, 278, 282, 287. Nat. Archeol.
Arch., Nat. Mus. Natural Hist., Smithsonian
Instit., Wash. D.C.

Downing, R. L. 1980. Survey of interior Least Tern
nesting populations. Amer. Birds 34:209–211.

Dumont, P. A. 1933. An old specimen of hybrid
flicker from Central Arkansas. Auk 50:362.

Durham, J. H., and G. L. Kizzia. 1964. A deep burial
in Crenshaw mound "C," Miller County, Arkansas. Cent. States Archeol. J. 2:44–67.

Dusi, J. L. 1967. Migration in the Little Blue Heron.
Wilson Bull. 79:223–235.

Dykstra, J. N. 1965. The role of eggs and nestlings in
regulating the nesting activities of the Robin, Turdus migratorius L.. M.S. thesis, Univ. Ark., Fayetteville, 65 p.

Dykstra, J. N. 1968. The role of nests, eggs, and nestlings in regulating the stimulus-response mecha-
nisms in the nesting behavior of the Robin, Turdus
migratorius L.. Doctoral dissertation, Univ. Ark.,
Fayetteville, 65 p.

Eaton, R. J. 1934. The migratory movements of certain colonies of Herring Gulls in eastern North
America, Part III. Bird-Banding 5:70–84.

*Eisenmann, E. 1970. A review of: A distributional
survey of the birds of Honduras. Wilson Bull.
82:106–108.

*Eyster-Smith, N. M. 1983. The prairie-forest ecotone
of the western interior highlands: an introduction
to the tallgrass prairies. Proc. 8th N. Amer. Prairie
Conf., Western Mich. Univ., p. 73–80.

Fankhauser, D. P. 1968. A comparison of migration
between blackbirds and Starlings. Wilson Bull.
80:225–227.

Farner, D. S. 1945. The return of Robins to their
birthplaces. Bird-Banding 16:81–99.

Featherstonhaugh, G. W. 1835. Geological report
of an examination made in 1834, of the elevated
country between the Missouri and the Red Rivers.
U.S. 23rd Cong., 2nd Sess. House Exec. Doc.
151:1–97, Public Doc. 274.

Featherstonhaugh, G. W. 1844. Excursion through
the slave states, from Washington on the Potomac

to the frontier of Mexico. Harper, New York. 168 p.

Fisher, R. B., and G. Gill. 1946. A cooperative study of the White-throated Sparrow. Auk 63:402–418.

Fleeman, E. D. 1968. A study of breeding birds of man-made reservoirs in Woodruff County, Arkansas. Graduate paper, Ark. State Univ., 25 p.

Flint, T. 1826. Recollections of the last ten years passed in occasional residences and journeyings in the valley of the Mississippi. Cummings, Hillard, & Co., Boston, 395 p.

Floyd, M. D., and G. A. Heidt. 1979. Modifications and improvements in the formax method of preparing small avian study specimens. Ark. Acad. Sci. Proc. 30:76–77.

Ford, A. 1967. Journal of John James Audubon. Univ. Okla. Press, Norman, 409 p.

Foti, T. 1971. The Grand Prairie. Ozark Soc. Bull. 5(4):6–11.

Foti, T. 1974. Natural divisions of Arkansas, p. 11–37 in Arkansas Natural Area Plan. Ark. Dept. Planning, Little Rock.

Fritz, G. J., and R. H. Ray. 1982. Rock art sites in southern Arkansas Ozarks and Arkansas River Valley, p. 240–276 in N. L. Trubowitz and M. D. Jeter (eds.), Arkansas archeology in review, Ark. Archeol. Surv., Research Series No. 15.

Funk, E. 1958. Rogers and the mystery of the Passenger Pigeon. Pioneer, Benton Co., Ark., May issue, p. 15–17.

Gaines, B. 1972. The eastern Wild Turkey in Arkansas. Ark. Game & Fish 5(1):2–5.

Ganier, A. F. 1930. Breeding of the Least Tern on the Mississippi River. Wilson Bull. 42:103–107.

Ganier, A. F. 1931. Facts about eagles in Tennessee. Tenn. Acad. Science 6:49–57.

Ganier, A. F. 1932. Nesting of the Bald Eagle. Wilson Bull. 44:3–9.

Ganier, A. F. 1951. Some notes on Bald Eagles. Migrant 22:37–39.

Gary, D. L. 1970. Bioenergetics during night-roosting in the Slate-colored Junco, Junco hyemalis (Linnaeus). M.S. thesis, Univ. Ark., Fayetteville, 20 p.

Gault, B. T. 1896. Some Bluebird notes. Nidiologist 3:84–85.

Gerstaecker, F. W. C. 1859. Wild sports in the far west. Crosby, Nichols & Co., Boston, 396 p.

Gipson, P. S. 1968. A study of mainland and island populations of small mammals and game animals in northwestern Arkansas. M.S. thesis, Univ. Ark., Fayetteville, 76 p.

Graves, G. R. 1972. Shorebirds of the Scott-Lonoke area. Ark. Audubon Soc. Newsletter 17(4):4–5.

Gray, D. L. 1962. Quail management in Arkansas. Univ. Ark. Agric. Ext. Serv., Leaflet No. 331, 12 p.

Gray, H. R. 1948. Banding data from Wilton, North Dakota. Bird-Banding 19:159–162.

Greenleaf, P. A. 1978. Nocturnal roosting behavior of blackbirds and starlings in northwestern Arkansas. M.S. thesis, Univ. Ark., Fayetteville, 29 p.

Gregg, H. R. 1935. White-throated Swift at Hot Springs National Park, Arkansas. Auk 52:452.

*Griffin, J. B. 1967. Eastern North American archeology, a summary. Science 156:175–191.

Grömbeck. 1890. Arkansas Wild Turkeys. Forest & Stream 34:169.

Gross, A. O. 1940. The migration of the Kent Island gulls. Bird-Banding 11:129–155.

Guilday, J. E., and P. W. Parmalee. 1971. Thirteen-lined ground squirrel, prairie chicken, and other vertebrates from an archeological site in northeastern Arkansas. Amer. Midl. Nat. 86:227.

Guilday, J. E., and P. W. Parmalee. 1977. Identifiable zooarcheological remains 1968–1969 field season, p. 259–260 in D. G. Anderson (ed.), Zebree appendixes 1977. Ark. Archeol. Surv., Fayetteville.

Hahn, P. 1963. Where is that vanished bird? Univ. Toronto Press, Toronto, 347 p.

Halberg, E. M. 1976. The Evening Grosbeak invasion. Ark. Audubon Newsletter 21(3):1–2 (suppl.).

Halberg, H. N. 1971. How we counted forty million blackbirds. Amer. Birds 25:515.

*Hall, G. A. 1964. Breeding-bird censuses—why and how. Audubon Field Notes 18:413–416.

Hanebrink E. L. 1965. A study of bird populations in selected habitats in Northeast Arkansas. Doctoral dissertation. Okla. State Univ., Stillwater, 87 p.

Hanebrink, E. L. 1968a. Two albino icterids collected from northeastern Arkansas. Migrant 39:14–15.

Hanebrink, E. L. 1968b. A survey of albino birds in Arkansas. Ark. Acad. Sci. Proc. 22:17–28.

Hanebrink, E. L. 1968c. A comparison of three heronries in the Mississippi valley. Migrant 39:50–52.

Hanebrink, E. L. 1969a. An albino Loggerhead Shrike collected from Drew County, Arkansas. Migrant 40:61.

Hanebrink, E. L. 1969b. Fall migrants associated with fish ponds and flats. Migrant 40:53–56.

Hanebrink, E. L. 1971a. Dilute albinism in a Western Meadowlark collected in Mississippi County, Arkansas. Migrant 42:82, 85.

Hanebrink, E. L. 1971b. Food, feeding behavior and extension of range of the Cattle Egret. Migrant 42:49–53, 56.

Hanebrink, E. L. 1972. A check list of birds from northeastern Arkansas. Div. Biol. Sci., Ark. State Univ., 4 p.

Hanebrink, E. L. 1980. Birds of northeastern Arkansas. Stuart Rockwell Publ., 48 p.

Hanebrink, E. L., and J. K. Beadles. 1971. Abnormality in the beak of a juvenal Little Blue Heron. S.W. Naturalist 15:495–496.

Hanebrink, E. L., and R. Cochran. 1966. An inland nesting record for the Glossy Ibis in Arkansas. Auk 83:474.

Hanebrink, E. L., and G. Denton. 1969. Feeding behavior and analysis of regurgitated food collected from the Cattle Egret *Bubulcus ibis* and the Little Blue Heron *Florida caerulea*. Ark. Acad. Sci. Proc. 23:74–79.

Hanebrink, E. L., and A. Posey. 1979. Seasonal abundance and habitat distribution of birds in northeastern Arkansas. Ark. Acad. Sci. Proc. 33:38–42.

Hanebrink, E. L., A. F. Posey, and K. Sutton. 1979. A note on the food habits of selected raptors from northeastern Arkansas. Ark. Acad. Sci. Proc. 33:79–80.

Hanebrink, E. L., and A. Rhodes. 1969. A study of fall migratory bird populations in sewage ponds. Migrant 40:73–78.

Hanebrink, E. L., and B. R. Singleton. 1971. Crossbeak anomaly in the Mockingbird. Migrant 42:4–5.

Hanebrink, E. L., K. Sutton, and A. F. Posey. 1978. Species composition and diversity of hawk populations in northeastern Arkansas. Ark. Acad. Sci. Proc. 32:51–54.

Hanson, H. C., and R. E. Griffith. 1952. Notes on the south Atlantic Canada Goose population. Bird-Banding 23:1–22.

Hardy, J. W. 1957. The Least Tern in the Mississippi valley. Mich. State Univ. Museum, Biological Series 1(1):1–60.

Harrington, M. R. 1960. The Ozark bluff-dwellers. Mus. Amer. Indian, Heye Foundation, New York, p. 34–35, 60.

Harris, R., and E. L. Hanebrink. 1980. Growth patterns, behavior, and food items fed to nestling Great Horned Owls (*Bubo virginianus*). Ark. Acad. Sci. Proc. 34:118–119.

*Harris, R. S. 1958. Harry Edgar Wheeler 1874–1952. Paleontological Research Institution Memorials, Ithaca, N.Y., 11 Oct. 1958.

Hart, D. L. 1982. Home range and foraging habitat requirements of two Red-cockaded Woodpecker clans at the Felsenthal N.W.R., Arkansas. M.S. thesis, Univ. Ark., Fayetteville, 74 p.

Harvey, F. L. 1880. Voraciousness of *Chordeiles popetue* Baird. Amer. Naturalist 14:896.

Harvey, F. L. 1882. Habits of the Woodcock. Amer. Naturalist 16:737–738.

Hasbrouck, E. M. 1891a. The present status of the Ivory-billed Woodpecker (*Campephilus principalis*). Auk 8:174–186.

Hasbrouck, E. M. 1891b. The Carolina Paroquet (*Conurus carolinensis*). Auk 8:369–379.

Hay, O. P. 1882. A list of birds from the Lower Mississippi Valley observed during the summer of 1881,

with brief notes. Bull. Nuttall Ornith. Club 7:89–94.

Haynes, R. J. 1969. The effects of 100 ppm DDT in the diet and of food deprivation on lipid and glycogen storage in the Bobwhite, *Colinus virginianus* (Linnaeus). M.S. thesis, Univ. Ark., Fayetteville, 106 p.

Haynes, R. J. 1972. Effects of DDT on glycogen and lipid levels in Bobwhites. J. Wildl. Mgmt. 36:518–523.

Hermann, K. F. 1900. Chronik der aus Ibra (Churhessen) Stammenden Familie Johann Heinrich Hermann, 1650 bis 1900. Merseburger & Walther, Leipzig. 223 p.

Hickey, J. J. 1951. Mortality records as indices of migration in the Mallard. Condor 53:284–297.

Hickey, J. J. 1956. Autumnal migration of ducks banded in eastern Wisconsin. Trans. Wisc. Acad. Sci. Arts & Letters 45:59–76.

*Hickey, J. J. (ed.) 1969. Peregrine Falcon populations; their biology and decline. Univ. Wisc. Press, Madison, 596 p.

Hildreth, S. P. 1842. History of our early voyage on the Ohio and Mississippi Rivers, with historical sketches of the different points along them, etc., Amer. Pioneer 1(1):89–105, (4):128–145, March and April.

Hoffman, R. W. 1981. Animal resource exploitation patterns at the Toltec site: a zooarcheological study. M.A. thesis, Univ. Ark., Fayetteville, table 6.

Hoffman, R. W. 1983. Preliminary faunal analysis on the Albertson site, 3BE174 *in* appendix to Albertson site report by D. Dickson, Ark. Archeol. Surv. Research Series (in preparation).

Hofslund, P. B. 1959. Fall migration of Herring Gulls from Knife Island, Minnesota. Bird-Banding 30:104–114.

Hoiberg, A. J. 1951. Southern mature oak-pine stream bottomland. Audubon Field Notes 5:323–324.

Hoiberg, A. J. 1952. Southern mature oak-pine botomland. Audubon Field Notes 6:310.

Hoiberg, A. J. 1953a. Upland pine and pine-oak woodland. Audubon Field Notes 7:343–344.

Hoiberg, A. J. 1953b. Southern oak-pine stream bottomland. Audubon Field Notes 7:345–346.

Hoiberg, A. J. 1954a. Upland pine and pine-oak woodland. Audubon Field Notes 8:368–369.

Hoiberg, A. J. 1954b. Oak-pine stream bottomland. Audubon Field Notes 8:369.

Hoiberg, A. J. 1955a. Upland pine and pine-oak woodland. Audubon Field Notes 9:304–305.

Hoiberg, A. J. 1955b. Southern oak-pine stream bottomland. Audubon Field Notes 9:421–422.

Hoiberg, A. J. 1955c. Upland pine and pine-oak woodland. Audubon Field Notes 9:422.

Hoiberg, A. J. 1956a. Upland pine and pine-oak woodland. Audubon Field Notes 10:298–299.

Hoiberg, A. J. 1956b. Southern oak-pine stream bottomland. Audubon Field Notes 10:426.

Hoiberg, A. J. 1956c. Upland pine and pine-oak woodland. Audubon Field Notes 10:426–427.

Hoiberg, A. J. 1957a. Comments and comparisons, counts 20 and 21. Audubon Field Notes 11:304–305.

Hoiberg, A. J. 1957b. Southern oak-pine bottomland. Audubon Field Notes 11:442–444.

Hoiberg, A. J. 1957c. Upland pine and pine-oak woodland. Audubon Field Notes 11:444–447.

Hoiberg, A. J., and J. A. Hoiberg. 1952. Southern mature oak-pine bottomland. Audubon Field Notes 6:225–226.

Hoiberg, A. J., and J. A. Hoiberg. 1953a. Upland pine and pine-oak woodland. Audubon Field Notes 7:247–248.

Hoiberg, A. J., and J. A. Hoiberg. 1953b. Southern oak-pine stream bottomland. Audubon Field Notes 7:248–249.

Hoiberg, A. J., and J. A. Hoiberg. 1954a. Upland pine and pine-oak woodland. Audubon Field Notes 8:282–283.

Hoiberg, A. J., and J. A. Hoiberg. 1954b. Southern oak-pine stream bottomland. Audubon Field Notes 8:283.

Hoiberg, A. J., and J. A. Hoiberg. 1955. Southern oak-pine bottomland. Audubon Field Notes 9:305.

Hoiberg, A. J., and J. A. Hoiberg. 1956. Southern oak-pine bottomland. Audubon Field Notes 10:299.

Hoiberg, A. J., and J. A. Hoiberg. 1957. Southern oak-pine bottomland. Audubon Field Notes 11:303–304.

Hoiberg, A. J., and S. Hoiberg. 1957. Upland pine and pine-oak woodland. Audubon Field Notes 11:302–303.

Holder, T. H. 1951. A survey of Arkansas game. Ark. Game & Fish Comm., Little Rock, 155 p.

*Holder, T. H. 1970. Disappearing wetlands in eastern Arkansas. Ark. Planning Comm., Little Rock, 72 p.

Hollister, N. 1902. Notes on the winter birds of Arkansas. Wilson Bull. 9:10–15.

Holroyd, G. L., and J. G. Woods. 1975. Migration of the Saw-whet Owl in eastern North America. Bird-Banding 46:101–105.

Holt, J. G. 1979. Purple Sandpiper in West Tennessee. Migrant 50:63.

House, J. H. 1982. Powell Canal: Baytown period occupation on Bayou Macon in southeast Arkansas. Ark. Archeol. Surv. Research Series No. 19, p. 33.

Howell, A. H. 1911. Birds of Arkansas. U.S. Dept. Agric., Biol. Surv. Bull. No. 38, 100 p.

Howell, A. H. 1924. Bibliography of Arkansas birds, p. 167–171 in H. E. Wheeler, The Birds of Arkansas. Ark. Bureau Mines, Manufacturers, Agric., Little Rock.

*Hudson, C. M. 1976. The southeast Indians. Univ. Tennessee Press, Knoxville, 573 p.

Hudson J. E. 1972. A comparison of breeding bird populations at selected sites in the southern Appalachians and in the Boston Mountains. Dissertation Abstr. International 33B(10):4768.

Hunt, C. J. 1920. Sunlight and shadow. Condor 22:186.

Hunt, C. J. 1921a. Notes of the winter and early spring birds of southeastern Arkansas. Auk 38:370–381.

Hunt, C. J. 1921b. Additional notes on Arkansas birds. Auk 38:610–611.

Hunt, C. J. 1931. Notes on the winter birds of Arkansas. Auk 48:235–239.

Hunter, C. 1954. The value of bicolor and sericea field border plantings to quail in Arkansas. J. Wildl. Mgmt. 18:343–347.

Hunter, S., L. Allred, L. B. Barber II, E. G. H. Clark, G. G. Hawks, Jr., M. J. Lockerd, R. A. S. Lockerd, T. A. Nigh, M. A. Paulissen, and D. James. 1979. Environmental evaluation: use and expansion of the Graber method (a student-originated study of the Buffalo National River in Arkansas). Final Report for Nat. Sci. Foundation No. NSF SPI 79-05277, 298 p.

*Imhof, T. A. 1962. Alabama birds. Univ. Alabama Press. University, Ala., 591 p.

Jackson, J. A. 1971. The evolution, taxonomy, distribution, past populations and current status of the Red-cockaded Woodpecker, p. 4–29 in R. L. Thompson (ed.), The ecology and management of the Red-cockaded Woodpecker. Bur. Sport. Fish. & Wildlf., U.S. Dept. Interior and Tall Timbers Res. Sta., Tallahassee, Florida.

Jackson, J. A. 1977. Determination of the status of Red-cockaded Woodpecker colonies. J. Wildl. Mgmt. 41:448–452.

James, D. 1955. Immature oak-pine forest. Audubon Field Notes 9:420–421.

James, D. 1956a. Immature oak-pine forest. Audubon Field Notes 10:299.

James, D. 1956b. Mixed flood plain forest. Audubon Field Notes 10:299–300.

James, D. 1959. The changing seasons, a summary of the winter season. Audubon Field Notes 13:268–274.

James, D. 1960. Some recent findings concerning the avifauna of Arkansas. Ark. Acad. Sci. Proc. 14:8–13.

James, D. 1962. Winter 1961–1962: dominated by movements of boreal birds and marked by still low numbers of Eastern Bluebirds. Audubon Field Notes 16:306–311.

James, D. 1963. Winter 1962–1963: late arriving northern finches, interregional mixing of other faunas, and rising bluebird and eastern House Finch populations. Audubon Field Notes 17: 300–304.

James, D. 1964. Arkansas avifauna: some recent findings, 1960 to 1964. Ark. Acad. Sci. Proc. 28: 50–54.

James, D. 1967. Source and dispersal of migratory Arkansas birds. Final Report for National Institutes of Health, Res. Grants Nos. AI-05832-01 & AI-05832-02, 92 p.

James, D. 1969. The big grosbeak fly in. Ark. Audubon Newsletter 14(2):7.

James, D. 1972a. Failure to establish feral *Coturnix* Quail populations in Arkansas in the late 1950's. Ark. Acad. Sci. Proc. 31:27–29.

James, D. 1972b. Leatherwood Creek. Nature Conservancy News 22:7–9.

James, D. 1975. Avian movements between North and South America. Final Report for National Institutes of Health, Res. Grants Nos. AI-07365-01 & AI-07365-02, 125 p.

*James, D. 1980. In memorium, William J. Baerg, 1885–1980. Ark. Audubon Newsletter 25(2):1.

James, D. 1982. Checklist of the birds sighted in Arkansas. Ark. Acad. Sci. Biota Checklist No. 33, 9 p.

James, D., and F. L. Burnside, Jr. 1979a. Status of the Red-cockaded Woodpecker at the Felsenthal National Wildlife Refuge in Arkansas. Ark. Acad. Sci. Proc. 33:43–45.

James, D., and F. Burnside. 1979b. A study of the Red-cockaded Woodpecker in Arkansas. Ann. Report for Ark. Game & Fish Comm., Project No. E-1-2 (Job 11-A), 94 p.

James, D., E. E. Dale, Jr., M. J. Lockerd, D. Schick, and C. R. Preston. 1979. Appraisal of the avifauna, mammalian fauna, and plant communities at developmental sites proposed for the Buffalo National River. Final Report for National Park Service, SW Region, Contract No. CX702980013, 80 p.

James, D., and K. B. Davis, Jr. 1965. The effect of sublethal amounts of DDT on the discrimination ability of the Bobwhite. Amer. Zoologist 5:229.

James, D., L. G. Fooks, and J. R. Preston. 1983. Success of native-trapped compared to captivity-raised birds in restoring Wild Turkey populations to northwestern Arkansas. Ark. Acad. Sci. Proc. 37:38–41.

James, D. A., D. L. Hart, and F. L. Burnside. 1981. Study of the Red-cockaded Woodpecker in Arkansas. Final Report for Ark. Game & Fish Comm., Project E-1-5 (Job II), 143 p.

James, D., and F. C. James. 1964. The seasonal occurrences of Arkansas birds. Ark. Acad. Sci. Proc. 18:20–30.

James, D., M. J. Lockerd, C. R. Preston, and K. G. Smith. 1980. Avian community relationships at the Buffalo National River in Arkansas. Proc. 2nd Conf. on Scientific Res. in National Parks 12: 53–70. (National Park Serv.).

James, D., A. F. Posey, and D. H. White. 1975. Communities, continua, and ecotopes. Bull. Ecol. Soc. Amer. 56:21.

James, D., and J. R. Preston. 1959. An inventory in 1957 of the distribution of the Wild Turkey (*Meleagris gallopavo silvestrius Vieillot*) in the Ozark Plateau region of Arkansas. Ark. Acad. Sci. Proc. 13: 83–90.

James, D., and J. D. Rising. 1985. Identifying perplexing chickadee specimens from skeletal material. Ark. Acad. Sci. Proc. 39 (in press).

James, F. C. 1968a. A more precise definition of Bergmann's rule. Amer. Zoologist 8:815–816.

James, F. C. 1968b. Robins in early winter in the Ozarks. Ozark Soc. Bull. 2(1):5, 9.

James, F. C. 1968c. The Roadrunner. Ozark Soc. Bull. 2(4):7, 11.

James, F. C. 1970a. Geographic size variation in birds and its relationship to climate. Doctoral dissertation, Univ. Ark., Fayetteville, 61 p.

James, F. C. 1970b. Geographic size variation in birds and its relationship to climate. Ecology 51:365–390.

James, F. C. 1971. Ordinations of habitat relationships among breeding birds. Wilson Bull. 83: 215–236.

James, F. C. 1972. The Scissor-tailed Flycatcher. Ozark Soc. Bull. 32(3):3.

James, F. C. 1974. Threatened native birds of Arkansas, p. 107–122 *in* Ark. Natural Area Plan. Ark. Dept. Planning, Little Rock.

*James, F. C. 1983. Environmental component of morphological differentiation in birds. Science 221: 184–186.

James, F. C., R. F. Johnston, N. O. Wamer, G. J. Niemi, and W. J. Boecklen. 1984. The Grinnellian niche of the Wood Thrush. Amer. Naturalist 124:17–47.

James, F. C., and H. H. Shugart, Jr. 1970. A quantitative method of habitat description. Audubon Field Notes 24:727–736.

Jay, C. 1935. Eureka Springs, Ark., 1935 data. Oologist 52:68–69.

Johnsgard, P. A. 1967. Sympatry changes and hybridization incidence in Mallards and Black Ducks. Amer. Midland Naturalist 77:51–63.

Johnsgard, P. A., and R. E. Wood. 1968. Distributional changes and interaction between Prairie Chickens and Sharp-tailed Grouse in the Midwest. Wilson Bull. 80:173–188.

Johnson, D. M. 1979. Birds of Faulkner County,

Arkansas. Ark. Valley Audubon Soc., Conway, Ark., 16 p.

Joutel, H. 1966. The last voyage perform'd by de la Sale. Univ. Microfilms, Ann Arbor, Mich., 205 p.

Jurney, D. H. 1978. The Ridge house cellars: using faunal analysis to reconstruct meat diet. M.A. thesis, Univ. Ark., Fayetteville, p. 93–96.

Kaffka, J. 1970. White River Refuge: oasis in an ecological desert. Ark. Game & Fish 3(2):7–9.

Keener, R. W. 1969. A three-year comparison of breeding bird populations in Mississippi, Randolph and Clay counties of northeastern Arkansas. M.S. paper, Ark. State Univ., Jonesboro, 26 p.

Kennard, J. H. 1975. Longevity records of North American birds. Bird-Banding 46:55–73.

Kennerly, C. B. R. 1859. Report on birds collected on the route, p. 19–35 in U.S. War Dept., Explorations and surveys for a railroad route. Vol. 10, Pt. 6, Zoological Report, No. 3, (Whipple report).

Kessel, B. 1953. Distribution and migration of the European Starling in North America. Condor 55:49–67.

*Klinger, T. C. 1975–1978. An exceptional example of carved bone technology from the Lower Mississippi Valley. Ark. Archeol. 16–18:93–98.

*Kolb, H. 1965. The Audubon winter bird-population study. Audubon Field Notes 19:432–434.

*Küchler, A. W. 1964. Potential natural vegetation of the conterminous United States. Amer. Geographical Soc., Spec. Publ. No. 36, 116 p.

Lano, A. 1913. Greater Snow Goose in Arkansas. Auk 30:579.

Lano, A. 1921a. Prairie Chicken (*Tympanuchus americanus*) in Arkansas. Auk 38:112.

Lano, A. 1921b. American Osprey in Arkansas. Auk 38:113.

Lano, A. 1926a. Ring-billed Gull in Arkansas. Auk 43:87.

Lano, A. 1926b. Krider's Hawk in Arkansas. Auk 43:368.

Lano, A. 1927. Great Blue Heron electrocuted. Auk 44:246.

Latrobe, C. J. 1835. The rambler in North America. Harper & Bros., N.Y. 2 vols.

Lavers, N. 1979. Hovering flight in Red-tailed Hawks (*Buteo jamaicensis*). Ark. Acad. Sci. Proc. 33:84.

Lavers, N. 1980. Sage Thrasher (*Oreoscoptes montanus*), a new state record. Ark. Acad. Sci. Proc. 34:122.

Lawrence, L. 1976. Grassland ecology of wintering and nesting species of birds at the Jonesboro airport. M.S. thesis, Ark. State Univ., Jonesboro, 31 p.

Lawrie, A. 1944. Lawrie's trip to northeastern Texas, 1854–1855. S. W. Historical Quart. 48:238–253.

Le Page du Pratz, A. S. 1763. The history of Louisiana. T. Becket and P. A. De Hondt, London. 2 vols.

*Lesquereux, L. 1860. Botanical and palaeontological report of the geological state survey of Arkansas, p. 295–400 in D. D. Owen, Second report of a geological reconnoissance of the middle and southern counties of Arkansas. C. Sherman & Son, Philadelphia.

Lewis A. 1932. La Harpe's expedition on the Arkansas, p. 61–85 in Along the Arkansas. Southwest Press, Dallas.

Lincoln, F. C. 1922. Trapping ducks for banding purposes. Auk 39:322–334.

Lincoln, F. C. 1924. Returns from banded birds, 1920–1923. U.S. Dept. Agric., Dept. Bull. No. 1268, 55 p.

Lincoln, F. C. 1927. Returns from banded birds 1923 to 1926. U.S. Dept. Agric., Tech. Bull. No. 32, 95 p.

Lincoln, F. C. 1932. State distribution of returns from banded birds. Bird-Banding 3:140–142.

Lincoln, F. C. 1933. State distribution of returns from banded ducks. Bird-Banding 4:19–32, 88–99, 132–146, 177–189.

Lincoln, F. C. 1936a. Recoveries of banded birds of prey. Bird-Banding 7:38–45.

Lincoln, F. C. 1936b. Returns from banded birds: second paper. Bird-Banding 7:121–128.

Lincoln, F. C. 1947. Bullock's Oriole in Arkansas. Auk 64:318–320.

Lockerd, R. S., M. J. Lockerd, S. Hunter, L. Allred, L. B. Barber II, E. G. H. Clark, G. G. Hawks, Jr., T. A. Nigh, and M. A. Paulissen. 1980. Environmental Evaluation of the Buffalo National River using the Graber method. Proc. 2nd Conf. on Scientific Res. in National Parks 7:397–421. (National Park Serv.).

Lowery, G. H., Jr. 1974. Louisiana birds, 3rd Ed. Louisiana State Univ. Press, Baton Rouge, 651 p.

Lowery, R., and E. L. Hanebrink. 1967. The subspecies and ecology of meadowlarks in northeast Arkansas. Ark. Acad. Sci. Proc. 21:26–32.

Ludwig, C. C. 1953. Bronzed Grackles. Bird-Banding 24:154–155.

MacArthur, R. H. 1959. On the breeding distribution pattern of North American migrant birds. Auk 76:318–325.

Madson, J. B. 1975. The crowd goes turkey hunting. Ark. Game & Fish 7(3):18–21.

Magee, M. J. 1932. Some banding results after eleven years of banding at Sault Ste. Marie, Michigan 1921 to 1931. Bird-Banding 3:111–113.

Magee, M. J. 1935. Eastern Purple Finch recoveries in and away from the eastern part of the upper peninsula of Michigan. Bird-Banding 6:102–103.

Marquette, J., and L. Joliet. 1673. An account of the discovery of some new countries and nations in North America in 1673, in Historical Collections of Louisiana. Compiled by B. F. French, part 2, Phila., 1850.

Mattocks, P., Jr. 1960a. Deciduous creek bottom with canebrake. Audubon Field Notes 14:490–491.

Mattocks, P., Jr. 1960b. Upland mixed forest. Audubon Field Notes 14:496–497.

Mattocks, P. W., Jr. 1961a. Upland mixed forest. Audubon Field Notes 15:364.

Mattocks, P. W., Jr. 1961b. Deciduous creek bottom with canebrake. Audubon Field Notes 15:368.

Mattocks, P. W., Jr. 1961c. Deciduous creek bottom with canebreak. Audubon Field Notes 15:502.

Mattocks, P. W., Jr. 1961d. Upland mixed forest. Audubon Field Notes 15:510–511.

Mattocks, P. W., Jr. 1962. Upland mixed forest. Audubon Field Notes 16:371.

Mattocks, P., Jr., and H. Shugart. 1962. Birds of South-Central Arkansas. S. Ark. Audubon Soc., El Dorado, Ark., 12 p.

McAtee, W. L. 1911. Local names of waterfowl and other birds. Forest & Stream 77:172–174.

McAtee, W. L. 1923. Ducks useful in Arkansas as scavengers of red rice. Auk 40:527–528.

McAtee, W. L. 1931. Local names of migratory game birds. U.S. Dept. Agric., Misc. Circ. No. 13, 95 p.

McDaniel, V. R., and J. E. Gardner. 1977. Cave fauna in Arkansas: vertebrate taxa. Proc. Ark. Acad. Sci. 31:68–71.

*McGimsey, C. R. 1969. Indians of Arkansas. Ark. Archeol. Surv. Popular Series No. 1, p. 4, 47.

McKinley, D. 1960. The Carolina Parakeet in pioneer Missouri. Wilson Bull. 72:274–287.

McKinley, D. 1964. History of the Carolina Parakeet in its southwestern range. Wilson Bull. 76:68–93.

*McKinley, D. 1980. The balance of decimating factors and recruitment in extinction of the Carolina Parakeet. Indiana Audubon Quart. 58(1): 8–18, (2):50–61, (3):103–104.

McKinley, D., and D. James. 1984. A summary account of the Carolina Parakeet in Arkansas. Ark. Acad. Sci. Proc. 38:64–67.

McKnight, E. T. 1929. Bird-Lore's twenty-ninth Christmas census. Rush, Ark. Bird-Lore 31:59.

Meanley, B. 1951. Vermilion Flycatcher in Arkansas rice district. Wilson Bull. 63:203–204.

Meanley, B. 1952a. Notes on nesting Traill's Flycatcher in eastern Arkansas. Wilson Bull. 64:111–112.

Meanley, B. 1952b. Notes of the ecology of the Short-billed Marsh Wren in the lower Arkansas rice fields. Wilson Bull. 64:22–25.

Meanley, B. 1953. Nesting of the King Rail in the Arkansas rice fields. Auk 70:262–269.

Meanley, B. 1954. Nesting of the Water-turkey in eastern Arkansas. Wilson Bull. 66:81–88.

Meanley, B. 1955. A nesting study of the Little Blue Heron in eastern Arkansas. Wilson Bull. 67:84–89.

Meanley, B. 1956a. Food habits of the King Rail in the Arkansas rice fields. Auk 73:252–258.

Meanley, B. 1956b. Banding blackbirds in a rice field reservoir roost. Bird-Banding 27:170–171.

Meanley, B. 1956c. Foods of the Wild Turkey in the White River bottomlands of southeastern Arkansas. Wilson Bull. 68:305–311.

Meanley, B. 1957. Notes on the courtship behavior of the King Rail. Auk 74:433–440.

Meanley, B. 1960. Fall food of the Sora Rail in the Arkansas rice fields. J. Wildl. Mgmt 24:339.

Meanley, B. 1963. Nesting ecology and habits of the Dickcissel on the Arkansas Grand Prairie. Wilson Bull. 75:280.

Meanley, B. 1964. Origin, structure, molt, and dispersal of a late summer Red-winged Blackbird population. Bird-Banding 35:32–38.

Meanley, B. 1965. The roosting behavior of the Red-winged Blackbird in the southern United States. Wilson Bull. 77:217–228.

Meanley, B. 1968. Singing behavior of the Swainson's Warbler. Wilson Bull. 80:72–77.

Meanley, B. 1969a. Natural history of the King Rail. U.S. Bur. Sport Fish & Wildl., North Amer. Fauna No. 67, 108 p.

Meanley, B. 1969b. Pre-nesting and nesting behavior of the Swainson's Warbler. Wilson Bull. 81:246–257.

Meanley, B. 1970. Molts and plumages of the Red-winged Blackbird with particular reference to fall migration. Bird-Banding 41:22–27.

Meanley, B. 1971a. Blackbirds and the southern rice crop. U.S. Fish & Wildl. Serv. Resource Publ. No. 100, 64 p.

Meanley, B. 1971b. Natural history of the Swainson's Warbler. U.S. Bur. Sport Fish & Wildl., North Amer. Fauna No. 69, 90 p.

Meanley, B. 1972. Swamps, river bottoms and canebrakes. Barre Publishers, Barre, Mass., 142 p.

Meanley, B. 1976. Distribution and ecology of blackbird and Starling roosts in the United States. Prog. Rep. under work units P-F-25.1, 25.2, Patuxent Wildl. Res. Center, U.S. Fish & Wildl. Serv., Laurel, Maryland. 82 p.

Meanley, B., and J. A. Neff. 1953a. Bird notes from the Grand Prairie of Arkansas. Wilson Bull. 65:200–201.

Meanley, B., and J. A. Neff. 1953b. Food habits of the Bobolink in Arkansas rice fields. Auk 70:211–212.

Meanley, B., and J. S. Webb. 1963. Nesting ecology and reproductive rate of the Red-winged Blackbird in tidal marshes of the upper Chesapeake Bay region. Chesapeake Science 4:90–100.

Meanley, B., and J. S. Webb. 1968. Nationwide population estimates of blackbirds and Starlings. Atlantic Naturalist 20:189–191.

Mehner, J. F. 1959. Distribution and migration of the

Robin in southern Michigan and western Pennsylvania. Jack Pine Warbler 37:68–73.

Mendall, H. L., and C. M. Aldous. 1943. The ecology and management of the American Woodcock. Maine Coop. Wildl. Res. Unit, Orono, Maine, 39 p.

Mengel, R. M., and J. A. Jackson. 1977. Geographic variation of the Red-cockaded Woodpecker. Condor 79:349–355.

Merrill, D. E. 1934. Starling in Benton County, Arkansas. Auk 52:191.

Miller, H. A., and N. R. Ax. 1940. Bird-Lore's fortieth Christmas bird census. White River Migratory Waterfowl Refuge, St. Charles, Ark. Bird-Lore 42:116.

Mitchell, R. H. 1894. Capture of Clarke's Nutcracker in Crittenden County, Arkansas. Auk 11:327.

Möllhausen, B. 1858. Diary of a journey from Mississippi to the coasts of the Pacific. Longman, Brown, Green, Longmans & Roberts, London. 2 vols.

Mondecar, M. C. 1982. The effect of pairing on activity pattern of the White-throated Sparrow, *Zonotrichia albicollis* (Gmelin). Doctoral dissertation, Univ. Ark., Fayetteville, 45 p.

Moore, C. B. 1911. Some aboriginal sites on Mississippi River. J. Acad. Nat. Science, Philadelphia, 14:414–449.

Morphew, L. R. 1907. Arkansas birds. Forest & Stream 68:536.

Morse, D. F. 1982. Regional overview of northeast Arkansas, p. 20–37 *in* Arkansas archeology in review, ed. by N. L. Trubowitz and M. D. Jeter. Ark. Archeol. Sur. Research Series, No. 15.

Morse, D. F. 1984. A Nodena Phase infant burial in northeast Arkansas. Field Notes, No. 200, p. 3–8 (Ark. Archeol. Soc. Newsletter).

Neal, J. 1981. In the noose of a shrinking habitat. Ark. Game & Fish 12(3):22–26.

Neal, J. 1983. Bird records for the Ozarks in northwestern Arkansas, an annotated list. N.W. Ark. Audubon Soc., Fayetteville, 28 p.

Neal, J. C. 1985. Pre-Peterson bird watchers of Arkansas. Field Notes, No. 203, p. 5–8 (Ark. Archeol. Soc. Newsletter).

Neal, J. C. 1986. Birds of the Western Arkansas Ozarks: an annotated list. N. W. Ark. Audubon Soc., Fayetteville, 49 p.

Neff, J. A. n.d. Migratory blackbirds and crop damage. U.S. Fish & Wildl. Serv. and Univ. Ark. Agric. Ext. Serv., 17 p.

Neff, J. A. 1949a. Frightening blackbirds from rice fields. U.S. Fish & Wildl. Serv. and Ark. Agric. Ext. Serv., Misc. Publ. 30, 7 p.

Neff, J. A. 1949b. Blackbird depredations on Arkansas rice fields. Trans. 14th N. Amer. Wildl. Conf., p. 556–566.

Neff, J. A., and B. Meanley. 1952. Experiences in banding blackbirds in eastern Arkansas. Bird-Banding 23:154–157.

Neff, J. A., and B. Meanley. 1957a. Blackbirds and the Arkansas rice crop. Univ. Ark. Agric. Exp. Sta. (and U.S. Fish & Wildl. Serv.) Bull. No. 584, 89 p.

Neff, J. A., and B. Meanley. 1957b. Status of Brewer's Blackbird on the Grand Prairie of eastern Arkansas. Wilson Bull. 69:102–105.

Nice, M. M. 1948. Late spring in Arkansas. Chicago Naturalist 10:42–49.

Nice, M. M., and R. H. Thomas. 1948. A nesting of the Carolina Wren. Wilson Bull. 60:139–158.

*Norris, D. J., and W. H. Elder. 1982. Decline of the Roadrunner in Missouri. Wilson Bull. 94:354–355.

Nuttall, T. 1821. A journal of travels into the Arkansa Territory, during the year 1819. T. W. Palmer, Philadelphia, 296 p.

Nuttall, T. 1832. A manual of the ornithology of the United States and Canada. The Land Birds, Hilliard & Brown, Cambridge, 683 p.

Oberholzer, H. C. 1917. Critical notes on the eastern subspecies of *Sitta carolinensis* Latham. Auk 34:181–187.

Oberholzer, H. C. 1918a. The migration of North American birds. Second Series. II. The Scarlet and Louisiana Tanagers. Bird-Lore 20:16–19.

Oberholzer, H. C. 1918b. The migration of North American birds. Second Series. III. The Summer and Hepatic Tanagers, Martins and Barn Swallow. Bird-Lore 20:145–152.

Oberholzer, H. C. 1918c. The migration of North American birds. Second Series. IV. The waxwings and Phainopepla. Bird-Lore 20:219–222.

Oberholzer, H. C. 1920. The migration of North American birds. Second Series. XIV. Cowbirds. Bird-Lore 22:343–345.

Oberholzer, H. C. 1921. The geographic races of *Cyanocitta cristata*. Auk 38:83–89.

Oberholzer, H. C. 1922. The migration of North American birds. Second Series. XX. Baltimore Oriole. Bird-Lore 24:338–341.

Oberholzer, H. C. 1923. The migration of North American birds. Second Series. XXI. Orchard Oriole. Bird-Lore 25:119–120.

*Ogden, J. C., and S. A. Nesbitt. 1979. Recent Wood Stork population trends in the United States. Wilson Bull. 91:512–523.

O'Halloran, P. L., and C. P. Stone. 1964. Intensive blackbird decoy trapping in northeastern Arkansas. U.S. Fish & Wildl. Serv., Patuxent Wildl. Res. Cent. Spec. Rept., 27 p.

Old-Timer. 1899. Duck hunting in Arkansas. Amer. Field 52:181.

Owen, C. M. 1935. Bay-breasted Warbler in Arkansas. Auk 52:314.

*Owen, D. D. 1858. First report of a geological reconnoissance of the northern counties of Arkansas.

Johnson & Yerkes, State Printers, Little Rock, 256 p.

*Owen, D. D. 1860. Second report of a geological reconnoissance of the middle and southern counties of Arkansas. C. Sherman & Son, Philadelphia, 433 p.

Owens, D. F. 1963. Polymorphism in the Screech Owl in eastern North America. Wilson Bull. 75:183–190.

Owens, L. 1972. Turkey bagged in '72. Ark. Game & Fish 5(2):15.

Paige, K. N., C. T. McAllister, and C. R. Tumlison. 1979. Unusual results from pellet analysis of the American Barn Own *Tyto alba pratincola* (Bonaparte). Ark. Acad. Sci. Proc. 33:88–89.

Parker, J. W., and J. C. Ogden. 1979. The recent history and status of the Mississippi Kite. Amer. Birds 33:119–129.

Parmalee, P. W. 1962. Identification of the faunal remains from the Lawhorn site, Appendix A, p. 95–96 *in* The Lawhorn site by J. Moselage. Missouri Archeol. 24.

Parmalee, P. W. 1966. Animal remains from the Banks site, p. 142–145 *in* G. Perino, The Banks Village Site, Crittenden Co., Arkansas. Mem. Missouri Archaeol. Soc., No. 4.

Peakall, D. B. 1970. The Eastern Bluebird: its breeding season, clutch size, and nesting success. Living Bird 9:239–255.

*Peck, W. B. 1981. W. J. Baerg, 1885–1980. J. Arachnol. 9:115–116.

Pell, B. 1983. The natural divisions of Arkansas: a revised classification and description. Natural Areas Journal 3:12–23.

Perino, G. 1966. The Banks village site. Mem. Missouri Archeol. Soc. No. 4, 161 p.

Perino, G. 1967. Report on field burials 24, 26, and 28 at the Haley Place, Miller County, Arkansas. Okla. Anthropol. Soc. Newsletter 15 (5):1–8.

Perkins, S. E., III. 1932. The Indiana Bronzed Grackle migration. Bird-Banding 3:85–94.

Pettingill, O. S., Jr. 1936. The American Woodcock. Memoirs Boston Soc. Nat. Hist. 9:167–391.

Pettingill, O. S., Jr. 1981. A guide to bird finding west of the Mississippi. Oxford Univ. Press, N.Y., 783 p.

Pharris, L. 1983. A different drummer in Arkansas. Ark Game & Fish 14(1):10–12.

Pharris, L. D., S. Chaney, and M. Cartwright. 1983. Preliminary evaluation of Ruffed Grouse restoration efforts in Arkansas. Proc. 37th Ann. Conf. S.E. Assoc. Fish & Wildl. Agencies (in press).

*Phillips, P., and J. A. Brown. 1978. Pre-Columbian shell engravings from the Craig mound at Spiro, Oklahoma, part 1, Peabody Mus., Cambridge, Plates 19, 86, 89, 112, 121, and Fig. 242, p. 186.

Phillips, P., J. Ford, and J. Griffin. 1951. Archeological survey of the Lower Mississippi Alluvial Valley, 1940–1947. Peabody Museum, Cambridge.

Philquist, G. E. 1932. Arkansas migration. Oologist 49:108.

Pierce, R. A., and R. T. Kirkwood. 1977. Evaluation of plantings for wildlife on a power line right of way in southern Arkansas. Proc. Ark. Acad. Sci. 31:83–89.

Pindar, L. O. 1924. Winter birds in eastern Arkansas. Wilson Bull. 36:201–207.

Pirnie, M. D. 1932. Fall migration of the Black Duck from northern Michigan. Papers Mich. Acad. Sci. Arts & Letters 15:485–490.

*Pitelka, F. 1950. Geographic variation and the species problem in the shorebird genus *Limnodromus*. U. Calif. Publ. Zool. 50:1–108.

Plank, W. 1911. Notes on the Olive-sided Flycatcher. Oologist 28:154.

Pleas, C. E. 1888. Van Buren County, Arkansas, Notes. Oologist 5:124–125.

Pleas, C. E. 1889. Arkansas notes. Oologist 6:130.

Pleas, C. E. 1890a. Chuck-will's-widow at Clinton, Arkansas. Oologist 7:142.

Pleas, C. E. 1890b. The Caprimulgidae in Arkansas. Oologist 7:155–156.

Pleas, C. E. 1890c. Fairies in a Fairyland. Oologist 7:215–218.

Pleas, C. E. 1892a. Spring openers. Oologist 9:142–143.

Pleas, C. E. 1892b. Some of our visitors and neighbors. Oologist 9:160–161.

Pleas, C. E. 1895. From a rusty pen. Oologist 12:155–156.

Pleas, C. E. 1896. The story of a find. Oologist 13:34–36.

Pleas, C. E. 1897. Carolina Rail at a high elevation. Osprey 1:67.

Pleas, L. 1891a. Feeding the birds in winter. Oologist 8:156–157.

Pleas, L. 1891b. The Screech Owl. Oologist 8:195–196.

Pleas, L. 1891c. The great Carolina Wren. Oologist 8:215–216.

Pleas, L. 1891d. The Pileated Woodpecker. Oologist 8:236–237.

Pleas, L. 1891e. The Blue-gray Gnatcatcher in Arkansas. Oologist 8:239–240.

Pleas, L. 1892. Our winter visitors. Oologist 9:44–45.

Pleas, L. 1897. A baby Ruby-throated Hummingbird. Osprey 1:136–137.

Posey, A. F. 1974. Vegetational habitats of breeding birds in Ozark shrubby old fields. Doctoral dissertation, Univ. Ark., Fayetteville, 42 p.

Preston, C. R. 1978. Ecological separation among color morphs of the Red-tailed Hawk wintering in northwestern Arkansas. M.S. thesis, Univ. Ark., Fayetteville, 25 p.

Preston, C. R. 1980. Differential perch site selection by color morphs of the Red-tailed Hawk (*Buteo jamaicensis*). Auk 97:782–789.

Preston, C. R. 1981. Environmental influence on soaring in wintering Red-tailed Hawks. Wilson Bull. 93:350–356.

Preston, C. R. 1982. Territoriality, space utilization, and autumn clan composition in the Tufted Titmouse (*Parus bicolor*). Doctoral dissertation, Univ. Ark., Fayetteville, 42 p.

Ragsdale, G. H. 1889. On the hiatus existing between the breeding ranges of the Loggerhead and White-rumped Shrikes. Auk 6:224–226.

Reynolds, H. S. 1877. Winter birds of Arkansas. Amer. Naturalist 11:307–308.

*Reynolds, J. H., and D. Y. Thomas. 1910. History of the University of Arkansas. Univ. Ark., Fayetteville, 555 p.

Rhinehart, R. R. 1984. Arthropod abundance and the distribution of forest birds breeding in the Ozarks. M.S. thesis, Univ. Ark., Fayetteville, 33 p.

*Robbins, C. S. 1979. Effect of forest fragmentation on bird populations, p. 198–212 *in* R. M. DeGraaf and K. E. Evans (eds.), Management of north central and northeastern forests for nongame birds. U.S. Dept. Agric. Forest Serv. Gen. Tech. Rpt. NC-51.

Roberts, R. W., G. C. Branner, and M. R. Owens (eds.). 1942. Arkansas' natural resources—their conservation and use. The disappearance of wild animal species. Democrat Printing & Lithographing Co., Little Rock, p. 294–296.

Robertson, J. M. 1929. Some results of bird banding in 1928. Condor 31:242–247.

Robinson, E. R. 1931. The pigeon roosts at Wattensas and Old Brownville, p. 174–176 *in* F. W. Allsopp, Folklore of romantic Arkansas. The Grolier Soc., vol. 1.

Rolingson, M. A. (ed.). 1982. Emerging patterns of Plum Bayou Culture. Ark. Archeol. Surv. Research Series No. 18, p. 60.

Rolingson, M. A., and F. F. Schambach. 1981. The Shallow Lake site. Ark. Archeol. Surv. Research Series No. 12, p. 57.

Roth, E. A. 1977. Faunal subsistence patterns, p. 23–3, 4 *in* D. F. and P. A. Morse (eds.), Excavation, data interpretation, and report on the Zebree homestead site, Mississippi County, Arkansas. Manuscript on file, Ark. Archeol. Surv., Fayetteville.

Roth, R. R. 1976. Effects of a severe thunderstorm on airborne ducks. Wilson Bull. 88:654–656.

Rowland, E. O. (Mrs. Dunbar Rowland). 1930. Life, letters and papers of William Dunbar. Miss. Historical Soc., Jackson, 410 p.

*Russell, R. P., Jr. 1983. The Piping Plover in the Great Lakes region. Amer. Birds 37:951–955.

*Sabo, G., D. B. Waddell, and J. H. House. 1982. A cultural resource overview of the Ozark-St. Francis National Forests. U.S. Dept. Agric. Forest Serv. South Region, p. 67–75.

Samson, F. B. 1971. Migration of resident and migrant Canada Geese banded at Necedah National Wildlife Refuge. Bird-Banding 42:115–118.

*Schantz, V. S. 1940. Arthur H. Howell (1872–1940). J. Mammology 21:384–388.

Schoolcraft, H. R. 1821. Journal of a tour into the interior of Missouri and Arkansaw. Printed for Sir R. Phillips & Co., London, 102 p.

Schorger, A. W. 1955. The Passenger Pigeon, its natural history and extinction. Univ. Wisc. Press, Madison, 424 p.

Shepherd, W. M. 1983. The migrant shrike. Ark. Audubon Newsletter 28(2):2.

Shepherd, W. M. 1985. Arkansas River surveyed for Least Terns. Directions 4 (4):4. Dept. of Ark. Heritage, Little Rock, p. 7.

Short, J. J. 1975. The relationships of breeding bird communities in North America based on species composition population levels, and diversity. M.S. thesis, Univ. Ark., Fayetteville, 55 p.

Short, J. J. 1979. Patterns of alpha-diversity and abundance in breeding bird communities across North America. Condor 81:21–27.

Shufeldt, R. W. 1913. Further studies of fossil birds with descriptions of new and extinct species. Bull. Amer. Mus. Nat. Hist. 33(Art. 16):285–306.

Shugart, H. 1959. Disturbed bottomland deciduous forest and edge. Audubon Field Notes 13:472.

Shugart, H. 1960a. Deciduous creek bottom. Audubon Field Notes 14:490.

Shugart, H. 1960b. Bottomland deciduous forest and edge. Audubon Field Notes 14:501–502.

Shugart, H. 1961a. Deciduous creek bottom. Audubon Field Notes 15:501–502.

Shugart, H. 1961b. Bottomland deciduous forest and edge. Audubon Field Notes 15:522.

Shugart, H. H., Jr. 1968. Ecological succession of breeding bird populations in northwestern Arkansas. M.S. thesis, Univ. Ark., Fayetteville, 62 p.

Shugart, H. H., Jr., and D. James. 1973. Ecological succession of breeding bird populations in northwestern Arkansas. Auk 90:62–77.

Shugart, H. H., Jr., and D. James. 1975. Errata and addenda for ecological succession of breeding bird populations in northwestern Arkansas. Auk 92:428.

Shugart, H., L. Goodwin, and R. Harris. 1958. Bottomland deciduous forest and edge. Audubon Field Notes 12:454–455.

Singleton, R. 1973. Species composition and behavior of herons and egrets at the Burdette heronry in northeastern Arkansas. M.S. thesis, Ark. State Univ., 45 p.

Smith, A. P. 1915. Birds of the Boston Mountains, Arkansas. Condor 17:41–51.

Smith, B. D. 1975. Middle Mississippi exploitation of animal populations. Mus. Anthropology, Univ. Mich., Anthropological Papers no. 57, Appendix B, p. 171–173.

Smith, J. M. 1844–1886. Personal journal, 2 vols. Univ. Ark. Library Spec. Coll., Fayetteville.

Smith, J. W. 1959. Movements of Michigan Herring Gulls. Bird-Banding 30:69–104.

Smith, K. G. 1975. Distribution of summer birds along a forest moisture gradient in an Ozark watershed. M.S. thesis, Univ. Ark., Fayetteville, 34 p.

Smith, K. G. 1977. Distribution of summer birds along a forest moisture gradient in an Ozark watershed. Ecology 58:810–819.

Smith, K. G. 1985. Wintering of Spotted Sandpiper at a thermal reservoir in northwest Arkansas. S.W. Naturalist 30:310–311.

Smith, K. G. 1986a. Population dynamics of Red-headed Woodpecker, Blue Jay, and Northern Mockingbird in the Ozarks. Am. Midland Naturalist 115:52–62.

Smith, K. G. 1986b. Downy Woodpecker feeding on mud-dauber wasp nests. S.W. Naturalist 31:134.

Smith, K. L. 1984. Animal species, pp. 48–70 in B. Shepherd (ed.), Arkansas's Natural Heritage. August House, Little Rock, Ark.

Smith, N. C. 1966. Populations of game animals and small animals in the forest and old field habitats in northwestern Arkansas. M.S. thesis, Univ. Ark., Fayetteville, 50 p.

Smith, R. A., and E. L. Hanebrink. 1982. Analysis of regurgitated Short-eared Owl (*Asio flammeus*) pellets from the Roth Prairie, Arkansas County, Arkansas. Ark. Acad. Sci. Proc. 36:106–107.

Smith, W. P. 1942. A White-crowned Sparrow recovery. Bird-Banding 13:182.

Stack, J. W., and R. L. Harned. 1944. Seventeen years of banding White-throated Sparrows and Slate-colored Juncos at Michigan State College. Bird-Banding 15:1–14.

Stephenson, L. M. 1895. Why are there so few bluebirds? Forest & Stream 45:510–511.

Stepney, P. H. R. 1975. Wintering distribution of Brewer's Blackbird: historical aspect, recent changes, and fluctuations. Bird-Banding 46:106–125.

Stevens, O. A. 1944. Fifteen years banding at Fargo, North Dakota. Bird-Banding 15:138–144.

Stevens, O. A. 1956. Harris' Sparrow transient return; other sparrow records. Bird-Banding 27:33.

Stewart, P. A. 1952. Dispersal, breeding behavior, and longevity of banded Barn Owls in North America. Auk 69:227–245.

Stewart, P. A. 1959. The "romance" of the Wood Duck. Audubon Magazine 61:62–65.

Stewart, P. A. 1977. Radial dispersal and southward migration of Wood Ducks banded in Vermont. Bird-Banding 48:333–336.

Stillwell, J., and N. Stillwell. 1952. Bird songs of dooryard, field and forest. Vol. 1. (33⅓ rpm record). Flicker Recording Service, Old Greenwich, Conn.

Stillwell, J., and N. Stillwell. 1953. Bird songs of dooryard, field and forest. Vol. 2. (33⅓ rpm record). Flicker Recording Service, Old Greenwich, Conn.

Stillwell, J., and N. Stillwell. 1958. The national network of bird songs. Three 30 cm 33⅓ rpm discs, C101, C107, and C109. Flicker Recording Service, Old Greenwich, Conn.

Stillwell, N. 1964. Bird songs. Doubleday, N.Y., p. 87–104, 125–126.

Stoner, D. 1936. Further evidence on Blue Jay migration. Bird-Banding 7:170–171.

Strait, L. E., and N. F. Sloan. 1975. Movements and mortality of juvenile White Pelicans from North Dakota. Wilson Bull. 87:54–59.

Styles, B. W., and J. R. Purdue. 1984. Faunal exploitation at the Cedar Grove site, p. 211–226 in Cedar Grove; N. L. Trubowitz, ed. Ark. Archeol. Surv. Research Series, No. 23.

Sullivan, J. 1978. The impact of lead poisoning in waterfowl. Ark. Game & Fish 10(3):2–5.

Sutton, G. M. 1967. Oklahoma Birds. Univ. Oklahoma Press, Norman, 674 p.

Sutton, G. M. 1974. A check-list of Oklahoma birds. Contrib. Stovall Mus., Univ. Okla., Norman, 48 p.

*Swanton, J. R. 1946. The Indians of the southeastern United States. Bull. Bur. Am. Ethnol., No. 137. Wash., D.C., p. 295, 298, 658–661.

Taber, W. B., Jr. 1930. The fall migration of Mourning Doves. Wilson Bull. 42:17–28.

Tanner, J. T. 1942. The Ivory-billed Woodpecker. Natl. Audubon Soc., N.Y., 111 p.

Thomas, R. A. 1969. Breckenridge: a stratified shelter in northwest Arkansas. M.A. thesis, Univ. Ark., Fayetteville, p. 119.

Thomas, R. A. 1975. Effects of variable brood size on growth and development of nestling Barn Swallows (*Hirundo rustica*). M.S. thesis, Univ. Ark., Fayetteville, 45 p.

Thomas, R. H. 1941a. "Anting" by Summer Tanager. Auk 58:102.

Thomas, Mrs. R. 1941b. Thrasher adjusts life habits to physical disability. Bird-Banding 12:72–73.

Thomas, R. H. 1941c. Ticks affecting birds' eyesight. Auk 58:590–591.

Thomas, R. H. 1946a. Return of winter-resident Mockingbirds in Arkansas. Wilson Bull. 58:53–54.

Thomas, R. H. 1946b. Catbird "anting" with a leaf. Wilson Bull. 58:112.

Thomas, R. H. 1946c. A study of Eastern Bluebirds in Arkansas. Wilson Bull. 58:143–183.

Thomas, R. H. 1946d. An Orchard Oriole colony in Arkansas. Bird-Banding 17:161–167.

Thomas, R. 1952. Crip, come home. Harper and Bros., N.Y., 175 p.

Thwaites, R. G. (ed.) 1896–1901. The Jesuit relations and allied documents. Burrows Bros., Cleveland. 73 vols.

Tomer, J. S. 1959. An Oklahoma record of the Yellow Rail. Auk 76:94.

Tulsa Audubon Society. 1973. Bird finding guide. Tulsa, Okla., p. 98–101.

Turner, J. E. 1966. The effects of DDT in the diet on group behavior, learning ability, and liver glycogen level in the Bobwhite Colinus virginianus (Linnaeus). M.S. thesis, Univ. Ark., Fayetteville, 74 p.

U.S. National Museum. 1949. Accession 168156, cat. no. 347764, Nov. 7, 1949.

Vaiden, M. G. 1940. The Starling in Mississippi. Oologist 57:43–44.

Vaiden, M. G. 1964. Notes on Mississippi birds. Occ. Pap. Miss. Nat. Club 1(8):1–4.

Wagner, G. 1933. Mortality in Marsh Hawks. Bird-Banding 4:50–51.

Wall, M. L., and W. H. Whitcomb. 1964. The effect of bird predators on winter survival of the southwestern and European corn borers in Arkansas. J. Kansas Entomol. Soc. 37:187–189.

Warner, A. C. 1966. Breeding-range expansion of the Scissor-tailed Flycatcher into Missouri and in other states. Wilson Bull. 79:289–300.

*Warren, L. O. 1980. William Baerg, 1885–1980. Bull. Entomol. Soc. Am. 26:136–137.

Watt, D. J. 1975. Comparison of the foraging behavior of the Carolina Chickadee and Tufted Titmouse in northwestern Arkansas. M.S. thesis, Univ. Ark., Fayetteville, 40 p.

Weaver, R. L. 1940. The Purple Finch invasion of northeastern United States and the maritime provinces in 1939. Bird-Banding 11:79–105.

Webb, J. S., and B. Meanley. 1963. Breeding Red-winged Blackbird populations of the Arkansas Grand Prairie. Ann. Prog. Report, Patuxent Wildl. Res. Center (1963), p. 117–118.

Wenger, J. D. 1975. Geographical variation and migratory movements in the Blue Jay (Cyanocitta cristata). Doctoral dissertation, Univ. Ark., Fayetteville, 56 p.

Wetherbee, D. K., and K. F. Jacobs. 1961. Migration of the common Coturnix in North America. Bird-Banding 32:85–91.

Wetmore, A. 1912. New records from Arkansas. Auk 29:112.

Wetmore, A. 1918. Bird-Lore's Christmas census. Bird-Lore 20:45.

Wetmore, A. 1940. A check-list of the fossil birds of North America. Smithsonian Misc. Collec. 99(4): 1–81.

Wetmore, A. 1959. Notes on certain grouse of the Pleistocene. Wilson Bull. 71:178.

Wharton, W. P. 1934. A Black-throated Green Warbler recovery. Bird-Banding 5:135.

Wharton, W. P. 1953. Recoveries of birds banded at Groton, Massachusetts, 1932–1950. Bird-Banding 24:1–7.

Wheeler, H. E. 1922a. Random notes from Arkansas. Wilson Bull. 34:221–224.

Wheeler, H. E. 1922b. The Fish Crow in Arkansas. Wilson Bull. 34:239–240.

Wheeler, H. E. 1923a. Random notes from Arkansas. Wilson Bull. 35:35–37.

Wheeler, H. E. 1923b. Finding an eagle's nest. The Haversack (Publ. by Methodist Episcopal Church, South), Nashville, June 10, 1923, p. 3, 8.

Wheeler, H. E. 1924. The birds of Arkansas. Ark. Bureau Mines, Manufacturers, Agric., Little Rock, 177 p.

Widmann, O. 1896. Bachman's Warbler (Helminthophila bachmani) in Greene County, Arkansas. Auk 13:264.

Widmann, O. 1897. The summer home of the Bachman's Warbler no longer unknown. Auk 14:305–310.

Widmann, O. 1907. A preliminary catalogue of the birds of Missouri. Trans. Acad. Sci. St. Louis 17(1):1–288.

Widmann, O. 1908. Another Clarke's Crow taken in Missouri. Auk 25:222.

Wier, D. B. 1881. An Arkansas game country. Forest & Stream 17:430.

Wier, D. B. 1882a. Habits of cormorants. Forest & Stream 18:27.

Wier, D. B. 1882b. On the "Ar-kan-saw" prairies. Forest & Stream 19:308.

Wier, D. B. 1882c. Sport on the "Arkansaw" prairies. Forest & Stream 19:386.

Wier, D. B. 1883. The carrion crow. Forest & Stream 20:45.

Wilhelm, E. J., Jr. 1960. March Hawk breeding in northwestern Arkansas. Wilson Bull. 72:401–402.

*Williams, A. B. 1936. The composition and dynamics of a beech-maple climax community. Ecol. Monogr. 6:319–408.

Williams, H. L. 1968. Market hunters in early Arkansas. Ark. Game & Fish 2(1):8–10.

*Williams, S. 1968. The Waring Papers. Peabody Mus., Cambridge, p. 40–47.

*Wilson, L. A. 1981. A possible interpretation of the bird-man figure found on objects associated with the Southern Cult of the southeastern United

States, A.D. 1200–1350, R6-18 *in* Phoebus 3, School of Art, Arizona State Univ., Tempe.

Wing, L. 1943. Relative distribution of Mallard and Black Duck in winter. Auk 60:438–439.

Wing, L. 1947. Christmas census summary, 1900–1939. Wash. State College, Pullman, 270 p. (mimeographed).

Wood, N. A. 1932. Harlan's Hawk. Wilson Bull. 44:78–87.

Wooten, C. W. 1982. Avian community composition and habitat associations in an upland deciduous forest in northwesten Arkansas. M.S. thesis, Univ. Ark., Fayetteville, 92 p.

Yell. 1880. Albino Robin and black opossum. Forest & Stream 14:44.

Yell. 1885. The big woodpecker. Forest & Stream 24:407.

Young, Howard. 1958. Some repeat data on the Cardinal. Bird-Banding 29:219–223.

Zammuto, R. M., and D. James. 1982. Relationships of environmental factors to onset of autumn morning vocalizations in an Ozark community. Wilson Bull. 94:74–79.

Index to Bird Names and Taxonomy

(Including the species accounts in boldface type and illustrations in italics)